Pro Apache Struts with Ajax

John Carnell
with Rob Harrop,
Edited by Kunal Mittal

Pro Apache Struts with Ajax

Copyright © 2006 by John Carnell, Rob Harrop, Kunal Mittal

ISBN-13 (pbk): 978-1-59059-738-5

ISBN-10 (pbk): 1-59059-738-9

Printed and bound in the United States of America 9 8 7 6 5 4 3 2 1

Lead Editor: Steve Anglin
Technical Reviewer: John Fallows
Editorial Board: Steve Anglin, Ewan Buckingham, Gary Cornell, Jason Gilmore, Jonathan Gennick, Jonathan Hassell, James Huddleston, Chris Mills, Matthew Moodie, Dominic Shakeshaft, Jim Sumser, Keir Thomas, Matt Wade
Project Managers: Beth Christmas, Elizabeth Seymour
Copy Edit Manager: Nicole Flores
Copy Editors: Ami Knox, Bill McManus
Assistant Production Director: Kari Brooks-Copony
Production Editor: Lori Bring
Compositor: Diana Van Winkle, Van Winkle Design
Proofreader: April Eddy
Indexer: Michael Brinkman
Cover Designer: Kurt Krames
Manufacturing Director: Tom Debolski

Distributed to the book trade worldwide by Springer-Verlag New York, Inc., 233 Spring Street, 6th Floor, New York, NY 10013. Phone 1-800-SPRINGER, fax 201-348-4505, e-mail orders-ny@springer-sbm.com, or visit http://www.springeronline.com.

For information on translations, please contact Apress directly at 2560 Ninth Street, Suite 219, Berkeley, CA 94710. Phone 510-549-5930, fax 510-549-5939, e-mail info@apress.com, or visit http://www.apress.com.

The source code for this book is available to readers at http://www.apress.com in the Source Code/ Download section.

Contents at a Glance

Contents

About the Authors

JOHN CARNELL is the president and owner of NetChange, a leading provider of enterprise architecture solutions and training. John has over nine years of experience in the field of software engineering and application development. Most of John's time has been spent working in Object-Oriented (OO) and Component-Based Development (CBD) software solutions.

John has authored, coauthored, and served as technical reviewer for a number of technology books and industry publications. Some of his works include

- *Professional Struts Applications: Building Web Sites with Struts, Object Relational Bridge, Lucene, and Velocity* (Apress, 2003)

- Coauthor, *J2EE Design Patterns Applied* (Apress, 2002)

- Coauthor, *Oracle 9i Java Programming: Solutions for Developers Using PL/SQL and Java* (Apress, 2001)

- Coauthor, *Beginning Java Databases* (Apress, 2001)

- Coauthor, *Professional Oracle 8i Application Programming with Java, PL/SQL, and XML* (Wrox Press, 2001)

- Technical reviewer, *J2EE Design and Deployment Practices* (Wrox Press, 2002)

In addition to his teaching, John travels the country on a regular basis speaking at nationally recognized conferences on a variety of Java development topics.

John lives in Green Bay, Wisconsin, with his wife, Janet; son, Christopher; and two dogs, LadyBug and Ginger. John always welcomes questions and comments from his readers and can be reached at john.carnell@netchange.us.

ROB HARROP is a software consultant specializing in delivering high-performance, highly scalable enterprise applications. He is an experienced architect with a particular flair for understanding and solving complex design issues. With a thorough knowledge of both Java and .NET, Rob has successfully deployed projects across both platforms. He also has extensive experience across a variety of sectors, retail and government in particular.

Rob is the author of five books, including *Pro Spring* (Apress 2005), a widely acclaimed, comprehensive resource on the Spring Framework.

Rob has been a core developer of the Spring Framework since June 2004 and currently leads the JMX and AOP efforts. He cofounded UK-based software company Cake Solutions Limited, in May 2001, having spent the previous two years working as Lead Developer for a successful dotcom start-up. Rob is a member of the JCP and is involved in the JSR-255 Expert Group for JMX 2.0.

About the Editor

KUNAL MITTAL serves as the Director of Technology for the Domestic TV group at Sony Pictures Entertainment. He is responsible for the technology strategy and application development for the group. Kunal is very active in several enterprise initiatives such as the SOA strategy and roadmap and the implementation of several ITIL processes within Sony Pictures.

Kunal has authored and edited several books and written over 20 articles on J2EE, WebLogic, and SOA. Some of his works include

- *Pro Apache Beehive* (Apress, 2005)

- *BEA WebLogic 8.1 Unleashed* (Wrox, 2004)

- "Build your SOA: Maturity and Methodology," a three-part series (SOAInstitute.com, 2006)

For a full list of Kunal's publications, visit his web site at http://www.kunalmittal.com/html/publications.shtml.

Kunal holds a master's degree in software engineering and is a licensed private pilot.

About the Technical Reviewers

JAN MACHACEK started with microelectronics in 1992 and then moved on to computer programming a few years later. During his studies at Czech Technical University in Prague and University of Hradec Kralove in the Czech Republic, Jan was involved in the development of distributed applications running on Windows, Linux, and Unix using each platform's native code and Java.

Currently, Jan is Lead Programmer of UK-based software company Cake Solutions Limited (http://www.cakesolutions.net), where he has helped design and implement enterprise-level applications for a variety of UK- and US-based clients. In his spare time, he enjoys exploring software architectures, nonprocedural and AI programming, as well as playing with computer hardware.

As a proper computer geek, Jan loves the *Star Wars* and *The Lord of the Rings* series. Jan lives with his lovely housemates in Manchester in the UK and can be reached at jan@cakesolutions.net.

JOHN R. FALLOWS is a Java architect at TXE Systems. Originally from Northern Ireland, John graduated from Cambridge University in the United Kingdom and has worked in the software industry for more than ten years. Prior to joining TXE Systems, John worked as a JavaServer Faces technology architect at Oracle. John played a lead role in the Oracle ADF Faces team to influence the architecture of the JavaServer Faces standard and to enhance the standard with Ajax functionality in the ADF Faces project.

John is a popular speaker at international conferences such as JavaOne and JavaPolis, and has written numerous articles for leading IT magazines such as *Java Developer's Journal*. John is coauthor of the highly popular book, *Pro JSF and Ajax: Building Rich Internet Components* (Apress, 2006).

Acknowledgments

When people pick up a book, they often think of only the effort the author put into writing the text. However, creating any book is a team effort that involves the endeavors of many individuals. I would like to first thank Gary Cornell, who had enough confidence in my work to ask me to work on a second edition of this book. His confidence, especially coming from someone with his background and experiences, meant a lot.

I also want to thank the following people:

- Beth Christmas, my Apress project editor, for her tireless effort in keeping this book on track.

- Ami Knox, my copy editor, whose keen eyes and attention to detail has made sure that I come across as an intelligent and grammatically correct author. Thanks, Ami!

- Jan Machacek, my technical editor. Your comments and careful insight kept me honest and made sure this book was always the best it could be.

- Rob Harrop, my coauthor. Rob, you brought a lot of energy back into this book. Your insights and the work you did for this book will always be appreciated.

John Carnell

Many people don't realize just how much work goes on behind the scenes when making a book like this. First, I want to thank my coauthor, John Carnell, who has an amazing ability to explain even the most difficult of topics to absolute beginners. Thanks also to our technical reviewer and my colleague, Jan Machacek, undoubtedly one of the best Struts programmers in the world. Thanks to everyone at Apress, especially Beth Christmas and Ami Knox; without the support of such a great team, writing this book would have been an absolute nightmare. A final word of thanks goes to my girlfriend, Sally, for putting up with me through all the nights I spent sitting in front of the computer and for listening to all the "cool" stories about Struts.

Rob Harrop

I would like to thank John, Rob, and the entire Apress team for giving me the opportunity to edit this book. Steve, Elizabeth, Lori, Bill, and many others who have worked behind the scenes on this edition, I owe you one! I would also like to thank my wife, Neeta, and my pooches, Dusty and Snowie, for letting me ignore them over the weekends and focus on this book.

Kunal Mittal

Preface for This Edition

Apache Struts 1.2.x is still the de facto Java industry-standard MVC-based Web framework despite challenges from JavaServer Faces (JSF), Spring MVC, WebWork, Wicket, and other APIs and frameworks.

Pro Apache Struts with Ajax is essentially a revision of the previously published *Pro Jakarta Struts, Second Edition* that accounts for changes to the open source Apache Struts MVC web framework in the following ways:

- The Struts web framework in this edition is based on final Struts 1.2.x.

- This edition acknowledges the graduation of Struts from Jakarta to Apache within the Apache Software Foundation.

- This edition provides a new chapter that shows how to integrate Ajax (Asynchronous JavaScript and XML) with Apache Struts.

While this book addresses the above matters, it does not address the evolving and still nascent Apache Shale nor Struts 2.0, also known as Struts Action Framework 2.0, which combines Struts 2 and WebWork. However, future Apress books likely will address these areas.

Sincerely,
Editors of this revision

Preface from Previous Edition
(*Pro Jakarta Struts, Second Edition*)

One of the questions I always get from people when they find out I am an author is "Why did you get into writing?" While it is fundamentally a simple question to ask, the answer is not so clear or concise.

If I had to summarize into one sentence why I wrote this book, it would have to be for one reason and one reason alone: I love technology and I love building things with it. I have been coding since I was 12 years old. I have worked with dozens of technologies, and for the last four years I have had the opportunity to build enterprise-level software using several different open source projects.

I have been consistently blown away with the quality and functionality these technologies bring to the table. One of my favorite open source technologies is the Apache Group's Struts development framework. The Struts framework is a powerful Java development framework that really allows Java web developers to focus on building applications and not infrastructure.

When I worked on the first edition of this book, I had two goals in mind: First, I wanted to write a book that would introduce readers to the Struts development framework, but would not overwhelm them with all of the nitty-gritty details associated with writing Struts applications. I personally think most people, even advanced developers, learn best by doing and seeing rather than reading through tons of details.

Second, I wanted people to see how Struts could be used to solve everyday problems they encounter in building their own web applications. That is why there is such a focus throughout the book on the concept of identifying common design mistakes (aka antipatterns) and looking at how Struts can be used to solve these problems.

However, this book always sticks to the core tenet that a framework never absolves the developer of the responsibility of designing an application. The Struts framework, like any framework, is a tool, and like any tool can be used inappropriately. That is why this book emphasizes the importance of good design even when using a framework like Struts. Good code is never something that unexpectedly appears. It is something that evolves from fore-thought and clean design.

This book has been designed with both the intermediate and advanced developer in mind. The application being built in this book is very simple and easy to follow, so anyone with a basic understanding of JSPs and servlets should be able to very quickly follow along. However, at every point my coauthor and I always try to call out how simple design decisions and design patterns can have a significant impact on the long-term health of extensibility.

In the second edition of this book, we have updated all of the material to Struts 1.1. We have included entire chapters on many of the new Struts 1.1 features (like the Tiles and Validator frameworks). In addition, we explore a host of other open source technologies, like ObjectRelationalBridge, Lucene, and Velocity, that when used in tandem with Struts can significantly reduce the amount of time and effort it takes to build common pieces of application functionality.

I guess in the end, I do not consider this book a one-way narrative where you read my thoughts on a particular topic. Instead, this book is part of an ongoing conversation that I have had since I fell in love with my first Commodore 64. As such, I always welcome comments (both positive and negative) from my readers. If you have any questions, comments, or just want to vent, please feel free to contact me at john.carnell@netchange.us. I hope you enjoy reading this book, and I look forward to hearing from you.

Sincerely,
John Carnell

## CHAPTER 1

What We Do Wrong: Web Antipatterns Explained

Everything in the universe moves to chaos. What is ordered becomes disordered, what is created becomes destroyed. This phenomenon has long been observed in the field of physics and carries the name of *entropy*.

■Definition *Webster's New World Dictionary* defines *entropy* as a measure of the degree of disorder in a substance or system: entropy always increases and available energy diminishes in a closed system as in the universe.

Entropy is a phenomenon that is also observed in the field of software development. How many times have you worked on an application whose initial code base started out neat and organized, or met your own personal coding and documentation styles, guidelines, and standards, only to see over time the code base became more and more chaotic as the application evolved and was maintained? You probably yourself cut corners on your standards due to time pressures, or while making minor enhancements or bug fixes.

Entropy and the ensuing chaos it brings is the same whether it is being applied to the laws of physics or a software development project. In a software development project, the more entropy present within the application and its code base, the less energy available to write software that meets end-user requirements or overall business goals. Every hour that a developer spends dealing with hard-to-maintain and nonextensible code reduces the time available for that developer to write useful software by one hour. This does not even include the risk of writing buggy code when the original code is not well written in the first place.

Why are software development efforts so prone to move from an ordered state to almost absolute chaos? There are many reasons that can be given, but all reasons often point back to one root cause: complexity. Some other common reasons are time pressures, changing or unclear requirements, or just pure bad habits.

The act of writing code for an application is an attempt to impose structure and order on some process. These processes can be mundane (for example, determining whether or not individuals have enough money in their bank accounts to make requested withdrawals) or very complicated (for example, a missile fire control system trying to ascertain whether an incoming airplane is a commercial airliner or a military fighter jet). We know this is a stretch to imagine, but you get the point.

Most software development professionals have learned that the processes they try to capture in their code rarely have neatly defined boundaries. These processes are often nonlinear in nature. They cannot be easily described in terms of discrete steps. Instead these processes often have multiple decision points that can result in completely different outcomes.

Almost all software is constantly in a state of flux. It is almost always being changed and updated to meet new end-user requirements. The general perception is that the functionality of an application can easily be changed without affecting its overall quality and integrity.

The nonlinear nature of software, combined with ever-changing end-user requirements and perceptions of software malleability, makes it extremely difficult to avoid complexity within an application. In a software development project, the relationship between entropy and complexity can be stated as follows: The more complexity a developer has to deal with, the higher the level of entropy present in the application. This complexity leaves developers with less time to do what they were hired to do: write software to solve a particular problem faced by an organization.

Unmanaged complexity results in poorly designed software that is often full of bugs, hard to maintain, and even harder to extend and reuse. The development team that is responsible for maintaining the application's code base will build workarounds and patches onto the software until the source code is completely unmanageable. Oftentimes, the chaos surrounding the application's implementation and maintenance will force the organization to throw away the code without ever realizing the full business benefits the software was supposed to give.

At this point, with all of the problems involved with implementing quality software, you might be questioning why you would even become involved in the field of software development.[1] Things are not as bleak as they might appear. Many of us in the software development profession do successfully deliver applications that bring value to the organizations we work for.

However, even when we are successful in building applications, we are often left with the nagging feeling that there should be a better way of building and delivering software. It is possible to build high-quality software on time and on budget. However, in order to do this, the software needs to be built on a solid foundation.

Software built without a plan, without a well-laid-out architecture, will soon collapse under its own weight. However, say the word architecture to many business managers and developers and you will see a look of pain cross their faces. The word architecture is one of the most abused words in the software engineering lexicon.

For many business managers, the word architecture invokes images of a whole team of software developers (often a very expensive team) going off to write code that is very intellectually stimulating for them, but has no value to the business. They see a lot of development time and resources spent without getting a well-defined Return On Investment (ROI).

For developers, the term architecture often invokes feelings of guilt and longing: guilt, because many developers realize that there are better ways to write software; longing, because frankly with enough time and resources a development team could put together a development framework that would enable them to write better software.

However, the simple truth is this: Writing a development framework is hard work that requires dedicated time from senior development resources. Quantifying the value of a development framework to the business managers in an organization is an even tougher challenge.

---

1. One of the authors of this book did so because his criminology degree did not pay nearly as well as his computer science degree.

What This Book Is About

This book will demonstrate the use of freely available *Java Open Source* (JOS) development frameworks for building and deploying applications. Specifically, we will focus on the JOS development frameworks available from the Apache Software Foundation (http://apache.org) as well as its Jakarta group (http://jakarta.apache.org).

While most books are heavy on explanation and light on actual code demonstration, this book emphasizes approachable code examples. The authors of this book want to provide a roadmap of JOS development tools to build your applications. Our intent in this book is not to present each of the frameworks in minute detail. Frankly, many of the development frameworks presented in this book could have entire books written about them.

This book will build a simple application using the following Apache technologies, except for XDoclet:

Struts Web Development framework: A Model-View-Controller–based development framework that enables developers to quickly assemble applications in a pluggable and extensible manner. This book will highlight some of the more exciting pieces of the Struts 1.2 framework. These pieces are described next.

Tiles: A new user interface framework that allows a development team to "componentize" a screen into granular pieces of code that can be easily built and updated.

Dynamic ActionForms and Validator framework: A new set of tools for alleviating many of the more monotonous tasks of writing web-based data collection screens.

Lucene: A powerful indexing and search tool that can be used to implement a search engine for any web-based application.

Jakarta Velocity: A templating framework that allows a development team to easily build "skinnable" applications, whose "look and feel" can be easily modified and changed.

ObjectRelationalBridge (OJB): An object/relational mapping tool that significantly simplifies the development of data access code against a relational database. ObjectRelationalBridge can literally allow a development team to build an entire application without ever having to write a single line of JDBC code.

XDoclet: A metatag-based, code-generation tool that eliminates the need for a developer to support the usual plethora of J2EE (web.xml, ejb-jar.xml, etc.) and Struts (struts-config.xml, validation.xml, etc.) configuration files. It is important to note that XDoclet is not an Apache technology. However, XDoclet has strong support for Struts and has been included as a topic of discussion for this book.

Ant: An industry-accepted Java build utility that allows you to create sophisticated application and deployment scripts.

In addition, this book includes a quick introduction and overview of Asynchronous JavaScript and XML (Ajax). Ajax is a technology that addresses a very common problem in web application development. Let me introduce this with the help of an example.[2]

---

2. The example described here is also a good example of the Tier Leakage antipattern.

Assume you have a web site that accepts information about a customer—typical information like name, address, telephone number, etc. Some drop-down fields that you are likely to have are State, City, and Country. Let's assume that when the customer selects their Country, you want to automatically refresh the State drop-down with appropriate values, and once they select a State, you want to refresh the City drop-down. In a typical web application, this requires a round trip to the server, and causes the entire page to refresh. Based on the amount of information on the page, this might take a few seconds. In addition, you have to decide which validations to execute at this stage (most likely none, because the user has not clicked Save yet). With Ajax, this sort of an operation happens behind the scenes, or asynchronously, avoiding the page refresh and improving the performance. Only the required information is sent to the server and a small packet of information is received back and populated onto the page.

Don't worry if this is a little confusing at the moment. We will spend a lot of time on this concept at the end of the book.

What This Chapter Is About

This chapter will not go into the details of the technologies just listed. Instead, it will highlight some of the challenges in building web applications and explore some common design mistakes and flaws that creep into web-based application development efforts.

The truth is that, while all developers would like to write new applications from scratch, most of their time is spent performing maintenance work on existing software. Identifying design flaws, referred to as *antipatterns* throughout this book, and learning to use JOS development frameworks to refactor or fix these flaws can be an invaluable tool.

Specifically, the chapter will explore how the following web-based antipatterns contribute to entropy within an application:

- Concern Slush

- Tier Leakage

- Hardwired

- Validation Confusion

- Tight-Skins

- Data Madness

The chapter will end with a discussion of the cost savings associated with building your own application development framework versus using the JOS development framework.

Challenges of Web Application Development

In the mid-nineties, the field of software development was finally achieving recognition as being a discipline that could radically change the way business was conducted. The Internet was quickly recognized as a revolutionary means for companies to communicate their data and processes to not only their employees but also their customers.

Fueling the Internet explosion was the World Wide Web and the web browser. Web browsers offered an easy-to-use graphical interface that was based on the standards and allowed easy access to data on a remote server. Originally, the web browser was viewed as a means of allowing end users to access static content of a web server. Early web applications were often nothing more than "brochures" that provided users browsing information about a company and the products and services it offered.

However, many software developers realized that the web browser was a new application development platform. The web browser could be used to build applications that provided customers with direct and easy access to corporate applications and data sources. This was a revolutionary concept because for many businesses, it eliminated the need to have a large customer service department to handle routine customer requests. It allowed them to make their processes more efficient and develop a more intimate relationship with their customers.

The "thin" nature of the web browser meant that software could be quickly written, deployed, and maintained without ever touching the end user's desktop. Moreover, the web browser had a naturally intuitive interface that most end users could use with very little training. Thus, the Internet and the web browser have become a ubiquitous part of our computing lives and a primary application development platform for many of today's applications.

The transition of the web from being electronic "brochureware" to an application development platform has not been without growing pains. Writing anything more than a small web application often requires a significant amount of application architecture before even a single line of real business logic is written.

The additional overhead for implementing a solid web application is the result of several factors, such as

The stateless nature of the web: Hypertext Transfer Protocol (HTTP), the communication protocol for the web, was built around a request/response model. The stateless nature means a user would make a request and the web server would process the request. But the web server would not remember who the user was between any two requests. Some development teams build elaborate schemes using hidden form fields or manually generated session cookies that tie back to state data stored in a database. These schemes, while meeting the functional needs of the application, are complex to implement and difficult to maintain over the long term.

The limited functionality of a web browser–based user interface: The web originally started as a means to share content and not perform business logic. The *Hypertext Markup Language* (HTML) used for writing most web pages only offers limited capabilities in terms of presentation. A web-based interface basically consists of HTML forms with a very limited number of controls available for capturing user data.

The large number of users that the web application would have to support: Many times a web application has thousands of concurrent users, all hitting the application using different computing and networking technologies.

The amount of content and functionality present in the web application: In equal proportion to the number of end users to be supported, the amount of content and navigability of a web-based application is staggering. Many companies have web-based applications in which the number of screens the user can interact with and navigate to is in the thousands. Web developers often have to worry about presenting the same content to diverse audiences with a wide degree of cultural and language differences (also known as *internationalization*).

The number of systems that must be integrated so that a web application can give its end users a seamless, friction-free experience: Most people assume that the front-end application that a user interacts with is where the majority of development work takes place. This is not true. Most web application development often involves the integration of back-office applications, built on heterogeneous software and hardware platforms and distributed throughout the enterprise. Furthermore, extra care must be taken in securing these back-end systems so that web-based users do not inadvertently get access to sensitive corporate assets.

The availability of web-based applications: Web-based applications have forced enterprises to shift from a batch-process mentality to one in which their applications and the data they use must be available 365 days a year.

Early web-based development was often chaotic and free flowing. Little thought was given to building web applications based on application frameworks that abstracted away many of the "uglier" aspects of web development. The emphasis was on being first to market, not on building solid application architectures. However, the size and complexity of web applications grew with time, and many web developers found it increasingly difficult to maintain and add additional functionality to their applications.

Most experienced software developers deal with this complexity by abstracting various pieces of an application's functionality into small manageable pieces of code. These small pieces of code capture a single piece of functionality, and when taken together as a whole form the basis for an application development framework.

Definition An *application development framework* can be defined as follows: A collection of services that provides a development team with a common set of functionality, which can be reused and leveraged across multiple applications.

For web applications these services can be broken down into two broad categories:

- Enterprise services

- Application services

Enterprise Services

Enterprise services consist of the traditional "plumbing" code needed to build applications. These services are extremely difficult to implement correctly and are outside the ability of most corporate developers.

Some examples of enterprise services include

- Transaction management, to make sure any data changes made to an application are consistently saved or rolled back across all the systems connected to the application. This is extremely important in a web application that might have to process the updates across half a dozen systems to complete an end user's request.

- Resource pooling of expensive resources like database connections, threads, and network sockets. Web applications oftentimes have to support thousands of users with a limited amount of computing resources. Managing the resources, like the ones just named, is essential to have a scalable application.

- Load balancing and clustering to ensure that the web application can scale gracefully, as the number of users using the application increases. This functionality also ensures that an application can continue to function even if one of the servers running the application fails.

- Security to ensure the validation of the users (authentication) and that they are allowed to carry out the action they have requested (authorization). While security is often considered an administrative function, there are times when application developers need to be able to access security services to authenticate and authorize an action requested by a developer.

Fortunately, the widespread acceptance of building applications based on application servers has taken the responsibility for implementing these services out of the hands of corporate developers. Enterprise-level development platforms, like Sun's J2EE specification and Microsoft's .NET, offer all of the functionalities listed previously as ready-to-use services that developers can use in their applications. Application servers have eliminated much of the plumbing code that an application developer traditionally has had to write.

This book will not be focusing on the services provided by J2EE and .NET application servers, rather it will be focusing heavily on the next topic, application services.

Application Services

The enterprise-level development platforms, such as J2EE or .NET, simplify many of the basic and core development tasks. While the services offered solve many enterprise issues (security, transaction management, etc.), they do not help the application architect with the often daunting task of building web applications that are maintainable and extensible. To achieve the goals of maintainability and extensibility, several challenges need to be overcome:

Application navigation: How does the end user move from one screen to the next? Is the navigation logic embedded directly in the business logic of the application? Web applications, having a primitive user interface, can allow users to access and navigate through thousands of pages of content and functionality.

Screen layout and personalization: As web applications run in a thin-client environment (with a web browser), the screen layout can be personalized to each user. Since user requirements are constantly changing, web developers need to adapt the look and feel of the application quickly and efficiently. Design decisions made early in the application design process can have a significant impact on the level of personalization that can be built into the application at a later date.

Data validation and error handling: Very few web development teams have a consistent mechanism for collecting data, validating it, and indicating to the end user that there is an error. An inconsistent interface for data validation and error handling decreases the maintainability of the application and makes it difficult for one developer to support another developer's code.

Reuse of business logic: This is one of the most problematic areas of web application development, the reason being that the development team does not have a disciplined approach for building its business logic into discrete components that can be shared across applications. The developers couple the business logic too tightly to the web application, and resort to the oldest method of reuse, cut and paste, when they want to use that code in another application. This makes it difficult to maintain the business rules in a consistent fashion across all of the web applications in the organization.

Data abstraction services: The majority of web application development efforts involve integrating the front-end web application with back-office data stores. However, data retrieval and manipulation logic is tedious code to write, and when poorly implemented, ties the front-end application to the physical structure of the back-office data stores.

Unfortunately, most developers either do not have the expertise or are not given the time to properly address these issues before they begin application development. With the pressure to deliver the application, they are forced to "design on the fly" and begin writing code with little thought to what the long-term implications of their actions are. This may result in antipatterns being formed within their applications.

These antipatterns contribute to the overall complexity of the application and ultimately increase the presence of entropy within the code base. Many times, developers do not realize the impact of these antipatterns until they have implemented several web applications and subsequently try to support these applications while developing new code.

In the following sections, we are going to introduce you to the concept of patterns and antipatterns. We will then identify some common antipatterns in web application development, based on the preceding discussion.

An Introduction to Patterns and Antipatterns

You cannot open a software development journal or go to the bookstore without seeing some reference to software design patterns. While many software architects love to enshroud patterns in a cloak of tribal mysticism, the concept of a software development pattern is really quite simple.

Design patterns capture software development patterns in a written form. The idea behind design patterns is to identify and articulate these best practices so as to help other developers avoid spending a significant amount of time reinventing the wheel. The notion of the design pattern did not originate in the field of software development.

Design patterns originated in the field of architecture. In 1977, an architect by the name of Christopher Alexander was looking for a method to identify common practices in the field of architecture that could be used to teach others. The concept of design patterns was first applied to the field of software engineering in 1987 by Kent Beck and Ward Cunningham (http://c2.com/doc/oopsla87.html).

However, the embracing of software development design patterns really occurred with the publishing of the now infamous Gang of Four (GOF) book, *Design Patterns: Elements of Reusable Object Oriented Software* (Gamma, Helm, Johnson, and Vlissides, Addison-Wesley, ISBN: 0-20163-361-2). First published in 1995, this classic book identified 23 common design patterns used in building software applications. Over a decade later, this is still one of the most interesting books in the software space today and is still a best seller.

The concept of the antipattern was first introduced in the groundbreaking text, *AntiPatterns: Refactoring Software, Architectures, and Projects in Crisis* (Brown et al., John Wiley & Sons, ISBN: 0-47119-713-0). The book examined common patterns of misbehavior in system architecture and project management. As you are going to explore various antipatterns associated with web application development, it is useful to look at the original definition (from the aforementioned book) of the antipattern:

■**Definition** An *antipattern* is a literary form that describes a commonly occurring solution to a problem that generates decidedly negative consequences. The antipattern might be the result of a manager or developer not knowing any better, not having sufficient knowledge or experience in solving a particular type of problem, or having applied a perfectly good pattern in the wrong context.

An antipattern is a means of establishing a common language for identifying poor design decisions and implementations within your application. Antipatterns help identify poor design decisions and help give suggestions on how to refactor or improve the software. However, the suggestions associated with an antipattern are only that. There is no right or wrong way of refactoring any antipattern, because every instance of an antipattern is different. Each instance of an antipattern will often have a unique set of circumstances that caused the pattern to form. Web antipatterns focus on poor design decisions made in web-based applications.

It is not an uncommon experience for a developer studying an antipattern to stop and say, "I have seen this before," or to feel a sense of guilt and think, "I have done this before." Antipatterns capture common development mistakes and provide suggestions on how to refactor these mistakes into workable solutions. However, there is no single way to refactor an antipattern. There are dozens of solutions. In this book, we merely offer you guidance and advice, not dogmatic principles.

The web development antipatterns that are identified and discussed throughout this book are not purely invented by the authors. They are based on our experience working with lots of development teams on a wide variety of projects.

Web Application Antipatterns

For the purpose of this book, we have identified six basic antipatterns that most Java developers will encounter while building web-based applications. The web development antipatterns to be discussed are Concern Slush, Tier Leakage, Hardwired, Validation Confusion, Tight-Skins, and Data Madness.

Since the original definition of an antipattern is a literary form of communication, we will discuss antipatterns in general. In addition, symptoms of the antipattern are identified along with suggested solutions. However, the solutions described in this chapter are only described at a very high level. Specific solutions for the antipatterns will be demonstrated, throughout this book, by the application of JOS development frameworks.

We wrote this book with the following key points in mind:

- Most developers are not architects. They do not have the time and energy to write the application architecture from the ground up and provide constant maintenance to it. Therefore, practical solutions using an existing application's framework are more valuable than the code snippets demonstrating one part of the application architecture. So try to leverage other people's code. Every feature you use in application architecture is one less feature you have to write and maintain yourself.

- There are already several open source development frameworks ready for immediate use. Writing architecture code might be intellectually challenging for some developers, but it is often a waste of time, resources, and energy for the organization employing them.

- Focus on the business logic. The job of most developers is to solve business problems. Every time they are confronted with writing a piece of code that is not directly related to solving a business problem, they should try to build a business case for writing that code. An architecture without a business case is nothing more than an esoteric, academic coding exercise.

- Keep it simple. The most extensible and maintainable systems are ones that always focus on and strive for simplicity.

■**Tip** Architecture is done right when it has been implemented in the most straightforward fashion. Simplicity, above everything else, will guarantee the long-term maintainability and extensibility of an application.

Now let's discuss the different web antipatterns in more detail.

Concern Slush

The Concern Slush antipattern is found in applications when the development team has not adequately separated the concerns of the application into distinct tiers (that is, the presentation, business, and data logic). Instead, the code for the applications is mixed together in a muddy slush of presentation, business, and data tier logic. While development platforms like J2EE help developers separate their application logic into distinct tiers, it is ultimately how the application is designed that determines how well defined the application tiers are. Technology can never replace good design and a strong sense of code discipline.

The Concern Slush antipattern makes the code extremely brittle. Changing even a small piece of functionality can cause a ripple effect across the entire application. In addition, every time a business rule needs to be modified or the structure of a data store changes, the developers have to search the application source code looking for all the areas affected by the change. This leads to a significant amount of time being wasted.

REFACTORING

Martin Fowler wrote a classic book on refactoring existing software code. The book, *Refactoring: Improving the Design of Existing Code* (Fowler et al., Addison-Wesley, ISBN: 0-201-48567-2), is a must-have on any developer's bookshelf.

Unfortunately, he did not cover one of the most common and most unmanageable forms of refactoring: refactoring through *search and replace*. One of the most common symptoms of the Concern Slush antipattern is that when a change has to be made to a piece of code, developers have to open their editor, search for all occurrences of that code within the application, and modify the code.

A good example of this would be when platform-specific database code is embedded in the business tier. If a new requirement comes along that requires the application to support multiple database platforms, developers must go through each of the business objects in their application hunting for references to the platform-specific code and refactor the code. This can be a huge amount of work and might require extensive retesting of the application. After all, every time code is touched, it is considered broken until a unit test proves otherwise.

This type of "refactoring" occurs because developers oftentimes do not separate their application into cleanly divided tiers of functionality. Instead, the application code evolves and when reuse is needed, rather than refactor the code out into a single unit that can be called by anyone, the developers employ the oldest form of reuse: reuse through cut and paste.

This antipattern also tends to lead to insidious bugs creeping into the application, because invariably the developer will miss some code that needs to be modified. The bugs resulting from these missed changes might not manifest themselves for several months after the change to the original code was made. Hence, the development team has to spend even more time tracking down the missed code and fixing, testing, and redeploying it.

Most of the time, the Concern Slush antipattern will emerge for one of the following reasons:

Lack of an application architect: The development team does not have a senior developer playing the role of an application architect. The application architect's primary role is to provide high-level design constructions for the application. The architect establishes the boundaries for each of the application tiers. They enforce development discipline within the team and ensure that the overall architectural integrity of the application stays in place.

Inexperience of the development team: Members of the development team are new to enterprise development and write their web applications without a thorough understanding of the technology they are working with. Many times the developers are used to writing code in a procedural language (such as C or Visual Basic) and are suddenly appointed to write web-based applications with an object-oriented language like Java. Development team members continue to rely on their original training and continue to write code in a procedural fashion, never fully embracing multitiered, object-oriented design techniques.

Extreme time pressures: Team members realize their mistakes during the development phase of a project, but they have been given an aggressive deadline to meet. They toss caution to the wind and begin coding. They often do not realize how poorly designed the application is until they begin the maintenance phase of the project.

Using an application prototype as the base for development: Often, the development team will work together on a quick prototype for an application as a proof of concept. The code for the prototype is poorly designed. However, upon demonstrating the prototype, it becomes a huge success. The developers now fall victim to this success as they are put under heavy pressure to deliver the prototyped application quickly. Therefore, they decide to use the prototype code as the basis for the application.

Symptoms

For web applications based on the Java platform, the symptoms for this antipattern will usually manifest in one of two ways:

- Overloading of responsibilities

- Indiscrete mixing of presentation, business, and data logic

The first symptom, overloading of responsibilities, occurs when a single or small group of servlets or JSP pages is responsible for all actions carried out by the application. A basic tenet of object-oriented design is that each class within the system should have a small, well-defined, and discrete set of responsibilities.

A class, in this case a servlet or JSP page, is overloaded when the exact responsibilities of the class are not clear. Servlets and JSP pages that do not have well-defined responsibilities are often said to be *fat* or *heavy*. The call to such a page always includes a number of control parameters that are used by the servlet or JSP page. These control parameters are used by conditional logic embedded by the servlet or JSP page to determine the code to be executed within the page.

In the second symptom, a servlet or JSP page mixes together presentation, business, and data logic into one massive procedure call. An example of this particular symptom is out.write() statements mixed with business logic and data logic. JSP pages are even more prone to this abuse because JSP scriptlets make it extremely easy, for even a novice web developer, to quickly build an application.

In the second symptom, you should assume that no session Enterprise JavaBeans (EJBs) are being used in the application. When EJBs are used in an application, most developers will gravitate toward putting the business logic in the EJBs. The Concern Slush antipattern manifests itself in EJBs, when developers indiscriminately mix data access logic with the application's business logic in the EJB.

Solution

The solution is to provide software constructs that adequately separate the application's code into readily recognizable presentation, business, and data logic. For Java-based applications, the JSP Model-2 architecture is the recommended architectural model for building web applications. The JSP Model-2 architecture is based on the concept of a Model-View-Controller (MVC) framework.

In an MVC framework, all requests made by the end user are routed through a controller class (usually a servlet) that determines the business object used to carry out the request. The data that the users request and the corresponding business object are considered to be a model piece of the framework. After the business object has processed the user's request, the results are forwarded by the controller to the view portion of the framework. The view portion of the framework is responsible for the presentation logic that renders the results of the user's request to the end user. Figure 1-1 presents a conceptual view of an MVC framework.

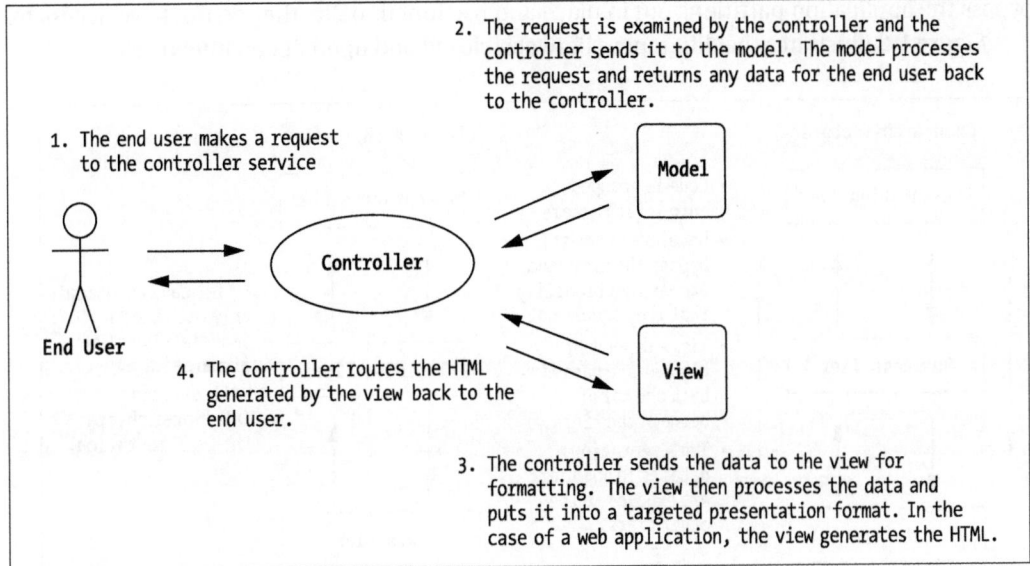

Figure 1-1. *An overview of the Model-View-Controller (MVC) framework*

The two key features of the MVC framework are as follows:

- *The clean separation of the presentation, business, and data logic into self-contained software constructs:* The MVC framework acts as a natural roadmap that helps software developers ensure that they keep their application's logic broken into distinct pieces.

- *The emphasis on building an application through declarative programming:* Since all the access to presentation, business, and data logic is controlled through a single entity (that is, the controller), the developer can easily change the behavior of the application by changing the configuration data being fed to the controller. The application developer can completely "rewire" the code to display a different presentation interface or apply different business logic without having to touch the source code for the application.

Tier Leakage

The Tier Leakage antipattern occurs in applications that have been separated into three distinct layers of application logic (presentation, business, and data). Tier leakage occurs when code and functionality from one tier are exposed to the other tiers.

This antipattern occurs when the application architect does not enforce the principle of "closed" tier architecture. A closed tier architecture allows each tier to communicate only with the tier immediately below it. In other words, the presentation tier can only communicate with the business tier. It should never bypass the business tier and access data directly. The communication between the tiers happens via well-defined interfaces that do not expose the underlying implementation details of that tier to the one above.

In the case of tier leakage, application architects break the application into three tiers, but they also allow communication between the tiers to be open. This means the presentation tier can still call and invoke services on the data access tier. In addition, even if there is encapsulation of services, the underlying tier details still remain exposed. This allows the developers to bypass the application partitions put in place and use functionality they do not have access to.

Figure 1-2 illustrates the differences between closed and open tier architectures.

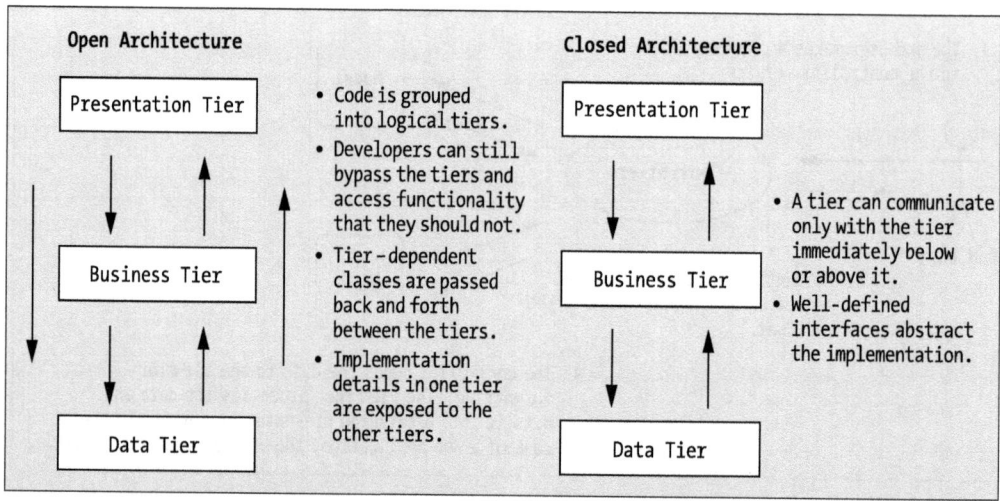

Figure 1-2. *Characteristics of open versus closed multitiered architectures*

The end result of not enforcing a closed tier architecture is that while various classes within the web application can be identified and grouped together in distinct tiers, dependencies still exist between the tiers. This means that the changes to one tier can have side effects that ripple through the code in the other tiers.

This antipattern occurs when the development team has not defined discrete interfaces that hide the implementation details of one application tier from another. The causes for the Tier Leakage antipattern are very similar to those of the Concern Slush antipattern: developer inexperience, compressed delivery dates, and inappropriate reuse of an application prototype.

Symptoms

Some of the symptoms of tier leakage include the following:

- Changes to one tier break the code in other tiers.

- You find that you cannot easily reuse a piece of code in one tier because of dependencies on a class in another tier.

The first symptom is a common mistake. Instead of wrapping data retrieved from the data tier, the business tier exposes the details about the data tier, by allowing the data tier objects to be passed back to the presentation tier. This results in the presentation class being unnecessarily exposed to the data access technology being used to retrieve data (that is, JDBC, JDO, entity beans). It also tightly couples the presentation code to the physical column names, data types, and data relationships from the database. If physical details of the database change, developers need to walk through all of the code in the application to reflect the database changes.

The second symptom occurs when the developer allows tier-specific classes to be passed back and forth between the different tiers. For example, you may have several classes, responsible for the business logic within your web application, that you may want to reuse in a Swing-based application. However, you cannot easily reuse the business logic, as it accesses an HttpSession object passed to it. The developer, rather than pulling the data out of the session object and then passing it to the business class, passes the HttpSession object directly to the class.

Solution

You can take three steps to avoid tier leakage:

1. Ensure that all the communication between the different tiers of an application takes place behind well-defined interfaces. Again, this means that one tier (say, the presentation tier) should only be able to access the tier immediately below it (say, the business logic tier). In a Java-based web application, this can be accomplished through the judicious application of J2EE design patterns. (We will be covering certain details of specific J2EE design patterns. For more information about this, you may refer to *J2EE Design Patterns Applied* [Juric et al., Wrox Press, ISBN: 1-86100-528-8].) J2EE design patterns like the Business Delegate, Data Access Object, and Value Object patterns all do an excellent job of wrapping the implementation details of the classes within a particular tier. These design patterns will be described in greater detail in Chapters 4 and 5.

2. Perform frequent code reviews. If you are using a version control system, establish a process where nothing is checked into the version control system without another developer reviewing it. Provide a checklist of elements in the code that must be architecturally compliant. Make developers who want to check the code walk through the code changes they have made and have the reviewer compare this against the compliancy checklist. This review is designed to be very short (no more than five minutes long). It forces the developers to verbalize exactly what they have written and gives the reviewer a chance to catch tier leakage mistakes before they creep into the overall code base.

3. Leverage JOS development frameworks, such as Struts, to abstract away the implementation details of one tier from the other. These frameworks provide services that allow you to minimize dependencies between the application tiers.

While any one of these steps can help minimize the risk of tier leakage, you will probably find that using all three steps combined is the most effective. As you will see in later chapters, even with application frameworks such as Struts, you will still need to apply the J2EE design patterns within your application.

Using a development framework can still create dependencies in your code if you are not careful. You can still end up having your application being too tightly bound to the application development framework. Chapter 5 will look at how you can leverage various J2EE design patterns to cleanly separate your application code from the development framework.

Hardwired

While the Tier Leakage antipattern deals with dependencies being created at the architectural level of the application, the Hardwired antipattern occurs when developers create dependencies at the application level. Hardwiring arises when the developer does not provide configurable plug-in points for screen navigation and application business rules. These items are hard coded into the application source code; thus, any changes to functionality require the source code to be altered, recompiled, and redeployed.

The Hardwired antipattern makes maintenance of web applications difficult because

- Web applications can have thousands of pages of functionality. Hardwiring the pages that a user can navigate to directly in the application source code creates tight dependencies between the pages. This makes it difficult to rearrange the order in which screens are accessed. It also makes it nearly impossible to break screens into independent entities that can be reused across multiple applications.

- The business rules for a web application are in a constant state of flux. There is an unrelenting demand by organizations to provide a personalized web experience to their customers. Therefore, hardwiring the creation and invocation of business rules directly to a particular page demands the constant modification of the application source code by the web development team of the organization.

The Hardwired antipattern develops because the web development team does not use a declarative approach to build its applications. A declarative design approach separates the application's "what happens" functionality from the application's "how it happens" functionality.

In a declarative architecture, the application is broken into small pieces of functionality that can be configured together using metadata. Metadata is essentially data about data. In most application frameworks, metadata is used to define how a user's request is to be carried out and processed by the framework.

Metadata is usually stored in configuration files, independent of the application source code. When the application development team needs to change the behavior of the application, it does it by changing the metadata configuration. By using a declarative architecture, new functionality can be added or existing behavior modified by changing the metadata. Thus the behavior of the application is not hard coded and does not require a recompilation and redeployment for the changes to take place.

The advantage of a declarative architecture is that it allows the development team to introduce new functionality into the application, while minimizing the risk of ripple effects that the change will have throughout the system. The disadvantage is that it can be overdone to the point where the application becomes overabstracted and hard to maintain because of the complex configuration rules, and suffers from poor performance.

Symptoms

The symptoms for the Hardwired antipattern begin to manifest themselves when changes to the application require functionality that was not in its original scope. The symptoms of hardwiring include the following:

- Navigation logic is hard coded directly within the application's source code. If your development team has to search through all of the application's source code to change a link, your application is showing signs of the Hardwired antipattern.

- The workflow of the application cannot be changed without a significant amount of refactoring of the application's source code. If the application you are writing always assumes that data captured from the end user is always entered in a certain screen order, then the application is hardwired.

- There is no consistency in how or when a particular screen invokes the business rules. This inconsistency makes it difficult to maintain the application's code and also means that new logic or functionality cannot be "swapped" into the application. This symptom is particularly common in projects with large development teams.

One of the true indications of whether or not your application is suffering from the Hardwired antipattern is when a small navigation or business rule change causes major headaches for you or your development team.

Solution

The Hardwired antipattern can be refactored by taking the responsibility of writing the code for screen navigation and business rule invocation out of the hands of the application developer. Instead, this logic should reside as a service within the application architecture. Since this service is no longer a responsibility for the developer, consistency can be enforced among the entire development team, and much of the application's navigation, workflow, and business rule invocation functionality can be described as metadata.

The MVC pattern is again an excellent tool for refactoring this antipattern. The controller of the MVC is responsible for application navigation. The business logic for the application is cleanly separated from the presentation logic. Metadata is used to tie all of these different pieces together.

Even if an MVC development framework is used, the only true way to guarantee that a Hardwired antipattern does not develop is through strong software development practices. These practices include the following:

- Use design patterns judiciously to ensure that hardwiring does not occur between your application code and the development framework you are using to build the application. We will explore these design patterns in greater detail in Chapters 4 and 5.

- Write an application framework development guide that explains to your development team how the application framework is partitioned into different pieces. Clearly identify the architectural best practices and identify those practices that violate the integrity of the framework. The framework developer's guide must be constantly updated, to ensure that material contained within it matches the current implementation of the framework. Depending on the complexity of the project, your development guide might be something as simple as a set of UML diagrams explaining the major framework components along with some notes about any design patterns used. Do not always rely on the JOS framework documentation. JOS projects can have haphazard documentation.

- Use the application framework development guide as a tool during code and design reviews. Hold these review sessions frequently and make the developers accountable for adhering to standards defined in the guide.

Do not become overzealous while avoiding hardwiring in your applications. It is easy to want to make everything in the application configurable.

Tip Good application architecture lies in its simplicity. You always have to negotiate between the need to generalize and abstract framework functionality and the need to avoid tight dependencies. In the end, overabstraction or tight dependencies both lead to the same problem: code that is too complex to understand and maintain easily.

The Struts development framework takes a declarative approach to writing applications. This framework allows you to change the behavior of the application by modifying configuration files. In both of these frameworks, application configuration is very easy and is designed to avoid the overabstraction problems mentioned previously.

Validation Confusion

The Validation Confusion antipattern revolves around the inconsistent application of validation and business logic in an application. Many web application developers do not clearly separate the application's validation logic from its business logic in an organized fashion.

The end result is the application consisting of a mess of JavaScript and server-side code for handling data validations. The data validation code is split between the front-end screens and also embedded within the business rules that carry out end-user requests. Logic for handling end-user errors is often inconsistently applied and mixed with the business logic.

For the purpose of this book, validation logic is defined as any type of user interface code that involves the following:

- Formatting of data being presented or collected from the end user.

- Checking to ensure the user entered the required data.

- Type checking to ensure that the data entered is the appropriate type. For instance, you want to make sure that when users are asked to enter numerical data in a field, they do not enter a nonnumeric character or nonnumeric string.

- Simple bound-checking logic to ensure that the data collected falls within a certain range (whether it is numeric or date data being collected).

Validation logic is considered extremely "lightweight." Validation rules are considered light, because changing them should not have a significant amount of impact on the overall business processes supported by the application. Business logic is the "heavyweight" cousin of validation logic. Business logic supports business processes. Changing this logic can have a significant impact on how a business is operated.

Why worry about the separation of validation logic from business logic? Failure to separate these two types of logic from one another makes it difficult to support the code. Since the validation logic is not centralized, developers have multiple spots to check when modifying a business rule.

More importantly, not cleanly partitioning the application's validation logic from its business logic can make it more difficult to reuse that business logic in another application. How validation rules are enforced and communicated to the end user is often very specific to an application. Business logic can be abstracted, generalized, and reused across multiple applications. However, with validation rule invocations specific to the application embedded inside of the business logic, a tight dependency is created that makes code reuse problematic.

A clean validation logic approach can help avoid the antipatterns mentioned previously, namely Concern Slush and Tier Leakage. The validation layer can be responsible for adapting the input provided by the user interface to the input required by the business logic. This can help prevent the user interface details from leaking down into the business logic.

This antipattern occurs when members of the web development team have not clearly defined how they are going to handle the validation of the data collected from the end user. They pass all of the data directly to the business rules in their application, without first putting the data through some kind of filter that ensures data validity.

Symptoms

Validation Confusion can be spotted in any of the following cases:

- When asked where a particular validation rule for a screen resides, a developer has to search through presentation (that is, a language like JavaScript or JSP scriptlets) and business tier code to find the exact spot of the validation rule.

- The development team needs to constantly refactor code, because application-specific validation rules are embedded inside of the business logic this team wants to reuse.

- There is no consistent mechanism for how validation errors are handled. End users encounter different formats for presenting error messages. For example, in an application with validation confusion, some of the errors might be displayed directly in the web browser, while other errors will pop up in JavaScript alert windows. In short, there is no consistency in the error handling that the end user experiences.

Solution

Refactoring the Validation Confusion antipattern can be accomplished by defining a consistent set of services used for form validation in the web application. These validation services are invoked before any of the business logic for the application is invoked. Any validation errors that occur are immediately processed, and the end user is notified in a consistent and repeatable fashion.

This means that the validation for the application only resides in one tier of the application, using a consistent mechanism, for invoking the validation rules. This might mean having all of the application validation logic reside in a standard set of JavaScript class libraries, or, as is the case with Struts, moving all validation logic for a form to a set of Java classes that are invoked whenever the user submits data.

In Chapter 3, we will discuss the mechanism provided by Struts for handling form validation and error.

Tight-Skins

Web-based applications have the ability to deliver unprecedented amounts of personalized content to the end user. Traditionally, companies pushed information out to their customers in a mass-marketing approach. In this approach, customers were categorized into broad groups who shared similar interests and backgrounds. The company would then direct different advertising messages about its products to these groups. This mass-marketing approach was considered successful if the organization running the marketing campaign received a response rate of 1 percent.

The web development platform, with its thin-client, easy-to-use, personalizable interface, has turned the mass-marketing concept on its head. Web-based applications can deliver tightly focused information and functionality to individual users, with very specific preferences and interests. Many of the sophisticated web applications currently online have the following characteristics:

- End users can choose the information and content that they want to see.

- End users can also personalize the color, font, and layout of the web application user interface to reflect their personal choices.

- A global audience is reached by presenting the web application in various languages, using a look and feel appropriate for a particular end user's culture.

However, the ability to deliver a customizable user interface to the end user requires some careful planning in the design phase of a project. The Tight-Skins antipattern is a presentation tier antipattern. It forms when the development team has not built its presentation tier to be flexible enough to handle personalized content for individual end users.

This antipattern can occur for a number of reasons:

- The original requirements of the application did not include an extensible user interface. However, requirements for the application changed. Since the development team had not planned interface flexibility up front, it now has to face the challenge of refactoring the presentation tier of the application to support it.

- The development team was too focused on reuse at the business and data tier. The team wrote the presentation tier in a monolithic fashion that did not have a component structure. Most developers are very comfortable thinking in terms of generalization, abstraction, and extensibility for server-side logic. However, the presentation code is often written with no real attempt to "templatize" it into components that can be easily swapped in and out of the application.

- The development team used the presentation code from the application prototype (if there is one) for the production application. This is usually done to save time and is again a reflection of the lack of design consideration for the user interface.

Unfortunately, the only way to combat the Tight-Skins antipattern, after it is formed, is to rewrite the user interface from scratch. This is why it is critical to identify personalization requirements for the application before any serious development work begins.

Symptoms

This antipattern has a number of symptoms including the following:

- The application's content is not separate from the application code. If you need to modify your application's source code to change the content delivered to the end user, this is a definite sign of a Tight-Skins antipattern. A common example would be when a JSP page has a significant amount of JSP scriptlet code and HTML mixed together. Tight coupling could exist between some of the contents of the page and the JSP scriptlets.

- The application screens are not based on templates. You have not designed your application's screen so that it is divided into discrete components (that is, the header, the footer, navigation bars, etc.), without which you will find yourself propagating the same change across multiple screens.

- The presentation tier is hard coded in one language. Many web applications start out supporting only one group of people. All content for the application is written in only that language. If the development team has to support multiple languages, it usually has to scour all code for any content that will be displayed to the end user and then translate it over to the new language. This is especially painful if more than two languages have to be supported.

Solution

The solution for the Tight-Skins antipattern involves cleanly separating application content from your Java source code. This way the content can be presented in multiple formats without having to wade through code. This also makes it easier to change how the content is to be displayed to the end user. Some ways of separating the application's content from its source include the following:

- Use JSP tag libraries to completely abstract any Java code from a JSP page. This way presentation content can easily be changed without having to wade through Java application code.

  - The Struts framework makes heavy use of custom JSP tag libraries. Some of the Struts tag libraries will be covered in greater detail in Chapter 3.

  - In addition to Struts, a developer can use a templating framework like Jakarta's Velocity framework to avoid embedding Java code inside the application. Chapter 12 of this book will introduce you to the Velocity templating language and its various uses.

- Separate the application's content by making it external to the application's source code. Struts allows you to separate screen content and messages in a file independent of the application. This way, content can be changed without having to change the actual JSP page. This material will be covered in Chapter 4.

- Build your application's screens using a template. The Struts 1.1 framework now allows developers to build screen templates, based on a collection of tiles. Each individual tile within a screen template represents a small component that can be easily plugged in, pulled out, or even shared across multiple screens. Tiles also allow common elements in the presentation to be shared across all of the screens in the application.

Data Madness

Most web developers know that embedding data access logic inside of presentation code is poor design. Applications written in this fashion are difficult to maintain, and are tightly coupled with the underlying data structure of the database that they are manipulating. A change to the database can cause many elements of the user interface to be visited and often modified.

Many Java-based web development teams never allow the presentation layer of an application to directly obtain a database connection and use it to access a data store. Instead, they always wrap these calls inside of the business tier. The development team never breaks out the Create, Retrieve, Update, and Delete (CRUD) logic associated with manipulating the data into a distinct set of classes. Instead, the team intermixes business and data access logic together inside the business tier.

The Data Madness antipattern forms when the application's architect does not decide how data access logic is to be abstracted away from the other tiers in the application. When building a data access tier, the following items have to be considered:

- How data is going to be accessed and manipulated

- Mapping relational data to Java-based objects

- Abstracting away physical details and relationships of the underlying data store

- Wrapping nonportable, vendor-specific database extensions

- How transactions are going to be managed, particularly transactions that cross multiple objects manipulating data from a data source

As most developers do not think of the data access tier while designing, the formation of a Data Madness antipattern can significantly increase the amount of time and effort needed to complete a project. Consider the following:

- Most database access in Java is accomplished via the JDBC standard.

- The JDBC standard uses standard SQL code to retrieve and manipulate data from a relational database. It is very easy to write poorly behaving SQL. Furthermore, JDBC and SQL code can be fairly tedious, in that oftentimes it requires a significant amount of code to perform even small data access tasks like retrieving data from or inserting data into a table.

- The JDBC API, while using Java objects in the actual API, does not take an object-oriented approach to data access. JDBC uses a relational model that retrieves data in a very row-oriented relational manner. This method of access is very clumsy and time consuming for a Java developer to work with.

- In a medium to large application, a significant amount of a developer's time can be spent doing nothing more than writing JDBC code to access data.

A significant amount of the development team's time is taken up writing data access code (usually SQL code). Code that does not fit an object-oriented development model is prone to be coded improperly, and is scattered haphazardly through an application's business tier. This is the crux of the Data Madness antipattern.

Symptoms

Most development teams do not see the symptoms of the Data Madness antipattern until they are well along in their development efforts. The first symptoms of the Data Madness antipattern include the following:

- The same data access logic is repeated within several business logic classes. This symptom is particularly prevalent in large development projects where very little development work is being done in the database (there are no stored procedures, triggers, or queries being executed inside the database). Developers are left to write their own data access code, and often two developers will go after the same data for use in two different areas in the application and end up with almost identical data access code.

- Members of the development team suddenly realize that they are seriously behind schedule on the project. Upon examination, they find that most of their efforts are spent writing database code.

- Data access helper classes and "homegrown" persistence frameworks suddenly appear within the application source code. These helper classes might help reduce the amount of code the developer is writing, but they do not solve the overall architectural issues of not having a well-defined data access tier.

- The development team is unable to define the data access tier in anything other than database or data access technology. Many development teams put a significant amount of thought into how their application's middle tier is designed. However, most development teams treat the data access tier in physical rather than logical terms.

- A database has to be reorganized for performance reasons. If several table relationships need to be changed, the development team faces a daunting refactoring project, as it has to pour through all of the source code and make modifications to reflect the underlying database change.

- The developers try to port the application to a new database platform and find that several key pieces of logic are relying on vendor-specific functionality. For example, one of the most common problem areas is the generation of primary keys for a database. Without a well-designed data access tier, moving an application from SQL Server to Oracle can be a coding nightmare. SQL Server features auto-incrementing columns, while Oracle uses sequence objects. This means to port the code you need to find every SQL statement that uses sequences and change it. This is not a small task in a large project. With a well-defined data access strategy in place, the development team could have abstracted how primary keys are generated, and centralized all of this logic in one class responsible for primary key generation.

- The development team wants to refactor the application to use the latest and greatest technology (Java Data Objects, Web services—you choose the buzzword). Since the technology used to retrieve and manipulate data is not abstracted away from the classes using the data, the development team must again perform search-and-replace missions to find all code that uses the existing technology, and replace it.

Solution

Two steps can be taken to refactor the Data Madness antipattern:

1. Include a clearly defined data access tier, which provides services that the business tier can use to access data. These services should abstract away the physical details of the database being accessed, any vendor-specific APIs being used, and how the data is actually being retrieved.

2. Avoid writing data access code, whenever possible. Use technologies that will let the developer map the underlying database tables to Plain Old Java Objects (POJOs). These significantly reduce the amount of code that development team members must write and let them more clearly focus on the functionality of the application.

The first step is a design-based approach involving the use of common J2EE data tier patterns, like the Data Access Object and Value Object patterns, to abstract away database and data access details. These patterns are extremely easy to implement and when used, help the development team maintain data tier code without affecting the rest of the application.

The second step is a technology-based approach. Java is an object-oriented language that is not well suited to deal with the table-centric structure of relational databases. Instead of having the development team write its own SQL code, use an Object Relational (O/R) mapping tool to perform CRUD actions on behalf of the developers.

O/R mapping tools allow the development team to declare how data retrieved from the database maps to Java objects. O/R mapping is not a new concept. The J2EE API supports the concept of *Container Managed Persistence* (CMP) based entity beans. CMP-based entity beans allow the developer to provide O/R mappings to the J2EE application server, and in turn, the application server generates all of the SQL code needed to access the database.

An alternative to entity beans is to use commercial O/R mapping tools. These tools have been available for years to C++ developers and have started gaining a significant amount of acceptance from the Java development community.

Commercial O/R mapping tools, while being very powerful, often carry long and expensive licensing agreements. They are often complicated to use and, being commercial products, require a heavy investment in training before the development team becomes proficient in their use.

However, over the last two years, JOS O/R mapping tools have started gaining more and more acceptance as an alternative means of building data access tiers. In Chapter 5 of this book, we are going to examine how one such JOS O/R mapping tool, ObjectRelationalBridge, can be used to solve many of the problems created by the Data Madness antipattern.

Antipatterns, JOS Frameworks, and Economics

When web antipatterns form in an application, the cost of building and maintaining that application grows substantially. The development team's time is eaten up with the complexity that has crawled its way into the application. Less time is available to write real code, and the code that is written is usually of mediocre quality.

Why are these antipatterns allowed to form? Very few developers purposely write poorly designed applications. We believe that web development frameworks can significantly reduce the occurrences of web antipatterns forming within an application. Antipatterns sometimes appear because applications are extremely complex to build and implement.

Again, developers do not purposely go out and introduce these antipatterns. These antipatterns often occur because the developers try to manage the complexity of just implementing the application's business logic. At times, they do not realize that the decisions they make now will come at a high price later when an antipattern manifests itself.

A well-designed web development framework will promote consistency and structure for the development team. A framework will provide core application services for screen navigation, data validation, error handling, business rule management, and data persistence. With all of these benefits, why haven't more Java web developers adopted the use of web development frameworks in their application development efforts? The reasons vary:

- Writing a web development framework is expensive.

- Writing a development framework usually requires senior developers and architects with a significant amount of design expertise.

- Development teams have not been able to build a business case for spending the money necessary to build an application framework.

- The development team had to spend the time necessary to maintain the development framework.

Until recently, open source development frameworks have not been readily available to developers. This meant that if a development team wanted to use a framework, they needed to build it themselves. Writing a homegrown development framework can be an expensive undertaking. It usually requires a group of senior developers several months of uninterrupted time to design, implement, and thoroughly test the development framework.

Most IT organizations do not have senior developers and architects sitting around with nothing to do. Usually these individuals are extremely overallocated, and giving them the time to focus on one problem requires commitment from the highest level of management. Even after the framework is completed, additional ramp-up time is needed as the framework developers begin training the development teams in how to use the framework.

For example, the Struts framework has a significant number of services embedded in it. To write an in-house version that offers even a fraction of the services offered by Struts, you have to take into consideration the resources that have contributed to the Struts framework:

- The Struts framework was built by some of the finest developers currently in the industry. Many of these individuals are senior Java developers who command extremely high salaries.

- The Struts framework has had literally hundreds of individuals testing and debugging the framework. Most organizations could not even begin to provide a quality assurance (QA) team that could thoroughly debug a framework like Struts.

- Struts is now a mature framework that has literally hundreds of client implementations all running on a wide variety of hardware and Java platforms.

For an organization to build a framework like Struts for internal use with the same level of sophistication and quality assurance could literally cost between a half a million and a million dollars.

Let's not forget that even after a custom framework has been built, the costs of the framework continue to accumulate, as you begin to factor in the development resources needed to maintain and support the framework code base.

For organizations building their own application frameworks, it can take a year to a year and a half before the organizations start seeing firm ROI from their framework development efforts. (This includes the time needed to develop the framework and actually build two or three applications using the framework.) This is simply too large of a leap of faith for most companies to make.

Java Open Source development frameworks offer a viable alternative to building your own application architecture. These frameworks provide the following advantages:

They are free to use. Most JOS frameworks have a liberal licensing agreement that lets you use the framework free of charge for building your applications. The only real restrictions that come into play with open source development tools is that the group sponsoring the tools places restrictions on repackaging the tools and selling them as your own.

They are well supported. All of the open source development frameworks covered in this book enjoy a significant amount of support. High-priority bugs that are discovered within the framework are usually fixed and made available for general use within hours. In addition, mailing lists and Internet newsgroups offer a wealth of information on how to solve common development problems encountered with JOS development frameworks.

The information is free of charge and, unlike most commercial software products, does not require an annual support contract. Some open source projects have groups willing to sell support for the product. JBoss (http://jboss.org) not only builds the JBoss Application Server, but also offers different levels of paid support for the project.

They are extensible. If you find there are features lacking in the framework you have chosen, there is nothing stopping you or your development team from extending it. The source code is readily available for modification. Many of the features found in open source frameworks started out as the result of challenges encountered by developers using the framework. The developers extended the framework to handle their problems and then donated their solutions back to the framework's code base.

There are a couple of downsides with open source development frameworks that should be noted:

Documentation for an open source framework can be extremely vague. People writing the frameworks are donating most of their time and energy to do something that they love: write code. But the same level of attention is not paid to the mundane but equally important task of writing documentation. Occasionally, a JOS development framework does require the developer to crack open a debugger to figure out what the framework is doing.

Open source frameworks tend to be very Darwinistic when it comes to features in the framework. High-priority bugs in the JOS frameworks are often found and fixed immediately. However, bugs that are of a low priority for the JOS framework developers might never be fixed. This can be problematic for a development team using the framework that needs that particular bug fixed.

JOS development frameworks are relatively new technology. Things can still go wrong with them, and they cause unexpected behavior in your application. It is imperative that if your development team is going to write mission-critical software with a JOS framework, it needs to perform a significant amount of testing. In addition, the developers need to ensure that the framework that they have chosen to use is supported by a vibrant development group that actively supports their code.

Open source frameworks free a development team from having to invest its time in writing infrastructure code. Infrastructure code is the entry price you must pay before you can seriously begin writing an application. From the authors' anecdotal experiences, in many projects, up to 40 to 60 percent of development effort involves the implementation of infrastructure code. For the "we don't have time for architecture" development teams, that 40 to 60 percent of infrastructure development effort is usually spent in increased maintenance of the application over the course of its lifetime.

Note Trying to cut costs by implementing complex architectures shifts the up-front architect and infrastructure costs to the maintenance phase of the application.

Ultimately, leveraging the functionality in open source frameworks translates into three direct benefits:

- Less complexity for application developers in writing their applications

- More focus on writing code that has a direct benefit to the organization

- A significant cost savings, by allowing the development team to access a significant amount of functionality without having to pay a dime for it

These benefits allow the developers to produce higher quality code and deliver their applications more quickly to their end users.

From a management perspective, there are still some items to consider before you use a JOS development framework on your projects:

- *Using a Java Open Source framework does not eliminate the need to have an application architect or architecture team.* You still need individuals who can support JOS framework questions and issues.

- *The initial adoption of a JOS framework does require extra time to be built into a project plan.* The development team is going to need time to learn how to effectively use the JOS framework. This means that the first one or two applications built on the framework might take more time than what they would have taken without using the framework.

- *For the first application built on the framework, you should have someone who is experienced with the framework to mentor your team.* This might require bringing in outside consulting resources. Consulting costs will be market rate if the JOS framework chosen is widely known and used (that is, Struts). For more obscure JOS frameworks, consulting costs could be significantly higher.

The JavaEdge Application

As stated earlier in this chapter, the purpose of this book is to provide a simple and straightforward roadmap that demonstrates how to successfully use the Apache web development frameworks. To do this, we are going to show you how to build a simple *weblog* application (also known as a *blog*). A weblog, in its simplest form, is an electronic bulletin board on which one user can post a story and other users can comment on it. Often, a weblog ends up being a combination of reports on real-world events with a heavy dose of editorial bias from the story-writers and their commentators. The example weblog is called JavaEdge.

The requirements for the JavaEdge application are as follows:

Visitor registration: Individuals who visit the JavaEdge blog can register themselves to be the members of the JavaEdge community. By registering, users can receive the weekly JavaEdge newsletter.

Browse stories: Visitors of the JavaEdge web site will be able to see the latest top ten stories posted by the JavaEdge community. When browsing the stories, the JavaEdge user will be able to see a short summary of the story. Clicking a link next to each story will bring up the complete story listing.

Browse comments: When users click a link next to each story, they will be presented with not only a complete listing of the story they have chosen, but also all of the comments associated with that particular story. Each posted comment will display the comment text, when the comment was posted, and who posted it.

Post stories and comments: Individuals can post a story or comments for an already existing story. If the individuals choose to register themselves as JavaEdge members, any stories or comments posted by them will show the name they provided during the registration process. If they do not register as JavaEdge members, they can still post stories and comments, but their name will not appear next to the story. Instead, the story will appear to be posted by an anonymous user.

User registration: Users can register to become members of the JavaEdge community by providing some simple information (such as name, e-mail, user ID, password, etc.).

Search capabilities: A user can search all the stories posted on the JavaEdge web site using a simple keyword search engine. Any hits found by the search engine will be displayed as a list of URLs.

The application code for JavaEdge is relatively sparse because we wanted to focus more on the underlying open source frameworks than building a full-blown application. In addition to demonstrating the capabilities of the Apache Java development frameworks, the application will illustrate some basic design principles that will ensure the long-term maintainability and extensibility of the JavaEdge code base.

Summary

Not every application developer needs to be an architect. However, all application developers need to have some basic understanding of software architecture. Otherwise, it is easy to bypass common design mistakes that form antipatterns that can make code difficult to support and extend.

This chapter has identified six common antipatterns that often spring up in web-based application development. These antipatterns include

- Concern Slush

- Tier Leakage

- Hardwired

- Validation Confusion

- Tight-Skins

- Data Madness

Along with descriptions of these antipatterns, we discussed general solutions to these antipatterns. A common theme that has formed throughout the discussions of solutions is that JOS development frameworks offer a structured mechanism to develop applications and minimize the amount of infrastructure code being written. Developing an application framework is an expensive proposition. Open source frameworks have the advantage of being

- Free of charge

- Supported by a large and enthusiastic development community

- Easily extended to support new features and functionality

We also discussed the requirements of the JavaEdge application that we are going to develop in this book.

The rest of this book will demonstrate the technique to use the following open source frameworks to refactor the antipatterns discussed earlier:

- Struts web development framework

- ObjectRelationalBridge (OJB)

- XDoclet

- Velocity template engine

After reading this book, you should have

- A working definition of what an application framework is, the knowledge of the costs and efforts of building an application development framework, and the attractiveness of the open source framework.

- The ability to identify web antipatterns within your own projects. You should be able to understand the root causes of these antipatterns and the long-term architectural implications of the antipatterns.

- An understanding of what steps needs to be taken to refactor the antipatterns.

- The ability to use common JOS development frameworks, like Struts, to refactor these antipatterns out of your applications.

- A comprehensive set of best practices for each of the frameworks discussed in this book. These best practices will cover a range of topics including what are common development mistakes when using the framework and what design patterns can be used to supplement the services offered by the framework.

CHAPTER 2

■ ■ ■

Struts Fundamentals

Building a web-based application can be one of the most challenging tasks for a development team. Web-based applications often encompass functionality and data pulled from multiple IT systems. Most of the time, these systems are built on a variety of heterogeneous software and hardware platforms. Hence, the question that the team always faces is, how do we build web applications that are extensible and maintainable, even as they get more complex?

Most development teams attack the complexity by breaking the application into small, manageable parts that can communicate with one another via well-defined interfaces. Generally, this is done by breaking the application logic into three basic tiers: the presentation tier, business logic tier, and data access tier. By layering the code into these three tiers, the developers isolate any changes made in one tier from the other application tiers. However, simply grouping the application logic into three categories is not enough for medium to large projects. When coordinating a web-based project of any significant size, the application architect for the project must ensure that all the developers write their individual pieces to a standard framework that their code will "plug" into. If they do not, the code base for the application will be in absolute chaos, because multiple developers will implement their own pieces using their own development style and design.

The solution is to use a generalized development framework that has specific plug-in points for each of the major pieces of the application. However, building an application development framework from the ground up entails a significant amount of work. It also commits the development team to build and support the framework. Framework support forces the development team to exhaust resources that could otherwise be used for building applications.

The next three chapters of this book introduce you to a readily available alternative for building your own web application development framework, the *Apache Struts* development framework. These chapters do not cover every minute detail associated with the Struts development framework; instead, they are a guide on how to use Struts to build the JavaEdge application, introduced in Chapter 1.

This chapter is going to focus on installing the Struts framework, configuring it, and building the first screen in the JavaEdge application. We cover the following topics in this chapter:

- A brief history of the Struts development framework.

- A Struts-based application walkthrough.

- Setting up your first Struts project, including the physical layout of the project, and an explanation of all the important Struts configuration files.

- Configuring a Struts application. Some of the specific configuration issues that will be dealt with here include

  - Configuring the Struts `ActionServlet`

  - Configuring Struts actions in the struts-config.xml file

- Best practices for Struts configuration

In addition to our brief Struts configuration tutorial, we are going to discuss how Struts can be used to build a flexible and dynamic user interface. We will touch briefly on some, but not all, of the custom JSP tag libraries available to the Struts developer. Some of the things you can do with tag libraries that will be covered in this chapter include

- Manipulating JavaBeans by using the Struts Bean tag library

- Making JSP pages dynamic by leveraging the conditional and iterating power of the Struts Logic tag library

Let's begin our discussion with some of the common problems faced while building an application.

The JavaEdge Application Architecture

The JavaEdge application, which we are going to show you how to develop, is a very simple weblog (that is, a blog) that allows the end users to post their stories and comment on the other stories. We have already discussed the requirements of the JavaEdge application in Chapter 1 in the section called "The JavaEdge Application." The application is going to be written completely in Java. In addition, all the technologies used to build this application will be based on technology made available by the Apache Software Foundation.

In this section, we'll focus on some of the architectural requirements needed to make this application extensible and maintainable. This application is built by multiple developers. To enforce consistency and promote code reuse, we will use an application development framework that provides plug-in points for the developers to add their individual screens and elements.

The framework used should alleviate the need for the JavaEdge developers to implement the infrastructure code normally associated with building an application. Specifically, the development framework should provide

- *A set of standard interfaces for plugging the business logic into the application*: A developer should be able to add and modify new pieces of functionality using the framework while keeping the overall application intact (that is, a small change in the business logic should not require major updates in any part of the application).

- *A consistent mechanism for performing tasks*: This includes tasks such as end-user data validation, screen navigation, and invocation of the business logic. None of these tasks should be hard coded into the application source code. Instead, they should be implemented in a declarative fashion that allows easy reconfiguration of the application.

- *A set of utility classes or custom JSP tag libraries that simplify the process in which the developer builds new applications and screens*: Commonly repeated development tasks, such as manipulating the data in a JavaBean, should be the responsibility of the framework and not the individual developer.

The chosen development framework must provide the scaffolding in which the application is to be built. Without this scaffolding, antipatterns such as Tier Leakage and Hardwired will manifest themselves. We will demonstrate how Struts can be used to refactor these antipatterns in this chapter. Now, let's start the discussion on the architectural design of the JavaEdge application.

The Design

We will use a Model-View-Controller (MVC) pattern as the basis for the JavaEdge application architecture. The three core components of the MVC pattern, also known as a Model-2 JSP pattern by Sun Microsystems, are shown in Figure 2-1.

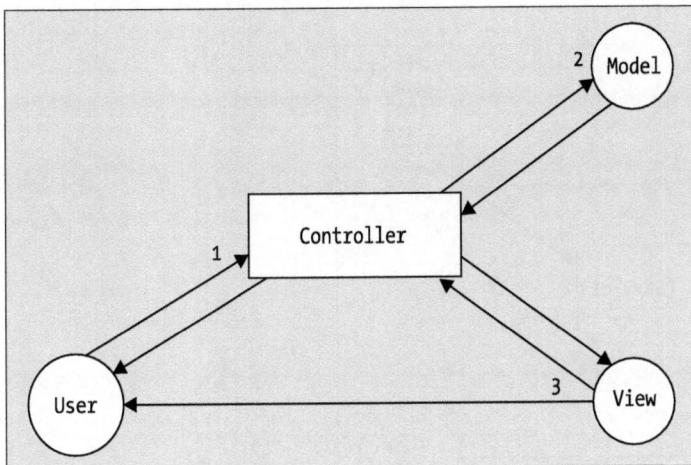

Figure 2-1. *A Model-View-Controller pattern*

The numbers shown in the diagram represent the flow in which a user's request is processed. When a user makes a request to an MVC-based application, it is always intercepted by the controller (step 1). The controller acts as a traffic cop, examining the user's request and then invoking the business logic necessary to carry out the requested action.

The business logic for a user request is encapsulated in the model (step 2). The model executes the business logic and returns the execution control back to the controller. Any data to be displayed to the end user will be returned by the model via a standard interface.

The controller will then look up, via some metadata repository, how the data returned from the model is to be displayed to the end user. The code responsible for formatting the data, to be displayed to the end user, is called the *view* (step 3). Views contain only the presentation logic and no business logic. When the view completes formatting the output data returned from the model, it will return execution control to the controller. The controller, in turn, will return control to the end user who made the call.

The MVC pattern is a powerful model for building applications. The code for each screen in the application consists of a model and a view. Neither of these components has explicit knowledge of the other's existence. These two pieces are decoupled via the controller, which acts as intermediary between these two components. At runtime, the controller assembles the required business logic and the view associated with a particular user request. This clean decoupling of the business and presentation logic allows the development team to build a pluggable architecture. As a result, new functionality and methods to format end-user data can easily be written while minimizing the chance of any changes disrupting the rest of the application.

New functionality can be introduced into the application by writing a model and view and then registering these items to the controller of the application. Let's assume that you have a web application whose view components are JSP pages generating HTML. If you want to rewrite this application for a mobile device, or in something like Swing instead of standard web-based HTML for users' requests, you would only need to modify the view of the application. The changes you make to the view implementation will not have an impact on the other pieces of the application. At least in theory!

In a Java-based web application, the technology used to implement an MVC framework might look as shown in Figure 2-2.

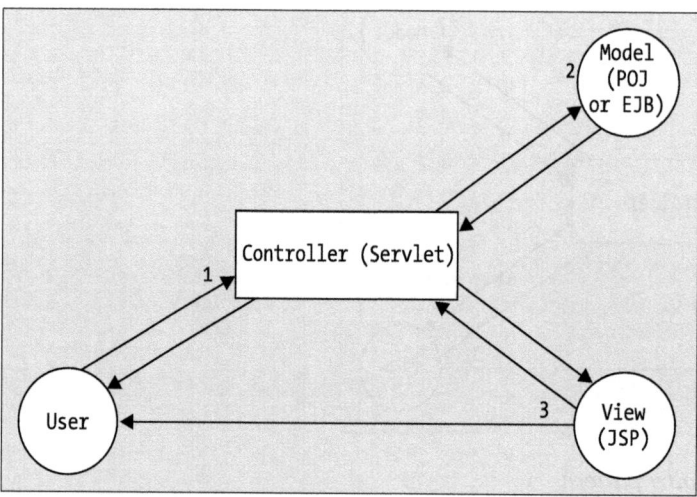

Figure 2-2. *The Java technologies used in an MVC*

An MVC-based framework offers a very flexible mechanism for building web-based applications. However, building a robust MVC framework infrastructure requires a significant amount of time and energy from your development team. It would be better if you could leverage an already existing implementation of an MVC framework. Fortunately, the Struts development framework is a full-blown implementation of the MVC pattern.

In the next section, we are going to walk through the major components of the Struts architecture. While Struts has a wide variety of functionalities available in it, it is still in its most basic form, which is an implementation of an MVC pattern.

Using Struts to Implement the MVC Pattern

The Struts development framework (and many of the other open source tools used in this book) is developed and managed by the Apache Software Foundation (ASF). The ASF has its roots in the Apache Group. The Apache Group was a loose confederation of open source developers who, in 1995, came together and wrote the Apache Web Server. (The Apache Web Server is the most popular web server in use and runs over half of the web applications throughout the world.) Realizing that the group needed a more formalized and legal standing for protecting their open source intellectual property rights, the Apache Group reorganized as a nonprofit organization—the Apache Software Foundation—in 1999.

The Struts development framework was initially designed by Craig R. McClanahan. Craig, a prolific open source developer, is also one of the lead developers for another well-known Apache project, the Tomcat servlet container. He wrote the Struts framework to provide a solid underpinning for quickly developing JSP-based web applications. He donated the initial release of the Struts framework to the ASF, in May 2002.

All of the examples in this book are based on Struts release 1.2, which is the latest stable release. It is available for download from `http://struts.apache.org/`.

With this brief history of Struts complete, let's walk through how a Struts-based application works.

Walking Through Struts

Earlier in this chapter, we discussed the basics of the MVC pattern, on which the Struts development framework is based. Now, let's explore the workflow that occurs when an end user makes a request to a Struts-based application. Figure 2-3 illustrates this workflow.

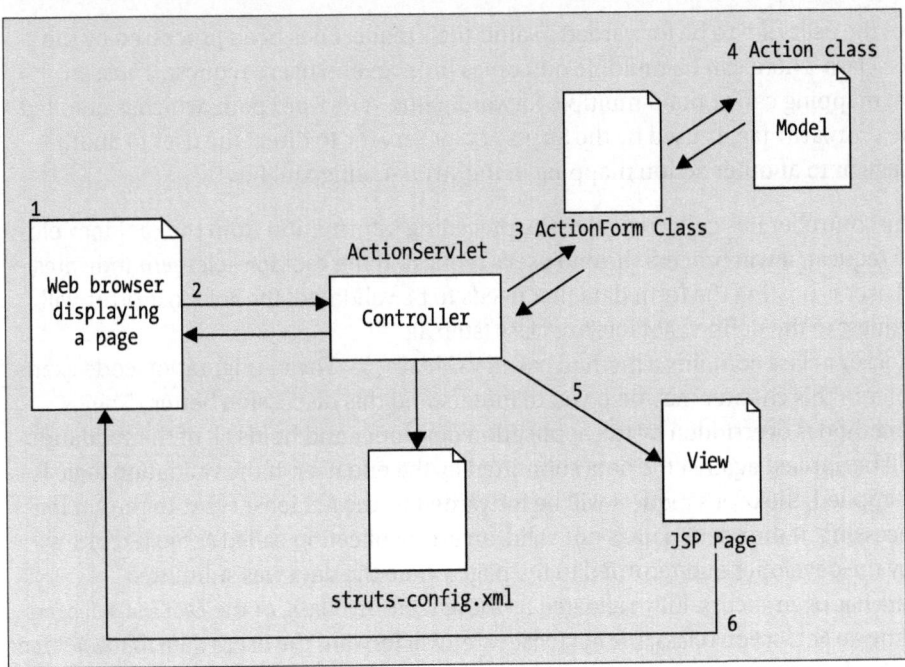

Figure 2-3. *The Struts implementation of an MVC pattern*

Imagine an end user looking at a web page (step 1). This web page, be it a static HTML page or a JavaServer Page, contains a variety of actions that the user may ask the application to undertake. These actions may include clicking a hyperlink or an image that takes them to another page, or perhaps submitting an online form that is to be processed by the application. All actions that are to be processed by the Struts framework will have a unique URL mapping (that is, /execute/*) or file extension (that is, *.do). This URL mapping or file extension is used by the servlet container to map all the requests over to the Struts `ActionServlet`.

The Struts `ActionServlet` acts as the controller for the Struts MVC implementation. The `ActionServlet` will take the incoming user request (step 2) and map it to an action mapping defined in the struts-config.xml file. The struts-config.xml file contains all of the configuration information needed by the Struts framework to process an end user's request. An `<action>` is an XML tag defined in the struts-config.xml file that tells the `ActionServlet` the following information:

- The `Action` class that is going to carry out the end user's request. An `Action` class is a Struts class that is extended by the application developer. Its primary responsibility is to contain all of the logic necessary to process an end user's request.

- An `ActionForm` class that will validate any form data that is submitted by the end user. It is extended by the developer. It is important to note that not every action in a Struts application requires an `ActionForm` class. An `ActionForm` class is necessary only when the data posted by an end user needs to be validated. An `ActionForm` class is also used by the `Action` class to retrieve the form data submitted by the end user. An `ActionForm` class will have `get()` and `set()` methods to retrieve each of the pieces of the form data. This will be discussed in greater detail in Chapter 3.

- Where the users are to be forwarded to after their request has been processed by the `Action` class. There can be multiple outcomes from an end user's request. Thus, an action mapping can contain multiple forward paths. A forward path, which is denoted by the `<forward>` tag, is used by the Struts `ActionServlet` to direct the user to another JSP page or to another action mapping in the struts-config.xml file.

Once the controller has collected all of the preceding information from the `<action>` element for the request, it will process the end user's request. If the `<action>` element indicates that the end user is posting the form data that needs to be validated, the `ActionServlet` will direct the request to the defined `ActionForm` class (step 3).

An `ActionForm` class contains a method called `validate()`. (The configuration code examples given later in this chapter may help you to understand this discussion better.) The `validate()` method is overridden by the application developer and holds all of the validation logic that will be applied against the data submitted by the end user. If the validation logic is successfully applied, the user's request will be forwarded by the `ActionServlet` to the `Action` class for processing. If the user's data is not valid, an error collection called `ActionErrors` is populated by the developer and returned to the page where the data was submitted.

If the data has been successfully validated by the `ActionForm` class, or the `<action-mapping>` does not define an `ActionForm` class, the `ActionServlet` will forward the user's data to the `Action` class defined by the action mapping (step 4). The `Action` class has three public methods and several protected ones. For the purpose of this discussion, we will consider only the `execute()` method of the `Action` class. This method, which is overridden by the application developer, contains the entire business logic necessary for carrying out the end-user request.

Once the `Action` has completed processing the request, it will indicate to the `ActionServlet` where the user is to be forwarded. It does this by providing a key value that is used by the `ActionServlet` to look up from the action mapping. The actual code used to carry out a forward will be shown in the section called "Configuring the homePageSetup Action Element" later in this chapter. Most of the time, users will be forwarded to a JSP page that will display the results of their request (step 5). The JSP page will render the data returned from the model as an HTML page that is displayed to the end user (step 6).

In summary, a typical web screen, based on the Struts development framework, will consist of the following:

- An action that represents the code that will be executed when the user's request is being processed. Each action in the web page will map to exactly one `<action>` element defined in the struts-config.xml file. An action that is invoked by an end user will be embedded in an HTML or a JSP page as a hyperlink or as an `action` attribute inside a `<form>` tag.

- An `<action>` element that will define which `ActionForm` class, if any, will be used to validate the form data submitted by the end user. It will also define which `Action` class will be used to process the end user's request.

- An `Action` class can use one or more forwards. A forward is used to tell the `ActionServlet` which JSP page should be used to render a response to the end user's request. A forward is defined as a `<forward>` element inside of the `<action>` element. Multiple forwards can be defined within a single `<ActionMapping>` element.

Now that we have completed a conceptual overview of how a single web page in a Struts application is processed, let's look at how a single page from the JavaEdge blog is written and plugged into the Struts framework.

Getting Started: The JavaEdge Source Tree

Before diving into the basics of Struts configuration, we need to enumerate the different pieces of the JavaEdge application's source tree. The JavaEdge blog is laid out in the directory structure shown in Figure 2-4.

The root directory for the project is called waf. There are several key directories underneath it, as listed here:

- *src*: Contains the entire JavaEdge source code of the application. This directory has several subdirectories, including

  - *java*: All Java source files for the application.

  - *ojb*: All ObjectRelationalBridge configuration files. These files are discussed in greater detail in Chapter 5.

  - *web*: The entire source code of the application that is going to be put in the WEB-INF directory. Files in this directory include any image file used in the application along with any JSP files.

  - *sql*: All of the MySQL-compliant SQL scripts for creating and prepopulating the waf database used by the JavaEdge application.

- *build*: Contains the Ant build scripts used to compile, test, and deploy the application.

- *lib*: Contains the jar files for the various open source projects used to build the JavaEdge application.

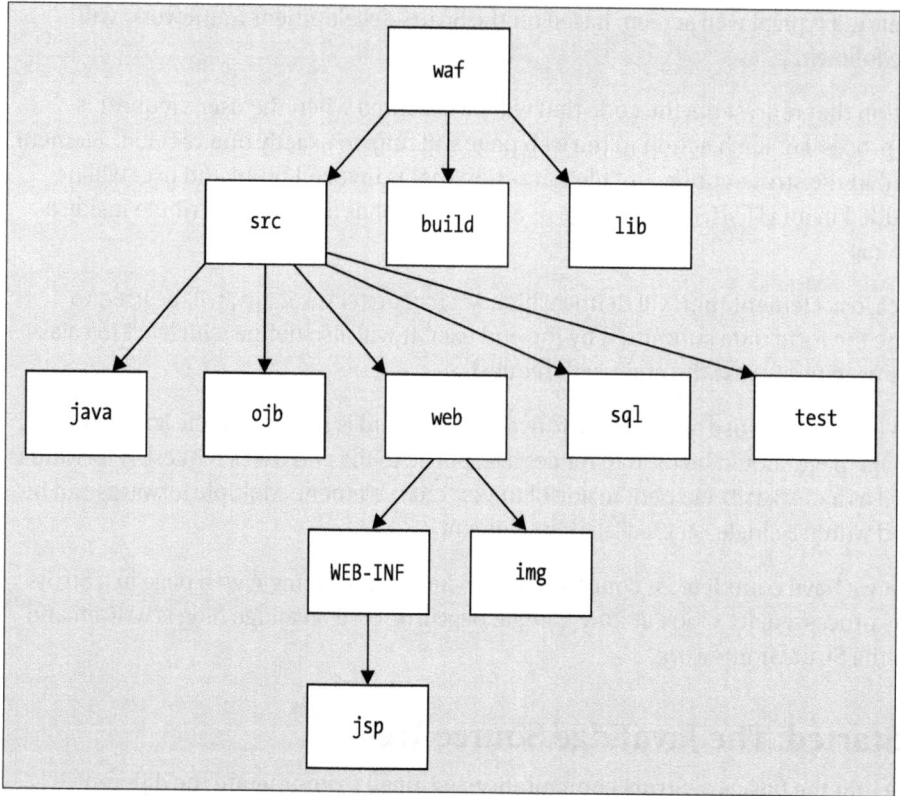

Figure 2-4. *The JavaEdge directory structure*

The JavaEdge application is built, tested, and deployed with the following software:

Tomcat 5.5.16: Tomcat is an implementation of Sun Microsystems' Servlet and JSP speci-fications. It is considered by Sun Microsystems to be the reference implementation for its specifications. The JavaEdge application is built and deployed around Tomcat. In Chapter 4, the open source application server bundle, JBoss 3/Tomcat 5.5.16, is used to run the appli-cation. Tomcat is available for download at http://tomcat.apache.org/. JBoss is an open source J2EE application server produced by JBoss. It can be downloaded at http://jboss.org.

MySQL: MySQL was chosen because it is one of the most popular open source databases available today. It is highly scalable and extremely easy to install and configure. MySQL 5.0 is available for download at http://www.mysql.com.

Ant: Version 1.6.5 of the Apache Software Foundation's Ant build utility can be down-loaded at http://ant.apache.org/.

Lucene: Lucene is a Java-based open source search engine. Version 1.9.1 can be down-loaded at http://lucene.apache.org.

Velocity: Version 1.4 of this alternative templating framework to JSP is available at http://jakarta.apache.org/velocity/.

ObjectRelationalBridge (OJB) 1.0.4: OJB is an open source Object Relational mapping tool available from the Apache DB Project. It can be downloaded from http://db.apache.org/ojb.

■**Note** All of the source code used in this book can be downloaded from the Apress web site (http://
www.apress.com). We will not be discussing how to configure any of the development tools listed previously
in this chapter. For information on how to configure these tools to run the code examples in this book, please
refer to the readme.txt file packaged with the source code.

We will start the JavaEdge Struts configuration by demonstrating how to configure the
application to recognize the Struts ActionServlet.

Configuring the ActionServlet

Any application that is going to use Struts must be configured to recognize and use the Struts
ActionServlet. Configuring the ActionServlet requires that you manipulate two separate configuration files:

web.xml: Your first task is to configure the Struts ActionServlet as you would any other
servlet by adding the appropriate entries to the web.xml file.

struts-config.xml: Your second task is to configure the internals of the ActionServlet.
Since version 1.1 of the Struts framework, the recommended mechanism for this configuration is to use the struts-config.xml file. You can still configure the ActionServlet using
the init-param tag in web.xml, but this feature will be removed at a later date and is now
officially deprecated.

An example of the <servlet> tag that is used to configure the ActionServlet for the
JavaEdge application is shown here:

```
<?xml version="1.0" encoding="ISO-8859-1"?>

<!DOCTYPE web-app
  PUBLIC "-//Sun Microsystems, Inc.//DTD Web Application 2.3//EN"
  "http://java.sun.com//dtd/web-app_2_3.dtd">

<web-app>

  <!--Setting up the MemberFilter-->
  <filter>
    <filter-name>MemberFilter</filter-name>
    <filter-class>com.apress.javaedge.common.MemberFilter</filter-class>
  </filter>

  <filter-mapping>
    <filter-name>MemberFilter</filter-name>
    <url-pattern>/execute/*</url-pattern>
  </filter-mapping>
```

```xml
<!-- Standard Action Servlet Configuration (with debugging) -->
<servlet>
  <servlet-name>action</servlet-name>
  <servlet-class>org.apache.struts.action.ActionServlet</servlet-class>
  <init-param>
        <param-name>config</param-name>
        <param-value>/WEB-INF/struts-config.xml </param-value>
   </init-param>
   <init-param>
        <param-name>validating</param-name>
        <param-value>true </param-value>
   </init-param>
   <load-on-startup>2</load-on-startup>
</servlet>

<!-- Standard Action Servlet Mapping -->
<servlet-mapping>
  <servlet-name>action</servlet-name>
  <url-pattern>/execute/*</url-pattern>
</servlet-mapping>

<!-- The Usual Welcome File List -->
<welcome-file-list>
  <welcome-file>default.jsp</welcome-file>
</welcome-file-list>

<taglib>
  <taglib-uri>/taglibs/struts-bean</taglib-uri>
  <taglib-location>/WEB-INF/taglibs/struts-bean.tld</taglib-location>
</taglib>

<taglib>
  <taglib-uri>/taglibs/struts-html</taglib-uri>
  <taglib-location>/WEB-INF/taglibs/struts-html.tld</taglib-location>
</taglib>

<taglib>
  <taglib-uri>/taglibs/struts-logic</taglib-uri>
  <taglib-location>/WEB-INF/taglibs/struts-logic.tld</taglib-location>
</taglib>

<taglib>
  <taglib-uri>/taglibs/struts-template</taglib-uri>
  <taglib-location>/WEB-INF/taglibs/struts-template.tld</taglib-location>
</taglib>
```

```
<taglib>
  <taglib-uri>http://jakarta.apache.org/taglibs/veltag-1.0</taglib-uri>
  <taglib-location>/WEB-INF/taglibs/veltag.tld</taglib-location>
</taglib>

<!-- Tiles Tage Library Descriptors -->
<taglib>
    <taglib-uri>/taglibs/struts-tiles</taglib-uri>
    <taglib-location>/WEB-INF/taglibs/struts-tiles.tld</taglib-location>
</taglib>
</web-app>
```

Anyone who is familiar with Java servlet configuration will realize that there is nothing particularly sophisticated going on here. The `<filter>` and `<filter-mapping>` tags define a filter that checks if the user has logged in to the application. If the user has not yet logged in, they will automatically be logged in as an anonymous user. This filter is called every time the Struts ActionServlet is invoked. The `<servlet>` tag defines all the information needed to use the Struts ActionServlet in the JavaEdge application. The `<servlet-name>` tag provides a name for the servlet. The `<servlet-class>` tag indicates the fully qualified Java class name of the Struts ActionServlet.

From the preceding example, you will notice that not all configuration settings have been moved into the struts-config.xml file. Mainly, the configuration parameters that are still specified using the `<init-param>` tag are those that are required to either find or read the struts-config.xml file. Specifically, you are left with the parameters in Table 2-1.

Table 2-1. *The ActionServlet's web.xml Configuration Parameters*

Parameter Name	Parameter Value
config	This parameter provides the ActionServlet with the location of the struts-config.xml file. By default the ActionServlet looks for struts-config.xml at /WEB-INF/struts-config.xml. If you place your struts-config.xml at this location, then you can omit this parameter, although we recommend that you always specify the location. That way if the default value for this parameter changes in a later release of Struts, then your application won't be broken.
validating	You should always leave this parameter set to true. Setting this parameter to true causes the struts-config.xml file to be read by a validating XML parser. This *will* at some point in your development career save you from tearing your hair out trying to debug your application only to find there is a rogue angle bracket in your config file.

The other important part of configuring the ActionServlet is setting up the mapping so the container passes the correct requests to the Struts framework for processing. This is done by defining a `<servlet-mapping>` tag in the web.xml file. The mapping can be done in one of two ways:

- URL prefix mapping
- Extension mapping

In URL prefix mapping, the servlet container examines the URL coming in and maps it to a servlet. The `<servlet-mapping>` for the JavaEdge application is shown here:

```
<web-app>
...
  <servlet-mapping>
    <servlet-name>action</servlet-name>
    <url-pattern>/execute/*</url-pattern>
  </servlet-mapping>
</web-app>
```

This servlet mapping indicates to the servlet container that any request coming into the JavaEdge application, which has a URL pattern of /execute/*, should be directed to the `ActionServlet` (defined by the `<servlet-name>` shown previously) running under the JavaEdge application. For example, if you want to bring up the home page for the JavaEdge application, you would point your browser to http://localhost:8080/JavaEdge/execute/homePageSetup, where JavaEdge is the application name, execute is the URL prefix, and homePageSetup is the Struts action.

Note It is important to note that all URLs shown in our code examples are case sensitive and must be entered exactly as they appear.

The servlet container, upon getting this request, would go through the following steps:

1. Determine the name of the application. The user's request indicates that they are making a request for the JavaEdge application. The servlet container will then look in the web.xml file associated with the JavaEdge application.

2. The servlet container will find the servlet that it should invoke. For this, it looks for a `<servlet-mapping>` tag that matches a URL pattern called execute. In the JavaEdge web.xml file, this `<servlet-mapping>` tag maps to the `ActionServlet` (that is, the Struts `ActionServlet`).

3. The user's request is then forwarded to the `ActionServlet` running under the JavaEdge application. The homePageSetup in the preceding URL is the action the user would like the Struts framework to carry out. Remember, an action in Struts maps to an `<action>` element in the struts-config.xml file. (Note that we will be going through how to set up an `<action>` element in the section "Configuring the homePageSetup Action Element.") This `<action>` element defines the Java classes and JSP pages that will process the user's request.

The second way to map the user's request to the `ActionServlet` is to use extension mapping. In this method, the servlet container will take all URLs that map to a specified extension and send them to the `ActionServlet` for processing. In the example that follows, all of the URLs that end with an *.st extension will map to the Struts `ActionServlet`:

```
<web-app>
  <servlet-mapping>
```

```
    <servlet-name>action</servlet-name>
    <url-pattern>*.st</url-pattern>
  </servlet-mapping>
</web-app>
```

If you use extension mapping to map the user's requests to the ActionServlet, the URL to get to the JavaEdge home page would be http://localhost:8080/ JavaEdge/homePageSetup.st, where JavaEdge is the application name, homePageSetup is the Struts action, and .st is the extension.

For the JavaEdge application being built in the next four chapters, we will be using the URL prefix method (this is the best practice for setting up and prepopulating the screens).

Once the ActionServlet is configured within the container, all that is left to do is config-ure the actual parameters for the Struts environment. The most important piece of configuration needed is specifying the controller. Since version 1.1, the actual processing of requests has been refactored from the ActionServlet and placed in a controller object. This pattern, called the *Application Controller pattern*, provides a simple mechanism to decouple the processing of the Struts request from the actual physical request mechanism, in this case the ActionServlet. To configure the controller, you simply add this entry to the struts-config.xml file:

```
<controller
    processorClass="org.apache.struts.action.RequestProcessor">
```

Although this entry in the configuration file is entirely optional, RequestProcessor is the default controller, and adding it means that any changes to the Struts framework in the future, such as a change in the default controller, will not affect your application. The controller ele-ment has a wide variety of parameters for configuring the Struts request controller, the most widely used being those in Table 2-2.

Table 2-2. *Configuration Parameters for the Struts Request Controller*

Parameter Name	Parameter Value
className	Using this parameter, you can define a separate configuration bean to handle the configuration of the Struts controller. By default this parameter is set to org.apache.struts.config.ControllerConfig.
contentType	Using this parameter, you can configure the default content type to use for each response from the Struts controller. The default for this is text/html and the default can be overridden by each action or JSP within your application as needed.
locale	Set this parameter to true (which is the default) to store a Locale object in the user's session if there isn't one already present.
maxFileSize	If you are taking advantage of the Struts file-upload capabilities, then you can configure the maximum file size allowed for upload. You specify an integer value to represent the maximum number of bytes you wish to allow. Alternatively you can suffix the number with K, M, or G to represent kilobytes, megabytes, or gigabytes, respectively. The default for this is 250 megabytes.
multipartClass	By default, the org.apache.struts.upload.CommonsMultipartRequestHandler class is used to handle multipart uploads. If you have your own class to handle this behavior or you want to override the behavior of the default class, then you can use this parameter to do so.

The final part of this configuration is to configure a resource bundle to enable you to externalize the application's resources such as error messages, label text, and URLs. The Struts framework provides support for resource bundles in almost all areas, and its support is central to delivering a successfully internationalized application. To configure the resource bundle, you simply specify the name of the properties file that stores your externalized resources:

```
<message-resources
    parameter="ApplicationResources"
    null="false" />
```

The `parameter` attribute is the name of the properties file without the file extension that contains the application resources. For example, if your resource bundle is named ApplicationResources.properties, then the value of the parameter attribute is `ApplicationResources`.

Additional configuration parameters for both the `<controller>` and `<message-resource>` tags can be found at `http://struts.apache.org/1.x/userGuide/configuration.html`.

As the servlet configuration is complete for the JavaEdge application, let's focus on setting up and implementing your first Struts action, the `homePageSetup` action. This action sends the user to the JavaEdge home page. However, before the user actually sees the page, the action will retrieve the latest postings from the JavaEdge database. These postings will then be made available to the JSP page, called homePage.jsp.

Note If you look at homePage.jsp, you will notice that it is very small and that it does not seem to contain any content. homePage.jsp describes the physical layout of the page in terms of individual screen components. The actual content for the JavaEdge home page is contained in homePageContent.jsp. Chapter 6 will go into greater detail on how to "componentize" your application's screens.

This page displays the latest ten stories in a summarized format and allows the user to log in to JavaEdge and view their personal account information. In addition, the JavaEdge reader is given a link to see the full story and any comments made by the other JavaEdge readers.

To set up the `homePageSetup` action, the following steps must be undertaken:

1. A Struts `<action>` element must be added in the struts-config.xml file.

2. An `Action` class must be written to process the user's request.

3. A JSP page, in this case homePage.jsp, must be written to render the end user's request.

It is important to note that the Struts framework follows all of Sun Microsystems' guidelines for building and deploying web-based applications. The installation instructions, shown here, can be used to configure and deploy Struts-based applications in any J2EE-compliant application server or servlet container.

Configuring the homePageSetup Action Element

Setting up your first struts-config.xml file is a straightforward process. This file can be located in the WEB-INF directory of the JavaEdge project, downloaded from the Apress web site (http://www.apress.com). The location of the struts-config.xml file is also specified in the config attribute, in the web.xml entry of the ActionServlet.

The struts-config.xml file has a root element, called <struts-config>:

```
<?xml version="1.0" encoding="ISO-8859-1"?>
<!DOCTYPE struts-config
   PUBLIC "-//Apache Software Foundation//DTD Struts Configuration 1.1//EN"
          "http://struts.apache.org/dtds/struts-config_1_1.dtd">
<struts-config>
...
</struts-config>
```

All actions for the JavaEdge application are contained in a tag called <action-mappings>. Each action has its own <action> tag. To set up homeSetupAction, you would add the following information to the struts-config.xml file:

```
<?xml version="1.0" encoding="ISO-8859-1"?>
<!DOCTYPE struts-config
   PUBLIC "-//Apache Software Foundation//DTD Struts Configuration 1.1//EN"
          "http://struts.apache.org/dtds/struts-config_1_1.dtd">
<struts-config>
  <action-mappings>
    <action
      path="/homePageSetup"
      type="com.apress.javaedge.struts.homepage.HomePageSetupAction"
      unknown="true">
      <forward name="homepage.success" path="/WEB-INF/jsp/homePage.jsp"/>
    </action>
  </action-mappings>
</struts-config>
```

An action has a number of different attributes that can be set. In this chapter, we will only be concerned with the path, type, and unknown attributes of the <action> element. The other <action> element attributes are discussed in Chapter 3. Let's now discuss the previously mentioned attributes briefly.

- path: Holds the action name. When an end-user request is made to the ActionServlet, it will search all of the actions defined in the struts-config.xml file and try to make a match, based on the value of the path attribute.

  If the ActionServlet finds a match, it will use the information in the rest of the <action> element to determine how to fulfill the user's request. In the preceding example, if users point their web browser to http://localhost:8080/JavaEdge/homePageSetup, the ActionServlet will locate the action by finding the <action> element's path attribute that matches /homePageSetup. It is important to note that all path names are case sensitive.

■**Note** Note that all values in the path attribute for an action must start with a forward slash (/) to map to the attribute. If you fail to put this in your path attribute, Struts will not find your action.

- type: Holds the fully qualified name of the Action class. If the user invokes the URL shown in the preceding bullet, the ActionServlet will instantiate an Action subclass of type com.apress.javaedge.struts.homepage.HomePageSetupAction. This class will contain all of the logic to look up the latest ten stories that are going to be displayed to the end user.

- unknown: Can be used by only one <action> element in the entire struts-config.xml file. When set to true, this tag tells the ActionServlet to use this <action> element as the default behavior whenever it cannot find a path attribute that matches the end user's requested action. This prevents the user from entering a wrong URL and, as a result, getting an error screen. Since the JavaEdge home page is the starting point for the entire application, we set the homePageSetup action as the default action for all unmatched requests. Only one <action> tag can have its unknown attribute set to true. The first one encountered, in the struts-config.xml file, will be used and all others will be ignored. If the unknown attribute is not specified in the <action> tag, the Struts ActionServlet will take it as false. The false value simply means that Struts will not treat the action as the default action.

An <action> tag can contain one or more <forward> tags. A <forward> tag is used to indicate where the users are to be directed after their request has been processed. It consists of two attributes, name and path. The name attribute is the name of the forward. Its value is the user-defined value that can be arbitrarily determined. The path attribute holds a relative URL, to which the user is directed by the ActionServlet after the action is completed. The value of the name attribute of the <forward> tag is a completely arbitrary name. However, this attribute is going to be used heavily by the Action class defined in the <action> tag. Later in this chapter, when we demonstrate the HomePageSetupAction class, you will find out how an Action class uses the <forward> tags for handling the screen navigation. When multiple <forward> tags exist in a single action, the Action class carrying out the processing can indicate to the ActionServlet that the user can be sent to multiple locations.

Exception handling has been greatly improved since the Struts 1.1 release. Struts now allows developers to register unchecked exceptions raised in the Struts action with the Struts ActionServlet. This concept, known as *exception handlers*, relieves developers of the need to clutter up their Action code with what is essentially the same application exception logic. Refer to Chapter 4 for more details on handling exceptions in Struts.

Sometimes, you might have to reuse the same <forward> tag across multiple <action> tags. For example, in the JavaEdge application, if an exception is raised in the business tier, it is caught and rewrapped as an ApplicationException.

In Struts version 1.0x of the JavaEdge application, when an ApplicationException is caught in an Action class, the JavaEdge application will forward the end user to a properly formatted error page. Rather than repeating the same <forward> tag in each Struts action defined in the application, you can define it to be global. This is done by adding a <global-forwards> tag at the beginning of the struts-config.xml file:

```
<?xml version="1.0" encoding="ISO-8859-1"?>
<!DOCTYPE struts-config
  PUBLIC "-//Apache Software Foundation//DTD Struts Configuration 1.1//EN"
       "http://struts.apache.org/dtds/struts-config_1_1.dtd">
<struts-config>
```

```
<global-forwards type="org.apache.struts.action.ActionForward">
  <forward name="system.error" path="/WEB-INF/jsp/systemError.jsp"/>
</global-forwards>
<action-mappings>
     ...
</action-mappings>
</struts-config>
```

The `<global-forwards>` tag has one attribute, called type, which defines the `ActionForward` class that forwards the user to another location. Struts is an extremely pluggable framework, and it is possible for a development team to override the base functionality of the Struts `ActionForward` class with its own implementation. If your development team is not going to override the base `ActionForward` functionality, the type attribute should always be set to `org.apache.struts.action.ActionForward`. After the `<global-forwards>` tag is added to the struts-config.xml file, any `Action` class in the JavaEdge application can redirect a user to `systemError.jsp` by indicating to the `ActionServlet` that the user's destination is the `system.error` forward.

Now let's discuss the corresponding `Action` class of the `homePageSetup`, that is, `HomePageSetupAction.java`.

Building HomePageSetupAction.java

The `HomePageSetupAction` class, which is located in the src/java/com/apress/javaedge/struts/homepage/HomePageSetupAction.java file, is used to retrieve the top postings made by JavaEdge users. The code for this `Action` class is shown here:

```java
package com.apress.javaedge.struts.homepage;

import com.apress.javaedge.common.ApplicationException;
import com.apress.javaedge.story.StoryManagerBD;
import com.apress.javaedge.story.IStoryManager;
import org.apache.struts.action.Action;
import org.apache.struts.action.ActionForm;
import org.apache.struts.action.ActionForward;
import org.apache.struts.action.ActionMapping;

import javax.servlet.http.HttpServletRequest;
import javax.servlet.http.HttpServletResponse;
import java.util.Collection;

/**
 *  Retrieves the top ten posting on JavaEdge.
 */
public class HomePageSetupAction extends Action {

    /** The execute() method comes from the base Struts Action class. You
     * override this method and put the logic to carry out the user's
     * request in the overridden method.
```

```
        */
        public ActionForward execute(ActionMapping mapping,
                                     ActionForm    form,
                                     HttpServletRequest request,
                                     HttpServletResponse response) {


            IStoryManager storyManagerBD = StoryManagerBD.getStoryManagerBD();
            Collection topStories = storyManagerBD.findTopStory();
            request.setAttribute("topStories", topStories);

            return (mapping.findForward("homepage.success"));
        }
    }
```

Before we begin with the discussion on the HomePageSetupAction class, let's have a look at the Command design pattern.

The Power of the Command Pattern

The Action class is an extremely powerful development metaphor, because it is implemented using the Command design pattern.

DESIGN PATTERNS IN STRUTS

This chapter introduces the Command pattern. According to the Gang of Four's (Erich Gamma, Richard Helm, Ralph Johnson, and John Vlissides) definition, a Command pattern

Encapsulates a request as an object, thereby letting you parameterize clients with different requests . . .

—Design Patterns, Elements of Reusable Object-Oriented Software
(Addison-Wesley, ISBN: 0-20163-361-2), p. 233

A Command pattern lets the developer encapsulate a set of behaviors in an object and provides a standard interface for executing that behavior. Other objects can also invoke the behavior, but they have no exposure to how the behavior is implemented. This pattern is implemented with a concrete class and either an abstract class or an interface.

The JavaEdge application uses different J2EE design patterns such as the Business Delegate and Value Object patterns. Chapters 4 and 5 will explore these patterns in greater detail.

The parent class or interface contains a single method definition (usually named perform() or execute()) that carries out some kind of action. The actual behavior for the requested action is implemented in a child class (which, in this example, is HomePageSetupAction), extending the Command class. The Struts Action class is the parent class in the Command pattern implementation. Figure 2-5 illustrates the relationship between the Action and HomePageSetupAction classes.

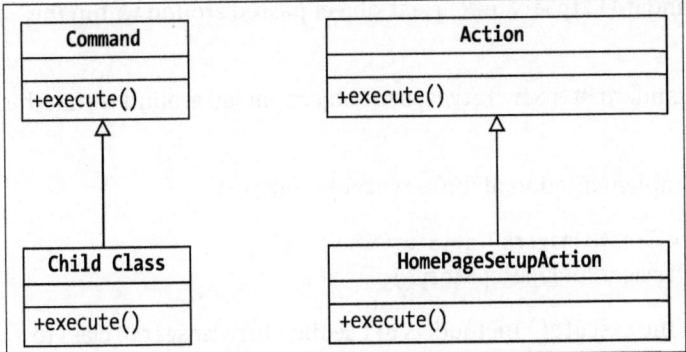

Figure 2-5. *A simple object model of the Action and HomePageSetupAction classes*

The use of the Command design pattern is one of reasons why Struts is so flexible. The ActionServlet does not care how a user request is to be executed. It only knows that it has a class that descends from Action and will have an execute() method. When the end user makes a request, the ActionServlet just executes the execute() method in the class that has been defined in struts-config.xml. If the development team wants to change the way in which an end-user request is processed, it can do it in two ways: either rewrite the code for the already implemented Action class or write a new Action class and modify the struts-config.xml file to point to the new Action class. The ActionServlet never knows that this change has occurred. Later in this section, we will discuss how Struts' flexible architecture can be used to solve the Hardwired antipattern. For the sake of this discussion on the Command pattern, let's go back to the HomePageSetupAction class.

The first step in writing the HomeSetupAction class is to extend the Struts Action class:

```
public class HomePageSetupAction extends Action
```

Next, the execute() method for the class needs to be overridden. (In the Action class source code, several execute() methods can be overridden, some of which are deprecated as of version 1.1. Other methods allow you to make requests to Struts from a non-HTTP-based call. For the purpose of this book, we will be dealing with only HTTP-based execute() methods.)

```
public ActionForward execute(ActionMapping mapping,
                    ActionForm form,
                    HttpServletRequest request,
                    HttpServletResponse response){

}
```

The execute() method signature takes four parameters:

- ActionMapping: Used to find an ActionForward from the struts-config.xml file and return it to the ActionServlet. This ActionForward class contains all the information needed by the ActionServlet to forward end users to the next page in the application.

- ActionForm: A helper class that is used to hold any form data submitted by the end user. The ActionForm class is not being used in the HomePageSetupAction class shown earlier. This class will be discussed in greater detail in Chapters 3 and 4.

- HttpServletRequest: A standard HttpServletRequest object passed around within the servlet.

- HttpServletResponse: A standard HttpServletResponse object passed around within the servlet.

Now let's look at the actual implementation of the execute() method:

```
IStoryManager storyManagerBD = StoryManagerBD.getStoryManagerBD();
Collection topStories = storyManagerBD.findTopStory();
```

The first step, carried out by the execute() method, is to use the StoryManagerBD class to retrieve a business delegate of type IStoryManager. The storyManagerBD variable is then used to retrieve a Collection, called topStories, of the top stories currently submitted to the JavaEdge application. The topStories collection holds up to ten instances of type StoryVO. A StoryVO is based on the J2EE design pattern called the *Value Object pattern*. A value object is used to wrap data retrieved from a data source in a Java-based implementation-neutral interface. Each StoryVO in the topStories collection represents a single row of data retrieved from the JavaEdge database's story table.

The Business Delegate pattern is a J2EE design pattern used to abstract away how a piece of business logic is actually being invoked and carried out. In the preceding example, the HomePageSetupAction class does not know how the StoryManagerBD class is actually retrieving the collection of stories. The StoryManagerBD could be using an EJB, Web service, or a Plain Old Java Object to carry out the requested action.

Note The term *J2EE patterns* is a bit of a misnomer. The Business Delegate pattern and Value Object pattern—also known as the Data Transfer Object pattern—were used in other languages before Java. However, they were called J2EE patterns when the patterns were explained in the book *Core J2EE Design Patterns: Best Practices and Design Strategies* (Alur et al., Prentice Hall, ISBN: 0-13064-884-1).

After the storyManagerBD.findTopStory() method is executed, the topStories object will be placed as an attribute of the request object:

```
request.setAttribute("topStories", topStories);
```

When the ActionServlet forwards this to the homePage.jsp page (as defined in the struts-config.xml file), the homePage.jsp will be able to walk through each item in the topStories Collection and display the data in it to the end user.

Once the story data has been retrieved, an ActionForward will be generated by calling the findForward() method in the mapping object passed into the execute() method:

```
return (mapping.findForward("homepage.success"));
```

We have finished showing you how to configure the struts-config.xml file and build an Action class to prepopulate the JavaEdge's home screen with story data. Before we look at the JSP file, homePage.jsp, let's discuss how to refactor the Hardwired antipattern.

Refactoring the Hardwired Antipattern

The declarative architecture of the Struts development framework provides a powerful tool for avoiding or refactoring a Hardwired antipattern. (Refer to Chapter 1 for the discussion of Hardwired and other antipatterns.)

All activities executed by the user in a Struts-based application should be captured within an <action> tag defined in the struts-config.xml file. Using an <action> tag gives the developer flexibility in the way in which the screen navigation and application of business rules are carried.

The advantage of using the <action> tag is that it forces the development team members to take a declarative approach to writing their applications. It decouples the various pieces of code associated with building out a screen from one another. For instance, when JSP developers build an application without the Struts framework, they oftentimes will have a JSP page directly invoke a piece of business logic to process a user's request.

This essentially "hardwires" the JSP page to that piece of business logic. If you want to change the behavior of the application, you need to either rewrite the class containing the business logic or have the JSP call a completely different method or class containing the new business logic. The problem is that modifying the relationship between the calling code (the JSP) and the called code (the Java class containing the business logic) is easy to do when dealing with one or two applications. However, maintaining this type of relationship in an enterprise environment where the same caller/called relationship might occur in 10 to 20 applications can be extremely difficult.

What the <action> tag allows is for the development team to extract the caller/called relationship out of the code into a metadata file (struts-config.xml). The development team describes caller/called relationships in a declarative fashion, rather than programmatically. If the development team wants to change the behavior of a screen in an application, it can modify the <action> tag to describe a new Struts Action class to carry out users' requests. The development team still has to write code to implement the new functionality, but there are now fewer touchpoints in the existing application that it has to modify.

This all ties back to the following:

■Note If you touch the code, you break the code. The less code you have to modify to implement new functionality, the less chance there is that existing functionality will be broken and cause a ripple of destructive behavior through your applications.

According to our experience, while building a Struts application, <action> elements defined within the application fall into three general categories:

- *Setup actions*: Used to perform any activities that take place before the user sees a screen. In the JavaEdge home page example, you use the /HomePageSetup action to retrieve the top stories from the JavaEdge database and place them as an attribute in the HttpServletRequest object.

- *Form actions*: Actions that will process the data collected from the end user.

- *Tear-down actions*: Can be invoked after a user's request has been processed. Usually, this type of action carries out any cleanup needed after the user's request has been processed.

These three types of actions are purely conceptual. There is no way in the Struts `<action>` tag to indicate that the action being defined is a setup, form, or tear-down action. However, this classification is very useful for your own Struts applications. A setup action allows you to easily enforce "precondition" logic before sending a user to a form. This logic ensures that, before the user even sees the page, certain conditions are met. Setup actions are particularly useful when you have to prepopulate a page with data. In Chapters 3 and 4, when we discuss how to collect the user data in Struts, you will find several examples of a setup action used to prepopulate a form. In addition, putting a setup action before a page gives you more flexibility in maneuvering the user. This setup action can examine the current application state of end users, and based on this state navigate them to any number of other Struts actions or JSP pages.

A form action is invoked when the user submits the data entered in an HTML form. It might insert a record into a database or just perform some simple data formatting on the data entered by the user.

A tear-down action is used to enforce "postcondition" logic. This logic ensures that after the user's request has been processed, the data needed by the application is still in a valid state. Tear-down actions might also be used to release any resources previously acquired by the end user.

As you become more comfortable with Struts, you will prefer chaining together the different actions. You will use the setup action to enforce preconditions that must exist when the user makes the initial request. The setup action usually retrieves some data from a database and puts it in one of the different JSP page contexts (that is, page, request, session, or application context). It then forwards the user to a JSP page that will display the retrieved data. If the JSP page contains a form, the user will be forwarded to a form action that will process the user's request. The form action will then forward the user to a tear-down action that will enforce any postcondition rules. If all postcondition rules are met, the tear-down action will forward the user to the next JSP page the user is going to visit.

It's important to note that by using the strategies previously defined, you can change an application's behavior by reconfiguring the struts-config.xml file. This is a better approach than to go constantly into the application source code and modify the existing business logic.

With this discussion on the Hardwired antipattern wrapped up, let's have a look at home-Page.jsp and the Struts tag libraries that are used to render the HTML page that users will see after the request has been processed.

Constructing the Presentation Tier

Now we are going to look at how many of the Struts custom JSP tag libraries can be used to simplify the development of the presentation tier. With careful design and use of these tag libraries, you can literally write JSP pages without ever writing a single Java scriptlet. The Struts development framework has four sets of custom tag libraries:

- Bean
- Logic
- HTML
- Tiles

We will not be discussing the Struts HTML or the Struts Tiles tag libraries in this chapter. Instead, we will discuss these tags in Chapters 4 and 6, respectively.

Before we begin our discussion of the individual tag libraries, the web.xml file for the JavaEdge application has to be modified to include the following Tag Library Definitions (TLDs):

```
<web-app>
  ...
  <taglib>
      <taglib-uri>/taglibs/struts-bean</taglib-uri>
      <taglib-location>/WEB-INF/taglibs/struts-bean.tld</taglib-location>
  </taglib>

  <taglib>
      <taglib-uri>/taglibs/struts-html</taglib-uri>
      <taglib-location>/WEB-INF/taglibs/struts-html.tld</taglib-location>
  </taglib>

  <taglib>
      <taglib-uri>/taglibs/struts-logic</taglib-uri>
      <taglib-location>/WEB-INF/taglibs/struts-logic.tld</taglib-location>
  </taglib>

  <taglib>
      <taglib-uri>http://jakarta.apache.org/taglibs/veltag-1.0</taglib-uri>
      <taglib-location>/WEB-INF/taglibs/veltag.tld</taglib-location>
  </taglib>

  <taglib>
      <taglib-uri>/taglibs/struts-tiles</taglib-uri>
      <taglib-location>/WEB-INF/taglibs/struts-tiles.tld</taglib-location>
  </taglib>
</web-app>
```

With these TLDs added to the web.xml file, we next look at the first page in the JavaEdge application that an end user will encounter: the JavaEdge home page.

The JavaEdge Home Page

All of the pages in the JavaEdge application are broken into three core components: a header, footer, and page body. All of the pages share the same header and footer. Let's look at the header and footer JSP files (header.jsp and footer.jsp) for all JavaEdge JSP pages and the source code for the homePageContent.jsp. We are not going to go into the actual page in great deal in this section. Instead, we will explore the different Struts tags and demonstrate their use throughout the rest of this book as we construct the JavaEdge application.

Note There are two sets of JSP files in the JavaEdge application. When using the URLs listed in the book for the JavaEdge application, you are going to be using JSP files using the `<template>` tags found in Struts 1.0x. These files were kept in here for backward compatibility with the first edition of this book. The `<template>` tags are going to be deprecated in future of releases of Struts.

In Chapter 6, we look at a second set of JSP files based on the Tiles framework; these replaced the `<template>` tags. The JSP files in the first set use the exact same set of JSP code, with the only difference being how the screens are componentized. So anything you see in this chapter and the following regarding the JSP tag libraries is applicable to the code seen in Chapter 6.

header.jsp

Following is the code for the header JSP file:

```
<%@ page language="java" %>
<%@ taglib uri="/taglibs/struts-bean" prefix="bean" %>
<%@ taglib uri="/taglibs/struts-html" prefix="html" %>
<%@ taglib uri="/taglibs/struts-logic" prefix="logic" %>
<%@ taglib uri="/taglibs/struts-template" prefix="template" %>

<font size="7"><bean:message key="javaedge.header.title"/></font></p>

<div align="center">
  <center>
  <html:form action="login">
  <table border="0" cellpadding="0"
            cellspacing="0" style="border-collapse: collapse"
            bordercolor="#111111" width="100%" id="AutoNumber1"
            bgcolor="#FF66FF">
    <tr>
      <logic:notEqual scope="session"
            name="memberVO" property="memberId" value="1">
        <td width="16%" bgcolor="#99CCFF" align="center">
          <bean:message key="javaedge.header.logout"/>
        </td>
      </logic:notEqual>
      <logic:notEqual scope="session"
            name="memberVO" property="memberId" value="1">
        <td width="17%" bgcolor="#99CCFF" align="center">
          <bean:message key="javaedge.header.myaccount"/>
        </td>
      </logic:notEqual>

      <td width="17%" bgcolor="#99CCFF" align="center">
        <bean:message key="javaedge.header.postastory"/>
      </td>

      <td width="17%" bgcolor="#99CCFF" align="center">
        <bean:message key="javaedge.header.viewallstories"/>
      </td>

      <td width="17%" bgcolor="#99CCFF" align="center">
```

```
              <bean:message key="javaedge.header.search"/>
          </td>

        <logic:equal scope="session" name="memberVO" property="memberId" value="1">
          <td width="17%" bgcolor="#99CCFF" align="center">
            <bean:message key="javaedge.header.signup"/>
          </td>
        </logic:equal>
    </tr>
    <tr>
        <logic:equal scope="session" name="memberVO" property="memberId" value="1">
          <td width="16%" bgcolor="#99CCFF" align="left" colspan="4">
            <bean:message key="javaedge.header.userid"/>
                    <input type="text" name="userId"/>
            <bean:message key="javaedge.header.password"/>
                    <input type="password" name="password"/>
            <html:submit property="submitButton" value="Submit"/>
            <html:errors property="invalid.login"/>
          </td>
        </logic:equal>
    </tr>

  </table>
  </html:form>
  </center>
</div>
```

footer.jsp

Next is the code for the footer JSP file:

```
<%@ page language="java" %>
<%@ taglib uri="/taglibs/struts-bean" prefix="bean" %>
<%@ taglib uri="/taglibs/struts-html" prefix="html" %>
<%@ taglib uri="/taglibs/struts-logic" prefix="logic" %>
<%@ taglib uri="/taglibs/struts-template" prefix="template" %>

<table border="0" cellpadding="0"
          cellspacing="0" style="border-collapse: collapse"
          bordercolor="#111111" width="100%"
          id="AutoNumber1" bgcolor="#FF66FF">
    <tr bgcolor="#99CCFF">
        <td>
            
        </td>
    </tr>
</table>
```

homePageContent.jsp

Here is the code for homePageContent.jsp:

```
<%@ page language="java" %>
<%@ taglib uri="/taglibs/struts-bean" prefix="bean" %>
<%@ taglib uri="/taglibs/struts-html" prefix="html" %>
<%@ taglib uri="/taglibs/struts-logic" prefix="logic" %>
<%@ taglib uri="/taglibs/struts-template" prefix="template" %>

<BR/><BR/>
<H1>Today's Top Stories</H1>
<TABLE>
      <logic:iterate id="story" name="topStories"
            scope="request" type="com.apress.javaedge.story.StoryVO">
        <TR bgcolor="#99CCFF">
            <TD>

                <bean:write name="story" scope="page" property="storyTitle"/><BR/>
                <FONT size="1">
                   Posted By: <bean:write name="story"
                                           property="storyAuthor.firstName"/>
                   <bean:write name="story" property="storyAuthor.lastName"/>
                   on <bean:write name="story" property="submissionDate"/>
                </FONT>
            </TD>
        </TR>
        <TR>
          <TD>
            <bean:write name="story" property="storyIntro"/>
          </TD>
        </TR>
        <TR>
          <TD align="right">
            <a href='/JavaEdge/execute/storyDetailSetup?storyId=③
               <bean:write name="story" property="storyId"/>'>
                        Full Story</a><BR/><BR/>
          </TD>
        </TR>
      </logic:iterate>
  </TABLE>
```

Now let's break these different pages apart and see how the Struts JSP tag libraries were used to build the pages. Let's start with the Struts bean tags.

Bean Tags

Well-designed JSP pages use JavaBeans to separate the presentation logic in the application from the data that is going to be displayed on the screen. A JavaBean is a regular class that can contain the data and logic. In the JavaEdge home page example, the HomePageSetupAction class retrieves a set of StoryVO objects into a collection and puts them into the session. The StoryVO class is a JavaBean that encapsulates all of the data for a single story posted in the JavaEdge database. Each data element, stored within a StoryVO object, has a getXXX() and setXXX() method for each property. The code for the StoryVO class is shown here:

```
package com.apress.javaedge.story;

    import com.apress.javaedge.common.ValueObject;
    import com.apress.javaedge.member.MemberVO;

    import java.util.Vector;

    /**
     * Holds story data retrieved from the JavaEdge database.
     */
    public class StoryVO extends ValueObject {

        private Long storyId;
        private String storyTitle;
        private String storyIntro;
        private byte[] storyBody;
        private java.sql.Date submissionDate;
        private Long memberId;
        private MemberVO storyAuthor;
        public Vector comments = new Vector(); // of type StoryCommentVO


        public Long getStoryId() {
            return storyId;
        }

        public void setStoryId(Long storyId) {
            this.storyId = storyId;
        }

        public String getStoryTitle() {
            return storyTitle;
        }

        public void setStoryTitle(String storyTitle) {
            this.storyTitle = storyTitle;
        }
```

```java
    public String getStoryIntro() {
        return storyIntro;
    }

    public void setStoryIntro(String storyIntro) {
        this.storyIntro = storyIntro;
    }

    public String getStoryBody() {
        return new String(storyBody);
    }

    public void setStoryBody(String storyBody) {
        this.storyBody = storyBody.getBytes();
    }


    public java.sql.Date getSubmissionDate() {
        return submissionDate;
    }

    public void setSubmissionDate(java.sql.Date submissionDate) {
        this.submissionDate = submissionDate;
    }


    public Vector getComments() {
        return comments;
    }

    public void setComments(Vector comments) {
        this.comments = comments;
    }

    public MemberVO getStoryAuthor() {
        return storyAuthor;
    }

    public void setStoryAuthor(MemberVO storyAuthor) {
        this.storyAuthor = storyAuthor;
    }
} // end StoryVO
```

The JSP specification defines a number of JSP tags that give the developer the ability to manipulate the contents of a JavaBean.

The Struts Bean tag library offers a significant amount of functionality beyond that offered by the standard JSP tag libraries. The functionality provided by the Bean tag library can be broken into two broad categories of functionality:

- Generating output from an existing JavaBean residing in the page, request, or session scope.

- Creating new JavaBeans. These new JavaBeans can hold the data specified by the developer or retrieved from web artifacts, such as a cookie or a value stored in an HTTP header.

We are going to begin with the most common use of the Struts bean tag, the retrieval and display of data from a JavaBean.

Two bean tags are available for generating output in the Struts Bean tag library:

- <bean:write>

- <bean:message>

The <bean:write> tag retrieves a value from a JavaBean and writes it to the web page being generated. Examples of this tag can be found throughout the homePageContent.jsp file. For example, the following code will retrieve the value of the property (storyTitle) from a bean, called story, stored in the page context:

```
<bean:write name="story" scope="page" property="storyTitle"/><BR/>
```

To achieve the same result via a Java scriptlet would require the following code:

```
<%
  StoryVO story = (StoryVO) pageContext.getAttribute("story");

  if (story != null){
    out.write(story.getStoryTitle());
  }
  else{
    //Throw an exception unless the <bean:write> ignore attribute is
    // set to true.
  }
%>
```

The <bean:write> tag supports the concept of the nested property values. For instance, the StoryVO class has a property called storyAuthor. This property holds an instance of a MemberVO object. The MemberVO class contains the data about the user who posted the original story. The homePageContent.jsp page retrieves the values from a MemberVO object by using a nested notation in the <bean:write> tag. For instance, to retrieve the first name of the user who posted one of the stories to be displayed, the following syntax is used:

```
<bean:write name="story" property="storyAuthor.firstName"/>
```

In the preceding example, the <bean:write> tag is retrieving the storyAuthor by calling story.getStoryAuthor() and then the firstName property by calling storyAuthor.getFirstName().

The <bean:write> tag has the attributes listed in Table 2-3.

Table 2-3. *Attributes for the <bean:write> Tag*

Attribute Name	Attribute Description
filter	Determines whether or not characters that are sensitive in HTML should be replaced with their & counterparts. For example, if the data retrieved from a call to StoryVO.getTitle() contains an & symbol, setting the filter attribute to true would cause the <bean:write> tag to write the character as &amp. The default value for this attribute is true.
ignore	When set to true, this attribute tells the <bean:write> not to throw a runtime exception, if the bean name cannot be located in the scope specified. The <bean:write> tag will simply generate an empty string to be displayed in the page. (If scope is not specified, the same rules apply here, as specified previously.) If this attribute is not set or is set to false, a runtime exception will be thrown by the <bean:write> tag, if the requested bean cannot be found.
name	The name of the JavaBean to be retrieved.
property	The name of the property to be retrieved from the JavaBean. The <bean:write> tag uses the reflection to call the appropriate get() method of the JavaBean from which you are retrieving the data. Therefore, your JavaBean has to follow the standard JavaBean naming conventions (that is, a get prefix followed by the first letter of the method name capitalized).
scope	The scope in which to look for the JavaBean. Valid values include page, request, and session. If this attribute is not set, the <bean:write> tag will start searching for the bean at the page level and continue until it finds the bean.

The second type of tag for generating output is the Struts <bean:message> tag. The <bean:message> tag is used to separate the static content from the JSP page in which it resides. All the contents are stored in a properties file, independent of the application. The properties file consists of a name-value pair, where each piece of the text that is to be externalized is associated with a key. The <bean:message> tag will use this key to look up a particular piece of text from the properties file.

To tell the name of the properties file to the ActionServlet, you need to make sure that the application parameter is set in the web.xml file. The properties file, usually called ApplicationResources.properties, is placed in the classes directory underneath the WEB-INF directory of the deployed applications. In the JavaEdge source tree, the ApplicationResources. properties file is located in working directory/waf/src/web/WEB-INF/classes (where working directory is the one in which you are editing and compiling the application source).

For the purpose of the JavaEdge application, an <init-param> tag must be configured as shown here:

```
<servlet>
  ...
  <init-param>
    <param-name>application</param-name>
    <param-value>ApplicationResources</param-value>
  </init-param>
</Servlet>
```

The static content for the JavaEdge application has not been completely externalized using the `<bean:message>` functionality. Only the header.jsp file has been externalized. The following `<bean:message>` example, taken directly from header.jsp, will return the complete URL for the JavaEdge login page:

```
<bean:message key="javaedge.header.logout"/>
```

When this tag call is processed, it will retrieve the value for the `javaedge.header.logout` key from the ApplicationResources.properties file. All of the name-value pairs from the ApplicationResources.properties file used in the header.jsp file are shown here:

```
javaedge.header.title=The Java Edge
javaedge.header.logout=<a href="/JavaEdge/execute/LogoutSetup">Logout</a>
javaedge.header.myaccount=<a href="/JavaEdge/execute/MyAccountSetup">My Account</a>
javaedge.header.postastory=<a href="/JavaEdge/execute/postStorySetup">
     Post a Story</a>
javaedge.header.viewallstories=<a href="/JavaEdge/execute/ViewAllSetup">
     View All Stories</a>
javaedge.header.signup=<a href="/JavaEdge/execute/signUpSetup">Sign Up</a>
javaedge.header.search=<a href="/JavaEdge/execute/SearchSetup">Search</a>
```

If the `<bean:message>` tag cannot find this key in the ApplicationResources.properties file, the `<bean:message>` tag will throw a runtime exception.

The `<bean:message>` tag has the attributes listed in Table 2-4.

Table 2-4. *Attributes for the <bean:message> Tag*

Attribute Name	Attribute Description
arg0	Parameter value that can be passed into the text string retrieved from the properties file. For instance, if a property had the value hello.world=Hi {0}!, using `<bean:message key="hello.world" arg="John"/>` would return the following text to the output stream: Hi John!. The `<bean:message>` tag can support at most five parameters being passed to a message.
arg1	Second parameter value that can be passed to the text string retrieved from the properties file.
arg2	Third parameter value that can be passed to the text string retrieved from the properties file.
arg3	Fourth parameter value that can be passed to the text string retrieved from the properties file.
arg4	Fifth parameter value that can be passed to the text string retrieved from the properties file.
bundle	The name of the application scope bean in which the MessageResources object containing the application messages is stored.
key	Key in the properties file for which the `<bean:message>` tag is going to look.
locale	The name of the session scope bean in which the Locale object is stored.

Next we'll have an interesting discussion on the Tight-Skins antipattern before moving on to bean creation.

The Tight-Skins Antipattern

Recollecting our discussion in Chapter 1, the Tight-Skins antipattern occurs when the development team does not have a presentation tier whose look and feel can be easily customized. The Tight-Skins antipattern is formed when the development team embeds the static content in the JSP pages. Any changes to the static content result in having to hunt through all of the pages in the application and making the required changes.

As you saw earlier, the <bean:message> tag can be used to centralize all the static content in an application to a single file called ApplicationResources.properties. However, the real strength of this tag is it makes it very easy to write internationalized applications that can support multiple languages. The JavaEdge header toolbar is written to support only English. However, if you want the JavaEdge's header toolbar to support French, you need to follow these steps:

1. Create a new file called ApplicationResources_fr.properties.

   The _fr extension to the ApplicationResources.properties file is not just a naming convention followed here. This extension is part of the ISO-3166 standard. For a complete list of all of the country codes supported by this standard, please visit http://www.ics. uci.edu/pub/ietf/http/related/iso639.txt.

2. Copy all of the name-value pairs from the JavaEdge's application into the new ApplicationResources_fr.properties file. Translate all of the static contents in these name-value pairs to French. Also, if the JavaEdge application is going to support only French, you may rename the file from ApplicationResources_fr.properties to ApplicationResources.properties and replace the existing ApplicationResources.properties file. However, if you want to support English and French at the same time, you to need to tell Struts which java.util.Locale is to be used for the user. A Locale object is part of the standard Java SDK and is used to hold the information about a region. For more details on the Locale object, please refer to the Sun JDK documentation (available at http://java.sun.com).

3. To support both English and French concurrently, you could ask the users the language in which they want to see the site when they are registering for a JavaEdge account. Their language preference could be stored in the JavaEdge database. If a user chooses French as their language preference, then anytime that user logs in to the JavaEdge application, the following code could be executed in any Action class to switch the language preference from English over to French:

```
HttpSession session = request.getSession();
session.setAttribute(org.apache.struts.action.Action.LOCALE_KEY,
                 new java.util.Locale(LOCALE.FRENCH, LOCALE.FRENCH) );
```

Struts stores a Locale object in the session as the attribute key org.apache.struts.action.Action.LOCALE_KEY. Including a new Locale object (which is instantiated with the values for French) will cause Struts to reference the ApplicationResources_fr.properties file for the time for which the user's session is valid (or at least until a new Locale object containing another region's information is placed in the user's session).

Accessing Indexed or Mapped Data

The Struts JSP tag libraries allow you to directly access a Java object stored inside of an `Array`, `List`, or `Map` object. For example, say you modified the `MemberVO` class to contain an array of all of the addresses associated with the JavaEdge user. This modification would get() and set() a `String` array containing all of the address information:

```
public String[] getAddresses(){
    return addresses;
}

public void setAddresses(String[] addresses){
    this.addresses=addresses;
}
```

As you will see later in the chapter, you can walk through the returned array by using the `<logic:iterate>` tag to retrieve each individual address stored in the array or `Collection`. However, if you wanted to directly access an address via an array index, you can use the following syntax:

```
<bean:write name="memberVO" scope="request" property="addresses[1] "/>
```

Behind the scenes, the preceding code would be the equivalent of the following JSP code:

```
<%
    MemberVO memberVO = (MemberVO) request.getAttribute("memberVO");

    String[] addresses = memberVO.getAddresses();
    out.write(addresses[1]);
%>
```

Now let's make the address code a little bit more sophisticated. Let's create a value object, called `AddressVO`, to hold the entire address record. The code for `AddressVO` is shown here:

```
package com.apress.javaedge.member;

public class AddressVO {
    public static final String HOME_ADDRESS="HOME";
    public static final String BUSINESS_ADDRESS="BUS";
    public static final String TEMPORARY_ADDRESS="TEMP";

    private String addressId;
    private String addressType;
    private String street1;
    private String street2;
    private String street3;
    private String city;
    private String state;
    private String zip;
    private String country;
```

```java
    public String getCountry() {
        return country;
    }

    public void setCountry(String country) {
        this.country = country;
    }

    public String getZip() {
        return zip;
    }

    public void setZip(String zip) {
        this.zip = zip;
    }

    public String getAddressId() {
        return addressId;
    }

    public void setAddressId(String addressId) {
        this.addressId = addressId;
    }

    public String getAddressType() {
        return addressType;
    }

    public void setAddressType(String addressType) {
        this.addressType = addressType;
    }

    public String getStreet1() {
        return street1;
    }

    public void setStreet1(String street1) {
        this.street1 = street1;
    }

    public String getStreet2() {
        return street2;
    }

    public void setStreet2(String street2) {
        this.street2 = street2;
    }
```

```
    public String getStreet3() {
        return street3;
    }

    public void setStreet3(String street3) {
        this.street3 = street3;
    }

    public String getCity() {
        return city;
    }

    public void setCity(String city) {
        this.city = city;
    }

    public String getState() {
        return state;
    }

    public void setState(String state) {
        this.state = state;
    }
}
```

Let's rewrite the getAddress() and setAddress() methods to return a specific AddressVO. The getAddress() and setAddress() methods would "wrapper" a HashMap object and allow the user to return a specific address by a type: BUSINESS, HOME, or TEMPORARY. The getAddress() and setAddress() methods on the MemberVO for retrieving the addresses would look something like this:

```
public void setAddress (String addressType, Object address){
  addresses.put(addressType, address);
}

public Object getAddress(String addressType)
  Object holder = addresses.get(addressType);

  if (holder==null) return "";

  return holder;
}
```

If you want to use a Struts custom tag library to access directly a property on the business address for a JavaEdge member, the syntax would look something like this:

```
<bean:write name="memberVO" scope="request"
            property="address(BUSINESS).street1"/>
```

The preceding code translates into the following JSP code:

```
<%
    MemberVO memberVO = (MemberVO) request.getAttribute("memberVO");
    out.write(memberVO.getAddress("BUSINESS").getStreet1());
%>
```

One thing to be concerned about is ensuring the value returned from the HashMap is actually a valid object. If the object being requested is not found, the getAddress() method must decide how to handle the returned NULL value.

The concept of accessing mapped properties is an extremely powerful one. We will explore it in greater detail in Chapter 3, where we will examine how to use the HashMap and the ActionForm classes to build dynamic ActionForms.

Bean Creation

Struts offers a number of helper tags (bean creation tags) for creating the JavaBeans to be used within a JSP page. With these tags, a number of tasks can be carried out within the JSP page, without the need to write Java scriptlet code. These tasks include

- Retrieving a value from a cookie and creating a new JavaBean to hold the cookie's contents

- Retrieving an HTTP parameter and storing its value in a new JavaBean

- Retrieving a configuration element of Struts (such as a forward, mapping, or form bean) and storing its information in a JavaBean

- Retrieving an object from the JSP page context (that is, the application, request, response, or session objects)

- Defining a new JavaBean from scratch and placing a value in it

- Copying the contents of a single property from an existing JavaBean into a new JavaBean

Table 2-5 gives a brief summary of the different bean creation tags available.

Table 2-5. *The Different Struts Bean Creation Tags*

Bean Name	Bean Description
<bean:cookie>	Creates a new JavaBean to hold the contents of the specified cookie. To retrieve a cookie named shoppingCart into a bean, you use the following syntax: <bean:cookie id="cart" name="shoppingCart" value="None"/>. This call creates a new JavaBean called cart, which will hold the value stored in the cookie shoppingCart. The value attribute tells the bean to store the string None, if the cookie cannot be found. Essentially, the value attribute allows you to define a default value for a cookie if no cookie with the correct name can be found. If the value attribute is not specified and the cookie cannot be found, a runtime exception will be raised.
<bean:define>	Creates a new JavaBean and populates it with a string value defined by the developer. The following <bean:define> tag creates a JavaBean called hello that will hold the ever ubiquitous phrase, "Hello World": <bean:define id="hello" value="Hello World" scope="session"/>. This bean will be placed in a session of the application.

Bean Name	Bean Description
`<bean:header>`	Creates a new JavaBean and populates it with an item retrieved from the HTTP header. In the following example, the `referer` property is being pulled out of the HTTP header and placed in a bean called `httpReferer`: `<bean:header id="httpReferer" name="referer"/>`. However, since no `value` attribute is being defined, a runtime exception will be thrown if the `referer` value cannot be found in the HTTP header.
`<bean:include>`	Creates a JavaBean to hold the content returned from a call to another URL. The following example will take the content retrieved from a call to the /test.jsp page and place it in a JavaBean called `testInclude`: `<bean:include id="testInclude" name="/test.jsp"/>`.
`<bean:page>`	Creates a new JavaBean to hold an object retrieved from the JSP page context. The following example will retrieve the session object from the `HttpServletRequest` object and place it as a JavaBean called `hSession`: `<bean:page id="hSession" property="session"/>`.
`<bean:parameter>`	Creates a new JavaBean to hold the contents of a parameter retrieved from the `HttpServletRequest` object. To retrieve a request parameter, called `sendEmail`, from the `HttpServletRequest`, you use the following code: `<bean:parameter id="sendEmailFlag" name="sendEmail" value="None"/>`. Like the `<bean:cookie>` tag, if the value attribute is not specified and the requested parameter is not located, a runtime exception will be raised.
`<bean:resource>`	Retrieves the data from a file located in a web application resource file. This data can be retrieved as a string or an `InputStream` object by the tag. The following code will create a new JavaBean, called `webXmlBean`, which will hold the contents of the web.xml file as a string: `<bean:resource id="webXmlBean" name="/web.xml"/>`.
`<bean:struts>`	Creates a new JavaBean to hold the contents of a Struts configuration object. The following `<bean:struts>` tag will retrieve the `homePageSetup` action and place the corresponding object into a JavaBean called `homePageSetupMap`: `<bean:struts id="homePageSetupMap" forward="/homePageSetup"/>`.

We have not used any of the bean creation tags in the JavaEdge application. There is simply no need to use them for any of the pages in this application. Also, in our opinion, most of the bean creation tags can be included in an `Action` class using Java code. According to our experience, the overuse of the bean creation tags can clutter up the presentation code and make it difficult to follow.

Logic Tags

The Logic tag library gives the developer the ability to add a conditional and interactive control to the JSP page without having to write Java scriptlets. These tags can be broken into three basic categories:

- Tags for controlling iteration.

- Tags for determining whether a property in an existing JavaBean is equal to, not equal to, greater than, or less than another value. In addition, there are logic tags that can determine whether or not a JavaBean is present within a particular JSP page context (that is, page, request, session, or application scope).

- Tags for moving (that is, redirecting or forwarding) a user to another page in the application.

Iteration Tags

The Logic tag library has a single tag, called <logic:iterate>, which can be used to cycle through a Collection object in the JSP page context. Recollect that in the HomePageSetupAction class, a collection of StoryVO objects is placed into the request. This collection holds the latest ten stories posted to the JavaEdge site. In the homePageContent.jsp page, you cycle through each of the StoryVO objects in the request by using the <logic:iterate> tag:

```
<logic:iterate id="story" name="topStories" scope="request"
                type="com.apress.javaedge.valueobject.StoryVO">
  <TR bgcolor="#99CCFF">
    <TD>
      <bean:write name="story" scope="page" property="storyTitle"/><BR/>
      ...
</logic:iterate>
```

In the preceding code snippet, the <logic:iterate> tag looks up the topStories collection in the request object of the JSP page. The name attribute defines the name of the collection. The scope attribute defines the scope in which the <logic:iterate> tag is going to search for the JavaBean. The type attribute defines the Java class that is going to be pulled out of the collection, in this case, StoryVO. The id attribute holds the name of the JavaBean, which holds a reference to the StoryVO pulled out of the collection. When referencing an individual bean in the <logic:iterate> tag, you use the <bean:write> tag. The name attribute of the <bean:write> tag must match the id attribute defined in the <logic:iterate>.

```
<bean:write name="story" scope="page" property="storyTitle"/>
```

Keep in mind the following points while using the <logic:iterate> tag:

- Multiple types of collections can be supported by the <logic:iterate> tag. These types include

  - Java Collection objects

  - Java Map objects

  - Arrays of objects or primitives

  - Java Enumeration objects

  - Java Iterator objects

- If your collection can contain NULL values, the <logic:iterate> tag will still go through the actions defined in the loop. It is the developer's responsibility to check if a NULL value is present by using the <logic:present> or <logic:notPresent> tags. (These tags will be covered in the next section, "Conditional Tags.")

Conditional Tags

The Struts development framework also provides a number of tags to perform basic conditional logic. Using these tags, a JSP developer can perform a number of conditional checks on the common servlet container properties. These conditional tags can check for the presence of the value of a piece of data stored as one of the following types:

- Cookie

- HTTP header

- HttpServletRequest parameter

- JavaBean

- Property on a JavaBean

The Struts conditional tags <logic:equal> and <logic:notEqual> can be used to test the equality or nonequality of a value sitting in a cookie, header variable, or JavaBean. For instance, the JavaEdge application always has a memberVO placed in the session of the user using the application.

If the user has not logged in, their session will hold a memberVO object whose memberId property is equal to "1". If they are logged in, the memberVO will hold the data retrieved from the member table. In the header.jsp file, the <logic:equal> and <logic:notEqual> tags are used to determine whether or not a login or logout link should be displayed to the end user:

```
<logic:notEqual scope="session" name="memberVO"
                          property="memberId" value="1">
    <td width="16%" bgcolor="#99CCFF" align="center">
        <bean:message key="javaedge.header.logout"/>
    </td>
</logic:notEqual>
<logic:notEqual scope="session" name="memberVO"
property="memberId" value="1">
    <td width="17%" bgcolor="#99CCFF" align="center">
        <bean:message key="javaedge.header.myaccount"/>
    </td>
</logic:notEqual>
```

Alternatively, you could modify how security is handled in the JavaEdge application and only place a memberVO in the user's session when they have actually logged in. Then you could use the <logic:present> and <logic:notPresent> tags to determine if the user has logged in and then display the corresponding login/logout links:

```
<logic:notPresent scope="session" name="memberVO" >
  <td width="16%" bgcolor="#99CCFF" align="center">
    <bean:message key="javaedge.header.login"/>
  </td>
</logic:notPresent>
```

```
<logic:present scope="session" name="memberVO">
  <td width="16%" bgcolor="#99CCFF" align="center">
    <bean:message key="javaedge.header.logout"/>
  </td>
</logic:present>
```

In this JSP code, a column containing a link to the login URL will be rendered only if the JavaEdge user has not yet logged in to the application. The `<logic:notPresent>` checks the user's session to see if there is a valid memberVO object present in the session. The `<logic:present>` tag in the preceding code checks if there is a memberVO object in the user's session. If there is one, a column will be rendered containing a link to the logout page.

The `<logic:present>` and `<logic:notPresent>` tags are extremely useful, but in terms of applying the conditional logic are extremely blunt instruments. Fortunately, Struts provides you with a number of other conditional logic tags.

Conditional Logic and Cookies

Suppose that the user authentication scheme was again changed and the JavaEdge application set a flag indicating that the user was authenticated by placing a value of true or false in a cookie called userloggedin. You could rewrite the preceding code snippet as follows to use the `<logic:equals>` and `<logic:notEquals>` tags:

```
<logic:notEquals cookie="userloggedin" value="true">
  <td width="16%" bgcolor="#99CCFF" align="center">
    <bean:message key="javaedge.header.login"/>
  </td>
</logic:notEquals>

<logic:equals cookie="userloggedin" value="true">
  <td width="16%" bgcolor="#99CCFF" align="center">
    <bean:message key="javaedge.header.logout"/>
  </td>
</logic:equals>
```

You can use the `<logic:equals>` and `<logic:notEquals>` tags to even check a property in a JavaBean. For instance, you could rewrite the authentication piece of the JavaEdge application to set an attribute (called authenticated) in the memberVO object to a hold a string value of true or false. You could then check the property in the memberVO JavaBean using the following code:

```
<logic:notEquals name="memberVO" property="authenticated" scope="session"
                 value="true">
  <td width="16%" bgcolor="#99CCFF" align="center">
    <bean:message key="javaedge.header.login"/>
  </td>
</logic:notEquals>

<logic:equals name="memberVO" property="authenticated" scope="session"
              value="true">
  <td width="16%" bgcolor="#99CCFF" align="center">
```

```
    <bean:message key="javaedge.header.logout"/>
  </td>
</logic:equals>
```

When applying the conditional logic tags against a property on a JavaBean, keep two things in mind:

- *The scope that you are looking for the JavaBean in*: If you do not define a scope attribute, all of the contexts in the JSP will be searched. If you define this attribute and the value you are looking for is not there, a runtime exception will be thrown by the Java tag.

- *Chaining the property values of a JavaBean using dot (.) notation*: You can find examples of dot notation in the "Bean Output" section in this chapter.

Some other conditional logic tags are available:

- `<logic:greaterThan>`: Checks if the value retrieved from a JavaBean property, HttpServletRequest parameter, or HTTP header is greater than the value stored in the value attribute of the `<logic:greaterThan>` tag.

- `<logic:lessThan>`: Checks if the value retrieved from a JavaBean property, HttpServletRequest parameter, or HTTP header value is less than the value stored in the value attribute of the `<logic:lessThan>` tag.

- `<logic:greaterEqual>`: Checks if the value retrieved from a JavaBean property, HttpServletRequest parameter, or HTTP header value is greater than or equal to the value stored in the value attribute of the `<logic:greaterEqual>` tag.

- `<logic:lessEqual>`: Checks if the value retrieved from a JavaBean property, HttpServletRequest parameter, or HTTP header value is less than or equal to the value stored in the value attribute of the `<logic:lessEqual>` tag.

The logic tags just shown will try to convert the value they are retrieving to a float or double and perform a numeric comparison. If the retrieved value cannot be converted to a float or double, these tags will perform the comparisons based on the string values of the items being retrieved.

Movement Tags

These logic tags in the Struts tag library offer the developer the ability to redirect the user to a new URL. The two movement logic tags are

- `<logic:forward>`: Forwards the user to a specified global `<forward>` tag defined in the struts-config.xml file

- `<logic:redirect>`: Performs a redirect to a URL specified by the developer

Let's see how these two tags can be used. To bring up the JavaEdge application, users need to point the browser to http://localhost:8080/JavaEdge/homePageSetup. This forces users to know they have to go to the /homePageSetup action. An easier solution would be to allow them to go to http://localhost:8080/JavaEdge.

In a non–Struts-based application, this could be accomplished by setting up a `<welcome-file-list>` tag in the application's web.xml file. This tag allows you to define the default JSP or HTML file, which is presented when users come to the application and do not define a specific page. However, this is the problem for the Struts application. The `<welcome-file-list>` allows you to specify only filenames and not URLs or Struts actions.

However, using the movement logic tags provides you with the ability to work around this shortcoming. First, we will walk you through a solution using a `<logic:forward>` tag. You still need to set up the `<welcome-file-list>` tag in the web.xml file of JavaEdge. You are going to set up a file, called default.jsp, for the default file to be executed:

```
<web-app>
  ...
  <welcome-file-list>
    <welcome-file>default.jsp</welcome-file>
  </welcome-file-list>
</web-app>
```

Next, you add a new `<forward>` tag, called `default.action`, to the `<global-forwards>` tag in the struts-config.xml file for the JavaEdge application:

```
<struts-config>
  <global-forwards type="org.apache.struts.action.ActionForward">
    <forward name="system.error" path="/WEB-INF/jsp/systemError.jsp"/>
    <forward name="default.action" path="/execute/homePageSetup"/>
  </global-forwards>
  ...
</struts-config>
```

The last step is to write the default.jsp file. This file contains the following two lines of code:

```
<%@ taglib uri="/taglibs/struts-logic.tld" prefix="logic" %>
<logic:forward name="default.action"/>
```

You can perform the same functionality with the `<logic:redirect>` tag. If you implement default.jsp using a `<logic:redirect>` tag, you still need to set up the default.jsp in the web.xml file. However, you do not need to add another `<forward>` tag to the `<global-forwards>` tag located in struts-config.xml. Instead, you just need to write the default.jsp in the following manner:

```
<%@ taglib uri="/taglibs/struts-logic.tld" prefix="logic" %>
<logic:redirect page="/execute/homePageSetup"/>
```

This code will generate a URL relative to the JavaEdge application (http:// localhost:8080/ Javaedge/execute/HomePageSetup). You are not restricted, while using the `<logic:redirect>`, to redirect to a relative URL. You can also use a fully qualified URL and even redirect the user to another application. For instance, you could rewrite the default.jsp as follows:

```
<%@ taglib uri="/taglibs/struts-logic.tld" prefix="logic" %>
<logic:redirect
 href="http://localhost:8080/JavaEdge/execute/homePageSetup"/>
```

Using `<logic:redirect>` and `<logic:forward>` is the equivalent of calling the `sendRedirect()` method on the `HttpServletResponse` class in the Java Servlet API. The difference between the two tags is that the `<logic:forward>` tag will let you forward only to a `<global-forward>` defined in the struts-config.xml file. The `<logic:redirect>` tag will let you redirect to any URL.

The `<logic:redirect>` tag has a significant amount of functionality. However, you have had just a brief introduction to what the `<logic:redirect>` tag can do. A full listing of all the attributes and functionalities of this tag can be found at `http://struts.apache.org/1.x/struts-el/tlddoc/logic/redirect.html`.

Summary

In this chapter, we explored the basic elements of a Struts application and how to begin using Struts to build the applications. To build a Struts application, you need to know the following:

- The basic components of a Struts application:

  - `ActionServlet`: Represents the controller in the Struts MVC implementation. It takes all user requests and tries to map them to an `<action>` entry in the struts-config.xml file.

  - `action`: Defines a single task that can be carried by the end user. Also, it defines the class that will process the user's request and the JSP page that will render the HTML the user sees.

  - `Action` class: Contains the entire logic to process a specific user request.

  - `ActionForm`: Is associated with an `<action>` tag in the struts-config.xml file. It wraps all the form data submitted by the end user and also can perform validation on the data entered by the user.

  - *JSP pages*: Used to render the HTML pages that the users will see as a result of their request to the `ActionServlet`.

- The configuration files necessary to build a Struts application:

  - *web.xml*: This file contains the entire `ActionServlet` configuration, the mapping of user requests to the `ActionServlet`, and all the Struts Tag Library Definitions.

  - *struts-config.xml*: This file contains all the configuration information for a Struts-based application.

  - *ApplicationResources.properties*: This file is a central location for static content for a Struts application. It allows the developer to easily change the text or internationalize an application.

- The different Struts tag libraries for building the presentation piece of the application, including the following:

  - *Bean*: Provides the developer with JSP tags for generating output from a JavaBean and creating a JavaBean from common JSP web artifacts.

  - *Logic*: Can be used to apply the conditional logic in the JSP page through `Collections` stored in the user's JSP page context and redirect the user to another page.

  - *HTML*: These tags are not discussed in this chapter. However, they offer a significant amount of functionality and are discussed in greater detail in Chapters 3 and 4.

Also, we identified some different areas where Struts can be used to refactor the web antipatterns that might form during the design and implementation of web-based applications. Refactoring of the following antipatterns was discussed:

- *Hardwired*: We looked at how to chain together Struts actions to perform the precondition, form processing, and postcondition logic. This segregation of the business logic into the multiple applications provides a finer control over the application of the business logic and makes it easier to redirect the user to different Struts actions and JSP pages.

- *Tight-Skins*: While examining this antipattern, we looked at how to use the bean and logic tags to implement role-based presentation logic.

This chapter lays the foundation for the material covered in Chapters 3 and 4. In the next chapter, we are going to cover how to implement web-based forms using the Struts form tags. We will also look at the Struts HTML tag library and how it simplifies form development. Finally, the next chapter will focus on how to use the Struts `ActionForm` class to provide a common mechanism for validating the user data and reporting validation errors back to the user.

■ ■ ■

Form Presentation and Validation with Struts

In the previous chapter, all of our Struts examples were built around very simple screens that were populated with data retrieved from the JavaEdge application. However, most web applications require a high degree of interaction, with end users often submitting the data via HTML forms.

This chapter is going to look at how to simplify the construction of HTML forms and form-handling code using the Struts development framework. We are going to discuss, from both a conceptual and an implementation point of view, how the Struts framework can provide a configurable and consistent mechanism for building web forms. This chapter is going to cover the following topics:

- Validating HTML form data using the `ActionForm` class

- How the `validate()` method of the `ActionForm` class is used to validate data against the user

- Error handling when a validation rule is violated

- Prepopulating an HTML form with data

- Configuring Struts for processing HTML form data

- Simplifying the development of HTML form pages using the Struts HTML tag libraries

- Using `Map`-backed `ActionForms` to build flexibility into your application

- Best practices associated with using the Struts `ActionForm` class

Problems with Form Validation

Most web development teams do not have a consistent strategy for collecting data from the end user, validating it, and returning any error messages that need to be displayed. They use a hodgepodge of different means of collecting and processing the user's data. Two commonly used validation mechanisms include embedding JavaScript in the HTML or JSP page rendering the form, and/or mixing the validation logic for the screen with the business logic in the business tier of the application.

This inconsistency in how data is collected and validated often results in the following:

- Customers, whether they are internal (such as employees) or external (such as purchasers), having a disjointed experience while using the web-based applications of the organization. Each application requires the customer to have a different set of skills and an understanding of how the application works and how to respond to errors. In larger applications, this inconsistency can exist even between different pages in the same application.

- Validation logic is strewn through the different layers of the application. This increases the amount of time required to perform application maintenance. The maintenance developer, who is rarely the same as the code developer, often has to hunt for the location of the validation logic and know multiple development languages (JavaScript for validation rules enforced in the browser, Java for validation logic in the middle tier, and a stored procedure language for validation logic in the database).

- Validation logic is used differently across different browsers. JavaScript, though "standardized," is implemented differently across browsers. Developers of a web browser take great liberties in the way in which they implement the JavaScript European Computer Manufacturers Association (ECMA) standard. Often, they provide their own browser-specific extensions, which make cross-browser viewing (and portability) of the application difficult.

- The application code is difficult to reuse. With validation logic strewn throughout the tiers of an application, it is difficult to pick up that validation code and reuse it in another application. The developer has to take care of the dependencies being present before reusing the validation code, because there is no clean separation between the validation and business logic.

All the problems just identified are the symptoms of the Validation Confusion antipattern. Recollecting the discussion in Chapter 1, the Validation Confusion antipattern occurs due to one of the following reasons:

- No clear distinction between the validation logic of the form data and the business logic that processes the user's request

- Lack of a pluggable interface, which allows the developer to easily modify the validation logic for a particular screen

- No standardized mechanism for identifying the validation violations and notifying the end user of them

Fortunately, the Struts framework provides a rich set of software services for building and managing the form data. These services allow a developer to handle the form validation in a consistent fashion. Much of the logic, normally associated with capturing and presenting the errors, becomes the responsibility of the Struts framework and not of the application developer.

Using Struts for Form Validation

To build an HTML form, in Struts, you need to have the following pieces in place:

- A Struts ActionForm class, which is used to hold the data collected from the end user and perform any validations on that data. This class provides a simple-to-use "wrapper" that eliminates the need for developers to pull the submitted data out of the HttpServletRequest object, associated with the end user's request.

- A Struts Action class to carry out the user's request. In the process of carrying out the user's request, any business rules that should be enforced will be executed, and any database inserts, updates, or deletes will be performed.

- A JSP page that uses the Struts HTML tag libraries to render the form elements that are going to appear on the page.

Tying all of these pieces together is the struts-config.xml file. This file will have entries in it for defining the Struts ActionForm classes used in the application, which ActionForm classes are going to be used with which action, and whether an ActionForm class is going to enforce the validation against the submitted data. Each Struts action processing the form data must have its corresponding <action> tag modified, to indicate which ActionForm class will be used by the action.

Let's discuss what happens when the user submits the data in an HTML form. Figure 3-1 shows what happens when the user submits the form data to a Struts-based application, as described next:

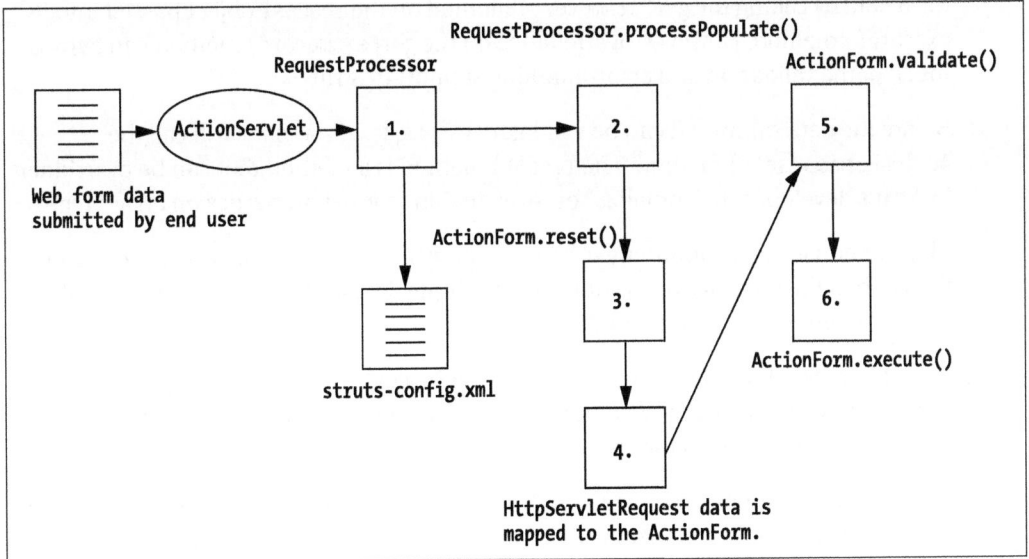

Figure 3-1. *The flow of a user request through Struts*

1. The ActionServlet will examine the incoming URL mapping or extension to determine what action the user submitting the data wants to take. The ActionServlet will create an instance of an org.apache.struts.action.RequestProcessor class and hand over responsibility for processing the user's request to it.

   The RequestProcessor will look at the data for the action requested in the struts-config. xml file. It will then determine whether or not an ActionForm has been defined for the action and, if so, what scope the ActionForm resides in.

   Once a scope has been determined for an ActionForm, the RequestProcessor will check to see if the ActionForm already exists in that scope. If the desired ActionForm class does exist in the defined scope, the RequestProcessor will retrieve it and pass it to the RequestProcessor.processPopulate() method.

   If the desired ActionForm does not exist in the scope, the RequestProcessor will create an instance of it, put it into the scope defined inside of the <action> tag in the struts-config.xml file, and then pass the created ActionForm instance to the processPopulate() method.

2. The processPopulate() method is responsible for mapping the form data passed into it via the HttpServletRequest object to the Struts ActionForm defined for the action being processed. It does this by first calling the reset() method on the ActionForm and then populating the ActionForm with data from the HttpServletRequest object.

   An ActionForm simplifies the form processing, but it is not required to access the form data submitted by the end user. An Action class can still access the submitted form data by calling the getParameter() method on the request object passed into its execute() method. However, overreliance on the getParameter() method can bypass much of the validation and error-handling support in Struts.

3. Before the data submitted can be validated, the RequestProcessor will call the ActionForm's reset() method. The reset() method is a method that can be overridden by Struts developers to "initialize" or "override" individual properties on an ActionForm.

   This method is most commonly used to properly handle a web form's radio checkbox fields when the form has been submitted multiple times. The reset() method will be covered in greater detail later in the chapter.

4. Once the reset() method has been called, the RequestProcessor will populate the ActionForm with data from the request by using the org.apache.struts.util. RequestUtil's populate() method.

5. Once the form data has been mapped from the HttpServletRequest object to the ActionForm, the submitted data will be validated. The RequestProcessor will validate the form data by calling the ActionForm's validate() method.

If a validation error occurs, the `RequestProcessor` will inform the `ActionServlet` to redirect users back to the screen where data was submitted. Users will then have to correct the validation violations before they can continue. We will be covering how Struts is notified of a validation error in the section called "Validating the Form Data."

6. If the data contained in the `ActionForm` successfully passes all validation rules defined in the `validate()` method, the `RequestProcessor` will invoke the `execute()` method on the `Action` class. The `execute()` method contains the business logic needed to carry out the end user's request.

Remember that the Java class, which carries out the end user's request, is defined via the type attribute in the `<action>` element. We suggest that you refer to Chapter 2 to understand how to configure a Struts action before continuing.

Implementing Form Validation with Struts

Let's begin the discussion of form handling by Struts by looking at how an HTML form is processed by Struts when a user submits it. We are going to use the Post a Story page from the JavaEdge application as our example.

This page can be accessed by either clicking the Post a Story link in the menu bar at the top of every JavaEdge page or pointing your browser to `http://localhost:8080/javaedge/execute/postStorySetup`. The Post a Story page is used by a JavaEdge user to submit a story, which the other users visiting this page can read.

If you have successfully reached this page, you will see the screen in Figure 3-2.

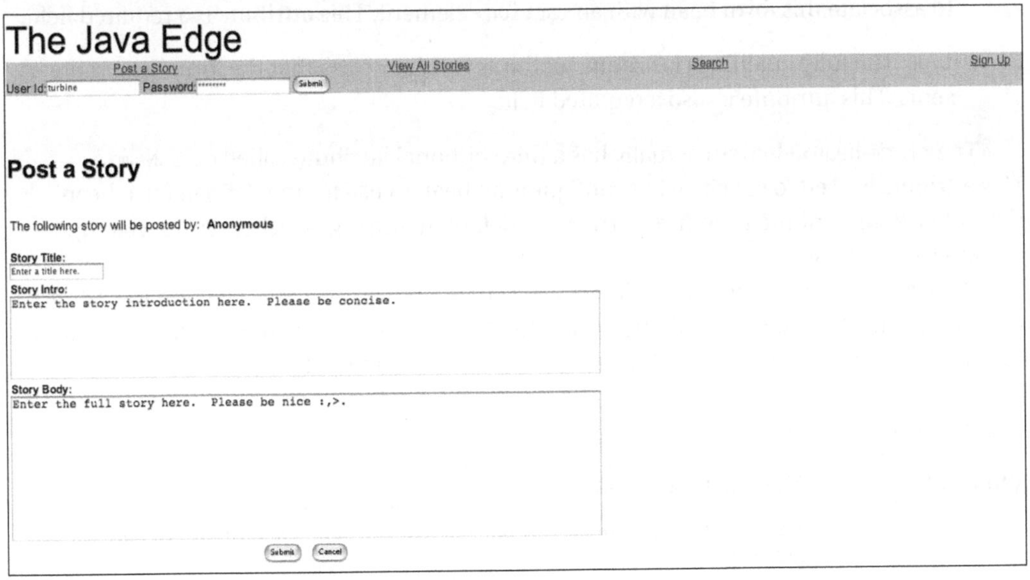

Figure 3-2. *The Post a Story page*

Let's begin by looking at how to set up the struts-config.xml file to use ActionForm objects.

The struts-config.xml File

To use an ActionForm class to validate the data collected from a user form, the struts-config.xml file for the application must be modified. These modifications include

- Adding a <form-beans> tag, which will define each of the ActionForm classes used in the application

- Modifying the <action> tag processing the user's request to indicate that before the user's request is processed, it must be validated by an ActionForm class

The <form-beans> tag holds one or more <form-bean> tags within it. This tag appears at the top of the struts-config.xml file. Each <form-bean> tag corresponds to only one ActionForm class in the application. For the JavaEdge application, the <form-beans> tag looks as shown here:

```
<form-beans>
  <form-bean name="postStoryForm"
            type="com.apress.javaedge.struts.poststory.PostStoryForm"/>
  ...
  <form-bean> //More form-bean definitions.
</form-beans>
```

The <form-bean> element has two attributes:

- name: A unique name for the form bean being defined. Later on, this name will be used to associate this form bean with an <action> element. This attribute is a required field.

- type: The fully qualified class name of the ActionForm class that the form bean represents. This attribute is also a required field.

The <form-bean> element actually has a third optional attribute called className. This attribute is used to specify what configuration bean to use for the defined form bean. If the className attribute is omitted, Struts will default to the org.apache.struts.config. FormBeanConfig class.

Once a <form-bean> has been defined, you can use it in an <action> element to perform validation of the form data. To add the validation to a <form-bean>, you must supply the four additional attributes described in Table 3-1 in an <action> element.

Table 3-1. *Attributes of the Form Bean Tag*

Attribute Name	Attribute Description
name	Maps to the name of the <form-bean> that will be used to process the user's data.
scope	Defines whether or not the ActionForm class will be created in the user's request or session context. The scope attribute can be used only when the name attribute is defined in the <action> tag. If the name attribute is present, the scope attribute is an optional tag. The default value for the scope attribute is request.

Attribute Name	Attribute Description
validate	A Boolean attribute that indicates whether or not the submitted form data will be validated. If it's true, the validate() method in the ActionForm class and the execute() method in the Action class will be invoked. If it's false, then the validate() method will not be invoked, but the execute() method in the Action class defined in the tag will be executed. The validate attribute is used only when the name attribute has been defined in the tag. The default value for the validate attribute is true.
input	Used to define where the user should be redirected, if a validation error occurs. Usually, the user is redirected back to the JSP page where the data was submitted. It is not required if the name attribute is not present.

The /postStory action processing the data entered by the user in the postStory.jsp page is shown here:

```
<action path="/postStory"
        input="/WEB-INF/jsp/postStory.jsp"
        name="postStoryForm"
        scope="request"
        validate="true"
        type="com.apress.javaedge.struts.poststory.PostStory">
    <forward name="poststory.success" path="/execute/homePageSetup"/>
</action>
```

Struts ActionForm Class

The Struts ActionForm class is used to hold the entire form data submitted by the end user. It is a helper class that is used by the ActionServlet to hold the form data that it has pulled from the end user's request object. The application developer can then use the ActionForm to access the form through get() and set() method calls.

The ActionForm class not only provides a convenient wrapper for the request data but also validates the data submitted by the user. However, an Action class is not required to have an ActionForm class. An Action class can still access the form data submitted by the end user by calling the getParameter() method in the request object passed into its execute() method.

To build an ActionForm class, the developer needs to extend the base Struts ActionForm class and override two methods in it, reset() and validate().

Just to review, the reset() method is overridden by the developer when an ActionForm class for an action is to be stored in the user's session context. The reset() method clears the individual attributes in the ActionForm class to ensure that the ActionForm class is properly initialized before it is populated with the user's form data. The validate() method is overridden by the developer. This method will contain all of the validation logic used in validating the data entered by the end user.

In addition, the application developer needs to define all the form elements that are going to be collected by the ActionForm class and stored as private properties in the class. For each defined property, there must be corresponding get() and set() methods that follow the standard JavaBean naming conventions.

Note You must implement a get() and set() method for each form element captured off the web form. These get() and set() methods should follow the standard JavaBean naming conventions. The first letter of the word after get()/set() should be capitalized along with the first letter of each word in the method thereafter. All other letters in the method name should be lowercase. The Struts framework uses Java reflection to read the data from and write data to the ActionForm class. An exception will be raised if the get() or set() method is not present for a piece of data submitted.

For the Post a Story page, you are going to write a Struts ActionForm class called PostStoryForm.java. This class will hold the story title, the story intro, and the body of the story. In addition, it will contain the validation code for the data being submitted by the user.

The class diagram shown in Figure 3-3 illustrates the class relationships, methods, and attributes for the Struts ActionForm class and the PostStoryForm class.

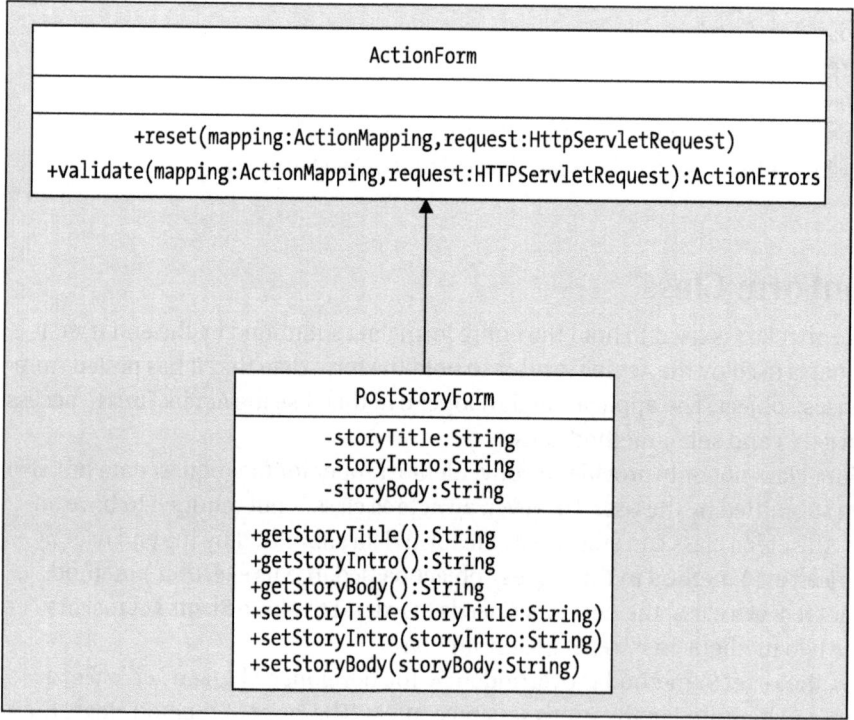

Figure 3-3. *PostStoryForm's relationship to the ActionForm class*

It is very easy to fall into the mind-set that there must be one ActionForm class for each HTML form from which the data is collected. In small-to-medium size applications, there is nothing wrong in using a single ActionForm placed in the user's session. All the forms in the application will use this ActionForm to hold the data collected from the user.

This simplifies the collection of the data because your application has only one ActionForm instance that you have to work with. By using a single ActionForm class and placing it in the user's session, you can very easily implement a wizard-based application that will remember each piece of user information entered. As the user steps back and forth through the wizard, the data can easily be retrieved from the single ActionForm class.

The problem with using a single ActionForm class in the user's session is that the application will not scale as well. Remember, the objects placed in the user's session have a held reference until the session times out and the objects are garbage collected.

Do not place ActionForm objects in the session merely as a convenience. The other problem with this method occurs if the users are carrying out a long-lived transaction. If the users lose their connection or close their browser, any of the data entered till then will be lost.

To ensure that as much of the user's data is captured and persisted as possible, break the application into smaller transactions. Use an ActionForm class for each application screen and persist the data in the ActionForm class as soon as the users submit their data. Place the ActionForm class into the request so that server resources are not unnecessarily used.

The code for the PostStoryForm class is shown next. However, the reset() and validate() methods for this class are not displayed. They will be discussed in the sections "Using the reset() Method" and "Validating the Form Data," respectively.

```
package com.apress.javaedge.struts.poststory;

import com.apress.javaedge.common.VulgarityFilter;
import com.apress.javaedge.common.ApplicationException;
import com.apress.javaedge.story.StoryVO;
import com.apress.javaedge.member.MemberVO;
import org.apache.struts.action.*;
import org.apache.struts.util.MessageResources;
import org.apache.commons.beanutils.BeanUtils;
import org.apache.struts.action.Action;
import javax.servlet.http.HttpServletRequest;
import javax.servlet.http.HttpSession;
import java.util.Vector;
import java.lang.reflect.InvocationTargetException;
import org.apache.struts.Globals;

/**
 * Standard Struts class that collects data
 * submitted by the end-user.
 * @author jcarnell
 *
 * ----------XDoclet Tag----------------
 * @struts.form name="postStoryForm"
 * -------------------------------------
 */
public class PostStoryForm extends ActionForm {


    String storyTitle = "";
    String storyIntro = "";
    String storyBody  = "";
```

```java
//Checks to make sure field being checked is not null
private void checkForEmpty(String fieldName, String fieldKey,
    String value, ActionErrors errors){
    if (value.trim().length()==0){
      ActionError error = new
        ActionError("error.poststory.field.null", fieldName);
      errors.add(fieldKey, error);
    }
}


//Checks to make sure the field being checked does
// not violate our vulgarity list
private void checkForVulgarities(String fieldName, String fieldKey,
    String value, ActionErrors errors){
    VulgarityFilter filter = VulgarityFilter.getInstance();

    if (filter.isOffensive(value)){
      ActionError error =
        new ActionError("error.poststory.field.vulgar", fieldName);
      errors.add(fieldKey, error);
    }
}


//Checks to make sure the field in question
//does not exceed a maximum length
private void checkForLength(String fieldName,
    String fieldKey, String value, int maxLength, ActionErrors errors){
    if (value.trim().length()>maxLength){
      ActionError error =
        new ActionError("error.poststory.field.length", fieldName);
      errors.add(fieldKey, error);
    }
}

public ActionErrors validate(ActionMapping mapping,
                          HttpServletRequest request) {
    ActionErrors errors = new ActionErrors();

    checkForEmpty("Story Title", "error.storytitle.empty",
        getStoryTitle(),errors);
    checkForEmpty("Story Intro", "error.storyintro.empty",
        getStoryIntro(), errors);
    checkForEmpty("Story Body",  "error.storybody.empty",
        getStoryBody(), errors);

    checkForVulgarities("Story Title", "error.storytitle.vulgarity",
        getStoryTitle(), errors);
```

```
        checkForVulgarities("Story Intro", "error.storyintro.vulgarity",
            getStoryIntro(), errors);
        checkForVulgarities("Story Body",  "error.storybody.vulgarity",
            getStoryBody(), errors);

        checkForLength("Story Title", "error.storytitle.length",
            getStoryTitle(), 100, errors);
        checkForLength("Story Intro", "error.storyintro.length",
            getStoryIntro(), 2048, errors);
        checkForLength("Story Body", "error.storybody.length",
            getStoryBody(),  10000, errors);

        return errors;
    }

    /**
     * @see org.apache.struts.action.ActionForm#reset
      (org.apache.struts.action.ActionMapping,
     javax.servlet.http.HttpServletRequest)
     */
    public void reset(ActionMapping mapping,
                      HttpServletRequest request) {
            // deprecated 1.1
      //ActionServlet servlet =  this.getServlet();
      //MessageResources messageResources = servlet.getResources();

        // new for 1.2
        MessageResources messageResources =
            (MessageResources) request.getAttribute(Globals.MESSAGES_KEY);

        storyTitle = messageResources.getMessage(
            "javaedge.poststory.title.instructions");
      storyIntro = messageResources.getMessage(

    /** Getter for property storyTitle.
     * @return Value of property storyTitle.
     */
    public java.lang.String getStoryTitle() {
        return storyTitle;
    }

    /** Setter for property storyTitle.
     * @param storyTitle New value of property storyTitle.
     */
    public void setStoryTitle(java.lang.String storyTitle) {
        this.storyTitle = storyTitle;
    }
```

```
    /** Getter for property storyIntro.
     * @return Value of property storyIntro.
     */
    public java.lang.String getStoryIntro() {
        return storyIntro;
    }

    /** Setter for property storyIntro.
     * @param storyIntro New value of property storyIntro.
     */
    public void setStoryIntro(java.lang.String storyIntro) {
        this.storyIntro = storyIntro;
    }

    /** Getter for property storyBody.
     * @return Value of property storyBody.
     */
    public java.lang.String getStoryBody() {
        return storyBody;
    }

    /** Setter for property storyBody.
     * @param storyBody New value of property storyBody.
     */
    public void setStoryBody(java.lang.String storyBody) {
        this.storyBody = storyBody;
    }
}
```

Using the reset() Method

The reset() method is used to ensure that an ActionForm class is always put in a "clean" state before the ActionServlet populates it with the form data submitted in the user's request. In the struts-config.xml file, the developer can choose to place an ActionForm for a specific Struts action in either the user's session or request.

The reset() method was originally implemented to allow developers to deal with one of the more annoying HTML form controls: checkboxes. When a form is submitted with unchecked checkboxes, no data values are submitted for the checkbox control in the HTTP request.

Thus, if an ActionForm is sitting in the user's session and the user changes a checkbox value for the ActionForm from true to false, the ActionForm will not get updated because the value for the checkbox will not be submitted. Remember, the HTML <input> tag does not send a value of false on an unchecked checkbox.

The reset() method can be used to initialize a form bean property to a predetermined value. In the case of a form bean property that represents a checkbox, the reset() method can be used to set the property value always to false.

Since the reset() method is called before the form is populated with data from the HttpServletRequest object, it can be used to ensure that a checkbox is set to false. Then if the user has checked a checkbox, the false value set in the reset() method can be overridden with the value submitted by the end user.

The Struts development team typically recommends the reset() method only be used for the preceding purpose. However, as you will see in the next section, the reset() method can be useful for prepopulating a JSP page with data.

A Word on the reset() Method

Among Struts developers, the use of the reset() method to prepopulate form data can be the cause of rigorous debate. The Struts JavaDoc advises to not use the reset() method. The main reason the Struts development team gives is that the reset() method maybe deprecated at some point in the future (even though this has yet to be even mentioned anywhere).

In the next several sections, we will be demonstrating how to prepopulate a web page by using the reset() method and a "setup" action. We give our reason for using both methods and have seen both methods work rather successfully in production-level systems. That being said, please do not deluge our mailboxes with angry e-mails if it is deprecated in the future.

Implementing the reset() method for the PostStoryForm will set all its properties to an empty string. The reset() method for the PostStoryForm class is shown here:

```
public void reset(ActionMapping mapping,
                    HttpServletRequest request) {
    storyTitle = "";
    storyIntro = "";
    storyBody  = "";
}
```

Prepopulating an ActionForm with Data

So far, we have talked about using the reset() method to ensure that the contents of an ActionForm class are cleared before the ActionServlet places data in it from the user request. However, an ActionForm class can also be used to prepopulate an HTML form with data. The data populating the form might be text information retrieved from a properties file or a database.

To prepopulate an HTML form with data, you need to have the following Struts elements in place:

- A Struts setup action that will be called before a user is redirected to a JSP page, displaying an HTML form prepopulated with the data. The concept of setup actions is discussed in Chapter 2.

- An ActionForm class whose reset() method will prepopulate the form fields with data retrieved from the ApplicationResources.properties file. The ApplicationResources.properties file is discussed in Chapter 2.

- A JSP page that uses the Struts HTML tag library to retrieve the data from the ActionForm class.

For example, you can prepopulate the HTML form for the Post a Story page with some simple instructions on what data is supposed to go in each field. For this example, you are going to use the following files:

- PostStoryForm.java

- PostStorySetupAction.java

- postStoryContent.jsp

We are only going to show you the PostStoryForm and the PostStorySetupAction Java classes. The postStoryContent.jsp file will use the Struts HTML tag library to read the values out of the PostStoryForm object stored in the request and display them in each field. The post-StoryContent.jsp file and Struts HTML tag library are discussed later in the chapter, in the section "The Struts HTML Tag Library."

PostStoryForm.java

Writing the reset() method for a PostStoryForm to prepopulate the ActionForm with the instructions for each field in the form is a straightforward task:

```
public void reset(ActionMapping mapping,
                   HttpServletRequest request) {
    MessageResources messageResources =
        (MessageResources) request.getAttribute(Globals.MESSAGES_KEY);

  storyTitle =
    messageResources.getMessage("javaedge.poststory.title.instructions");
  storyIntro =
    messageResources.getMessage("javaedge.poststory.intro.instructions");
  storyBody =
    messageResources.getMessage("javaedge.poststory.body.instructions");
}
```

The reset() method just shown reads values from the ApplicationResources.properties file and uses them to populate the properties of the PostStoryForm object.

Note In the preceding reset() method, the error messages being looked up by the call to getMessage() have a string literal being passed in as a parameter. This string literal is the name of the message being looked up from the resource bundle used for the JavaEdge application (that is, the ApplicationResources.properties file).

This was done for clarity in reading the code. A more maintainable solution would be to replace the individual string literals with corresponding static final constant values.

The Struts development framework provides an easy-to-use wrapper class, called MessageResources, for directly accessing the data in the ApplicationResources.properties file.

■**Note** We use the name ApplicationResources.properties for the name of the message resource bundle used in the JavaEdge application because this is traditionally what this file has been called in the Struts application. However, the name of the file used as the message resource bundle can be set in the `parameter` attribute of the `<message-resources>` tag contained within the struts-config.xml file. For a review of the `<message-resources>` tag, please review Chapter 2.

After getting an instance of a `MessageResources` object, you can pass the message key of the item that you want to retrieve to `getMessage()`. The `getMessage()` method will retrieve the desired value.

```
messageResources.getMessage("javaedge.poststory.title.instructions");
```

If the key passed to the `getMessage()` method cannot be found, a value of `null` will be returned. The following are the name-value pairs from the ApplicationResources.properties file used to prepopulate the `PostStoryForm`:

```
javaedge.poststory.title.instructions=Enter a title here.
javaedge.poststory.intro.instructions=
Enter the story introduction here. Please be concise.
javaedge.poststory.body.instructions=Enter the full story here. Please be nice.
```

The `PostStoryForm.reset()` method is a very simple example of how to prepopulate a form with the data contained in an `ActionForm` class. In reality, many applications retrieve their data from an underlying relational database rather than from a properties file. How the `reset()` method on the `PostStoryForm` is invoked is yet to be explored.

■**Note** A common mistake by beginning Struts and JSP developers is to try to use the `ActionForm` class to manage Struts form data without using the Struts HTML tag library.

It is important to note that all of the techniques shown for prepopulating a web form will only work with the Struts HTML JSP tag libraries.

Let's take a look at the PostStorySetupAction.java file and see how we can trigger the `reset()` method.

PostStorySetupAction.java

Triggering the `PostStoryForm.reset()` method does not require any coding in the PostStorySetupAction.java file. All that the `PostStorySetupAction` class is going to do is forward the user's request to the postStoryContent.jsp file. So what role does the PostStorySetupAction.java file play, if its `execute()` method just forwards the user on to a JSP page? How is the `reset()` method in the `PostStoryForm` class called?

If you set a Struts <action> tag in the struts-config.xml file to use an ActionForm and tell the ActionServlet to put the PostStoryForm in the user's request, the reset() method in the PostStoryForm class will be invoked.

When users click the Post a Story link in the JavaEdge header, they are asking the ActionServlet to invoke the /postStorySetup action. This action is configured to use the ActionForm class of PostStoryForm. The PostStoryForm is going to be put in the users' request context by the ActionServlet.

Since the ActionForm class for the /postStorySetup action is the PostStoryForm class and the PostStoryForm class is going to be placed into the users' request context, the reset() method in the PostStoryForm class will be invoked. The reset() method is going to initialize each of the attributes in the PostStoryForm class to hold a set of simple instructions pulled from the ApplicationResources.properties file.

After the reset() method has been invoked, the ActionServlet will place any submitted form data in the PostStoryForm instance. Since the user has not actually submitted any data, the PostStoryForm class will still hold all of the values read from the ApplicationResources. properties file. The ActionServlet will then invoke the execute() method in the PostStorySetupAction class, which will forward the user to the postStoryContent.jsp page. This page will display a form, prepopulated with instructions.

In summary, to prepopulate the form, you need to perform the following two steps:

1. Write a Struts Action class called PostStorySetupAction. The execute() method of this class will pass the user on to postStoryContent.jsp.

2. Set up an action called /postStorySetup in the struts-config.xml file. This action will use the PostStoryForm class.

The code for PostStorySetupAction.java is shown here:

```
package com.apress.javaedge.struts.poststory;

import org.apache.struts.action.Action;
import org.apache.struts.action.ActionMapping;
import org.apache.struts.action.ActionForm;
import org.apache.struts.action.ActionForward;
import javax.servlet.http.HttpServletRequest;
import javax.servlet.http.HttpServletResponse;
import javax.servlet.http.HttpSession;

public class PostStorySetupAction extends Action {
  public ActionForward execute(ActionMapping mapping,
                               ActionForm form,
                               HttpServletRequest request,
                               HttpServletResponse response){

    return (mapping.findForward("poststory.success"));
  }
}
```

The execute() method just forwards the user to the postStoryContent.jsp page by returning an ActionForward mapped to this page:

```
return (mapping.findForward("poststory.success"));
```

The poststory.success mapping corresponds to the <forward> element, defined for the following <action> tag of /postStorySetup:

```
<action path="/postStorySetup"
        type="com.apress.javaedge.struts.poststory.PostStorySetupAction"
        name="postStoryForm"
        scope="request"
        validate="false">
    <forward name="poststory.success" path="/WEB-INF/jsp/postStory.jsp"/>
</action>
```

The name attribute shown here tells the ActionServlet to use an instance of PostStoryForm whenever the user invokes the /postStorySetup action:

```
name="postStoryForm"
```

Remember, the value of the name attribute must refer to a <form-bean> tag defined at the beginning of the struts-config.xml file.

The scope attribute tells the ActionServlet to place the PostStoryForm as an attribute in the HttpServletRequest object:

```
scope="request"
```

Setting the validate attribute to false in the preceding tag will cause the ActionServlet not to invoke the validate() method of the PostStoryForm. This means the reset() method in the PostStoryForm object is going to be invoked and placed in the user's request, but no data validation will take place.

Since no data validation takes place, the execute() method of PostStorySetupAction will be invoked. Remember, the Action class that carries out the end user's request is defined in the type attribute:

```
type="com.apress.javaedge.struts.poststory.PostStorySetupAction"
```

Another Technique for Prepopulation

Another technique exists for prepopulating an ActionForm with data. It is discussed here because implementing your Struts application using this technique can cause long-term maintenance headaches.

In the PostStorySetupAction.java file, you could implement the execute() method so that it creates an instance of PostStoryForm and invokes its reset() method directly. After the reset() method is invoked, the PostStoryForm can then be set as an attribute in the request object passed in the execute() method.

The following code demonstrates this technique:

```
public class PostStorySetupAction extends Action {
  public ActionForward execute(ActionMapping mapping,
                               ActionForm form,
                               HttpServletRequest request,
                               HttpServletResponse response){

    PostStoryForm postStoryForm = new PostStoryForm();
    postStoryForm.setServlet(this.getServlet());
    postStoryForm.reset(mapping, request);
    request.setAttribute("postStoryForm", postStoryForm);

    return (mapping.findForward("poststory.success"));
  }
}
```

Note If you find yourself working around the application framework, consider redesigning the task you are trying to execute. Stepping outside the application framework, as in the example shown previously, can lead to long-term maintenance and upgrade issues. The Struts architecture tries to remain very declarative, and controlling the application flow programmatically breaks one of Struts' fundamental tenets.

Prepopulating a Form the Correct Way

If you are going to use a setup action and not the reset() method on an ActionForm to prepopulate a form with data, then you should do all of the work directly in the setup action. The code that follows demonstrates this:

```
public class PostStorySetupAction extends Action {
  public ActionForward execute(ActionMapping mapping,
                               ActionForm form,
                               HttpServletRequest request,
                               HttpServletResponse response){

    ActionServlet servlet = this.getServlet();
    PostStoryForm postStoryForm = new PostStoryForm();
    postStoryForm.setServlet(this.getServlet());

        MessageResources messageResources =
            (MessageResources) request.getAttribute(Globals.MESSAGES_KEY);

postStoryForm.setStoryTitle(
    messageResources.getMessage("javaedge.poststory.title.instructions"));
postStoryForm.setStoryIntro(
    messageResources.getMessage("javaedge.poststory.intro.instructions"));
postStoryForm.setStoryBody(
```

```
        messageResources.getMessage("javaedge.poststory.body.instructions"));
    request.setAttribute("postStoryForm", postStoryForm);

        return (mapping.findForward("poststory.success"));
    }
}
```

If you look at this code, you will notice that you can directly retrieve and set Struts
ActionForm classes in the user's request or session context:

```
storyTitle =
    messageResources.getMessage("javaedge.poststory.title.instructions");

    storyBody =
    messageResources.getMessage("javaedge.poststory.body.instructions");
    request.setAttribute("postStoryForm", postStoryForm);
```

At some point as a Struts developer you will need to retrieve, create, or manipulate an
ActionForm manually.

Note The Struts framework always uses the value stored in the name attribute of an <action> element
as the key to storing the ActionForm class as the user's request or session.

Validating the Form Data

As discussed earlier, a common mistake in web application development is for no clear distinction to exist between the application's business logic and validation logic. The ActionForm
class helps the developers to solve this problem by allowing them to enforce lightweight validation rules against the data entered by a user. By encapsulating these validation rules in the
ActionForm class, the developer can clearly separate the validation rules from the business
logic that actually carries out the request. The business logic is placed in the corresponding
Action class for the end user's request.

Web developers can override the validate() method and provide their own validation
rules for the submitted data, while writing their own ActionForm class. If the developers do not
override the validate() method, none of the data submitted will have any validation logic run
against it.

The validate() method for the PostStoryForm class is going to enforce three validation rules:

- The users must enter a story title, story introduction, and story body. If they leave any
  field blank, they will receive an error message indicating that they must enter the data.

- The users are not allowed to put vulgarity in their application. The validate() method
  will check the data entered by the user for any inappropriate phrases.

- Each field in the Post a Story page is not allowed to exceed a certain length; otherwise,
  the user will get an error message.

It is important to note that in all the cases, the users will not be allowed to continue until
they correct the validation violation(s).

The `validate()` method for the `PostStoryForm` class is as shown here:

```
public ActionErrors validate(ActionMapping mapping,
                            HttpServletRequest request) {
  ActionErrors errors = new ActionErrors();

  checkForEmpty("Story Title", "error.storytitle.empty",
                getStoryTitle(), errors);
  checkForEmpty("Story Intro", "error.storyintro.empty",
                getStoryIntro(), errors);
  checkForEmpty("Story Body",  "error.storybody.empty",
                getStoryBody(), errors);

  checkForVulgarities("Story Title", "error.storytitle.vulgarity",
                    getStoryTitle(), errors);
  checkForVulgarities("Story Intro", "error.storyintro.vulgarity",
                    getStoryIntro(), errors);
  checkForVulgarities("Story Body",  "error.storybody.vulgarity",
                    getStoryBody(), errors);

  checkForLength("Story Title", "error.storytitle.length", getStoryTitle(),
                100, errors);
  checkForLength("Story Intro", "error.storyintro.length", getStoryIntro(),
                2048, errors);
  checkForLength("Story Body", "error.storybody.length", getStoryBody(),
                2048, errors);

  return errors;
}
```

The first step in the `validate()` method is to instantiate an instance, called errors, of the `ActionErrors` class:

```
ActionErrors errors = new ActionErrors();
```

The `ActionErrors` class is a Struts class that holds one or more instances of an `ActionError` class. An `ActionError` class represents a single violation of one of the validation rules being enforced in the `ActionForm` class.

■**Note** The Struts framework's `ActionError` class is used throughout all of the code examples in this book. As of Struts 1.2.1, the `ActionError` class will be deprecated and replaced by the `ActionMessage` class.

The upgrade of Struts 1.0.2 to Struts 1.1 took over a year to release to production. Struts 1.2 contains minor bug fixes with no major new functionality. As such, new and existing applications using Struts 1.1 have a while before they need to be upgraded. To use the code with this edition of the book, some code has been modified to take advantage of the changes in APIs in Struts 1.2 and remove code that has been deprecated since Struts 1.1.

If a form element submitted by an end user violates a validation rule, an ActionError will be added to the errors object.

When the validate() method completes, the errors object will be returned to the ActionServlet:

```
return errors;
```

If the errors object is null or contains no ActionErrors, the ActionServlet will allow the business logic to be carried out, based on the end user's request. This is done by invoking the execute() method in the Action class associated with the request.

Let's look at the checkForVulgarities() method to see how an ActionError class is actually created when a validation rule is violated. The checkForEmpty() and checkForLength() methods will not be discussed in detail, but the code for these methods is shown here:

```
private void checkForEmpty(String fieldName, String fieldKey, String value,
                           ActionErrors errors) {
  if (value.trim().length() == 0) {
    ActionError error = new ActionError("error.poststory.field.null",
                                        fieldName);

    errors.add(fieldKey, error);
  }
}
```

```
private void checkForLength(String fieldName, String fieldKey, String value,
                            int maxLength, ActionErrors errors){
  if (value.trim().length() > maxLength){
    ActionError error = new ActionError("error.poststory.field.length",
                                        fieldName);

    errors.add(fieldKey, error);
  }
}
```

Creating an ActionError

The checkForVulgarities() method is as shown here:

```
private void checkForVulgarities(String fieldName, String fieldKey,
                                 String value, ActionErrors errors) {

  VulgarityFilter filter = VulgarityFilter.getInstance();

  if (filter.isOffensive(value)){
    ActionError error = new ActionError("error.poststory.field.vulgar",
                                        fieldName);
    errors.add(fieldKey, error);
  }
}
```

The first line in this method retrieves an instance of the VulgarityFilter into a variable called filter.

```
VulgarityFilter filter = VulgarityFilter.getInstance();
```

The VulgarityFilter class is implemented using a Singleton design pattern and wraps a collection of words that are considered to be offensive. The code for the class is shown here:

```
package com.apress.javaedge.common;

public class VulgarityFilter {

  private static VulgarityFilter filter = null;

  private static String[] badWords = {"Stupid", "Idiot", "Moron", "Dummy",
                          "Flippin", "Ninny"};

  static {
    filter = new VulgarityFilter();
  }

  public static VulgarityFilter getInstance(){
    return filter;
  }

  public boolean isOffensive(String valueToCheck){
    String currentWord = "";

    for (int x = 0; x <= badWords.length - 1; x++){
      if (valueToCheck.toLowerCase().indexOf(badWords[x].toLowerCase())
          != -1) {
        return true;
      }
    }

  return false;
  }
}
```

The VulgarityFilter class has a single method called isOffensive(), which checks if the text passed in is offensive. A value of true returned by this method indicates the user has entered data that contains offensive text:

```
if (filter.isOffensive(value))
```

When a vulgarity is found, a new ActionError is created and added to the errors object passed to the checkForVulgarity() method:

```
ActionError error = new ActionError("error.poststory.field.vulgar",
                          fieldname);
errors.add(fieldKey, error);
```

There are five constructors that can be used to instantiate an ActionError class. The first parameter of each of these constructors is a lookup key that Struts uses to find the text of the error message displayed to the end user. Struts will look for all error messages in the ApplicationResources.properties file associated with the application. The error messages for the Post a Story page are shown here:

```
error.poststory.field.null= The following field: {0} is a required field.
error.poststory.field.vulgar=  You have put a vulgarity in your {0} field.
error.poststory.field.length=Your {0} field is too long.<br/>
```

When the user violates the vulgarity validation rule and the checkForVulgarity() method creates an ActionError, the lookup key error.poststory.field.vulgar will be used to return the following error message:

```
The following field: {0} is a required field. Please provide a value for {0}.<br/>
```

The error message can contain at most four distinct parameter values. The parameter values are referenced by using the notation {number}, where number is between zero and three. In the preceding example, only one parameter is inserted into the error message. A summary of the five constructors in the ActionError class is given in Table 3-2.

Table 3-2. *ActionError Attributes*

ActionError Constructor	Description
ActionError(String lookupKey)	Retrieves the error message from the ApplicationResources.properties file
ActionError(String lookupKey, String param0)	Retrieves the error message from the ApplicationResources.properties file and passes in one parameter
ActionError(String lookupKey, String param0, String param1)	Retrieves the error message from the ApplicationResources.properties file and passes in two parameters
ActionError(String lookupKey, String param0, String param1, String param2)	Retrieves the error message from the ApplicationResources.properties file and passes in three parameters
ActionError(String lookupKey, String param0, String param1, String param2, String param3)	Retrieves the error message from the ApplicationResources.properties file and passes in four parameters

After the error object has been created, it is later added to the errors object by calling the add() method in errors:

```
errors.add(fieldKey, error);
```

The add() method takes two parameters:

- A key that uniquely identifies the added error within the ActionErrors class. This key must be unique and can be used to look up a specific error in the ActionErrors class.

- An ActionError object containing the error message.

Viewing the Errors

The Struts ActionServlet checks if there are any errors in the returned ActionErrors object to determine if a validation error was returned by the validate() method. If the value returned from the validate() method is null or contains no ActionError objects, no validation errors were found.

If the Struts ActionServlet finds that there are errors present in the ActionError object, it will redirect the user to the path set in the input attribute for the action.

■**Note** Remember, the input attribute on the <action> tag is a required field if the name attribute is also defined on the tag. The name attribute is used to define the name of the ActionForm that will hold the form data being submitted.

Failure to include an input attribute when using an ActionForm will result in an exception being thrown.

Most of the time, the value in this input tag is the JSP page where the data was entered. The ActionForm object holding the user's data will still be in the request. Thus, any data entered by the user in the form will appear prepopulated in the form. How does Struts present the user with all the errors raised in the validate() method? It does this using the <html:errors/> tag. This tag is found in the Struts HTML custom JSP tag library. (Several other form-related custom tags are contained in the HTML tag library. We will be discussing the full HTML tag library in the section "The Struts HTML Tag Libraries.") There are two ways of using this tag:

- To write each error message stored within the ActionErrors class to the JSP PrintWriter class

- To retrieve a specific error from the ActionErrors class and place it next to the specific fields

Writing All Error Messages to the JSP Page

To perform the first action, you must import the Struts HTML tag library and place the <html:errors/> tag where you want the errors to appear. For instance, in postStoryContent.jsp, you use this tag in the following manner:

```
<%@ page language="java" %>
<%@ taglib uri="/WEB-INF/struts-html.tld" prefix="html" %>

<BR/><BR/>
<H1><bean:message key="javaedge.poststory.text.header"/></H1>

<html:errors/>
```

This code will write all the errors in the ActionErrors class returned by the validate() method of the PostStoryForm immediately below the header of the page. The following example shows the type of error messages that can be presented to the end user:

You have put a vulgarity in your Story Title field.
Please refer to our <a href="/javaedge/policy.html">terms
of use policy.</a>
The following field: Story Intro is a required field.
Please provide a value for Story Intro.
The following field: Story Body is a required field.
Please provide a value for Story Body.

It is extremely important to note that the <html:errors/> tag will write the error text exactly as it has been defined in the ApplicationResources.properties file. This means that the developer must provide HTML tags to format the appearance of the error message. This also includes putting any <br/> tags for the appropriate line breaks between the error messages. The <html:errors/> tag allows the application developer to define a header and footer for a collection of error messages. Headers and footers are defined by including an errors.header property and errors.footer property in the ApplicationResources.properties file. These two properties can contain text (and HTML code) that will appear immediately before and after the errors written by the <html:errors/> tag. The following snippet shows these properties for the JavaEdge application:

```
errors.header=<h3><font color="red">Important Message</font></h3><ul>
errors.footer=</ul><hr>
```

The <html:errors/> tag provides a very simple and consistent error-handling mechanism. Front-end screen developers only need to know that they have to put an <html:errors/> tag in their JSP form pages to display any validation errors. The job of the server-side developers is simplified because they can easily validate the form data submitted by the end user and communicate the errors back to the user by populating an ActionErrors object.

Keeping in mind all the discussion that we had so far, when the end users violate a validation rule on the Post a Story page, they will see the output shown in Figure 3-4.

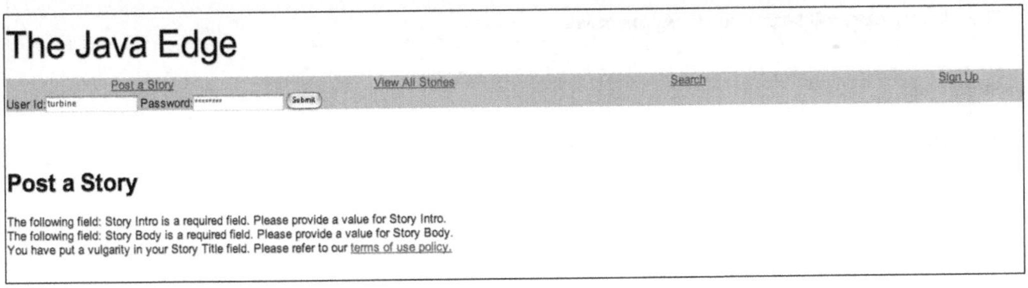

Figure 3-4. *The end result of a validation rule violation*

Retrieving a Single Error Message

The <html:errors/> tag by itself is somewhat inflexible, because you have to present all the validation errors caused by the end user at a single spot on the screen. Many application developers like to break the validation errors apart and put them next to the field that contains the invalid data.

Fortunately, the <html:errors/> tag allows you to pull a single error message from an ActionErrors object. It has an attribute called property. This attribute will let you retrieve an

error message, using the key value that was used while adding the error message to the
ActionErrors object. For example, when a user enters a word that violates the vulgarity filter,
you add that validation error to the errors object by calling

```
errors.add(fieldKey, error);
```

The fieldKey variable passed to the errors.add() method is the name we have chosen to
represent that particular error. For example, if the user typed the word *dummy* into the Story
Title field, this would violate the vulgarity validation rule and a new ActionError class would
be instantiated. The new ActionError would be added to the errors class and would have a
fieldKey value of error.storytitle.vulgarity.

If you wanted to put that specific error message directly above the Story Title field label,
you could rewrite postStoryContent.jsp with the following code:

```
<TR>
  <TD>
    <font size="1" color="red">
      <html:errors property="error.storytitle.vulgarity"/>
    </font>
    <bean:message key="javaedge.poststory.form.titlelabel"/>
    <html:text name="postStoryForm" property="storyTitle"/>
  </TD>
</TR>
```

By using the <html:errors/> tag in the manner shown, you can cause postStoryContent.jsp
to generate an error message that may look like the one shown in Figure 3-5.

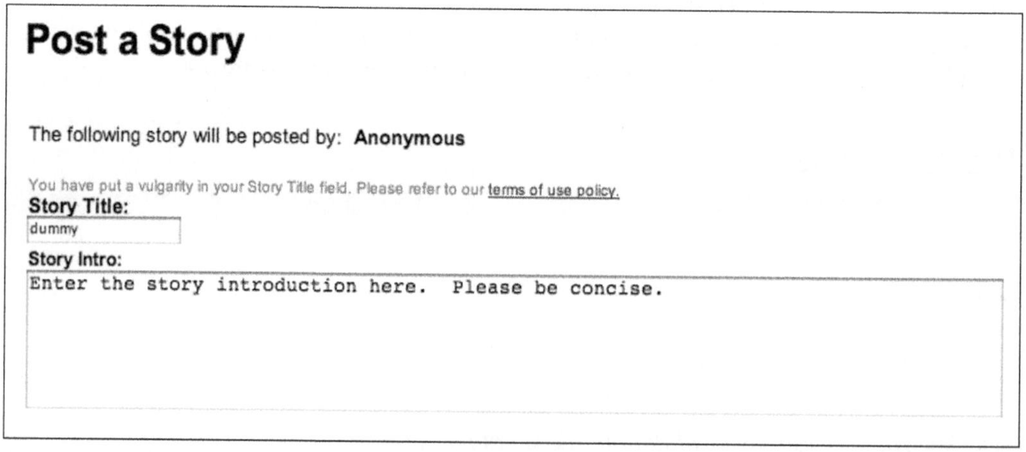

Figure 3-5. *Displaying a single validation error message*

If you want to automatically format the individual error messages, you need to use
error.prefix and error.suffix rather than the error.header and error.footer properties in
the ApplicationResources.properties file:

```
error.prefix=<font size="1" color="red">
error.suffix=</font>
```

Error Handling and Prepopulation

After discussing how HTML errors are handled in Struts, you might be a little bit confused. Why does the form show up with all of the fields prepopulated with the data that the user just entered? Why doesn't the `reset()` method in the `ActionForm` class reset all the values?

The reason is simple. When the `validate()` method is invoked and if there are validation errors, the `ActionServlet` is going to look at the value of the `input` attribute in the `<action>` tag. The `input` attribute almost invariably points back to the JSP where the user entered the data. Remember, the `reset()` method gets called only when an action is invoked. Redirecting the user back to a JSP page will not invoke the `reset()` method. If the JSP page to which the user is redirected uses the Struts HTML tag library and an `ActionForm` in the user's request or session, it will pull the data out of the `ActionForm` and prepopulate the form elements with that data. Thus, when a validation error occurs, the user sees the validation errors and a pre-populated form.

If you want to force the reset of all the elements in a form, after the validation occurs, you need to point the `input` attribute in the `<action>` element to a setup action that will repopulate the data.

On Validations and Validation Libraries

One of the biggest complaints that we have heard from development teams using Struts is that it seems wrong to separate the validation logic from the actual business logic. After all, the same validation logic is going to be applied regardless of where the actual business logic is being executed. For example, a parameter that is required by a piece of business logic to be non-null is going to have the same requirement regardless of which application is executing the business logic.

The strength of the `ActionForm` class's `validate()` method is that it provides a clean mechanism for performing validation *and* handling errors that are found during validation. The examples in this chapter have shown the validation rules for the code embedded directly in the `ActionForm` class doing the validation. This has been to simplify the reading of code and allow the reader to follow the examples without having to wade through multiple layers of abstraction and generalization.

The problem with embedding the validation logic inside the `ActionForm` class is that it ties the code to a Struts-specific class and makes the embedded validation code difficult to reuse in a non-Struts application.

Oftentimes, development teams will leverage a number of approaches to help generalize validation and avoid tying it to a Struts `ActionForm` class. These include

- Separating all of the validation logic used in an application into a set of validation "helper" classes that can be reused across multiple applications.

- Moving the validation code into the value objects being used to move data back and forth across the application tiers. The base value object class extended by all of the value objects in the application has a `validate()` method that can be overridden to contain validation code. If you are not familiar with the Value Object pattern, please refer to Chapter 5.

- Moving all of the validation code into the business logic layer. Each object in the business logic layer has a private `validate()` method that is called before the actual business logic is processed.

- Using a validation framework, like the Validator framework in Struts, to externalize the validation logic from the business logic and make them as declarative as possible.

Each of the items listed have their advantages and disadvantages. Moving all of the validation logic to a set of "helper" classes is simple, but oftentimes leads to the development team creating a cumbersome set of low-level data validation calls that they must maintain and support. There are already plenty of open source libraries and frameworks that do this type of low-level validation. The question becomes, Why waste time on something others have already done?

Moving the validation logic to the Value Object pattern has the advantage of putting the validation logic very close to the data. The same validation logic for data can be applied over and over again by simply invoking the `validate()` method on the value object. The problem with this approach is that the value objects are supposed to be lightweight "wrappers" for data being passed across the different application boundaries (presentation, business, and data). At any given time there can be a large number of value objects being used with only a small fraction of them actually being validated. This is a lot of extra overhead for nothing.

Moving the validation logic to the business layer and embedding it inside of a business object makes sense. After all, one of the first rules of object-oriented programming is that all data and the code that acts on that data should be self-contained within a single discrete class. Oftentimes when validation rules are built into a business layer class, nonbusiness layer details that deal with error handling and error presentation are also embedded in the class. This results in tight dependencies being created on the business object and violates another tenet of OOP, the concept of Single Responsibility.

Classes and the methods contained within them should have a discrete set of responsibilities that reflect on the domain being modeled by the class. When other pieces of nondomain-specific logic start creeping into the class, it becomes bloated and difficult to maintain. This is one of the principal reasons why the Struts `ActionForm` class is useful: It allows a developer to write validation logic without getting the business logic used in the class too tightly tied to the application.

The last option is our favorite. If you can use a framework that specifically is built for validation, you can save a lot of time. The Struts `ActionForm` class's `validate()` method is only meant to be a plug-in point from which validation logic is called. However, if you start from the premise that validation logic is lightweight and will consist of no more than a handful of standard checks, using a declarative validation framework where you have to write little to no code for performing validation is the best approach. The Struts 1.1 framework now integrates with the Validator framework. This framework lets you declare a set of validation rules that can be processed against data contained within an `ActionForm` class.

The validation rules in the Validator framework cover most of the validation rules a developer is going to need while building an application. In addition, the Validator framework is extensible enough to allow you to build your own validation rules. The Validator framework will be covered in greater detail in Chapter 7.

The Struts HTML Tag Library

As we have seen earlier in this chapter, Struts provides the ActionForm and Action classes as the means of validating and processing the data submitted by the end user. The Struts development framework also provides a JSP tag library, called the HTML tag library, that significantly simplifies the development of HTML-based forms. The HTML tag library allows the developer to write JSP pages that tightly integrate with an ActionForm class.

The Struts HTML tag library can be used to generate HTML form controls and read data out of an ActionForm class in the user's session or request. It also helps developers avoid writing significant amounts of scriptlet code to pull the user data out of JavaBeans (that is, the ActionForm objects) in the user's request and/or session. When combined with the other Struts tag libraries, as discussed in Chapter 2 (see the section called "Building the homepage.jsp"), a developer can write very dynamic and data-driven web pages without ever having to write a single line of JSP scriptlet code.

The Struts HTML tag library contains a wide variety of tags for generating HTML form controls. We are not going to cover every tag in the Struts HTML tag library. Instead, we are going to go through the most commonly used tags and explore their usage. For a full list of the different tags available in the Struts HTML tag library, you can visit http://struts.apache.org/. The tags discussed in this chapter are listed and described in Table 3-3.

Table 3-3. *Commonly Used HTML Tags*

Tag Name	Tag Description
<html:form>	Renders an HTML <form> tag
<html:submit>	Renders a submit button
<html:cancel>	Renders a cancel button
<html:text>	Renders a text field
<html:textarea>	Renders a textarea field
<html:select>	Renders an HTML <select> tag for creating drop-down boxes
<html:option>	Renders an HTML <option> control that represents a single option in a drop-down box
<html:checkbox>	Renders an HTML checkbox
<html:radio>	Renders an HTML radio control

Let's begin the discussion of the Struts HTML tag library by looking at the postStoryContent.jsp page:

```
<%@ page language="java" %>
<%@ taglib uri="/taglibs/struts-bean.tld" prefix="bean" %>
<%@ taglib uri="/taglibs/struts-html.tld" prefix="html" %>
<%@ taglib uri="/taglibs/struts-logic.tld" prefix="logic" %>
<%@ taglib uri="/taglibs/struts-tiles.tld" prefix="tiles" %>
```

```
<BR/>
<BR/>
<H1>
  <bean:message key="javaedge.poststory.text.header"/>
</H1>

<html:errors/>

<html:form action="postStory">
  <TABLE>
    <TR>
      <TD>
        <bean:message key="javaedge.poststory.text.intro"/>
        <logic:present scope="session" name="memberVO">
          <B>
            <bean:write name="memberVO" scope="session"
                        property="firstName"/> 
            <bean:write name="memberVO" scope="session"
                        property="lastName"/>
          </B><BR/>
        </logic:present>

        <logic:notPresent scope="session" name="memberVO">
          <B>Anonymous</B>
        </logic:notPresent>
</html:form>
```

Setting Up a Struts HTML Form

Before using the individual Struts HTML tag within a JSP page, you must take three steps:

1. Import the Struts HTML Tag Library Definitions (TLDs).

2. Define an <html:form> tag, within the page that will map to an <action> tag defined in the struts-config.xml file.

3. Define an <html:submit> button to allow the user to submit the entered data.

The Struts HTML TLD is imported as shown here:

```
<%@ taglib uri="/taglibs/struts-html.tld" prefix="html" %>
```

Next, you use the Struts HTML tags. Just as in a static HTML page, you need to define a <form> tag that will encapsulate all the HTML form controls on the page. This is done by using the <html:form> tag.

```
<html:form action="postStory">
    ...
</html:form>
```

The <html:form> tag has a number of different attributes associated with it. However, we will not be discussing every <html:form> attribute in detail. Some of the <html:form> attributes are given in Table 3-4.

Table 3-4. *Attributes of the HTML Form Tag*

Attribute Name	Attribute Description
action	Maps to the <action> tag that will carry out the user's request when the form data is submitted. This is a required field.
method	Determines whether the form will be sent as a GET or POST. This is not a mandatory field and if not specified, it will generate the <form> tag to use a POST method.
name	The name of the JavaBean that will be used to prepopulate the form controls. The <html:form> tag will check if this bean is present in the user's session or request. The scope attribute defines whether to look into the user's session or request. If no JavaBean is found in the context defined in the scope attribute, the <html:form> tag will create a new instance of the bean and place it into the scope defined by the scope attribute. The class type of the created JavaBean is determined by the type attribute.
scope	Determines whether the tag should look in the user's session or request for the JavaBean named in the name attribute. The value for this attribute can be either "session" or "request".
type	Fully qualified Java class name for the JavaBean being used to populate the form.
onsubmit	Lets the developer define a JavaScript onSubmit() event handler for the generated form.
onreset	Lets the developer define a JavaScript onReset() event handler for the generated form.
focus	Name of the field that will have focus when the form is rendered.

The most important of these attributes is the action attribute. It maps to an <action> element defined in the struts-config.xml file. If no name, scope, or type attribute is specified in the <html:form> tag, the ActionForm that will be used to populate the form, its fully qualified Java name, and the scope in which it resides will be pulled from the <action> tag in the struts-config.xml file.

In the <html:form> tag used in the postStoryContent.jsp, all the ActionForm information would be retrieved by the ActionServlet, by looking at the name attribute in the <action> tag of the postStory action in the struts-config.xml file:

```
<action path="/postStory"
  input="/WEB-INF/jsp/postStory.jsp"
  name="postStoryForm"
  scope="request"
  validate="true"
  type="com.apress.javaedge.struts.poststory.PostStory">
  <forward name="poststory.success" path="/execute/homePageSetup"/>
</action>
```

Since the value of name (postStoryForm) is defined as a <form-bean> element in the struts-config.xml file, the ActionServlet can figure out its fully qualified Java class name and instantiate an instance of that class.

Note It is a good practice to use the action attribute rather than the name, scope, and type attributes to define the JavaBean that will populate the form. Using this attribute gives you more flexibility by allowing you to change the ActionForm class in one location (struts-config.xml) rather than searching multiple JSP pages.

Let's look at the HTML generated by the <html:form> tag shown earlier:

```
<form name="postStoryForm" method="POST"
      action="/javaedge/execute/postStory">
```

The name attribute generated tells the ActionServlet of Struts that the postStoryForm bean, defined in the <form-beans> tag of the struts-config.xml file, is going to be used to hold all the data posted by the user. The default method of the form (since you did not define one in the <html:form> tag) is going to be a POST method. The action attribute contains the URL to which the form data is going to be submitted. Since the action of the <html:form> tag was postStory, the <html:form> generated the action attribute (for the corresponding <form> tag) as /javaedge/execute/postStory.

The last step in setting up an HTML form is using the Struts <html:submit> tag to generate an HTML submit button:

```
<html:submit property="submitButton" value="Submit"/>
```

In addition to the <html:submit> tag, the Struts HTML tag library has HTML tags for creating cancel buttons. When an <html:cancel> tag is used, an HTML button will be rendered, which when clicked will cause the ActionServlet to bypass the validate() method in the ActionForm that is associated with the form.

Even though the validate() method is bypassed, the execute() method for the Action class (in this case PostStory.java) linked with the form will be invoked. This means if you want to use an <html:cancel> button in your page, the execute() method must detect when the cancel button is invoked and act accordingly. For instance, let's say the following <html:cancel> tag was added to the postStoryContent.jsp file:

```
<html:cancel value="Cancel"/>
```

The validate() method in the PostStoryForm class would not be called. However, the execute() method on the PostStory class will be invoked. The execute() method taken from the PostStory class could be written in the following manner:

```
public ActionForward execute(ActionMapping mapping,
                             ActionForm form,
                             HttpServletRequest request,
                             HttpServletResponse response){
```

```
if (this.isCancelled(request)){
    System.out.println("*****The user pressed cancel!!!");
    return (mapping.findForward("poststory.success"));
}

//Add the story data to the database.
...
return (mapping.findForward("poststory.success"));
}
```

If you did not want the code in the execute() method to be executed, you will have to use a method called isCancelled() to detect if the user pressed a cancel button. The isCancelled() method is inherited from the base Struts Action class. This method looks for a parameter in the user's request, called org.apache.struts.taglib.html.CANCEL. If it finds this parameter, it will return true, indicating to the developer writing the execute() method code that the user clicked the cancel button.

The parameter name, org.apache.struts.taglib.html.CANCEL, maps to the name attribute in the <input> tag generated by the <html:cancel> button. The HTML button generated by the <html:cancel> tag shown earlier looks like this:

```
<input type="submit" name="org.apache.struts.taglib.html.CANCEL"
       value="Cancel">
```

Unlike the <html:submit> tag, the property attribute on the <html:cancel> tag is rarely set.

Note If you set the property attribute in the <html:cancel> button, it will override the default value generated, and you will not be able to use the isCancelled() method to determine if the user wants to cancel the action.

Using Text and TextArea Input Fields

The postStoryContent.jsp files use text <text> and <textarea> tags to collect the data from the end user. The <html:text> and <html:textarea> tags are used to generate the text and textarea <input> tags, respectively. For instance, the postContent.jsp page uses the <html:text> tag to generate an HTML text <input> tag by using the following:

```
<html:text property="storyTitle"/>
```

The <html:text> tag has a number of attributes, but the most important are name and property. The name attribute defines the name of the ActionForm bean that the input field is going to map to. The property attribute defines the property in the ActionForm bean that is going to map to this input field. You should keep in mind two things while working with the property attribute:

- The property attribute will map to a get() and set() method in the ActionForm bean. This means that value must match the standard JavaBean naming conventions. For instance, the value storyTitle is going to be used by the ActionServlet to call the getStoryTitle() and setStoryTitle() methods in the ActionForm.

- The value in a `property` attribute can be nested by using a "`.`" notation. Let's assume that the `ActionForm` method had a `property` called `member` that mapped to a `MemberVO` object containing the user data. The developer could set the value of the `property` attribute to be `member.firstName`. This would translate into a call to the `getMember()`. `getFirstName()` and `getMember().setFirstName()` methods of the `PostStoryForm` class.

■**Note** If you refer to the Struts documentation on the Apache web site, you will notice that almost every Struts HTML tag has a `name` attribute in it. This attribute is the name of the JavaBean that the HTML tag will read and write data to. You do not have to supply a `name` attribute for the HTML form attributes we are describing in the following sections. If you do not supply a `name` attribute and if the `<html:*>` control is inside an `<html:form>` tag, the `<html:*>` control will automatically use the `ActionForm` associated with the `<html:form>` tag.

The `<html:textarea>` input tag behaves in a similar fashion to the `<html:text>` tag. The `<html:textarea>` tag uses the `cols` and `rows` attributes to define the width and length of the textarea the user can type in:

```
<html:textarea name="postStoryForm" property="storyIntro" cols="80" rows="5"/>
```

The preceding tag will generate a `<textarea>` tag called `storyIntro` that will be 80 columns wide and five rows long.

Drop-Down Lists, Checkboxes, and Radio Buttons

Most HTML forms are more than just a collection of the simple text field controls. They use drop-down lists, checkboxes, and radio buttons to collect a wide variety of information. While the postStoryContent.jsp file did not contain any of these controls, it is important to understand how the Struts framework renders these controls using the HTML tag library. Let's begin the discussion by the looking at drop-down lists.

Drop-Down Lists

An HTML drop-down list control provides a list of options that a user can select from. However, the user sees only the item that has been selected. All of the other items are hidden until the user clicks the drop-down box. On clicking the box, the rest of the options will be displayed and the user will be able to make a new choice.

Since the Post a Story page does not have a drop-down box, we will have to step away from it briefly. Using the Struts HTML tag library, there are two ways of rendering a drop-down box:

- Use an `<html:select>` tag and build a static list of options by hard coding a static list of `<html:option>` tags in the code.

- Use an `<html:select>` tag and dynamically build the list by reading the data from a Java collection object using the `<html:options>` tag.

The `<html:select>` tag renders a `<select>` tag in HTML. The `<html:option>` tag renders a single option for the placement in the drop-down list. If you want to display a drop-down list containing a list of name prefixes, you would write the following code in your JSP file:

```
<html:select property="someBeanProperty">
  <html:option value="NS">Please select a prefix</html:option>
  <html:option value="Mr.">Mr.</ html:option>
  <html:option value="Ms.">Ms.</ html:option>
  <html:option value="Mrs.">Mrs.</ html:option>
  <html:option value="Dr.">Dr.</ html:option>
</html:select>
```

This code snippet would generate the following HTML:

```
<select name="someBeanProperty">
  <option value="NS">Please select a prefix</option>
  <option value="Mr.">Mr.</option>
  <option value="Ms.">Ms.</option>
  <option value="Mrs.">Mrs.</option>
  <option value="Dr.">Dr.</option>
</select>
```

The `<html:select>` tag has one important attribute, the property attribute. It is the name of the property of the ActionForm bean that will store the item selected from the drop-down list. The `<html:option>` tag must always be contained within an `<html:select>` tag. The value attribute in the `<html:option>` tag specifies the value that will be sent in the users' request for the selected item from the drop-down list when they hit the submit button.

The `<html:select>` and `<html:option>` tags work well while generating a drop-down list that does not change. However, if you want to create a drop-down list based on data that is dynamic, such as data pulled from a database, you need to the use the `<html:options>` tag. The `<html:options>` tag allows you to generate an `<option>` list from a Java Collection object.

Let's assume that in a SetupAction class, you created a Vector object and populated it with the prefix codes. You then put that code in the request object as shown here:

```
Vector prefixes = new Vector();
prefixes.add("NS");
prefixes.add("Mr.");
prefixes.add("Ms.");
prefixes.add("Mrs.");
prefixes.add("Dr.");
request.setAttribute("prefixes", prefixes);
```

You could then render this collection into a drop-down list using the following code:

```
<html:select property="someBeanProperty">
  <html:options name="prefixes">
</html:select>
```

Checkboxes

Setting up a checkbox to appear on an HTML form is easy to do. It just requires the use of a checkbox flag. To create a checkbox on a form, you can use the following syntax:

```
<html:checkbox property="someBeanProperty" value="true"/>
```

The `property` attribute for the checkbox matches the name of the `property` in the `ActionForm` that the checkbox is going to get and set data from. The `value` attribute is the value that will be sent in the HTTP request if the user checks the checkbox. If no value is specified, then the default value will always be `on`.

One important thing to remember is that when a checkbox is not checked, no value will be passed in the HTTP request. This also means that the value that was already set in the `ActionForm` property associated with the checkbox will not change. You have to check the `request` to see if the checkbox is present in the request. If it is not, you have to set the `ActionForm` property to a `false` or `off` value:

```
if (request.getAttribute("someBeanProperty") == null) {
  this.setSomeBeanProperty(false);
}
```

This is important because if the submitted data has a validation error and the `ActionServlet` returns the user to the screen where they entered data, any checkboxes that had been moved from a checked to an unchecked state will still show up on the screen as checked.

So in the `validate()` method of your `ActionForm` bean you must check the `request` object for the checkbox parameter. If the checkbox parameter has not been submitted as part of the request, you must set the corresponding property in the `ActionForm` to be `false`. This has to be done before you start doing any validation of the form data, or else you will end up with your form data inconsistently handling the checkbox information passed to it. This also means that if you want to prepopulate a form with checkboxes set in an off status, the `reset()` method of the `ActionForm` being used to populate the page must set the properties in the `ActionForm` (that map to checkboxes) to a `false` value.

Radio Buttons

To render a radio button in a form, you use the `<html:radio>` tag. This tag has two core attributes: `property` and `value`. These two attributes are similar in behavior to the `<html:checkbox>` tag. The `property` attribute defines the name of the property in the `ActionForm` that the radio button maps to. The `value` attribute is the value that will be sent, if the radio button is selected when the user submits the form.

Caution If you do not preset a radio button and no radio button is selected by the user, the property on the `ActionForm` representing the radio button will not have a value set on it. Use one of the `ActionForm` prepopulation techniques described earlier if you require the radio button to have some default value associated with it.

To group a set of radio button controls together so that only one of a group of radio buttons can be set, you set each radio button's property attribute to point to the same ActionForm property.

If you wanted to use a radio button instead of the drop-down list to show a selection of prefixes to the user, you could write the following code:

```
<LI>Mr. <html:radio property="someBeanProperty" value="Mr."/>
<LI>Ms. <html:radio property="someBeanProperty" value="Ms."/>
<LI>Mrs. <html:radio property="someBeanProperty" value="Mrs."/>
<LI>Dr. <html:radio property="someBeanProperty" value="Dr."/>
The HTML generated by this code would look as shown here:
<LI>Mr. <input type="radio" name="someBeanProperty" value="Mr.">
<LI>Ms. <input type="radio" name="someBeanProperty" value="Ms.">
<LI>Mrs. <input type="radio" name="someBeanProperty" value="Mrs.">
<LI>Dr. <input type="radio" name="someBeanProperty" value="Dr.">
```

Building More Dynamic ActionForms

The concept of wrapping data within an ActionForm is a powerful one because it allows the application developer to retrieve and manipulate data submitted by the end user without having to litter their code with the gory details of accessing an HttpRequest object. However, as most developers will quickly discover, for large projects that collect significant amounts of data, building ActionForm classes can be extremely tedious.

Writing individual get()/set() methods for each attribute being submitted by the end user is a time-consuming and thus error-prone process. Fortunately, Struts 1.1 now provides two mechanisms to simplify the process of building ActionForm classes:

- Dynamic ActionForm

- Map-backed ActionForm

Dynamic ActionForms allow the developer to declare a Struts form bean and its corresponding attributes in the application's struts-config.xml file. We are not going to go into any greater detail on Dynamic ActionForms in this chapter. Instead, we will cover them in greater detail in Chapter 7.

Map-backed ActionForms are an exciting new addition to the Struts framework. A Map-backed ActionForm allows the developer to wrap a Map object (that is, HashMap, TreeMap, etc.) and expose it on the ActionForm class.

Shown next is the PostStoryForm rewritten as a Map-backed ActionForm:

```
package com.apress.javaedge.struts.poststory;

import com.apress.javaedge.common.VulgarityFilter;
import org.apache.struts.action.*;
import org.apache.struts.util.MessageResources;

import javax.servlet.http.HttpServletRequest;
import java.util.HashMap;
import java.util.Map;
```

```java
public class PostStoryMapForm extends ActionForm{
    private HashMap attributeMap = new HashMap();


    private Map getMap(){
        return attributeMap;
    }

    public void setAttribute(String attributeKey, Object attributeValue){
        getMap().put(attributeKey, attributeValue);
    }

public Object getAttribute(String attributeKey){

        Object holder = getMap().get(attributeKey);

        if (holder==null) return "";

        return holder;
    }

    private void checkForEmpty(String fieldName, String fieldKey,
                               String value, ActionErrors errors){
        //Same implementation as the PostStoryForm.
    }

    private void checkForVulgarities(String fieldName, String fieldKey,
                                     String value, ActionErrors errors){
        //Same implementation as the PostStoryForm.
    }

    private void checkForLength(String fieldName, String fieldKey,
                                String value, int maxLength,
                                ActionErrors errors){
        //Same implementation as the PostStoryForm.
    }

public ActionErrors validate(ActionMapping mapping,
                                 HttpServletRequest request) {
        ActionErrors errors = new ActionErrors();

        checkForEmpty("Story Title", "error.storytitle.empty",
                    (String)getAttribute("storyTitle"),errors);
        checkForEmpty("Story Intro", "error.storyintro.empty",
                    (String)getAttribute("storyIntro"), errors);
        checkForEmpty("Story Body",  "error.storybody.empty",
                    (String)getAttribute("storyBody"), errors);

        checkForVulgarities("Story Title", "error.storytitle.vulgarity",
                    (String)getAttribute("storyTitle"), errors);
```

```
        checkForVulgarities("Story Intro", "error.storyintro.vulgarity",
                    (String)getAttribute("storyIntro"), errors);
        checkForVulgarities("Story Body",  "error.storybody.vulgarity",
                    (String)getAttribute("storyBody"), errors);

        checkForLength("Story Title", "error.storytitle.length",
                    (String)getAttribute("storyTitle"), 100, errors);
        checkForLength("Story Intro", "error.storyintro.length",
                    (String)getAttribute("storyIntro"), 2048, errors);
        checkForLength("Story Body", "error.storybody.length",
                    (String)getAttribute("storyBody"),  10000, errors);

        return errors;
    }

        public void reset(ActionMapping mapping,
                    HttpServletRequest request) {
        ActionServlet servlet =  this.getServlet();
        MessageResources messageResources = servlet.getInternal();

        setAttribute("storyTitle",
    messageResources.getMessage③
            ("javaedge.poststory.title.instructions"));
        setAttribute("storyIntro", messageResources.getMessage③
                    ("javaedge.poststory.intro.instructions"));
        setAttribute("storyBody" , messageResources.getMessage③
                    ("javaedge.poststory.body.instructions"));
    }
}
```

The first thing you should notice about the PostStoryMapForm class is that there is no get() and set() for individual attributes. All attributes for the form bean are stored in a HashMap called attributeMap:

```
private HashMap attributeMap = new HashMap();
```

All access to the attributeMap variable is controlled by a pair of methods called getAttribute() and setAttribute():

```
public void setAttribute(String attributeKey, Object attributeValue){
  getMap().put(attributeKey, attributeValue);
}

public Object getAttribute(String attributeKey){

  Object holder = getMap().get(attributeKey);

  if (holder==null) return "";

  return holder;
}
```

These methods do nothing more than provide an entry point for Struts to perform a retrieval and insertion of objects into the attributeMap variable, as shown in Figure 3-6.

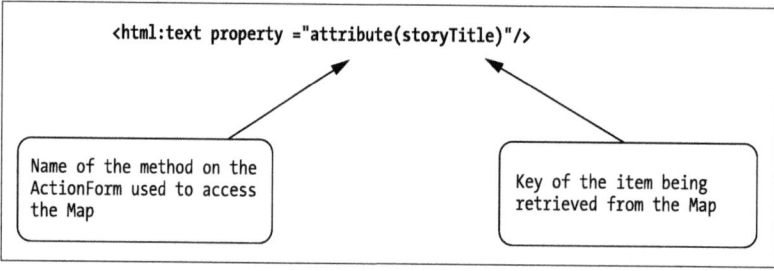

Figure 3-6. *Map-backed ActionForm*

■**Note** The method names getAttribute() and setAttribute() are arbitrary names. You can call your "wrapper" method to an internal HashMap anything you want as long as the method names follow standard JavaBean naming conventions and they have the same method signatures shown in the preceding code.

Keep in mind that entry methods like getAttribute() and setAttribute() do not have to perform straight calls into the Map object. You can place code in the entry methods to ensure that form attributes being retrieved out of and set in the internal Map object are formatted in a particular manner. In the PostStoryMapForm class, the getAttribute() call always returns an empty String object if the attribute from the attributeMap is null:

```
Object holder = getMap().get(attributeKey);

if (holder==null) return "";

return holder;
```

When data is accessed from the PostStoryMapForm class, the getAttribute() and setAttribute() methods are used. You can see this in the PostStoryMapForm's validate() method:

```
public ActionErrors validate(ActionMapping mapping,
                             HttpServletRequest request) {
  ActionErrors errors = new ActionErrors();

  checkForEmpty("Story Title", "error.storytitle.empty",
                (String)getAttribute("storyTitle"),errors);
  checkForEmpty("Story Intro", "error.storyintro.empty",
                (String)getAttribute("storyIntro"), errors);
  checkForEmpty("Story Body",  "error.storybody.empty",
                (String)getAttribute("storyBody"), errors);

  . . .

  return errors;
}
```

At this point you might be wondering how the individual attributes in the `PostStoryMapForm` class are accessed in a JSP page. Before Struts 1.1, there was no way a Struts custom tag could directly access an element contained within an `Array` or a `Map` object. Sure, you could always use a combination of `<logic:iterate>` and `<logic:equals>` tags to find a value, but you could never tell the Struts tag to directly access element X contained within a particular attribute on a form bean.

Since the release of Struts 1.1, you can now do this. Code examples often speak volumes, so let's look at a rewritten version of the Post a Story page that uses the `PostStoryMapForm` class to retrieve and set form data. This new page, called postStoryMapContent.jsp, is shown here:

```
<%@ page language="java" %>
<%@ taglib uri="/taglibs/struts-bean" prefix="bean" %>
<%@ taglib uri="/taglibs/struts-html" prefix="html" %>
<%@ taglib uri="/taglibs/struts-logic" prefix="logic" %>
<%@ taglib uri="/taglibs/struts-tiles" prefix="tiles" %>


<BR/><BR/>
<H1><bean:message key="javaedge.poststory.text.header"/></H1>


<html:errors/>
<html:form action="postStory">

<TABLE>
  <TR>
    <TD>
      <bean:message key="javaedge.poststory.text.intro"/>

      <logic:present scope="session" name="memberVO">
        <B><bean:write name="memberVO" scope="session"
            property="firstName"/> <bean:write name="memberVO"
            scope="session" property="lastName"/></B><BR/>
      </logic:present>
      <logic:notPresent scope="session" name="memberVO">
        <B>Anonymous</B>
      </logic:notPresent>

    </TD>
    <TD>
      <BR/><BR/> 
    </TD>
  </TR>
  <TR>
    <TD>
      <font size="2"><b>
<bean:message
    key="javaedge.poststory.form.titlelabel"/>: 
</b></font><br/>
```

```
        <html:text property="attribute(storyTitle)"/>
      </TD>
    </TR>
    <TR>
      <TD>
        <font size="2"><b>
          <bean:message
            key="javaedge.poststory.form.introlabel"/>: 
          </b></font><br/>
        <html:textarea property="attribute(storyIntro)" cols="80" rows="5"/>
      </TD>
    </TR>
    <TR>
      <TD>
        <font size="2"><b>
          <bean:message
            key="javaedge.poststory.form.bodylabel"/>: 
          </b></font><br/>
        <html:textarea  property="attribute(storyBody)" cols="80" rows="10"/>
      </TD>
    </TR>
    <TR>
      <TD align="center">
        <html:submit property="submitButton" value="Submit"/>  
        <html:cancel value="Cancel"/>
      </TD>
    </TR>
  </TABLE>
</html:form>
```

To use this new ActionForm, you need do the following:

- Add a new <form-bean> tag to the JavaEdge application's struts-config.xml file for the PostStoryMapForm.

- Modify the /postStorySetup and /postStory actions in the struts-config.xml file to use the newly created <form-bean>.

- Modify the PostStory.java file to cast to a PostStoryMapForm class instead of the PostStoryForm class. You also need to remove any references to PostStoryForm's get()/set() method class and replace them with calls to PostStoryMapForm's getAttribute() and setAttribute() methods.

- Modify the postStory.jsp to use the postStoryMapContent.jsp file instead of the postStoryContent.jsp file.

ActionForm Best Practices

ActionForm classes provide a very clean mechanism for abstracting the implementation details of getting and setting data in the HttpServletRequest object passed into the Struts ActionServlet. There are some best practices associated with using ActionForm classes. These best practices have evolved, as development teams using Struts have had to maintain and extend applications in a production environment.

Two of these best practices are documented here:

- Make all of the public attributes on your ActionForm of type String.

- Cleanly separate all of your ActionForm classes from your application's business logic. Do not pass ActionForm classes directly into your application's business logic.

Strings and the ActionForm

While a Struts ActionForm can expose any data type using a get()/set() method on the interface, it's a good idea to only use Strings as the data types being passed in and out of the ActionForm. The reason for this is that when a user submits form data to a Struts application, the Struts ActionServlet is going to pull all of the data out of the HTTP request and match that data to a get()/set() attribute on an ActionForm.

The problem arises when the user submits a piece of data in a form field that does not match the data type of its corresponding attribute on the ActionForm. This problem is encountered most often when dealing with numeric (that is, Integer, Float, etc.), Date/Timestamps, and Boolean data types. For example, suppose you expose an attribute on ActionForm with a get()/set() pair of methods that accept and return an Integer class. The user enters a value of "a" in the form field that is expecting an Integer object.

When this value is submitted, the Struts ActionServlet will try to set the value of "a" on an attribute that has been defined to be of type Integer. When this happens, an exception will be thrown and the user will usually end up with a big white screen full of informative Java error messages. You cannot catch this problem in the validate() method on the ActionForm, because the data is copied out of the HTTP request before the validate() method is invoked.

How do you deal with this kind of problem? You could try to point JavaScript code to the HTML where the form data is being captured. The problem is that you can easily end up creating a Validation Confusion antipattern because you have effectively split your validation logic for the form into two different locations, and that is what you are trying to avoid. In addition, you lose a great deal of control when using JavaScript validation. End users can easily disable the JavaScript validation by configuring their web browser to not execute JavaScript code.

The best way to deal with this type of problem is to keep all of the properties on your ActionForm class as type String. By doing this, you can then capture all of the data entered by the user without running the risk of a type mismatch. Then in the ActionForm's validate() method you can perform type checking on the data contained within these strings and cleanly throw validation errors using Strut's ActionError objects.

ActionForms and Business Logic

The ActionForm class is used to hold data submitted by the end user. It is passed into the execute() method on an Action class, where its data can then be used by the action to carry out the business logic associated with the request. Ideally, business logic for the application should not be embedded inside of the Action class code itself.

Instead, the business logic for the application should be contained in a POJO or an EJB that is completely independent of the Action class. Unfortunately, for many developers using Struts for the first time, the temptation to pass the ActionForm class from the Action class to the corresponding business logic is a very strong one. After all the ActionForm class is already holding the data submitted by the end user, so why not just pass it directly to the POJO or EJB containing the business logic?

The problem with this approach is that you are introducing the Tier Leakage antipattern into your application. You are letting an implementation detail from your presentation tier, the ActionForm class, be passed to your business tier. This creates a dependency on a Struts-specific class, with an unintended consequence if you want to reuse that piece of business logic outside of a Struts-based application: You have to refactor the code to not have this dependency or instantiate a Struts ActionForm class and populate it with data, even if you are not building a web-based application.

To avoid this problem, you should copy the data contained within your ActionForm class to a framework-independent class called a value object. The concept of a value object is covered in greater detail in Chapter 5. For now, think of a value object as being nothing more than a class that holds data.

There are two ways you can copy data from an ActionForm. The first mechanism is to brute force the copy and set the attributes on a value object by calling the individual get() methods on the ActionForm class. For example, in the PostStory.execute() method, you need to copy data from the ActionForm to the StoryVO object:

```
public ActionForward execute(ActionMapping mapping,
                             ActionForm     form,
                             HttpServletRequest request,
                             HttpServletResponse response){


    PostStoryForm postStoryForm = (PostStoryForm) form;

    HttpSession session = request.getSession();

    MemberVO  memberVO     = (MemberVO) session.getAttribute("memberVO");
    StoryVO storyVO = new StoryVO();

    storyVO.setStoryIntro(postStoryForm.getStoryIntro());
    storyVO.setStoryTitle(postStoryForm.getStoryTitle());
    storyVO.setStoryBody(postStoryForm.getStoryBody());

    storyVO.setStoryAuthor(memberVO);
    storyVO.setSubmissionDate(new java.sql.Date(System.currentTimeMillis()));
```

```
    storyVO.setComments(new Vector());

    //Rest of the code
    . . . . .
}
```

As you can guess, on an `ActionForm` with a lot of data, you can end up cluttering your `Action` class with a lot of code that does nothing more than copy data from the `ActionForm` to the value object.

The Struts framework does provide some utility classes that enable you to more quickly copy data from the `ActionForm` to the value object. These two classes are part of the Apache Commons BeanUtils project (`http://jakarta.apache.org/commons`). These classes are distributed with Struts in the commons-beanutils.jar file. The classes are

- `org.apache.commons.beanutils.BeanUtils`

- `org.apache.commons.beanutils.PropertyUtils`

Both of these classes simplify many of the most common tasks associated with manipulating a JavaBean. In the code example, we are going to show you how to use the `copyProperties()` method on the `BeanUtils` class to copy data from `postStoryForm` to `storyVO`:

```
public ActionForward execute(ActionMapping mapping,
                             ActionForm     form,
                             HttpServletRequest request,
                             HttpServletResponse response){


    PostStoryForm postStoryForm = (PostStoryForm) form;

    HttpSession session = request.getSession();

    MemberVO  memberVO      = (MemberVO) session.getAttribute("memberVO");
    StoryVO storyVO = new StoryVO();


    try{
      BeanUtils.copyProperties(storyVO, postStoryForm);
    }
    catch(IllegalAccessException e) {
      throw new ApplicationException("IllegalAccessException " +
        " in PostStory.execute",e);
    }
    catch(InvocationTargetException e){
      throw new ApplicationException(
        "InvocationTargetException in PostStory.execute",
        e);
    }
```

```
        storyVO.setStoryAuthor(memberVO);
        storyVO.setSubmissionDate(new java.sql.Date(System.currentTimeMillis()));
        storyVO.setComments(new Vector());

        //Rest of the code
        . . . . .
}
```

When the copyProperties() method is invoked, it will use Java reflection to call each of the get() methods on the postStoryForm object:

```
try{
    BeanUtils.copyProperties(storyVO, postStoryForm);
}
catch(IllegalAccessException e) {
    throw new ApplicationException("IllegalAccessException in
                            PostStory.execute",e);
}
catch(InvocationTargetException e){
    throw new ApplicationException("InvocationTargetException in
                            PostStory.execute",e);
}
```

When BeanUtils.copyProperties() is called, it will invoke each of the get() methods on the object passed in as the first parameter. As copyProperties() calls each get() method, it will try to call a corresponding set() method that has the same name on the object passed as the second parameter.

The BeanUtils.copyProperties() can be a significant time saver when you are trying to copy data from an ActionForm to a value object. However, it still litters up the Action class's execute() method with exception-handling code.

■ **Note** The BeanUtils.copyProperties() method will try to do type conversions between properties being copied from one JavaBean to another.

This means that if an application is trying to use the copyProperties() method to copy a property defined as type Integer to a property of type String on another bean, the copyProperties() method will attempt to do a type conversion. If the copyProperties() method cannot do the type conversion, it will throw an exception of type java.lang.reflect.InvocationTargetException.

■ **Note** If you know that there are going to be no type conversions when copying the contents of one JavaBean to another JavaBean, you can use the PropertyUtils.copyProperties() method. This copyProperties() method on PropertyUtils does the same function as the corresponding method on BeanUtils, but does not attempt to do type conversion of properties.

As you will see later, in Chapter 4, one of the design goals of a Struts application should be to minimize the amount of code present in the Action class.

What if you were to encapsulate all the logic for copying data to and from a value object inside of the ActionForm class itself? This way, the Action class would just need to invoke a method on the ActionForm to get a value object that would be passed to Action's business logic. The concept of building a value object factory method into ActionForm is not new and was first documented in the book *Struts in Action* (Ted Husted et al., Manning Press, ISBN: 1-930-11050-2).

Let's add a new method to the PostStoryForm class called buildStoryVO:

```
public StoryVO buildStoryVO(HttpServletRequest request)
  throws ApplicationException{
  HttpSession session = request.getSession();

  MemberVO      memberVO      = (MemberVO) session.getAttribute("memberVO");
  StoryVO storyVO = new StoryVO();

  /*Example of how to use the BeanUtils class to populate a valueobject.*/
  try{
    BeanUtils.copyProperties(storyVO, this);
  }
  catch(IllegalAccessException e) {
    throw new ApplicationException("IllegalAccessException in
                            PostStoryForm.execute",e);

  }
  catch(InvocationTargetException e){
    throw new ApplicationException("InvocationTargetException in
                            PostStoryForm.execute",e);

  }

  storyVO.setStoryAuthor(memberVO);
  storyVO.setSubmissionDate(new java.sql.Date(System.currentTimeMillis()));
  storyVO.setComments(new Vector());

  return storyVO;
}
```

The buildStoryVO() method on the PostStoryForm class cleanly encapsulates all of the details associated with building out a StoryVO based on the data contained within the PostStoryForm. When this method is used in the execute() method on the PostStory class, you end up with a much cleaner method:

```
public ActionForward execute(ActionMapping mapping,
                        ActionForm      form,
                        HttpServletRequest request,
                        HttpServletResponse response)
          throws ApplicationException {
```

```
  if (this.isCancelled(request)){
    return (mapping.findForward("poststory.success"));
  }

  PostStoryForm postStoryForm = (PostStoryForm) form;
  StoryVO storyVO = postStoryForm.buildStoryVO(request);

  StoryManagerBD storyManager = new StoryManagerBD();
  storyManager.addStory(storyVO);
  return (mapping.findForward("poststory.success"));
}
```

You may have noticed that the execute() method just shown throws an ApplicationException. However, nowhere in the code is a try{}/catch{} block to handle the exception. So, how does the JavaEdge application deal with the ApplicationException if the exception is raised?

The JavaEdge application uses the Struts 1.1 exception-handler functionality to process the ApplicationException. Struts exception handlers allow a development team to declare how an Exception is to be thrown without cluttering up the Action class. This new exception-handling functionality is described in greater detail in the next chapter.

Summary

This chapter focuses on how to use Struts to collect and process the data submitted in an HTML form. The following four pieces must be present to use the Struts-based form processing:

- ActionForm class

- Action class

- JSP page that uses the Struts HTML tag library to generate the HTML <input> fields used to collect the user information

    - name attribute in an <action> tag in the struts-config.xml file

- Tags used for building the base HTML form:

    - <html:form>: Used to render a <form> tag

    - <html:submit>: Renders a submit button

    - <html:cancel>: Renders a cancel button

    - <html:errors>: Renders any validation errors that have been raised during processing

CHAPTER 4

■ ■ ■

Managing Business Logic
with Struts

So far you've seen how to use the Struts framework to facilitate the construction of an application. You've also had a chance to examine the basic workflow of a Struts-based request along with the different components needed to carry out a user's requested action. However, while the Struts framework is a powerful tool for building applications, it is still only a tool. Using the Struts framework does not relieve you of the responsibility of architecting your application.

A framework like Struts is meant to promote rapid application development as well as ease the maintenance and extensibility of an application. However, if no forethought is given to how the business logic for an application is going to be built, it becomes very easy to "lock" an application's business logic into the Struts framework.

As a result, a development team using Struts might be able to quickly build the initial applications, but later, the team will find that it cannot easily reuse the functionality in a non-Struts framework. A framework provides structure, but it also defines boundaries, constraints, and dependencies, which will cause a significant number of problems if they are not considered early on.

This chapter demonstrates how to use several common J2EE design patterns to ensure that an application's business logic is not too tightly coupled with the Struts framework. Specifically we are going to show you

- Common implementation mistakes made while implementing a Struts `Action` class. We will discuss how, even with the use of the Struts development framework, the Concern Slush and Tier Leakage antipatterns can still form. (Refer to Chapter 1 for our discussion on the various antipatterns.)

- How to refactor these antipatterns into a more maintainable framework, which will allow you to reuse business logic across both Struts and non-Struts applications.

The design patterns that will be covered in this chapter include

- The Business Delegate pattern

- The Service Locator pattern

- The Session Facade pattern

All of these design patterns will be implemented with the help of the JavaEdge application code.

In addition, we will look at how to properly handle application exceptions thrown from your business logic.

Business Logic Antipatterns and Struts

The Struts framework's Model-View-Controller implementation significantly reduces the chance that the Concern Slush or Tier Leakage antipattern will form. Recollecting the discussion from Chapter 1, the Concern Slush antipattern forms when the system architect does not provide a framework separating the presentation, business, and data access logic into well-defined application tiers. As a result, it becomes difficult to reuse and support the code.

The Tier Leakage antipattern occurs when an application developer exposes the implementation details of one application tier to another tier—for example, when the presentation logic of the application, that is, a JSP page, creates an EJB to invoke some business logic on its behalf. Although the business logic for the page has been cleanly separated from the JSP code, the JSP page is exposed to the complexities of locating and instantiating the EJB. This creates a tight dependency between the presentation tier and the business tier.

The Struts framework does an excellent job of enforcing a clean separation of presentation and business logic within an application. All the presentation logic is encapsulated in JSP pages using Struts tag libraries to simplify the development effort. All business logic is placed in a Struts `Action` class. The JSP pages in the application are never allowed to invoke the business logic directly. It's the responsibility of the `ActionServlet`.

However, in a Struts-based application, the way in which the business logic is implemented is still decided by the application developer. Often, developers who are new to the Struts framework will place all of the business and data access logic for the application into a Struts `Action` class. They need to consider the long-term architectural consequences of doing this. Without careful forethought and planning, antipatterns such as Concern Slush and Tier Leakage can still manifest themselves within an application.

At this point, you might be asking the question, "I thought the Struts development framework was supposed to refactor these antipatterns?" The answer is yes, to a point.

Note Using a development framework does not mitigate or relieve development teams of the responsibility of architecting the application. Development teams need to ensure that their use of a framework does not create dependencies that make it difficult to reuse application logic outside of the framework. Application architects are still responsible for enforcing the overall integrity of the application's architecture. A development framework is a tool, not a silver bullet.

When development teams make the decision to adopt a development framework, they often rush in and immediately begin writing code. They have not cleanly separated the "core" business logic from the framework itself. As a result, they often find themselves going through all sorts of contortions to reuse the code in nonframework-based applications.

Let's look at two code examples that can be precursors to the formation of the Concern Slush and Tier Leakage antipatterns in Struts.

Concern Slush and Struts

The Concern Slush antipattern can manifest itself in a Struts-based application when the developer fails to cleanly separate the business and data access logic from the Struts Action class. Let's revisit the Post a Story page that was explored in Chapter 3. The following is an example of how the PostStory action (as defined in PostStory.java file) can be implemented:

```java
package com.apress.javaedge.struts.poststory;

import org.apache.struts.action.*;
import org.apache.struts.*;
import javax.servlet.http.*;
import javax.naming.*;
import java.sql.*;
import javax.sql.*;

import com.apress.javaedge.story.*;
import com.apress.javaedge.member.*;
import com.apress.javaedge.story.ejb.PrizeManager;

public class PostStory extends Action {

  public ActionForward execute(ActionMapping mapping,
                               ActionForm form,
                               HttpServletRequest request,
                               HttpServletResponse response) {

    PostStoryForm postStoryForm = (PostStoryForm) form;
    HttpSession session = request.getSession();

    MemberVO memberVO = (MemberVO) session.getAttribute("memberVO");

    if (this.isCancelled(request)) {
      return (mapping.findForward("poststory.success"));
    }

    Connection conn = null;
    PreparedStatement ps = null;

    try {
      Context ctx = new InitialContext();
      DataSource ds = (DataSource) ctx.lookup("java:/MySQLDS");
      conn = ds.getConnection();
      conn.setAutoCommit(false);

      StringBuffer insertSQL = new StringBuffer();
```

```
    /*
     * Please note that this code is only an example. The SQL code assumes
     * that the story table is using an auto-generated key. However, in
     * the JavaEdge application we use ObjectRelationalBridge's Sequence
     * capabilities to generate a key. This code will not work unless you
     * modify the story table to use an auto-generated key for the
     * story_id column.
     */
    insertSQL.append("INSERT INTO story(              ");
    insertSQL.append("  member_id              ,     ");
    insertSQL.append("  story_title            ,     ");
    insertSQL.append("  story_into             ,     ");
    insertSQL.append("  story_body             ,     ");
    insertSQL.append("  submission_date              ");
    insertSQL.append(")                              ");
    insertSQL.append("VALUES(                        ");
    insertSQL.append("  ?                      ,     ");
    insertSQL.append("  ?                      ,     ");
    insertSQL.append("  ?                      ,     ");
    insertSQL.append("  ?                      ,     ");
    insertSQL.append("  CURDATE()              )     ");

    ps = conn.prepareStatement(insertSQL.toString());

    ps.setLong(1, memberVO.getMemberId().longValue());
    ps.setString(2, postStoryForm.getStoryTitle());
    ps.setString(3, postStoryForm.getStoryIntro());
    ps.setString(4, postStoryForm.getStoryBody());

    ps.execute();
    conn.commit();

    checkStoryCount(memberVO);

} catch(SQLException e) {
  try{
    if (conn != null) conn.rollback();

  } catch(SQLException ex) {}

  System.err.println("A SQL exception has been raised in " +
                "PostStory.execute(): " + e.toString());

  return (mapping.findForward("system.failure"));
} catch(NamingException e) {
  System.err.println("A Naming exception has been raised in " +
                "PostStory.execute(): " + e.toString());
```

```
      return (mapping.findForward("system.failure"));
    } finally {
      try {
        if (ps != null) ps.close();
        if (conn != null) conn.close();
      } catch(SQLException e) {}

  }

  return (mapping.findForward("poststory.success"));
}

private void checkStoryCount(MemberVO memberVO)
    throws SQLException, NamingException {
  Connection conn = null;
  PreparedStatement ps = null;
  ResultSet rs = null;

  try {
    Context ctx = new InitialContext();
    DataSource  ds = (DataSource) ctx.lookup("java:/MySQLDS");
    conn = ds.getConnection();

    StringBuffer selectSQL = new StringBuffer();

    selectSQL.append("SELECT                     ");
    selectSQL.append("  count(*) total_count     ");
    selectSQL.append("FROM                        ");
    selectSQL.append("  story where member_id=?  ");

    ps = conn.prepareStatement(selectSQL.toString());
    ps.setLong(1, memberVO.getMemberId().longValue());

    rs = ps.executeQuery();
    int totalCount = 0;

    if (rs.next()) {
      totalCount = rs.getInt("total_count");
    }

    boolean TOTAL_COUNT_EQUAL_1000 = (totalCount==1000);
    boolean TOTAL_COUNT_EQUAL_5000 = (totalCount==5000);

    if (TOTAL_COUNT_EQUAL_1000 || TOTAL_COUNT_EQUAL_5000) {
    //Notify Prize Manager
      PrizeManager prizeManager = new PrizeManager();
      prizeManager.notifyMarketing(memberVO, totalCount);
```

```
      }
   } catch(SQLException e) {
      System.err.println("A SQL exception has been raised in " +
                        " PostStory.checkStoryCount(): " + e.toString());

      throw e;
   } catch(NamingException e) {
      System.err.println("A Naming exception has been raised in " +
                        " PostStory.checkStoryCount(): " +
                        e.toString());
      throw e;
   } finally {
      try {
         if (rs != null) rs.close();
            if (ps != null) ps.close();
            if (conn != null) conn.close();
      } catch(SQLException e) {}
   }
  }
}
```

The preceding execute() method performs two very simple functions:

- It inserts the data submitted by the user on the Post a Story page using the standard JDBC and SQL calls. From the discussions in Chapter 3, you know that the submitted data has already been validated by the validate() method on the PostForm class.

- It checks, via a call to checkStoryCount(), if the total number of stories submitted by a JavaEdge member is at the 1000th or 5000th mark. On the 1000th and 5000th story submitted by the user, the marketing department is notified via the PrizeManager class.

The PrizeManager class integrates several legacy systems throughout the organization and ultimately sends the user $100 to spend at the bookstore on the JavaEdge site.

From a functional perspective, the code for the execute() method works well. However, from an architectural viewpoint, the implementation for the PostStory class shown previously is a mess. Several problems are present in the preceding code that will eventually cause significant long-term maintenance and extensibility problems. These problems include the following:

- The entire business logic for adding a story and checking the total number of stories submitted by a user is embedded in the Struts Action class. This has several architectural consequences:

   • If the development team wants to reuse this logic, it must use the PostStory class (even if it does not really fit into the other application); refactor the business logic into a new Java class; or perform the oldest form of reuse: cut and paste. This operation leads to either usage of more code than what is needed or, plainly put, bugs.

   • The business logic for the application is tied directly to the Struts framework. If the development team decides to move the application from the Struts framework into something else, say Apache Beehive or Shale, it is looking at a significant amount of rework.

- There is no clean separation of the business and data access logic. While these two pieces of logic are cleanly separated by Struts from the presentation tier, a significant number of dependencies are still being created between the business logic and the data access logic:

  - The `Action` class has intimate knowledge of which data access technology is being used to access the data used by the JavaEdge application. If the development team wants to switch to a new data access technology at some point, it must revisit every single place in the application that is interacting with a database.

  - The `Action` class has SQL Data Definition Language (DDL) embedded in it. Any changes to the underlying table structures that the JavaEdge application is using can send ripple effects throughout the system.

Definition A *ripple effect* is when there are such tight dependencies between application modules or application code and data structures that a change to one piece of code sends you hunting throughout the rest of the application for other areas that must be modified to reflect that change.

For example, if a data relationship between two tables were to change, such as a one-to-many relationship being refactored into a many-to-many relationship, any SQL code embedded in the application that accessed these tables would need to be visited and probably refactored.

Abstraction is the key to avoiding a ripple effect. If the SQL logic for the application was cleanly hidden behind a set of interfaces that did not expose the actual structure of the database table to the application, the chance of a ripple effect occurring is much less. In the next chapter, we will demonstrate how to use some basic data access design patterns to achieve this goal.

Note Ultimately, the `Action` class should be a plug-in point where business logic is invoked but not contained.

The code shown previously is difficult to follow and maintain. Even though the business logic for the Post a Story page is very simplistic, it still took a large amount of code to implement. Keep the following in mind, while building your first Struts-based application:

Note Development frameworks like Struts are used for building applications. However, the business logic in applications often belongs to the enterprise and not just a single application. How many times have you seen the business logic cut across multiple applications within an organization? Be wary of embedding too much business logic directly within Struts. Otherwise you might find that reuse of business logic becomes extremely difficult.

Tier Leakage and Struts

Many development teams will get an uneasy feeling about the amount of business logic being placed in the Struts Action class. They might have already run into situations where they have the same business logic being reused in many of their applications.

The natural tendency is to refactor the Struts code and move it into a component-based architecture (such as Enterprise JavaBeans) or a services-based architecture (such as Web services). This moves the business logic out of the Struts Action class and makes it more readily accessible to the other applications. Let's refactor the PostStory class and move all of the business logic into an Enterprise JavaBean called StoryManager. The code for the rewritten PostStory class is shown here:

```
package com.apress.javaedge.struts.poststory;

import org.apache.struts.action.*;
import javax.servlet.http.*;
import javax.naming.*;
import javax.ejb.*;
import java.rmi.*;
import javax.rmi.*;

import com.apress.javaedge.common.*;
import com.apress.javaedge.story.*;
import com.apress.javaedge.member.*;
import com.apress.javaedge.story.ejb.*;

public class PostStory extends Action {

  public ActionForward execute(ActionMapping mapping,
                               ActionForm form,
                               HttpServletRequest request,
                               HttpServletResponse response){

    if (this.isCancelled(request)) {
      return (mapping.findForward("poststory.success"));
    }

    PostStoryForm postStoryForm = (PostStoryForm) form;
    HttpSession session = request.getSession();

    MemberVO memberVO = (MemberVO) session.getAttribute("memberVO");

    try {
      Context ctx = new InitialContext();
      Object ref = ctx.lookup("storyManager/StoryManager");
```

```
    StoryManagerHome storyManagerHome =
      (StoryManagerHome) PortableRemoteObject.narrow(ref,
        StoryManagerHome.class);
    StoryManager storyManager = storyManagerHome.create();
    storyManager.addStory(postStoryForm, memberVO);

  } catch(ApplicationException e){
    System.err.println("An Application exception has been raised in " +
                  "PostStory.execute(): " + e.toString());
    return (mapping.findForward("system.failure"));

  } catch(NamingException e) {
    System.err.println("A Naming exception has been raised in " +
                  "PostStory. execute (): " + e.toString());
    return (mapping.findForward("system.failure"));

  } catch(RemoteException e) {
    System.err.println("A Remote exception has been raised in " +
                  "PostStory. execute (): " + e.toString());
    return (mapping.findForward("system.failure"));

  } catch(CreateException e) {
    System.err.println("A Create exception has been raised in " +
                  "PostStory. execute (): " + e.toString());
    return (mapping.findForward("system.failure"));
  }

  return (mapping.findForward("poststory.success"));
  }
}
```

The preceding code appears to solve all the problems defined earlier. It is much easier to read and understand. The Concern Slush antipattern, which was present earlier, has been refactored. By moving the business logic out of the PostStory.execute() method and into the StoryManager EJB, the business logic can be reused more easily across multiple applications.

However, the rewritten PostStory class just shown still has flaws in it that can lead to a Tier Leakage antipattern. The refactored execute() method has intimate knowledge of how the business logic is being invoked. The entire business logic is contained within the EJB, and the application developer has to perform a JNDI lookup and then retrieve a reference to the EJB by invoking its create() method.

What happens if the development team later wants to rewrite the business logic and wrap it to use a Web service instead of an EJB? Since the PostStory Action class has direct knowledge that the business logic it needs is contained within an EJB, the class must be rewritten to now invoke a Web service instead of an EJB.

Note As you will see shortly, what is needed here is some kind of proxy that will sit between the framework class (the `PostStory` class) and the actual business logic (the EJB). The proxy should completely abstract how the business logic is being invoked. This proxy, also known as the Business Delegate pattern, will be discussed shortly.

Another problem with the preceding code is that the addStory() method is taking the PostStoryForm class as an input parameter:

```
storyManager.addStory(postStoryForm, memberVO);
```

This creates a dependency between the business logic, which is responsible for adding a story to the JavaEdge application, and the Struts framework in which the application is built. If the developers want to use the StoryManager EJB in a non-Struts–based application, they would not be able to do so easily.

Note Even when choosing to use a Java open source development framework, it is important not to create tight dependencies between the framework and business logic. Applications rarely exist in a vacuum. They often have to be integrated with the other systems being maintained by the IT department. This integration often means reusing code that has already been written. Tight coupling of business logic with the framework can limit your ability to reuse that business logic in applications that are not built with your chosen framework.

This is why it is still extremely important to apply the architectural principles of abstraction and encapsulation, even when building Struts-based applications. Antipatterns are a subtle beast. It is rare for developers to feel the full impact of an antipattern in the first application that they build. Instead, the problems caused by an antipattern will suddenly manifest themselves when the development team has already deployed several applications and needs to integrate or reuse the code in these applications. That is when the antipattern and the full scope of the necessary rework are revealed.

Separating Business Logic from Struts

The challenge is to build your Struts application in such a way that the business logic for the application becomes independent of the actual Struts framework. The Action classes in your Struts application should only be a plug-in point for the business logic.

Fortunately, common J2EE design patterns provide a readily available solution. These patterns are particularly well suited for solving many of the dependencies between the framework and the business logic as were discussed earlier. In this chapter, we are not going to cover all the J2EE design patterns in great detail. Instead, we are going to discuss the patterns that are most appropriate for use in building Struts-based applications.

The design patterns that are going to be discussed include

- The Business Delegate pattern

- The Service Locator pattern

- The Session Facade pattern

Figure 4-1 demonstrates how these J2EE design patterns can be assembled to partition the business logic used in the application from the Struts development framework.

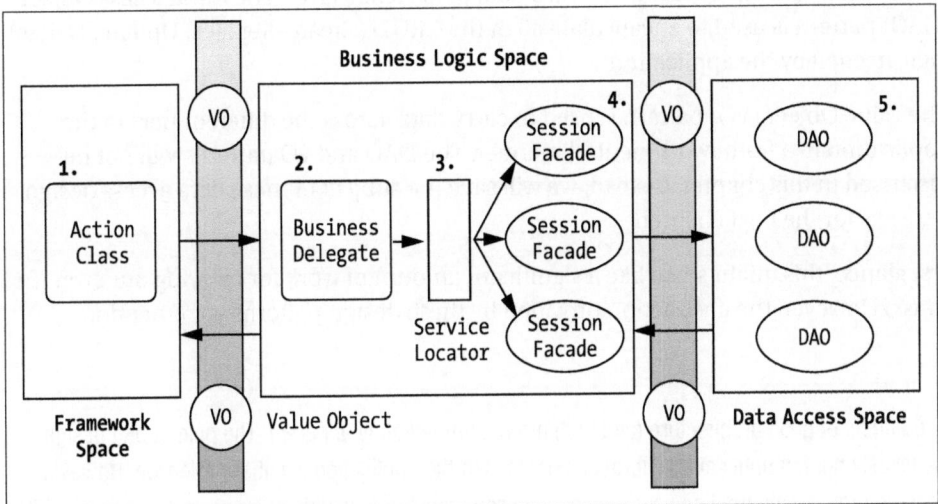

Figure 4-1. *Struts and the J2EE design patterns—a conceptual view*

Let's revisit the whole process of how an end user adds a new story to the JavaEdge application, using the architectural model shown in Figure 4-1:

1. The user makes a request to add a story. The execute() method in the PostStory Action class is invoked. However, in this model, the PostStory action does not contain the actual code for adding the user's story and checking the number of stories submitted by the user. Instead, the PostStory class instantiates a business delegate that carries out this business logic.

2. The business delegate is a Java class that shields the PostStory Action class from knowing how the business logic is created and executed. In the section "Tier Leakage and Struts" earlier, the code for adding a story was moved to the StoryManager EJB. The business delegate class would be responsible for looking up this EJB via JNDI. All the public methods in the StoryManager EJB should be available to the business delegate. All the public method calls in the business delegate would be forwarded to the StoryManager EJB.

3. The business delegate does not have the direct knowledge of how to look up the StoryManager EJB. Instead, it uses a class called the ServiceLocator. The ServiceLocator is used to look up the various resources within the application. Examples of resources looked up and returned by a ServiceLocator class include the home interface for EJBs and DataSource objects for retrieving JDBC connections.

4. The EJBs returned by the ServiceLocator class are known as session facades. A *session facade* is an EJB that wraps a complex business process involving multiple Java objects behind a simple-to-use coarse-grained interface. In the PostStory example, the StoryManager EJB is a session facade that hides all of the steps involved in adding a story to the JavaEdge application.

5. The business objects are responsible for carrying out the individual steps in the business action requested by the end user. Business logic classes should never be allowed to talk directly to any of the databases used by the application. Instead, these classes should interact with the database via a data persistence layer. The Data Access Object (DAO) pattern is used to encapsulate all of the CRUD (Create, Replace, Update, Delete) logic needed by the application.

   The Value Object (VO) pattern is used to carry data across the different tiers in the application in a framework-neutral manner. The DAO and VO patterns will not be discussed in this chapter. Instead, we will save the subject of these data access design patterns for the next chapter.

At first glance, this might seem like a significant amount of work for carrying out even the simplest task. However, the abstraction provided by these design patterns is tremendous.

■**Note** The effects of good architecture (and bad) are not immediately apparent. The pain of bad design decisions is usually not felt until several iterations past when the application is initially released. However, the time spent in properly abstracting your applications can have huge payoffs in terms of the maintainability and extensibility of your code.

The J2EE design patterns, demonstrated in Figure 4-1, completely separate the business logic from the Struts framework and ensure that the business logic for the application has no intimate knowledge of the data access code being used.

Implementing the Design Patterns

The remaining sections of this chapter discuss the implementations of the J2EE design patterns discussed so far. We will be refactoring the PostStory Action class so that it uses a business delegate to invoke the logic, which it needs to carry out the user request.

Figure 4-2, which looks similar to the previous diagram, demonstrates the actions that take place when the execute() method of the PostStory class is invoked.

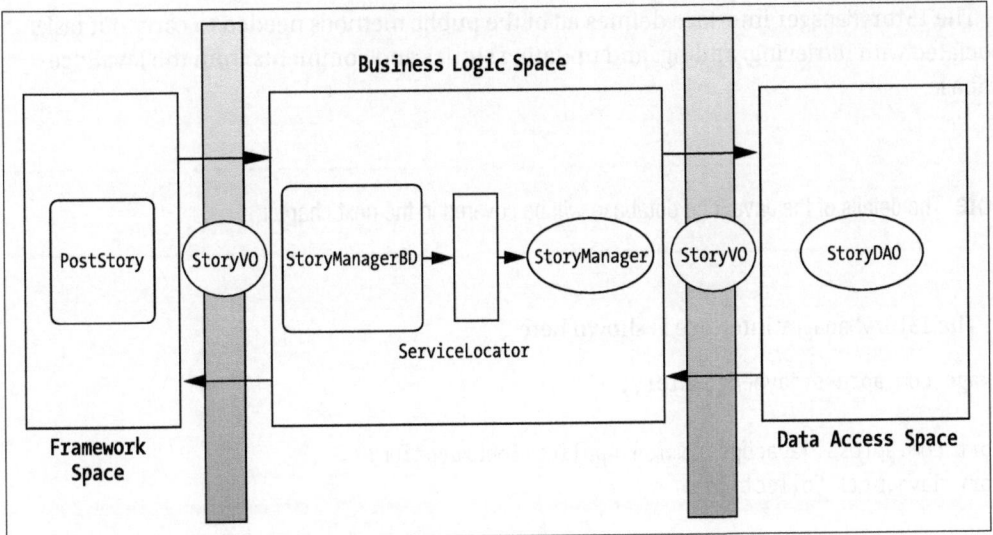

Figure 4-2. *An example of J2EE design patterns in action*

Implementing the Business Delegate Pattern

A Business Delegate pattern hides the complexity of instantiating and using the enterprise
services such as EJBs or Web services from the application consuming the service. A Business
Delegate pattern is very straightforward. It is implemented by wrapping an already existing
service behind a plain Java class. Each public method available in the service is mapped to a
public method in the business delegate.

The code for StoryManagerBD.java that follows demonstrates how to wrap the business
logic associated with managing story data. For demonstration purposes, the StoryManagerBD.
java class does not simply delegate all calls to a Plain Old Java Object (POJO) or an EJB. Instead,
the StoryManagerBD provides a single method, getStoryManagerBD(), that returns a reference
to a class that implements the IStoryManager interface.

```
package com.apress.javaedge.story;

import com.apress.javaedge.common.ApplicationException;
import com.apress.javaedge.common.DataAccessException;
import com.apress.javaedge.story.dao.StoryDAO;

import java.util.Collection;


public class StoryManagerBD {

    public static final IStoryManager getStoryManagerBD() {
        return new StoryManagerPOJOImpl();
    }

}
```

The IStoryManager interface defines all of the public methods needed to carry out tasks associated with retrieving, adding, and updating stories and comments from the JavaEdge database.

Note The details of the JavaEdge database will be covered in the next chapter.

The IStoryManager interface is shown here:

```
package com.apress.javaedge.story;

import com.apress.javaedge.common.ApplicationException;
import java.util.Collection;


public interface IStoryManager {

    public void addStory(StoryVO storyVO) throws ApplicationException;
    public Collection findTopStory() throws ApplicationException;
    public StoryVO retrieveStory(String primaryKey);
    public void updateStory(StoryVO storyVO) throws ApplicationException;
}
```

In the StoryManagerBD, we provide two different implementations that could possibly be returned by the class. One implementation, StoryManagerPOJOImpl, uses POJO-based objects to execute all requested actions against a JavaEdge story:

```
package com.apress.javaedge.story;

import com.apress.javaedge.common.ApplicationException;
import com.apress.javaedge.common.DataAccessException;
import com.apress.javaedge.story.dao.StoryDAO;

import java.util.Collection;

public class StoryManagerPOJOImpl implements IStoryManager {
    StoryDAO storyDAO = new StoryDAO();

    public void addStory(StoryVO storyVO) throws ApplicationException {
        try {
            storyDAO.insert(storyVO);
        } catch (DataAccessException e) {
            throw new ApplicationException(
                    "DataAccessException Error in StoryManagerBean.addStory(): "
                    + e.toString(),
                    e);
        }
    }
```

```java
    }

    public Collection findTopStory() throws ApplicationException {
        Collection topStories = null;

        try {

            topStories = storyDAO.findTopStory();

        } catch (DataAccessException e) {
            e.printStackTrace();
            String msg = "Data access exception raised in " +
                            "StoryManagerBD.findTopStory ()";
            throw new ApplicationException(msg, e);
        }

        return topStories;
    }

    public StoryVO retrieveStory(String primaryKey) throws ApplicationException {
        try {
            return (StoryVO) storyDAO.findByPK(primaryKey);
        } catch (DataAccessException e) {
            throw new ApplicationException(
                    "DataAccessException Error in " +
                    "StoryManagerBean.retrieveStory(): "
                    + e.toString(),
                    e);
        }
    }

    public void updateStory(StoryVO storyVO) throws ApplicationException {
        try {
            storyDAO.insert(storyVO);
        } catch (DataAccessException e) {
            throw new ApplicationException(
                    "DataAccessException Error in StoryManagerBean.updateStory(): "
                    + e.toString(),
                    e);
        }
    }
}
```

The second implementation of our StoryManager business delegate, called StoryManagerEJBImpl, passes all requests to an EJB called StoryManager:

```
package com.apress.javaedge.story;

import com.apress.javaedge.story.ejb.StoryManager;
import com.apress.javaedge.story.ejb.StoryManagerHome;
import com.apress.javaedge.common.ApplicationException;
import com.apress.javaedge.common.ServiceLocator;
import com.apress.javaedge.common.ServiceLocatorException;

import javax.ejb.CreateException;
import javax.naming.Context;
import javax.naming.InitialContext;
import javax.naming.NamingException;
import javax.rmi.PortableRemoteObject;
import java.rmi.RemoteException;

public class StoryManagerEJBImpl {

    StoryManager storyManager = null;

    public StoryManagerEJBImpl() throws ApplicationException {
        try {
            Context ctx = new InitialContext();
            Object ref = ctx.lookup("storyManager/StoryManager");

            StoryManagerHome storyManagerHome = (StoryManagerHome)
                    PortableRemoteObject.narrow(ref, StoryManagerHome.class);
            storyManager = storyManagerHome.create();
        } catch (NamingException e) {
          throw new ApplicationException("A Naming exception has been raised in " +
                    "StoryManagerBD constructor: " +
                    e.toString());
        } catch (RemoteException e) {
          throw new ApplicationException("A Remote exception has been raised in " +
                    "StoryManagerBD constructor: " +
                    e.toString());
        } catch (CreateException e) {
          throw new ApplicationException("A Create exception has been raised in " +
                    "StoryManagerBD constructor: " +
                    e.toString());
        }
    }
```

The StoryManagerEJBImpl class looks up the home interface of the StoryManager EJB in its constructor. Using the retrieved home interface, the StoryManager EJB is created. A reference to the newly created bean will be stored in the private attribute, called storyManager. The StoryManagerBean being retrieved by StoryManagerEJBImpl has the same code being executed as the StoryManagerPOJOImpl class. Thus, in an effort to save space, the StoryManagerBean's code will not be shown.

Avoiding Dependencies

Another noticeable part of this implementation of the StoryManagerBD class is that each of the public methods is just a simple pass-through to the underlying service (in this case, a stateless EJB). However, none of these public methods takes a class that can tie the business logic to a particular front-end technology or development framework.

A very common mistake while implementing the first Struts application is to pass an ActionForm or HttpServletRequest object to the code executing the business logic. Passing in a Struts-based class, such as ActionForm, ties the business logic directly to the Struts framework. Passing in an HttpServletRequest object creates a dependency whereby the business logic is only usable by a web application. Both of these situations can be easily avoided by allowing "neutral" objects, which do not create these dependencies, to be passed into a business delegate implementation.

After the StoryManagerBD has been implemented, the PostStory class changes, as shown here:

```java
package com.apress.javaedge.struts.poststory;

import com.apress.javaedge.story.IStoryManager;
import com.apress.javaedge.story.StoryManagerBD;
import com.apress.javaedge.story.StoryVO;
import org.apache.struts.action.Action;
import org.apache.struts.action.ActionForm;
import org.apache.struts.action.ActionForward;
import org.apache.struts.action.ActionMapping;

import javax.servlet.http.HttpServletRequest;
import javax.servlet.http.HttpServletResponse;

import com.apress.javaedge.common.ApplicationException;

public class PostStory extends Action {
        public ActionForward execute(ActionMapping mapping,
                    ActionForm      form,
                    HttpServletRequest request,
                    HttpServletResponse response) throws ApplicationException {

        if (this.isCancelled(request)){
            return (mapping.findForward("poststory.success"));
        }
```

```
        PostStoryForm postStoryForm = (PostStoryForm) form;

        StoryVO storyVO = postStoryForm.buildStoryVO(request);

        IStoryManager storyManager = StoryManagerBD.getStoryManagerBD();
        storyManager.addStory(storyVO);


        return (mapping.findForward("poststory.success"));
    }
}
```

The code in the PostStory class just shown is much simpler and cleaner than the PostStory implementation shown earlier. Let's make a couple of observations here:

- The code has absolutely no business logic embedded it in it. All business logic has been moved safely behind the StoryManager business delegate. This business logic can easily be called from a non-Struts–based application, web or otherwise.

- The code in the preceding execute() method has no idea how the business logic is being invoked. It is using a simple Java interface, IStoryManager, to hide the actual business logic invocation. By changing a single line in the StoryManagerBD, you can plug in a new business delegate implementation that invokes its logic in a completely different manner.

- All exceptions thrown from the business logic layer are now safely captured and rethrown as a generic exception, ApplicationException. This code is using a Struts global exception handler to process all ApplicationExceptions thrown from the Action classes. Exception handlers will be discussed shortly.

Now we have to admit, the preceding StoryManagerBD implementation is a little contrived. A more common implementation of a Business Delegate pattern is to have a class that "wraps" all actual business logic invocations. If that logic were to change, a developer would go and rewrite, recompile, and redeploy the newly modified business delegate.

The example shown is meant to demonstrate how quickly and easily a new method of invoking business logic could be implemented without breaking any of the applications that are consuming the services of that business logic component. For example, it would be extremely easy for you to write a new StoryManager business delegate that invoked Web services to carry out the end-user request. Even with this new implementation, the PostStory class would never know the difference.

In both of the StoryManagerBD implementations, the PostStoryForm class is no longer passed in as a parameter on any of its method implementations. This small piece of refactoring avoids creating a dependency on a Struts-specific class.

Note Abstraction, when applied appropriately, gives your applications the ability to evolve gracefully as the business and technical requirements of the application change over time.

Implementing the Service Locator Pattern

Implementing a business delegate can involve a significant amount of repetitive coding. Every business delegate constructor has to look up the service, which it is going to wrap, via a JNDI call. The Service Locator pattern mitigates the need for this coding and, more importantly, allows the developer to hide the implementation details associated with looking up a service. A service locator can be used to hide a variety of different resources such as the following:

- JNDI lookups for an `EJBHome` interface

- JNDI lookups associated with finding a JDBC `DataSource` for retrieving a database connection

- Object creation associated with the following:

  - Looking up an Apache Axis `Call` class for invoking a Web service

  - Retrieving Persistence Broker/Manager for Object Relational Management tools, such as the open source package ObjectRelationalBridge (OJB) or Oracle's TopLink

In addition, the implementation of a Service Locator pattern allows you to implement optimizations to your code without having to revisit multiple places in your application.

For instance, performing a JNDI lookup is expensive. If you allow your business delegate classes to directly invoke a JNDI lookup, implementing a caching mechanism that minimizes the number of JNDI calls would involve a significant amount of rework. However, if you centralize all of your JNDI lookup calls behind a Service Locator pattern, you would be able to implement the optimizations and caching and only have to touch one piece of code. A Service Locator pattern is easy to implement. For the time it takes to implement the pattern, the reduction in overall maintenance costs of the application can easily exceed the costs of writing the class.

The business delegate class also allows you to isolate vendor-specific options for looking up JNDI components, thereby limiting the effects of "vendor lock-in."

Shown next is a sample service locator implementation that abstracts how an `EJBHome` interface is looked up via JNDI. The service locator implementation for the JavaEdge application provides the methods for looking up `EJBHome` interfaces and JDBC database connections.

```
package com.apress.javaedge.common;

import org.apache.ojb.broker.PBFactoryException;
import org.apache.ojb.broker.PersistenceBroker;
import org.apache.ojb.broker.PersistenceBrokerFactory;
import org.apache.commons.logging.Log;
import org.apache.commons.logging.LogFactory;

import javax.ejb.EJBHome;
import javax.naming.Context;
import javax.naming.InitialContext;
import javax.naming.NamingException;
import javax.rmi.PortableRemoteObject;
import javax.sql.DataSource;
import java.sql.Connection;
```

```java
import java.sql.SQLException;
import java.util.Hashtable;

public class ServiceLocator{
  private static ServiceLocator serviceLocatorRef = null;
  private static Hashtable      ejbHomeCache       = null;
  private static Hashtable      dataSourceCache   = null;

  /*Enumerating the different services available from the service locator*/
  public static final int STORYMANAGER          = 0;
  public static final int JAVAEDGEDB             = 1;

  /*The JNDI Names used to look up a service*/
  private static final String STORYMANAGER_JNDINAME =
                          "storyManager/StoryManager";

  private static final String JAVAEDGEDB_JNDINAME="java:/MySQLDS";

  /*References to each of the different EJB Home Interfaces*/
  //private static final Class STORYMANAGERCLASSREF = StoryManagerHome.class
  private static final Class STORYMANAGERCLASSREF = null;

  static {
    serviceLocatorRef = new ServiceLocator();
  }

  /*Private Constructor for the ServiceLocator*/
  private ServiceLocator(){
    ejbHomeCache    = new Hashtable();
    dataSourceCache = new Hashtable();
  }

  /*
   * The ServiceLocator is implemented as a Singleton. The getInstance()
   * method will return the static reference to the ServiceLocator stored
   * inside of the ServiceLocator Class.
   */
  public static ServiceLocator getInstance(){
    return serviceLocatorRef;
  }

  /*
   * The getServiceName will retrieve the JNDI name for a requested
   * service.  The service is indicated by the ServiceId passed into
   * the method.
   */
  static private String getServiceName(int pServiceId)
```

```
     throws ServiceLocatorException{
     String serviceName = null;
     switch (pServiceId){
       case STORYMANAGER:      serviceName = STORYMANAGER_JNDINAME;
                               break;
       case JAVAEDGEDB:        serviceName = JAVAEDGEDB_JNDINAME;
                               break;
       default:                throw new ServiceLocatorException(
                               "Unable to locate the service requested in " +
                               "ServiceLocator.getServiceName() method.  ");

     }
     return serviceName;
   }

   static private Class getEJBHomeRef(int pServiceId)
     throws ServiceLocatorException{
     Class homeRef = null;
     switch (pServiceId){
       case STORYMANAGER:      homeRef = STORYMANAGERCLASSREF;
                               break;
       default:                throw new ServiceLocatorException(
                               "Unable to locate the service requested in " +
                               "ServiceLocator.getEJBHomeRef() method.  ");

     }
     return homeRef;
   }

public EJBHome getEJBHome(int pServiceId)
     throws ServiceLocatorException{

       /*Trying to find the JNDI Name for the requested service*/
        String serviceName = getServiceName(pServiceId);
        EJBHome ejbHome    = null;

     try {
       /*Checking to see if we can find the EJBHome interface in cache*/
       if (ejbHomeCache.containsKey(serviceName)) {
         ejbHome = (EJBHome) ejbHomeCache.get(serviceName);
         return ejbHome;
       } else {
         /*
          * If we could not find the EJBHome interface in the cache, look it
          * up and then cache it.
          * */
         Context ctx = new InitialContext();
         Object jndiRef    = ctx.lookup(serviceName);
```

```
            Object portableObj =
              PortableRemoteObject.narrow(jndiRef, getEJBHomeRef(pServiceId));

            ejbHome = (EJBHome) portableObj;

            ejbHomeCache.put(serviceName, ejbHome);
            return ejbHome;
          }
      } catch(NamingException e) {
          String msg = "Naming exception error in ServiceLocator.getEJBHome()";
          throw new ServiceLocatorException( msg ,e );
      } catch(Exception e) {
          String msg = "General exception in ServiceLocator.getEJBHome";
          throw new ServiceLocatorException(msg,e);
      }


    }

  public Connection getDBConn(int pServiceId)
      throws ServiceLocatorException{
       /*Getting the JNDI Service Name*/
       String      serviceName = getServiceName(pServiceId);
       Connection conn         = null;
       try {
           /*Checking to see if the requested DataSource is in the Cache*/
         if (dataSourceCache.containsKey(serviceName)) {
           DataSource ds = (DataSource) dataSourceCache.get(serviceName);
            conn = ((DataSource)ds).getConnection();

       return conn;
         } else {
         /*
          * The DataSource was not in the cache. Retrieve it from JNDI
          * and put it in the cache.
          */
         Context ctx = new InitialContext();
           DataSource newDataSource = (DataSource) ctx.lookup(serviceName);
           dataSourceCache.put(serviceName, newDataSource);
           conn = newDataSource.getConnection();
           return conn;
         }
      } catch(SQLException e) {
         throw new ServiceLocatorException("A SQL error has occurred in " +
                                    "ServiceLocator.getDBConn()", e);
      } catch(NamingException e) {
         throw new ServiceLocatorException("A JNDI Naming exception has "+
                                    "occurred in "+
                                    "ServiceLocator.getDBConn()" , e);
```

```
  } catch(Exception e) {
    throw new ServiceLocatorException("An exception has occurred "+
                                "in ServiceLocator.getDBConn()"   ,e);

  }
}

public PersistenceBroker findBroker() throws ServiceLocatorException{
  PersistenceBroker broker = null;
  try{
    broker = PersistenceBrokerFactory.createPersistenceBroker();
  }
  catch(PBFactoryException e) {
  e.printStackTrace();
  throw new ServiceLocatorException("PBFactoryException error " +
        "occurred while parsing the repository.xml file in " +
        "ServiceLocator constructor",e);
}


  return broker;
}
 public Log getLog(Class aClass) {
      return LogFactory.getLog(aClass);
 }
}
```

The service locator implementation just shown is built using the Singleton design pattern. This design pattern allows you to keep only one instance of a class per Java Virtual Machine (JVM). This instance is used to service all the requests for the entire JVM.

Because looking up the resources such as EJBs or DataSource objects is a common activity, implementing the Service Locator pattern as a Singleton pattern prevents the needless creation of multiple copies of the same object doing the same thing. To implement the service locator as a singleton, you need to first have a private constructor that will instantiate any resources being used by the ServiceLocator class:

```
private ServiceLocator() {
  ejbHomeCache = new Hashtable();
  dataSourceCache = new Hashtable();
}
```

The default constructor for the ServiceLocator class just shown is declared as private so that a developer cannot directly instantiate an instance of the ServiceLocator class. (You can have only one instance of the class per JVM.)

A Singleton pattern ensures that only one instance of an object is present within the virtual machine. The Singleton pattern is used to minimize the proliferation of large numbers of objects that serve a very narrow purpose. In the case of the Service Locator pattern, its sole job is to look up or create objects for other classes. It does not make sense to have a new service locator instance being created every time a user needs to carry out one of these tasks.

■**Note** The Singleton pattern is a very powerful design pattern, but it tends to be overused. Inexperienced architects will make everything a singleton implementation. Using a Singleton pattern can introduce reentrancy problems in applications that are multithreaded.

■**Note** One thread can alter the state of a singleton implementation while another thread is working. A Singleton pattern can be made thread-safe through the use of Java synchronization blocks. However, synchronization blocks represent potential bottlenecks within an application, as only one thread at a time can execute the code surrounded by a synchronization block.

The example service locator implementation is going to use two Hashtables, ejbHomeCache and dataSourceCache, which respectively store EJBHome and DataSource interfaces. These two Hashtable instances are initialized in the default constructor of the ServiceLocator.

The constructor is called via an anonymous static block that is invoked the first time the ServiceLocator class is loaded by the JVM:

```
static {
  serviceLocatorRef = new ServiceLocator();
}
```

This anonymous static code block invokes the constructor and sets a reference to a ServiceLocator instance, which is declared as a private attribute in the ServiceLocator class.

You use a method called getInstance() to retrieve an instance of the ServiceLocator class stored in the serviceLocatorRef variable:

```
public static ServiceLocator getInstance(){
  return serviceLocatorRef;
}
```

To retrieve an EJBHome interface, the getEJBHome() method in the ServiceLocator class is invoked. This method takes an integer value (pServiceId) that represents the EJB being requested. For this service locator implementation, all the available EJBs have a public static constant defined in the ServiceLocator class. For instance, the StoryManager EJB has the following constant value:

```
public static final int STORYMANAGER = 0;
```

The first action taken by the getEJBHome() method is to look up the JNDI name that will be used to retrieve a resource, managed by the service locator. The JNDI name is looked up by calling the getServiceName() method, in which the pServiceId parameter is passed:

```
String serviceName = getServiceName(pServiceId);
```

Once the JNDI service name is retrieved, the ejbHomeCache is checked to see if that EJBHome interface is already cached. If a hit is found, the method immediately returns with the EJBHome interface stored in the cache:

```
if (ejbHomeCache.containsKey(serviceName)) {
    ejbHome = (EJBHome) ejbHomeCache.get(serviceName);
    return ejbHome;
```

If the requested EJBHome interface is not located in the ejbHomeCache Hashtable, the getEJBHome() method will look up the interface, add it to the ejbHomeCache, and then return the newly retrieved interface back to the calling application code:

```
} else {
  Context ctx = new InitialContext();
  Object jndiRef = ctx.lookup(serviceName);

  Object portableObj =
    PortableRemoteObject.narrow(jndiRef, getEJBHomeRef(pServiceId));

  ejbHome = (EJBHome) portableObj;
  ejbHomeCache.put(serviceName, ejbHome);
  return ejbHome;
}
```

The getDBConn() method is designed in a very similar fashion. When the user requests a JDBC connection via the getDBConn() method, the method checks the dataSourceCache for a DataSource object before doing a JNDI lookup. If the requested DataSource object is found in the cache, it is returned to the method caller; otherwise, a JNDI lookup takes place.

Let's revisit the constructor of the StoryManagerEJBImpl class and see how using a service locator can significantly lower the amount of work involved in instantiating the StoryManager EJB:

```
package com.apress.javaedge.story;

import com.apress.javaedge.story.ejb.StoryManager;
import com.apress.javaedge.story.ejb.StoryManagerHome;
import com.apress.javaedge.common.ApplicationException;
import com.apress.javaedge.common.ServiceLocator;
import com.apress.javaedge.common.ServiceLocatorException;

import javax.ejb.CreateException;
import javax.naming.Context;
import javax.naming.InitialContext;
import javax.naming.NamingException;
import javax.rmi.PortableRemoteObject;
import java.rmi.RemoteException;
```

```java
public class StoryManagerEJBImpl {

    StoryManager storyManager = null;

    public StoryManagerEJBImpl() throws ApplicationException {
        try{
            ServiceLocator serviceLocator = ServiceLocator.getInstance();
            StoryManagerHome storyManagerHome =
            (StoryManagerHome)
            serviceLocator.getEJBHome(ServiceLocator.STORYMANAGER);
            storyManager = storyManagerHome.create();
        }
        catch(ServiceLocatorException e){
          throw new ApplicationException("A ServiceLocator exception " +
              " has been raised in StoryManagerEJBImpl constructor: " +
              e.toString ());
        }
        catch(CreateException e){
          throw new ApplicationException("A Create exception has been " +
          " raised in StoryManagerEJBImpl constructor: " + e.toString ());

        }
        catch(RemoteException e){
          throw new ApplicationException("A remote exception " +
                "has been raised in StoryManagerEJBImpl constructor: "
                + e.toString ());

        }
    }
}
```

This service locator implementation has significantly simplified the process of looking up and creating an EJB.

The Service Locator Pattern to the Rescue

We ran into a situation just this past year in which we were building a web-based application that integrated to a third-party Customer Relationship Management (CRM) system.

The application had a significant amount of business logic, embedded as PL/SQL stored procedures and triggers, in the Oracle database it was built on. Unfortunately, the third-party application vendor had used an Oracle package, called DBMS_OUTPUT, to put the trace code through all of their PL/SQL code. This package never caused any problems because the end users of the CRM package used to enter the database data via a "fat" GUI, which always kept the database transactions very short.

However, we needed to build a web application that would collect all of the user's data and commit it all at once. The transaction length was significantly longer than what the CRM vendors had anticipated. As a result, the message buffer, which the DBMS_OUTPUT package used for writing out the log, would run out of space and the web application would fail at what appeared to be random intervals.

At this point we were faced with the choice of going through every PL/SQL package and trigger and stripping out the DBMS_OUTPUT code (which should have never been put in production code). However, the DBA informed us that if we started every session with a call to DBMS_OUTPUT.DISABLE, we would be able to disable the DBMS_OUTPUT package. This would disable the DBMS_OUTPUT package for that particular session, but would not cause any problems for other application users.

If we had allowed a direct JNDI lookup to retrieve DataSource objects for getting a JDBC connection, we would have had the daunting task of going through every line in the application and making the call to DBMS_OUTPUT.DISABLE every time a new Connection object was created from the retrieved DataSource. However, since we had implemented a Service Locator pattern and used it to retrieve all the database connections, there was only one place in which the code had to be modified.

This example illustrates that you might not appreciate the abstraction that the Service Locator pattern provides until you need to make a change in how a resource is requested, which will affect a significant amount of your code base.

The Service Locator Revisited

We built the service locator example using Hashtable classes to store the EJB and DataSource instances. We used Hashtable because we wanted to keep the service locator example simple and thread-safe. A Hashtable is thread-safe solution, but does not offer any kind of intelligence regarding the actual number of items being stored within it. There are no caching algorithms (for example, a Least-Recently-Used algorithm) built into the Hashtable that allow the developer to control how many items are loaded into the Hashtable instance or when items should be unloaded from it.

Fortunately, the Jakarta Commons project offers a number of "enhanced" Collections classes that allow for a more intelligent caching solution.

Note The Collections classes discussed in this section can be downloaded from the Jakarta Commons project at http://jakarta.apache.org/commons/collections.

One of these Collections is the LRUMap class. The LRUMap class is a HashMap implementation that is built around a Least-Recently-Used (LRU) algorithm. The LRU algorithm built into the LRUMap class allows the developer to restrict the number of objects that can be held within it.

This means that if the maximum number of objects is reached with the LRUMap and another object is added to it, the LRUMap will unload the least accessed object from the map and then add the new object to it.

Let's make the service locator implementation a little bit more intelligent by using the Jakarta Common's LRUMap to allow it to hold only five references to an EJB or a data source at any given time. The code for this is shown here and the areas in the code where the LRUMap is being used appear in bold:

```
package com.apress.javaedge.common;

import org.apache.commons.logging.Log;
import org.apache.commons.logging.LogFactory;
import org.apache.ojb.broker.PBFactoryException;
import org.apache.ojb.broker.PersistenceBroker;
import org.apache.ojb.broker.PersistenceBrokerFactory;
import org.apache.commons.collections.LRUMap;
import java.util.Collections;
import java.util.Map;


import javax.ejb.EJBHome;
import javax.naming.Context;
import javax.naming.InitialContext;
import javax.naming.NamingException;
import javax.rmi.PortableRemoteObject;
import javax.sql.DataSource;
import java.sql.Connection;
import java.sql.SQLException;

public class ServiceLocatorLRU{
  private static ServiceLocatorLRU serviceLocatorRef = null;
  private static LRUMap          ejbHomeCache       = null;
  private static LRUMap          dataSourceCache    = null;

  /*Enumerating the different services available from the service locator*/
  public static final int STORYMANAGER       = 0;
  public static final int JAVAEDGEDB         = 1;

  /*The JNDI Names used to look up a service*/
  private static final String STORYMANAGER_JNDINAME =
                        "storyManager/StoryManager";

  private static final String JAVAEDGEDB_JNDINAME="java:/MySQLDS";

  /*References to each of the different EJB Home Interfaces*/
  //private static final Class STORYMANAGERCLASSREF = StoryManagerHome.class
  private static final Class STORYMANAGERCLASSREF = null;

  static {
    serviceLocatorRef = new ServiceLocatorLRU();
  }
```

```java
    /*Private Constructor for the ServiceLocator*/
    private ServiceLocatorLRU(){
       ejbHomeCache    = new LRUMap(5);
       dataSourceCache = new LRUMap(5);
    }

public static ServiceLocatorLRU getInstance(){
    return serviceLocatorRef;
    }

static private String getServiceName(int pServiceId)
    throws ServiceLocatorException{
    String serviceName = null;
    switch (pServiceId){
      case STORYMANAGER:        serviceName = STORYMANAGER_JNDINAME;
                                break;
      case JAVAEDGEDB:          serviceName = JAVAEDGEDB_JNDINAME;
                                break;
      default:                  throw new ServiceLocatorException(
                                "Unable to locate the service requested in " +
                                "ServiceLocator.getServiceName() method.  ");

    }
    return serviceName;
  }

static private Class getEJBHomeRef(int pServiceId)
    throws ServiceLocatorException{
    Class homeRef = null;
    switch (pServiceId){
      case STORYMANAGER:        homeRef = STORYMANAGERCLASSREF;
                                break;
      default:                  throw new ServiceLocatorException(
                                "Unable to locate the service requested in " +
                                "ServiceLocator.getEJBHomeRef() method.  ");

    }
    return homeRef;
  }

  /
  public EJBHome getEJBHome(int pServiceId)
    throws ServiceLocatorException{

       /*Trying to find the JNDI Name for the requested service*/
       String serviceName = getServiceName(pServiceId);
       EJBHome ejbHome    = null;

       Map ejbMap = Collections.synchronizedMap(ejbHomeCache);
```

```java
        try {
          /*Checking to see if we can find the EJBHome interface in cache*/
          if (ejbMap.containsKey(serviceName)) {
            ejbHome = (EJBHome) ejbMap.get(serviceName);
            return ejbHome;
          } else {
           /*
            * If we could not find the EJBHome interface in the cache, look it
            * up and then cache it.
            * */
           Context ctx = new InitialContext();
           Object jndiRef    = ctx.lookup(serviceName);

           Object portableObj =
             PortableRemoteObject.narrow(jndiRef, getEJBHomeRef(pServiceId));

           ejbHome = (EJBHome) portableObj;

           ejbMap.put(serviceName, ejbHome);
           return ejbHome;
         }
       } catch(NamingException e) {
           throw new ServiceLocatorException("Naming exception " +
               " error in ServiceLocator.getEJBHome()" ,e);

       } catch(Exception e) {
           throw new ServiceLocatorException("General exception " +
               " in ServiceLocator.getEJBHome",e);

       }

     }


     public Connection getDBConn(int pServiceId)
       throws ServiceLocatorException{
        /*Getting the JNDI Service Name*/
        String     serviceName = getServiceName(pServiceId);
        Connection conn         = null;
        Map        dsMap        = Collections.synchronizedMap(dataSourceCache);

        try {
             /*Checking to see if the requested DataSource is in the Cache*/
           if (dataSourceCache.containsKey(serviceName)) {
             DataSource ds = (DataSource) dsMap.get(serviceName);
             conn = ((DataSource)ds).getConnection();
```

```
      return conn;
        } else {
      /*
       * The DataSource was not in the cache.  Retrieve it from JNDI
       * and put it in the cache.
       */
      Context ctx = new InitialContext();
        DataSource newDataSource = (DataSource) ctx.lookup(serviceName);
        dsMap.put(serviceName, newDataSource);
        conn = newDataSource.getConnection();
        return conn;
      }
    } catch(SQLException e) {
      throw new ServiceLocatorException("A SQL error has occurred in " +
                                "ServiceLocator.getDBConn()", e);
    } catch(NamingException e) {
      throw new ServiceLocatorException("A JNDI Naming exception has "+
                              "occurred in "+
                              "ServiceLocator.getDBConn()" , e);
    } catch(Exception e) {
     throw new ServiceLocatorException("An exception has occurred "+
                              "in ServiceLocator.getDBConn()"   ,e);
    }
  }


  public PersistenceBroker findBroker() throws ServiceLocatorException{
......
  }

  public Log getLog(Class aClass) {
      ......
  }

}
```

The difference between the ServiceLocator.java and ServiceLocatorLRU.java implementations is that the LRUMap is being used in place of the Hashtable:

```
private static LRUMap        ejbHomeCache      = null;
private static LRUMap        dataSourceCache   = null;
```

To set the maximum number of objects allowed to be stored in the ejbHomeCache and dataSourceCache objects, an integer value is passed into the constructor on the LRUMap:

```
    ejbHomeCache    = new LRUMap(5);
    dataSourceCache = new LRUMap(5);
```

Remember, the `Hashtable` is a synchronized Java class and can be accessed safely by multiple threads. The `LRUMap` is not. To make it thread-safe, you must get a synchronized `Map` instance by calling the `java.util.Collections`'s `synchronizedMap()` method and passing in an instance of an `LRUMap`:

```
Map         dsMap      = Collections.synchronizedMap(dataSourceCache);
```

With the addition of the `LRUMap`, the service locator used in the JavaEdge application has become sophisticated. More importantly, this was accomplished without the need to write your own LRU algorithm implementation. The "take-away" thought from this should be the following:

Note Whenever you start finding yourself or your development team writing low-level code, you should take a step back. Most problems that a development team faces have already been overcome before. Look to open source projects like the Jakarta Commons project for solutions before implementing your own.

EJBs and Struts

Since the release of the J2EE specifications, it has been incessantly drilled into every J2EE developer that all business logic for an application should be placed in the middle tier as session-based Enterprise JavaBeans (EJB). Unfortunately, many developers believe that by putting their business logic in EJBs, they have successfully designed their application's middle tier.

The middle tier of an application often captures some of the core business processes used throughout the enterprise. Without careful forethought and planning, many applications end up with a middle tier that is too tightly coupled to a specific application. The business logic contained within the application cannot easily be reused elsewhere and can become so complex that it is not maintainable.

The following are symptoms of a poorly designed middle tier:

The EJBs are too fine-grained: A very common mistake when building Struts-based applications with EJBs is to have each `Action` class have a corresponding EJB. This results in a proliferation of EJBs and can cause serious performance problems in a high-transaction application. The root cause of this is that the application developer is treating a component-based technology (that is, EJB) like an object-oriented technology (that is, plain old Java classes).

In a Struts application, you can often have a small number of EJBs carrying out the requests for a much larger number of `Action` classes. If you find a one-to-one mapping between `Action` classes and EJBs, the design of the application needs to be revisited.

The EJBs are too fat: Conversely, some developers end up placing too much of their business logic in an EJB. Putting too much business logic into a single EJB makes it difficult to maintain and reuse it in other applications. "Fat" EJBs are often implemented by developers who are used to programming with a module development language, such as C or Pascal, and are new to object-oriented analysis and design.

We have encountered far more of the latter design problem, "fat" EJBs, when building Struts-based applications. Let's look at the "fat" EJB problem in more detail.

On "Fat" EJBs

"Fat" EJBs are monolithic "blobs" of code that do not take advantage of object-oriented design.

■ **Note** The term *blob* is not our term. It is actually an antipattern that was first defined in the text *AntiPatterns: Refactoring Software Architectures and Projects in Crisis* (Brown et al., John Wiley & Sons, ISBN: 0-471-19713-0). The Blob antipattern is an antipattern that forms when a developer takes an object-oriented language like C++ or Java and uses it in a procedural manner.

In a Struts application, an extreme example of this might be manifested by a single EJB that contains one method for each of the Action classes present in the Struts application. The execute() method for each Action class would invoke a corresponding method on the EJB to carry out the business logic for the action.

This is an extreme example of a "fat" EJB. A more typical example of a "fat" EJB is one in which the EJBs are designed along functional breakdowns within the application. In the JavaEdge application, you might have a Member EJB and a Story EJB that encapsulate all of the functionality for that specific set of application tasks.

This kind of functional breakdown into individual EJBs makes sense. EJBs are coarse-grained components that wrap processes. The EJB model does offer the same type of object-oriented features (polymorphism, encapsulation, etc.) as their more fine-grained counterparts: plain Java classes. The problem arises when the EJB developer does not use the EJB as a wrapper around more fine-grained objects but instead puts all of the business logic for a particular process *inside* the EJB.

For example, if you remember earlier in the chapter we talked about how many developers will push all of their business logic from their Struts Action class to an EJB. We demonstrated how if your Struts did not use a Business Delegate pattern to hide the fact you were using EJBs, you could end up creating tight dependencies between Struts and the EJB APIs.

What we did not talk about is how blindly moving your business logic out of the PostStory Action class and into an EJB can result in a "fat" EJB. Shown here is the StoryManagerBean.java class:

```
package com.apress.javaedge.story.ejb;

import javax.naming.*;
import java.rmi.*;
import javax.ejb.*;
import java.sql.*;

import com.apress.javaedge.common.*;
import com.apress.javaedge.story.*;
```

```java
import com.apress.javaedge.member.*;
import com.apress.javaedge.story.dao.*;
import com.apress.javaedge.struts.poststory.*;

public class StoryManagerBean implements SessionBean {
  private SessionContext ctx;

  public void setSessionContext(SessionContext sessionCtx) {
    this.ctx = sessionCtx;
  }

  public void addStory(StoryVO storyVO)
      throws ApplicationException, RemoteException{
    Connection conn = null;
    PreparedStatement ps = null;

    try {
      conn = ServiceLocator.getInstance().getDBConn(ServiceLocator.JAVAEDGEDB);
      conn.setAutoCommit(false);

      StringBuffer insertSQL = new StringBuffer();

      insertSQL.append("INSERT INTO story(              ");
      insertSQL.append("  member_id                ,    ");
      insertSQL.append("  story_title              ,    ");
      insertSQL.append("  story_into               ,    ");
      insertSQL.append("  story_body               ,    ");
      insertSQL.append("  submission_date          ");
      insertSQL.append(")                          ");
      insertSQL.append("VALUES(                     ");
      insertSQL.append("  ?                    ,    ");
      insertSQL.append("  ?                    ,    ");
      insertSQL.append("  ?                    ,    ");
      insertSQL.append("  ?                    ,    ");
      insertSQL.append("  CURDATE()               )    ");

      ps = conn.prepareStatement(insertSQL.toString());

      ps.setLong(1, storyVO.getStoryAuthor().getMemberId().longValue());
      ps.setString(2, storyVO.getStoryTitle());
      ps.setString(3, storyVO.getStoryIntro());
      ps.setString(4, storyVO.getStoryBody());

      ps.execute();
      checkStoryCount(storyVO.getStoryAuthor());

    } catch(SQLException e) {
```

```
        throw new ApplicationException("SQL Exception occurred in " +
                            "StoryManagerBean.addStory()", e);

    } catch(ServiceLocatorException e) {
        throw new ApplicationException("Service Locator Exception occurred in " +
                            "StoryManagerBean.addStory()", e);

    } finally {
        try {
            if (ps != null) ps.close();
            if (conn != null) conn.close();
        } catch(SQLException e) {}

    }
}

private void checkStoryCount(MemberVO memberVO)
        throws SQLException, NamingException {
  ...
}



public void addStory(PostStoryForm postStoryForm, MemberVO memberVO)
        throws ApplicationException, RemoteException{
  ...
}

public void ejbCreate() { }
public void ejbRemove() { }
public void ejbActivate() { }
public void ejbPassivate(){ }


}
```

We have not included the full listing of the StoryManagerBean class for the sake of brevity. However, you should be able to tell that this EJB is going to be huge if all of the business logic associated with managing stories is put into it.

The JavaEdge application is an extremely simple application. In more real-world EJB implementations, the Struts amount of business logic that is put into the EJB can become staggering. Let's look at how the Session Facade design pattern can help you manage the business logic contained within an EJB.

The Session Facade Pattern

The Session Facade pattern is implemented as a stateless session EJB, which acts as a coarse-grained wrapper around finer-grained pieces of code. Typically, these finer-grained pieces of code are going to be plain old Java classes rather than the more component-oriented EJB architecture. In a component-based architecture, a component wraps the business processes behind immutable interfaces. The implementation of the business process may change, but the interface that the component presents to the applications (which invoke the business process) does not change.

Instead, the methods on an EJB implemented as a session facade should act as the entry point in which the business process is carried by more fine-grained Java classes. Figure 4-3 illustrates this.

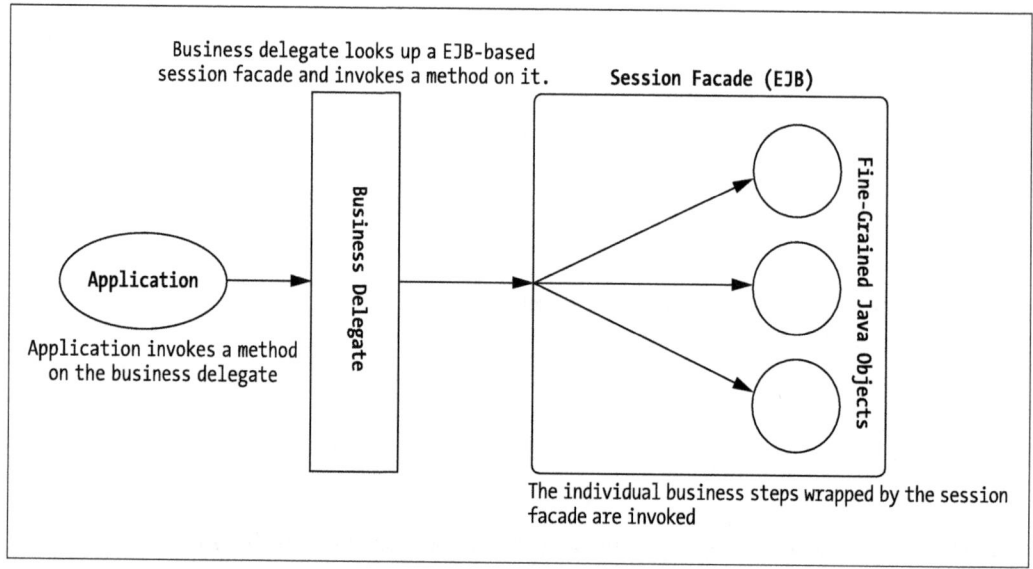

Figure 4-3. *Application invoking a session facade via a business delegate*

So if you were going to rewrite the StoryManagerBean's addStory() method to be less monolithic and more fine-grained, it might look something like this:

```java
public void addStory(StoryVO storyVO)
    throws ApplicationException, RemoteException {

  try {
    StoryDAO storyDAO = new StoryDAO();
    storyDAO.insert(storyVO);

    PrizeManager prizeManager = new PrizeManager();
    int numberOfStories =
      prizeManager.checkStoryCount(storyVO.getStoryAuthor());

    boolean TOTAL_COUNT_EQUAL_1000 = (numberOfStories==1000);
    boolean TOTAL_COUNT_EQUAL_5000 = (numberOfStories==5000);

    if (TOTAL_COUNT_EQUAL_1000 || TOTAL_COUNT_EQUAL_5000) {
      prizeManager.notifyMarketing(storyVO.getStoryAuthor(), numberOfStories);
    }
```

```
    } catch (DataAccessException e){
        throw new ApplicationException("DataAccessException Error in " +
                            StoryManagerBean.addStory(): " +
                            e.toString(), e);
    }
}
```

The addStory() method is much more manageable and extensible. All of the data access logic for adding a story has been moved to the StoryDAO class (which will be covered in more detail in the next chapter). All of the logic associated with prize management has been moved to the PrizeManager class.

As you can see, you also need to refactor the code associated with the checkStoryCount() method. The checkStoryCount() method is only used when trying to determine whether or not the individual qualifies for a prize. So you move the checkStoryCount() method to the PrizeManager. You could also move this method to the StoryDAO class. By moving it out of the StoryManager EJB, you avoid having "extraneous" code in the session facade implementation.

Implementing the Session Facade pattern is not difficult. It involves looking at your EJBs and ensuring that the individual steps for carrying out a business process are captured in fine-grained Java objects. The code inside of the session facade implementation should act as the "glue" that strings these individual steps together into a complete process.

Any method on a session facade EJB should be short. If it's over 20 to 30 lines, you need to go back and revisit the logic contained within the method to see if it can be refactored out into smaller individual classes. Remember, one of the core concepts behind object-oriented design is division of responsibility. Always keep this in mind as you are building your EJBs.

What About Non-EJB Applications?

All of the examples presented so far in this chapter have made the assumption that you are using EJB-based J2EE to gain the benefits offered by these design patterns. However, it is very easy to adapt these patterns to a non-EJB Struts-based application. We have worked on many successful Struts applications using these patterns and just a web container.

For non-EJB Struts implementations, you should still use the Business Delegate pattern to separate the Struts Action class from the Java classes that carry out the business logic. You need not implement a Session Facade pattern in these situations. Instead, your business delegate class will perform the same function as the session facade class. The business delegate would act as a thin wrapper around the other Java objects carrying out a business process.

You might ask the question, "Why go through all of this extra work even in a non-J2EE application?" The reason is simple: By cleanly separating your Action class from the application's business logic (using a Business Delegate pattern), you provide a migration path for moving your applications to a full J2EE environment.

At some point, you might need to move the Struts applications to a full-blown J2EE application server and not just a JSP/servlet container. You can very easily move your business logic to session facades and EJBs, without rewriting any of your Struts applications. This is because you have separated your Struts applications from your business logic.

Your Struts applications only invoke the business logic through a plain Java interface. This abstraction allows you to completely refactor the business tier of your applications without affecting the applications themselves.

A DECISION POINT IN THE JAVAEDGE APPLICATION

We struggled when trying to determine whether or not we should build the JavaEdge application as an EJB-based application. In the end, we decided not to because JavaEdge is such a simple application that it didn't require the power (and the complexity) that comes with implementing an EJB solution.

Since the logic for the JavaEdge application is simple, we embedded most of it as calls to Data Access Objects (covered in the next chapter) directly inside of the business delegate implementations. The business logic was not broken out into session facades and was instead kept inside of the business delegate classes.

However, even though the JavaEdge application does not use EJBs in its implementation, we felt that this material was an important piece to cover when looking at using Struts for your own EJB-based applications.

As the Struts `Action` classes only talk to business delegates, we could have easily refactored the code into an EJB-based solution without having to touch any of the Struts code.

The design patterns discussed in this chapter cleanly separate the Struts framework from how the business logic for the application is being invoked. This allows you to evolve the application over time while minimizing the effects of these changes on the application.

Remember, design patterns are a powerful tool for abstraction and reuse, but when used improperly become common causes of overabstraction and complexity.

Handling Exceptions in the Action Class

For the development team, unanticipated behavior in the application code is a byproduct of the nonlinear, fuzzy, and complex business processes that are being modeled with the application code. One of the most common mistakes developers make when building multitiered applications, like web applications, is not understanding or appreciating how poorly designed exception-handling code can cause implementation details from one tier to be exposed to the tier immediately above it.

For example, the Business Delegate pattern is supposed to abstract away all implementation details of how the business logic in an application is actually invoked from the presentation tier. However, we have seen many instances where development teams have implemented their business delegate implementations and had the methods on the delegate throwing technology-specific implementation details like a `RemoteException`.

The end result is that even though the business delegate implementation hides the fact that an EJB is being invoked, the classes using the business delegate have to still catch the `RemoteException` or rethrow it. This creates a dependency that must be reworked if the development team ever changes the underlying implementation for the business delegate away from something other than EJBs.

The best way to deal with any exceptions thrown from the business tier is to establish two practices:

- *Catch, process, and log all exceptions thrown in the business tier before the exception leaves the business tier*: This is important because by the time an application exception gets to the presentation layer and to a Struts `Action` class, all of the heavy lifting associated with processing the exception should be done. The Struts framework should merely be catching the exception and directing the user to a nicely formatted error page.

- *When an exception is caught in the business tier, rethrow the exception as a single generic exception type*: That way, the presentation tier consuming the services of the business logic tier only needs to know that it has to catch one type of exception. Catching an exception and rethrowing it as a generic type completely abstracts away the implementation details associated with the exception.

  If your application truly needs to be able to differentiate different types of exceptions being thrown from the business logic tier, then you should consider building some simple type of exception hierarchy that minimizes the number of specific exception types that need to be caught.

All the Action classes in the JavaEdge application are set to process a generic exception called ApplicationException. An ApplicationException is a generic exception that is used to "level" all exceptions thrown by the business logic tier to a single type of exception.

Without the ApplicationException being thrown from the StoryManagerBD, the development team would have to rewrite its Action classes every time the underlying implementation of the business delegate changed.

For instance, without a generic ApplicationException being thrown, if you wanted to change the underlying logic for story management to be contained within an EJB rather than a POJO, the PostStory class would need to be rewritten to have to catch the CreateException, RemoteException, and NamingException that could be thrown from the StoryManagerEJBImpl class. This would give the PostStory class the intimate knowledge of how the business logic for the request was being carried out.

Tip Never expose an application that uses a business delegate to any of the implementation details wrapped by the delegate. This includes any exceptions that might be raised during the course of processing a request.

The ApplicationException is used to notify the application, which consumes a service provided by the business delegate, that some kind of error has occurred. It is up to the application to decide how it will respond to an unexpected exception.

There are two different ways exception handling with ApplicationException can be implemented. Each method is dependent on the version of Struts being used. Let's start by looking at how exception handling can be implemented in the older Struts 1.0.x releases.

Exception Handling in Struts 1.0.x

When building web applications using Struts 1.0.x, we have found that the best approach for clear and uniform exception handling in the Action classes is to implement the following:

- Write an ApplicationException class that will represent all exceptions thrown from the business tier layer.

- Implement a single global forward via the <global-forwards> tag in the application's struts-config.xml file. This global forward will be used to redirect the end user to a neatly formatted error page rather than a web page full of Java code stack traces.

- Ensure that all Action classes within the application catch the ApplicationException and redirect the user to the error page defined in the global forward.

To build the JavaEdge application's ApplicationException class, some of the functionality in the Jakarta Commons lang project (http://jakarta.apache.org/commons/lang) was used. All the classes from the Jakarta Common's lang project are located in the commons-lang.jar file.

For the Struts 1.0.x framework, we are going to demonstrate the use of the org.apache. commons.lang.exception.NestableException class. The NestableException class provides a nice mechanism to ensure that the call stack for the exception being caught is being maintained if the application chooses to rethrow the exception. The reason why the NestableException is used is that before JDK 1.4 the propagation of the exception call stack was not built into the core Java language.

Shown here is the ApplicationException class used specifically to build the JavaEdge application in Struts version 1.0.x:

```
package com.apress.javaedge.common;
import org.apache.commons.lang.exception.NestableException;

public class ApplicationException extends NestableException {
    Throwable exceptionCause = null;

    /** Creates a new instance of ApplicationException */
    public ApplicationException(String msg) {
        super(msg);
    }

    public ApplicationException(String msg, Throwable exception){
        super(msg, exception);
        exceptionCause = exception;
    }

    /**Overriding the printStackTraceMethod*/
    public void printStackTrace(){
      if (exceptionCause!=null){
        System.err.println("An exception has been caused by: " +
                                    exceptionCause.toString());
        exceptionCause.printStackTrace();
      }
    }
}
```

When an application exception is thrown, the user should always be directed to a nicely formatted error page. To achieve this redirection, we are going to show you how to set up a <global-forwards> tag in the JavaEdge application's struts-config.xml file. Shown here is the tag used, but we are not going to walk through the details of the <global-forwards> tag as this information was covered in Chapter 2:

```
<global-forwards type="org.apache.struts.action.ActionForward">
  <forward name="system.error" path="/WEB-INF/jsp/systemError.jsp"/>
  <forward name="default.action" path="/execute/homePageSetup"/>
</global-forwards>
```

Once these two elements are set up, it is a straightforward process to capture an ApplicationException and redirect the user to the error page. Shown here is the execute() method from the PostStory class:

```
public ActionForward execute(ActionMapping mapping,
                             ActionForm      form,
                             HttpServletRequest request,
                             HttpServletResponse response){

    if (this.isCancelled(request)){
        return (mapping.findForward("poststory.success"));
    }

    try{
        PostStoryForm postStoryForm = (PostStoryForm) form;

        StoryVO storyVO = postStoryForm.buildStoryVO(request);

        IStoryManager storyManager = StoryManagerBD.getStoryManagerBD();
        storyManager.addStory(storyVO);
    }        catch(ApplicationException e){
        return (mapping.findForward("system.error"));
    }

    return (mapping.findForward("poststory.success"));
}
```

Although this code is a clean mechanism for capturing all exceptions thrown in your Action classes, one issue should leap out at you. Capturing application exceptions and redirecting the user is very repetitive. The process of capturing these exceptions "clutters" up your Action classes, especially because the exception handling code is doing the same thing over and again. Fortunately, in Struts 1.1, the handling of exceptions thrown in an Action class has now been integrated as part of the Struts framework in what is known as *exception handlers*. Let's revisit the preceding ApplicationException code. We will look at how to use Struts version 1.1 exception handlers to automate the processing of the ApplicationException.

Exception Handling in Struts 1.1 and Later

The Struts version 1.1 framework introduced the concept of framework-based exception handlers. This concept has not changed in the current 1.2.x releases of Struts. Framework-based exception handlers allow you to handle application exceptions thrown in your Action classes declaratively. Using them, you can define in your application's struts-config.xml file what exceptions are to be caught by the Action class and where the user should be directed when the error occurs.

Implementing exception handlers in Struts 1.1 was very easy to do. For the JavaEdge application, you implement exception handling for the ApplicationException in the following manner:

- Modify the ApplicationException to be a NestableRuntimeException rather than a NestableException.

- Add a <global-exceptions> tag to the JavaEdge application's struts-config.xml file. This tag defines all of the exceptions that can be thrown and processed from a JavaEdge Action class.

- Modify all of the Action classes in the JavaEdge application to remove all try..catch statements that process the ApplicationException.

Rewriting the ApplicationException Class

The ApplicationException class is modified so that it extends the NestableRuntimeException rather than NestableException:

```
package com.apress.javaedge.common;
import org.apache.commons.lang.exception.NestableRuntimeException;
```

```
public class ApplicationException extends NestableException {
. . .
}
```

The rest of the code for the ApplicationException remains exactly the same. So why make the switch from NestableException to NestableRuntimeException? The reason is that NestableException is a "checked" exception. Even with the use of Strut's exception-handler capability, the Java compiler would complain if you did not catch the ApplicationException exception being thrown from your business delegate classes.

Since you want to delegate all exception-handling code to Struts, you make the ApplicationException class a "runtime" exception that does not require a try..catch block.

Setting Up the struts-config.xml File

Now to actually tell Struts that it should be looking for a particular exception you need to modify the application's struts-config.xml file. There are two types of exception handlers: global and local. A *global exception handler* uses the <global-exceptions> tag to define a list of exceptions that can be thrown by *all* of the Action classes within the application.

A *local exception handler* is defined inside of an <action> tag and specifies an exception that can be caught and processed specific to that Action class. Please note that there is nothing stopping a developer from redefining the same exception to be caught by simply redefining the same exception inside different <action> tags.

For the JavaEdge application, you define the following `<global-exceptions>` tag inside of the application's struts-config.xml file:

```
<global-exceptions>
        <exception key="error.system"
                   scope="request"
                   type="com.apress.javaedge.common.ApplicationException"
                   path="/WEB-INF/jsp/systemError.jsp"/>
</global-exceptions>
```

For each exception defined inside of the `<global-exceptions>` tag, there will be a corresponding `<exception>` tag. An `<exception>` tag can have a number of attributes associated with it. The four attributes you are most concerned about are key, scope, type, and path. We will walk you through each of these attributes with the understanding that the behavior described by these three attributes are the same whether you are defining a global exception handler or a local exception handler.

Note To conform to the struts-config-1.1 or the struts-config-1.2 DTD, you must make sure that the `<global-exceptions>` tag comes before the `<global-forwards>` tag. Otherwise, you might end up wasting a lot of time scouring the application's struts-config.xml file the first time you run this file through a validating XML parser.

When a defined exception is caught and processed, Struts provides a default exception handler whose fully qualified class name is org.apache.struts.action.ExceptionHandler. This exception handler will create an ActionError instance for the exception and store it in an ActionErrors collection. The corresponding resource key used to look up the error message when creating the ActionError instance is defined by the value in the key attribute. Remember, this resource key is used to pull out the error message from the ApplicationResources.properties file.

For instance, in the JavaEdge application, every time an ApplicationException is thrown in a Struts Action, the following text will be read out of the ApplicationResources.properties file:

```
error.system=A system error has occurred.  Please contact JavaEdge customer
                support at 262-555-1212 for support.
                The error to report is:<br/> <b>{0}
```

The actual exception message will be passed in as the first message parameter for the ActionError. This means if you have a JSP page that will display a neatly formatted message about the exception, you can get the text of the exception-thrown message by using the {0} parameter used in the error message defined in the ApplicationResources.properties file.

This also means that the <html:errors> tag and all of its corresponding formatting functions can be used to display the exception information for the exception thrown. A very simple example of this is shown here:

```
<%@page contentType="text/html"%>
<%@ taglib uri="/taglibs/struts-html" prefix="html" %>
<html>
<head><title>JSP Page</title></head>
<body>

<H1> A SYSTEM ERROR HAS OCCURRED</H1>
<html:errors/>
</body>
</html>
```

The type attribute provides the fully qualified Java class name of the exception that is to be caught. The path attribute is the relative URL that the end user will be directed to if the defined exception is caught. This URL can be another Struts action or a JSP page.

At this point, we have shown you how to implement a global exception handler. Implementing a local exception handler for a specific class involves nothing more than adding an <exception> tag to an <action> tag. Shown here is the PostStory action with the ApplicationException being handled by that tag:

```
<action path="/postStory"
        input="/WEB-INF/jsp/postStory.jsp"
        name="postStoryMapForm"
        scope="request"
        validate="true"
        type="com.apress.javaedge.struts.poststory.PostStory">
        <exception key="error.system"
                scope="request"
                type="com.apress.javaedge.common.ApplicationException"
                path="/WEB-INF/jsp/systemError.jsp"/>
        <forward name="poststory.success" path="/execute/homePageSetup"/>
</action>
```

Once the ApplicationException code has been rewritten to use the NestedRuntimeException and the <global-exceptions> tag setup, the PostStory class's execute() method shown earlier can be rewritten so that all try..catch information is removed:

```
public ActionForward execute(ActionMapping mapping,
                            ActionForm     form,
                            HttpServletRequest request,
                            HttpServletResponse response)
        throws ApplicationException {


        if (this.isCancelled(request)){
            return (mapping.findForward("poststory.success"));
        }
```

```
        PostStoryForm postStoryForm = (PostStoryForm) form;
        StoryVO storyVO = postStoryForm.buildStoryVO(request);

        IStoryManager storyManager = StoryManagerBD.getStoryManagerBD();
        storyManager.addStory(storyVO);

        return (mapping.findForward("poststory.success"));
}
```

Writing a Custom ExceptionHandler

Why would you want to write your own exception handler? The Struts ExceptionHandler does not provide any kind of functionality like logging, e-mail notification, etc. However, Struts, being the pluggable framework it is, allows you to write your own ExceptionHandler implementation and use it within the framework.

To write a custom ExceptionHandler, follow these guidelines:

- The custom ExceptionHandler must extend org.apache.struts.action.ExceptionHandler.

- The execute() method on ExceptionHandler must be overridden. The execute() method is where the custom exception-handling code is implemented. Shown here is the method signature for the execute() method:

```
public ActionForward execute(Exception ex,
                             ExceptionConfig ae,
                             ActionMapping mapping,
                             ActionForm formInstance,
                             HttpServletRequest request,
                             HttpServletResponse response)
throws ServletException {}
```

  The Exception parameter holds the instance of the Exception thrown by the Action class. The ExceptionConfig parameter holds the configuration information about the exception defined inside of the <exception> tag. The ActionMapping and ActionForm parameters are used to provide context on the Struts Action where the exception occurred. The HttpServletRequest and HttpServletResponse parameters should be self-explanatory.

- The custom ExceptionHandler can take any action as long as it returns an ActionForward that is used by the Struts ActionServlet to determine where the end user is to go next. There is no requirement that the path the ActionForward directs the user to has to be defined only from the <exception> tag in the struts-config.xml file.

- If you want to store the exception as an ActionError from within your custom exception handler, you need to make sure you invoke the storeException() method on the ExceptionHandler class.

- Once the custom ExceptionHandler has been implemented, you must add the handler attribute to the <exception> tag defining the exception handler. The handler attribute defines the fully qualified Java class name of the custom ExceptionHandler class being used to process the exception.

Following is an example custom exception handler called `MailExceptionHandler`. This exception handler will generate an e-mail every time an `ApplicationException` is thrown from a Struts Action class.

```
package com.apress.javaedge.common;

import org.apache.struts.action.ExceptionHandler;
import org.apache.struts.action.ActionForward;
import org.apache.struts.action.ActionMapping;
import org.apache.struts.action.ActionForm;
import org.apache.struts.config.ExceptionConfig;
import org.apache.log4j.Logger;

import javax.servlet.http.HttpServletRequest;
import javax.servlet.http.HttpServletResponse;
import javax.servlet.ServletException;
import javax.mail.internet.MimeMessage;
import javax.mail.internet.InternetAddress;
import javax.mail.Transport;
import java.util.Properties;

import javax.mail.Message;
import javax.mail.Transport;
import javax.mail.internet.InternetAddress;
import javax.mail.internet.MimeMessage;
import javax.mail.Session;


/**
 * Simple ExceptionHandler that sends an e-mail every time a Struts Action class
 * throws an ApplicationException.
 */
public class MailExceptionHandler extends ExceptionHandler{

    private static Logger logger = Logger.getLogger(MailExceptionHandler.class);

    public ActionForward execute(Exception e,
                                 ExceptionConfig ex,
                                 ActionMapping mapping,
                                 ActionForm    form,
                                 HttpServletRequest request,
                                 HttpServletResponse response)
        throws ServletException{


        ActionForward forward = super.execute(e, ex, mapping, form,
                                              request, response);
```

```java
Properties props = new Properties();

//Getting the name of the e-mail server.
props.put("mail.smtp.host", "netchange.us");
props.put("mail.from", "JavaEdgeApplication");

Session session = Session.getDefaultInstance(props,
                            null);
session.setDebug(false);

Message msg = new MimeMessage(session);

try{
  msg.setFrom();

  //Setting who is supposed to receive the e-mail
  InternetAddress to = new InternetAddress("john.carnell@netchange.us");

  //Setting the important text
  msg.setRecipient(MimeMessage.RecipientType.TO, to);
  msg.setSubject("Error message occurred in Action:" + mapping.getName());
  msg.setText("An error occurred while trying " + "
      to invoke execute() on Action:" +
      mapping.getName () +

              ". Error is: " + e.getMessage());

  Transport.send(msg);
}
catch(Exception exception){

logger.error("An error has occurred in the " +
    "MailExceptionHandler while trying to process Action: "
              + mapping.getName());
  logger.error("Exception raised is : " + exception.getMessage());
  logger.error("Original Exception: " + e.getMessage());
}

    return forward;
  }

}
```

The `MailExceptionHandler` class is pretty simplistic. All it is doing is extending the `ExceptionHandler` and overriding the `execute()` method on the class. The overridden `execute()` method immediately calls the `execute()` method on the `ExceptionHandler` to ensure the proper setup of the `ActionErrors` class:

```
public class MailExceptionHandler extends ExceptionHandler{
    public ActionForward execute(Exception e,
                                 ExceptionConfig ex,
                                 ActionMapping mapping,
                                 ActionForm    form,
                                 HttpServletRequest request,
                                 HttpServletResponse response)
        throws ServletException{

        //Calling the execute() method on the Struts ExceptionHandler class
        ActionForward forward = super.execute(e, ex, mapping, form,
                                              request, response);


    }
}
```

Once the `ActionForward` class has been retrieved from the call to `super.execute()`, the code sets up an e-mail message and sends it via the JavaMail API:

```
props.put("mail.smtp.host", "netchange.us");
props.put("mail.from", "JavaEdgeApplication");

javax.mail.Session session = javax.mail.Session.getDefaultInstance(props, null);
session.setDebug(false);

Message msg = new MimeMessage(session);

try{
  msg.setFrom();

  //Setting who is supposed to receive the e-mail
  InternetAddress[] to =
      {new InternetAddress("john.carnell@netchange.us")};

  //Setting the important text
  msg.setRecipients(MimeMessage.RecipientType.TO, to);
  msg.setSubject("Error message occurred in Action:" + mapping.getName());
  msg.setText("An error occurred while trying to invoke execute() on Action:" +
              mapping.getName() +
              ". Error is: " + e.getMessage());
  msg.setSentDate(new java.util.Date());
  Transport.send(msg);
}
catch(Exception exception){}
```

To keep life simple, the `MailExceptionHandler` class catches all exceptions thrown by the e-mail code and simply logs the error message. The forward instance returned by the `super.execute()` method call is then returned from the code. The `ActionServlet` will forward the user on to whatever request has been defined in the `<exception>` tag for the exception handler.

To tell the JavaEdge application to use the `MailExceptionHandler` to process any `ApplicationException` exceptions thrown from its `Action` classes, you need to add the `handler` attribute to the `<exception>` tag in JavaEdge's struts-config.xml file:

```
<global-exceptions>
        <exception key="error.system"
                   scope="request"
                   handler="com.apress.javaedge.common.MailExceptionHandler"
                   type="com.apress.javaedge.common.ApplicationException"
                   path="/WEB-INF/jsp/systemError.jsp"/>
</global-exceptions>
```

Summary

Often in an object-oriented and component-based environment, more value is gained from interface reuse and the abstraction it provides than the actual code reuse. The business logic for an application changes regularly. Well-defined interfaces that abstract away the implementation details help shield an application from this uncertainty. This chapter explored how to use common J2EE design patterns to cleanly separate the business logic from the Struts framework on which the application is built. This promotes code reuse and also gives the developer more flexibility in refactoring business logic at a later date.

This chapter covered the following J2EE design patterns:

Business Delegate pattern: Hides the details of how the business logic used by the Struts application is actually invoked. It allows the development team to refactor the business tier while minimizing its impact on the applications that use the business logic. It also hides the technology (EJBs, Web services, or just plain Java classes) used to implement the actual business logic. This chapter demonstrated how two different business delegate implementations could be plugged in without the JavaEdge application ever knowing the difference.

Service Locator pattern: Simplifies the process of requesting the commonly used resources like EJBs and `DataSource` objects within your business delegate.

Session Facade pattern: Represents an EJB that provides a coarse-grained interface that wraps a business process. Carrying out the individual steps for the business process, wrapped by the session facade, is left to much more fine-grained Java objects.

Finally, this chapter covered different approaches for managing exceptions thrown from the business tier in Struts. Our efforts mainly focused around making sure that all exceptions thrown from the business delegate classes were caught and rethrown as an ApplicationException. We demonstrated how to use the ApplicationException in Struts version 1.0.x.

We also discussed how to use the ApplicationException class and Struts version 1.1 and later exception handlers to refactor exception handling completely out of the Action classes. We demonstrated how to implement global and local exception handlers in the struts-config.xml file using the default Struts ExceptionHandler. Finally, we briefly touched on how to write a custom ExceptionHandler class to generate an e-mail every time an ApplicationException is thrown.

This chapter focused solely on modeling and implementing the business tier of a Struts-based application. However, we still need to focus on how data is retrieved and manipulated by the business logic tier. The next chapter is going to demonstrate how to use an open source object/relational mapping tool, called ObjectRelationalBridge, to build a data persistence tier. In addition, it will discuss how to use J2EE data access design patterns to hide the implementation details in the data persistence tier from the business tier.

Architecting the Data Access Tier with ObjectRelationalBridge

A well-defined data access tier, which provides a logical interface for accessing corporate data sources, is one of the most reused pieces of code in any system architecture. This statement, on the surface, may appear to be an overinflated claim, but it is made with the following two points in mind:

- Applications are developed according to the changing needs of the organization. However, the data used by these applications is used for a long time, even after the application has been replaced with some completely new piece of technology. The data possessed by an organization is often the only constant in any IT ecosystem.

- Any application does not exist all by itself. Most of an organization's development efforts involve integrating a newly built or bought application with the other existing systems. To maximize their value, most applications must exchange their data with other systems using a consistent interface, which abstracts away the "messy" technology details associated with accessing the data.

The previous three chapters have focused on building the presentation and business layers of the JavaEdge web site using the Struts development framework. In this chapter, we are going to change our perspective and move the focus off the Struts development framework and onto building the JavaEdge data access tier.

Building a data access tier is more than just using a particular technology to retrieve and manipulate data. The requirements of the data access tier are as follows:

- To minimize the need to write significant amounts of SQL and JDBC database code. Accessing data from a relational database using SQL is often a tedious and error-prone process. It involves writing a large amount of code that does not map well into the object-oriented model, in which most Java developers are used to working. Furthermore, poorly written data access code can bring the performance of any application to an unpleasant halt.

- To abstract away the underlying details of the data store used to hold the application data. These details include the specific database technology used to hold the data, physical details of how the data is stored, and the relationships that might exist between the data. Abstracting away these details provides the developers with more flexibility in changing the underlying data access tier, without having the impact of those changes on the presentation and business tiers of the application.

While building the JavaEdge data access tier, we are going to focus on

- Using the Apache group's Object/Relational (O/R) mapping tool: ObjectRelational-Bridge (OJB). OJB allows a developer to transparently map data pulled from a relational database to plain Java objects. Using OJB, you can significantly reduce the amount of data access code that needs to be written and maintained by the application team.

- Implementing two core J2EE data access design patterns that ensure that your business and presentation tiers are never exposed to the underlying data access technology used to retrieve your data. There is no need for a business component to know whether the data it is consuming is retrieved via JDBC, entity beans, or OJB. Specifically, we are going to explore the following J2EE data access patterns:

  - The Data Access Object (DAO) pattern

  - The Value Object (VO) pattern

Developing a Data Access Strategy

Although it is difficult to emphasize the importance of a data access tier, the fact is that most development teams do not have a coherent strategy defined for building one. Rather than having a well-defined set of services and interfaces for accessing their data, they will define their data access strategy in one of two ways:

- By the particular data access technology that they use to get the data

- By the database vendor that they use to hold their data

The problem with these two definitions is that the focus is on a purely technological solution.

Note A well-designed data access tier should transcend any one particular technology or data store.

Technologies change at a rapid rate; a new technology that appears to be a cutting-edge technology can quickly become obsolete. Development teams who couple their applications too tightly with a particular technology or technology vendor will find that their applications are not as responsive when new business requirements force an organization to adopt new data access technologies.

A data access tier should allow the business services to consume data without giving any idea of how or from where it is being retrieved. Specifically, a data access tier should have the following characteristics:

- *Allows a clean separation of data persistence logic from the presentation and business logic*: For instance, a business component should never be passed a Java ResultSet object or have to capture a SQLException. The entire data access logic should be central-ized behind a distinct set of interfaces, which the business logic *must* use to retrieve or manipulate data.

- *Decouples the application(s) from any knowledge of the database platform in which the data resides*: The objects in the business tier, requesting the data, need not know that they are accessing a relational database such as Oracle, an object-based database such as Poet, or an XML database such as the Apache Group's Xindice database.

- *Abstracts away the physical details of how data is stored within the database and the relationships that exist between entities in the database*: For instance, a business tier class should never know how the `Customer` object and the `Address` object manage their one-to-many relationship. These details should be handled by the data access tier and be completely hidden from the developer.

- *Simplifies the application development process by hiding the details associated with getting a database connection, issuing a command, or managing transactions*: Data access code can be very complicated even though it looks very easy to write. By putting all data access code behind a set of data access services, the development team can give the responsibility of writing that code to one or two developers who thoroughly understand the data access technology being used. All the other developers on the team only have to use the services provided by the data access tier to retrieve and manipulate data. They do not have to worry about the underlying details of the data access code. This significantly simplifies application development efforts and reduces the chance that a piece of poorly written data access code will inadvertently affect the application's code base.

As discussed in Chapter 1, the lack of planning for the data access tier results is the formation of the Data Madness antipattern. This antipattern manifests in a number of different manners including the following:

- *The creation of tight dependencies between the applications consuming the data and the structures of the underlying data stores*: Every time a change is made to the database structure, the developers have to hunt through the application code, identify any code that references the changed database structures (that is, the tables), and then update the code to reflect the changes. This is time consuming and error prone.

- *The inability to easily port an application to another database platform because of the dependencies on the vendor-specific database extensions*: Often, neglecting to abstract simple things, such as how a primary key is generated in the application's SQL code, can make it very difficult to port the application to another database platform.

- *The inability to easily change data access technologies without rewriting a significant amount of application code*: Many developers mix their data access code (that is, their SQL/JDBC or entity EJB lookups) directly in their application code. This intermixing will cause tight dependencies and an increase in the amount of code that needs to be touched up when you want to use a new data access technology.

- *The presence of a 2.5 tier architecture*: A 2.5 tier architecture is an architecture in which there is a well-defined presentation tier for the application, but the business logic is not clearly separated from the data access logic of the application. This particular symptom is sometimes very obvious.

You will find this symptom when you start studying the business logic of an application and find the SQL code scattered throughout the logic. (The code is found anywhere in the business logic and affects the flow. A good sign of this is when a database administrator asks the developers to look at all of the SQL code for an application and they have to search the entire application source code to find it.)

The presence of "data madness" can be easily found by knowing how the data access tier is designed. If the development team says that it is using JDBC, entity EJBs, SQLJ, Oracle, SQL Server, and so on, it is likely that there has been no real preplanning for the data access tier.

The JavaEdge Data Access Model

The data model for the JavaEdge application is very simple. It contains three entities: member, story, and story_comment. Figure 5-1 shows the JavaEdge database tables, the data elements contained within them, and the relationships that exist between them.

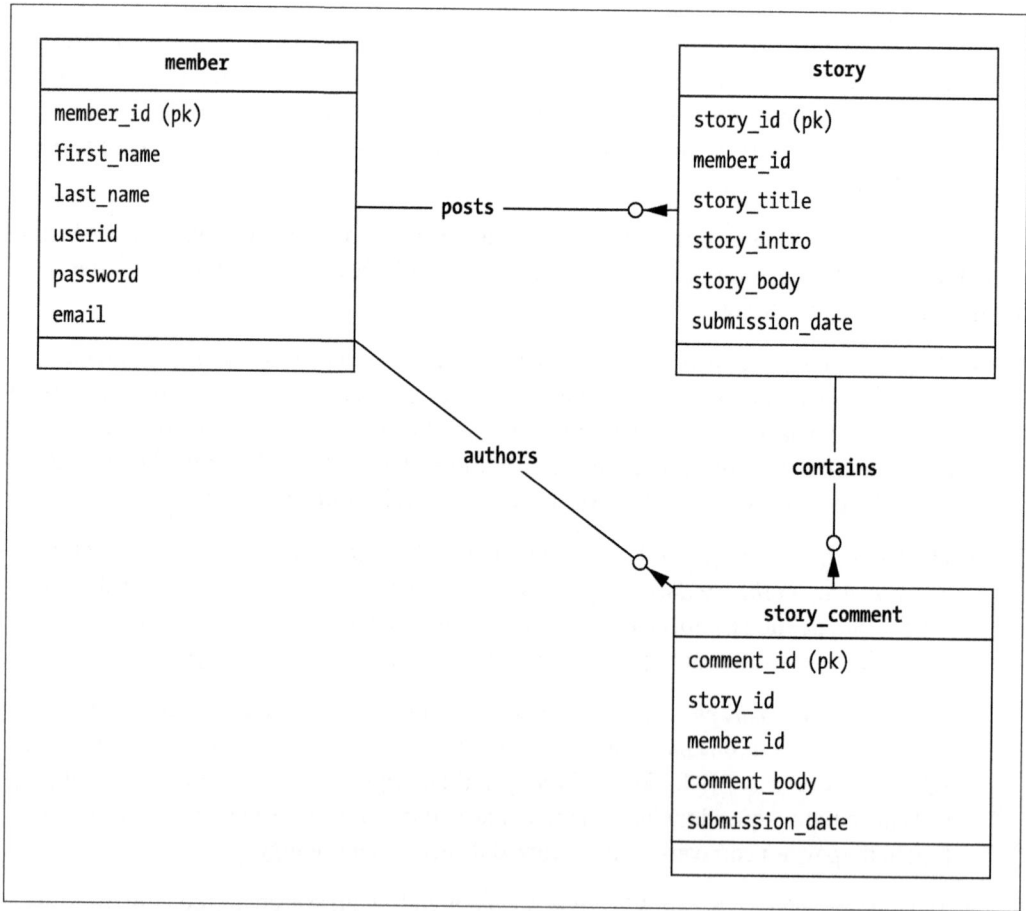

Figure 5-1. *The JavaEdge data model*

Figure 5-1 illustrates the following points:

- A JavaEdge member can post zero or more stories. A story can belong to one and only one member.

- A story can have zero or more comments associated with it. A story_comment can belong to one and only one story.

- A JavaEdge member can post zero or more comments on a particular story. A JavaEdge story_comment can be posted only by one member.

The JavaEdge data access tier is going to be built on one tenet:

Note The business code for the application will never be allowed to directly access the JavaEdge database.

All interactions with the JavaEdge database will be through a set of *Data Access Objects* (DAOs). DAO is a core J2EE design pattern that completely abstracts the *Create, Retrieve, Update, and Delete* (CRUD) logic needed to retrieve and manipulate the data behind the Java interface. One of the first examples of the Data Access Objects and Value Objects being articulated in a Java book is in *Core J2EE Patterns: Best Practices and Design Strategies* (Alur et al., Prentice Hall, ISBN 0-130-64884-1).

On Value Objects

The first edition of *Core J2EE Patterns: Best Practices and Design Strategies* used the term *Value Object* to describe a pattern for moving data between different tiers of an application's architecture. However, the use of this name has caused quite a bit of consternation in the patterns community because the term *Value Object* has also been used to describe another type of pattern implementation.

Many individuals feel that the name *Data Transfer Object* (DTO) is a more appropriate name for this pattern. The second edition of *Core J2EE Patterns: Best Practices and Design Strategies* has switched to this new name. For the sake of continuity with the previous edition of this book, we will continue to call this pattern the Value Object pattern.

However, for purposes of this discussion the terms *Value Object* and *Data Transfer Objects* are referring to the same type of pattern implementation.

The JavaEdge database is a relational database. Relational databases are row-oriented and do not map well into an object-oriented environment like Java. Even with the use of DAO classes, the question that needs to be solved is how to mitigate the need to pass row-oriented Java objects, such as the ResultSet class, back and forth between the business tier and DAO classes.

The answer is to use the Value Object (VO) pattern to map the data, retrieved and sent to a relational database, to a set of Java classes. These Java classes wrap the retrieved data behind simple get() and set() methods and minimize the exposure of the physical implementation details of the underlying database table to the developer. The underlying database structure can be changed or even moved to an entirely different platform with a very small risk of breaking any applications consuming the data.

Let's look at the diagram in Figure 5-2 and see how all of these pieces fit together.

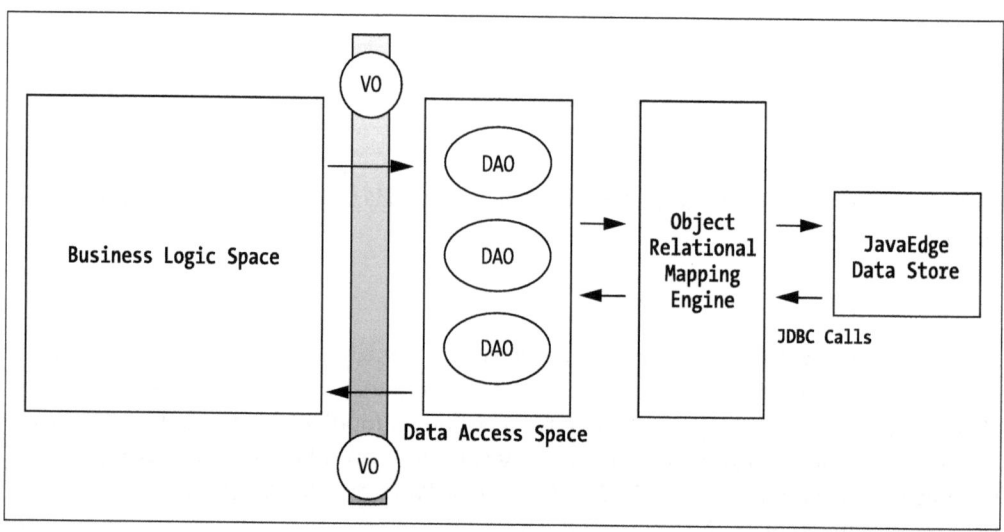

Figure 5-2. *The Data Access Object pattern in action*

The diagram in Figure 5-2 lays out the architecture for the example data access tier at a high level. As shown, the business tier uses the Data Access Objects to retrieve, insert, update, and delete data from the JavaEdge database. All data coming to and going from the DAOs is encapsulated in a Value Object. A Value Object represents a single record residing within the JavaEdge database. It abstracts away the physical database-specific details of the record and provides the Java programmer simple get()/set() methods for accessing individual attributes in a record. A Value Object can contain collections of other Value Objects. For example, the MemberVO class (in the JavaEdge application) contains a collection of stories. This collection represents the relationship that exists between a member record and its corresponding story records.

The DAOs never talk directly to the JavaEdge database. Instead, all the database access is done through an O/R mapping tool. The introduction of an O/R mapping tool is significantly time saving. This tool allows the developer to define declaratively, rather than programmatically, how data is to be mapped to and from the Value Objects in the application. This means that the developers do not have to write JDBC and SQL code to retrieve the JavaEdge data.

Now, let's cover the Data Access Objects and Value Objects being used for the JavaEdge application in more detail.

Data Access Objects

Data Access Objects are meant to wrap all the CRUD logic associated with entities within the JavaEdge database. DAOs provide an abstraction layer between the business tier and the physical data stores. Specifically, DAOs abstract

- The type of data store being accessed

- The database access technology being used to retrieve the data

- The physical location of data

Use of a set of DAOs removes the need for a developer to know whether the database is being stored in an Oracle server, a MySQL server, or a mainframe. This keeps the application database independent and minimizes the risk of exposing vendor-specific database extensions to the business tier. Database vendors provide a number of extensions that often make writing the data access code easy or offer performance enhancements above the standard SQL code. However, these extensions come at a price: portability. By abstracting away these database-specific extensions from the business tier, the development team can minimize the impact of vendor locking on its business code. Instead, only the data access tier is exposed to these details.

In addition, DAOs keep the business tier code from being exposed to the way in which the data is being accessed. This gives the development team a lot of flexibility in choosing data access technology. A beginning team of Java developers may choose to write the application code with JDBC. As they become more comfortable with the Java environment, they may rewrite their Data Access Objects using a much more sophisticated technology such as entity beans or Java Data Objects (JDO).

In many IT organizations, data is spread throughout various data stores. Hence, the developers have to know where all of this data is located and write the code to access it. DAOs allow the system architect to put together the data that is found in multiple locations and present a single logic interface for retrieving and updating it. The application consuming the data is location independent. For example, most organizations do not have all of their customer data in one location. They might have some of the data residing in the Customer Relationship Management (CRM) system, some of it in their order entry system, some of it in the contact management used by the sales department, and so on. Using a Data Access Object, a system architect can centralize all CRUD logic associated with the accessing of customer data into a single Java object. This relieves the developer from having to know where and how to access the customer data.

DAOs simplify the work for the development team because they relieve the majority of the team from knowing the "dirty" details of data access.

The JavaEdge Data Access Objects

All the DAOs in the JavaEdge application are going to extend a single interface class called DataAccessObject. This interface guarantees that all the Data Access Objects in the JavaEdge application have the following four base methods:

- findByPK()

- insert()

- update()

- delete()

If you want all of your DAOs to have a particular functionality, make the DataAccessObject an abstract class rather than an interface. The code for the DataAccessObject interface is shown here:

```
package com.apress.javaedge.common;

public interface DataAccessObject {

  public ValueObject findByPK(String primaryKey) throws DataAccessException;
  public void insert(ValueObject insertRecord) throws DataAccessException;
  public void update(ValueObject updateRecord) throws DataAccessException;
  public void delete(ValueObject deleteRecord) throws DataAccessException;
}
```

The findByPK() method is a *finder method* used to retrieve a record based upon its primary key. This method will perform a database lookup and return a ValueObject containing the data. A ValueObject is a Java class that wraps the data retrieved using get()/set() methods. We will discuss more about this class in the next section.

The DataAccessObject interface, shown previously, supports only primary key lookups using a single key. However, many times in a data model, the uniqueness of a row of data can be established only by combining two or more keys together. This is known as a *composite primary key*. To support this model, you could easily change the DataAccessObject interface to have a ValueObject passed in as a parameter. This ValueObject could then contain more than one value necessary to perform the database lookup.

The insert(), update(), and delete() methods correspond to different actions that can be taken against the data stored in the JavaEdge database. Each of these three methods has a ValueObject passed in as a parameter. The DAO will use the data contained in the ValueObject parameter to carry out the requested action (that is, a database insert, update, or delete).

The DataAccessObject interface contains method signatures that reflect the four basic actions associated with retrieving and manipulating data. If the developers want to add additional methods (that is, additional finder methods to perform specialized queries) these methods will usually go on the concrete implementation of the DAO. For example, the StoryDAO has an additional finder method called findTopStory().

All four of the methods in the DataAccessObject interface throw an exception called DataAccessException. The DataAccessException is a user-defined exception used to wrap any exceptions that might be thrown by the data access code contained within the DAO.

The whole purpose of a DAO is to hide how the data is accessed. This means the DAO should never allow a data-access-specific exception, such as a JDBC SQLException, to be thrown.

Many times, implementing a solid system architecture that is going to be easily maintainable and extensible may involve small decisions to be made early on in the design of the architecture. In the data access tier for our example application, small things such as wrapping the technology-specific exceptions with a more generic exception can have a huge impact. For instance, allowing a JDBC SQLException to be thrown from the DAO would unnecessarily expose the way in which the data is being accessed to application code using the DAO. The business code would have to catch the SQLException every time it wants to access a method in that DAO. Also, if the developers later want to rewrite the DAO to use something other than JDBC, they would have to go back to every place in the business tier that used the DAO and refactor the try..catch block for the SQLException. Wrapping the SQLException with the DataAccessException avoids this problem.

Note You often do not feel the pain of poor design decisions until the application has gone into production and you now have to maintain and extend it.

The JavaEdge application is going to have two DAOs: StoryDAO and MemberDAO. The class diagram in Figure 5-3 shows the DAOs and their corresponding methods.

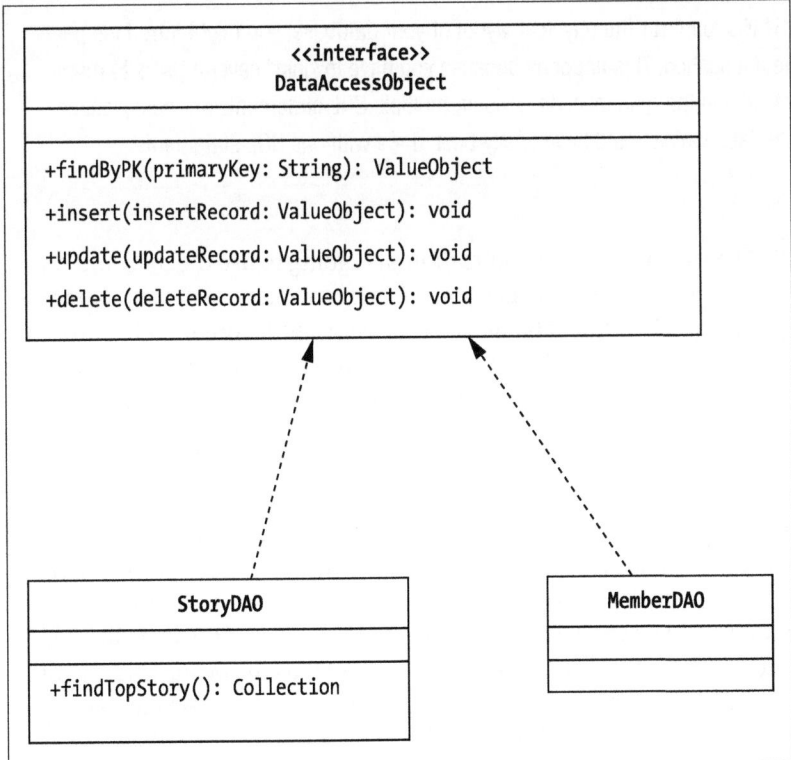

Figure 5-3. *The Data Access Object and its methods*

Two observations can be made from the class diagram in Figure 5-3. First, the DataAccessObject interface defines only the base methods that all DAO classes must implement. You can add any other methods to the classes implementing the DAO interface. For example, StoryDAO has an additional finder method called findTopStory(). This method will return a Java Collection of StoryVO Value Objects. A DAO implementation can have as many finder methods in it as needed. The additional methods added in a DAO implementation can do additional tasks, such as perform specialized queries or invoke a stored procedure.

The second observation from the diagram is that even though there are three database tables (member, story, and story_comment), only two DAOs (StoryDAO and MemberDAO) have been implemented for the JavaEdge application. There is no DAO present for handling the data logic associated with manipulating data in the story_comment table.

A common mistake that is made while implementing a data access tier using a Data Access Object pattern is to mimic the physical layout of the database. The application designer tends to create a DAO for each of the tables in the database schema. However, the designers have to consider the context in which their data is going to be used while modeling the DAOs.

In the JavaEdge application, the story and the story_comment table have a one-to-many relationship. Story comments have no context other than being associated with a story. So, the StoryDAO is responsible for managing both story and story_comment data. This may seem a little unclear now, but as we start discussing Value Objects, you will see that one Value Object can contain collections of other Value Objects.

Note If you model your DAOs to mirror the physical layout of your database, you might introduce performance problems into the application. This happens because you have to "join" several DAOs to mimic the relationships that might exist in the database. As a result, multiple SQL statements are being issued to retrieve, update, or delete data, which could have easily been done with one SQL statement.

By modeling your DAO based on how the application(s) is going to use the data and not just mimicking the physical layout of the database, you can often avoid unnecessary database calls. This is particularly true for relational databases, where with a little forethought you can leverage SQL "joins" to retrieve data (particularly the data that has a one-to-many relationship) in one SQL call inside one DAO, instead of multiple SQL calls involving multiple DAOs.

Value Objects

The Value Object pattern evolved in response to the performance problems inherent in the EJB 1.1 specification. In the EJB 1.1 specification, entity beans supported only remote interfaces. It was expensive to invoke methods in a remote interface. Each time a method was invoked, a significant amount of data marshaling had to take place, even if the code invoking the entity bean was located in the same Java Virtual Machine (JVM) as the bean. This meant that the fine-grained get() and set() method calls for retrieving individual data elements from an entity bean could quickly incur a performance hit.

The solution was to minimize the number of individual get()/set() methods being called on an entity bean. This is how the Value Object pattern evolved. A Value Object pattern is nothing more than a plain old Java class that originally held the data retrieved from an entity bean lookup. A Value Object contains no business logic and only has get()/set() to retrieve and alter data that it contains.

An entity bean populates a Value Object with the data it retrieved and then returns that Value Object to the caller as a serialized object. By putting all of the data in a Value Object, an entity bean developer could avoid the performance costs associated with multiple invocations on a remote interface. The application using the Value Object would use the get() methods in the object to retrieve the data looked up by the entity bean. Conversely, if the application wanted to insert or update via the entity bean, it would populate a new Value Object or update an already existing one and return it back to the entity bean to perform the database write.

The Value Object pattern was evolved to deal with the inherent performance problems in entity beans. With the release of the EJB 2.0 specification and the introduction of local interfaces, it would seem that the Value Object pattern would not be needed. However, this pattern is also very useful for abstracting physical database details and moving data back and forth between the data tier and the other tiers in a web-based application.

Value Objects provide a mechanism in which the data being used by the application can be decoupled from the data store that holds the data. By using Value Objects in your data access tier, you can do the following:

- *Easily pass data to and from the presentation and business tiers without ever exposing the details of the underlying data store*: The Value Objects become the transport mechanism for moving data between the presentation framework (that is, Struts), the business tier (that is, your business delegates and session facades), and the data tier.

- *Hide the physical details of the underlying data store*: Value Objects can be used to hold your data; as a result, the developer would not know the physical data types being used to store data in the database. For instance, one of your database tables may contain a Binary Large Object (BLOB). Rather than forcing the developer to work with the JBDC Blob type, you can have the developer work with a String data type on the Value Object and make the DAO using that Value Object be responsible for converting that String to the JDBC Blob data type.

- *Hide the details of the relationships that exist between the entities within your data store*: An application using a Value Object is exposed to only the cardinality between entities through a get() method that returns a Collection of objects. They have no idea of whether or not that cardinality is a one-to-many or many-to-many relationship. In this example, if you want to restructure the story and story_comment table to have a many-to-many relationship, only the StoryDAO would need to be modified. None of the applications using the Story data would be affected.

Let's look at the Value Objects that are implemented for the JavaEdge application.

The JavaEdge Value Objects

Three Value Objects are used in the JavaEdge application: MemberVO, StoryVO, and
StoryCommentVO. All of these classes extend an abstract class called ValueObject. (The Value
Object pattern can be implemented in a number of ways.) The code for the ValueObject class
is shown here:

```
package com.apress.javaedge.common;
import  org.apache.commons.lang.builder.ReflectionToStringBuilder;

public abstract class ValueObject {

    /** Creates a new instance of ValueObject */
    public ValueObject() {
    }

    public String toString() {
        return ReflectionToStringBuilder.toString(this);
    }
}
```

The Jakarta Commons Project to the Rescue Again

The ValueObject class serves as a good base class for putting methods that are going to be
shared across all Value Objects in the application. Oftentimes while building out the JavaEdge
application, the authors needed to dump the contents of a JavaBean. Rather than writing their
own method to do this, they used the ReflectionToStringBuilder class from the Jakarta Commons lang project. The Commons lang project provides several "helper" utilities for carrying
out most low-level tasks related to the core java.lang classes. The ReflectionToStringBuilder
classes use Java reflection to build a string containing all of the properties within a class.

By overriding the toString() method on the base ValueObjects and using the
ReflectionToStringBuilder class, in three lines of code we were able to have a consistent
mechanism for dumping the contents of a JavaBean. The preceding example only shows a
very simple use of the ReflectionToStringBuilder class. For more in-depth examples of how
to use this functionality, please visit the Jakarta Commons lang project's web site at
http://jakarta.apache.org/commons/lang.

For a different implementation of the Value Object pattern, you may want to refer to
J2EE Design Patterns Applied (Juric et al., Wrox Press, ISBN: 1-861-00528-8). It is common
for the Value Object base call to be either an interface or a class. If you are going to pass your
Value Objects between different Java Virtual Machines, they should at least implement the
Serializable interface.

In the JavaEdge application, the ValueObject interface is used as a *marker* interface to
indicate that the class is a Value Object. This interface has no method signatures and provides
a generic type for passing data in and out of a DAO. By passing only ValueObjects in the
DataAccessObject interface, you can guarantee that every DAO in the JavaEdge application
supports a base set of CRUD functionality. It is the responsibility of the DAO to cast the
ValueObject to the type it is expecting.

The class diagram in Figure 5-4 shows the details of the Value Objects used in the JavaEdge application.

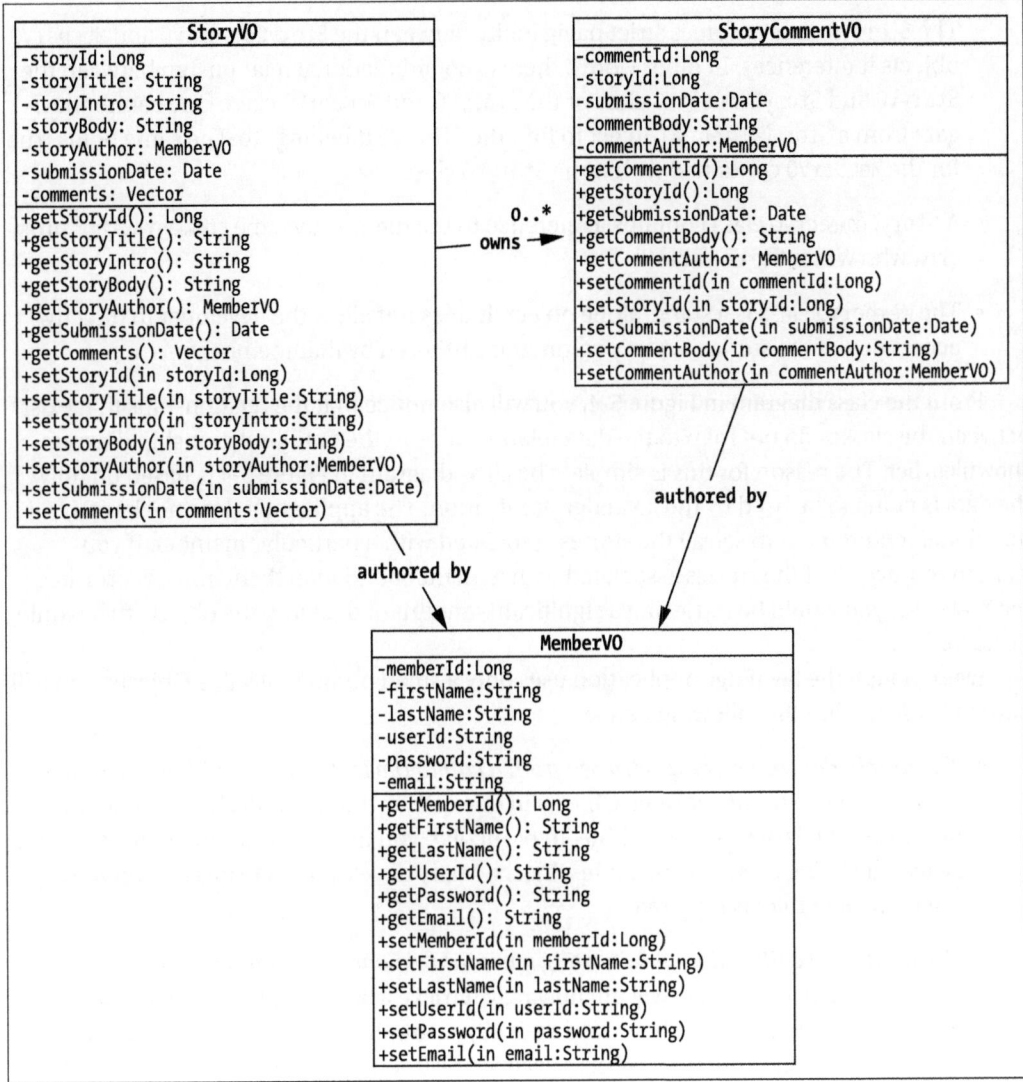

Figure 5-4. *The JavaEdge Value Objects*

All of the classes in this diagram implement the ValueObject interface. Based on the class diagram, you can see the following relationships among the classes: A StoryVO class can contain zero or more StoryCommentVO objects. The StoryCommentVO classes are stored in a Vector inside the StoryVO class. A StoryVO object contains a reference, via the storyAuthor property, to the JavaEdge member who authored the original story.

Child objects can be returned from a parent object in a number of ways. For the JavaEdge application, a Vector was chosen to return "groups" of Value Objects because a Vector enforces thread-safety by synchronizing the access to the items stored within the Vector. This means two threads cannot simultaneously add or remove items from the Vector.

If you are trying to maximize the performance and know that multiple threads in your application are not going to add or remove items from the collection, you can use a nonsynchronized `Collection` object like an `ArrayList`.

- The `StoryVO` class enforces strict navigability between the `StoryCommentVO` and `MemberVO` objects it references. In other words, there is no bidirectional relationship between the `StoryVO` and `StoryCommentVO` class or the `StoryVO` and `MemberVO` class. One cannot navigate from a `StoryCommentVO` object to find the `StoryVO` it belongs to. The same holds true for the `MemberVO` contained within the `StoryVO` class.

- A `StoryCommentVO` class contains a reference to the member, via the `commentAuthor` property, who wrote the comment.

- The `MemberVO` class is a stand-alone object. It does not allow the developer to directly access any of the stories or story comments authored by that member.

From the class diagram in Figure 5-4, you will also notice that the relationships that exist between the classes do not map to the data relationships in the entity-relationship diagram shown earlier. The reason for this is simple. The class diagram in Figure 5-4 is based on how the data is going to be used by the JavaEdge application. The application does not have a functional requirement to see all the stories associated with a particular member. If you want to retrieve all of the stories associated with a member and map them into a `Vector` in the `MemberVO`, you would be retrieving a significant amount of data into the objects that would never be used.

Even though the JavaEdge application uses only a small number of Value Objects, you will have to keep in mind the following items:

- *The number of values being retrieved from a call to the DAOs*: You would not want to retrieve large amounts of Value Objects in one call, as this can quickly consume memory within the Java Virtual Machine. In particular, you need to be aware of the data that is actually being used in your Value Objects. Many development teams end up retrieving more data than is required.

- *The number of child Value Objects being retrieved by a parent*: Often, while building the data access tier, developers will unknowingly retrieve a large number of Value Objects because they do not realize how deep their object graphs are. For instance, if you retrieve 10 stories in a call to the `StoryDAO` and each `StoryVO` contains 20 `StoryCommentVOs`, you end up retrieving

  10 stories * 20 story comments + 10 story authors + 20 story comment authors = 230 objects for one call

The primary design principle that was embraced while designing the Value Objects used in the JavaEdge application was this:

Note Understand how the data in your application is going to be used. A Value Object is nothing more than a view of the data, and there is nothing inappropriate about having a DAO return different types of Value Objects, all showing a different perspective of the same piece of data.

Using an O/R Mapping Tool

It has been said that 40 to 60 percent of a development team's time is spent writing the data access code. For most Java developers, this means writing significant amounts of SQL and JDBC code. As the developers of the JavaEdge application, we decided that we wanted to significantly reduce the amount of work needed to implement the data access tier. We decided to use an O/R mapping tool that would allow us to dynamically generate SQL requests and map any data operations needed from plain Java objects.

O/R mapping tools have been available for quite a while and actually have predated the language. Even though these tools offer fine solutions, they are expensive. Hence we had to use a single vendor's proprietary toolset.

Fortunately, several open source O/R mapping tools are now available and gaining widespread acceptance in the development community. O/R mapping tools fall into two broad categories in terms of how they are implemented:

- *Code generators*: O/R mapping tools in the code generator category require the development team to map out the structure of its database tables and Java objects. These tools then generate all of the Java and JDBC code needed to carry out database transactions. The development team can use these generated classes in the applications. Examples of open source O/R code generators include

  - *The Apache Group's Torque project:* Torque originally started as a component of the Apache Group's Turbine project. Torque is a very powerful persistence tool that can convert an existing database into a set of usable persistence-aware Java classes. Torque can even be used to develop a database from scratch and then generate the entire database DDL and Java classes via an Ant Task. Torque uses proprietary API for performing database queries. More details on Torque are available at `http://db.apache.org/torque`.

  - *The Middlegen project*: Middlegen, another in this category, takes a slightly different approach than Torque. It can take an existing database and generate either Container-Managed Persistence–based (CMP) entity beans or Java Data Objects (JDO). Both CMP entity beans and JDO are industry-accepted standards and are not solely "owned" by a vendor. Middlegen can even generate the EJB 2.0 vendor-specific deployment descriptors for many of the leading application servers. More information on Middlegen can be found at `http://boss.bekk.no/boss/middlegen`.

- *Dynamic SQL generators*: The other category of O/R mapping tools is the dynamic SQL generators. These O/R tools allow you to define your database according to Java object mappings. However, these tools do not generate the Java classes for you. Instead, the developer is responsible for writing the mapped Java objects (usually implemented as Value Objects). The O/R tools' runtime engine will then transparently map data to and from the Java object.

An example of a dynamic SQL generator is the Apache Group's ObjectRelationalBridge (OJB). Three main reasons for choosing this tool for implementing the JavaEdge project are as follows:

- *OJB is very lightweight and extremely easy to set up and use.* A simple data persistence tier can be implemented by just configuring two files: repository.xml and OJB.properties. You can start using OJB without having to modify existing Java class files.

- *Since OJB does not perform the code generation, it makes it extremely easy to use with existing applications.* This is a key consideration while evaluating O/R mapping tools. It is better to use O/R mapping tools that generate code while developing a project from scratch. However, they can be an absolute nightmare to implement while retrofitting the O/R tool into an existing application. If the developers want to tweak the code generated by the tool, they must remember to reimplement their changes every time they regenerate their persistence tier code.

  In addition, code generator O/R mapping tools require you to set up the generation process as part of your development environment and/or build process. This itself can be a time-consuming and error-prone process.

- *OJB has a unique architecture that allows it to embrace multiple industry standards for data persistence.* As explained in the section "About ObjectRelationalBridge," OJB implements a micro-kernel architecture that allows it to use its own proprietary APIs for making persistence calls and the JDO and Object Data Management Group (ODMG) 3.0 standards. This makes it easier to move the applications off of OJB and onto other O/R mapping tools, if the OJB is not working out.

  As with all of the tools talked about so far, OJB is open source.

In addition, OJB supports a number of features that are normally found in its more expensive commercial cousins. Some of these features include

- An object cache, which greatly enhances the performance and helps guarantee the identities of multiple objects pointing to the same data row.

- Transparent persistence. The developer does not need to use OJB-generated classes or extend or implement any additional classes to make the state of the objects persistable to a database.

- Automatic persistence of child objects. When a parent object is saved, updates are made to all persistence-aware child objects that the parent references.

- An architecture that can run in a single JVM or in a client/server mode that can service the needs of multiple application servers running in a cluster.

- The ability to integrate in an application server environment, including participation in container-managed transactions and JNDI data source lookups.

- Multiple types of locking support, including support for optimistic locking.

- A built-in sequence manager.

This is just a small list of the features currently supported by OJB. Let's discuss OJB in more detail.

About ObjectRelationalBridge (OJB)

ObjectRelationalBridge is one of the newest Apache Group projects. It is a fully functional O/R mapping tool. OJB is based on micro-kernel architecture. A *micro-kernel architecture* is the one in which a core set of functionality is built around a very minimalist and concise set of APIs. Additional functionality is then layered around the kernel APIs. Micro-kernel APIs are very flexible because different implementations of a technology can be built around a single set of APIs.

Figure 5-5 illustrates this architecture.

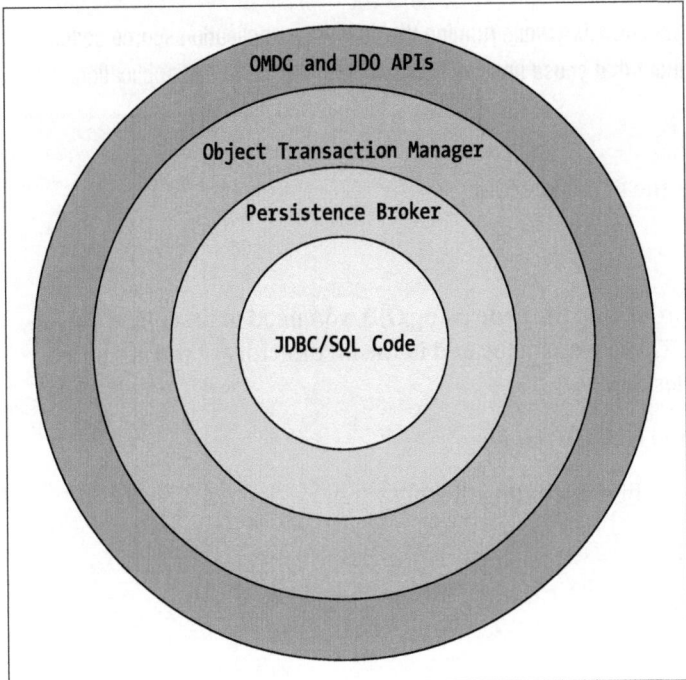

Figure 5-5. *The OJB micro-kernel architecture*

At the heart of OJB is the Persistence Broker (PB) API. This API defines a number of standard calls for interacting with a data store. The PB API supports making calls only against a relational database (as designated by the Persistence Broker API shown in Figure 5-5). It uses JDBC 1.0 database calls and a subset of SQL to guarantee the maximum amount of database support. In future releases, the OJB development team is planning to implement additional JDBC support along with support for Object, LDAP, and XML-based databases.

Since OJB is designed using micro-kernel architecture, OJB uses a very basic kernel API (that is, the PB API) and then builds on that API to implement multiple data access APIs. OJB currently supports both JDO and the ODMG's Object Data Standard (version 3.0). Both of these APIs are built on top of OJB's PB API and interact with it.

OJB is an extremely configurable and tunable product. It is built on a set of pluggable components, so that if you find that some feature in OJB does not meet your needs (such as its caching model), you can easily replace that component with your own implementation.

The JavaEdge application uses the following technology to build the data access tier:

- *MySQL MaxDB*: Available at `http://mysql.com`.

- *Connector/J 3.1 (a MySQL JDBC Driver)*: Available at `http://mysql.com`. Connector/J 5.0 is in development and might be in Generally Available (GA) release by the time this book is published.

- *OJB 1.0.4*: Available at `http://db.apache.org/ojb`.

■**Caution** Please use at least OJB version 1.0.4 while running the JavaEdge application source code. Earlier releases of OJB have bugs in them that cause unusual behavior with the JavaEdge application.

Now, we will walk through some of the key files.

The Core OJB Files

OJB is very easy to set up. To begin writing the code using OJB, you need to first place the following jar files in your classpath. These files are located in the lib directory of the unzipped OJB distribution. The required files are

- db-ojb-1.0.4.jar, which is the core OJB jar file

- Several Jakarta Commons jar files, including the following:

    - commons-beanutils.jar

    - commons-collections.jar

    - commons-lang-2.0.jar

    - commons-logging.jar

    - commons-pool.jar

Once these jar files are included in your classpath, you are ready to begin mapping your Java class files. In the JavaEdge application, these will be the MemberVO, StoryVO, and StoryCommentVO classes, mapped to your database tables.

Setting Up the Object/Relational Mappings

Setting up your O/R mappings using OJB is a straightforward process that involves creating and editing two files: OJB.properties and repository.xml. The OJB.properties file is used to customize the OJB runtime environment.

By modifying the OJB.properties file, a developer can control whether OJB is running in single virtual machine or client/server mode, the size of the OJB connection pool, lock management, and the logging level of the OJB runtime engine. We will not be going through a step-by-step description of the OJB.properties file. Instead, we are going to review the relevant material.

The repository.xml file is responsible for defining the database-related information. It defines the JDBC connection information that is going to be used to connect to a database. In addition, it defines all of the Java class-to-table definitions. This includes mapping the class attributes to the database columns, and the cardinality relationships that might exist in the database (such as one-to-one, one-to-many, and many-to-many).

The JavaEdge repository.xml

The JavaEdge repository.xml file is quite simple. It only maps three classes to three database tables. A repository.xml file for a medium-to-large size database would be huge. Right now, the OJB team is working on a graphical O/R mapping tool, but it could take some time before it is stable.

The following code is the JavaEdge repository.xml file:

```xml
<?xml version="1.0" encoding="UTF-8"?>


<!-- defining entities for include-files -->

<!DOCTYPE descriptor-repository SYSTEM "repository.dtd" [

<!ENTITY internal SYSTEM "repository_internal.xml">
]>

<descriptor-repository version="1.0" isolation-level="read-uncommitted">

<!-- The Default JDBC Connection. If a class-descriptor does not specify its own
     JDBC Connection, the Connection specified here will be used. -->

<jdbc-connection-descriptor
               jcd-alias="strutsdb"
               default-connection="true"
                       platform="MySQL"
                       jdbc-level="2.0"
                       driver="org.gjt.mm.mysql.Driver"
                       protocol="jdbc"
                       subprotocol="@OJB_DB_URL@"
                       dbalias="waf"
                       username="waf_user"
                       password="password"
                       />

<class-descriptor class="com.apress.javaedge.member.MemberVO" table="member">
    <field-descriptor name="memberId" column="member_id"
        jdbc-type="BIGINT"  primarykey="true" autoincrement="true"/>
```

```
            <field-descriptor name="firstName" column="first_name" jdbc-type="VARCHAR"/>
            <field-descriptor name="lastName"  column="last_name"  jdbc-type="VARCHAR"/>
            <field-descriptor name="userId" column="userid" jdbc-type="VARCHAR"/>
            <field-descriptor name="password" column="password" jdbc-type="VARCHAR"/>
            <field-descriptor name="email" column="email" jdbc-type="VARCHAR"/>
        </class-descriptor>

        <class-descriptor class="com.apress.javaedge.story.StoryVO" table="story">
            <field-descriptor name="storyId" column="story_id" jdbc-type="BIGINT"
                            primarykey="true" autoincrement="true"/>
            <field-descriptor name="memberId" column="member_id" jdbc-type="BIGINT"/>
            <field-descriptor name="storyTitle" column="story_title"
                            jdbc-type="VARCHAR"/>
            <field-descriptor name="storyIntro"  column="story_intro"
                            jdbc-type="VARCHAR"/>
            <field-descriptor name="storyBody" column="story_body"
                            jdbc-type="LONGVARBINARY"/>
            <field-descriptor name="submissionDate" column="submission_date"
                            jdbc-type="DATE"/>
            <collection-descriptor name ="comments"
                    element-class-ref="com.apress.javaedge.story.StoryCommentVO"
                    auto-retrieve="true" auto-update="true" auto-delete="true">
                    <inverse-foreignkey field-ref="storyId"/>
            </collection-descriptor>

            <reference-descriptor name="storyAuthor"
                class-ref="com.apress.javaedge.member.MemberVO" auto-retrieve="true">
                    <foreignkey field-ref="memberId"/>
            </reference-descriptor>
        </class-descriptor>

        <class-descriptor class="com.apress.javaedge.story.StoryCommentVO"
                        table="story_comment">
            <field-descriptor name="commentId" column="comment_id"
                            jdbc-type="BIGINT"
                            primarykey="true" autoincrement="true"/>
            <field-descriptor name="storyId" column="story_id" jdbc-type="BIGINT"/>
            <field-descriptor name="memberId" column="member_id" jdbc-type="BIGINT"/>
            <field-descriptor name="commentBody" column="comment_body"
                            jdbc-type="LONGVARBINARY"/>
            <field-descriptor name="submissionDate" column="submission_date"
                            jdbc-type="DATE"/>
            <reference-descriptor name="commentAuthor"
                class-ref="com.apress.javaedge.member.MemberVO" auto-retrieve="true">
                    <foreignkey field-ref="memberId"/>
            </reference-descriptor>
        </class-descriptor>
```

```
<!-- include ojb internal mappings here -->
&internal;

</descriptor-repository>
```

The root element of the repository.xml file is the deployment descriptor called
`<descriptor-repository>`. This element has two attributes defined in it: `version` and
`isolation-level`. The `version` attribute is a required attribute and indicates the version of
the repository.dtd file used for validating the repository.xml file. The `isolation-level` attribute
is used to indicate the default transaction level used by all of the `class-descriptor` elements
in the file. A `class-descriptor` element is used to describe a mapping between a Java class
and a database table, and we discuss this element in the section "Setting Up a Simple Java
Class-to-Table Mapping."

The values that can be set for the `isolation-level` attribute include

- `read-uncommitted`

- `read-committed`

- `repeatable-read`

- `serializable`

- `optimistic`

If no value is set for the `isolation-level` attribute, it will default to `read-uncommitted`.

In the next several sections, you are going to get the chance to study the individual pieces
of the repository.xml file. We will start by discussing how to configure OJB to connect to a database. We will then look at how to perform a simple table mapping, and finally work our way up
to the more traditional database relationships, such as one-to-one, one-to-many, and many-
to-many.

Setting Up the JDBC Connection Information

Setting up OJB to connect to a database is a straightforward process. It involves setting up a
`<jdbc-connection-descriptor>` element in the repository.xml file. The `<jdbc-connection-
descriptor>` for the JavaEdge application is shown here:

```
<jdbc-connection-descriptor
          jcd-alias="strutsdb"
          default-connection="true"
                    platform="MySQL"
                    jdbc-level="2.0"
                    driver="org.gjt.mm.mysql.Driver"
                    protocol="jdbc"
                    dbalias="waf"
                    username="waf_user"
                    password="password"
                    />
```

The repository.xml file can contain multiple database connections defined within it. Each database connection can be assigned a unique name using the jcd-alias attribute on the <jdbc-connection-descriptor/> tag for the database connection. The default-connection attribute is used to tell OJB which of the <jdbc-connection-descriptor/> tags in the repository.xml file is the default connection. The value for the default-connection attribute can be true or false. There can be only one default JDBC connection for a repository.xml file.

The rest of the attributes in the <jdbc-connection-descriptor/> tag map closely to the properties used to configure a data source in any J2EE application. These attributes include the following:

- driver: The fully qualified class name of the JDBC driver being used by OJB to connect to the database.

- dbalias: The name of the database being connected to.

- username/password: The user name and password OJB will use to log in to the database. These values do not need to be set in the repository.xml file and instead can be used in the conjunction with the org.apache.ojb.broker.PBKey and org.apache.ojb.broker. PersistenceBroker classes to perform database authentication dynamically at runtime. These classes will be covered in greater detail in the section "OJB in Action."

The two attributes that are not standard to JDBC and particular to OJB are the platform and jdbc-level attributes. The platform attribute tells OJB the database platform that the repository.xml file is being run against. OJB uses a pluggable mechanism to handle calls to a specific database platform. The value specified in the platform attribute will map to a PlatformxxxImpl.java (located in the org.apache.ojb.broker.platforms package).

The following databases are supported officially by OJB:

- DB2

- Hsqldb (HyperSonic)

- Informix

- MS Access (Microsoft Access)

- MS SQL Server (Microsoft SQL Server)

- MySQL

- Oracle

- PostgresSQL

- SapDB

- Sybase

The jdbc-level attribute is used to indicate the level of JDBC compliance at which the JDBC driver being used runs. The values currently supported by the jdbc-level attribute are 1.0, 2.0, and 3.0. If it is not set, OJB will use the default value of 1.0.

OJB can integrate with a JNDI-bound data source. To do this, you need to set up the `<jdbc-connection-descriptor>` element to use the `jndi-datasource-name` attribute. For example, you can rewrite the preceding `<jdbc-connection-descriptor>` to use a JNDI data source bound to the JBoss application server running JavaEdge, as follows:

```
<jdbc-connection-descriptor
          platform="MySql"
          jdbc-level="2.0"
          jndi-datasource-name="java:/MySqlDS"
/>
```

It is important to note that when a JNDI data source is defined in the `<jdbc-connection-descriptor>` tag, no `driver`, `protocol`, or `dbalias` is needed. All of this information is going to be defined via the application server's JNDI configuration. In the preceding example, the `username` and `password` attributes are not specified for the same reason.

Now, let's discuss how to map the JavaEdge classes to database tables stored in your database.

Setting Up a Simple Java Class-to-Table Mapping

Let's start with a simple mapping, the `MemberVO` class. The `MemberVO` class does not have any relationships with any of the classes in the JavaEdge application. The source code for the `MemberVO` class is shown here:

```java
package com.apress.javaedge.member;

import com.apress.javaedge.common.ValueObject;

public class MemberVO extends ValueObject implements java.io.Serializable{

    private Long memberId;
    private String firstName;
    private String lastName;
    private String userId;
    private String password;
    private String email;

    public MemberVO(String email,
    String firstName,
    String lastName,
    Long memberId,
    String password,
    String    userId){
        this.email = email;
        this.firstName = firstName;
        this.lastName  = lastName;
        this.memberId  = memberId;
        this.password  = password;
        this.userId    = userId;
```

```java
    }

    /////////////////////////////////////////
    // Access methods for attributes.

    public String getFirstName() {
        return firstName;
    }

    public void setFirstName(String firstName) {
        this.firstName = firstName;
    }

    public String getLastName() {
        return lastName;
    }

    public void setLastName(String lastName) {
        this.lastName = lastName;
    }

    public String getUserId() {
        return userId;
    }

    public void setUserId(String userId) {
        this.userId = userId;
    }

    public String getPassword() {
        return password;
    }

    public void setPassword(String password) {
        this.password = password;
    }

    public String getEmail() {
        return email;
    }

    public void setEmail(String email) {
        this.email = email;
    }

    public Long getMemberId() {
        return memberId;
```

```
    }

    public void setMemberId(Long memberId) {
        this.memberId = memberId;
    }

} // end MemberVO
```

As you can see, the MemberVO class consists of nothing more than get()/set() methods for member attributes. To begin the mapping, you need to set up a <class-descriptor> tag:

```
<class-descriptor class="com.apress.javaedge.member.MemberVO"
                  table="member">
...
</class-descriptor>
```

This <class-descriptor> has two attributes in it: class and table. The class attribute gives the fully qualified Java class name that is going to be mapped. The table attribute defines the name of the database table to which the class is mapping.

A <class-descriptor> tag contains one or more <field-descriptor> tags. These tags are used to map the individual class attributes to their corresponding database columns. The column mappings for the MemberVO are as shown here:

```
<field-descriptor name="memberId" column="member_id"
                  jdbc-type="BIGINT" primarykey="true"
                  autoincrement="true"/>
<field-descriptor name="firstName" column="first_name"
                  jdbc-type="VARCHAR"/>
<field-descriptor name="lastName" column="last_name"
                  jdbc-type="VARCHAR"/>
<field-descriptor name="userId" column="userid"
                  jdbc-type="VARCHAR"/>
<field-descriptor name="password" column="password"
                  jdbc-type="VARCHAR"/>
<field-descriptor name="email" column="email"
                  jdbc-type="VARCHAR"/>
```

Let's take the <field-descriptor> tag for the memberId and look at its components. This <field-descriptor> tag has five attributes. The first attribute is the name attribute, which defines the name of the Java attribute that is going to be mapped. The column attribute defines the name of the database column. By default, OJB directly sets the private attributes of the class using Java reflection. By using reflection, you do not need get() or set() methods for each attribute.

By having OJB set the mapped attributes directly via reflection, you do not need to make the mapped attributes public or protected.

It is a good programming practice to have all attributes accessed in an object have a get()/set() method. However, while performing O/R mappings via OJB, there are two advantages to setting the private mapped attributes of a class directly. First, you can implement read-only data attributes by having OJB directly setting private attributes of a class and then providing a get() method to access the data. If you have OJB for mapping data using get() and set() methods, you cannot have only a get() method for an attribute; you must also have a set() method because OJB requires it.

The second advantage is that you can hide the underlying details of how the data is stored in the database. For example, all stories in the JavaEdge database are stored as BLOBs. Their Java data type representation is an array of bytes. Rather than forcing the clients using the mapped Java class to convert the byte[] array to a String object, you can tell OJB to map directly to the private attribute (of type byte[]) of the Story class. Then, you provide get()/set() methods for converting that array of bytes to a String object. The application need not know that its data is actually being saved to the JavaEdge database as a BLOB.

If you were to tell OJB to map the data from the story table to the StoryVO object using the get()/set() methods of StoryVO, you would need to have a pair of get() and set() methods that would return an array of bytes as a return type and accept it as a parameter. This would unnecessarily expose the implementation detail.

However, it is often desirable to have OJB go through the get()/set() methods of the class. For example, in cases involving lightweight data transformation logic present in the get()/set() methods of the class, this ensures the data is always properly formatted. Sidestepping the get()/set() methods would be undesirable. Fortunately, OJB's field manipulation behavior can be customized.

OJB allows you to define your own field conversions so that if a mismatch occurs between an existing Java class (that is, domain model) and your database schema (that is, data model), you can implement your own FieldConversions class. The discussion of the FieldConversions class is outside the scope of this book. However, an excellent tutorial is provided with the OJB documentation that comes with the OJB distribution (ojb distribution/doc/jdbc-types.html).

The fourth attribute in the memberId tag is the primarykey attribute. When set to true, this attribute indicates that the field being mapped is a primary key field. OJB supports the concept of the composite primary key. Having more than one <field-descriptor> element with a primarykey attribute set to true tells OJB that a composite primary key is present.

The last attribute, autoincrement, tells OJB to automatically generate a sequence value whenever a database insert occurs for a database record that has been mapped into the class. If the autoincrement flag is set to false or is not present in the tag, it is the responsibility of the developer to set the primary key.

Let's see how to set up the OJB auto-increment feature. To use this feature, you need to install the OJB core tables. To install the OJB core tables, you need to perform the following steps:

1. Edit the ojb-distribution/build.properties file. At the top of the file you will see several different database profiles. Uncomment the mysql profile option (since that is the database being used for the JavaEdge application) and put any other database, already uncommented, in a comment.

2. Edit the ojb-distribution/profile/mysql.profile file. In this file, supply the connection information for the mysql database. For the JavaEdge application, these properties will look as follows:

```
dbmsName = MySql
jdbcLevel = 2.0
urlProtocol = jdbc
```

```
urlSubprotocol = mysql
urlDbalias = //localhost:3306/javaedge
createDatabaseUrl = ${urlProtocol}:${urlSubprotocol}:${urlDbalias}
buildDatabaseUrl = ${urlProtocol}:${urlSubprotocol}:${urlDbalias}
databaseUrl = ${urlProtocol}:${urlSubprotocol}:${urlDbalias}
databaseDriver = org.gjt.mm.mysql.Driver
databaseUser = jcarnell
databasePassword = netchange
databaseHost = 127.0.0.1
```

3. Run the `prepare-testdb` target in the build.xml file. This can be invoked by calling the following command at the command line:

   ```
   ant prepare-testdb
   ```

   This will generate the SQL scripts needed for the core tables and execute them against the JavaEdge database.

4. The OJB distribution comes with a number of unit tests and database tables. Running the `prepare-testdb` target will generate these additional unit test tables. In a production environment, the only tables needed by OJB are the following:

   - OJB_DLIST

   - OJB_DLIST_ENTRIES

   - OJB_DMAP

   - OJB_DMAP_ENTRIES

   - OJB_DSET

   - OJB_DSET_ENTRIES

   - OJB_HL_SEQ

   - OJB_LOCKENTRY

   - OJB_NRM

In addition to the attributes described in the preceding `MemberVO` example, a number of additional attributes can be defined in the `<field-descriptor>` tag:

- `nullable`: If set to `true`, OJB will allow `null` values to be inserted into the database. If set to `false`, OJB will not allow a `null` value to be inserted. This attribute is set to `true` by default.

- `conversion`: The fully qualified class name for any `FieldConversions` classes used to handle the custom data conversion.

- `length`: Specifies the length of the field. This must match the length imposed on the database column in the actual database scheme.

- `precision/scale`: Used to define the precision and scale for the float numbers being mapped to the database column.

In this section, we described how to implement a simple table mapping using OJB. However, the real power and flexibility related to OJB come into play while using OJB to cleanly capture the data relationships between entities in a database. The next several sections will demonstrate how to map common database relationships using OJB.

Sequence Generation, OJB, and Legacy Applications

Few developers have the luxury of using OJB to map to clean databases where they have absolute control over the structure of the database and how such a common task as sequence generation for primary keys is undertaken. Instead, the development team must map its Java objects to an existing set of database tables and use whatever sequence generation technique is already in place.

This means that OJB's database-independent primary key generator (as shown previously) cannot be used to generate primary keys. Oftentimes, the developers need to use the database's native primary key generation mechanism. For instance, if the database being mapped is Oracle, the development needs to map to an existing set of Oracle Sequence objects.

OJB provides strong support for integrating to a database's native sequence-generation mechanism. To tell OJB to use the database's native sequence-generation mechanism, you need to configure a `<sequence-manager/>` tag. The `<sequence-manager/>` tag is placed inside the `<jdbc-connector/>` tag in the repository.xml file. An example of this tag is shown here:

```
<descriptor-repository version="1.0" isolation-level="read-uncommitted">
    <jdbc-connection-descriptor
                  jcd-alias="strutsdb"
                  default-connection="true"
                        platform="MySQL"
                        jdbc-level="2.0"
                        driver="org.gjt.mm.mysql.Driver"
                        protocol="jdbc"
                        subprotocol="@OJB_DB_URL@"
                        dbalias="waf"
                        username="waf_user"
                        password="password">

    <sequence-manager className=
        "org.apache.ojb.broker.util.sequence.SequenceManagerNextValImpl">
                <attribute attribute-name="autoNaming" attribute-value="false"/>
            </sequence-manager>
        </jdbc-connection-descriptor>

    <class-descriptor class="com.apress.javaedge.story.StoryCommentVO"
                  table="story_comment"/>
. . .
</descriptor-repository>
```

The `<sequence-manager/>` tag has a single attribute on it, `className`. The `className` is used to define the fully qualified Java class name that is implementing the sequence manager. OJB currently has a number of sequence managers available for use. Three of the more common sequence managers include

- org.apache.broker.util.sequence.SequenceManagerNextValImpl

- org.apache.broker.util.sequence.SequenceManagerHighLowImpl

- org.apache.broker.util.sequence.SequenceManagerInMemoryImpl

The `SequenceManagerNextValImpl` class uses the native database's sequence generator to retrieve a value. The `SequenceManagerNextValImpl` class makes a database call every time it needs to retrieve a unique value from the database. In a high transaction environment, constant database calls to get a sequence value can represent unnecessary overhead.

The `SequenceManagerHighLowImpl` class does not query the database every time it needs a sequence. Instead, the `SequenceManagerHighLowImpl` class grabs a "batch" of sequences from the database and hands them out as needed. When the current batch of sequences is gone through, `SequenceManagerHighLowImpl` will grab another batch of sequences.

The `SequenceManagerInMemoryImpl` class is the most performant of the three sequence managers described. The `SequenceManagerInMemberImpl` class will grab its initial sequence value from a database sequence object. However, once the value is retrieved, all future requests for sequences by OJB will be incremented from that base number and maintained in memory.

Which Sequence Manager to Use?

When dealing with legacy applications in which you already have sequences being used, always use either the `SequenceManagerNextValImpl` or `SequenceManagerHiLoImpl` classes. Both of these sequence managers will always fetch a value from the database sequence object. `SequenceManagerHiLoImpl` is a bit more efficient because it will retrieve a bunch of sequence numbers from the database sequence object and cache them for use.

Never use the `SequenceManagerInMemoryImpl` class with legacy databases where you have non-OJB clients using the database sequence objects. The `SequenceManagerInMemoryImpl` class *only* reads a sequence value when the sequence manager is first loaded. This can be problematic because you can end up with situations in which the values managed by `SequenceManagerInMemoryImpl` can conflict with values being returned by the database sequence object. This can lead to duplicate primary keys being generated for a record.

All sequence managers accept various parameters to control their behavior. These parameters can be passed in via the `<attribute/>` tag placed inside of the `<sequence-manager/>` tag. In the interest of space, we are not going to go through all of the attributes available to the different sequence managers. For this information, please visit the OJB project site at `http://db.apache.org/ojb/`.

To use a database sequence for a field in a `<class-descriptor>` mapping, you need to add the `sequence-name` attribute to the column that is going to hold the sequence. If you were to use an Oracle database and you wanted to map the `memberId` column on the `MemberVO` to a sequence called `memberId_seq`, the mapping would look something like this:

```
<class-descriptor class="com.apressjavaedge.member.MemberVO" table="member">
  <field-descriptor name="memberId" column="member_id" jdbc-type="BIGINT"
          primarykey="true" autoincrement="true" sequence-name="memberId_seq"/>
  <field-descriptor name="firstName" column="first_name"
                      jdbc-type="VARCHAR"/>
  <field-descriptor name="lastName"  column="last_name"
                      jdbc-type="VARCHAR"/>
  <field-descriptor name="userId" column="userid" jdbc-type="VARCHAR"/>
  <field-descriptor name="password" column="password" jdbc-type="VARCHAR"/>
  <field-descriptor name="email" column="email" jdbc-type="VARCHAR"/>
</class-descriptor>
```

By using the `sequence-name` attribute on the preceding column when performing an insert for a `MemberVO` object, OJB will generate behind the scenes the following SQL statement:

```
SELECT memberId_seq.nextval FROM dual;
```

We have just gone through a whirlwind tour of OJB's different sequence generation capabilities. Let's now resume our discussion on mapping database tables and looking at the simplest form of mapping between two tables: a one-to-one mapping.

Mapping One-to-One Relationships

The first data relationship we are going to map is a one-to-one relationship. In the JavaEdge application, the `StoryVO` class has a one-to-one relationship with the `MemberVO` object (that is, one story can have one author that is a `MemberVO`).

We are not going to show the full code for the `StoryVO` class. Instead, here is an abbreviated version of the class:

```
package com.apress.javaedge.story;

import com.apress.javaedge.common.ValueObject;
import com.apress.javaedge.member.MemberVO;

import java.util.Vector;


public class StoryVO extends ValueObject {

    private Long storyId;
    private String storyTitle;
    private String storyIntro;
    private byte[] storyBody;
    private java.sql.Date submissionDate;
    private Long memberId;
```

```
    private MemberVO storyAuthor;
    public Vector comments = new Vector(); // of type StoryCommentVO

    public Vector getComments() {
        return comments;
    }

    public void setComments(Vector comments) {
        this.comments = comments;
    }

    public MemberVO getStoryAuthor() {
        return storyAuthor;
    }

    public void setStoryAuthor(MemberVO storyAuthor) {
        this.storyAuthor = storyAuthor;
    }

} // end StoryVO
```

The StoryVO class has an attribute called storyAuthor. The storyAuthor attribute holds a single reference to a MemberVO object. This MemberVO object holds all the information for the JavaEdge member who authored the story.

The following code is the <class-descriptor> tag that maps the StoryVO object to the story table and captures the data relationship between the story and member tables:

```
<class-descriptor class="com.apress.javaedge.story.StoryVO" table="story">
    <field-descriptor name="storyId" column="story_id"
            jdbc-type="BIGINT"  primarykey="true" autoincrement="true"/>
    <field-descriptor name="memberId" column="member_id" jdbc-type="BIGINT"/>
    <field-descriptor name="storyTitle" column="story_title"
            jdbc-type="VARCHAR"/>
    <field-descriptor name="storyIntro"  column="story_intro"
            jdbc-type="VARCHAR"/>
    <field-descriptor name="storyBody" column="story_body"
            jdbc-type="LONGVARBINARY"/>
    <field-descriptor name="submissionDate" column="submission_date"
            jdbc-type="DATE"/>

    . . .
    <reference-descriptor name="storyAuthor"
      class-ref="com.apress.javaedge.member.MemberVO" auto-retrieve="true">
        <foreignkey field-ref="memberId"/>
    </reference-descriptor>

</class-descriptor>
```

The preceding `<reference-descriptor>` tag maps a record, retrieved from the `member` table, to the `MemberVO` object reference called `storyAuthor`. This `<reference-descriptor>` tag has four attributes associated with it: `name`, `class-ref`, `auto-retrieve`, and `auto-update`.

The `name` attribute is used to specify the name of the attribute in the parent object to which the retrieved data is mapped. In the preceding example, the member data retrieved for the story is going to be mapped to the `storyAuthor` attribute.

The `class-ref` attribute tells OJB the type of class that is going to be used to hold the mapped data. This attribute must define a fully qualified class name for a Java class. This class must be defined in the `<class-descriptor>` element in the repository.xml file.

The remaining two attributes, `auto-retrieve` and `auto-update`, control how OJB handles the child relationships when a data operation is performed on the parent object. When set to `true`, `auto-retrieve` tells OJB to automatically retrieve the member data for the story. If it is set to `false`, OJB will not perform a lookup, and it will be the responsibility of the developer to ensure that child data is loaded.

Note If OJB cannot find a child record associated with a parent or if the `auto-retrieve` attribute is set to `false`, it will leave the attribute (which is going to be mapped) in the state that it was before the lookup was performed. For instance, in the `StoryVO` object, the `storyAuthor` property is initialized with a call to the default constructor of the `MemberVO` class. If OJB is asked to look up a particular story and no member information is found in the `member` table, OJB will leave the `storyAuthor` attribute in the state that it was before the call was made. It is extremely important to remember this if you leave child attributes to the `null` value.

You need to be careful about the depth of your object graph while using the `auto-retrieve` attribute. The indiscriminate use of the `auto-retrieve` attribute can retrieve a significant number of objects, because the child objects can contain other mapped objects that might also be configured to retrieve automatically any other child objects.

The `auto-update` attribute controls whether OJB will update any changes made to a set of child objects, after the parent object has been persisted. In other words, if the `auto-update` method is set to `true`, OJB will automatically update any of the changes made to the child objects mapped in the `<class-descriptor>` for that parent. If this attribute is set to `false` or is not present in the `<reference-descriptor>` tag, OJB will not update any mapped child objects.

OJB also provides an additional attribute, called `auto-delete`, that is not used in the `StoryVO` mapping. When set to `true`, the `auto-delete` method will delete any mapped child records when the parent object is deleted. This is the functional equivalent of a cascading delete in a relational database. You need to be careful while using this attribute, as you can accidentally delete the records that you did not intend to delete, or end up cluttering your database with "orphaned" records that have no context outside the deleted parent records.

Note Note that the `auto-update` and `auto-delete` attributes function only while using the low-level Persistence Broker API (which we use for these code examples). The JDO and ODMG APIs do not support these attributes.

One or more <foreignkey> tags are embedded in the <reference-descriptor> tag. The <foreignkey> tag is used to tell OJB the id attribute of the <field-descriptor> attribute, which the parent object is going to use to perform the join.

The field-ref attribute, contained inside the <foreignkey> tag, points to the <field-descriptor> tag of the parent's <class-descriptor> element.

Consider the following snippet of code:

```
<reference-descriptor name="storyAuthor"
                      class-ref="com.apress.javaedge.member.MemberVO"
                      auto-retrieve="true" auto-update="true">
  <foreignkey field-ref="memberId"/>
</reference-descriptor>
```

This code maps to the <field-descriptor> memberId. OJB will then use the memberId to map to the memberId attribute defined in the MemberVO <class-descriptor>. It is important to note that, while the preceding <reference-descriptor> tag is mapping to the storyAuthor attribute in the StoryVO class, the name of the attribute being mapped in the <foreignkey> element must match the name of a <field-descriptor> defined in another class.

Thus, in the preceding example, the <foreignkey> maps to the memberId attribute of the StoryVO class descriptor. This means that there must be a corresponding <field-descriptor> for memberId in the <class-descriptor> element that maps to the MemberVO object.

Mapping One-to-Many Relationships

Mapping a one-to-many relationship is as straightforward as mapping a one-to-one relationship. The story table has a one-to-many relationship with the story_comment table. This relationship is mapped in the StoryVO mappings via the <collection-descriptor> tag.

The <collection-descriptor> tag for the StoryVO mapping is shown here:

```
<collection-descriptor name ="comments"
    element-class-ref="com.apress.javaedge.story.StoryCommentVO"
    auto-retrieve="true" auto-delete="true">
  <inverse-foreignkey field-ref="storyId"/>
</collection-descriptor>
```

The name attribute for the tag holds the name of the attribute in the mapped class that is going to hold the child data retrieved from the database. In the case of the StoryVO mapping, this attribute will be the comments attribute. The comments attribute in the StoryVO code, shown in the earlier section, is a Java Vector class.

OJB can use a number of data types to map the child data in a one-to-many relationship. These data types include

- Vector

- Collection

- Arrays

- List

OJB also supports user-defined collections, but this subject is outside the scope of this book. For further information, please refer to the OJB documentation.

The element-class-ref attribute defines the fully qualified Java class that is going to hold each of the records retrieved into the collection. Again, the Java class defined in this attribute must be mapped as a <class-descriptor> in the repository.xml file.

The <collection-descriptor> also has attributes for automatically retrieving, updating, and deleting the child records. These attributes have the same name and follow the same rules as the ones discussed in the section "Mapping One-to-One Relationships." There are a number of additional attributes in the <collection-descriptor> tag. These attributes deal with using proxy classes to help improve the performance of data retrieved from a database. We will not be covering these attributes in greater detail.

A <collection-descriptor> tag can contain one or more <inverse-foreignkey> elements. The <inverse-foreignkey> element maps to a <field-descriptor> defined in the <class-descriptor> of the object that is being "joined."

Note It is very important to understand the difference between an <inverse-foreignkey> and a <foreignkey> element. An <inverse-foreignkey> element, used for mapping one-to-many and many-to-many relationships, points to a <field-descriptor> that is located outside the <class-descriptor> where the <inverse-foreignkey> is defined. A <foreignkey> element, which is used for one-to-one mapping, points to a <field-descriptor> defined inside the <class-descriptor> where the <foreignkey> element is located.

This small and subtle difference can cause major headaches if the developer doing the O/R mapping does not understand the difference. OJB will not throw an error and will try to map the data.

Mapping Many-to-Many Relationships

The JavaEdge database does not contain any tables that have a many-to-many relationship. However, OJB does support many-to-many relationships in its table mappings. Let's refactor the one-to-many relationship between story and story_comment to a many-to-many relationship. To refactor this relationship, you need to create a join table called story_story_comments. This table will contain two columns: story_id and comment_id. You need to make only a small adjustment to the StoryVO mappings to map the data retrieved via the story_story_comment table to the comments vector in the StoryVO.

The revised mappings are as shown here:

```
<class-descriptor class="com.apress.javaedge.story.StoryVO"
                  table="story">
  <field-descriptor name="storyId" column="story_id"
                    jdbc-type="BIGINT"  primarykey="true"
                    autoincrement="true"/>
```

```
<field-descriptor name="memberId" column="member_id"
                  jdbc-type="BIGINT"/>
<field-descriptor name="storyTitle" column="story_title"
                  jdbc-type="VARCHAR"/>
<field-descriptor name="storyIntro"  column="story_intro"
                  jdbc-type="VARCHAR"/>
<field-descriptor name="storyBody" column="story_body"
                  jdbc-type="LONGVARBINARY"/>
<field-descriptor name="submissionDate"
                  column="submission_date" jdbc-type="DATE"/>

<reference-descriptor name="storyAuthor"
                  class-ref="com.apress.javaedge.member.MemberVO"
                  auto-retrieve="true">
  <foreignkey field-id-ref="memberId"/>
</reference-descriptor>

<collection-descriptor name ="comments"
                  element-class-ref=
                         "com.apress.javaedge.story.StoryCommentVO"
                  auto-retrieve="true" auto-delete="true"
                  indirection_table="STORY_STORY_COMMENTS">

  <fk-pointing-to-this-class column="STORY_ID"/>
  <fk-pointing-to-this-class column="COMMENT_ID"/>
</collection-descriptor>

</class-descriptor>
```

There are two differences between this and the one-to-many mapping. The first is the use of the indirection_table attribute in the <collection-descriptor> tag. This attribute holds the name of the join table used to join the story and story_comment tables. The other difference is that the <collection-descriptor> tag does not contain an <inverse-foreignkey> tag. Instead, there are two <fk-pointing-to-this-class> tags. The column attribute in both these tags points to the database columns that will be used to perform the join between the story and story_comment tables.

You will notice that even though the mapping for the StoryVO has changed, the actual class code has not. As far as applications using the StoryVO are concerned, there has been no change in the data relationships. This gives the database developer a flexibility to refactor a database relationship while minimizing the risk that the change will break the existing application code.

Now, you will see how OJB is actually used to retrieve and manipulate the data.

OJB in Action

OJB was used to build all the DAOs included in the JavaEdge application. Using an O/R mapping tool like OJB allows you to significantly reduce the amount of time and effort needed to build the data access tier for the JavaEdge application. The following code is used to build the StoryDAO. All the DAOs are implemented using the OJB Persistence Broker API. The code for the other DAOs is available for download at http://www.apress.com.

```java
package com.apress.javaedge.story.dao;

import com.apress.javaedge.common.*;
import com.apress.javaedge.story.StoryVO;
import org.apache.ojb.broker.PersistenceBroker;
import org.apache.ojb.broker.PersistenceBrokerException;
import org.apache.ojb.broker.query.Criteria;
import org.apache.ojb.broker.query.Query;
import org.apache.ojb.broker.query.QueryByCriteria;
import org.apache.ojb.broker.query.QueryFactory;

import java.util.Collection;


/**
 *
 * StoryDAO is responsible for all CRUD logic associated with stories.
 *
 */
public class StoryDAO implements DataAccessObject {
    public static final int MAXIMUM_TOPSTORIES = 11;

    // Create Log4j category instance for logging.
    static private org.apache.log4j.Category log =
      org.apache.log4j.Category.getInstance(StoryDAO.class.getName());

    /**
     * Finds a single Story record by a story id passed into the method.
     * @see com.apress.javaedge.common.DataAccessObject#findByPK(java.lang.String)
     */
    public ValueObject findByPK(String primaryKey) throws DataAccessException {
        PersistenceBroker broker = null;
        StoryVO storyVO = null;

        try {
            broker = ServiceLocator.getInstance().findBroker();
            storyVO = new StoryVO();
            storyVO.setStoryId(new Long(primaryKey));
```

```java
            Query query = new QueryByCriteria(storyVO);
            storyVO = (StoryVO) broker.getObjectByQuery(query);
        } catch (ServiceLocatorException e) {
            log.error("PersistenceBrokerException thrown in StoryDAO.findByPK(): "
                    + e.toString());
            throw new DataAccessException("Error in StoryDAO.findByPK(): "
                    + e.toString(), e);
        } finally {
            if (broker != null) broker.close();
        }
        return storyVO;
    }



    /**
     * Returns a collection of the top latest stories.  The number of records to
     * be returned are controlled by the MAXIMUM_TOPSTORIES constant on this
     * class.
     * @return Collection
     * @throws DataAccessException
     */
    public Collection findTopStory () throws DataAccessException {
        PersistenceBroker broker = null;
        Collection results = null;

        Criteria criteria = new Criteria();
        criteria.addOrderByDescending("storyId");

        Query query = QueryFactory.newQuery(StoryVO.class, criteria);

        query.setStartAtIndex(1);
        query.setEndAtIndex(MAXIMUM_TOPSTORIES - 1);

        try {
            broker = ServiceLocator.getInstance().findBroker();
            results = (Collection) broker.getCollectionByQuery(query);
        } catch (ServiceLocatorException e) {
            log.error("PersistenceBrokerException thrown in " +
                    "StoryDAO.findTopStory(): "
                    + e.toString());
            throw new DataAccessException("Error in StoryDAO.findTopStory(): "
                    + e.toString(), e);
        } finally {
            if (broker != null) broker.close();
        }
        return results;
    }
```

```java
/**
 * Inserts a single story record into the database.
 *
 */
public void insert(ValueObject insertRecord) throws DataAccessException {
    PersistenceBroker broker = null;
    try {
        StoryVO storyVO = (StoryVO) insertRecord;

        broker = ServiceLocator.getInstance().findBroker();
        broker.beginTransaction();
        broker.store(storyVO);
        broker.commitTransaction();

    } catch (PersistenceBrokerException e) {
        // If something went wrong: rollback.
        broker.abortTransaction();
        log.error("PersistenceBrokerException thrown in StoryDAO.insert(): "
                + e.toString());
        e.printStackTrace();

        throw new DataAccessException("Error in StoryDAO.insert(): "
                + e.toString(), e);
    } catch (ServiceLocatorException e) {
        log.error("ServiceLocatorException thrown in StoryDAO.insert(): "
                + e.toString());
        throw new DataAccessException("ServiceLocatorException " +
                                      "thrown in StoryDAO.insert()", e);
    } finally {
        if (broker != null) broker.close();
    }
}

/**
 *   Deletes a single record from the story table using OJB.
 */
public void delete(ValueObject deleteRecord) throws DataAccessException {
    PersistenceBroker broker = null;

    try {
        broker = ServiceLocator.getInstance().findBroker();
        StoryVO storyVO = (StoryVO) deleteRecord;

        //Begin the transaction.
        broker.beginTransaction();
        broker.delete(storyVO);
        broker.commitTransaction();
```

```
    } catch (PersistenceBrokerException e) {
        // If something went wrong: rollback.
        broker.abortTransaction();
        log.error("PersistenceBrokerException thrown in StoryDAO.delete(): "
                + e.toString());
        e.printStackTrace();

        throw new DataAccessException("Error in StoryDAO.delete()", e);
    } catch (ServiceLocatorException e) {
        throw new DataAccessException("ServiceLocator exception in " +
                                    "StoryDAO.delete()", e);
    } finally {
        if (broker != null) broker.close();
    }
}


/**
 *  Updates a single record from the story table using OJB.
 */
public void update(ValueObject updateRecord) throws DataAccessException {
    PersistenceBroker broker = null;

    try {
        StoryVO storyVO = (StoryVO) updateRecord;

        broker = ServiceLocator.getInstance().findBroker();
        broker.beginTransaction();
        broker.store(storyVO);
        broker.commitTransaction();
    } catch (PersistenceBrokerException e) {
        // If something went wrong: rollback.
        broker.abortTransaction();
        log.error("PersistenceBrokerException thrown in StoryDAO.update(): "
                + e.toString());
        e.printStackTrace();

        throw new DataAccessException("Error in StoryDAO.update()", e);
    } catch (ServiceLocatorException e) {
        log.error("ServiceLocatorException thrown in StoryDAO.delete(): "
                + e.toString());
        throw new DataAccessException("ServiceLocatorException " +
                                        "error in StoryDAO.delete()",
                                                e);
    } finally {
        if (broker != null) broker.close();
    }
```

```
        }

        /**
         * Retrieves all stories in the database as a Collection.
         * Used by Search functionality.
         *
         * @return all stories in the app;
         */

        public Collection findAllStories() throws DataAccessException {
            PersistenceBroker broker = null;
            Collection results = null;

            try {
                Criteria criteria = new Criteria();
                criteria.addOrderByDescending("storyId");
                Query query = QueryFactory.newQuery(StoryVO.class, criteria);

                query.setStartAtIndex(1);

                broker = ServiceLocator.getInstance().findBroker();
                results = (Collection) broker.getCollectionByQuery(query);
            } catch (ServiceLocatorException e) {
                log.error("ServiceLocatorException " +
                            " thrown in StoryDAO.findAllStories(): "
                        + e.toString());
                throw new DataAccessException("ServiceLocatorException error in "
                    + StoryDAO.findAllStories()", e);
            } finally {
                if (broker != null) broker.close();
            }

            return results;

    }
```

Now, we will examine the preceding code and discuss how OJB can be used to

- Perform queries to retrieve data

- Insert and update data into the JavaEdge database

- Delete data from the JavaEdge database

Retrieving Data: A Simple Example

The first piece of code that we are going to look at shows how to retrieve a single record from the JavaEdge database. Let's take a look at the findByPK() method from StoryDAO:

```
public ValueObject findByPK(String primaryKey) throws DataAccessException {
    PersistenceBroker broker = null;
    StoryVO storyVO = null;

    try {
        broker = ServiceLocator.getInstance().findBroker();
        storyVO = new StoryVO();
        storyVO.setStoryId(new Long(primaryKey));

        Query query = new QueryByCriteria(storyVO);
        storyVO = (StoryVO) broker.getObjectByQuery(query);

    } catch (ServiceLocatorException e) {
        log.error("PersistenceBrokerException thrown in StoryDAO.findByPK(): "
                    + e.toString());
        throw new DataAccessException("Error in StoryDAO.findByPK(): "
                                        + e.toString(),e);
    } finally {
        if (broker != null) broker.close();
    }

    return storyVO;
}
```

The first step in the code is to get an instance of a PersistenceBroker object:

```
broker = ServiceLocator.getInstance().findBroker();
```

A PersistenceBroker is used to carry out all the data actions against the JavaEdge database. We have written the code for retrieving a PersistenceBroker in the findBroker() method of the ServiceLocator class (discussed in Chapter 4). The method, shown in the following code, will use the PersistenceBrokerFactory class to retrieve a PersistenceBroker and return it to the method caller:

```
public PersistenceBroker findBroker() throws ServiceLocatorException{
    PersistenceBroker broker = null;
    try{
        broker = PersistenceBrokerFactory.defaultPersistenceBroker();
    }
    catch(PBFactoryException e) {
        e.printStackTrace();
        throw new ServiceLocatorException("Error occurred while trying to " +
                "look up an OJB persistence broker: ",e);
    }
}
```

In the preceding method, the application is going to create a PersistenceBroker by calling the defaultPersistenceBroker() method in the PersistenceBrokerFactory without passing in a value. When no value is passed into the method, the PersistenceBrokerFactory will look at the root of the JavaEdge's classes directory for a repository.xml file (/WEB-INF/classes). If it cannot find the repository.xml file in this location, it will throw a PBFactoryException exception.

As mentioned early in the chapter, a repository.xml file can contain multiple database sources. These data sources are identified by the jcd-alias attribute on the <jdbc-connection-descriptor> tag. To look up a PersistenceBroker by a jcd-alias, you need to first instantiate an org.apache.ojb.broker.PBKey object and pass it into the PersistenceBrokeryFactory.createPersistenceBroker()'s method. The following code snippet demonstrates this:

```
PBKey pbKey = new PBKey("strutsdb");
PersistenceBroker broker = PersistenceBrokerFactory.createPersistenceBroker(pbKey);
```

After a broker has been retrieved in the findByPK() method, an empty StoryVO instance, called storyVO, is created. Since the findByPK() method is used to look up the record by its primary key, you call the setStoryId() method in which the primaryKey variable is passed:

```
storyVO = new StoryVO();
storyVO.setStoryId(new Long(primaryKey));
```

Once the storyVO instance has been created, it is going to be passed to a constructor in a QueryByCritieria object:

```
Query query = new QueryByCriteria(storyVO);
```

A QueryByCriteria class is used to build the search criteria for a query. When a "mapped" object, being mapped in the repository.xml file, is passed in as a parameter in the QueryByCriteria constructor, the constructor will look at each of the nonnull attributes in the object and create a where clause that maps to these values.

Because the code in the findByPK() method is performing a lookup based on the primary key of the story table (that is, story_id), the where clause generated by the QueryByCriteria constructor would look like this:

```
where story_id=?    /*Where the question mark would be the value set in the
                    setStoryId() method*/
```

If you want to perform a lookup for an object by the story title, you would call the setStoryTitle() method instead of setStoryID().

The QueryByCriteria object implements a Query interface. This interface is a generic interface for different mechanisms for querying OJB. Some of the other mechanisms for retrieving data via the OJB PB API include

- QueryBySQL: Lets you issue SQL calls to retrieve data

- QueryByMtoNCriteria: Lets you issue queries against the tables that have a many-to-many data relationship

For more details on QueryBySQL() and QueryByMToNCriteria(), please refer to the OJB JavaDocs.

We will not be covering these objects in any greater detail. Instead, we are going to focus on building the criteria using the QueryByCriteria object.

Once a query instance is created, you pass it to the getObjectByQuery() method in broker. This method will retrieve a single instance of an object based on the criteria defined in the Query object passed into the method:

```
storyVO = (StoryVO) broker.getObjectByQuery(query);
```

If the getObjectByQuery() method does not find the object by the presented criteria, a value of null is returned. If more than one record is found by the preceding call, PersistenceBrokerException is thrown. It is important to remember that you need to cast the value returned by the getObjectByQuery() method to the type you are retrieving.

If you are using a broker to carry out the data actions, you need to make sure the broker is closed. A broker instance is a functional equivalent of a JDBC database connection. Failure to close the broker can result in connection leaks. To ensure that the broker connection is closed, you put the following code in a finally block:

```
finally{
   if (broker != null) broker.close();
}
```

Retrieving Data: A More Complicated Example

In the previous section, we looked at a very simple example of retrieving data using OJB. OJB can be used to build some very sophisticated queries through its Criteria class. This class contains a number of methods that represent common components of a where clause. Some of these methods are listed in Table 5-1.

Table 5-1. *The Different Methods for Building a Criteria Object*

Method Name	Description
addEqualTo(String attribute, Object value)	Generates an equal-to clause in which attribute = value.
addGreaterThan(String attribute, Object value)	Generates a greater-than clause in which attribute > value.
addGreaterOrEqualThan(String attribute, Object value)	Generates a greater-than or equal-to clause in which attribute >= value.
addLessThan(String attribute, Object value)	Generates a less-than clause in which attribute < value.
addLessOrEqualThan(String attribute, Object value)	Generates a less-than or equals-to clause in which attribute <= value.
addIsNull(String attribute)	Generates an IS NULL clause.
addNotNull(String attribute)	Generates a NOT NULL clause.
addIsLike(String attribute, Object value)	Generates a LIKE clause.
addOrderByAscending(String fieldName)	Generates an ORDER BY ASCENDING clause.
addOrderByDescending(String fieldName)	Generates an ORDER BY DESCENDING clause.
addAndCriteria(Criteria criteria)	Uses AND to ensure that both the criteria objects are applied.
addOrCriteria(Criteria criteria)	Uses OR to ensure that one of the two criteria objects is applied.
addSql(String sqlStatement)	Adds a piece of a raw SQL to the criteria. This is extremely useful if you want to use a vendor-specific SQL extension.

Table 5-1 is by no means exhaustive, and it is highly recommended that you read the JavaDocs for the `Criteria` objects to see the full list of methods available in the class.

Based on the preceding methods, let's build a more complex query. Say you want to write an OJB query that would retrieve a `Collection` of JavaEdge member records whose last name is "Smith" and whose first name starts with a "*J.*" In addition, you want all of these records to be in ascending order of the first name. To do this, you would write the following code fragment:

```
Criteria criteriaEquals = new Criteria ();   //Criteria for the equals
Criteria criteriaLike = new Criteria ();     //Criteria for the like

criteriaEquals.addEqualTo("last_name", "Smith");
criteriaLike.addLike("first_name", "J%");

criteriaEquals.addAndCriteria(criteriaLike);    //Adding the two pieces
criteriaEquals.addOrderByAscending("first_name"); //Adding an order by
Query query = new QueryByCritieria(MemberVO.class, criteriaEquals);
Collection results = broker.getCollectionByQuery (Query);
```

In this code fragment, you first need to create `Criteria` objects for your query. You then need to set the behavior of each of the `Criteria` objects. The `criteriaEquals` instance sets the query clause to have the last name equal to `"Smith"`. It does this by calling the `addEqualTo()` method and passing the database column (`last_name`) and the value (`"Smith"`) as parameters into the method call:

```
criteriaEquals.addEqualTo ("last_name", "Smith");
```

Note Note that while building your database queries, you need to use the name of the database column and not the attribute in the Java class.

The second condition is implemented by calling the `addLike()` method in the `criteriaLike` object and passing the parameter values of `"first_name"` and `"J%"`:

```
criteriaLike.addLike ("first_name","J%");
```

Note The `addLike()` method on the `Criteria` object has the following behavior:

If an * or % is passed in, the `addLike()` method will create a wildcard search. So searching for "Sm*" or "Sm%" will return a value of Smith in the preceding example.

A ? passed into the `addLike()` method will match a single occurrence of a character within a string.

A \ will act as an escape character and allow the developer to search data for * and \ values.

To ensure that both the conditions are applied, the addAndCriteria() method of the criteriaEquals object is called and the criteriaLike object is passed as a parameter:

```
criteriaEquals.addAndCriteria (criteriaLike);    //Adding the two pieces
```

The last step is to add the OrderBy clause to your where statement. This is done by calling the addOrderByAscending() method and passing in the name of the database column:

```
criteriaEquals.addOrderByAscending ("first_name"); //Adding an order by
```

The where clause generated by building the preceding criteriaEquals object would look as shown here:

```
WHERE last_name="Smith" and first_name LIKE "J%" ORDER BY first_name ASCENDING
```

Note To see the SQL code generated by OJB, you need to set org.apache.ojb.broker.accesslayer. sql.SqlGeneratorDefaultImpl.LogLevel to DEBUG. All the SQL code generated by OJB will be written to System.out. Also, a number of other logging options are available that can be set in the OJB.properties file.

Once the criteria have been built out, they can be passed as parameters to the QueryCriteria constructor:

```
Query query = new QueryByCriteria (MemberVO.class, criteriaEquals);
```

Note that this time you pass in the MemberVO class and the criteriaEquals object that is built. Since you are retrieving more than one record, you are going to call the getCollectionByQuery() method in the broker instance as shown here:

```
Collection results = broker.getCollectionByQuery (Query);
```

The getCollectionByQuery() method will return a Collection of all of the records. The collection will be of the data type Class, passed in the QueryCriteria constructor.

Storing Data Using OJB

Inserting and updating data with OJB is very easy. Both of these data operations require the use of the store() method in a PersistenceBroker instance. The following code shows the insert() method for the StoryDAO method:

```
public void insert(ValueObject insertRecord) throws DataAccessException {
  PersistenceBroker broker = null;
  try {
    StoryVO storyVO = (StoryVO) insertRecord;

    broker = ServiceLocator.getInstance().findBroker();
    broker.beginTransaction();
    broker.store(storyVO);
    broker.commitTransaction();
```

```
  } catch (PersistenceBrokerException e) {
    // If something went wrong: rollback.
    broker.abortTransaction();
    System.out.println(e.getMessage());
    e.printStackTrace();

    throw new DataAccessException("Error in StoryDAO.insert(): "
                                  + e.toString(),e);
  } catch(ServiceLocatorException e) {
    System.out.println("ServiceLocatorException thrown in StoryDAO.insert():
                        " + e.toString());
    throw new DataAccessException("ServiceLocatorException thrown in " +
                                  "StoryDAO.insert()",e);
  } finally {
    if (broker != null) broker.close();
  }
}
```

■ Note You may have noticed that the code never checks to see if the object being passed into the
insert() method just shown is of type StoryVO. All of the DAOs in the JavaEdge application implement
the DataAccessObject interface that accepts a ValueObject as an interface. If you want to be more type
safe, you need to check the type passed in ValueObject by using instanceof.

The first step for saving the data is to retrieve a broker instance. Once a broker instance
is retrieved via the ServiceLocator.getInstance().findBroker() method, you need to set
a transactional boundary for your transaction. This is accomplished by calling the
beginTransaction() method on the broker instance:

```
broker.beginTransaction();
```

Now, you can actually insert or update the data into the database via a call to the store()
method of the broker instance and pass the object that is to be stored in the database:

```
broker.store(storyVO);
```

The OJB runtime engine will determine whether the data contained within the StoryVO
object needs to be inserted or updated. Depending on how the repository.xml mappings are
done, the store() method call will also persist any of the child objects associated with the
StoryVO instance.

The last step in the process is to commit the transaction via the broker.commitTransaction()
method call:

```
broker.commitTransaction();
```

If any exceptions are thrown while processing the user request, such as a
PersistenceBrokerException, a call to broker.abortTransaction will roll back any changes
currently made within that transactional context:

```
} catch (PersistenceBrokerException e){
  // If something went wrong: rollback.
  broker.abortTransaction();
  e.printStackTrace();

  throw new DataAccessException("Error in StoryDAO.insert(): "
                      + e.toString(),e);
}
```

If any exception is caught, the transaction is aborted and the exception is rethrown as a DataAccessException.

Deleting Data with OJB

The following code shows the delete() method from the StoryDAO:

```
public void delete(ValueObject deleteRecord) throws DataAccessException {
  PersistenceBroker broker = null;

  try {
    broker = ServiceLocator.getInstance().findBroker();
    StoryVO storyVO = (StoryVO) deleteRecord;

    //Begin the transaction.
    broker.beginTransaction();
    broker.delete(storyVO);
    broker.commitTransaction();
  } //Rest of the code has been omitted.
```

The delete() method in a broker instance will remove a record from the database, based on the object passed into the method. If you want to isolate the transaction, you must use the beginTransaction() and commitTransaction() or abortTransaction() methods shown in the previous section.

Bringing It All Together

So far, we demonstrated how to use the OJB to perform common data transactions. However, the business logic should never be exposed to data access code, whether implemented via JDBC or OJB. Therefore, you should wrap all the code using a Data Access Object pattern.

The following code is the implementation of the addStory() method of the StoryManagerBD class. It is being shown to demonstrate how a DAO is actually used.

```
public void addStory(StoryVO storyVO) throws ApplicationException {
  try {
    StoryDAO storyDAO = new StoryDAO();
    storyDAO.insert(storyVO);
  } catch (DataAccessException e) {
    throw new ApplicationException("DataAccessException Error in
```

```
        StoryManagerBean.addStory(): " + e.toString(), e);
   }
}
```

The preceding code is for inserting a StoryVO into the database. Note that in the entire code, you do not tie your business logic to a particular data access technology or database. You can easily rewrite the preceding StoryDAO to use JDBC or entity beans, and the application code would never know the difference. This small piece of abstraction can make a huge difference in terms of long-term maintainability and extensibility of the application.

For instance, you could easily write a different StoryDAO implementation using different data access technologies. The object diagram in Figure 5-6 illustrates this.

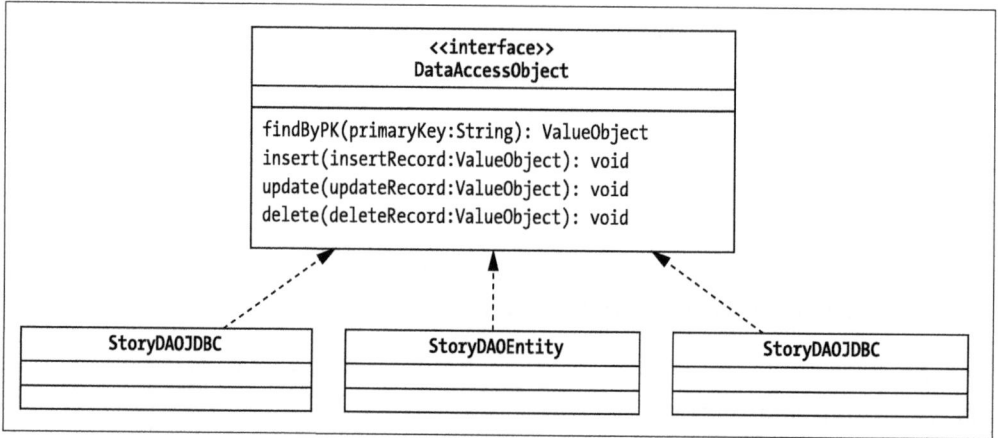

Figure 5-6. *StoryDAO implementations*

In this model, there could be three different implementations of the StoryDAO. The application using the DAO would never be allowed to directly create one of the three preceding classes. Instead, you could introduce a DAOFactory that would be responsible for creating the appropriate StoryDAO instance on behalf of the application. An example of the DAOFactory is shown here:

```
package com.apress.javaedge.common;

import java.io.FileInputStream;
import java.io.IOException;
import java.util.Properties;

public class DAOFactory {
    private static Properties classInfo =
            new Properties();
    private static DAOFactory daoFactory = null;
    public static final String MEMBERDAO = "dao.member.impl";
    public static final String STORYDAO  = "dao.story.impl";
```

```java
/**
 *   Private constructor that will load all of the fully qualified DAO
 *   class names from the datatier.properties file.
 */
private DAOFactory() {
    try{
        String daoFileName = System.getProperty("datatier.properties", "");

        classInfo.load(new FileInputStream(daoFileName));
    }
    catch(IOException e){
        System.out.println(e.toString());
    }
}


//Static block that creates a new DAO factory
//the first time a DAOFactory is created.
static{
    daoFactory = new DAOFactory();
}


/**
 * Returns a single instance of DAOFactory.
 */
public static DAOFactory getInstance(){
    return daoFactory;
}


/**
 *   The getDAO() method will retrieve a DAO requested by the user.
 */
public DataAccessObject getDAO(String desiredDAO) throws DataAccessException{
    Object dao = null;

    //If the classInfo properties object contains the key requested
    //by the user
    if (classInfo.containsKey(desiredDAO)){

        try{
            //Get the fully qualified class name.
            String className = (String) classInfo.get(desiredDAO);

            //Retrieve a Class object for the requested className.
            Class desiredClass = Class.forName(className);

            //Retrieve a new instance of the requested DAO.
            dao = desiredClass.newInstance();
```

```
        }
        catch(InstantiationException e){
            throw new DataAccessException("InstantiationException " +
            "in DAOFactory.getDAO(): " + desiredDAO,e);
        }
        catch(IllegalAccessException e){
            throw new DataAccessException("IllegalAccessException " +
            "in DAOFactory.getDAO(): " + desiredDAO,e);
        }
        catch(ClassNotFoundException e){
            throw new DataAccessException("DataAccessException " +
            "in DAOFactory.getDAO(): " + desiredDAO,e);
        }

        return (DataAccessObject) dao;
    }
    else{
        throw new DataAccessException("Unable to locate the DAO requested " +
        "in DAOFactory.getDAO(): " + desiredDAO);
    }
  }
}
```

We are not going to walk through the preceding code in great detail because we did not show you how to use a DAO Factory pattern in this JavaEdge implementation. Since this is a simple application and all of this data access code was going to be written in OJB, using the preceding DAOFactory implementation would be too heavy. However, the preceding DAOFactory implementation does allow you to declare DAO implementations that are going to be used for the application without directly hard coding the creation of that object in the application source. The addStory() method, shown earlier, rewritten to use the preceding DAOFactory implementation would be as follows:

```
public void addStory(StoryVO storyVO) throws ApplicationException{
  try {
    DAOFactory daoFactory.getInstance()
    StoryDAO storyDAO = (StoryDAO) daoFactory.getDAO(DAOFactory.STORYDAO);
    storyDAO.insert(storyVO);

  } catch (DataAccessException e) {
    throw new ApplicationException("DataAccessException Error in " +
                        "StoryManagerBean.addStory(): " +
                        e.toString(), e);
  }
}
```

The actual Java class that implements the StoryDAO is defined in a Java properties file. This Java properties filename and location is determined by a user-defined Java system property called datatier.properties. A user can define this property by setting the CATALINA_OPTS environment variable to be equal to -Ddatatier.properties=full name and path of the Java file containing the DAO class information.

The following example shows this properties file:

```
dao.member.impl=com.apress.javaedge.member.dao.MemberDAO
dao.story.impl=com.apress.javaedge.story.dao.StoryDAO
```

Summary

Building a data access tier is more than picking a particular data access or database technology. It needs basic design patterns that will allow the development team to abstract away the data access implementation details. In this chapter, we discussed the following two J2EE design patterns that help you accomplish these goals:

- The Data Access Object (DAO) pattern

- The Value Object (VO) pattern

The DAO pattern allows you to abstract away the CRUD logic associated with the data store interactions. You need to remember the following key points about the DAO pattern:

- DAOs should completely abstract away the details of how data is retrieved and manipulated.

- Watch the granularity of your DAOs. You need to understand how your data is used and make sure you do not model your DAOs solely based on your physical data model.

- DAOs afford the opportunity to combine the data from multiple data sources behind a single logical view. Do not write your DAOs to mirror the physical location of different pieces of the same customer data.

The VO pattern is used to wrap data retrieved from the database. It is an object-based representation of relational-oriented data. Key points of the Value Object pattern are the following:

- Watch the number of Value Objects returned by a DAO. Returning a large number of VOs results in a large amount of memory being consumed.

- Watch the level of your object graphs. Making the object graphs too deep will result in multiple levels of data for a single record.

- Value Objects merely represent a particular view of the data. It is not necessary that you have one Value Object return all of the data associated with a particular business entity. Understand how your data is being used and build your Value Objects accordingly.

We also discussed how O/R mapping tools could save a significant amount of developers' time for writing the data access tier. One of these tools, OJB, is an easy-to-use open source tool that offers almost all the features found in similar commercial products. In this chapter, we discussed how OJB can be used to

- Perform mappings between Java classes and database tables. The mappings demonstrated in the chapter include the following:

    - Simple table mappings

    - One-to-one mappings

    - One-to-many mappings

    - Many-to-many mappings

- Perform data-related tasks, including the following:

    - Managing sequences using both OJB-managed sequences and native database sequence objects

    - Retrieving data using OJB

    - Inserting and updating data using OJB

    - Deleting data with OJB

CHAPTER 6

■ ■ ■

Building Flexible Front-Ends with the Tiles Framework

Earlier in Chapter 1, we talked about the Tight-Skins antipattern and how the formation of this antipattern can lead to long-term difficulties in modifying the look and feel of web-based applications. The Tight-Skins antipattern usually forms when the development team fails to properly separate the content and look and feel of the application into discrete components that are independent of the code rendering the unique data being presented on the page.

Symptoms of the Tight-Skins antipattern manifest themselves in a number of ways, including the following:

- *The content of the screen is tightly integrated with page-specific code*: An example of this would be a JSP page that has HTML and JSP scriptlet code heavily intermixed throughout the page.

- *Common pieces of page content are not broken out into discrete components that can be maintained independently of the page*: Developers are always looking for opportunities for reuse. However, most development teams only focus on reuse at the business logic layer of an application and never really focus their efforts on the presentation tier.

In the earlier edition of this book, we demonstrated how the Struts `<template>` tag libraries allowed a developer to break an application screen into individual components. These components can then be easily assembled together to form a page. Any modifications to an individual component would be propagated to all of the pages using it.

While the Struts `<template>` tag library is very useful for building applications, after using it a while, developers will quickly run into some of the limitations of the tag library, which include the following:

- *No centralized mechanism for declaring templates*: In the JavaEdge application, every page built using the `<template>` tags must have two JSP pages. One JSP declares the layout of the page. The other declares the actual content of the page to be displayed. For example, the home page JSP page for the JavaEdge application consists of two pages: homePage.jsp (which defines the page layout) and homePageContent.jsp (which renders the content).

  For small applications that is not much of an issue. However, for larger applications this can become a huge problem. A 100-page application built using the Struts `<template>` tags is going to end up with 201 JSP pages: 100 JSP pages declaring the page templates, 100 contents pages, and 1 master template page. Wouldn't it be better to declare all of the page templates in a single location and reduce the total number of JSP pages to maintain in half?

- *No inheritance mechanism built into a* `<template>` *tag*: Every template built using the `<template>` tags is considered a unique entity. There is no way to declare a master template that can have existing features overridden or be extended to include a new look and feel.

- *Struts* `<template>` *tags very limited in how they can render information*: The `<template>` tags essentially take content from a source (for example, a JSP page) and include the rendered content into the page. They do not offer the capability to render content retrieved from a JavaBean.

Starting with Struts 1.1, the framework offered a new templating framework called *Tiles*. Tiles overcomes the limitations of the existing Struts `<template>` tag library. While the Struts `<template>` tag library is still available in Struts 1.2, the Tiles framework is being positioned to eventually replace it completely.

This chapter is going to look at the basics of using the Tiles framework. We will examine the core functionality of the framework and demonstrate how to refactor the existing JavaEdge application from a `<template>` tag approach to a pure Tiles one. Specifically, the following topics will be covered:

- The conceptual architecture of the Tiles framework

- How to configure Tiles for your Struts applications

- W riting your first Tiles-based page

- Moving beyond the basics and using Tiles definitions to build your Tiles templates

- C entralizing all of your template layouts in a single tiles-defs.xml file

- U sing inheritance and overriding in your Tiles pages

What Is the Tiles Framework?

The Tiles framework is a tool for defining how a page is going to be laid out using discrete presentation components. A page in Tiles is based on a template. A template is a JSP page that describes where different presentation components are going to be placed. Each presentation component defined in the template is called a *tile*. The best way to think of a template is that it generically describes how a page looks.

A tile represents a self-contained window in the web page that contains content that is rendered by using JSP tags and scriptlets. A single tile can be composed of other tiles. By breaking an application's pages into tiles, it is extremely easy to identify pieces of presentation code that can be shared across screens in your application. It also makes maintaining the look and feel of your application much easier because modifying a specific tile will cause that change to be propagated across all of the pages using it.

A tile can have zero or more attributes associated with it. A tile attribute is a parameter that can be passed into the tile and allows JSP tags and scriptlets to modify their behavior based on the attribute passed in. Tile attributes give the developer a great deal of control over how a tile is going to render itself.

■Note A Tiles template merely declares the layout of the page. A JSP page in the JavaEdge application will implement the template and define what JSP files will implement each of the different tiles defined within the template.

Figure 6-1 shows the relationship between templates, tiles, and attributes.

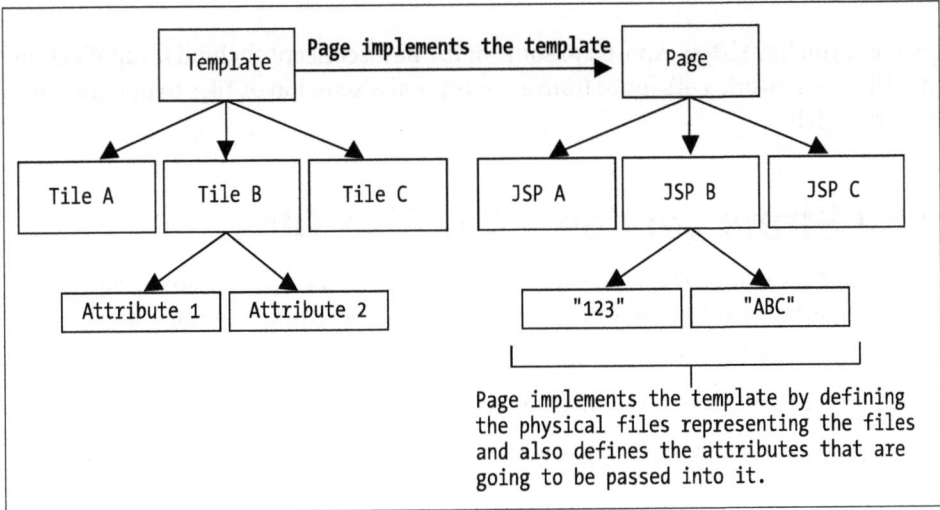

Figure 6-1. *Mapping a tile layout to JSP pages*

In the JavaEdge application, every page has been broken into three pieces: a header that contains the navigation links and the JavaEdge logo, a body consisting of any content or functionality that is going to be presented to the end user, and a footer containing a blue bar across the bottom of the page. This layout can easily be translated into three tiles for every page in the application, as you can see in Figure 6-2.

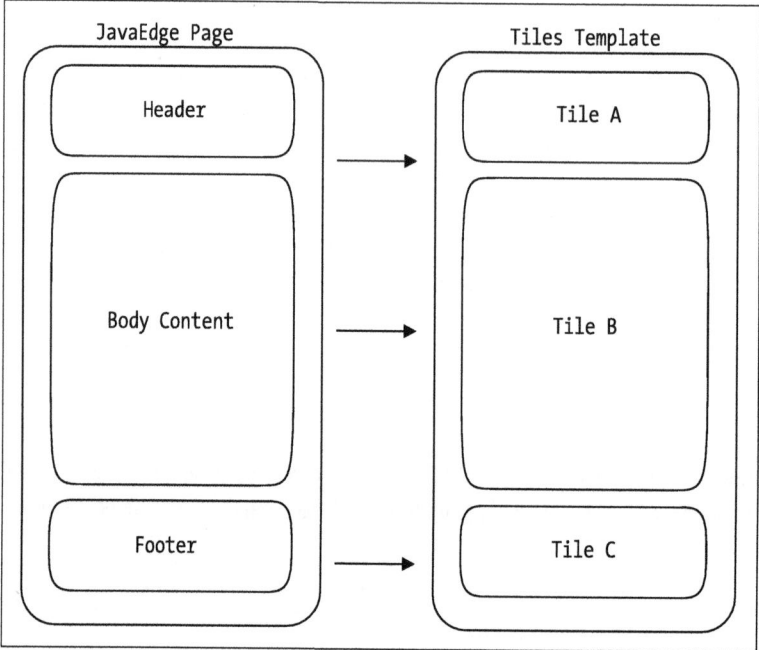

Figure 6-2. *The basic structure of a JavaEdge page*

At this point you have been exposed to some of the basic concepts behind an application built on the Tiles framework. Let's move from a conceptual discussion of Tiles to doing some hands-on work with it.

Enabling Struts Version 1.1 to Use Tiles

The Tiles framework is included with the Struts 1.2x distribution as a plug-in to the Struts framework. Configuring Struts version 1.2x to use the Tiles framework is a straightforward process that takes three steps:

1. Configure the struts-config.xml file to include the Tiles plug-in.

2. Write a tiles-defs.xml file to hold any Tiles definitions used by the Tiles framework.

3. Add the Tiles Tag Library Definitions (TLDs) to the web.xml file.

Configuring the Tiles Plug-In

To turn on the Tiles functionality, you need to configure the Tiles plug-in developed by the Struts development team. This plug-in is configured in the application's struts-config.xml file.

A NOTE ABOUT CONFIGURATION

To cleanly separate the Tiles-based JavaEdge application from the non-Tiles JavaEdge application, the struts-config.xml file for the Tiles-based application has been moved to the project root src/web/WEB-INF/jsp/tiles directory. The file has been renamed to struts-config-tiles.xml. All of the plug-in configuration information and any Struts actions for this chapter have been placed in this file.

Please remember to modify the `<init-parameters>` tag for the Struts ActionServlet in JavaEdge's web.xml file to use the struts-config-tiles.xml file.

The Tiles plug-in entry for the JavaEdge application is shown here:

```
<?xml version="1.0" encoding="ISO-8859-1"?>
<!DOCTYPE struts-config PUBLIC
    "-//Apache Software Foundation//DTD Struts Configuration 1.2//EN"
    http://struts.apache.org/dtds/struts-config_1_2.dtd>

<struts-config>

  <!--Form Bean Entries -->
    ....
    <!-- Global Forwards -->
    ....
    <!-- Actions -->
    ....
    <!--The tiles plug-in-->
    <plug-in className="org.apache.struts.tiles.TilesPlugin" >
        <set-property property="definitions-config"
                      value="/WEB-INF/jsp/tiles/tiles-defs.xml" />

        <set-property property="definitions-parser-validate"
                      value="true" />
        <set-property property="moduleAware "
                      value="false" />
    </plug-in>
</struts-config>
```

Each plug-in used by Struts version 1.2x is going to have a `<plug-in>` XML tag defined in the struts-config-tiles.xml file:

```
<plug-in className="org.apache.struts.tiles.TilesPlugin">
....
</plug-in>
```

This `<plug-in>` tag defines a single attribute called `className`. The `className` attribute holds the fully qualified Java class name of the class that is going to act as an entry point for all calls to that plug-in. The Java class used for the Tiles framework is the `org.apache.struts.tiles.TilesPlugin` class. This class file, along with the other Tiles Java classes, has been packaged up into the struts.jar file located in the lib of the JavaEdge project tree.

Note In early releases of Struts 1.1, the Tiles plug-in supported two properties for configuring logging within the Tiles framework: `definitions-debug` and `definitions-parser-details`. While these two properties are still supported in the stable release of Struts 1.1, they have been deprecated and should not be used. Struts 1.2 will be completely removing these parameters. To enable logging of the Tiles framework, please use the Jakarta Commons Logging integration with Struts. This information will be covered in Chapter 9.

A Struts plug-in can have zero or more properties that help configure the behavior of the plug-in. These properties are defined using a `<set-property>` tag contained with the defined `<plug-in>` tag. A `<set-property>` tag has two attributes in it: `property` and `value`. The preceding Tiles plug-in configuration has three properties set:

```
<set-property property="definitions-config"
              value="/WEB-INF/tiles-defs.xml"/>


<set-property property="definitions-parser-validate" value="true"/>
<set-property property="moduleAware"
                        value="true"/>
```

The `<set-property>` tag's `definitions-config` property tells the Tiles plug-in the name of the file that holds a description of all of the template layouts used in the Struts application. This file is said to hold the Tiles definitions of the different screen layouts. We will be covering the details of setting up these Tiles definitions later on in the chapter.

After the `definitions-config` `<set-property>` tag is the `definitions-parser-validate` `<set-property>` tag. The `definitions-parser-validate` property takes a value of `true` or `false`. If the property is set to `true`, the Struts framework will validate that the file designated earlier in the `definitions-config` (i.e., tiles-defs.xml) is well formed and conforms to the XML DTD file specified in the file. If the value is set to `false`, no DTD validation will take place.

Note It is a good practice during development to keep the value of this property set to `true`. Speaking from experience, nothing is more frustrating than discovering that the bug you were trying to fix was caused by a malformed or invalid XML file. The default value for the `definitions-parser-validate` file is `true`.

The last property tag is the `moduleAware` `<set-property>` tag. The `moduleAware` property is used to tell Tiles whether or not the Tiles framework can support multiple Struts applications modules. If the value of this property is set to `true`, then each module can have its own Tiles setup and configuration. If this value is `false`, then the Tiles definitions and setup is shared across all of the application modules.

For more information on Struts modules, please see Chapter 2.

The tiles-defs.xml File

As mentioned earlier, the tiles-defs.xml file can hold layout information related to the templates being used in Tiles. For the purposes of configuring Struts to use Tiles, create the following tiles-defs.xml file in the JavaEdge project's *project root/src/web/WEB-INF/jsp/tiles* directory:

```
<?xml version="1.0" encoding="ISO-8859-1"?>
 <!DOCTYPE tiles-definitions PUBLIC
       "-//Apache Software Foundation//DTD Tiles Configuration//EN"
       http://struts.apache.org/dtds/tiles-config.dtd>

<tiles-definitions>

</tiles-definitions>
```

At this point there is no real information present in the tiles-defs.xml file other than the XML version of the file, the location of the Tiles DTD that can be used to validate the file, and the root tags for the file, `<tiles-definitions>`. As this chapter unfolds, we will show you how to add more information to the tiles-defs.xml file.

Adding the Tiles TLDs

The last step in configuring the Tiles framework for use in a Struts version 1.2x application is to add the Tiles TLDs to the application's (in this case, JavaEdge's) web.xml file. This step will make the Tiles JSP tag libraries available to the JavaEdge application's pages. Shown here is the entry made in the JavaEdge application's web.xml:

```
<?xml version="1.0" encoding="ISO-8859-1"?>

<!DOCTYPE web-app
    PUBLIC "-//Sun Microsystems, Inc.//DTD Web Application 2.3//EN"
    "http://java.sun.com/j2ee/dtds/web-app_2_3.dtd">
```

```
<web-app>
    <!--The beginning of the web.xml file -->
     .....

    <!-- Tiles Tag Library Descriptors -->
    <taglib>
       <taglib-uri>/taglibs/struts-tiles</taglib-uri>
       <taglib-location>/WEB-INF/taglibs/struts-tiles.tld</taglib-location>
    </taglib>
</web-app>
```

Upon completion of this step, the Tiles framework should now be fully available to the JavaEdge application.

Your First Tiles Template

There are three methods for building web pages using the Tiles framework:

- U sing a Tiles-enabled JSP template to build JSP pages

- E mbedding Tiles definitions inside of a JSP page

- C entralizing your Tiles definitions into a single configuration file

Each of these methods has its own advantages and disadvantages.

Using Tiles-Enabled JSP Templates

The simplest method to begin working with the Tiles framework is to use JSP templates that leverage the <tiles> JSP tag libraries to implement a page. This process involves the following steps:

- C reating a JSP-based master template using the <tiles> JSP tag libraries to define what the generic components of a screen are going to be.

- W riting a JSP page that defines the concrete elements that correspond to the generic components described in the master template.

Note All of the Tiles-based JSP pages written in this chapter will be located under the project root/src/web/WEB-INF/jsp/tiles directory. These files have been broken out into a separate directory to clearly delineate them from the JSP pages used in the rest of the book.

Let's start by looking at how to refactor the existing JavaEdge home page to use the Tiles framework. The first step in this process is to rewrite the template.jsp page, which acts as the master template, for the Struts <template> implementation of the JavaEdge application to use the <tiles> JSP tags:

```
<%@ taglib uri="/taglibs/struts-tiles" prefix="tiles " %>

<html>
<head>
   <title><tiles:getAsString name="title "/></title>
</head>

  <body>
  <p>
  <tiles:insert attribute="header"/>
  <tiles:insert attribute="content"/>
  <tiles:insert attribute="footer"/>
</body>
</html>
```

The template.jsp file just shown has three distinct graphical components that are going to be part of each page: a header, page body, and footer.

The first line of the template.jsp file imports the Tiles tag libraries:

```
<%@ taglib uri="/taglibs/struts-tiles" prefix="tiles"%>
```

The header, page body, and footer components for the template are defined using the `<tiles:insert>` tag. The attribute parameter on the `<tiles:insert>` tag allows a developer to define a name for each part of an application's page layout:

```
<tiles:insert attribute= "header"/>
<tiles:insert attribute="content"/>
<tiles:insert attribute="footer"/>
```

The `<tiles:insert>` tag defines a runtime parameter that can be used by a page implementing the template to pass in the absolute or relative path of a JSP file that renders the body of the tile.

The `<tiles:getAsString>` tag also establishes a parameter in which the developer can pass in information. The example that follows defines a template parameter called `title`. This is set by setting the `<tiles:getAsString>` tag's name attribute equal to "title":

```
<title><tiles:getAsString name="title"/></title>
```

The difference between the `<tiles:insert>` and the `<tiles:getAsString>` tag is as follows: The `<tiles:insert>` tag will execute any JSP code it reads from the file defined in its attribute parameter. The `<tiles:getAsString>` tag will write the value passed directly to the page's `JspWriter` object. Since the value is written as is, any JSP scriptlets or tag libraries passed in will not be executed.

Now that you have set up the Tiles-based master template for the JavaEdge application, you want to rewrite the JavaEdge home page to use the template shown previously. To do this you need to write two additional files: homePage.jsp and homePageContent.jsp.

The homePage.jsp file implements the template and defines the JSP files that will render each of the components laid out in the template. The homePage.jsp file is shown here:

```
<%@ page language="java" %>
<%@ taglib uri="/taglibs/struts-tiles" prefix="tiles" %>

<tiles:insert page="/WEB-INF/jsp/tiles/template.jsp" flush="true">
  <tiles:put name="title" value="Todays Top Stories"/>
  <tiles:put name="header" value="/WEB-INF/jsp/tiles/header.jsp"/>
  <tiles:put name="content" value="/WEB-INF/jsp/tiles/homePageContent.jsp"/>
  <tiles:put name="footer" value="/WEB-INF/jsp/tiles/footer.jsp"/>
</tiles:insert>
```

The page implements the template by using the `<tiles:insert>` tag and passing in the name of the template file (in this case template.jsp) via its page attribute:

```
<tiles:insert page="/WEB-INF/jsp/tiles/template.jsp" flush="true">
  . . .
</tiles:insert>
```

The `<tile:insert>` tag's flush attribute indicates whether or not the JspWriter for the JSP is flushed. If the flush attribute is set to true, any characters currently residing in the JspWriter's output stream's buffer will be written out before any of the content for the template is written out. If the flush attribute is set to false, then the JspWriter is not flushed when the `<tiles:insert>` tag is processed.

The `<tiles:insert>` tag will contain one or more `<tiles:put>` tags. The `<tiles:put>` tag is used to provide the value for the `<tile:insert>` tag's attribute parameter defined in the template.jsp page. Four values are being passed to the template.jsp page:

```
<tiles:put name="title" value="Todays Top Stories">
<tiles:put name="header" value="/WEB-INF/jsp/tiles/header.jsp"/>
<tiles:put name="content" value="/WEB-INF/jsp/tiles/homePageContent.jsp"/>
<tiles:put name="footer" value="/WEB-INF/jsp/tiles/footer.jsp"/>
```

Each `<tiles:put>` tag defines two attributes within it: name and value. The name attribute defines the name of the attribute parameter that is going to be passed to the JSP template defined in the `<tiles:insert>` tag. The value attribute defines a value that is going to be passed to the template. Depending on how the attribute parameter is defined in the template.jsp page, the value passed in may be a simple string or a path to a JSP file.

A `<tiles:put>` tag in the homePage.jsp page must correspond to a `<tiles:insert>` tag defined in the template.jsp page. Table 6-1 shows the relationship between the attributes defined in the template.jsp page and the homePage.jsp page.

Table 6-1. *Mapping the Tags from template.jsp to homePage.jsp*

template.jsp	homePage.jsp
`<tiles:getAsString name="title"/>`	`<tiles:put name="title" value=....>`
`<tiles:insert attribute="header"/>`	`<tiles:put name="header" value=..../>`
`<tiles:insert attribute="content"/>`	`<tiles:put name="content" value=..../>`
`<tiles:insert attribute="footer"/>`	`<tiles:put name="footer" value=..../>`

The actual content of the JavaEdge home page resides in the homePageContent.jsp page. We will not be reviewing this page, as the code in this page is the exact same material presented in Chapter 2.

Once the JavaEdge home page is rewritten using Tiles, it can be viewed by adding a new <action> tag to JavaEdge's struts-config-tiles.xml file. Shown here is the <action> tag for the Tiles-based JavaEdge home page:

```
<action path="/homePageSetup"
        type="com.apress.javaedge.struts.homepage.HomePageSetupAction"
        unknown="true">
  <forward name="homepage.success" path="/WEB-INF/jsp/tiles/homePage.jsp"/>
</action>
```

To see the rewritten page, open a web browser and key in the text http://localhost:8080/ JavaEdge/execute/homePageSetup. Once you have done this, you should see the JavaEdge home page, fully populated with stories from its database.

What Are Tiles Definitions?

As noted earlier, the fashion in which you use the Tiles framework to refactor the JavaEdge home page is very similar in design and usage to the Struts 1.0x <template> tags.

The use of Tiles in this fashion also means that like the <template> tag example, the developer needs to write two JSP files to implement a single page: a file to implement the JSP template (i.e., homePage.jsp), and a file to implement the page's content (i.e., homePageContent.jsp).

Many times the page used to implement the JSP template is only changing one or two values. Let's revisit the homePage.jsp file:

```
<%@ page language="java" %>
<%@ taglib uri="/taglibs/struts-tiles" prefix="tiles" %>

<tiles:insert page="/WEB-INF/jsp/tiles/template.jsp" flush="true">
<!-- Value Changes Every Page--> <tiles:put name="title" ../>
<!-- Never Changes            --> <tiles:put name="header" ../>
<!-- Value Changes Every Page--> <tiles:put name="content" ../>
<!-- Never Changes            --> <tiles:put name="footer" ../>
</tiles:insert>
```

In the JavaEdge application, all pages share the exact same header and footer. The only thing that ever changes from page to page is the title of the page and the page body's content.

However, the developer still has to define a <tiles:insert> tag that maps every attribute being passed into a template via a <tiles:put> tag. Every attribute has to be declared, even if the value being passed into the template never changes (for example, the values specifying the header and footer).

Using Tiles, it is possible for the developer to define all of the attribute parameters that are to be passed into a template into a single unit of work with a unique ID. This uniquely identified collection of attributes is known as a *Tiles definition*.

Tiles definitions afford the developer a great deal of flexibility. Using them, a developer can do the following:

- *Reuse definitions across multiple JSP pages*: Using a definition, a developer does not have to redeclare the template and the attribute parameter values that are going to be passed into the template for every single page in the application.

- *Inherit the attribute values defined within an existing definition*: Since the majority of attribute values do not change from page to page, a developer using JSP templates can automatically inherit and use attribute values declared within a definition. Changing a value in the base definition will automatically propagate the change to all JSP pages using the definition.

- *Override the values of attributes declared within a declaration with values specific to that page*: For those pieces of a page that do change, using a Tiles definition, a developer can, on a page-by-page basis, choose to override an attribute value declared in the definition with a value specific to the page.

- *Extend an existing definition to include new attributes*: Definitions allow the developer to add new attributes to an existing definition. This extensibility allows the developer to build a hierarchy of Tiles definitions that share the same basic look and feel, but have their own unique characteristics.

There are two ways to declare definitions within the Tiles framework:

• D eclaring a definition in a JSP file

• D eclaring a definition in an XML file

In the next several sections, we will walk through how to use both techniques.

Tiles Definitions: A JSP-Based Approach

Writing a Tiles definition using JSPs is extremely easy. Let's start by writing a JSP fragment, called javaEdgeDef.jsp, that is going to define the base definition implemented by all of the pages in the JavaEdge application. Shown here is the javaEdgeDef.jsp page:

```
<%@ taglib uri="/taglibs/struts-tiles" prefix="tiles" %>

<tiles:definition id="baseDef"
                  page="/WEB-INF/jsp/tiles/template.jsp">
  <tiles:put name="title"    value="Base JavaEdge Template"/>
  <tiles:put name="header"   value="/WEB-INF/jsp/tiles/header.jsp"/>
  <tiles:put name="content"  value="/WEB-INF/jsp/tiles/baseContent.jsp"/>
  <tiles:put name="footer"   value="/WEB-INF/jsp/tiles/footer.jsp"/>
</tiles:definition>
```

To declare a JSP-based Tiles definition, the `<tiles:definition>` tag is used:

```
<tiles:definition id="baseDef"
                   page="/WEB-INF/jsp/tiles/template.jsp>
. . .
</tiles:definition>
```

The `<tiles:definition>` tag has a number of different attributes associated with it. Right now you only care about the id and the page attributes. The id attribute defines the name of the Tiles definition. The value placed in the id attribute will be the value passed by a JSP page when it indicates it wants to use a particular Tiles definition. The page attribute is used to define what template file is going to be used by the definition.

A Tiles definition can contain one or more `<tiles:put>` tags within it. The `<tiles:put>` tags can pass values to attribute parameters inside the template defined in the `<tile:definition>` tag's page attribute. The example Tiles definition shown previously defines four `<tiles:put>` tags that correspond to `<tiles:insert>` tags defined inside the template.jsp file:

```
<tiles:put name="title"   value="Base JavaEdge Template"/>
<tiles:put name="header"  value="/WEB-INF/jsp/tiles/header.jsp"/>
<tiles:put name="content" value="/WEB-INF/jsp/tiles/baseContent.jsp"/>
<tiles:put name="footer"  value="/WEB-INF/jsp/tiles/footer.jsp"/>
```

Let's look at how a Tiles definition is used. The file simplePage.jsp uses the preceding Tiles definition to define its layout. It does not override any of the attribute parameters being declared in the `<tiles:put>` tag for the javaEdgeDef.jsp file. The code contained within the simplePage.jsp file is shown here:

```
<%@ taglib uri="/taglibs/struts-tiles" prefix="tiles"%>
<%@ include file="javaEdgeDef.jsp"%>

<tiles:insert beanName="baseDef" flush="true"/>
```

The simplePage.jsp page includes the Tiles definition called baseDef by including the contents of javaEdgeDef.jsp using the `<%@ include %>` JSP page directive.

Once the contents of the javaEdgeDef.jsp file are included in the simplePage.jsp page, the definition is used by placing a `<tiles:insert>` tag into the page and passing the name of the definition, originally defined in the definition's id attribute, to the `<tile:insert>` tag's beanName attribute.

Let's take a look at the results of using the baseDef definition in simplePage.jsp. First, you need to set up a Struts action for the page in the struts-config.xml file. The new `<action>` entry is shown here:

```
<action path="/simplePage"
        type="com.apress.javaedge.struts.tiles.TilesTestAction">
  <forward name="tiles.success" path="/WEB-INF/jsp/tiles/simplePage.jsp"/>
</action>
```

To see the simplePage.jsp page, bring up a web browser and type `http://localhost:8080/JavaEdge/execute/tiles/simplePage` in the Address field. You should see the base content tile shown in Figure 6-3.

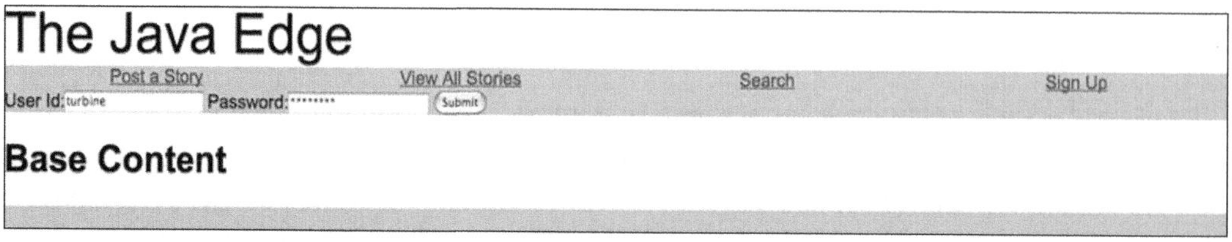

Figure 6-3. *The base content tile*

The Tiles definition example we have shown so far is very basic. It does not really do anything other than demonstrate some of the mechanics involved in setting a page up to use a Tiles definition.

The goal of the next section is to demonstrate how a Tiles definition can be reused across multiple web pages by including it in the page and then overriding individual values declared in the definition. To do this, we will show you how to rewrite the homePage.jsp page to override some of the attribute values declared in the baseDef Tiles definition with values that are specific to the JavaEdge home page.

Overriding the Attribute Values in a Tiles Definition

Overriding attributes in a Tiles definition is extremely easy. First you need to declare that you are going to use a definition by using the `<tiles:insert>` tag. To override individual attribute values on the declared Tiles definition, you need to place `<tiles:put>` tags inside the `<tiles:insert>` tag for each attribute in the declaration you want to override.

Shown next is a rewritten homePage.jsp file. This file has been modified to use the baseDef Tiles definition shown in the previous section. However, this example overrides two attribute parameters, `title` and `content`, with values that are specific to the JavaEdge home page.

```
<%@ page language="java" %>
<%@ taglib uri="/taglibs/struts-tiles" prefix="tiles" %>
<%@ include file="javaEdgeDef.jsp"%>

<tiles:insert beanName="baseDef" flush="true">
  <tiles:put name="title" value="Todays Top Stories"/>
  <tiles:put name="content" value="/WEB-INF/jsp/tiles/homePageContent.jsp"/>
</tiles:insert>
```

The `header` and `footer` attributes from the baseDef Tiles definition do not have to be overridden because they never change from page to page. The examples we are using in this chapter are obviously simplistic by design. However, you should be able to see that if you are using Tiles definitions with a great number of attributes that are *not* going to change, JSP-based Tiles definition can save the developer a lot of typing.

Using Dummy Values in Your Tiles Definition

Because the attribute values declared inside of a Tiles definition are automatically inherited and used by any page employing the definition, it is a good idea to place clearly marked dummy text in any of the attribute values that are going to be overridden on a regular basis. This is one of the reasons why the `title` and `content` attributes on the `baseDef` Tiles definition contain text indicating that it is fake."

We were working with a developer who had spent half of the day trying to figure out why the content of one of his pages was not showing up correctly. The page always showed the content of the application's home page. The developer kept insisting that it must be a problem with the Tiles framework.

On review of this developer's Tiles definition, we found that the `content` attribute in his base Tiles definition was set to point to the `content` on his home page. It turned out that he had forgotten to override the `content` attribute on the page he was working on. A little dummy text in the base Tiles definition would have prevented him from wasting his time on such a simple error.

Disadvantages of JSP Tiles Definitions

JSP-based Tiles definitions can save you a lot of time and effort by eliminating the need to redeclare a template implementation for each page in the application. Instead, you declare the template implementation as a Tiles definition inside of the JSP file that can then be included in each JSP page.

You can override individual attributes on a definition and can even add new attributes by declaring new Tiles definitions and extending off of an existing definition. This makes propagating changes to all of the pages in an application easy, as the Tiles definitions can be modified and all changes made to them are immediately available to all changes implementing the definitions.

While JSP-based Tiles definitions do offer a number of advantages to JSP page developers, using them also has two disadvantages. First, using JSP-based Tiles definitions, you are faced with either keeping all of the Tiles definitions in one JSP file or splitting the definitions into multiple JSP files. If the definitions are put in one JSP file, all pages that include the definitions will end up picking up definitions that they are not going to use. In a project with a large number of Tiles definitions and a high volume of users, the extra processing associated with executing the Tiles definitions can limit the overall response time and scalability of the application.

The alternative here is to break the Tiles definitions into multiple JSP files and then include them as needed into a page. This avoids the extra overhead associated with having too many Tiles definitions in a page that never uses them. However, it does introduce two problems:

- B reaking Tiles definitions into multiple JSP files can make maintaining the pages in an application more of a maintenance headache. The definitions are not located in one file, and members of the development team might have to hunt through multiple files before they find a definition they want to change.

- B reaking Tiles definitions into multiple JSP files, particularly in projects where a large number of definitions are present, makes it difficult for the development team to see commonalities that exist between Tiles definitions.

The second disadvantage to using JSP-based Tiles definitions is that if you want to build a completely component-based user interface, you must maintain at least two physical files for every page in the application:

- A JSP file that includes the Tiles definitions, declares which definitions are going to be used in a page, and overrides any of the attributes used in the definition

- A JSP file that holds the page's content

Fortunately, Tiles offers an alternative to using JSP-based Tiles definitions. The Tiles framework can centralize all of the Tiles definitions in a single XML file. Using this XML file, you can completely eliminate the need to write the JSP page that uses a Tiles definition.

The XML file that holds the Tiles definitions is declared as a property on the Tiles plug-in in the application's struts-config-tiles.xml file. The Tiles plug-in property that is set is definitions-config. For the JavaEdge application, the definitions-config property is set to the following value:

```
<set-property property="definitions-config"
              value="/WEB-INF/jsp/tiles/tiles-defs.xml"/>
```

Let's take a look at the structure and content of this file.

Anatomy of the tiles-defs.xml File

The tiles-defs.xml file will contain one or more definitions within it. The first definition to be declared is the base definition that is going to be inherited by all of the screens in the JavaEdge application. This definition is shown here:

```
<?xml version="1.0" encoding="ISO-8859-1"?>

<!DOCTYPE tiles-definitions PUBLIC
      "-//Apache Software Foundation//DTD Tiles Configuration//EN"
      "http://struts.apache.org/dtds/tiles-config.dtd">

<tiles-definitions>
  <definition name=".baseDef" path="/WEB-INF/jsp/tiles/template.jsp">
      <put name="title"    value="Base Template Page"/>
      <put name="header"   value="/WEB-INF/jsp/tiles/header.jsp"/>
      <put name="content"  value="/WEB-INF/jsp/tiles/baseContent.jsp"/>
      <put name="footer"   value="/WEB-INF/jsp/tiles/footer.jsp"/>
  </definition>
  . . .
</tiles-definitions>
```

The XML tag structure and format is almost exactly like that used in the JSP-based Tiles definitions. The tiles-defs.xml file's root tag is `<tile-definitions>`. Inside of the `<tiles-definitions>` tag will be one or more `<definition>` XML tags.

A `<definition>` tag delineates each Tiles definition. Each `<definition>` tag has a name attribute that is used to define the unique name of the definition within the tiles-defs.xml file. The name attribute plays the exact same role as the id attribute found in the `<tiles:definition>` JSP tag. The `<definition>` tag's path attribute defines the absolute or relative path of the JSP file that will act as a template for all of the pages using the definition.

Inside of the `<definition>` tag will be zero or more `<put>` tags that define the attribute values that will be passed to the template JSP declared for the definition:

```
<put name="title"    value="Base Template Page"/>
<put name="header"   value="/WEB-INF/jsp/tiles/header.jsp"/>
<put name="content"  value="/WEB-INF/jsp/tiles/baseContent.jsp"/>
<put name="footer"   value="/WEB-INF/jsp/tiles/footer.jsp"/>
```

The Tiles definition just shown, `.baseDef`, is the base definition for the JavaEdge application. Every page in the JavaEdge application will have its own unique `<definition>` tag that will inherit all of the attributes of the `.baseDef` Tiles definition. In the next section, we will demonstrate how to set up the other JavaEdge pages using the inheritance capabilities of the Tiles framework.

Inheritance Using Tiles Definitions

To inherit from an existing Tiles definition, the developer must create a new `<definition>` tag and then use the extends attribute with the name of the Tiles definition the new definition is inheriting from. The new definition inherits all of the attributes defined in the parent definition. Figure 6-4 illustrates this.

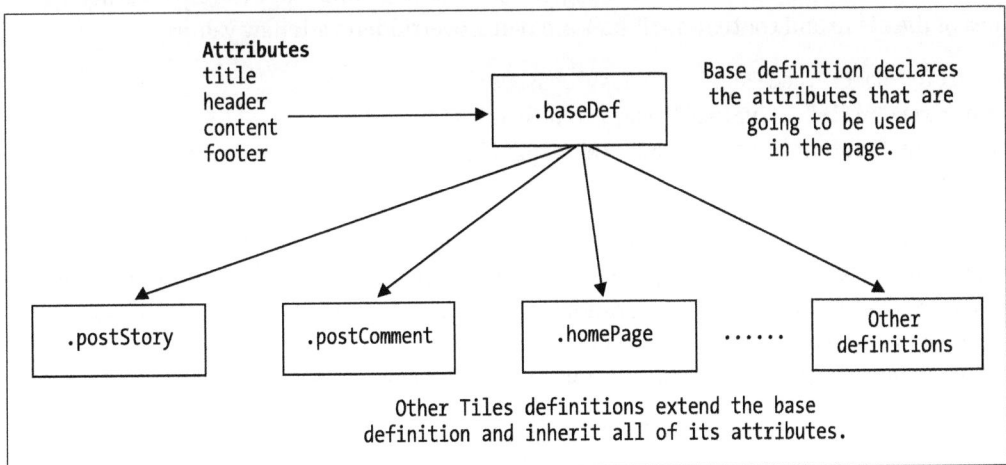

Figure 6-4. *A basic Tiles hierarchy*

To set up a Tiles definition for the JavaEdge home page, the following Tiles definition would need to be declared in the tiles-defs.xml file:

```
<?xml version="1.0" encoding="ISO-8859-1"?>

<!DOCTYPE tiles-definitions PUBLIC
      "-//Apache Software Foundation//DTD Tiles Configuration//EN"
      "http://struts.apache.org/dtds/tiles-config.dtd">

<tiles-definitions>
  <!-- Base Tile Definition from the previous section -->
  <definition name=".baseDef" path="/WEB-INF/jsp/tiles/template.jsp">
     . . .
  </definition>

  <definition name=".homePage" extends=".baseDef">
     <put name="title" value="Todays Top Stories"/>
     <put name="content"  value="/WEB-INF/jsp/tiles/homePageContent.jsp"/>
  </definition>


  . . .
</tiles-definitions>
```

Remember, each page in the JavaEdge application will have the same basic look and feel. The only thing that varies on each page is the page's title and content. Fortunately, like JSP-based Tiles definitions, XML-based definitions can override the values of an attribute inherited from the parent definition.

Overriding an attribute can be accomplished by placing a <put> tag for the attribute to be overridden inside a page's <definition> tag. In the JavaEdge home page example earlier, the values of the title and content attributes are being overridden with new values:

```
<definition name=".homePage" extends=".baseDef">
  <put name="title"    value="Todays Top Stories"/>
  <put name="content"  value="/WEB-INF/jsp/tiles/homePageContent.jsp"/>
</definition>
```

The header and footer attributes that are being inherited from the .baseDef definition do not have <put> tags in the .homePage definition. Thus, when the .homePage definition is rendered, the values for the .baseDef definition will be used when it is determined what is going to be used for the page's header and footer.

Shown here are the Tiles definitions for the rest of the pages in the JavaEdge application:

```
<?xml version="1.0" encoding="ISO-8859-1"?>

<!DOCTYPE tiles-definitions PUBLIC
      "-//Apache Software Foundation//DTD Tiles Configuration//EN"
      "http://struts.apache.org/dtds/tiles-config.dtd">
```

```xml
<tiles-definitions>
  <!-- Base Tile Definition from the previous section -->
  <definition name=".baseDef" path="/WEB-INF/jsp/tiles/template.jsp">
      . . .
  </definition>

  <definition name=".homePage" extends=".baseDef">
      . . .
  </definition>

  <definition name=".postComment" extends=".baseDef">
      <put name="title"  value="Post a Comment"/>
      <put name="content"
          value="/WEB-INF/jsp/tiles/postCommentContent.jsp"/>
  </definition>

  <definition name=".postStory" extends=".baseDef">
      <put name="title" value="Post a Story"/>
      <put name="content"
          value="/WEB-INF/jsp/tiles/postStoryContent.jsp"/>
  </definition>

  <definition name=".searchForm" extends=".baseDef">
      <put name="title" value="Search JavaEdge"/>
      <put name="content"
          value="/WEB-INF/jsp/tiles/searchFormContent.jsp"/>
  </definition>

  <definition name=".searchForm" extends=".baseDef">
      <put name="title" value="Search JavaEdge"/>
      <put name="content"
          value="/WEB-INF/jsp/tiles/searchFormContent.jsp"/>
  </definition>

  <definition name=".signUp" extends=".baseDef">
      <put name="title" value="Become a JavaEdge Member"/>
      <put name="content"  value="/WEB-INF/jsp/tiles/signUpContent.jsp"/>
  </definition>

  <definition name=".storyDetail" extends=".baseDef">
      <put name="title" value="View a specific story"/>
      <put name="content"
          value="/WEB-INF/jsp/tiles/storyDetailContent.jsp"/>
  </definition>
</tiles-definitions>
```

Extending a Tiles Definition

It is possible to declare a new Tiles definition that inherits all of the attributes of an existing Tiles definition and then adds new attributes that are unique to that tile. This is often done when you want to write a page that has the same basic look and feel as all the rest of the pages in an application, but has some additional visual elements that are unique.

Let's say that the marketing department has decided that they want to try and underwrite some of the costs of the JavaEdge site by selling ad space immediately below the header on the main page. However, the marketing department is also considering adding ads to other pages in the JavaEdge application at some later point in the future.

The easy approach would be to modify the homePageContent.jsp file to include the ad information. However, this is not very reusable because every time the marketing department wants to add more pages with ads, the advertisement code added to the homePageContent.jsp would need to be replicated.

A more flexible approach would be to use the inheritance and extensibility features found in Tiles definitions to build a hierarchy of definitions. The root Tiles definition for the JavaEdge application is still the .baseDef definition. All of the pages in the JavaEdge application, except for the home page, would use this definition.

A new definition is going to be created for the JavaEdge home page that will *extend* the .baseDef definition. This new definition, which will be called .baseWithOneAd, will include a new attribute parameter that defines what HTML or JSP file is going to be used for the ad that is going to be placed in the JavaEdge application.

Figure 6-5 shows the relationship between the .baseDef definition, the .baseWithOneAd definition, and the pages that implement these definitions.

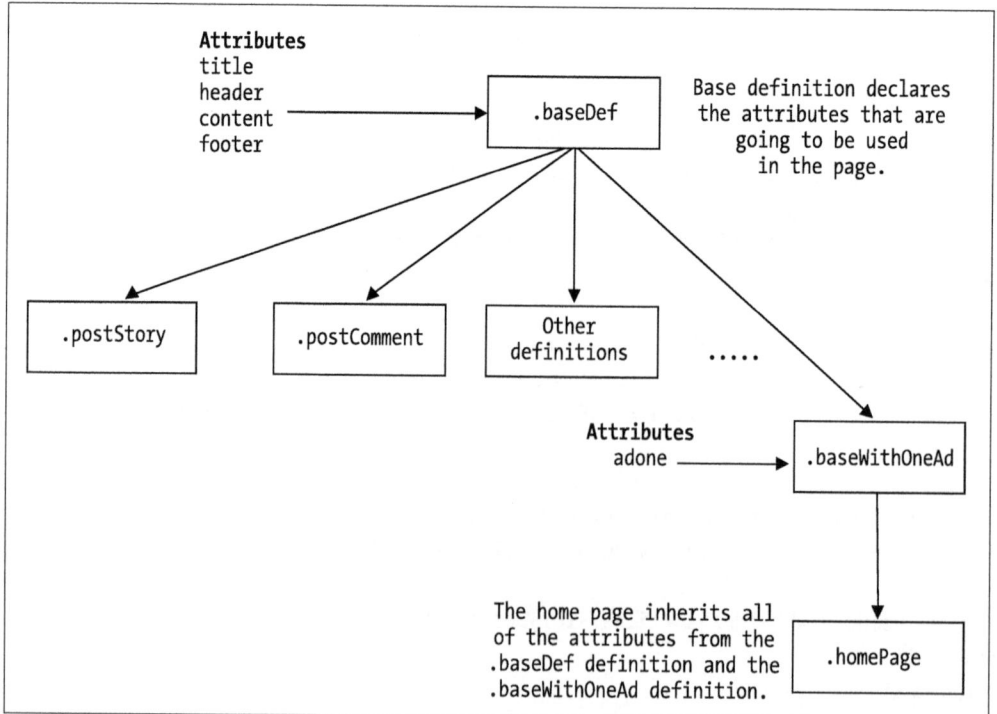

Figure 6-5. *Building a base definition*

To implement the Tiles definition hierarchy shown previously, the following steps need to be taken:

- The template.jsp that is being used by the JavaEdge application needs to be modified to include additional attributes that are only going to be implemented by the .baseWithOneAd Tiles definition.

- A new Tiles definition needs to be implemented in the tiles-defs.xml file that inherits and extends the attributes defined in .baseDef.

- The .homePage Tiles definition needs to be modified to use the .baseWithOneAd definition instead of the .baseDef definition.

Modifying the template.jsp File

All of the attributes defined in the template.jsp file are being passed values from the individual pages using the .baseDef Tiles definition. Every individual JavaEdge page that uses the .baseDef definition must override the attribute values defined in the definition. If the page does not override these values, the page will be rendered using the default values from the definition.

Implementing the condition that some pages in the JavaEdge application support advertisements requires a new attribute be added to the template.jsp page. This attribute, called adone, holds the path to a JSP file that contains the advertisement. The template.jsp file with the adone attribute declared is shown here:

```
<%@ taglib uri="/taglibs/struts-tiles" prefix="tiles" %>

<html>
<head>
    <title><tiles:getAsString name="title"/></title>
</head>

  <body>
  <p>
  <tiles:insert attribute="header"/>
  <tiles:insert attribute="adone" ignore="true"/>
  <tiles:insert attribute="content"/>
  <tiles:insert attribute="footer"/>
</body>
</html>
```

Typically when a Tiles definition uses a template, each attribute declared in the template must have a value passed into it. If a value is not passed into it, the Tiles framework will raise an exception.

However, with the introduction of the advertisement requirement, there is now an attribute, adone, in the template.jsp file that does not need to have a value passed to it by every Tiles definition using the template.

To make the adone attribute nonmandatory, the ignore XML attribute is added to the attribute's <tiles:insert> tag:

```
<tiles:insert attribute="adone" ignore="true"/>
```

The ignore XML attribute, when set to true, tells the Tiles framework to *not* throw an exception if the Tiles definition using the template does not pass a value for this attribute using a <tiles:put> tag. If the ignore XML attribute is set to false or is omitted altogether, every attribute defined in the template JSP must have a corresponding <tiles:put> tag defined in the Tiles definition implementing the template.

Now that the template.jsp has been modified, let's look at setting up the inheritance hierarchy for the JavaEdge Tiles definitions in the tiles-defs.xml file.

Adding the New Definition to tiles-defs.xml

Having one Tiles definition extend the attributes of another definition is straightforward. Shown here is the tiles-defs.xml file rewritten with an additional Tiles definition, .baseWithOneAd, added to it:

```
<?xml version="1.0" encoding="ISO-8859-1"?>

 <!DOCTYPE tiles-definitions PUBLIC
        "-//Apache Software Foundation//DTD Tiles Configuration//EN"
        "http://struts.apache.org/dtds/tiles-config.dtd">

<tiles-definitions>
   <definition name=".baseDef" path="/WEB-INF/jsp/tiles/template.jsp">
        <put name="title"     value="Base Template Page"/>
        <put name="header"    value="/WEB-INF/jsp/tiles/header.jsp"/>
        <put name="content"   value="/WEB-INF/jsp/tiles/baseContent.jsp"/>
        <put name="footer"    value="/WEB-INF/jsp/tiles/footer.jsp"/>
   </definition>

   <definition name=".baseWithOneAd" extends=".baseDef">
      <put name="adone" value="/WEB-INF/jsp/tiles/baseAd.jsp"/>
   </definition>
   . . .
</tiles-definitions>
```

The .baseWithOneAd Tiles definition looks very similar to the .baseDef definition. Both Tiles definitions use a <definition> tag to declare the definition. Both definitions also declare attributes the definitions are going to pass to the template via the <put> tag.

The key difference between the two different definitions is that the .baseWithOneAd definition does not use the path attribute to declare the path of the JSP file it is going to pass attribute values to. Instead, the .baseWithOneAd definition uses the extends attribute to indicate that it is inheriting all of the attributes from the .baseDef definition:

```
<definition id=".baseWithOneAd" extends=".baseDef">
```

By using the extends attribute, the .baseWithOneAd definition automatically inherits all of the attribute parameters declared in the .baseDef definition. The .baseWithOneAd definition can choose to override the attribute values declared in the .baseDef definition by redeclaring them via a <put> tag. Also remember, additional attributes can be added that are specific to the child definition.

The .baseWithOneAd Tiles definition has declared that it is going to pass a value to the adone attribute in the template.jsp file:

```
<tiles:put name="adone" value="/WEB-INF/jsp/tiles/baseAd.jsp"/>
```

Since the adone attribute is being declared in the .baseWithOneAd definition, only the JavaEdge pages using this definition will have the ad content included on the page.

Modifying the .homePage Definition

At this point, the .homePage definition can now be modified to use the .baseWithOneAd instead of the .baseDef Tiles definition:

```
<?xml version="1.0" encoding="ISO-8859-1"?>

<!DOCTYPE tiles-definitions PUBLIC
        "-//Apache Software Foundation//DTD Tiles Configuration//EN"
        "http://struts.apache.org/dtds/tiles-config.dtd">

<tiles-definitions>
  <definition name=".baseWithOneAd" extends=".baseDef">

    . . .
  </definition>

  <definition name=".homePage" extends=".baseWithOneAd">
      <put name="title" value="Todays Top Stories"/>
      <put name="content"  value="/WEB-INF/jsp/tiles/homePageContent.jsp"/>
      <put name="adone" value="/WEB-INF/jsp/tiles/ad.jsp"/>
  </definition>
    . . .

</tiles-definitions>
```

Let's look at the JavaEdge home page with the newly added ad at the top of the page. Bring up a web browser and go to http://localhost:8080/JavaEdge/execute/tiles/homePageSetup.

You should see the advertisement at the top of the screen immediately below the menu bar, as shown in Figure 6-6. The home page will be the only application that has this advertisement on it. However, it would be extremely easy to add the advertisement to other pages in the JavaEdge application. All that is required is to modify the extends attribute on the page to which you want to add the advertisement to use the .baseWithOneAd definition rather than the .baseDef definition.

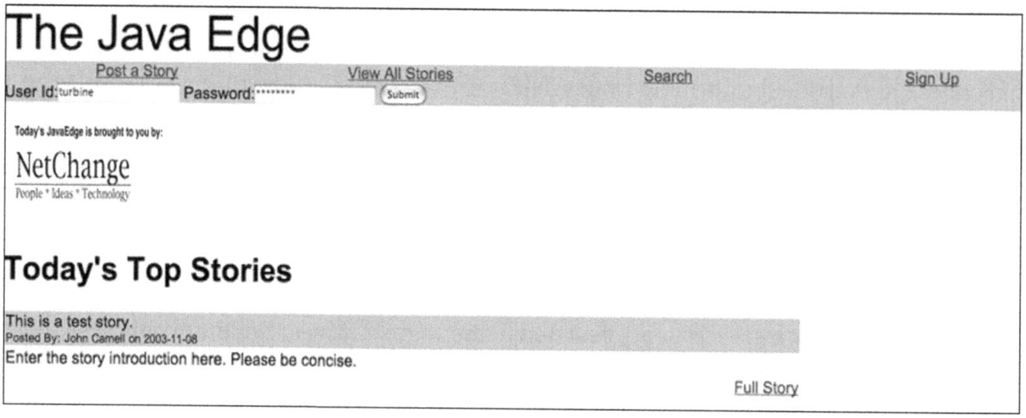

Figure 6-6. *The JavaEdge application with an ad on the screen*

The `.homePage` definition overrides attributes from the two different definitions, `.baseDef` and `.baseWithOneAd`. However, the `.homePage` definition has no knowledge that the title and content attributes come from the `.baseDef` definition.

Instead, as far as the `.homePage` definition is concerned, these attribute declarations are derived only from the `.baseWithOneAd` definition. The reason for this is that the Tiles inheritance model is a single-tree model. This means a definition can only inherit attributes from a single parent definition.

The Tiles framework does not support multitree inheritance, in which a definition can inherit from multiple definitions that have absolutely no relationship to one another. If you want a tile to inherit attributes from multiple definitions, the definitions must be organized into a hierarchical relationship where each definition inherits its attributes in a chain. The bottom of this chain will be the definition that is going to inherit all of the attributes.

Note It should be noted that while Tiles inheritance allows a great deal of flexibility in building the look and feel of a page, overusing and developing complex and/or deep inheritance hierarchies can cause performance problems and turn maintaining pages for the site into an absolute nightmare. We suggest never having a Tiles inheritance hierarchy more than two or three levels deep.

If you find yourself creating overly deep inheritance hierarchies, you should consider creating multiple base definitions based on the different distinct page types in your application.

Mapping Tiles Definitions to Action Forwards

Placing the Tiles definitions in a single file eliminates almost half of the JSP pages needed to build the JavaEdge application. However, the tiles-defs.xml file does not indicate how your Struts applications are supposed to actually navigate to the individual JSP pages. The question becomes, How does Struts map these Tiles definitions to JSP pages that can be reached from the Struts framework?

Struts uses the Tiles plug-in to map an XML-based Tiles definition to a Struts Action Forward defined in the application's struts-config.xml file.

To map a Tiles definition to a Struts Action Forward, the developer needs to use the value in the <definition> tag's name attribute in the <forward> tag for the Action. For example, to refactor the JavaEdge's /homePageSetup action to redirect the end user to the .homePage Tiles definition, the <action> tag for the /homePageSetup Struts action needs to be rewritten as shown here:

```
<?xml version="1.0" encoding="ISO-8859-1"?>
<!DOCTYPE struts-config PUBLIC
"-//Apache Software Foundation//DTD Struts Configuration 1.2//EN"
 "http://struts.apache.org/dtds/struts-config_1_2.dtd">

<struts-config>
  . . .
  <action-mappings>
    <action path="/homePageSetup"
            type="com.apress.javaedge.struts.homepage.HomePageSetupAction"
            unknown="true">
            <forward name="homepage.success" path=".homePage"/>
    </action>
    . . .
  </action-mappings>
</struts-config>
```

The key tag that needs to be modified is the <forward> tag. The path attribute in the <forward> tag must point to the name of the Tiles definition the user is going to be redirected to. With the Struts plug-in configured, the Struts framework will check to see if there is a Tiles definition defined that maps to the name specified in the path attribute.

If the Struts framework finds a match, it will assemble the contents of the page from its different component pieces and forward the user to the assembled page.

ON NAMING TILES

The "." naming convention that is being used by all of the JavaEdge Tiles definitions is not mandatory. You can still use "/" and a more traditional path structure to name the application's individual Tiles definitions.

However, even the refactored JavaEdge application uses Action Forwards that are not Tiles-based. Many of the Action Forwards in the JavaEdge application point to "pre-Actions" that do some work and then redirect the user to a Tiles-based JSP page. Using the "." notation for Tiles-based actions and the "/" notation for Struts-based Actions helps keep the struts-config.xml file manageable and easy to follow.

The idea of using the "." notation for Tiles-based Forwards is not ours. Cedric Dumoulin, one of the authors of *Struts in Action* (Ted Husted et al., Manning Publications Company, ISBN: 1-930-011050-2), first put forth this idea. We adopted it for our own Struts projects and have found it works well.

The homePageSetup Struts action does not submit any form data. However, when using XML-based Tiles definitions and Struts actions that submit form data, make sure that the input parameter on the action is mapped to the name of the Tiles definition for the page rather than the JSP where the data was entered.

For example, in the /login action shown here, the input parameter is set to the .homePage definition:

```
<action path="/login"
    input=".homePage"
    name="loginForm"
    scope="request"
    validate="true"
    type="com.apress.javaedge.struts.login.Login">
    <forward name="login.success" path="/execute/homePageSetup"/>
</action>
```

It is easy to overlook setting the input parameter to point to the Tiles definition. Missing this can result in hours of fun and debugging. Shown here are the rest of the JavaEdge action mappings converted to use XML-based Tiles definitions:

```
<action path="/storyDetailSetup"
        type="com.apress.javaedge.struts.storydetail.StoryDetailSetupAction">
    <forward name="storydetail.success" path=".storyDetail"/>
</action>

<action path="/signUpSetup"
        type="com.apress.javaedge.struts.signup.SignUpSetupAction"
        name="signUpForm"
        scope="request"
        validate="false">
    <forward name="signup.success" path=".signUp"/>
</action>

<action path="/signUp"
        input=".signUp"
        name="signUpForm"
        scope="request"
        validate="true"
        type="com.apress.javaedge.struts.signup.SignUp">
    <forward name="signup.success" path="/execute/homePageSetup"/>
</action>

<action path="/postStorySetup"
        type="com.apress.javaedge.struts.poststory.PostStorySetupAction"
        name="postStoryForm"
        scope="request"
        validate="false">
```

```
        <forward name="poststory.success" path=".postStory"/>
    </action>

    <action path="/postStory"
            input=".postStory"
            name="postStoryForm"
            scope="request"
            validate="true"
            type="com.apress.javaedge.struts.poststory.PostStory">
        <forward name="poststory.success" path="/execute/homePageSetup"/>
    </action>

    <action path="/postCommentSetup"
            type="com.apress.javaedge.struts.postcomment.PostCommentSetupAction"
            name="postCommentForm"
            scope="request"
            validate="false">
            <forward name="postcomment.success" path=".postComment"/>
    </action>

    <action path="/postComment"
            type="com.apress.javaedge.struts.postcomment.PostComment"
            name="postCommentForm"
            scope="request"
            validate="false">
        <forward name="postcomment.success" path="/execute/homePageSetup"/>
     </action>

    <action path="/SearchSetup"
            type="com.apress.javaedge.struts.search.SearchFormSetupAction"
            name="searchForm"
            scope="request"
            validate="false">
        <forward name="search.success" path=".searchForm"/>
    </action>

    <action path="/Search"
            type="com.apress.javaedge.struts.search.Search"
            input=".searchForm"
            name="searchForm"
            scope="request"
            validate="false">
      <forward name="search.success" path=".searchForm"/>
    </action>
```

Summary

This chapter went through the basics of using the Tiles framework to build a flexible presentation tier that can easily be modified as the business needs of your organization evolve. Some of the material that was covered in this chapter includes the following:

- Configuring Struts to use the Tiles framework:

    - Configuring the struts-config.xml file (or in the examples for this chapter, the struts-config-tiles.xml file) to activate the Tiles plug-in

    - Configuring the Tiles plug-in to recognize where the tiles-defs.xml file is located and what level of debugging the Tiles plug-in should carry out

    - Laying out the skeleton tiles-defs.xml file.

- Writing a simple JSP page to leverage the `<tiles>` tag libraries.

- Exploring how Tiles definitions can be used to build the JavaEdge applications. This chapter looked at the two different types of Tiles definitions (JSP-based and XML-based) and how they could be used to do the following:

    - Group together related page attributes into unique entities that could be reused across multiple screens

    - Demonstrate how to override individual attributes in a definition to allow customization of the basic look and feel of an individual page or tile

    - Use XML-based Tiles definitions to centralize all of the screen layouts into a single file that can be easily managed and modified

    - Leverage the inheritance and extensibility features of XML-based Tiles definitions to add new elements to an existing application screen

- Modifying the struts-config-tiles.xml file so that XML-based Tiles definitions can be used in a Struts Action Forward rather than the traditional JSP page.

Our advice is not to get caught up in the pure mechanics of the Tiles framework. It is more important to understand how the Tiles framework can help a development team avoid the Tight-Skins and Hardwired antipatterns. The Tiles framework allows the development team to break the presentation layer into discrete and reusable components that can be managed from a single location.

Let's quickly review some of the changes made to the JavaEdge application during the course of this chapter. It should become pretty apparent that we made some fundamental changes to the application's structure without having to rewrite a great deal of code.

- *Reconfigured the application to use a completely different set of JSP files without having to modify any of the existing files*: By modifying the JavaEdge's web.xml file to point to a new Struts configuration file (struts-config-tiles.xml file), you could move the JavaEdge application to a new presentation framework (Tiles) without having to touch any of the existing application source code.

- *Centralized all template and layout information into a single configuration file*: All template and layout information was centralized into the tiles-defs.xml file. By centralizing all of the template information into one file, you could eliminate half of the original JSP pages needed in the application.

- *Added the capability to modify or add new screen elements without visiting each application page*: By leveraging the Tiles framework's inheritance, overriding, and extension features, you could add new screen elements (for example, the ad on the JavaEdge home page) without having to actually go in and modify each screen.

Normally, to take an existing application that is not built around a framework and undertake the changes enumerated by the preceding three bullet points would require a tremendous amount of rework. However, by using Struts and Tiles, these tasks become trivial.

When a development team first begins using the Tiles framework, there can be a steep learning curve. The development team will have to design the initial application templates and write each of the Tiles definitions that are going to be used in the application. However, once this work has been completed, it becomes extremely easy to modify the core structure of the application, while minimizing the risk that changes to the code will break the application.

This chapter shows that you can easily move existing applications to Tiles, but it also shows that if you do that, you aren't using the full power of Tiles. Don't get me wrong: It'll still work and it's a good investment for the future, but it's like using Windows 2000 on a FAT file system. You get the power of a new system, but you're still dragging old limitations with you. Also, if you add Tiles to a sizable non-Tiles project, you can easily break existing pages.

Because Tiles tags can insert output of any action into the target tile, your presentation layer is not limited to only JSP pages. You can just as easily use Velocity, for example (see Chapter 11).

CHAPTER 7

∎ ∎ ∎

Dynamic Forms and the Struts Validator Framework

The current stable release of Struts, version 1.2.9, provides powerful development metaphors for capturing, processing, and validating form data submitted by an end user. ActionForm classes allow us to capture and validate data in a uniform manner. However, in medium-to-large projects, it quickly becomes apparent that writing the ActionForm classes for the application is a tedious, repetitive, and error-prone process.

The reason for this is twofold. First, the ActionForm class is used to scrape data submitted by the user from the HttpServletRequest object and place it into a more developer-friendly and type-safe Java object. However, the majority of the work involved with writing the ActionForm class is writing get()/set() methods for each of the attributes being captured from a submitted form. The hand coding of these get()/set() methods is usually reserved as punishment for the individual whose code broke the build for the previous evening.

Secondly, in most applications, when data is collected from the end user, the same validation rules are usually applied against the data. For example, in the real world, just about every HTML form submitted has some fields that are required to be populated. In addition, some fields, like an e-mail address or a credit card number, are going to be required to be a certain length and/or have a very specific format.

Using the ActionForm class and the validate() method requires the developer to invoke these rules over and over against the individual form attributes in this class. The smart developer will often break the validation rules out into a set of classes that can be reused over and over again. However, even by breaking the validation rules out into a set of reusable classes, the developer writing the ActionForm class must still write Java code to invoke the rules.

Ultimately, the issue here is such developers are repeating the same type of code over and over again throughout their application. Dave Thomas and Andrew Hunt, in their book *The Pragmatic Programmer* (Addison-Wesley, ISBN: 0-201-61622-X), articulated this problem and devised a simple yet powerful principle to battle it. This principle is called the D.R.Y. principle, or "Don't Repeat Yourself."

The main point of the D.R.Y. principle is that "every piece of knowledge must have a single, unambiguous, authoritative representation within a system."

Dave Thomas and Andrew Hunt are big proponents of using code generators and development frameworks to enforce the D.R.Y. principle. Starting with Struts version 1.1 and higher, you can use two new features of the framework to solve the problems of repetitive code in implementing ActionForm classes and validating the data contained within them.

These two features are *Dynamic Forms* and the *Jakarta Commons Validator framework*. This chapter is going to explore the functionality and capabilities of these exciting new additions to the Struts framework. Specifically, we will be discussing the following:

- An introduction to Dynamic Forms

- Declaring Dynamic Forms within the struts-config.xml file

- Using Dynamic Forms within your Struts `Action` classes

- The Jakarta Commons Validator framework

- Configuring Struts to use the Validator framework

- The different validation rules available in the framework

- Declaring validation rules in applications using Dynamic Forms

- Implementing validation rules in applications using traditional Struts `ActionForm` classes

- Writing your own validation rules for use within the Validator framework

Let's begin our discussion by looking at how you can use Struts Dynamic Forms to refactor the `PostStoryForm.java` `Action` class.

Introducing Dynamic Forms

Dynamic Forms allow a development team to declaratively define the attributes of an application's `ActionForm` classes in the struts-config.xml file. By declaring the attributes for an `ActionForm` class in a file, the development team can significantly reduce the amount of repetitive and tedious code that needs to be written. Furthermore, new fields can be added to the other form without having to rewrite the existing `ActionForm` classes.

To use Dynamic Forms within a Struts version 1.2x application, you need to perform two steps:

1. Define a `<form-bean>` tag for each Dynamic Form that is going to be used inside the application's struts-config.xml file.

2. Rewrite your `ActionForm` classes to extend the `DynaActionForm` class instead of the `ActionForm` class.

We will begin this discussion by looking at how you would define the Struts `postStoryForm` as a Dynamic Form.

Defining the postStoryForm Struts Form Bean

A `<form-bean>` tag for a Dynamic Form, like a `<form-bean>` tag for the more traditional Struts form, is declared in the struts-config-validator.xml.[1] However, unlike the more traditional

---

1. As in the previous chapter, we have opted to break out the Validator configuration into a separate struts-config.xml file. This file is called struts-config-validator.xml. Please remember to modify the parameters for the ActionServlet in your web.xml file.

Struts ActionForms that declare attributes via get()/set() methods inside the specific Java class implementations, the individual form attributes for a Dynamic Form are declared as <form-property> tags inside the <form-bean> tag.

Shown here is the <form-bean> entry used to define the Dynamic Form postStoryForm used in the Post a Story page:

```
<struts-config>
   <form-beans
      <form-bean name="postStoryForm"
                 type="com.apress.javaedge.poststory.PostStoryDynaForm">
         <form-property name="storyIntro" type="java.lang.String"/>
         <form-property name="storyBody"  type="java.lang.String"/>
         <form-property name="storyTitle" type="java.lang.String"/>
      </form-bean>

      <!-- Rest of the ActionForm definitions-->
   </form-beans>
   <!-- Rest of the struts-config.xml file -->
</struts-config>
```

Once you have defined the postStoryForm <form-bean> tag, you need to define the individual properties on the <form-bean>. This is the equivalent of writing a get()/set() method on a nondynamic ActionForm class:

```
<form-property name="storyIntro" type="java.lang.String"/>
<form-property name="storyBody"  type="java.lang.String"/>
<form-property name="storyTitle" type="java.lang.String"/>
```

Just like the nondynamic example shown earlier in Chapter 3, this dynamic post StoryForm ActionForm definition has three properties: storyIntro, storyBody, and storyTitle. Each of these properties has a corresponding <form-property> tag.

A <form-property> tag can have three attributes in it. We are only using two of the three attributes for the example declaration shown earlier, as listed in Table 7-1.

Table 7-1. *Attributes of the <form-property> Tag*

Attribute Name	Attribute Description
name	The name attribute is the name of the property and is the value that will be referenced by the Struts HTML tag libraries when accessing and setting form data. This is a mandatory attribute.
type	The type attribute is the fully qualified Java class name of the attribute being set. This is a mandatory attribute.

Now that the postStoryForm has been declared as a Dynamic Form, let's take a look at the actual implementation of the PostStoryDynaForm class.

Writing the PostStoryDynaForm.java Implementation

At face value, the PostStoryDynaForm class looks very similar to the PostStoryForm class shown earlier. However, subtle differences exist between the implementations. Shown here is the code for the PostStoryDynaForm class:

```java
package com.apress.javaedge.struts.poststory;

import org.apache.struts.action.ActionMapping;
import org.apache.struts.action.DynaActionForm;
import org.apache.struts.action.ActionForward;
import javax.servlet.http.HttpServletRequest;
import javax.servlet.http.HttpServletResponse;
import org.apache.struts.action.ActionErrors;
import org.apache.struts.action.ActionError;
import org.apache.struts.action.ActionServlet;
import org.apache.struts.util.MessageResources;

import com.apress.javaedge.common.VulgarityFilter;

public class PostStoryDynaForm extends DynaActionForm {
    //Checks to make sure field being checked is not null.
    private void checkForEmpty(String fieldName,
                String fieldKey, String value,
                ActionErrors errors){
        if (value.trim().length()==0){
          ActionError error =
          new ActionError("error.poststory.field.null",
          fieldName);
          errors.add(fieldKey, error);
        }
    }

    //Checks to make sure the field being checked
    //does not violate our vulgarity list.
    private void checkForVulgarities(String fieldName,
            String fieldKey,
            String value,
        ActionErrors errors){
        VulgarityFilter filter = VulgarityFilter.getInstance();

        if (filter.isOffensive(value)){
          ActionError error =
            new ActionError("error.poststory.field.vulgar",
            fieldName);
          errors.add(fieldKey, error);
        }
    }
```

```
//Checks to make sure the field in question
//does not exceed a maximum length.
private void checkForLength(String fieldName,
    String fieldKey,
    String value,
    int maxLength,
    ActionErrors errors){
     if (value.trim().length()>maxLength){
       ActionError error =
       new ActionError("error.poststory.field.length",
                          fieldName);
       errors.add(fieldKey, error);
     }
}

public ActionErrors validate(ActionMapping mapping,
                         HttpServletRequest request) {
   ActionErrors errors = new ActionErrors();


   checkForEmpty("Story Title",
               "error.storytitle.empty",
               (String) super.get("storyTitle"),errors);
   checkForEmpty("Story Intro",
                "error.storyintro.empty",
                (String) super.get("storyIntro"), errors);
   checkForEmpty("Story Body",
               "error.storybody.empty",
               (String) super.get("storyBody"), errors);

   checkForVulgarities("Story Title",
      "error.storytitle.vulgarity",
      (String) super.get("storyTitle"),errors);
   checkForVulgarities("Story Intro",
      "error.storyintro.vulgarity",
      (String) super.get("storyIntro"),
                                errors);
   checkForVulgarities("Story Body",
      "error.storybody.vulgarity",
      (String) super.get("storyBody"),
      errors);

   checkForLength("Story Title",
      "error.storytitle.length",
      (String) super.get("storyTitle"), 100,
      errors);
   checkForLength("Story Intro", "error.storyintro.length",
```

```
                        (String) super.get("storyIntro"), 2048,
                        errors);
            checkForLength("Story Body",
                "error.storybody.length",
                (String) super.get("storyBody"),
                10000,
                errors);

            return errors;
        }

        public void reset(ActionMapping mapping,
                          HttpServletRequest request) {
            ActionServlet servlet = super.getServlet();
            MessageResources messageResources = servlet.getResources();

            super.set("storyTitle",
                messageResources.getMessage("javaedge.poststory.title.instructions"));
            super.set("storyIntro",
                messageResources.getMessage("javaedge.poststory.intro.instructions"));
            super.set("storyBody",
                messageResources.getMessage("javaedge.poststory.body.instructions"));
        }
    }
```

The first thing to notice about the PostStoryDynaForm class is that it extends the Struts import org.apache.struts.action.DynaActionForm class rather than the Struts org.apache. struts.action.ActionForm class:

```
public class PostStoryDynaForm extends DynaActionForm {
    . . .
}
```

The DynaActionForm class extends the ActionForm. The DynaActionForm class is used to tell the Struts framework that the class is a Dynamic Form and that its attributes need to be read from the struts-config.xml file.

Because the DynaActionForm class extends the ActionForm class, it inherits the validate() and reset() method from the parent. These methods are invoked by the Struts framework in the exact same manner as their nondynamic ActionForm counterparts.

The PostStoryDynaForm's validate() and reset() implementation looks almost exactly like the PostStoryForm's implementation. The only difference is how these methods retrieve and set attributes when executing. Take a look at a code fragment from the PostStoryDynaForm's validate() method:

```
public ActionErrors validate(ActionMapping mapping,
                             HttpServletRequest request) {
    ActionErrors errors = new ActionErrors();

    checkForEmpty("Story Title", "error.storytitle.empty",
                        (String) super.get("storyTitle"),errors);
```

```
checkForEmpty("Story Intro", "error.storyintro.empty",
                        (String) super.get("storyIntro"), errors);
checkForEmpty("Story Body",  "error.storybody.empty",
                        (String) super.get("storyBody"), errors);

. . . . .
return errors;
}
```

When using Dynamic Forms, individual attributes are accessed by calling the DynaActionForm's get() method and passing in the name of the attribute that is to be retrieved:

```
checkForEmpty("Story Title",
            "error.storytitle.empty",
            (String) super.get("storyTitle"),
            errors);
```

The DynaActionForm's get() method will retrieve all values as objects. It is the responsibility of the developer to cast the returned object to its appropriate type. If the get() method cannot find the property requested, it will throw a NullPointerException.

To set an attribute on a Dynamic Form, you need to call the set() method on the DynamicActionForm, passing in the name of the attribute to be set, along with the value to be associated with that attribute. The set() method will accept only objects and not primitive values.

The reset() method demonstrates how to set an attribute for a form:

```
public void reset(ActionMapping mapping,
                    HttpServletRequest request) {
    ActionServlet servlet =  super.getServlet();
    MessageResources messageResources = servlet.getResources();
    super.set("storyTitle",
            messageResources.getMessage("javaedge.poststory.title.instructions"));

    ....
}
```

The DynaActionForm's set() method does do type checking on the value being passed into it. It does this by looking at the type attribute defined in the form attribute's <form-property> tag. If the set() finds that the object passed in does not match the type declared in the <form-property>, it will throw an org.apache.commons.beanutils.ConversionException. A ConversionException is an unchecked Java exception and does not have to be explicitly caught within a try{}..catch{} block.

Note Dynamic Forms allow the developer to quickly build forms without having to write extraneous Java code. The only disadvantage with them is that the attributes are not type safe. A careless keystroke by a developer can result in many hours of trying to debug this rather nefarious and difficult problem. However, careful unit testing can help mitigate this risk. A great reference for unit testing is *Java Development with Ant* by Erik Hatcher and Steve Loughran (Manning Publications, ISBN: 1-930-11058-8). While the book is not entirely on unit testing, it does have some great chapters covering the topic.

Once a Dynamic Form's <form-bean> tag and its corresponding <form-property> tags have been declared, you've done all the work you need to do to tell Struts to use a dynamic ActionForm class. The postStoryContent.jsp page that pulls data from the postStoryForm form bean does not have to be modified. It does not care if you are using a nondynamic or dynamic ActionForm.

Shown here is the rewritten PostStory Action class, pulling data from the dynamic postStoryForm form bean defined earlier:

```java
package com.apress.javaedge.struts.poststory;

import java.util.Vector;

import javax.servlet.http.HttpServletRequest;
import javax.servlet.http.HttpServletResponse;
import javax.servlet.http.HttpSession;

import org.apache.struts.action.Action;
import org.apache.struts.action.ActionForm;
import org.apache.struts.action.ActionForward;
import org.apache.struts.action.ActionMapping;
import org.apache.struts.action.DynaActionForm;

import com.apress.javaedge.common.ApplicationException;
import com.apress.javaedge.member.MemberVO;
import com.apress.javaedge.story.StoryManagerBD;
import com.apress.javaedge.story.StoryVO;
import com.apress.javaedge.story.dao.StoryDAO;

public class PostStory extends Action {

    public ActionForward perform(ActionMapping mapping,
                                 ActionForm     form,
                                 HttpServletRequest request,
                                 HttpServletResponse response){

        if (this.isCancelled(request)){
            return (mapping.findForward("poststory.success"));
        }


        DynaActionForm postStoryForm = (DynaActionForm) form;

        HttpSession session = request.getSession();

        MemberVO     memberVO = (MemberVO) session.getAttribute("memberVO");

        try{
```

```
        StoryVO storyVO = new StoryVO();

        storyVO.setStoryIntro((String)postStoryForm.get("storyIntro"));
        storyVO.setStoryTitle((String)postStoryForm.get("storyTitle"));
        storyVO.setStoryBody((String)postStoryForm.get("storyBody"));
        storyVO.setStoryAuthor(memberVO);
        storyVO.setSubmissionDate(new
                java.sql.Date(System.currentTimeMillis()));
        storyVO.setComments(new Vector());

        StoryManagerBD storyManager = new StoryManagerBD();
        storyManager.addStory(storyVO);
    }
    catch(Exception e){
        System.err.println("An application exception" +
        " has been raised in PostStory.perform(): " +
        e.toString());
        return (mapping.findForward("system.failure"));
    }

    return (mapping.findForward("poststory.success"));
    }
}
```

There are really two differences between the PostStory class and the earlier PostStory implementation shown in Chapter 3. First, the PostStory class just shown no longer casts the ActionForm being passed into the perform() method on the class to the PostStoryForm class shown earlier in the chapter. Instead, it casts the incoming ActionForm parameter to be of type DynaActionForm:

```
DynaActionForm postStoryForm = (DynaActionForm) form;
```

Second, just like the validate() and reset() methods shown earlier, the PostStoryForm. java implementation just shown does not call an individual getXXX() method for each property on the ActionForm. Instead, it invokes the get() method on the class, passing in the name of the property it wants to retrieve.

Some Thoughts About BeanUtils and the Preceding Code

You might be wondering why we did not use the BeanUtils.copyProperties() method to populate the StoryVO class, as was shown in Chapter 4. In the example, we wanted to explicitly demonstrate how to access Dynamic Form properties.

However, BeanUtils.copyProperties() does allow you to copy the properties from a Map class into a JavaBean. The copyProperties() method will use the key of each value stored in the Map object and try to match that to a get()/set() method on a JavaBean for copying. The Map object that is to be copied must be passed in as the second parameter, the origin parameter, on the BeanUtils.copyProperties() method.

So if you wanted to be consistent with what was shown in Chapter 4, you would rewrite the buildStoryVO() method on the PostStoryForm class to look like this:

```
public StoryVO buildStoryVO(HttpServletRequest request)
    throws ApplicationException{
        HttpSession session = request.getSession();
        MemberVO      memberVO      =
            (MemberVO) session.getAttribute("memberVO");
        StoryVO storyVO = new StoryVO();
    try{
        BeanUtils.copyProperties(storyVO, this.getMap());
    }
    catch(IllegalAccessException e) {
        throw new ApplicationException("IllegalAccessException" +
        " in PostStoryForm.buildStoryVO()",e);
    }
    catch(InvocationTargetException e){
        throw new ApplicationException("InvocationTargetException " +
        " in PostStoryForm.buildStoryVO()",e);
    }

    storyVO.setStoryAuthor(memberVO);
    storyVO.setSubmissionDate(new java.sql.Date(System.currentTimeMillis()));
    storyVO.setComments(new Vector());

    return storyVO;
}
```

The only difference between the buildStoryVO() method shown here and the buildStoryVO() method shown in Chapter 4 is

```
BeanUtils.copyProperties(storyVO, this.getMap());
```

The Struts DynamicActionForm lets you access the underlying Map that stores its properties through the getMap() method. Otherwise the code is exactly the same.

Dynamic Form beans are a powerful feature of Struts. They allow you to easily implement and change form beans without having to write a single line of code. This new feature keeps very much in line with the philosophy of Struts: Let the framework do as much of the work as possible, while allowing the developer to focus on building business code rather than infrastructure code.

Dynamic Forms allow you to greatly reduce the amount of Java code that needs to be written for a Struts form bean. However, while the Struts form beans are great for collecting data, one of their biggest strengths lies in the fact that they allow the developer to easily separate the validation data for the data being collected from the actual business rules being executed on the data. However, as anyone with any web development experience can attest to, writing validation logic for form data is a tedious undertaking. Oftentimes it involves executing such basic tasks as checking to see if a web form field has been filled in by the end user, whether it is the proper data type or the proper format, and so on.

USING DYNAMIC FORMS TO DO RAPID PROTOTYPING

The introduction of Dynamic Forms in Struts version 1.1x has been incredibly useful for rapidly building prototypes. Ideally, when building an application prototype, you want to be able to write the shell of the application quickly. Then if you can get away with it, you want to use as much of the prototype code as possible in the application.

Unfortunately, most development teams rarely get the time needed to really build a quality application skeleton. The emphasis on speed to deliver the prototype often results in shoddy code that looks usable on the surface, but from an architectural perspective is a "train wreck."

Before Dynamic Forms, if the development team wanted to "shell" out the look and feel and navigation for an application using Struts, the team still needed to write out the individual ActionForm classes needed for each screen. This was a requirement because if you wanted to use the Struts tag libraries to mock up a web form, the development team needed to have a fully implemented ActionForm class with each of the get()/set() methods that were going to be displayed on the screen.

Development teams "under the gun" to build a prototype are not going to go through all of this extra work. Instead, they usually end up using a combination of HTML and JSP scriptlets to throw the prototype together. They end up meeting their goals, but then find themselves with little reusable code. Worse, their management has now seen a "working" prototype and as is often the case jumps to the conclusion that the application is almost done.

With Dynamic Forms, a development team can declare the form in the struts-config.xml file. However, rather than extending and writing its own DynaActionForm class implementation and then declaring it in the <form-bean> tag's type attribute, the team can simply use org.apache.struts.action. DynaActionForm for the type attribute's value.

Thus, they do not have to write a Java class implementation. For example, if you just wanted to quickly throw together a mock-up of the Post a Story screen using Struts, you could declare the following in the application's strut-config.xml file:

```
<struts-config>
    <form-beans>
        <form-bean name="postStoryForm"
                        type="org.apache.struts.validator.DynaActionForm">

        . . .

        </form-bean>


    . . .

</struts-config>
```

Once this <form-bean> has been declared using DynaActionForm, it can be immediately used throughout the prototype without having an actual class written. When the application is actually being built out, a Java class can be written for the postStoryForm action and the type attribute can be modified to point to the new class.

Fortunately, since Struts version 1.1x, a data validation framework called the Jakarta Commons Validator framework has been integrated as a plug-in. The Validator framework gives developers a rich library of common form validation tasks to immediately use in their applications. The Validator framework is also extensible so that development teams can easily add their own validation rules to the framework.

The Jakarta Commons Validator Framework

The Validator framework used in Struts did not originate in the Struts project. Rather, the Validator framework is part of the Apache Jakarta Group's Commons project (http://jakarta.apache.org/commons). The Struts development team chose to integrate the Jakarta Commons Validator as a Struts plug-in. The team also extended the Validator framework to make the generic validation rules used in the Validator framework fit smoothly into the Struts validation infrastructure.

The Struts developers did this because they found that after implementing several Struts-based applications, they were performing the same types of validation over and over again. Some of these common validations included

- Checking to see if the user has entered all required fields

- Checking to see if data is within a minimum or maximum size

- Checking to see if the data entered is of the right type

In the next several sections, we are going to show you how to use the Jakarta Commons Validator framework and the PostStoryDynaForm implementation we examined earlier to collect the Post a Story pages form data and apply the following validation rules:

- Check to make sure that the Story Title, Story Body, and Story Introduction fields on the Post a Story page are filled in by the end user.

- Validate that each field entered by the user does not exceed a certain character length.

- Check to see if there is any vulgarity present in the user's story.

The first two validation rules will be enforced using "out-of-the-box" validation rules that come with the Validator framework. The last validation rule, checking for vulgarity, will be implemented as a custom validation rule that is going to be added to the existing Struts framework. To use the Validator framework in the JavaEdge application, you must take the following steps:

1. Configure Struts to use the Validator plug-in.

2. Define a <formset> tag in the validations.xml file that lists the validation rules that are going to be fired off when validating the PostStoryForm.

3. Write a new JavaEdge validation rule that checks for vulgarity.

4. Add a new entry to the validator-rules.xml file to tell the Validator framework about the new vulgarity rule.

Let's begin our discussion by looking at how the Validator framework is set up and configured.

Validator Framework Setup

The Validator framework requires a modification to the struts-config.xml file and the addition of two new configuration files: validator-rules.xml and validation.xml. Struts version 1.1 now allows new functionality to be added the framework via a *plug-in*. The Validator framework is one such plug-in.

To make Struts aware of the Validator framework, you need to add the following entry to the end of the JavaEdge struts-config.xml file:

```
<plug-in className="org.apache.struts.validator.ValidatorPlugIn">
  <set-property property="pathnames" value="/WEB-INF/validator-rules.xml,
                                  /WEB-INF/validation.xml"/>

</plug-in>
```

The <plug-in> tag goes at the end of your struts-config.xml file. It defines the fully qualified Java class that represents the plug-in point between Struts and the third-party software. The <set-property> tag is used to set a plug-in–specific property. In the preceding example, the pathnames property contains a comma-separated list telling the Validator framework where to find the validator-rules.xml file and the validation.xml file.

The validator-rules.xml file contains individual XML tags that describe the rules that come with the Validator framework. The validator-rules.xml file that comes with the Struts distribution will contain descriptions of all of the predefined validation rules that come as part of the Validator framework. A partial listing of the validation rules defined in the validator-rules.xml file is shown in Table 7-2.

Table 7-2. *Validator Rules*

Rule Name	Rule Description
required	Validates that the field has been filled in by the end user
requiredif	Deprecated; use validwhen
validwhen	Checks one field with another
minlength	Checks to ensure that the value entered is of a minimum length
maxlength	Checks to ensure that the value entered is of a maximum length
range	Deprecated; use intRange, doubleRange, or floatRange
mask	Validates that the field entered is of a particular format
byte	Validates that the field entered is of type byte
short	Validates that the field entered is of type short
integer	Validates that the field entered is of type integer
long	Validates that the field entered is of type long
float	Validates that the field entered is of type float
double	Validates that the field entered is of type double
date	Validates that the field entered is of type date
creditcard	Validates a credit card format
email	Validates that the field entered is a properly formatted e-mail address
intRange	Validates whether an integer is within a particular range
floatRange	Validates whether a float is within a particular range
doubleRange	Validates whether a double is within a particular range

The validation.xml file contains the mappings to each form bean in the application that is going to use the Validator framework. The validation.xml file maps each form bean field to the validation rule that is going to be invoked against it. We will be going through some of the validation.xml details shortly.

Implementing the Required Fields Validation

In the Post a Story page, Story Title, Story Introduction, and Story Body are all required fields. To use the Validator to enforce these rules, you must create a file called validation.xml. Shown here is the validation.xml file that is used for enforcing required fields validation:

```
<form-validation>
  <formset>
    <form name="postStoryForm">
        <field property="storyTitle" depends="required">
                <msg name="required" key="error.poststory.field.null"/>
                <arg0 key="javaedge.poststory.form.titlelabel"/>
        </field>
        <field property="storyIntro" depends="required">
           <msg name="required" key="error.poststory.field.null"/>
           <arg0 key="javaedge.poststory.form.introlabel"/>
        </field>
        <field property="storyBody" depends="required">
           <msg name="required" key="error.poststory.field.null"/>
           <arg0 key="javaedge.poststory.form.bodylabel"/>
        </field>
    </form>
  </formset>
</form-validation>
```

The <form-validation> tag is the root element for the validation.xml file. The <formset> tag represents a collection of forms for the application. A <formset> tag can contain one or more <form> tags. A <form> tag represents one particular form bean in the application.

```
<form name="postStoryForm">
```

The name attribute on the <form> tag is the name of the form bean defined in the struts-config.xml file. Each <form> tag has one or more <field> tags associated with it:

```
<field property="storyTitle" depends="required">
   <msg name="required" key="error.poststory.field.null"/>
   <arg0 key="javaedge.poststory.form.titlelabel"/>
</field>
```

The <field> tag represents a single attribute from the form that is going to be validated by the Validator framework. A <field> tag has two attributes:

- property: The name of the field that is going to be validated. This must match the name of a field defined in the <form-bean> on the struts-config.xml file. This is a mandatory attribute.

- depends: The depends attribute lists, from left to right, all of the validation rules that are going to be invoked on the field. These rules will be fired off in the order they are listed. In the preceding example, only the required rule is being applied against the field. This is a mandatory attribute.

A <field> tag can contain one or more <msg> tags. The <msg> tag is used by the Validator framework to determine what message should be displayed to the end user when a rule is violated:

```
<msg name="required" key="error.poststory.field.null"/>
```

A <msg> tag has three attributes on it. The attributes available on the <msg> tag include the following:

- name: The name attribute is the name of the rule the message is associated with. In the preceding example, the value of name points to the required rule.

- key: The key attribute is the key for the message in the Struts resource bundle (that is, ApplicationResources.properties) file. In the preceding example, the value of error. poststory.field.null would be pulled from the ApplicationResources.properties file as

```
The following field: {0} is a required field.
Please provide a value for{0}.
```

The key attribute is a required attribute on the <form> tag.

- resource: The resource attribute tells the Validator framework that it should use the resource bundle to look up an error message based on the value in the key attribute. If the value of resource is set to true, then the resource bundle is used. If the value of resource is set to false, the default Struts resource bundle will not be used and the value in the key attribute will be taken as a literal string. The default value of the resource attribute is true.

A <field> tag can also contain argument tags appropriately called <arg0>, <arg1>, <arg2>, <arg3>, and <arg4>. These tags are used to pass arguments into the <msg> tags. The <argX> tag allows developers to pass in values to a message defined in the Struts resource bundle. The postStoryForm validation has one argument being passed into each of the messages on the field.

For example, the Story Title field uses the following <arg0> tag to indicate that whenever a validation error occurs on the storyValidation field of the postStoryForm, the following key will be used to look up a value from the ApplicationResources.properties file and perform a string substitution on the message:

```
<arg0 key="javaedge.poststory.form.titlelabel"/>
```

So, if users do not enter a value in the Story Title field, they get the following error message presented to them:

```
The following field: Story Title is a required field.
Please provide a value for Story Title.
```

The `<argX>` tags have three attributes available to them:

- name: The `name` attribute defines the name of the validation rule this argument is associated with. For example, if you only wanted the first argument of the message to be available when the `required` rule is invoked for the `storyTitle` field, you would write the `<arg0>` tag as follows:

```
<arg0 name="required" key="javaedge.poststory.form.titlelabel"/>
```

If a name is not provided, this argument will be available to every validation rule that fires off a validation exception for that particular field.

- key: The `key` attribute is the key for the message in the Struts resource bundle (that is, ApplicationResources.properties) file.

- resource: The `resource` attribute tells the Validator framework that it should use the resource bundle to look up an argument based on the value in the `key` attribute. If the value of `resource` is set to `true`, then the resource bundle is used. If the value of `resource` is set to `false`, the default Struts resource bundle will not be used and the value in the `key` attribute will be taken as a literal string value. The default value of the `resource` attribute is `true`.

Once you have defined all of the form and field mappings in the validation.xml file, you still need to make one last change in order to validate your Dynamic Form bean against the rules you have defined.

At this point, we have demonstrated how to set up a very simple validation rule using the Validator framework. Let's look at setting up a slightly more complicated rule using the `maxlength` validation rule.

The maxlength Validation Rule

The next rule you want to implement for the rewritten Post a Story page is to put some maximum size limits on what the user can enter in each field on the page. To do this, you need to set up the `maxlength` validation rule on each field.

Shown here is the revised validation.xml file, containing the new rule definitions:

```
<form-validation>
  <formset>
    <form name="postStoryForm">
      <field property="storyTitle" depends="required,maxlength">
        <msg name="required" key="error.poststory.field.null"/>
        <msg name="maxlength" key="error.poststory.field.length"/>
        <arg0 key="javaedge.poststory.form.titlelabel"/>
        <arg1 name="maxlength" key="${var:maxlength}" resource="false"/>
        <var>
            <var-name>maxlength</var-name>
            <var-value>100</var-value>
        </var>
      </field>
      <field property="storyIntro" depends="required,maxlength">
```

```
                <msg name="required" key="error.poststory.field.null"/>
                <msg name="maxlength" key="error.poststory.field.length"/>
                <arg0 key="javaedge.poststory.form.introlabel"/>
                <arg1 name="maxlength" key="${var:maxlength}" resource="false"/>
                <var>
                    <var-name>maxlength</var-name>
                    <var-value>2048</var-value>
                </var>
            </field>
            <field property="storyBody" depends="required,maxlength">
                <msg name="required" key="error.poststory.field.null"/>
                <msg name="maxlength" key="error.poststory.field.length"/>
                <arg0 key="javaedge.poststory.form.bodylabel"/>
                <arg1 name="maxlength" key="${var:maxlength}" resource="false"/>
                <var>
                    <var-name>maxlength</var-name>
                    <var-value>100000</var-value>
                </var>
            </field>
        </form>
    </formset>
</form-validation>
```

To set up each field with the maxlength validation rule, you need to add the rule to the value of the depends attribute on each <field> tag. For the Story Title field, this would look like the following:

```
<field property="storyIntro" depends="required,maxlength">
```

Remember, rules are invoked from the left to the right. In the validation.xml file shown previously, the required validation rule will be invoked before the maxlength rule.

Now that there are two rules associated with each field, you need to add <msg> tags that will reflect different messages for each rule. In the Story Title field, you have two <msg> tags with the name attribute of each <msg> tag being tied to a name defined in the <field> tag's depends attribute:

```
<msg name="required" key="error.poststory.field.null"/>
<msg name="maxlength" key="error.poststory.field.length"/>
```

In addition, each message is going to have two arguments passed to it. Thus, an <arg0> and an <arg1> tag are defined in each <field> tag. For the Story Title field, this looks like the following:

```
<arg0 key="javaedge.poststory.form.titlelabel"/>
<arg1 name="maxlength" key="${var:maxlength}" resource="false"/>
```

The first argument, <arg0>, is going to be shared across all messages being thrown by the validation field. To do this, we do *not* define a name attribute on the <arg0> tag. However, the second argument, <arg1>, is only going to be available to the maxlength validation rule. We indicate this by setting the name attribute on the <arg1> tag to be maxlength.

Many of the validation rules in the Validator framework require values to be defined to help enforce the validation rule. For instance, with the `maxlength` validation rule, you need to tell the rule what the acceptable maximum length of the field being validated is. This value can be set by using the `<var>` tag to define a value to pass into the validation rule.

Note The `<arg>` tag is used to pass arguments to the error message being returned from a validation. The `<var>` tag is used to pass values to the validation rule that is being used. This is brought up because it is extremely easy to confuse how these two tags are used.

The `maxlength` validation rule takes a single parameter, `maxlength`, as an input value:

```
<var>
    <var-name>maxlength</var-name>
    <var-value>10</var-var>
</var>
```

The `<var>` tag contains two other tags: `<var-name>` and `<var-value>`. The `<var-name>` tag holds the name of the input parameter being passed into the validation rule. The `<var-value>` tag holds the value that is to be set for that variable.

Table 7-3 lists a few of the Validator rules that accept input parameters.

Table 7-3. *A Few Validator Rules That Accept Input Parameters*

Rule Name	Parameter Names	Parameter Description
minlength	minlength	Integer value representing the minimum size of the field
maxlength	maxlength	Integer value representing the maximum size of the field
intRange	min, max	Integer value representing the minimum and maximum values for the field
mask	mask	Regular expression indicating the mask to be applied to the field
url	allowallschemes, allow2slashes, nofragments, schemes	Controls how the URL is validated
date	datePattern	Date pattern that is to be applied against the field to determine whether or not the user has entered a proper date

On the `<arg1>` tag you should have noticed the unusual syntax of the key attribute. The `<arg1>` tag is set to the value ${var:maxlength}. This value will pull whatever value is defined for the `<var>` tag whose `<var-name>` is equal to `maxlength`. You should note though that the value of this variable will only be pulled if the resource attribute on the `<arg1>` tag is set to `false`.

At this point you now have two validation rules defined for the `postStoryForm` form bean. Let's take a look at how you can modify the `PostStoryDynaForm` class shown earlier to leverage these two rules and still call the code that checks for the vulgarities within the story submission.

Use the Validator Framework Within an ActionForm Class

We are going to show you how to rewrite the PostStoryDynaForm class to use the Validator framework. This new class is called PostStoryDynaValidatorForm.java and is shown here:

```
package com.apress.javaedge.struts.poststory;

import org.apache.struts.action.ActionMapping;
import org.apache.struts.validator.DynaValidatorForm;
import org.apache.struts.action.ActionForward;
import javax.servlet.http.HttpServletRequest;
import javax.servlet.http.HttpServletResponse;
import javax.servlet.http.HttpSession;
import org.apache.struts.action.ActionErrors;
import org.apache.struts.action.ActionError;
import org.apache.struts.action.ActionServlet;
import org.apache.struts.util.MessageResources;

import com.apress.javaedge.common.VulgarityFilter;

public class PostStoryDynaValidatorForm extends DynaValidatorForm {

    private void checkForVulgarities(String fieldName,
        String fieldKey, String value,
        ActionErrors errors){
        VulgarityFilter filter = VulgarityFilter.getInstance();

         if (filter.isOffensive(value)){
           ActionError error =
            new ActionError("error.poststory.field.vulgar",
                        fieldName);
           errors.add(fieldKey, error);
         }
    }

    public ActionErrors validate(ActionMapping mapping,
                              HttpServletRequest request) {

        ActionErrors errors = super.validate(mapping, request);

        checkForVulgarities("Story Title", "error.storytitle.vulgarity",
                                    (String) super.get("storyTitle"),
                                  errors);
        checkForVulgarities("Story Intro", "error.storyintro.vulgarity",
                                    (String) super.get("storyIntro"),
                                  errors);
```

```
checkForVulgarities("Story Body",  "error.storybody.vulgarity",
                                (String) super.get("storyBody"),
                                errors);

    return errors;
    }
}
```

The refactored postStoryForm Struts form bean is significantly smaller than its predecessors. The original PostStoryForm.java class is 131 lines of code. The PostStoryDynaValidatorForm class is 59 lines of code. By using Dynamic Forms and the Validator framework, a little over half the code, give or take a few comment lines, for the postStoryForm form bean has been eliminated.

Modifying a Dynamic Form class to use the Validator framework requires the following three steps to be undertaken:

1. Modify the Struts Action class in question to extend the DynamicValidatorForm class instead of the DynaActionForm.

2. Call the validate() method on the parent DynamicValidatorForm class as the first action in the Struts Action class's validate() implementation.

3. Create a <form> tag in the validation.xml file to define the validation rules that are going to be fired off when the form is validated.

The DynamicValidatorForm class is part of the org.apache.struts.validator package:

```
public class PostStoryDynaValidatorForm extends DynaValidatorForm {
}
```

To invoke the Validator framework from an existing validate() method on a Struts ActionForm, you need to invoke the validate() method on the parent DynaValidatorForm class, passing in the child class's mapping and request object:

```
public ActionErrors validate(ActionMapping mapping,
                            HttpServletRequest request) {
    ActionErrors errors = super.validate(mapping, request);
    . . .
}
```

The DynaValidatorForm's validate() method will look up the validation rules that are to be applied to this form (if any) and invoke each of the rules. The DynamicValidatorForm's validate() method will return an ActionErrors collection for any Validation errors found by the Validator Form class:

```
public ActionErrors validate(ActionMapping mapping,
                            HttpServletRequest request) {

    ActionErrors errors = super.validate(mapping, request);

    checkForVulgarities("Story Title", "error.storytitle.vulgarity",
                                (String)super.get("storyTitle"), errors);
    . . .
}
```

Using the Validator framework with Dynamic Forms significantly reduces the amount of code that needs to be written for an `ActionForm` implementation. Furthermore, the Struts framework is flexible enough to allow you to combine both "off-the-shelf" validation rules from the Validator framework with your own custom code.

It is possible to use the Validator with nondynamic forms. To use an `ActionForm` class employing `get()`/`set()` methods, have your `ActionForm` implementation extend the `org.apache.validator.ValidatorForm` class rather than the standard Struts `ActionForm` class. Then, like the Dynamic Form, have the first line of the `ActionForm` implementation call the parent `ValidatorForm`'s `validate()` method (that is, `super.validate(mapping, request);`). Finally, modify the `<form-bean>` tag's `type` attribute to point to your class.

By mixing the Validator framework in with existing `ActionForm` implementations, you can slowly start converting an existing Struts-based application over to these new features slowly and methodically. This will allow you to manage the risk associated with using a new technology feature and also give you the opportunity to evaluate how useful the Validator framework is going to be in your environment.

Writing Your Own Validation Rules

One of the most powerful features of the Validator framework is the ability to extend it with your own custom validation rules. In the JavaEdge application, any field on the Post a Story or Post a Comment page must be checked for vulgarity.

Since this task is repeated over and over again, it makes sense to extend the Validator framework and add the vulgarity checker as a validation rule. To create your own validation rule and then use it in a Struts Dynamic Form, you need to perform the following steps:

1. Implement the rule using a method signature that the Struts/Validator framework understands.

2. Modify the validation-rules.xml file to describe the new rules and the arguments that should be passed to it.

3. Add a new `<form>` tag or modify an existing tag to indicate that the vulgarity rule is to be applied when the form is validated.

Implementing the Vulgarity Rule

Writing a new validation rule is extremely easy and involves nothing more than providing an "entry" method on a Java class that the Validator framework can call to invoke the validation rule. However, there are two rules that must be followed when writing this entry method.

The first rule is that the entry method has to be declared as public and static. This rule is in place because the Validator framework does not try to create a new instance of the Java class–containing rule each time it tries to invoke the validation. This would be extremely inefficient, because in a high-transaction environment this would lead to the creation of large numbers of temporary objects.

The second rule is that the entry signature for the method must always be the following:

```
public static boolean methodName(
                    Object              targetObject     ,
                    ValidatorAction validatorAction      ,
                    Field               field            ,
                    ActionErrors        actionErrors     ,
                    HttpServletRequest request){ . . . }
```

The targetObject parameter represents the Struts ActionForm class that is being processed by the validation rule. The validatorAction parameter is a class that is part of the Validator framework. The validatorAction parameter holds all of the metadata for the validation rule. This metadata is described in the validator-rules.xml file inside of a <form> tag. Some of this metadata includes what message arguments and variable parameters (for example, the maximum length of a field for the maxlength validation rule) and any dependencies the validation rule might have on other fields in its <form>. The field parameter is of class type Field. The Field class is also found in the Jakarta Commons Validator framework. The Field class is used to represent the form field that the validation rule is firing against. This value will correspond to a <field> tag defined inside a <form> in the validation.xml file.

The actionErrors parameter is passed to hold any errors that are raised during the execution of the validation rule. The request parameter is a standard HttpServletRequest object that can be used by the validation rule to obtain any additional information that might need to be used during the execution of the validation rule.

Finally, a method acting as a validation rule must return a Boolean value. If the value returned by the method is true, the form field that is being validated by the method successfully passed the validation. If the value returned is false, the field being validated has violated the validation rule.

Shown here is the implementation of the vulgarity rule as a Validator validation rule. It has been refactored to take advantage of several features of the Validation framework (of which we will get to shortly).

```
package com.apress.javaedge.common;

import javax.servlet.http.HttpServletRequest;
import org.apache.commons.validator.Field;
import org.apache.commons.validator.ValidatorAction;
import org.apache.struts.action.ActionErrors;
import org.apache.commons.validator.GenericValidator;
import org.apache.commons.validator.ValidatorUtil;
import org.apache.struts.validator.Resources;

import java.util.StringTokenizer;
import java.util.Enumeration;


public class VulgarityRule {


    private static boolean isOffensive(String badWords, String value){
      StringTokenizer tokenizer = new StringTokenizer(badWords,",");

      while (tokenizer.hasMoreTokens()){
        String badWord = tokenizer.nextToken().toLowerCase().trim();
        if (value.toLowerCase().indexOf(badWord)!=-1){
          return true;
        }
      }
```

```
    return false;
  }

  /*
    Method that checks to see if the text contains a vulgarity.
  */
  public static boolean isOffensive(Object            targetObject      ,
                                    ValidatorAction validatorAction   ,
                                    Field             field             ,
                                    ActionErrors      actionErrors      ,
                                    HttpServletRequest request){

  /*Checking to see if the target is null.*/
  boolean TARGET_OBJECT_IS_NULL = (targetObject == null);
  if (TARGET_OBJECT_IS_NULL) return true;

  /*Checking to see if the field is null.*/
  String fieldValue =
    ValidatorUtil.getValueAsString(targetObject,
    field.getProperty());
  boolean FIELD_IS_NULL_OR_BLANK = GenericValidator.isBlankOrNull(fieldValue);
  if (FIELD_IS_NULL_OR_BLANK) return true;

  /*Getting the bad word list.*/
  String vulgarities = field.getVarValue("vulgarities");

  /*Checking to see if the value is offensive.*/
  boolean RULE_INVALID = isOffensive(vulgarities, fieldValue);

  if (RULE_INVALID){
    actionErrors.add(field.getKey(),
              Resources.getActionError(request,
                                            validatorAction,field)));

    return false;
  }

  return true;
  }

}
```

The public isOffensive() method is the entry point into the vulgarity checker validation rule. The first thing this method does is determine whether or not the ActionForm (that is, the targetObject parameter) is null and whether or not the field that is being validated by the rule is null:

```
  /*Checking to see if the target is null.*/
  boolean TARGET_OBJECT_IS_NULL = (targetObject == null);
  if (TARGET_OBJECT_IS_NULL) return true;
```

```
/*Checking to see if the field is null.*/
String fieldValue =
  ValidatorUtil.getValueAsString(targetObject,
  field.getProperty());
boolean FIELD_IS_NULL_OR_BLANK = GenericValidator.isBlankOrNull(fieldValue);
if (FIELD_IS_NULL_OR_BLANK) return true;
```

If either of these variables is null, you are going to return true. A null value cannot contain a vulgarity.

To get the actual value of the field being called, you are going to use the getValueAsString() method on the ValidatorUtil class:

```
String fieldValue =
  ValidatorUtil.getValueAsString(targetObject,
  field.getProperty());
```

The getValueAsString() method takes the ActionForm class and the name of the form field, retrieved via the field.getProperty() method, as parameters.

Once the value of the submitted field is retrieved and placed into the fieldValue variable, the value will be checked to see if it is null by calling the isBlankOrNull() method on the GenericValidator class:

```
boolean FIELD_IS_NULL_OR_BLANK = GenericValidator.isBlankOrNull(fieldValue);
```

The GenericValidator class is part of the org.apache.common.validator package and contains a set of base routines for performing basic types of validations. These validation methods are only used as building blocks for writing more complex Validator validation rules.

After the ActionForm and field have been checked as to whether or not they are null, the isOffensive() method is going to retrieve the list of words that are considered to be vulgarities:

```
/*Getting the bad word list.*/
String vulgarities = field.getVarValue("vulgarities");
```

This is one place where we improved upon the functionality in the vulgarity checker. In the original vulgarity checker class, all of the offensive words have been hard coded into the class as an array of strings. If you want to modify the list, you need to modify the code, recompile it, and redeploy.

Recall that earlier in our discussion about setting up a validation rule in the validation.xml file, we mentioned validation rules can have parameters passed into them. That is what the call to field.getVarValue("vulgarities") is doing. It is retrieving a comma-separated list of vulgarities that have been defined specifically for the field being validated.

Once the vulgarity list has been retrieved, it and the field value that is going to be validated are sent to the private method isOffensive():

```
boolean RULE_INVALID = isOffensive(vulgarities, fieldValue);
```

The private isOffensive() method will tokenize the comma-separated list and check to see if vulgarities are present. If a vulgarity is found in the submission, the private isOffensive()

method will return true; otherwise it will return false. If the field being validated does contain a vulgarity, then a new ActionError is going to be created and placed into the actionErrors variable passed into the isOffensive() method.

```
if (RULE_INVALID){
        actionErrors.add(field.getKey(),
                  StrutsValidatorUtil.getActionError(request,
                                                      validatorAction,field));

        return false;
}
```

If a validation rule does fail, an ActionError class must be added to the actionErrors parameter or the user will not see an error message displayed back to them. In the preceding code snippet, an ActionError class is retrieved by calling the getActionError() method on the StrutsValidatorUtil class. The getActionError() method will retrieve the ActionError object based on the <msg> tag defined for the field in the validation.xml file. In summary, the code you just saw demonstrates how to write a simple validation rule that is configurable via a parameter.[2] Let's now look at how to let the Validator framework know that this vulgarity rule exists and is available for use.

Adding the Vulgarity Rule to the validator-rules.xml File

To make the vulgarity rule available to the Validator framework, a description of the validation rule needs to be added to the validator-rules.xml file. This new rule will be described with a <validator> tag. Shown here is the <validator> tag for the vulgarity rule:

```
<validator
          name="vulgaritychecker"
          classname="com.apress.javaedge.common.VulgarityRule"
          method="isOffensive"
          methodParams="java.lang.Object,
                        org.apache.commons.validator.ValidatorAction,
                        org.apache.commons.validator.Field,
                        org.apache.struts.action.ActionErrors,
                        javax.servlet.http.HttpServletRequest"
          msg="errors.vulgarity"
        />
```

The <validator> tag contains a number of attributes that describe different facets of the validation rule. The name attribute is the logical name that the validation rule will be referred to when being used in a <form>:

```
name="vulgaritychecker"
```

---

2. For other examples of how to write validation rules, download the Struts source code from the Jakarta project and look at the FieldChecks.java file in the source directory/share/org/_apache/struts/validator directory.

The classname attribute is the fully qualified Java class name that holds the validation rule. In this case, the classname attribute contains the following value:

```
classname="com.apress.javaedge.common.VulgarityRule"
```

The method attribute contains the name of the method that will be invoked by the Validator framework:

```
method="isOffensive"
```

Remember, the method name must be declared as both public and static. The methodParams attribute lists the parameter types that will be passed into the method declared in the method attribute:

```
methodParams="java.lang.Object,
              org.apache.commons.validator.ValidatorAction,
              org.apache.commons.validator.Field,
              org.apache.struts.action.ActionErrors,
              javax.servlet.http.HttpServletRequest"
```

The parameters listed here must be in the exact same order as the parameters listed in the actual method.

Note The Jakarta Commons Validator framework allows you to build validation rules that have different method signatures. If you are going to write custom validation rules for use with the Struts/Validator plug-in, the validation rules must use the parameter list shown in the preceding methodParams attribute. Struts invokes validation rules using the preceding method signature. If your entry in the validation-rules.xml file does not match this signature, your validation rule will not be properly recognized by Struts and the Validator framework will not invoke the rule.

The final attribute in the <validator>, the msg attribute, defines the key of the error message that will be displayed when the validation rule is violated.

This key, along with its corresponding message, is defined in the ApplicationResources. properties file. The text of the error message from the ApplicationResources.properties file is shown here:

```
error.vulgarity=The following field {0} has a vulgarity present in it.
Please correct this.<br/>
```

If you review the other validation rules in the validator-rules.xml file, you will find that all of the <validation> tags that come with the Validator framework have a <javascript> tag inside of them. The Struts Validator framework allows you to generate JavaScript validation rules for web-form fields.

The <javascript> tag inside of each <validation> tag contains JavaScript code that is the functional equivalent of the Java code for the validation rule. For example, shown here is the <validation> tag for the maxlength validation rule:

```
<validator name="maxlength"
          classname="org.apache.struts.util.StrutsValidator"
             method="validateMaxLength"
        methodParams="java.lang.Object,
                    org.apache.commons.validator.ValidatorAction,
                    org.apache.commons.validator.Field,
                    org.apache.struts.action.ActionErrors,
                    javax.servlet.http.HttpServletRequest"
           depends="required"
               msg="errors.maxlength">
        <javascript><![CDATA[
           function validateMaxLength(form) {
              var bValid = true;
              var focusField = null;
              var i = 0;
              var fields = new Array();
              oMaxLength = new maxlength();
              for (x in oMaxLength) {
                 if (form[oMaxLength[x][0]].type == 'text' ||
                    form[oMaxLength[x][0]].type == 'textarea') {
                    var iMax = parseInt(oMaxLength[x][2]("maxlength"));
                    if (!(form[oMaxLength[x][0]].value.length <= iMax)) {
                       if (i == 0) {
                          focusField = form[oMaxLength[x][0]];
                       }
                       fields[i++] = oMaxLength[x][1];
                       bValid = false;
                    }
                 }
              }
              if (fields.length > 0) {
                 focusField.focus();
                 alert(fields.join('\n'));
              }
              return bValid; }]]>
        </javascript>
     </validator>
```

The vulgarity rule does not contain any JavaScript code within it, nor will this chapter be discussing how to use or implement client-side JavaScript validation rules.

Struts Validation and Potential Long-Term Consequences

The main reason for not using or demonstrating the JavaScript validation rules is that while JavaScript is a powerful tool, based on industry experience it tends to be abused and can often have cross-platform execution issues. Furthermore, JavaScript can be easily turned off by end users in their browser. This can quickly break an application that is dependent on JavaScript for validation.

As discussed earlier, the inappropriate mixing of validation logic in JavaScript and Java code often leads to the Validation Confusion antipattern. We would prefer that all validation code be kept in a set of centralized Java classes (for example, `ActionForms`) where it can be easily maintained and modified.

The Struts framework's validation mechanism is a powerful tool for building a consistent interface for dealing with application validation errors. However, you do need to be aware of two potential long-term architectural consequences of leveraging this functionality for your applications. First, you are moving your validation logic for a business application into code that is very framework specific. If you use the `ActionForm`'s `validate()` method and/or the Struts Validator framework, you are tightly coupling your validation logic to the Struts framework.

Secondly, Struts is a presentation framework for building *web-based* applications. If you need to reuse your validation and business logic in a nonweb application, like a Swing application, you are not going to be able to do it without rewriting code.

One solution to this would be to use the Validator framework in a stand-alone model, independent of the Struts framework, and then move all of the validation logic to either the value objects in the application or to your business objects. Then you could have the Struts `ActionForm.validate()` method invoke the validation on the value object or the business object and map the results back to an `ActionErrors` collection.

Another solution would be to implement your application's validation logic in a set of framework-independent validation classes that can be invoked from the `ActionForm`'s `validate()` method *or* your business logic. These validation classes would throw an `ApplicationException` if the rules were violated. Your application's presentation layer, whether it be Struts or some other kind of presentation layer (for example, a Swing interface), would then catch the exception and process it accordingly.

While this does achieve long-term independence from the Struts framework of your validation logic, it requires infrastructure coding that you would not otherwise have to do if you use the validation infrastructure already in Struts. In the end, it really comes down to what is going to be right for your applications and application teams.

Implementing the Vulgarity Rule in a Form

Once the validator-rules.xml file has been modified to include a description of the vulgarity rule, you are now able to use that rule in an actual field validation. Shown next is the `<field>` tag for the `storyTitle` attribute for the `postStoryForm` form bean. The elements that appear in bold are the new values that have to be added to activate the vulgarity rule.

```
<form-validation>
  <formset>
    <form name="postStoryForm">
      <field property="storyTitle" depends="required,maxlength,vulgaritychecker">
        <msg name="required" key="error.poststory.field.null"/>
        <msg name="maxlength" key="error.poststory.field.length"/>
        <msg name="vulgaritychecker" key="error.vulgarity"/>

        <arg0 key="javaedge.poststory.form.titlelabel"/>
        <arg1 name="maxlength" key="${var:maxlength}" resource="false"/>
```

```
                <var>
                    <var-name>maxlength</var-name>
                    <var-value>100</var-value>
                </var>
                <var>
                    <var-name>vulgarities</var-name>
                    <var-value>dummy, stupid, ninny</var-value>
                </var>
            </field>
    . . .
    </form>
</formset>
</form-validation>
```

When you compare the preceding field/validation mapping to the example shown earlier in the chapter, you will see that adding the vulgarity checker to the mapping involves very little effort. First you must add the rule vulgaritychecker to the comma-separated list of rules in the property attribute:

```
<field property="storyTitle" field property="storyTitle"
    depends="required,maxlength,vulgaritychecker">
```

You then declare the message that will be used by the Validator framework if an error is raised:

```
<msg name="vulgaritychecker" key="error.vulgarity"/>
```

Since no arguments are going to be passed to the message, you will not need an <argX> tag. The last XML element that needs to be defined is the list of the vulgarities that you are going to be checking for. You do this by defining a <var> tag that contains the name of the variable along with the list of vulgarities:

```
<var>
    <var-name>vulgarities</var-name>
        <var-value>dummy, stupid, ninny</var-value>
</var>
```

Once this mapping has been completed, you have now removed the need to have any code in the validate() method on the PostStoryDynaActionForm class.

An ActionForm Without Java

Combining the power of Dynamic Forms with the Validator framework can allow the developer to completely eliminate the need to write any Java code for an ActionForm. For the postStoryForm bean, all of the attributes for the bean have been as XML inside of the struts-config.xml file.

All of the postStoryFrom form bean validation rules are either part of the existing Validator framework (that is, the required and maxlength rules) or have been added as extensions to the framework (for example, the vulgarity rule).

To completely eliminate the need for a custom form bean for the Post a Story page, you need to make one more modification to the postStoryForm <form-bean> tag in the struts-config-validator.xml file. This modification is shown here:

```
<form-bean name="postStoryForm"
    type="org.apache.struts.validator.DynaValidatorForm">
        <form-property name="storyIntro" type="java.lang.String"/>
        <form-property name="storyBody"  type="java.lang.String"/>
        <form-property name="storyTitle" type="java.lang.String"/>
</form-bean>
```

In the preceding XML snippet, you see that you need to change the type of the class to be of type DynaValidatorForm rather than of type PostStoryDynaActionForm. Whereas the earlier example had the PostStoryDynaActionForm class extending the DynaValidatorForm class and then overriding the DynaValidatorForm's validate() method, you now use the DynaValidatorForm class directly in your <form-bean> definition.

By configuring your <form-bean> in this manner, no Java class has to be written to perform validations. Instead, the DynaValidatorForm class executes all validations. Remember, all of the validation rules for the postStoryForm form bean are defined in the validation.xml file.

When to Use the Validator Framework

The Validator framework is a very powerful tool that can empower your development team and focus its energies on quickly delivering applications. However, like any framework, the Validator framework is useful in some situations and in other situations causes more harm than good.

The real power of the Validator framework comes into play when your development team is building a large number of web-based forms that use the basic validation rules that come with the framework. You can quickly leverage these validation rules and reduce the amount of code needed to build out an application screen. The question becomes, what happens when you have a set of validation rules that need to be applied against web forms that do not exist in the Validator framework?

You have two choices in this situation: You can write a new validation rule and extend the Validator framework, or you can embed the validation code inside of the validate() method and keep it independent of the Validator framework.

We usually use the following questions to help us determine where a validation rule should go:

- Is the validation rule going to be reused across multiple screens?

- How complex is the validation rule?

- Is the validation rule in question really a validation rule, or has some business logic slipped into the validation layer?

The first question is a very valid question and should be considered carefully. If the validation code being written is going to be used in only one application screen, it does not make sense to extend the Validator framework. One-time-use code is better served in the validate()

method of an `ActionForm` class. Otherwise, you will find that over time your application's validation rules will be extremely cluttered with single-use rules. As your validator-rules.xml file becomes bigger and bigger, you will have a hard time tracking what rules can be reused.

The second question deals with complexity. The Validator framework allows you to build dependencies between different validation rules and the fields that are being validated. Based on our experiences, validation rules work best when they are used to validate a single field at any given time. The more complexities and interrelationships that exist between rules and fields, the more difficult it is to build a maintainable application. If you are building a custom validation rule, if you find yourself having to code these dependencies into your rule, you probably should consider leaving that validation rule out of the Validator framework and keeping it in a `validate()` method.

The third question, "Is the logic really a validation rule or is it business logic?" is very much related to the second question. Developers building validation rules for the first time with the Validator framework oftentimes let logic that is better located in the business application tier "slip" into the validation logic.

Always keep the following mind:

- Validation rules are meant to validate data within a field. While you capture interdependencies between field values, do not allow yourself to get carried away with your implementation.

- The Validator framework is supposed to allow you to quickly build web forms. If you find yourself getting bogged down in writing the validation rules for a form, you are probably going beyond the intent of the framework.

- Use the tools like the Validator framework to quickly build your applications, but do not let the structure of your applications become confined by the restrictions imposed by the tools.

- The Validator framework should be extended only when the rule being written is "lightweight" and can be reused across multiple business objects and applications.

Summary

This chapter has introduced you to some of the core pieces of functionality found in the Struts Dynamic Forms and the Jakarta Commons Validator framework features. For Dynamic Forms, we showed you how to

- Declare Dynamic Form beans in the struts-config.xml file.

- Use different implementations of Dynamic Forms, including the following:

  - Extending the `DynamicValidatorForm` to write a Dynamic Form eliminates the need to write individual `get()`/`set()` methods while still allowing the developer to override the `validate()` and `reset()` methods of the `ActionForm`.

  - Using the `DynamicValidatorForm` class without validations allows the development team to use Struts to quickly build a prototype that can then be iteratively converted to an actual application.

We also introduced you to the Struts Jakarta Commons Validator framework and how, when combined with Dynamic Forms, a development team could build web form applications with little-to-no Java code. Specifically, we discussed

- How to set up and configure the Struts/Jakarta Commons Validator plug-in.

- The configuration files used by the Validator plug-in. These files include the following:

  - *validator-rules.xml*: Defines all of the validation rules that are available for use by an application. By default, the Validator framework comes with a number of prepackaged rules. In addition, custom validation rule definitions can be added to this file.

  - *validator.xml*: Defines the Struts form-to-validation rules mapping. Individual fields on a Struts form are mapped to validation rules within this file.

- Mapping a form's fields to validation rules defined in the validator-rules.xml file. Some of the steps involved with mapping validation rules include the following:

  - Set up a `<formset>` tag to define a web form.

  - Define a `<field>` tag to map individual form fields to validation rules.

- Passing additional information to individual field-validation rules, including

  - The error message keys, defined by the `<msg>` tag, used to locate the error messages that will be passed to the end user

  - Any arguments, defined via the `<argX>` tags, that are going to be passed to the error messages when an error is raised

  - Metadata, defined via the `<var>` tags, that help define how the rule is to behave

- Some examples of field-to-validation rule mappings. The two rules that were demonstrated were `required` and `maxlength`.

- How to use the Validator framework in a number of different scenarios, including

  - Using the Validator framework to define validation in combination with a Dynamic Form's `validate()` method

  - Using the Validator framework and Dynamic Forms to eliminate the need for a Java `ActionForm` implementation

- How to extend the Validator framework with custom validation rules. The steps involved with implementing a custom validation rule include the following:

  1. Write the validation rule using a Validation framework–compliant method signature.

  2. Describe the new validation rule in the validator-rules.xml file.

  3. Modify the validation.xml file so the forms actually implement the rule.

We finished the chapter by discussing when it is appropriate to extend the Validator framework with your custom validation rules. We identified three questions that should be asked when trying to make this decision:

- Is the validation rule going to be reused across multiple screens?

- How complex is the validation rule?

- Is the validation rule in question really a validation rule or has some business logic slipped into the validation layer?

In the end, the decision to use Dynamic Forms and the Validator framework comes down to whether or not these tools will work within the architectural context of your application. Not every piece of Struts is going to be right for the project you are working on. Trying to leverage every piece of functionality of the Struts framework will oftentimes lead to a significant increase in the amount of time and energy needed to implement an application.

CHAPTER 8

■■■

Speeding Struts Development with XDoclet

One of the most common complaints voiced by J2EE developers is that writing a J2EE application, even a small application, is a complicated process. These complaints are valid because writing a J2EE application, even a simple JSP/servlet-based application using Plain Old Java Objects (POJOs), requires more than just writing the logic that carries out the user's request. It requires the developer to set up and configure a number of deployment descriptors and configuration files in order for the application to be deployed.

Look at the configuration steps needed to build a JSP/servlet-based application like the JavaEdge application used in this book. Before the JavaEdge application can even be run in a servlet engine like Tomcat, a web.xml file must be written that describes the servlet and maps any calls to the servlet to a URL. Since the JavaEdge application uses a number of third-party JSP tag libraries, the web.xml file must also include the Tag Library Definitions (TLDs) for the tags in the JavaEdge application's web.xml file.

One can argue that setting up a single configuration file like the web.xml file is not a cumbersome burden for a development team to undertake. Now, let's say that you wanted to use stateless session Enterprise JavaBeans (EJBs) to encapsulate the JavaEdge application's business logic and entity EJBs to retrieve and access data. In order to implement the EJBs for the application, you must write for each EJB being used three Java classes (the home and remote interfaces and the bean class that executes the business logic or retrieves and manipulates data), and two deployment descriptors: the application server–independent ejb-jar.xml file and an application server–specific file that describes the EJB to the application server it is running in.

Even if the JavaEdge application used only three stateless session EJBs, the extra overhead involved with writing and implementing the EJBs translates into a total of six Java classes (the remote and home interfaces) and six deployment descriptors. All of this "extra" code and deployment descriptors are needed to deploy the JavaEdge application, but in the end they really amount to nothing more than overhead. Furthermore, the difficulty of writing these EJB deployment descriptors can vary. Writing the deployment descriptors for a stateless session EJB takes very little effort. However, trying to implement the deployment descriptors for an entity EJB using Container Managed Persistence (CMP) and Container Managed Relations (CMR) can turn into an effort of Herculean proportions.

Looking at the JavaEdge application, all of the configuration files and deployment descriptors that have been described are J2EE-specific files. If you start adding in the configuration files needed for using frameworks like Struts (such as struts-config.xml, validation.xml, etc.) and ObjectRelationalBridge (ojb.properties and repository.xml), the complexity of building and deploying the JavaEdge application grows significantly.

One of the fundamental problems of the J2EE development platform is that it has *poor complexity scalability.*

Definition Complexity scalability is the ability for a development platform to remain simple to use even in the face of multiple technologies and development paradigms (thin-client, multitiered, object-oriented). As most J2EE developers will tell you, because J2EE has to remain platform and vendor independent, building enterprise applications on the J2EE platform often requires tremendous amounts of metadata on the application server to run the application.

A development platform has poor complexity scalability as the application becomes more complex; the amount of information needed to get the application running becomes almost unmanageable.

As the number of pieces of a J2EE application increases, the complexity of building and deploying the application does not grow in a proportional manner to the amount of code being written. Instead, the complexity of the application skyrockets because of the additional overhead introduced with all of the configuration and deployment descriptor files. Any J2EE developer who has paid penance in deployment descriptor purgatory[1] can attest to the amount of time and energy wasted on a project that can be traced back to a mistyped entry in a configuration file or a missing deployment descriptor.

What is needed here is a process that allows J2EE application code to be self-describing, so that deployment descriptors and support class files can be generated in a repeatable and consistent fashion. The process needs to be *self-describing* so that metadata needed to deploy the application can be contained within the application code. The process needs to be *repeatable* so that developers can use the same process and procedures to generate their applications. They should not have to jump through hoops to generate the metadata for their application. Whatever is generated should have the same *consistent* look and feel. This makes maintaining the application easier and ensures that every type of deployment descriptor in the application looks the same.

Fortunately, the Java Open Source community has developed a Java code generator that meets these three criteria: XDoclet. XDoclet allows developers to embed custom, non-Sun JavaDoc tags inside of their individual classes that, when run through the XDoclet engine, can be used to generate many of the "support" files need for a J2EE application.

---

1. *Deployment descriptor purgatory* is a state of staring at a screen full of error messages for days only to realize it was not the code that was causing the problem, but the configuration. It is not as bad as Microsoft's DLL hell, but it comes close.

Going through a complete and thorough examination of XDoclet is outside the scope of this book. However, we are going to show you how XDoclet can be used to help simplify many of the common tasks associated with building a Struts-based application. Specifically, this chapter will look at

- How to obtain and install XDoclet

- A conceptual view of how XDoclet generates code and configuration files

- How to use XDoclet to perform such common tasks as

  - Generating an application's web.xml file

  - Automating the creation of common Struts files including the struts-config.xml file and the Struts/Validator framework validation.xml file

Let's begin this exploration of XDoclet by looking at where to obtain and install the XDoclet tool.

Installing XDoclet

To install and use XDoclet, you need to first download the XDoclet distribution from http:// xdoclet.sourceforge.net/xdoclet/index.html. From this site you can download XDoclet in the following forms:

- *The source code distribution*: This distribution includes the XDoclet source code, build scripts, and documentation needed to build the XDoclet tool. This distribution includes several useful samples of how to use various XDoclet tags.

- *The binary distribution*: The binary distribution includes all of the XDoclet libraries already compiled and in a jar format. In addition, all of the documentation and sample source code is included in this distribution.

- *The library distribution*: The library distribution has nothing in it but the XDoclet core and contributor jar files.

All distributions include the considerable number of contributor extensions that have been built around the core XDoclet engine.

The XDoclet engine is invoked from within an Ant script. XDoclet includes several Ant Tasks that allow a developer to control its behavior. However, before just going out and using XDoclet, there are some dependencies that you must take into consideration:

- XDoclet requires the use of Ant 1.5 and higher.

- The tools.jar file from the JDK being used in your project must be in your Ant build script's classpath.

- XDoclet requires the presence of the XJavaDoc engine. XJavaDoc is a clone of the JavaDoc engine included with the JDK distribution. XJavaDoc can be downloaded from http://xdoclet.sourceforge.net/xjavadoc/. The jar file for XJavaDoc must be in your Ant build script's classpath.

- The XDoclet jar files must be visible to your Ant build script's classpath. You can accomplish this in one of three ways:

    - You can copy the XDoclet jar files to your Ant distributions lib directory.

    - You can set the classpath in your Ant build script to point to your unzipped XDoclet directory.

    - You can copy the XDoclet jars to the JavaEdge application's lib/build directory. We chose this route because the JavaEdge Ant script was written to automatically include any jar files present in the lib directory.

Once your XDoclet distribution has been downloaded and placed in a location visible to your Ant build scripts, you can begin using it. However, we are not going to jump right into all of the "gory" details associated with XDoclet. Instead, we will start our conversation about XDoclet with a high-level overview of the tool.

What Exactly Is XDoclet?

XDoclet is built around the concept of Attribute-Oriented Programming (AOP).[2] Simply put, the concept of AOP is to embed metadata, called *attributes* by the XDoclet team, inside of the actual Java source code for an application. This metadata is then read by the XDoclet engine and used to generate additional Java code, configuration files, and/or deployment descriptors.

Note The concepts of metadata attributes are built into the .NET platform. Metadata attributes help developers control the complexity of their applications by providing contextual information about the application to its runtime environment. XDoclet implements metadata attributes by parsing the source code. In JDK 1.5, metadata attributes will be included as part of the base language.

The XDoclet team extended Sun's built-in JavaDoc engine and added several new @ tags that can be used to define application metadata. The best way to understand XDoclet's approach to using JavaDoc-based tags to implement AOP-based programming is to see an example.

If you remember, the MemberFilter class is a servlet filter that checks each incoming HTTP request to see if the user has logged in. In order for the JavaEdge application to use the MemberFilter class, the web.xml file must be configured with two entries. The first entry is a <filter/> tag that describes the Java class that is going to be used to implement the filter. The second tag, <filter-mapping/>, maps the filter described in the <filter/> tag to a URL.

Shown next is the MemberFilter.java class file. This class has been modified to include the XDoclet tags that can be used to generate the <filter/> and <filter-mapping/> tags found inside of the JavaEdge application's web.xml file.

---

2. Attribute-Oriented Programming (AOP) should not be confused with the concept of Aspect-Oriented Programming (AOP). Unfortunately, AOP is often bandied around as an acronym for both concepts even though they really are two separate subjects.

```
package com.apress.javaedge.common;

import java.io.IOException;
import javax.servlet.Filter;
import javax.servlet.FilterChain;
import javax.servlet.FilterConfig;
import javax.servlet.RequestDispatcher;
import javax.servlet.ServletException;
import javax.servlet.ServletRequest;
import javax.servlet.ServletResponse;
import javax.servlet.http.HttpServletRequest;
import javax.servlet.http.HttpSession;

import com.apress.javaedge.member.MemberVO;
import com.apress.javaedge.member.dao.MemberDAO;

/**
 * This MemberFilter will check to see if the user is currently logged in. If
 * they are not logged in, the user will automatically be set up with an
 * anonymous login. This login is defined as the first record in the
 * database.
 *
 * Filter information
 *
 * @author John Carnell
 *
 * ----------------------XDoclet Tags ------------------------------
 * @web.filter name="MemberFilter"
 *     description="Filter for determining who the JavaEdge user is."
 *     display-name="Member Login Filter"
 * @web.filter-mapping servlet-name="MemberFilter"
 *      url-pattern="/execute/*"
 * ----------------------XDoclet Tags ------------------------------
public class MemberFilter implements Filter{

   . . .

}
```

The MemberFilter class just shown is using two XDoclet tags in the preceding source code to generate the <filter/> and <filter-map/> entries: @web.filter and @web.filter-mapping. When this code is run through the XDoclet engine, the following entry is generated in the web.xml file:

```
<?xml version="1.0" encoding="UTF-8"?>
<!DOCTYPE web-app PUBLIC "-//Sun Microsystems, Inc.//DTD Web Application 2.3//EN
" "http://java.sun.com/dtd/web-app_2_3.dtd">

<web-app >
   <distributable/>
```

```
<!--
To use non XDoclet filters, create a filters.xml file that
contains the additional filters (eg Sitemesh) and place it in your
project's merge dir.  Don't include filter-mappings in this file,
include them in a file called filter-mappings.xml and put that in
the same directory.
-->

<filter>
    <filter-name>MemberFilter</filter-name>
    <display-name>Member Login Filter</display-name>
    <description><![CDATA[Filter for determining who the JavaEdge user is.]]><
/description>
    <filter-class>com.apress.javaedge.common.MemberFilter</filter-class>
</filter>

<filter-mapping>
    <filter-name>MemberFilter</filter-name>
    <url-pattern>/execute/*</url-pattern>
</filter-mapping>


    . . .
</web-app>
```

Based on the simple XDoclet example just shown, we can make the following observations:

- To use XDoclet, you do not have not modify any of the actual Java source code. You just need to add some XDoclet tags.

- The XDoclet tags fit cleanly into the application's comments. The metadata for the MemberFilter class is very easy to read and conveys a significant amount of information in a very human readable fashion.[3]

- The inclusion of the web filter XDoclet tags allows you to significantly reduce the complexity of writing the <filter/> and <filter-map/> tags in the web.xml file. Five lines of XDoclet tags allow you to avoid writing ten lines of web.xml text.

These three points should demonstrate that using XDoclet allows a development team to more effectively scale the complexity of their applications. Let's now look at the individual steps that are involved with marking up the example application source code and generating the resulting web.xml file using XDoclet.

---

3. While XML, the format that most configuration files and deployment descriptors are now based on, is human readable, it is oftentimes very obtuse and difficult to follow.

From XDoclet to Source, and All the Steps in Between

Figure 8-1 gives a walkthrough of the steps involved with translating XDoclet metadata tags into Java source code and/or configuration files.

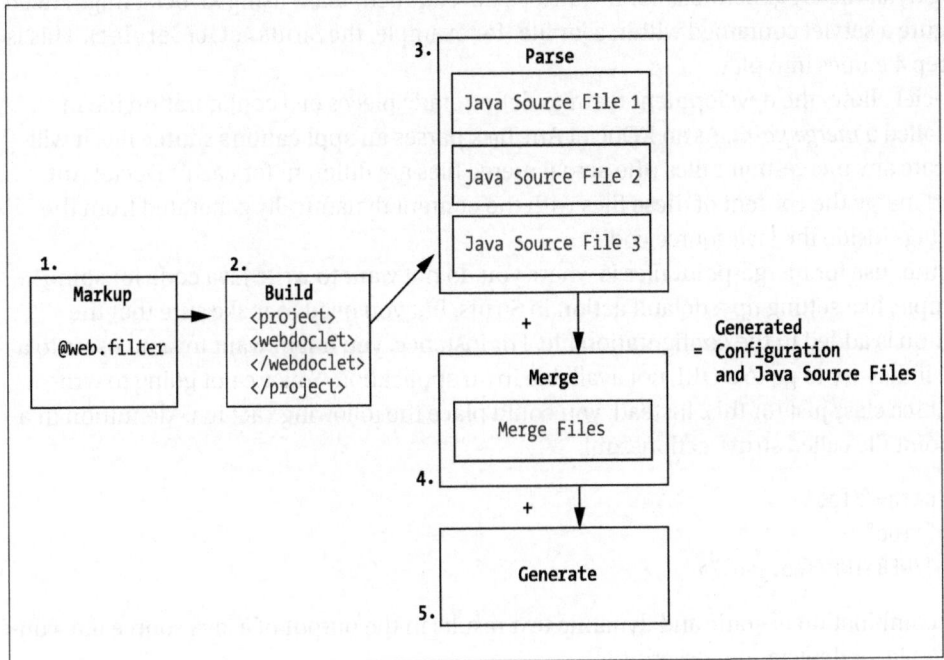

Figure 8-1. *The XDoclet process*

As you saw earlier, step 1 of the process involves the development team marking their Java classes up with XDoclet tags. XDoclet is not a stand-alone code generator; it must be used as part of Ant build script.

■Note We assume you already know how to use Ant. For further information on Ant, please visit http://ant.apache.org.

So in addition to marking up their application code, a development team using XDoclet must modify their Ant build scripts to include an XDoclet Ant Task. (We will be covering some of these build tags later on in the chapter.)

In step 2 of the preceding process, an Ant build script is going to be executed. One or more targets within the Ant build script will contain XDoclet Ant Tasks that will be used to fire off the XDoclet engine. Whenever an XDoclet Ant Task is encountered, the task will kick off two basic processes.

The first process, which is step 3 in Figure 8-1, is the parse process. The XDoclet Ant Task, based on the configuration information contained within it, will search through all of the Java source files and look for the specific set of XDoclet tags associated with the XDoclet task. It will then begin generating either deployment descriptors, configuration files, or source code based on the XDoclets embedded in the application's source code.

Let's not forget though that XDoclet is a code generator. Oftentimes when writing up a configuration file, like a web.xml file, you might need to include static content as part of the file being dynamically generated. For instance, a development team using XDoclet might need to configure a servlet contained within a jar file (for example, the Struts ActionServlet). This is where step 4 comes into play.

XDoclet allows the development team to define static pieces of a configuration file in what is called a *merge point*. As an XDoclet Ant Task parses an application's source file, it will try to locate any merge-point files (the actual merge files are different for each XDoclet Ant Task) and merge the content of these files with the content dynamically generated from the XDoclet tags inside the Java source code.

Another use for merge-point files is where you do not want to write Java code for something simple, like setting up a default action in Struts, but you need to make sure that the information is added to the configuration file. For instance, you might want to send users to a JSP page if they try to go to a URL not available in an application. You are not going to write a Struts Action class just for this. Instead, you could place the following <action> definition in a merge-point file called struts-actions.xml:

```
<action path="/foo"
unknown="true"
forward="/WEB-INF/foo.jsp"/>
```

The combination of static and dynamic text results in the output of a Java source file, configuration file, or deployment descriptor.

Note Remember that XDoclet does not just generate configuration files. Several XDoclet tags (for example, <ejbdoclet....>) actually generate source code. There are even instances where that generated source code can include source from a merge-point file.

If the output is Java source code, the Ant script can compile the source. If the output is a configuration file or a deployment descriptor, the Ant script can then package it and deploy it as a jar, war, or ear file.

We have now walked you through the conceptual process of using XDoclet. Let's revisit the web filter example used earlier in the chapter. We will explore in greater detail

- The available XDoclet tags

- The anatomy of an XDoclet tag

- Setting up and configuring Ant to parse and process XDoclet tags

After we go through this explanation, we will start looking at the Struts XDoclet tags.

The Available XDoclet Tags

The number of XDoclet markup tags and the corresponding functionality they provide is breathtaking and a bit overwhelming. Shown in Table 8-1 is a partial list of the technologies supported by XDoclet.

Table 8-1. *The Different XDoclet Tag Groups*

Technology/Product	Tag Prefixes	Description
Apache SOAP and Apache Struts	@soap @struts	Tags for generating SOAP descriptors, Tstruts-config.xml, and validation.xml
JSP and servlets	@web @jsp	Tags for generating the web.xml and the TTLDs for custom JSP tags
Enterprise JavaBeans	@ejb	Tags for generating EJB remote interfaces, home interfaces, and EJB deployment descriptors
BEA WebLogic	@weblogic	Tags used to generate WebLogic-specific deployment descriptor information
Borland Enterprise Application Server	@bes	Tags used to generate Borland Enterprise Application Server–specific deployment descriptor information
Oracle Container (OC4J)	@oc4j	Tags used to generate Oracle for Java Container for Java–specific deployment descriptor information
IBM WebSphere	@web	Tags used to generate WebSphere-specific deployment descriptor information
JBoss Application Server	@jboss	Tags used to generate JBoss-specific deployment descriptor information
Macromedia's JRun	@jrun	Tags used to generate JRun-specific Application Server deployment descriptor information
Resin JSP/Servlet Engine	@resin	Tags used to generate Resin-specific deployment descriptor information
ExoLab's Castor	@castor	Tags used to generate O/R Mapping Tool Object/Relational mappings for Castor
Hibernate O/R	@hibernate	Tags used to generate Mapping Tool Object/Relational mappings for Hibernate

This list only shows the tag prefixes for each different product or technology set. Each group of products can have literally dozens of XDoclet tags in them. For a full listing of these tags, please visit the XDoclet project site.

While there are literally hundreds of XDoclet tags available for use, they all follow the same basic rules and structures. So let's examine the basic anatomy of an XDoclet tag.

Anatomy of an XDoclet Tag

Three levels of XDoclet tags can be embedded within the source:

- Class-level tags

- Method-level tags

- Field-level tags

Class-level tags are placed outside of the actual Java class definition. They provide meta-data about the entire class. In the MemberFilter.java example shown at the beginning of the chapter, the @web.filter tags are class-level tags.

Method-level tags are tags used to generate configuration information about individual methods in a class. An example of a method-level XDoclet tag would be @struts.validator. This tag is used to map validation rules from the Validator framework to individual setter methods on an ActionForm class.[4] We will be going through the details of @struts.validator and other @struts tags later on in the chapter.

Field-level XDoclet tags are used to provide metadata information about individual properties within Java classes. Frankly, field-level tags are pretty uncommon. We are only aware of one set of XDoclet tags (the @jdo tags) that actually use field-level tags.

Although there are three levels of XDoclet tags, the individual XDoclet tags have the same structure. An XDoclet tag will always consist of a tag name followed by one or more tag attributes. Shown in Figure 8-2 is the @web.filter tag taken from the MemberFilter.java class.

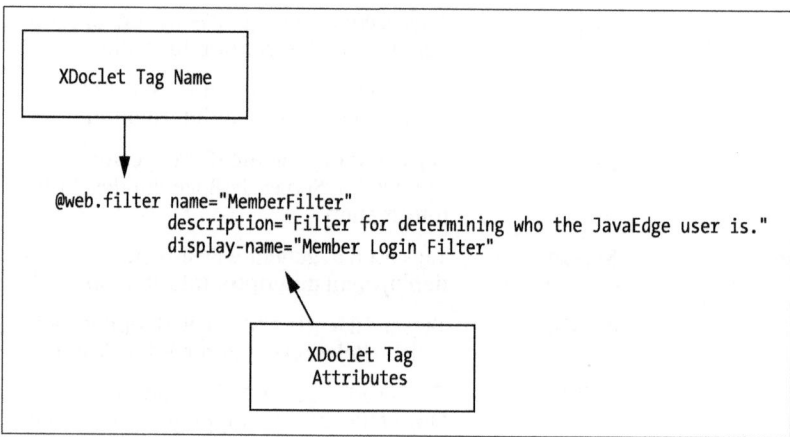

Figure 8-2. *Anatomy of an XDoclet tag*

In the MemberFilter.java example shown earlier in the chapter, we used only a subset of the @web.filter tags and attributes available. Table 8-2 provides a brief summary of all of the @web.filter tags.

---

4.   If you are not familiar with the Validator framework, please review Chapter 7.

Table 8-2. *The @web Tags and Their Descriptions*

Tag Name	Tag Attributes	Tag Description
@web.filter	name: A unique name for the filter. This is a mandatory attribute. display-name: The human-readable display name of the filter. icon: The path and filename of the graphical icon used to represent the filter. description: Description of the filter.	Generates a `<filter>` tag in the web.xml file.
@web.filter-init-param	name: Name of an initialization parameter used by the filter. This is a mandatory attribute. value: The value associated with the parameter. description: Description of the initialization parameter.	Generates an `<init-param>` tag inside of a `<filter>` tag.
@web.filter-mapping	servlet-name: Name of the servlet the web filter is going to be used with. url-pattern: URL pattern that the filter will be used against.	Generates a `<filter-mapping>` tag with the appropriate `<filter-name>` and `<url-pattern>` tags.

This table only shows the @web tags used for building filter entries in the JavaEdge application's web.xml file. There are a number of additional XDoclet tags in the @web tags collection that we have not covered. For full details, please visit the XDoclet site for a complete listing of these tags.

Up until this point, we have looked at how to use the @web.filter tags to mark up the MemberFilter.java class. Let's look at how to actually integrate XDoclet into the JavaEdge application. The integration of Ant and XDoclet, along with the @web tag material we just covered, will lay the foundation for our discussions about the XDoclet @struts tags.

Integrating Ant and XDoclet

XDoclet currently has seven Ant Tasks that can be used for code generation. Each of these tasks has a number different properties and nested elements available in them, including those listed in Table 8-3.

Table 8-3. *The Different XDoclet Tag Groups*

Task Name	Task Description
`<doclet.../>`	The `<doclet/>` task is the base Ant Task for all of the preceding tasks. It can be used to execute an XDoclet template that is not covered by any of the other tasks. XDoclet allows developers to write their own code-generation templates. For further information on writing your own XDoclet templates, please refer to the XDoclet web site (http://xdoclet.sourceforge.net/xdoclet/index.html).
`<ejbdoclet..../>`	Used for carrying out various EJB-related tasks, including generating EJB remote interfaces, EJB home interfaces, and EJB deployment descriptors for a wide variety of application servers.

Continued

Table 8-3. *Continued*

Task Name	Task Description
`<hibernatedoclet..../>`	Generates Object/Relational (O/R) mappings for the open source tool Hibernate (`http://www.hibernate.org/`).
`<jdodoclet..../>`	Tasks for generating Java Data Objects (JDO) O/R mappings. JDO is a Sun Microsystems vendor-neutral specification for building a persistence tier. For more information on JDO, please visit `http://java.sun.com/products/jdo`.
`<jmxdoclet..../>`	Specifies tasks for generating Java Management Extensions (JMX) classes. JMX is a Sun Microsystems API for building monitoring, instrumenting, and managing Java-based devices, applications, and networks. For more information on JMX, please visit `http://java.sun.com/products/JavaManagement/index.html`.
`<mockdoclet..../>`	Generates mock objects for use in testing. Mock objects provide a testing framework that allows developers to test to common Java interfaces. Mock objects allow a developer to simulate the behavior of an object without having to actually fire off an implementation.
`<webdoclet..../>`	Used for generating a number of web application–related tasks. This Ant Task can generate multiple application-specific web.xml files. In addition, this task is used by the `@struts` library to generate struts-config.xml and validation.xml files.

Obviously, we cannot cover all of the details associated with the tasks listed in Table 8-3. Instead, we will pick one tag, `<webdoclet..../>`, and demonstrate how it is used. The `<webdoclet..../>` tag can be used to generate not only an application's web.xml file, but also a Struts-based application's struts-config.xml and validation.xml file.

Let's start by writing a simple Ant target called `generate-source`. The `generate-source` target will use the `<webdoclet..../>` tag to parse through all of the Java source files in the JavaEdge application and generate a web.xml file based on the `@web` tags found within the source.

Shown here is the `generate-source` target:

```
<target name="generate-source">
    <mkdir dir="${build.generated.dir}"/>
    <taskdef name="webdoclet" classname="xdoclet.modules.web.WebDocletTask"
            classpathref="compile.classpath"/>

    <webdoclet
      destdir="${build.generated.dir}"
      mergedir="${src.web.dir}/WEB-INF/mergedir"
      force="true">

      <fileset dir=""${src.java.dir}">
         <include name="**/*.java"/>
      </fileset>
      <deploymentdescriptor servletspec="2.3" destdir="${build.generated.dir}">
         <taglib uri="http://java.sun.com/jstl/ea/core"
                location="/WEB-INF/c.tld" />
```

```
        </deploymentdescriptor>
      </webdoclet>
</target>
```

The first thing the generate-source target does is create a temporary directory where the generated files are stored. This temporary directory is set in the Ant property build.generated. property.

Tip The temporary directory that is built by XDoclet is not deleted after each run. If you are using CVS, you will see it note these files every time you run a cvs diff command against your source directory. To avoid this, make sure you include the temporary directory used by XDoclet in the .cvsignore file.

This Ant property is defined at the beginning of the JavaEdge build.xml script.

Next, you define the <webdoclet....> tag using the Ant <taskdef> tag:

```
<taskdef name="webdoclet" classname="xdoclet.modules.web.WebDocletTask"
            classpathref="compile.classpath"/>
```

The <taskdef> tag just shown defines a new tag, <webdoclet..../>, that can be used within the generate-src task. The name of the tag is defined by the <taskdef> tag's name attribute. The classname attribute (in this case xdoclet.modules.web.WebDocletTask) is used to define the fully defined Java class name of the Java class that will be executed when the <webdoclet..../> tag is seen within the generate-src task. The <taskdef/> tag's classpathref defines an Ant reference that holds the classpath for the script. The jar files from the XDoclet distribution must be part of this classpath.

Note Remember, XDoclet is not part of the Apache Ant distribution. By using the Ant Task <taskdef>, you expose the various XDoclet Java classes that are used to implement an Ant Task to your Ant build scripts.

The sample directory in the XDoclet source and binaries distribution contains a build.xml file that demonstrates how to set up not only the <webdoclet..../> Ant Task, but also all of the other XDoclet Ant Tasks.

The <webdoclet..../> task has a number of attributes that must be set in order to use the tag:

```
<webdoclet
        destdir="${build.generated.dir}"
        mergedir="${src.web.dir}/WEB-INF/mergedir"
        force="true">

    . . .

</webdoclet>
```

The first attribute, destdir, tells the <webdoclet..../> task where to place all of the files generated. The mergedir attribute is used to tell XDoclet the location of all the merge-point files that hold the static content that needs to be included in the generated web.xml file when the <webdoclet..../> task executes.

The <webdoclet..../> task's force attribute tells the <webdoclet..../> tag to always parse and generate its source and configuration files. Normally, the <webdoclet/> tag will compare the time stamp on the source files against the generated files. If the time stamps are the same and the force attribute is not set or is set to false, the <webdoclet..../> task will not generate any files.

Tip You don't need to set the force attribute to true, because you can still use the previously generated files. Having this attribute set to true does not hurt for smaller projects, but once the number of files to be processed increases, the time for XDoclet to process them gets unpleasantly long. Set the force attribute to true only when you want to always guarantee you have the latest generated files.

A <webdoclet..../> task can contain a number of different nested elements. We are only going to examine the nested elements currently shown in the generate-src Ant target. The first nested element is a <fileset/> element:

```
<fileset dir="${src.java.dir}">
    <include name="**/*.java"/>
</fileset>
```

The <fileset> element tells the <webdoclet..../> task where and what source files should be parsed when the <webdoclet..../> task is executed. The <fileset/> element used in the generate-src task tells the <webdoclet..../> tag to parse all files located in the JavaEdge source directory.

The <webdoclet..../> tag can generate many different files. If you want the <webdoclet..../> tag to generate the web.xml file for an application, you need to embed the <deploymentdescriptor/> element inside of it:

```
<deploymentdescriptor servletspec="2.3" destdir="${build.generated.dir}">
  <taglib uri="http://java.sun.com/jstl/ea/core" location="/WEB-INF/c.tld" />
</deploymentdescriptor>
```

The preceding <deploymentdescriptor/> element tells the <webdoclet..../> tag to generate a web.xml file that is compliant with the 2.3 version of the servlet specification. The generated web.xml file is placed in the directory defined by the build.generated.dir property.

Both the <webdoclet..../> and <deploymentdescriptor/> tags have a significant number of additional parameters and nested elements. Please refer to the XDoclet documentation for further details.

Using Merge Points

As explained earlier, XDoclet is a code generator. However, there are several instances where you need to incorporate static content into the files being generated. This static content is located as fragments of text stored inside of various files called merge-point files. The actual names of the individual merge-point files will vary for each different XDoclet task and their corresponding nested elements. For the `<webdoclet..../>` tag, you can have the merge-point files listed in Table 8-4.

Table 8-4. *The XDoclet Merge-Point Files*

Filename	File Description
filter-mappings.xml	Contains all non–XDoclet-generated filter mappings
filters.xml	Contains all non–XDoclet-generated filter definitions
listeners.xml	Contains all non–XDoclet-generated servlet listener definitions
mime-mapping.xml	Contains all of the MIME-type mappings for a web.xml file
error-page.xml	Contains any error page mappings used for the application
welcomefiles.xml	Contains the welcome file definitions used for the application
web-security.xml	Contains all non–XDoclet-generated security mappings for the application
servlet-mappings.xml	Contains all non–XDoclet-generated servlet mappings
servlets.xml	Contains all non-XDoclet servlet definitions

XDoclet and Struts

The Struts framework is an extremely powerful tool for building applications. Its use of metadata gives you an unprecedented amount of flexibility in building applications that are modular, easy to change, and more importantly extensible. However, the creation and maintenance of the metadata files needed by a Struts application (that is, the struts-config.xml file, the validation.xml file, etc.) can be a tedious, time-consuming, and error-prone process.

The reason for this again ties back to the idea of *complexity scalability*. The bigger and more complex the application being built around the Struts framework, the more metadata that is needed. This increase in the amount of metadata leads to greater opportunities for configuration errors and in turn lost evenings and weekends.

Fortunately, the XDoclet tool provides you with a number of XDoclet tags that can be embedded inside of your Struts classes (that is, the `Action` and `ActionForm` classes) to simplify the process of generating your Struts configuration files. Over the next several sections in this chapter, we will be looking at how to use the XDoclet Struts tags to perform such common tasks as

- Declaring Struts form beans within the struts-config.xml file

- Declaring Struts actions within the struts-config.xml file

- Declaring application exceptions within the struts-config.xml file

- Mapping validation rules from the Validator framework to a Struts `Action` class

- Modifying the `<webdoclet..../>` tag to generate the Struts metadata files

Declaring Struts Form Beans

As you saw in Chapter 3, in order to set up a web form to collect data from an end user, you need to write an ActionForm class to hold the data submitted by the user and then add a `<form-bean/>` tag to the application's struts-config.xml file. Once this `<form-bean/>` entry has been added, it can be used in an `<action/>` tag's name attribute.

You can automate the creation of the `<form-bean/>` entry in the struts-config.xml file by using the XDoclet's @struts-form tag. This tag is a class-level tag and is extremely easy to implement within an ActionForm class. Following is the PostStoryForm.java class using the @struts-form tag:

```
package com.apress.javaedge.struts.story;

/**
 * Standard Struts class that collects data submitted by the end user.
 * @author jcarnell
 *
 * ----------XDoclet Tag----------------
 * @struts.form name="postStoryForm"
 * -----------------------------------
 */
public class PostStoryForm extends ActionForm {}
```

In the preceding example, the @struts.form will generate a `<form-bean/>` in the JavaEdge application's struts-config.xml file that looks something like this:

```
<form-beans>
  <form-bean name="postStoryForm" type=③
     "com.apress.javaedge.struts.story.PostStoryForm"/>
     ....
</form-beans>
```

The name attribute in the preceding `<form-bean/>` entry corresponds to the name attribute set on the @strut.form XDoclet tag. XDoclet picks up the `<form-bean/>` tag's type attribute when the tool is parsing the PostStoryForm.java file.

If you have any `<form-bean/>` tags that are not generated by XDoclet, they can be defined as a merge-point file called struts-forms.xml. The content of this merge-point file will be included immediately following any `<form-bean/>` tags generated by XDoclet.

Now that you have seen how to generate `<form-bean/>` tags using XDoclet, we will show you how to use the @struts.action tag embedded within your Action classes to generate `<action/>` tags within the JavaEdge application's struts-config.xml file.

Declaring Struts Actions

The XDoclet @struts.action tag can be a bit intimidating when you first encounter it within the XDoclet documentation. Although it does have a large number of attributes, you will find that many of these attributes map to attributes that already have to be defined for a Struts `<action/>` tag. If you look at the PostStoryAction class shown here, you will see that this is the case:

```
/**
 * @author jcarnell
 *
 * Struts Action class used to submit a story by the end user.
 *
 *---------------XDoclet Tags--------------------
 * @struts.action path="/postStory"
 *                input="/WEB-INF/jsp/postStory.jsp"
 *                name="postStoryForm"
 *                scope="request"
 *                validate="true"
@struts.action-forward name="poststory.success" path="/execute/homePageSetup"
*@struts.action-exception *type="com.apress.javaedge.common.ApplicationException"
*path="/WEB-INF/jsp/systemError.jsp"
 *                                              key="error.system"
 *---------------XDoclet Tags--------------------
 */
public class PostStory extends Action {}
```

To generate an `<action/>` tag, you need to use two different XDoclet @struts tags: @struts.action and @struts.action-forward.

The @struts.action tag generates the `<action/>` tag and its corresponding attributes. All of the attributes on the @struts.action tag map to the corresponding attributes on the `<action/>` tag.[5]

```
* @struts.action path="/postStory"
*                input="/WEB-INF/jsp/postStory.jsp"
*                name="postStoryForm"
*                scope="request"
*                validate="true"
```

In addition to the @struts.action tag just shown, a @struts.action-forward tag is also defined. The @struts.action-forward tag will generate a `<forward/>` tag inside of the `<action/>` tag for the class.

```
* @struts.action-forward name="poststory.success" path="/execute/homePageSetup"
```

A class using the @struts.action tag can also have multiple @struts.action-forward tags defining different forwards that the `<action/>` tag can redirect the user to. Now, when the PostStory.java class is processed by XDoclet, it will generate the following `<action/>` and `<forward/>` tag entries:

```
<action
      path="/postStory"
      type="com.apress.javaedge.struts.poststory.PostStory"
      name="postStoryForm"
      scope="request"
```

5. If you need to review the attributes available on the `<action/>` tag, please refer to Chapter 2.

```
        input="/WEB-INF/jsp/postStory.jsp"
        unknown="false"
        validate="true"
    >
    <forward name="poststory.success"
             path="/execute/homePageSetup"
             redirect="false"/>
</action>
```

One question you might have at this point is how to generate `<global-forwards/>` tags for an application's struts-config.xml file. The short answer is you cannot use XDoclet tags to accomplish this. Instead, you must place all of your tag definitions inside of a merge-point file called `global-forwards.xml`.

XDoclet and Java Inheritance

One thing you need to be aware of when using the Struts tags is that when using an object hierarchy in your actions, you cannot define XDoclet tags on the superclass, because XDoclet will not allow you to change the tasks on subclasses. Consider this source code:

```
/**
 * @struts.action...
 */
public class FooSetupActionBase extends Action { }
and
/**
 * @struts.action tags will not be processed correctly.
 */
public class FooSetupAction extends FooSetupActionBase { }
```

This is not very common, but it can be very annoying when the application is not working because the struts-config.xml is not being generated properly.

Declaring Application Exceptions

Remember from our discussion in Chapter 4 that it is possible to tell the Struts framework to capture and process exceptions on your behalf. This frees your development team from having to clutter their Action classes with try..catch{} blocks that do nothing more than redirect the end user to an error page.

Remember, you can declare two types of exception handlers in Struts. The first type is a global exception handler that will be used to catch registered exceptions against all Action classes within the application. The second type is a local exception handler that can cause Struts to capture and process a specific exception on a specific Action class. If you want to use global exception handlers with XDoclet, you have to place them in a merge-point file called global-exceptions.xml.

You can use the @struts.action-exception XDoclet tag to mark up individual Action classes where you want to use the local exception handlers. In the XDoclet markup for the PostStory class, you can see this XDoclet tag in use:

```
*@struts.action-exception
* type="com.apress.javaedge.common.ApplicationException"
* path="/WEB-INF/jsp/systemError.jsp"
* key="error.system"
```

When the @struts.action-exception just shown is processed via XDoclet, the following code is generated. The code from the @struts.action-exception tag appears in bold.

```
<action path="/postStory"
        type="com.apress.javaedge.struts.poststory.PostStory"
        name="postStoryForm"
        scope="request"
        input="/WEB-INF/jsp/postStory.jsp"
        unknown="false"
        validate="true">
    <exception key="error.system"
    type="com.apress.javaedge.common.ApplicationException"
    path="/WEB-INF/jsp/systemError.jsp"/>

    <forward name="poststory.success"
             path="/execute/homePageSetup"
             redirect="false"/>
</action>
```

The @struts.action-exception tag has a number of different attributes associated with it. We only show three of these attributes (type, path, and key), but Table 8-5 summarizes all of the attributes in the @struts.action-exception tag.

Table 8-5. *The Attributes in the @struts.action-exception XDoclet Tag*

Attribute Name	Attribute Description
className	The fully qualified Java class name for the configuration bean for your ExceptionHandler. This is not a mandatory attribute and is usually only used when you write your own custom handler to process exceptions. If you do not write your own custom ExceptionHandler, the default Struts ExceptionHandler will be used for the exception handler in the generated struts-config.xml file.
handler	The fully qualified Java class name for a custom exception handler. This attribute is only used if you subclass the Struts ExceptionHandler to provide your own exception processing.
key	Name of the resource bundle that will retrieve the error message associated with this exception. This is a mandatory field.
path	A relative URL that the end user will be directed to if this exception is raised. Usually this will be some kind of neatly formatted error screen.
scope	The context in which the ActionError class for this object is accessed. The value can be either request or session.
type	The fully qualified Java class name of the exception that is going to be caught and processed when thrown by the action. This is a mandatory field.

Building struts-config.xml Using

At this point, we have examined the majority of the XDoclet @struts tags and how they can be used to mark up the Struts classes. Now, let's modify the generate-src Ant target shown earlier in the chapter to actually generate the struts-config.xml file for the JavaEdge application.

To do this, you need to add a new nested element to the task inside the generate-src target. This nested element, called , appears in bold in the following code example:

```
<target name="generate-src">
     <mkdir dir="${build.generated.dir}"/>
     <taskdef name="webdoclet" classname="xdoclet.modules.web.WebDocletTask"
                classpathref="compile.classpath"/>

     <webdoclet
       destdir="${build.generated.dir}"
       mergedir="${src.web.dir}/WEB-INF/mergedir"
       force="true">

       <fileset dir="${src.java.dir}">
          <include name="**/*.java"/>
       </fileset>
       <deploymentdescriptor servletspec="2.3" destdir="${build.generated.dir}">
            <taglib uri="http://java.sun.com/jstl/ea/core"
                    location="/WEB-INF/c.tld" />
       </deploymentdescriptor>

       <strutsconfigxml
         destdir="${build.generated.dir}"
         validatexml="true"
         version="1.1"/>
     </webdoclet>
</target>
```

The presence of the <strutsconfigxml> tag tells the <webdoclet..../> tag to parse all of the Java source files and generate a struts-config.xml file. The <strutsconfigxml/> tag has a large number of attributes associated with it. However, for the purposes of our discussion, we will only focus on the three attributes shown previously.

The <strutsconfigxml/> tag's destdir attribute tells the <strutsconfigxml/> tag where to generate the struts-config.xml file. The validatexml attribute indicates to the <strutsconfigxml/> tag whether or not to validate the form using XML or DTD for the struts-config.xml file. The version of the XML or DTD file is specified in the version attribute for the <strutsconfigxml/> tag.

The <strutsconfigxml/> file has a number of merge-point files where static and non–XDoclet-generated code can be placed. These files are listed in Table 8-6.

Table 8-6. *The Merge-Point Files for the @struts XDoclet Tags*

Filename	Description
global-exceptions.xml	Holds any global exceptions for the application. Remember, XDoclet can only generate local exception handlers. Any global exceptions for your applications must go in this file.
global-forwards.xml	Holds any of the global forwards needed within the Struts application.
struts-actions.xml	Holds any non–XDoclet-generated action definitions that the developer wants to be included in the struts-config.xml file.
struts-actions.xml	Holds any non–XDoclet-generated XDoclet `<action>` tags.
struts-data-sources.xml	Defines any data sources made available through Struts. We do not use the Struts data source capability for the JavaEdge application. For further information on this, please refer to the Struts documentation.
struts-forms.xml	Holds any form bean information not generated by XDoclet. Any `DynamicActionForms` defined in a Struts application must be placed in here.
struts-plugins.xml	Holds all `<plug-in>` information that needs to be included in the struts-config.xml file.

XDoclets and the Validator Framework

Another area in which the `@struts` XDoclet tags can be used is for generating the validation.xml files for use by the Validator framework. The `@struts` XDoclet tags can be embedded inside of an application's Struts form beans and used to indicate which Validator validation rules should be enforced against a particular property on an `ActionForm`.

If you have read the previous chapter on the Validator framework and actually tried to use the code examples, you quickly get a sense for how much configuration work needs to be done to set up a large number of `ActionForm` classes in an application. The Validator framework is a powerful framework, but the configuration files used to run it can quickly become very large and unmanageable.

There are two `@struts` XDoclet tags that are used in marking up a Struts form bean for Validator functionality. All of these tags are method-level tags that are placed on the `setter()` tags of the form bean:

- `@struts.validator`: Used to indicate what validation rules will be enforced against the property. This XDoclet tag will generate the `<field/>` tag for a `<form/>` tag inside of the validation.xml file.

- `@struts.validator-var`: Used to generate the `<var/>` tags for a `<form/>` tag inside of the validation.xml file.

Shown here is the `PostStoryValidatorForm` class using the `@struts.validator` and `@struts.validator-var` tag. In the interest of space and trees, we are only going to show the markup for the `storyTitle` attribute.

```
package com.apress.javaedge.struts.poststory;

import javax.servlet.http.HttpServletRequest;
```

```
import org.apache.struts.action.ActionError;
import org.apache.struts.action.ActionErrors;
import org.apache.struts.action.ActionMapping;
import org.apache.struts.action.ActionServlet;
import org.apache.struts.util.MessageResources;
import org.apache.struts.validator.ValidatorForm;
import com.apress.javaedge.common.VulgarityFilter;


/**
 * @author   John Carnell
 * @struts.form name="postStoryValidatorForm"
 */
public class PostStoryValidatorForm extends ValidatorForm {


    . . . .


/** Setter for property storyTitle.
     * @param storyTitle New value of property storyTitle.
     * @struts.validator type="required"
     *                   msgkey="error.poststory.field.null"
     *
     * @struts.validator type="maxlength"
     *                   msgkey="error.poststory.field.length"
     *                   arg1value="${var:maxlength}"
     *
     * @struts.validator type="vulgaritychecker"
     *                        msgkey="error.vulgarity"
     *
     * @struts.validator-var name="maxlength" value="100"
     * @struts.validator-var name="vulgarities" value="dummy,stupid,ninny"
     */
    public void setStoryTitle(java.lang.String storyTitle) {
        this.storyTitle = storyTitle;
    }
}
```

The first thing that should be pointed out is that if you want to use the @struts Validator XDoclet tags, you need to make sure that you extend the ValidatorForm class:

```
public class PostStoryValidatorForm extends ValidatorForm {}
```

The @struts Validator tags will only be processed on classes that extend the ValidatorForm class. You cannot use these tags with dynamic action forms. Even if you mark up a DynaActionForm class with the @struts.validator tags, XDoclet will ignore the embedded XDoclet tags.

The @struts Validator tags are method-level tags and are defined *only* on the set() methods of the Struts form bean being marked up. Three validation rules are being applied against the storyTitle attribute: required, maxlength, and vulgaritychecker. Each validation rule is represented by one @strut.validator tag:

```
* @struts.validator type="required"
*                    msgkey="error.poststory.field.null"
*
* @struts.validator type="maxlength"
*                    msgkey="error.poststory.field.length"
*                    arg1value="${var:maxlength}"
*
*
* @struts.validator type="vulgaritychecker"
*                    msgkey="error.vulgarity"
```

The type attribute for the @struts.validator tag is used to indicate the name of the validation rule that is going to be executed against the form bean property. The value that is placed in this attribute is not cross-referenced with the actual validation-defined rules in the validator-rules.xml file. You need to be careful here because a typo while entering the validation rule name will be propagated to the validation.xml file.

The msgkey attribute defines the key inside of the ApplicationResources.properties file that will be used to look up the text returned to the user if an error arises. Each @struts.validator tag can define arguments to be passed to the error message being raised by using the argXresource and argXvalue attributes.

Remember from our discussion in Chapter 7 on the Validator framework that you can pass in up to four arguments to an error message being raised by a validation rule. The actual names of the attributes are

- arg0resource/arg0value

- arg1resource/arg1value

- arg2resource/arg2value

- arg3resource/arg3value

These arguments allow you to customize the message being raised. When you are writing your @struts.validate tag, you should specify either the argXresource *or* the argXValue, but not both. The reason why is that the argXresource tag is used to define a key of an argument value residing in the application's resource bundle (that is, the ApplicationResources.properties file). If you use the argXvalue attribute, you are telling the @struts.validate tag to pass in the literal value being defined in the tag. In the case of the maxlength validation rule, by setting the arg1value attribute equal to "${var:maxlength}", an entry in the validation.xml file will be generated that tells the Validator framework *not* to look in the ApplicationResources.properties file for the value to pass to the error message. Instead, the value set in the <var> tag for the maxlength variable, which we will be discussing shortly, will be passed in.

ARGUMENT ANNOYANCES

In the Validator framework, if you do not specify a `name` attribute on the `<argX>` tag inside of `<field>`, the value of that argument would be passed to all of the error messages raised during the validation of that particular field. Typically, this "global" argument would be used for the first argument, `<arg0>`, to define the name of the field being validated.

Unfortunately, there is no way of defining a global argument using `@struts.validator` XDoclet tags. The `@struts.validator` tags will automatically generate a `name` attribute on the `<argX>` tag, thereby tying the argument to the particular validation rule being generated for the field.

Now here is where things really get irritating. If you do not define an `arg0resource` or `arg0value` on a field, the `@struts.validator` tag will automatically generate a global `<arg0>` tag for the field tag with the key attribute being `classname.propertyname`. *There is no way to override this* `key` *attribute*. Remember from Chapter 7 that all of the `<arg0>` tags were defined with no `name` attribute, which made the argument global to all validation rules on the field, and then a `key` attribute was used to look up the name of the field in the ApplicationResources.properties file.

The reason we bring this up is because one of us spent several hours wondering why the name of his fields would not show up in his error messages. So, for the `<arg0>` tag contained within your `<field>` tag, you have two choices. You can choose to let the `@struts.validator` XDoclet generate your `<arg0>` tag by not supplying an `arg0resource` or `arg0value` attribute for any of the `@struts.validator` tags for the field. However, you then need to make sure that you have a key in your ApplicationResources.properties file that matches the key generated by the `@struts.validator` tag.

The alternative, if you do not want to have the `@struts.validator` tag generate the name of the resource key used to look up `arg0`, is to define an `arg0resource` attribute for each one of the `@struts.validator` tags associated with the field.

Table 8-7 shows a summary of all of the attributes for the `@struts.validator` XDoclet tag.

Table 8-7. *Attributes of the @struts-validator XDoclet Tag*

Tag Attribute	Description
arg0resource	The first argument that can be passed into the error message for the validation rule. The value passed in is the key to look up the argument from the application's resource bundle. The first argument should always be the name of the field being validated.
arg0value	The first argument that can be passed into the error message for the validation rule. This will pass in a literal value to the error message and not use the application's resource bundle.
arg1resource	The second argument that can be passed into the error message for the validation rule. The value passed in is the key to look up the argument from the application's resource bundle.
arg1value	The second argument that can be passed into the error message for the validation rule. This will pass in a literal value to the error message and not use the application's resource bundle.
arg2resource	The third argument that can be passed into the error message for the validation rule. The value passed in is the key to look up the argument from the application's resource bundle.

Tag Attribute	Description
arg2value	The third argument that can be passed into the error message for the validation rule. This will pass in a literal value to the error message and not use the application's resource bundle.
arg3resource	The fourth argument that can be passed into the error message for the validation rule. The value passed in is the key to look up the argument from the application's resource bundle.
arg3value	The fourth argument that can be passed into the error message for the validation rule. This will pass in a literal value to the error message and not use the application's resource bundle.
msgkey	The key in the application's resource bundle that will be used to look up the error message when the validation rule for the field is violated.
type	The name of the validation rule that is going to be fired off.

When the Validator framework is validating a field, there can be zero or more variables that are passed into the validation rules. These variables are used to control the behavior of the validation rules. For example, when associating the maxlength validation rule within a <field> tag in the validation.xml file, you need to define a <var> tag that contains the name of the variable via a <var-name> tag and a numeric value defined in the <var-value> tag that represents the maximum length to be enforced.

XDoclet provides the @struts.validator-var tag to help generate all of these tags. In the example shown earlier, two variables, maxlength and vulgarities, were defined that will be made available to all validations being fired against the storyTitle attribute:

```
* @struts.validator-var name="maxlength" value="100"
* @struts.validator-var name="vulgarities" value="dummy,stupid,ninny"
```

The @struts.validator tag has two attributes associated with it: name and value. The @struts.validator-var will generate the <var> tag inside of a <field> tag and its two attributes, name and value, will generate the <var-name> and <var-value> tags inside of the <var> tag.

Generating the Validator Tags from Ant

Once you have marked up the Java source files in your project, you need to modify your <webdoclet..../> task to tell it to generate the validation.xml file. This can be accomplished by adding <strutsvalidationxml/> to the <webdoclet..../> target. Shown here is the revised <webdoclet..../> target for the generate-src tag:

```
<target name="generate-src">
    <mkdir dir="${build.generated.dir}"/>
    <taskdef name="webdoclet" classname="xdoclet.modules.web.WebDocletTask"
            classpathref="compile.classpath"/>

    <webdoclet
      destdir="${build.generated.dir}"
      mergedir="${src.web.dir}/WEB-INF/mergedir"
      force="true">
```

```
            <fileset dir="${src.java.dir}">
                <include name="**/*.java"/>
            </fileset>
            <deploymentdescriptor servletspec="2.3" destdir="${build.generated.dir}">
                <taglib uri="http://java.sun.com/jstl/ea/core"
                        location="/WEB-INF/c.tld" />
            </deploymentdescriptor>

            <strutsconfigxml validatexml="true" version="1.1"/>
            <strutsvalidationxml/>
        </webdoclet>
    </target>
```

On the `<strutsvalidationxml/>` tag, you can define the `destdir` and `mergedir` attributes to tell the tag where to generate the validation.xml file and the location of any merge files.[6] If you do not define these attributes, as in the preceding example, the `<strutsvalidationxml/>` tag will automatically read the values for these attributes from the `<webdoclet..../>` tag.

After adding the `<strutsvalidationxml/>` tag to the `<webdoclet..../>` tag, you can invoke the generate-src target in your Ant script. If you look in your destination directory, you should now see a validation.xml file. The file should look like this:

```
<?xml version="1.0" encoding="ISO-8859-1" ?>
<!DOCTYPE form-validation
PUBLIC "-//Apache Software Foundation//DTD ③
  Commons Validator Rules Configuration 1.0//EN"③
  "http://jakarta.apache.org/commons/dtds/③
  validator_1_0.dtd">

<form-validation>
  <!--
    Define global validation config in validation-global.xml
  -->
  <formset>
      <form name="postStoryValidatorForm">
            <field property="storyTitle"
                   depends="required,maxlength,vulgaritychecker">
                <msg name="required" key="error.poststory.field.null"/>
                <msg name="maxlength" key="error.poststory.field.length"/>
                <msg name="vulgaritychecker" key="error.vulgarity"/>

                <arg0 key="postStoryValidatorForm.storyTitle"/>
                <arg1 name="maxlength" key="${var:maxlength}"
                resource="false"/>
                <var>
                  <var-name>maxlength</var-name>
```

---

6. The `@struts.validate` tags only have one merge file called validation-global.xml. This file contains Ant validation rules that are global to all forms in the application.

```
                   <var-value>100</var-value>
               </var>
               <var>
                   <var-name>vulgarities</var-name>
                   <var-value>dummy,stupid,ninny</var-value>
               </var>
           </field>
            ..
       </form>
   </formset>
</form-validation>
```

Summary

Ultimately, the goal of XDoclet is to simplify the process of application development by making the metadata associated with J2EE application development self-contained inside of the actual Java source.

This greatly simplifies the management of any configuration files needed by the application. For example, developers who are not using XDoclet and need to rename an Action class within their application must manually check the application's struts-config.xml file. As developers who have paid the price of deployment descriptor hell, we can say without a doubt that sooner or later you are bound to miss at least one reference to that action and spend inordinate amounts of time debugging the application.

In addition, using XDoclet greatly simplifies the management of configuration files by a team of individuals. Nothing is more boring or annoying than having to resolve all of the conflicts in a web.xml file being committed to CVS because all the developers in a team have each modified the file.

The XDoclet team built XDoclet so that it was easily extensible and customizable. At its core the XDoclet engine is a templating engine that allows developers to write their own code "templates" and Java classes to process their own customer JavaDoc-style @ tags. Because of the extensible nature of XDoclet's architecture, XDoclet can automate most J2EE development tasks across a number of different application servers and provide additional functionality for a wide variety for Java Open Source development frameworks.

It is impossible to capture all of the intricacies of XDoclet in a single chapter. However, we have given you a brief overview of XDoclet and how it can be used to build Struts-based applications.

Specifically, we covered the following topics:

- The basic XDoclet architecture. We looked at how tags were processed and also looked at the three different XDoclet tag levels:

  - Class-level tags

  - Method-level tags

  - Field-level tags

- How to install and configure XDoclet

- How to build your web.xml file using XDoclet. We specifically looked at using XDoclet to

  - Generate filter entries in the web.xml file

  - Use merge-point files to include static and non–XDoclet-generated content in the web.xml file

- How to build your struts-config.xml file using XDoclet. Specifically, we looked at how to generate:

  - The `<form-bean>` tag entries using the `@struts.form-bean` XDoclet tags

  - The `<action>` tag entries using the `@struts.action` XDoclet tags

  - The `<action-forward>` tags for an `<action>` by using the `@struts.action-forward` tag

  - Local action exception handlers using the `@struts.action-exception` tags

- Generating a validation.xml file for use with the Validator framework. The XDoclet tags we looked at included

  - The `@struts.validator` tag for generating a field/validation rule mapping

  - The `@struts.validator-arg` tag for generating `<args>` tags within a `<field>` tag in the validation.xml file

  - The `@struts.validator-var` tag for generating `<var>` tags for passing information into a field/validation rule mapping

- Using Ant and the `<webdoclet..../>` tag to actually carry out the source code generation. In addition to covering the `<webdoclet..../>` tag, we also looked at how the following nested tag elements could be used to generate Struts configuration files:

  - `<strutsconfigxml/>` tells XDoclet to process any `@struts` tags and generate a struts-config.xml file.

  - `<strutsvalidationxml/>` tells XDoclet to process any `@struts.validation` tags and generate a validation.xml file.

CHAPTER 9

■ ■ ■

Logging and Debugging

For a web application of any size, there tends to be a large number of participating classes, views, and controllers, all performing their individual little bits. Using Struts is no different. A typical request in Struts involves the `ActionServlet`, your chosen controller such as `RequestProcessor`, your `Action` class, maybe an `ActionForm`, and of course your JSP view. If any of these individual components has an error, especially a spurious one such as `NullPointerException`, then narrowing down where this error occurs can be a nightmare. To solve this, you need to have flexible mechanisms for debugging your application and monitoring its behavior.

In this chapter, we are going to introduce you to two separate but associated topics. First we are going to address how you can leverage an effective logging mechanism within the JavaEdge application to enable you to debug an application easily and also to monitor the application while it is in production. Second, we are going to show you how you can use the Eclipse debugger capabilities to attach to the JBoss application server to debug the JavaEdge application.

For the most part, this chapter focuses on logging, since you are probably already familiar with debugging practices. Specifically, our discussion of logging will cover these topics:

- *Logging using* `ServletContext`: Part of the Servlet specification, the ability to write log messages to the container log file is the most basic form of logging available in a web application. No chapter on logging in a web application would be complete without a discussion of this topic.

- *Jakarta Commons Logging*: The Jakarta Commons Logging project provides a light-weight abstraction around many different logging tools and is the linchpin of many open source applications, including Struts. This chapter focuses extensively on this tool and how it is used.

- *Java logging API*: The standard Java logging API, available with version 1.4 of Java and onwards, is covered for the sake of completeness; more focus is given to Commons Logging and log4j.

- *Apache log4j*: This is an extremely powerful logging tool available from Apache that, when coupled with Commons Logging, is almost unbeatable. The latter part of the logging section of this chapter is pretty much focused on log4j and its associated features.

- *Logging best practices*: Logging is one of those things that is very easy to get wrong. In this section, we discuss some of the practices that we have found make logging in our applications easier to work with and easier to maintain with minimal impact on our application's performance.

- *Configuring Struts logging*: In this section, we draw on information from the previous section to show how you can configure Commons Logging and log4j to capture the Struts log messages to make debugging your Struts applications so much simpler.

In the final part of this chapter, we look at how you can use the debugging features of the Eclipse IDE coupled with the JBoss IDE plug-ins to get full debugging of your web application, including source-level debugging of Struts itself.

Why Use Logging?

Logging tends to be one of those things that is added to an application as an afterthought, yet you will often find the same application with `System.out.println()` statements scattered throughout the code, usually as a primitive means of debugging. When we talk about logging, we tend to look at it from two separate angles. First, we like to use logging as part of our debugging process. It is useful to be able to run through a process without having the debugger stop you at every juncture, yet still have a log of what occurred in the process. Usually during development this is done, as we said, with the `System.out.println()` method. The main drawback of this comes when you want the log output to go somewhere other than stdout. Sure, you can redirect stdout, but can you redirect it easily to a database or e-mail? No. The second aspect of logging is its use to monitor the status of a live application. Any web application with more than a few screens will have some kind of process or data that needs to be monitored. A good logging technology can take care of both of these aspects in one simple, lightweight solution.

So what makes a good logging technology? Three things really:

- *Flexibility of output*: A good logging technology allows for log messages to be output to a variety of destinations and to more than one destination at a time.

- *Different levels of logging*: Not all log messages are created equal. Some log messages are simply informational, such as logging the value of a variable at a certain point in a process. Others are more serious, perhaps indicating a system or an application error. A good logging solution can differentiate between message levels and allow for log messages for each level to be selectively turned on or off without touching the source code of the application.

- *Performance*: Any logging solution that you choose to employ should not adversely affect the performance of the application. Logging is meant to be an unintrusive part of your application; you certainly can't have your application competing for CPU cycles with the logging tool.

Another aspect of a good logging tool, in fact any tool used within an application, is its ability to stay loosely coupled to the application itself. This is quite an important factor that many of the best logging implementations do not take into consideration. In fact, the Apache project team considered this to be such a limiting factor that it started a specific project dedicated to mitigating this problem.

During this chapter you will see that not all logging implementations available to you fulfill these key points, but they are useful in their own ways. We will, of course, look at logging tools that offer all the functionality discussed previously, and we will demonstrate how such functionality has been integrated into the JavaEdge application. Also, don't think we've forgotten about Struts. The logging tool that we have chosen to use for the JavaEdge application is the same one used by Struts, and we will demonstrate how you can configure the Struts logging capabilities to get more information about what is happening under the hood of your application.

Log Message Levels

Before we start looking at any other methods of logging, we want to take a look at a concept that is common to almost all logging implementations: *log message levels.* One of the three main requirements of a good logging implementation is that it must be able to differentiate between messages. Sometimes called *message priority*, the message level indicates how important the message is and can be used by some logging implementations as a means to filter out unwanted messages. Thankfully, there seems to be an agreement on what the levels of logging should be, resulting in the following six levels being defined in all of the logging implementations in which you are interested:

- FATAL: Indicates that a fatal condition, usually some Exception or Error, has occurred and the application will be terminated.

- ERROR: Indicates an error or unexpected runtime behavior.

- WARN: Used to warn of the use of deprecated APIs conditions within the application that are undesirable but not necessarily an error. This is useful for flagging issues related to performance and security.

- INFO: Gives general information about the application such as startup and shutdown messages.

- DEBUG: Specifies detailed data about the operation of your application. This is useful when you want to be able to monitor the internals of application state in a production application.

- TRACE: Provides even more detailed information than the DEBUG level.

Effective use of these various message levels will allow you to filter out different messages into different log destinations and selectively activate and deactivate certain log output.

Simple Web Application Logging

Before we jump into exploring the more complex logging tools, let's take a quick look at what can be accomplished using the standard J2EE tools.

Logging with ServletContext

All servlet containers provide an implementation of the ServletContext interface that you can use to write a log entry to the containers' log file. The ServletContext interface declares two overloads for the log() method. The first accepts a single String parameter that is the message you want to log, and the second accepts a String parameter for the message and a Throwable parameter so you can log the details of an error. For example:

```
public class LoggingServlet extends HttpServlet {

protected void doGet(
    HttpServletRequest request,
    HttpServletResponse response)
        throws ServletException, IOException {

        process(request, response);
    }

    protected void doPost(
        HttpServletRequest request,
        HttpServletResponse response)
        throws ServletException, IOException {

        process(request, response);
    }

    private void process(
        HttpServletRequest request,
        HttpServletResponse response)
        throws IOException {

        ServletContext context = this.getServletContext();
        context.log("Hello World!");

    }
}
```

The important part of this code is the process() method. As you can see, you get access to the current ServletContext instance using the getServletContext() of the Servlet superclass. Once you have the ServletContext instance, you call the log() method to write to the servlet log file.

In Struts, you can get access to the current ActionServlet from within your actions by calling getServlet(), and from there you can access the ServletContext using getServletContext().

While using the built-in logging capabilities of the servlet container provides a quick and easy way for you to add logging to your application, there is no easy way to turn off the log messages without going back to the source code and removing the calls to the log method. Also, not only will you find that the location of the log file differs from container to container, but you are also limited to sending your log messages to a file that may be fine for a development environment yet lacks the sophistication necessary for your production requirements.

Using Commons Logging

The Java logging API isn't the only API available for adding logging capabilities to your application. In fact, a wide variety of logging APIs are available, but which one to use can prove a difficult decision. Thankfully, you don't need to make that decision up front. Commons

Logging from the Apache Jakarta project provides a lightweight wrapper around the most well-known logging implementations, as well as providing its own simple logging tool. Commons Logging includes a rich toolset and allows you to seamlessly plug in new logging implementations without having to touch your source code. Not only can you use the wrappers provided for the most well-known logging tools, but you can quite easily write a Commons Logging wrapper for your own logging tools as well.

So why use Commons Logging, when Java now has logging support built in (since the Java 1.4 release)? Well, Java logging hasn't got the widest range of features, and if you find in the future that you need to perform some other logging that Java 1.4 or Java 1.5 is not capable of, then you have to revisit your code to add the new capability. Also, Java 1.x logging is, quite obviously, available only on JVM version 1.4 and above, whereas Commons Logging can be used with any JVM version 1.2 or above. That is not to say that you shouldn't use the Java logging API when building applications targeted at a JVM version 1.4 or above, but in this case it would be wise to use the Commons Logging wrapper for JDK 1.4 logging so as to decouple your application from the logging implementation. Besides, when you see the wide range of features available when you combine Commons Logging with the Apache log4j project, you will probably decide that using JDK 1.4 is quite pointless.

Commons Logging in Other Applications

Before we jump into looking at Commons Logging, we want to show you which other applications use Commons Logging for logging. As we already mentioned, Struts uses Commons Logging, as do most other Apache projects. However, Commons Logging isn't just restricted to Apache projects; it's being used by many other projects in the Java world including JBoss, Hibernate, and Axion.

Learning how to use Commons Logging and the associated logging implementations means that you need to be familiar with the logging tool employed in most Java tools you will use, especially any that are open source. Most of these projects use Commons Logging not because of its logging abilities, since on its own it is no comparison to the likes of log4j or Avalon LogKit, but because by using Commons Logging they can maintain a consistent code base for logging while not being tied to any particular logging implementation.

Commons Logging Basics

Okay, now we are going to give you the lowdown on how Commons Logging works in isolation and then we will move on to looking at Commons Logging in conjunction with other logging tools, specifically log4j and JDK 1.4 logging.

The first thing you will need to do to get up and running with Commons Logging is obtain the distribution. You can download the latest version of Commons Logging from http://jakarta.apache.org/commons/logging/. You will also find that the Commons Logging jar file is included with the Struts distribution. For the purpose of this book, we have used the latest stable release of Commons Logging, which is currently 1.0.4.

Log and LogFactory

Let's start with a discussion of how logging is structured when using Commons Logging. The main two participating classes/interfaces in Commons Logging are Log and LogFactory. The Log class acts as a wrapper around the actual log implementation and is used by your application to write log messages. Each class that implements Log may write the actual log messages to multiple destinations such as a file, a system log, or an e-mail, but this is dependent on the configuration of the underlying logging implementation. You don't actually create an instance of Log directly; instead you use LogFactory to create your Log instance based on the data in your configuration file. The LogFactory class is the key to decoupling your application from the logging implementation. Since all the data about your logs is stored in an external configuration file, changing your logging implementation does not require any changes to the code. Because you don't have to change the code, you can change the logging behavior of your application while it is in production use, which as you'll see is very important when you start to leverage the different levels of log messages.

So consider this simple example:

```
import org.apache.commons.logging.Log;
import org.apache.commons.logging.LogFactory;

public class SimpleExample {

    public static void main(String[] args) {
        Log log = LogFactory.getLog("com.apress.commons.logging.SimpleExample");
        log.info("Hello Log!");
    }
}
```

What happens when you run this from the command line? You get the following message written to stdout:

```
[INFO] SimpleExample - Hello Log!
```

Notice the inclusion of [INFO] in this log message. This is the level of message created by the info() method of the Log instance. There are corresponding methods on the Log class for all six of the log levels discussed earlier.

No doubt you may be wondering what happened to the configuration of the logging implementation that we talked about. Unless you specify otherwise, Commons Logging will look for logging implementations in the following order:

- A pache log4j

- JDK 1.4 and above logging

- S impleLog

If log4j is found on your classpath, then Commons Logging will use that; however, you will need to configure it separately. If log4j is unavailable, Commons Logging will try to use JDK 1.4 logging. If you are using JVM 1.3 or below and do not have log4j on your classpath, then Commons Logging will default to its own internal logging implementation, called SimpleLog.

If you decide to create a wrapper for your own logging implementation, then you can tell Commons Logging to use that instead by setting the org.apache.commons.logging.Log system property to the full name of your log class. Extending the Commons Logging framework is outside the scope of this book, but you can find more details in the book *Pro Jakarta Commons* by Harshad Oak (Apress, ISBN: 1-59059-283-2).

Log Names

If you look back at the previous example, you will see that in the call to `LogFactory.getLog()` you pass in a `String` parameter. This is the name of the log that you want to retrieve. Most logging implementations support the notion of multiple logs for an application and use some form of naming scheme to retrieve each individual log. Commons Logging itself does not use the logging name for anything other than to pass to the underlying logging implementation. Also note that you do nothing to configure a log called `SimpleExample`. Instead, the underlying logger, in this case SimpleLog, provides a default log instance.

SimpleLog

Since we know that you may not have a JVM version 1.4 available to run JDK 1.4 logging, and you may not be able to use log4j within your applications, we want to cover the internal Commons Logging logging implementation, SimpleLog.

SimpleLog is a very lightweight logging provider that comes standard with Commons Logging. It doesn't support any log destinations other than the console, but when you are unable to use either JDK 1.4 logging or log4j, it makes a great alternative to using `System.out.println()`.

SimpleLog is configured by specifying system properties either directly with a call to `System.setProperty()` or by specifying them in the simplelog.properties file. We prefer to use the simplelog.properties file simply because it allows us to change the settings for our logs without having to touch our code.

The first set of configuration parameters for SimpleLog, listed here, applies to all logs within the application:

- `org.apache.commons.logging.simplelog.defaultlog`: Sets the default logging level for all logs. By default this is set to `INFO`.

- `org.apache.commons.logging.simplelog.showlogname`: Enables you to have the full name of the log displayed next to a log message. Set this to `true` to enable this behavior. The default value of this is `false`.

- `org.apache.commons.logging.simplelog.showShortLogname`: When set to `true`, displays the last component of the log name. For instance, in a log called `com.apress.logging.MyLog`, the name `MyLog` would be displayed. This is the default behavior for SimpleLog.

- `org.apache.commons.logging.simplelog.showdatetime`: When set to `true`, displays the time and date the log message was created alongside the log message. The default for this property is `false`.

Next, try building a simple example that uses a few of these properties to change the default log output. To do this, create the simplelog.properties file and place it in the root of your classpath. For this example, you also change the name of your log to `com.apress.logging.SimpleExample`. Add the following entries to the simplelog.properties file:

```
org.apache.commons.logging.simplelog.showdatetime=true
org.apache.commons.logging.simplelog.showlogname=true
org.apache.commons.logging.simplelog.showShortLogname=false
```

When this example is run, you now get this output:

```
2003/11/07 14:05:20:738 GMT [INFO] com.apress.logging.SimpleExample - Hello Log!
```

As you can see, you now have the time and date of the log message along with the full name of the log. Notice in the configuration parameters that you have to turn off the short-name logging and turn on the full-name logging. It is not enough to simply set showlogname to true; you must also set showShortLogname to false.

Now we want to move on and demonstrate how to perform multiple logs within your application. To do this, you simply have to set the org.apache.commons.logging.simplelog.log.xxx parameter to the maximum log level you wish to allow for a particular log, where xxx is the name of the log. Here is an extended example that uses two different logs:

```java
public class LogLevelExample {

    public static void main(String[] args) {
        Log log1 = LogFactory.getLog("log1");
        Log log2 = LogFactory.getLog("log2");

        log1.error("this is an error message");
        log1.info("this is an info message");
        log1.debug("this is a debug message");

        log2.error("this is an error message");
        log2.info("this is an info message");
        log2.debug("this is a debug message");
    }
}
```

For this example, all you do is load two separate logs into the application and then write three log messages of differing levels to each one. When you run this application, it should yield output like the following:

```
2003/11/07 14:14:23:615 GMT [ERROR] log1 - this is an error message
2003/11/07 14:14:23:630 GMT [INFO] log1 - this is an info message
2003/11/07 14:14:23:667 GMT [ERROR] log2 - this is an error message
2003/11/07 14:14:23:697 GMT [INFO] log2 - this is an info message
```

Notice that both the ERROR- and INFO-level messages have been outputted for each log, but the DEBUG-level messages have been omitted. If this surprises you, think back to when we showed you the configuration parameters for SimpleLog. By default, the log level is set to INFO. What this means is that only messages of INFO level or above will be outputted. You may be slightly confused by what we mean by "INFO level or above."The logging levels aren't just named; they are also structured into a hierarchy with one level more important than the other. The hierarchy is arranged as follows from most important to least important:

1. FATAL

2. ERROR

3. WARN

4. INFO

5. DEBUG

6. TRACE

So in the previous example, any DEBUG and TRACE messages would be discarded because they fall below the default INFO level. To change this behavior on a per-log-level basis, simply set the property corresponding to the log name to the lowest log level you want to allow for that log:

```
org.apache.commons.logging.simplelog.log.log1=WARN
org.apache.commons.logging.simplelog.log.log2=DEBUG
```

With these parameters, you are telling the SimpleLog engine to output only log messages of WARN level or above to log1 and only messages of DEBUG level or above to log2. When this example is run, the output looks like this:

```
2003/11/07 14:24:58:879 GMT [ERROR] log1 - this is an error message
2003/11/07 14:24:58:889 GMT [ERROR] log2 - this is an error message
2003/11/07 14:24:58:897 GMT [INFO] log2 - this is an info message
2003/11/07 14:24:58:905 GMT [DEBUG] log2 - this is a debug message
```

Now you can see that since the maximum level for log1 was set to WARN, only the ERROR-level message was outputted, but for log2 the maximum level was DEBUG, so all three log messages were outputted to the log window.

As you can see, SimpleLog is quite simple to use and offers the most flexibility across platforms, since you are not limited to having a JDK 1.4 JVM as you would be when using the JDK 1.4 logging tools. Also, Struts is distributed with Commons Logging and uses it internally. If you are not able to install another logging implementation such as log4j, then you may well have to work with SimpleLog for your log output. Hopefully now you are confident with configuring SimpleLog for your application.

In the next section, we will take you on a whirlwind tour of the JDK 1.4 logging API before moving on to a much more in-depth discussion of log4j.

The Java 1.4 Logging API

Newly introduced with the 1.4 release of Java 2 Standard Edition (J2SE) is the logging API. As you will see, Java 1.4 logging is very similar to log4j; it supports logger inheritance and a similar appender structure to log4j called *handlers* in Java 1.4 terminology. However, log4j has the upper hand slightly because it can run on older versions of Java, whereas Java 1.4 logging is, obviously, limited to running on a JVM version 1.4 or above. In terms of flexibility, log4j comes out on top again, as there is currently a wider range of appenders available for log4j than there are handlers for Java 1.4 logging.

Java 1.4 logging has completely different log levels from those described earlier. These are

- SEVERE: Corresponds to FATAL or ERROR in Commons Logging

- WARNING: Corresponds to WARN in Commons Logging

- INFO: Same as INFO in Commons Logging

- FINE: Corresponds to DEBUG in Commons Logging

- FINEST: Corresponds to TRACE in Commons Logging

- FINER: More detailed level; nothing corresponds to this in Commons Logging

- FINEST: Most detailed level; nothing corresponds to this in Commons Logging

- OFF: No explicit OFF state in Commons Logging

- ALL: No explicit ON state in Commons Logging

- CONFIG: No corresponding log level in Commons Logging

Fortunately, Commons Logging maps these levels to its own levels behind the scenes so you don't need to worry about changing the code you have created.

Commons Logging will use Java 1.4 logging only if you are running on a JVM version 1.4 or above, you have not specified that it must use another logger, and log4j is unavailable. We are not going to cover Java 1.4 logging separately; instead, we want to demonstrate how you can use Java 1.4 logging in conjunction with Commons Logging.

Let's start with a basic example:

```
public class JDK14Demo {
    public static void main(String[] args) {
        Log log = LogFactory.getLog("JDK14Demo");

        System.out.println("Log Type: " + log.getClass().getName());

        log.error("This is a FATAL message");
        log.error("This an ERROR message");
        log.warn("This is a WARN message");
        log.info("This is an INFO message");
        log.debug("This is a DEBUG message");
        log.trace("This is a TRACE message");

    }
}
```

To run this example correctly, make sure that you are on a JVM version 1.4 or above and you do *not* have log4j in your classpath. When you run this, you will get the following output:

```
Log Type: org.apache.commons.logging.impl.Jdk14Logger
15-Nov-2003 16:50:44 JDK14Demo main
SEVERE: This is a FATAL message
15-Nov-2003 16:50:44 JDK14Demo main
SEVERE: This an ERROR message
15-Nov-2003 16:50:44 JDK14Demo main
WARNING: This is a WARN message
15-Nov-2003 16:50:44 JDK14Demo main
INFO: This is an INFO message
```

Notice that the DEBUG and TRACE messages have not been outputted. This is because the default log supplied by the Java 1.4 logger writes only INFO-level messages and above, and always writes them to the console. You can change the log behavior in a similar way to SimpleLog by supplying configuration properties either as system properties or in a configuration file. Unlike SimpleLog, Java 1.4 logging does not look for a configuration file for your application; instead, you have to specify which file your configuration is stored in by setting the java.util.logging.config.file property. You can modify the code as follows to do this:

```
public class JDK14Demo {
    public static void main(String[] args) {
        System.setProperty("java.util.logging.config.file", "logging.properties");

        Log log = LogFactory.getLog("JDK14Demo");

        System.out.println("Log Type: " + log.getClass().getName());

        log.error("This is a FATAL message");
        log.error("This an ERROR message");
        log.warn("This is a WARN message");
        log.info("This is an INFO message");
        log.debug("This is a DEBUG message");
        log.trace("This is a TRACE message");

    }
}
```

Notice the call to System.setProperty() added as the first line. When you run this now, no log messages are outputted at all because the logging.properties file does not exist and therefore cannot supply any configuration details. Now create the basic configuration file and override the default log level:

```
# set the default level
.level = FINEST

# set the handlers
handlers = java.util.logging.ConsoleHandler
```

In the first line of this configuration file, you set the default log level to FINEST using the .level property. The second line configures the handlers that will be used by the log. In this case, the example specifies just the ConsoleHandler, but you could have provided a comma-separated list of handlers to send the log messages to.

When this is run, you would expect to see all the log messages outputted to the console, but this is not the case. Instead, you get the same output as before. This is because the default logging level for the ConsoleHandler is set to INFO, so you need to set the level of the handler as well. This is done by adding the following line to the configuration file:

```
java.util.logging.ConsoleHandler.level = FINEST
```

Running the example now will display all the log messages in the console.

We don't see any reason that would compel you to choose Java 1.4 logging as your logging implementation. You have much more flexibility with log4j and the structure of the logs, and the configuration works in a far more logical manner than with Java 1.4 logging; plus there are many more appenders available for log4j than there are handlers for Java 1.4 logging. However, you should always choose to use Commons Logging as your interface for logging. That way you are not tied to any particular logging technology, and you can easily change the logging provider without having to change your code.

Apache log4j

Apache log4j is a logging package available from the Apache Logging Services project. It differs from Commons Logging in many ways, not least because log4j is intended to be a full logging implementation, whereas Commons Logging is more of an abstraction layer around a logging provider. Apache log4j supports many advanced features that are not available with SimpleLog such as multiple log destinations and different formats for log messages; and unlike with Java 1.4, logging will run on older virtual machines. In this section, we are going to give you a quick look at log4j, although we won't be delving into the more advanced features offered, and we will also demonstrate how to configure Commons Logging to use log4j as the underlying provider.

Category or Logger

In the original version of log4j, the central class to the entire package was the Category class. The Category class represented a single log or category, such as com.apress.foo, and was used to write the actual log messages. In the more recent versions of log4j, this class has been superseded by the more intuitive Logger class. For all intents and purposes, while there are some subtle differences that we won't discuss here, the Category and Logger classes can be considered interchangeable. However, some of the log4j documentation still uses the term *category* in place of *logger*. More often than not, you will now see the term *category* refer to *log name*, which is deemed to be the log's category.

Appenders and Layouts

One of the main advantages of using log4j as your logging implementation is its ability to send log output to multiple destinations. The component that controls where log output is sent is called an *appender*. log4j has a wide variety of appenders provided to enable you to send log output to the console, log files, Unix Syslog, NT Event Log, JMS, or a GUI component. With log4j, you are not restricted to having to watch the console window of your application for log messages; something that may be acceptable during development but is certainly no use when your application is placed into production. You are not limited to the appenders available in the box with log4j; you can easily write your own custom appender to send log output to any destination you choose.

Not only is the destination of your log message flexible with log4j, but using layouts you can change the format of your messages as well. The use of this might not seem apparent when you are working in the development environment, but it can prove useful when you are in production. A prime example of where layouts can prove useful is when you have to provide log data to your clients. If you have to provide any kind of Service Level Agreement (SLA), they will probably want to be able to view the status and overall operation of the application. Using layouts, you can send your log messages as XML to a file, and after some XSLT wizardry you have a nice HTML page that you can allow your clients access to.

The standard distribution of log4j includes a wide selection of appenders, the most widely used being the following:

- `ConsoleAppender`: This is the basic appender that will send the log message to the console window.

- `FileAppender`: As the name implies, this appender writes the log message out to a file. This is useful if you want to keep a record of the log messages for a long time.

- `RollingFileAppender`: Similar to `FileAppender` in that log messages get written to a file, but `RollingFileAppender` limits the size of the file so that once the maximum size for a log is reached, the log file is moved to a backup location and the log file is started fresh.

- `SMTPAppender`: This appender broadcasts log messages to an e-mail address. This appender takes more time to process than the other appenders, and you should restrict the use of this to `FATAL`- or `ERROR`-level messages.

- `NTEventLogAppender`: When running your application on the Windows platform, you can use this appender to write the log messages to the NT Event Log.

- `SyslogAppender`: When running your application on the Unix platform, this appender can be used to write log messages to the Syslog.

- `JDBCAppender`: This appender will allow you to send log messages to a database so that they can be stored for retrieval at a later date.

As with appenders, the log4j distribution comes with a wide selection of layouts such as `SimpleLayout`, `PatternLayout`, and `XMLLayout`. These are discussed in more detail during the demonstration of log4j in the next section.

Both of these features are some, not all, of what sets log4j apart from logging implementations such as SimpleLog. These two simple concepts combine to provide massive flexibility that, with a small amount of configuration, can be leveraged from your Commons Logging–based application.

Using log4j with Commons Logging

We are not going to look at any examples of using log4j directly, as there is no real justification for doing so. Within our applications, we always use Commons Logging in the code, then we are free to configure whichever logging implementation we desire and that suits our purpose. If you are interested in how log4j works on its own, you can find out more in the book *Pro Jakarta Commons* (Oak, Apress, ISBN: 1-59059-283-2).

Okay, for this next example, use the code from the earlier SimpleLog example:

```
public class LogLevelExample {

    public static void main(String[] args) {
        Log log1 = LogFactory.getLog("log1");
        Log log2 = LogFactory.getLog("log2");

        log1.error("this is an error message");
        log1.info("this is an info message");
        log1.debug("this is a debug message");

        log2.error("this is an error message");
        log2.info("this is an info message");
        log2.debug("this is a debug message");
    }
}
```

This time, however, we are going to walk you through using log4j to handle the log output. The first thing you need to do to enable log4j within your Commons Logging application is to place the log4j.jar file in your classpath. Commons Logging will search the classpath for the log4j classes and use log4j as the implementation of preference if it is available. Once you have done that, you can try to run the application, but you will be presented with the following error:

```
log4j:WARN No appenders could be found for logger (log1).
log4j:WARN Please initialize the log4j system properly.
```

Before you can proceed, you need to configure log4j for use within your application. Configuring log4j is similar to configuring SimpleLog in that you have to specify system properties either directly, with a call to System.setProperty(), or via a configuration file, this time log4j.properties. That is where the similarities end, however. Configuring log4j is much more complicated than configuring SimpleLog, but with the extra level of complexity comes much more power.

Let's take a look at a simple properties file for the sample application:

```
#configure the default (root) logger
log4j.rootLogger=INFO, APP1

#configure the APP1 appender
log4j.appender.APP1=org.apache.log4j.ConsoleAppender
log4j.appender.APP1.layout=org.apache.log4j.SimpleLayout
```

The first line of this properties file sets the default logger (rootLogger) to display messages of INFO level or higher using the appender named APP1. In this case, the term *logger* is synonymous with the term *log* used in SimpleLog. The name APP1 is not a compulsory name for the appender, nor does it follow any kind of naming convention. The next two lines configure the appender APP1 to use the org.apache.log4j.ConsoleAppender class that writes log messages to the console and the org.apache.log4j.SimpleLayout layout class that simply writes the log level and the message. Running this example yields the following result:

```
ERROR - this is an error message
INFO - this is an info message
ERROR - this is an error message
INFO - this is an info message
```

As you can see, the log output is fairly basic, with no differentiation between the messages for each log. The SimpleLayout is just that simple. To improve the quality of the log output, you can use PatternLayout, which allows you to specify a pattern expression for log output similar to the functionality of the printf() function in C. Now set up PatternLayout as the layout for the APP1 appender. Notice this time that you specify another property, the pattern to use, which will be used by the PatternLayout class when building the output:

```
log4j.appender.APP1.layout=org.apache.log4j.PatternLayout
log4j.appender.APP1.layout.ConversionPattern=%-10c %d %-5p - [%t]: %m%n
```

Now when you run the example again, you get the following output:

```
log1      2003-11-07 11:40:38,395 ERROR - [main]: this is an error message
log1      2003-11-07 11:40:38,436 INFO  - [main]: this is an info message
log2      2003-11-07 11:40:38,441 ERROR - [main]: this is an error message
log2      2003-11-07 11:40:38,469 INFO  - [main]: this is an info message
```

The log messages are now much more descriptive and useful. The PatternLayout expressions are very flexible. You are free to insert any literal text you want into the pattern, plus you can take advantage of any of the % prefixed replacement variables such as %t in the example to output the thread name. Not only can you perform simple variable replacement, but you can perform advanced formatting on your replacements as well. In the pattern, you can see the expression %-5p outputs the log priority level, right-padded with spaces so that it equals five characters in length. The full list of replacement variables and formatting options can be found under the PatternLayout JavaDoc entry in the log4j documentation.

Now that the output of your log is improved, let's look at some of the other log4j configuration options. First you will notice that none of the DEBUG-level messages are being outputted and that both logs' messages are being sent to the same location: the console. Now we will show you how to modify your configuration so that only ERROR-level messages and above from log1 get outputted to the console and all error messages (TRACE and above) from log2 get outputted in XML format to a file.

The first step in the configuration is to define a second appender to output to a file in XML format. For this purpose, you can use org.apache.log4j.FileAppender to write the data to a file and `org.apache.log4j.xml.XMLLayout` to format the log messages in XML format. This is a simple matter of creating a new appender definition in the log4j.properties file:

```
#configure the APP2 (file) appender
log4j.appender.APP2=org.apache.log4j.FileAppender
log4j.appender.APP2.layout=org.apache.log4j.xml.XMLLayout
log4j.appender.APP2.File=log.txt
```

For this appender, you specify the appender and layout as discussed and also specify the `File` parameter for the appender so that the appender knows which file to place the log data in.

Now you need to create specific entries for the logs rather than using the default `rootLogger`, which is set to output to the console. To do this, you create entries similar to that of the `rootLogger`; however, this time you need to specify the log name:

```
# configure log1 and log2
log4j.logger.log1=ERROR, APP1
log4j.logger.log2=TRACE, APP2
```

If you run the example now, you get the following messages sent as XML format to the log.txt file:

```
<log4j:event logger="log2" timestamp="1068391735987" level="ERROR" thread="main">
<log4j:message><![CDATA[this is an error message]]></log4j:message>
</log4j:event>

<log4j:event logger="log2" timestamp="1068391736002" level="INFO" thread="main">
<log4j:message><![CDATA[this is an info message]]></log4j:message>
</log4j:event>

<log4j:event logger="log2" timestamp="1068391736010" level="DEBUG" thread="main">
<log4j:message><![CDATA[this is a debug message]]></log4j:message>
</log4j:event>
```

The XML log messages contain all the data about the message, including log name and log level. You should note that you cannot directly manipulate XML in this file using any of the Java XML APIs, because the XML is not well formed. There is no root node for the XML, so you will need to wrap the XML inside of a root node before it can be processed by an XML parser.

If you now look at the console messages, you will notice something strange—the messages from log2 are still being sent to the console even though the appender for log2 is set to send messages to a file. The reason for this is that all the logs are still inheriting the settings from the `rootLogger`. If you remove the `rootLogger` definition or comment out that line, then you will see that only the messages from log1 are sent to the console window.

log4j XML Configuration

In keeping with the current trend of making everything XML, log4j supports configuration using an XML file in place of the standard properties file. The log4j XML configuration file follows an Apache-created DTD called log4j.dtd. You will find this DTD file in the log4j download under the src directory.

Apache log4j doesn't look for any XML configuration by default; it still uses the log4j.properties file as the default configuration method. To use XML configuration, you need to set the `log4j.configuration` property to the file path of your XML configuration file. This file must end with the .xml suffix; otherwise log4j will not load the correct configuration class.

The XML configuration syntax is quite basic and self-descriptive. Here is the same configuration as in the previous example, this time in XML:

```xml
<?xml version="1.0" encoding="UTF-8" ?>
<!DOCTYPE log4j:configuration SYSTEM "log4j.dtd">
<log4j:configuration xmlns:log4j=http://logging.apache.org/log4j/docs/index.html
 debug="false">
    <root>
        <priority value="INFO" />
        <appender-ref ref="APP1" />
    </root>
    <appender name="APP1" class="org.apache.log4j.ConsoleAppender">
        <layout class="org.apache.log4j.SimpleLayout" />
    </appender>
    <appender name="APP2" class="org.apache.log4j.FileAppender">
        <param name="File" value="$log.txt" />
        <layout class="org.apache.log4j.xml.XMLLayout" />
    </appender>
    <category name="log1">
        <priority value="ERROR" />
        <appender-ref ref="APP1" />
    </category>
    <category name="log2">
        <priority value="TRACE" />
        <appender-ref ref="APP2" />
    </category>
</log4j:configuration>
```

Notice that in this case the root logger is specified using the `<root>` tag, and underneath the `<root>` you specify the priority and appender for the root log using the `<priority>` and `<appender>` tags, respectively:

```xml
<root>
        <priority value="INFO" />
        <appender-ref ref="APP1" />
    </root>
```

The appenders are defined using the `<appender>` tag, with the appender name and type being attributes of the tag. Nested in the `<appender>` tag are any `<param>` tags needed to pass parameters to the appender. In the case of `FileAppender`, you pass in the filename as the `File` parameter. Also nested log4j in the `<appender>` tag is the `<layout>` tag, which is used to define the layout for this particular appender. You can also pass parameters to the layout by nesting `<param>` under the `<layout>` tag.

```xml
<appender name="APP1" class="org.apache.log4j.ConsoleAppender">
        <layout class="org.apache.log4j.SimpleLayout" />
```

```
    </appender>
    <appender name="APP2" class="org.apache.log4j.FileAppender">
        <param name="File" value="$log.txt" />
        <layout class="org.apache.log4j.xml.XMLLayout" />
    </appender>
```

Finally comes the log configuration. Configuring the log is similar to configuring the `rootLogger`, but instead of using the `<root>` tag, you use the `<category>` tag and the name of the log is specified as an attribute:

```
<category name="log1">
        <priority value="ERROR" />
        <appender-ref ref="APP1" />
    </category>
    <category name="log2">
        <priority value="TRACE" />
        <appender-ref ref="APP2" />
    </category>
```

Log Inheritance

Log inheritance is a powerful concept that allows for the creation of extremely fine-grained logging within your application. Log inheritance is supported by both log4j and Java 1.4 logging, although we are only going to discuss log inheritance in the context of log4j.

The main premise behind log inheritance is that you create a log structure to match your package hierarchy. For instance, if you have two classes called com.apress.logging.Bar and com.apress.logging.Foo, then you should have two logs with identical names. This allows for extremely fine-grained control of your application logging. You are able to turn off logging on a per-class basis or just log for a selection of classes—the possibilities are endless. Log names in log4j are a lot more than simple identifiers and are used to build the inheritance structure for your logs. If you consider our previous statement that you should have a log for each class, then we are sure you have visions of a 1000-line configuration file—fortunately inheritance is in place to prevent that. When looking for settings for your log, log4j starts by looking for a log matching the actual name and will proceed up the hierarchy until it finds a match. Considering the previous example of com.apress.logging.Bar, log4j looks for the following logs in this order:

1. com.apress.logging.Bar

2. com.apress.logging

3. com.apress

4. com

5. log4j root logger

You can see from this example that log4j uses the period (.) character to separate levels of the hierarchy. You probably also realize that settings from the com, com.apress, and com.apress.logging levels will apply not only to the Bar class but also to the Foo class. So in this way, you can choose to apply settings to your entire package or to specific classes in the hierarchy—and you can do this all without touching your code. We realize that this is quite a complex concept, so we will walk you through an example before you proceed any further. For this example, you simply modify the previous example to use different log names and add a third log also:

```
import org.apache.commons.logging.Log;
import org.apache.commons.logging.LogFactory;

public class LogInheritance {

    public static void main(String[] args) {

        Log log1 = LogFactory.getLog("com.apress.logging.Bar");
        Log log2 = LogFactory.getLog("com.apress.logging.Foo");
        Log log3 = LogFactory.getLog("com.apress.logging.log4j.Foo");

        log1.error("this is an error message");
        log1.info("this is an info message");
        log1.debug("this is a debug message");

        log2.error("this is an error message");
        log2.info("this is an info message");
        log2.debug("this is a debug message");

        log3.error("this is an error message");
        log3.info("this is an info message");
        log3.debug("this is a debug message");
    }
}
```

As you can see in this example, you have three logs following a simple hierarchy—two directly under the com.apress.logging hierarchy branch and another under the com.apress.logging.log4j branch. Note that the log names are entirely fictional and are meant to mirror some imaginary class structure. To start with, create a simple configuration file aimed at all three logs:

```
# configure com.apress.logging logger
log4j.logger.com.apress.logging=ERROR, APP1

#configure the APP1 appender
log4j.appender.APP1=org.apache.log4j.ConsoleAppender
log4j.appender.APP1.layout=org.apache.log4j.PatternLayout
log4j.appender.APP1.layout.ConversionPattern= %-30c %-5p: %m%n
```

The appender declaration should be familiar; the important part is the log declaration. Notice that you specify the log name as com.apress.logging, which in this log hierarchy is a parent of all three logs in the code. When you run this example, you get the following output:

```
com.apress.logging.Bar              ERROR: this is an error message
com.apress.logging.Foo               ERROR: this is an error message
com.apress.logging.log4j.Foo        ERROR: this is an error message
```

Let's just take a second to digest what has happened. You set up a single log in the configuration with the name com.apress.logging to display log messages with a level of ERROR or above to the console. In the code, you have three logs: com.apress.logging.Foo, com.apress.logging.Bar, and com.apress.logging.log4j.Foo. When the code is run, you see that the settings for the single log com.apress.logging are applied to all three logs in your code. The reason for this is, of course, log inheritance. All the logs in your code are named with hierarchical names, each level separated by a period character, and all three share a common root in the hierarchy, namely com.apress.logging. Of course, you could have just specified com or com.apress as your log name, as they would also match the hierarchy of your logs. So what we are really saying is that log com.apress.logging.Foo inherits from com.apress.logging, which inherits from com.apress and so on up the tree.

So with log inheritance you can have a log for each class in your application, but you can configure all of those logs quite easily by specifying the settings for a log high up in the hierarchy. This is fine for the most part, but what happens when you need to be a little more specific about your logging? Perhaps you are in the throes of a big debugging session and want to get information about a particular class or subpackage. Fortunately this is easy. When searching for configuration details, log4j will look at the most specific part of the log hierarchy first and then gradually work its way up the tree until it finds a match—it will always use the least general match for your log as possible. So if you have settings for the com.apress and com.apress.logging logs in your configuration and a log called com.apress.logging.Foo in your code, then the settings for com.apress.logging are used, as this is the log furthest down the tree that matches your log.

As an example of this, you can set all logs in the com.apress.logging.log4j subpackage to display all log messages of INFO level and above by adding the following line to the configuration:

```
log4j.logger.com.apress.logging.log4j=INFO, APP1
```

When you run the example now, you get the following output:

```
com.apress.logging.Bar      ERROR: this is an error message
com.apress.logging.Foo      ERROR: this is an error message
com.apress.logging.log4j.Foo      ERROR: this is an error message
com.apress.logging.log4j.Foo      ERROR: this is an error message
com.apress.logging.log4j.Foo      INFO : this is an info message
com.apress.logging.log4j.Foo      INFO : this is an info message
```

Notice that the log messages for the `com.apress.logging.log4j.Foo` log are being output twice. This is because it matches both of the logs declared in the configuration file. You can, of course, specify configuration settings that apply to a single log. For instance, by adding the following line to the configuration file, you can cause the `com.apress.logging.Foo` log to output all messages of DEBUG level or higher:

```
log4j.logger.com.apress.logging.Foo=DEBUG, APP1
```

This now yields the following output:

```
com.apress.logging.Bar        ERROR: this is an error message
com.apress.logging.Foo        ERROR: this is an error message
com.apress.logging.Foo        ERROR: this is an error message
com.apress.logging.Foo        INFO : this is an info message
com.apress.logging.Foo        INFO : this is an info message
com.apress.logging.Foo        DEBUG: this is a debug message
com.apress.logging.Foo        DEBUG: this is a debug message
com.apress.logging.log4j.Foo   ERROR: this is an error message
com.apress.logging.log4j.Foo   ERROR: this is an error message
com.apress.logging.log4j.Foo   INFO : this is an info message
com.apress.logging.log4j.Foo   INFO : this is an info message
```

Log inheritance is a very important concept, as without it, maintaining a separate log for each class in an application would prove unwieldy and undesirable. As it is, log inheritance makes the configuration a breeze, so you are free to utilize this powerful logging mechanism. When we come to demonstrating how you can capture Struts debug messages, you will see how you can leverage Commons Logging and log4j to control the output of Struts log messages.

Logging Performance

Remember at the beginning of the chapter we told you one of the key features for any logging tool was that it must perform well. A slow logging application can cause more harm than good in your code, and you will no doubt find it hard to justify leaving your logging code in a production release if it slows down your application dramatically.

The whole point of a logging tool such as log4j being externally configurable is that you can leave the logging code in your production release and simply turn it on and off using configuration files. However, if the checks to see if logging is enabled are slow and logging itself is even slower, then you would be the first person to strip out the logging code and start again.

Thankfully, both Commons Logging and log4j are extremely fast, so you won't be seeing your application grind to a halt because of them. Apache has clocked log4j taking approximately 5 nanoseconds to check if a log message needs to be written and the actual log writing process taking between 21 and 37 microseconds depending on the layout. These figures were measured when running on an AMD Duron 800-MHz machine. Of course, the appender will have a lot to do with the performance—writing to the console is evidently going to be faster than writing to a file, which, in turn, should be faster than logging to e-mail.

Adding Commons Logging on top of log4j, you really won't notice much of a drop in performance, since in most cases all Commons Logging does is add a couple of extra calls to the call stack.

One thing you should always do, and this is especially true if you have your own custom appenders, is test your logging code. All logging code should be tested to make sure it is functional and not adversely affecting performance. There is nothing worse than seeing your logging code throw an exception or grind your application to a halt.

Logging Best Practices

In this section, we are going to discuss some best practices that you should follow when implementing logging to enable you to get the most out of your logging implementation.

Use Commons Logging

We know we have said this enough times already in this chapter, but you should really use Commons Logging in your code for logging. Although we currently can't think of any reason why you wouldn't use log4j as your logging provider, there may come a time when log4j is superseded by a better logging tool. If you use log4j directly within your code and you want to take advantage of a new implementation, then you had better break out your compiler and debugger and get ready for some fun. If, however, you used Commons Logging, chances are the new provider will come with a wrapper for Commons Logging, since it is the most widely used logging tool that we know of. Of course, if you can't use log4j for some reason, then using Commons Logging as a wrapper around your logging provider of choice (or not as the case may be!) provides you with an easy upgrade path to log4j in the future.

Don't just take our word for it. There is a reason that projects such as Struts, JBoss, and Hibernate use Commons Logging—you as a developer are not making preconceived ideas about how your application will be logged, just that it will.

Use Log Inheritance

This is an important one. When you have a large application, having one or two logs for the application can make debugging an absolute nightmare, not to mention making day-to-day monitoring a major chore. You really need to be keeping a separate log for each of your classes. This does not mean that you need a log file for each class, it simply means that you should have the ability to direct the log messages of a single class or subpackage to a destination separate from your standard log destination. This is where log inheritance comes in. Trying to implement and configure logging on a class-by-class basis without log inheritance is an absolute nightmare.

The LogFactory class in Commons Logging supports this behavior by providing an overload of getLog() that accepts a Class instance as opposed to a String instance representing the name. With this method, the full name of the class is used as the log name. For example:

```
package com.apress.logging;
import org.apache.commons.logging.Log;
import org.apache.commons.logging.LogFactory;

public class Foo {

    public static void main(String[] args) {
        Log log1 = LogFactory.getLog(Foo.class);
```

```
        log1.error("this is an error message");
        log1.info("this is an info message");
        log1.debug("this is a debug message");
    }
}
```

In the preceding example, the call to `LogFactory.getLog()` returns the log configuration closest to `com.apress.logging.Foo`. Notice that you don't use the name directly; instead, you pass in an instance of `Class` representing the `Foo` class.

For the most part, the requirement for log inheritance is going to mean you need to use log4j as the underlying log provider, but we don't see this being a major problem for you. Also don't forget that Java 1.4 logging supports log inheritance; so if you find that you can't use log4j for some reason, then consider that as an alternative.

Use External Configuration Files

Provided that your logging provider supports it, you should *always* use an external configuration file to configure your logs. Unless you provide a user interface in your application to configure the logging, you should always use a configuration file. There is absolutely nothing worse than having to recompile and redeploy an application just to change the logging behavior, especially if you have to deploy that application to a few different machines, and then test them to make sure you didn't inadvertently break the application.

External configuration files give you the flexibility to change your logging behavior whenever and however you need it. If you are getting unexpected errors in a certain class, then you can redirect the logging for all levels just for that class to e-mail without even having to touch the code. This makes fixing errors in a live application very easy, which makes for very happy clients. Break this rule at your own peril.

Consider Externalizing Log Messages

You should consider placing log messages in an external location such as a `ResourceBundle` so that you can change them without having to touch your application code.

This is useful for two reasons. First, if your application is considered more of a tool or middleware and you will have other developers using it, then chances are they may not speak your language. By externalizing the log messages, providing logging in another language won't require a massive overhaul of your code. Second, misspelled, misleading, or just plain wrong log messages are sometimes just as bad as or worse than no log messages at all, especially when you have other developers looking at the logs who won't be familiar with your errors. Correcting log messages when they are contained in a separate file is easy, but having to recompile your application and then redeploy just to correct an error in your log messages requires some degree of justification and a larger degree of effort.

If in Doubt, Log

If you aren't sure whether to log something or not, do. Chances are at some point you will need that information, and you don't want to be going back to your code to add in another log message. Just log anything that you aren't sure about under the `DEBUG` or `TRACE` level—that way it won't be displayed during normal logging, but a change in your configuration file will get it up and running with minimal fuss.

Use Code Guards

At first, this one might seem counterproductive, but you should always explicitly check the log level before performing some processing that is required to support the process of logging. For instance, consider this code:

```
import org.apache.commons.logging.Log;
import org.apache.commons.logging.LogFactory;

public class CodeGuards {

    public static void main(String[] args) {
        Log myLog = LogFactory.getLog("myLog");

        String name = "Darth Vader";

        myLog.error(name + " caused an error");
    }
}
```

In this example, the expression name + " caused an error" is always evaluated regardless of whether myLog is set to log ERROR-level messages or not. So even if this log message is not going to get written, you always have the overhead of creating a new String instance to pass into the Log.error() call. In this case, you should explicitly test that the log is set to log ERROR messages before building the log message, like this:

```
public class CodeGuards {

    public static void main(String[] args) {
        Log myLog = LogFactory.getLog("myLog");

        String name = "Darth Vader";

        if(myLog.isErrorEnabled()) {
            myLog.error(name + " caused an error");
        }
    }
}
```

When you use this mechanism, the String instance representing the log message will only be created if the log message will actually get written. You should note that there is no performance difference between using a code guard or not when the log message does not get written. The call to Log.isErrorEnabled() will always occur whether you perform it explicitly or whether it is done internally in the call to Log.error(). However, by calling it explicitly, the check is performed *before* the String instance for the log message is created as opposed to after. You should also note that two checks will occur when the ERROR level is enabled, resulting in a slight degradation in logging performance. However, this is an extremely small degradation that is greatly outweighed by the time you will save by using this method.

Use Log Levels Correctly

Log levels exist for a purpose, and you should use them accordingly. It is no use just making all log messages INFO level because it is easier to turn them on. Doing that means that you can't filter out important messages such as the inability to connect to the database from the fact that an e-mail was successfully sent. Even if you don't have a lot of log messages being written, you should remember that the log level classification will prove useful to others who will not be as familiar with the code as you will. Read our previous discussion on log levels for examples of situations to which each level is ideally suited.

Logging Exceptions

Logging exceptions can prove to be a difficult topic. There is a tendency to automatically log each exception using the ERROR log level, but this should not always be the case. Consider the FileNotFoundException. If your application expects this (as it always should), then you will probably have some kind of alternate action, perhaps by creating a default file or allowing the user to choose another location. Whatever the situation, a FileNotFoundException is rarely serious enough to warrant being logged at ERROR level. Our point here is you need to try and consider what situation the exception actually represents and then log it based on that. Doing this will allow you to differentiate easily between situations that are truly errors and those that are exceptional situations but are nonetheless expected.

Another issue with exceptions is where in the code to log them. With exceptions provided by the JDK or third-party tools, you are limited to logging them at the time they are caught in your code. With your own exceptions, you may want to consider performing the logging operation in the exception constructor. Using this practice you can easily reduce the amount of code you need to write to support your application's logging.

Capturing Struts Debug Messages

Now that we have most of the theory out of the way, we will show you how you can capture the Struts debug messages and write them to a log file.

Struts Log Structure

Internally, Struts uses Commons Logging as the interface for logging. Each Struts class that needs to write log messages has its own log that has the same name as the class. For this reason, you must use a logging provider that supports log inheritance, such as log4j, to enable simple configuration of the Struts log messages.

Since the Struts logs are structured to match the Struts package structure, you can leverage log inheritance to enable package-wide log configuration while still maintaining the flexibility to configure logging at the class level.

Configuring Logging

Configuring Struts to use log4j as the log provider is a fairly simple two-stage process that you should already be familiar with. First, you need to make sure that log4j is on the classpath of your application. For a web application, this simply means ensuring that the log4j jar file is in the lib directory of your application. Adding log4j to the JavaEdge classpath is simple; you will notice that it is included with the code download and that the Ant build script ensures that it is placed in the lib directory inside of the application war file.

The second configuration task is to create the log4j configuration file. You should already be familiar with the syntax of a log4j configuration file, so we won't be describing what each construct means. However, we want to discuss what you need to do to capture the Struts log messages. First, you configure an appender that will be used to write all the Struts log messages to a log file. You can choose to write the log messages to the console, but if your servlet container is running as a background process, then getting at the output won't be easy. A log file tends to be more flexible because you can view it whenever you please, even after you have shut down the process running your servlet container.

```
log4j.appender.STRUTS=org.apache.log4j.FileAppender
log4j.appender.STRUTS.FileName=c:\struts.log.txt
log4j.appender.STRUTS.layout=org.apache.log4j.PatternLayout
log4j.appender.STRUTS.layout.ConversionPattern=%d %-5p [%c] %m%n
```

Now all that remains is to configure a log for the Struts classes. This example demonstrates configuring a single log for the entire Struts package, org.apache.struts. If you want, you could make that more specific to catch log messages for just a single class, but in this case all you want to do is make sure you have some mechanism for seeing all the Struts log messages.

```
# Set root category priority to DEBUG and its only appender to A1.
log4j.logger.com.apress=TRACE, STRUTS
```

Notice that you set the log level to TRACE to make sure you catch all the messages that Struts outputs. Now that should get you up and running on most servlet containers, and we say 'most' because this does not work on all of them, including JBoss. In the next section, we will demonstrate how to configure log4j logging when using JBoss.

JBoss and log4j

As we mentioned earlier in the chapter, JBoss uses log4j for its own internal logging. Unfortunately, this causes a problem, as there is already a log4j configuration loaded into the JVM when your application starts. JBoss has its own log4j bootstrapper that loads log4j into memory well before your application is loaded. This means that even if you don't add log4j to your application's lib directory, your Commons Logging–enabled application will use it anyway because it is already loaded into your VM. At this point, you might be thinking, Great! I have log4j all ready to go.'It is, however, not that simple. The problem is that your log4j.properties file will be ignored because the instance of log4j that has been loaded into your application's VM has already been given a shiny new configuration by JBoss.

The log4j team has already realized that this is going to be a problem and has added features to the latest log4j release to enable the developers of applications such as JBoss to get around this limitation. However, in the current version of JBoss (3.2.2), this is not yet fixed.

Thankfully, it is not the end of the world—you can still configure logging for your application, you just have to do it a little differently. By default, you will find that any Struts log messages of INFO level or above are written to the JBoss console. Unfortunately, if you are using a Unix flavor like one of us does, then you will probably have the console stashed away in the background somewhere. To grab the Struts log messages and send them somewhere useful like a log file, you need to edit the JBoss log4j configuration file. JBoss uses XML configuration for log4j, and you will find the configuration file at {instance home}/conf/log4j.xml. To get all Struts error messages to output to a file when running in JBoss, you need to add the following code to your log4j.xml file:

```
<appender name="STRUTS" class="org.jboss.logging.appender.RollingFileAppender">
    <param name="File" value="${jboss.server.home.dir}/log/struts-log.log"/>

    <param name="DatePattern" value="'.'yyyy-MM-dd-HH"/>

    <layout class="org.apache.log4j.PatternLayout">
      <param name="ConversionPattern" value="%d %-5p [%c] %m%n"/>
      </layout>
  </appender>

<category name="org.apache.struts">
    <priority value="TRACE" />
    <appender-ref ref="STRUTS"/>
  </category>
```

This code creates an appender using `org.jboss.logging.appender.RollingFileAppender`, which will archive old logs and keep the main log to a sensible size. The `File` parameter specifies that the log will be stored in {instance home}/logs directly with the filename struts-log.log, and the `DatePattern` parameter is used to specify when the log will be archived (in this case hourly). The layout declaration should look familiar; it uses the standard log4j `PatternLayout` and passes in the required `ConversionPattern` parameter to define the layout of the log message. This particular pattern mimics the layout of JBoss's own log messages. The final part of the code creates a new log category for org.apache.struts, which will catch all log messages written by classes in the corresponding package or its subpackages. Set the log level to `TRACE` so that you get all the log messages and set the appender for this category to the previously defined `RollingFileAppender`.

Integrating Logging into JavaEdge

Now that you are up and running with the Struts log messages, it is time to add some log messages to the JavaEdge application. There are quite a few places to which you could add some logging code in your application, namely the following:

- *Data tier*: In the data tier, you are currently capturing all JRE and ObjectRelational-Bridge exceptions and wrapping them in `DataAccessExceptions`. You really want to capture the information about these exceptions and log them.

- *Business tier*: In the business tier, you have all your application-specific logic, making this the hardest tier to add logging to. You need a good understanding of what your application is doing and what information may be required by the major stakeholders to be able to add effective logging to this tier.

- *Web tier*: In the web tier, you have three specific areas that would benefit from being logged. First, you want to log any `ApplicationExceptions` that occur. Second, it would be useful to be able to log information about requests and responses, as this information can prove useful when you are trying to diagnose errors. And lastly, you want to log any information pertaining to security such as when a user logs in or logs out.

In this section, we are going to address all these logging requirements as well as look at some patterns that you can employ to reduce the amount of code you have to write and maintain to add logging to your application.

Extending Service Locator

An important part of logging in any application is getting an instance of the log class, in this case `org.apache.commons.logging.Log`. In Commons Logging, the usual method of obtaining a `Log` instance is to use the `LogFactory` class. When you are building your logging implementation, you can allow your classes to interact directly with the `LogFactory` class, or you can choose to provide some kind of internal helper class that wraps the `LogFactory`.

In Chapter 4, we discussed the use of the Service Locator pattern as a way to provide a simplified interface to application services. As it stands, obtaining a log instance directly from the `LogFactory` is a trivial amount of code; however, we prefer to encapsulate that logic within a service locator for three reasons:

- *Maintenance*: You are free to change the implementation of how you obtain your `Log` instance without affecting the rest of your code. Although it is unlikely, the method for obtaining a `Log` in Commons Logging may change, or more likely a better alternative will come along that you wish to use. If you have spread calls to `LogFactory.getLog()` throughout your code, then you will have a big job of changing to a new implementation, whereas if you have a single call to `LogFactory.getLog()` encapsulated within a service locator, then you are going to have a pretty easy time of it.

- *Code standards*: One thing we always insist on is that log names match class names. With `LogFactory`, developers are free to call the `getLog()` method and pass in a `String` parameter with any name they please. By using a service locator, you can force developers to use the full class name as the log name by only allowing them to retrieve `Log` instances using a `Class` instance.

- *Good practice*: Our final reason for advising you to use the Service Locator pattern is that it is just good practice. Experience has taught us that if we didn't encapsulate our `Log` sourcing in some form or another, we would end up having to change it, which generally means trawling through thousands of lines of code looking for our log code, or, worse still, resorting to the find-and-replace mechanism of code maintenance. Logging is an application service and therefore should be sourced through a service locator.

We are sure that you can understand the reasons for wrapping the mechanism for obtaining a `Log` instance inside a service locator, so now we will show you how to do it. First, you've already seen the `ServiceLocator` class in Chapter 4. Here, you simply add a single method to this class that allows for a `Log` to obtain a particular `Class` instance.

The code for this method is quite simple—it's just a wrapper around the `LogFactory.getLog()` from Commons Logging:

```
public Log getLog(Class aClass) {
    return LogFactory.getLog(aClass);
}
```

With this in place, you can proceed on to the actual logging.

Logging in the Data Tier

For the data tier, JavaEdge uses the Apache ObjectRelationalBridge (OJB) to manage the persistence and retrieval of data stored in the relational database, in this case MySQL. Within the application, any errors that occur with OJB or when retrieving `PersistenceBroker` instances from the `ServiceLocator` are wrapped inside a `DataAccessException` and passed up the stack, hiding the actual details of the underlying implementation from the business logic. Any occurrence of one of these exceptions is a fairly serious issue, since the rest of the application won't run if the data can't be loaded. For this reason, we have chosen to log any exceptions occurring in the DAOs as `ERROR`-level messages. This way they are of a suitably high priority that they will appear in most logs, including the default logs plus the classification is correct in this case, as these exceptions are errors. We are not going to include all the code for the data tier; instead, here is a standard method from the `StoryDAO` class:

```
public ValueObject findByPK(String primaryKey) throws DataAccessException {
    log.debug("************Entering the StoryDAO.findByPK**************");
    PersistenceBroker broker = null;
    StoryVO storyVO = null;

    try {
        broker = ServiceLocator.getInstance().findBroker();
        storyVO = new StoryVO();
        storyVO.setStoryId(new Long(primaryKey));

        Query query = new QueryByCriteria(storyVO);
        storyVO = (StoryVO) broker.getObjectByQuery(query);
    } catch (ServiceLocatorException e) {
        log.error(
            "PersistenceBrokerException thrown in StoryDAO.findByPK()",
            e);
        throw new DataAccessException(
                    "Error in StoryDAO.findByPK(): " + e.toString(), e);
    } finally {
        if (broker != null)
            broker.close();
    }

    log.debug("***********Done with the StoryDAO.findByPK()**************");
    return storyVO;
}
```

You will notice from the preceding code that `log.debug()` statements appear at the beginning and end of the method call. You may find these useful when debugging, as you can watch the activity of your data access layer to see how many times the commands are being executed. This is especially useful if you use some kind of caching in the middle tier and you want to verify that the data from the cache is being used and not the data from the database. With these messages set at DEBUG level, we can easily turn them off in the production system while still leaving the error tracing messages turned on.

Another area in which log messages can prove useful in the data tier is in tracing what your data access technology is doing. If you are using straight JDBC, this might involve logging the SQL commands that are issued to the database server so that you can make sure they are correct. In the case of OJB, the queries can get pretty complex, especially if you are building the query up using the Criteria object. In this case, it is useful to log exactly what the Criteria object is holding before the query is actually executed.

```java
public Collection findAllStories() throws DataAccessException {
    log.debug(
        "***********Entering the StoryDAO.findAllStories()**************");
    PersistenceBroker broker = null;
    Collection results = null;

    try {
        Criteria criteria = new Criteria();
        criteria.addOrderByDescending("storyId");

        if (log.isDebugEnabled()) {
            log.debug("Critiera:" + criteria.toString());
        }
        Query query = QueryFactory.newQuery(StoryVO.class, criteria);

        query.setStartAtIndex(1);
        broker = ServiceLocator.getInstance().findBroker();
        results = (Collection) broker.getCollectionByQuery(query);
    } catch (ServiceLocatorException e) {
        log.error(
            "ServiceLocatorException thrown in StoryDAO.findAllStories()",
            e);
        throw new DataAccessException(
            "ServiceLocatorException error in StoryDAO.findAllStories()", e);
    } finally {
        if (broker != null) broker.close();
    }

    log.debug(
        "***********Done with StoryDAO.findAllStories()**************");

    return results;

}
```

In a case like this, it is often tempting to watch this data in the debugger or to use `System.out.println()` during debugging before stripping it for deployment. If you use a low log priority level like `DEBUG`, you can turn the logging off for production, but you also have the ability to easily test the `Criteria` on your live platform.

For each DAOs, you simply declare the log as a static field:

```
private static Log log = ServiceLocator.getInstance().getLog(StoryDAO.class);
```

Logging in the Business Tier

Unlike logging in the data tier, there are no hard-and-fast rules for logging in the business tier. The business tier tends to be the part of the application that is most personalized for each application. You can use OJB for the data tier and Struts for the web tier in all of your web applications, but the chances of you using the same business logic in each application are rare.

When building a logging strategy for your business tier, you have to consider how important each particular piece of information is. If you have a particularly important process, then you are going to want to include log messages for all the major stages of the process. If something goes wrong during the process, you need to know about it. There is nothing worse than having your client breathing down your neck with a problem and not having the correct information to answer the question. Normally you should stick log messages that describe main parts of the business process under the `INFO` level. After all, the whole purpose of the application is to execute the business logic, so those log messages are information about the normal running of the application. If you have a particularly detailed process, you may want to log some of the more in-depth details as `DEBUG` or `TRACE` messages so that you can at least rerun the logic with the log messages activated. Try not to leave anything that you could possibly need unlogged. If it seems unlikely that you'll need the information often, just use a `DEBUG` or `TRACE` message—that way it is there if someone asks for it.

For less important logic, you can be a bit more restrained with your logging; but remember that the performance hit when a message is not going to be logged is very minimal, so you can afford to include a few extra log messages, provided you log them at the `DEBUG` or `TRACE` level.

When building the logging for the business tier, remember one fact: logging is a way of covering your own back and proving that the code you have written is functional. Not only that, but the quality of your logs directly affects your ability to diagnose and troubleshoot issues within the application. If you have detailed logs for your application, you can prove to your boss that your code is working, and your boss in turn can prove the same thing to the customer. This is really useful if you have to give your customer some kind of SLA for an application, and you need to make sure you can prove that you are meeting the agreed levels of service.

In the JavaEdge application, none of the processes are particularly complex, but you can include `DEBUG`-level messages to signal the start and end of each of the business methods in the `Story` and `Member` business delegate classes:

```
public void addStory(StoryVO storyVO) throws ApplicationException {
        log.debug("addStory() started");
        try {
            storyDAO.insert(storyVO);
        } catch (DataAccessException e) {
```

```
        log.error("DataAccessException in addStory()", e);
        throw new ApplicationException(
                "DataAccessException Error in StoryManagerBean.addStory(): "
                + e.toString(),
                e);
    }
    log.debug("addStory() finished");
}
```

Notice in the preceding code that you log not only the start and end of the method, but also any occurrences of DataAccessException. Although the root cause of these exceptions would already have been logged in the data tier, we don't want to make one tier dependent on another for logging. We would rather have each tier log the error encountered there and get multiple log entries than rely on the logging behavior of a different tier in the application and get no log messages.

Monitoring Application Security

One part of the business logic that should always be monitored is application security. You will no doubt have some kind of logic that you use to validate the users of your application. In this case, it is useful to audit the attempts to log in to the system so you can monitor any attempts to gain invalid access to your system. If you have a case in your log files where you see many attempts to log in using the same user name and many different passwords in a short space of time, it is very possible that someone is trying to guess the password for a user name they know exists. This certainly isn't the only measure you should be taking in your security, and more often than not you will find you can use the security logs to discount your manager's f ogue hacker against the establishment'theory when something goes wrong in the application.

The big issue with building a security log is where you should perform the actual logging. Should you do it in the web tier during the data entry, or should you do it in the business tier when performing the actual authentication? The answer to that question is, It depends. You most definitely want to build a log in the business tier since that is where the actual authentication takes place; and if you add more than one user interface tier, then you don't have to reproduce the logging. However, you may want to log more details about the attempted login such as the IP address the request came from. In that case, you can either log the request in the web tier as well or pass the IP address as a parameter to the business tier. We would recommend that you build a separate log in the web tier if you want to log the IP address of the request. Passing the IP address to the business tier is a case of the Tier Leakage antipattern detailed in Chapter 1. If you decide to use a Swing-based user interface, then the IP address really has no meaning.

For the JavaEdge application, you are only interested in maintaining a log of the login attempts, so you need to add some simple logging code to the MemberManagerBD.authenticate() method:

```
public MemberVO authenticate(String userId, String password)
        throws ApplicationException{
    log.debug("authenticate() started");
    MemberVO memberVO = new MemberVO();
```

```
        //Setting the query criteria.
        memberVO.setUserId(userId);
        memberVO.setPassword(password);

        MemberDAO memberDAO = new MemberDAO();

        try{
          memberVO = (MemberVO) memberDAO.findByCriteria(memberVO);

            if(memberVO == null) {
              if (log.isInfoEnabled()) {
                log.info(
                  "Failed Login Attempt. Username:" +
                  userId +
                  " Password:" + password);
              }
            } else {
              If (log.isInfoEnabled()) {
                  log.info("Successful Login Attempt for user:" + userId);
              }
            }
        }
        catch(DataAccessException e){
          log.error("Error in MemberManagerBD.authenticate()",  e);
          throw new ApplicationException(
                "Error in MemberManagerBD.validateUserId(): " +
                  e.toString(),e);
        }

        log.debug("authenticate() finished");
        return memberVO;
    }
```

Notice that for failed attempts you write both the user name and the password to the log file, whereas on successful attempts you write just the user name. The last thing you want to do is compromise the security of the JavaEdge application by storing valid user name and password combinations in a plain text file.

Logging in the Web Tier

Now to the section you've been waiting for!

Logging in Struts Actions or ActionForms

You can, of course, add any kind of logging you want to your Struts actions or ActionForms, but since most if not all of the logic in your application will reside in the business tier, there isn't really that much to log. Couple this with the extensive log output available from Struts, and you shouldn't need to perform any logging inside of your actions or ActionForms.

Logging ApplicationExceptions

The ApplicationException class derives indirectly from RuntimeException, making it an unchecked exception—that is, there is no need to either catch the exception within a method or declare it as thrown by that method. The JavaEdge application relies on Struts' ability to handle exceptions globally using a global exception handler. For the JavaEdge application, you build a global exception handler that sends the error details to an e-mail recipient. This is useful since it means that you can alert an administrator if something goes wrong in the application. However, you also want any ApplicationExceptions to be logged in the application log file. Since all ApplicationExceptions are caught and handled globally, this is a simple matter. All you need to do is add the logging code to the MailExceptionHandler:

```
public class MailExceptionHandler extends ExceptionHandler {
private static Log log =
        ServiceLocator.getInstance().getLog(MailExceptionHandler.class);
public ActionForward execute(Exception e,
                              ExceptionConfig ex,
                              ActionMapping mapping,
                              ActionForm    form,
                              HttpServletRequest request,
                              HttpServletResponse response)
        throws ServletException{


        ActionForward forward =
                super.execute(e, ex, mapping, form, request, response);

        Properties props = new Properties();

        //Getting the name of the e-mail server.
        props.put("mail.smtp.host", "netchange.us");
        props.put("mail.from", "JavaEdgeApplication");

        Session session = Session.getDefaultInstance(props, null);
        session.setDebug(false);

        // Write the exception details to the log file.
        log.error("An ApplicationException has occurred", e);

        Message msg = new MimeMessage(session);

        try{
          msg.setFrom();

          //Setting who is supposed to receive the e-mail.
          InternetAddress to = new InternetAddress("john.carnell@netchange.us");
```

```
            //Setting the important text.
            msg.setRecipient(MimeMessage.RecipientType.TO, to);
            msg.setSubject("Error message occurred in Action:" + mapping.getName());
            msg.setText(
                "An error occurred while trying to invoke execute() on Action:" +
                mapping.getName() +
                    ". Error is: " + e.getMessage());
            Transport.send(msg);
            if (log.isDebugEnabled()) {
                log.debug("E-Mail sent to:" + to);
            }
        }
        catch(Exception exception){
            log.error("  ===================================");
            log.error(
            "An error has occurred in the MailExceptionHandler" +
            "while trying to process Action:"
                + mapping.getName());
            log.error("Exception raised is : " + exception.getMessage());
            log.error("Original Exception: " + e.getMessage());
            log.error("===================================");

        }

        return forward;
    }
}
```

Notice that not only do you log the actual `ApplicationException`, but you also log when an e-mail is sent successfully and when one fails. This way you have proof that the administrator was notified of the error and you can also diagnose any errors with the mail delivery easily.

Debugging Struts Applications Using JBoss and Eclipse

So far, everything in this chapter has been focused on logging technologies and building and logging implementations for your application. In this final section, we are going to demonstrate how you can debug your Struts-based applications running in JBoss using the Eclipse open source IDE. We are not going to go into the details about what a debugger is and how to use one, since we assume you are already familiar with that topic. Instead, we want to give a practical demonstration of debugging Struts applications with JBoss and Eclipse, so that you will be able to use the knowledge in your own debugging.

JBoss IDE Eclipse Plug-Ins

We assume at this point you already have Eclipse and JBoss installed on your machine. If not, you will find more information on obtaining Eclipse in Appendix A and more information on obtaining and setting up JBoss in Appendix B.

Once you have those applications up and running, you need to obtain the JBoss IDE. JBoss IDE is a set of plug-ins developed by JBoss for use with Eclipse. Amongst other things, the JBoss IDE plug-ins add support for managing JBoss servers directly from the Eclipse IDE, hot code deployment, and application server debugging. You can download the JBoss IDE from http://www.jboss.org. Once you have the download, you need to unpack it and place the plug-ins in the appropriate directory in your Eclipse program directory.

Configuring the JBoss Server

Once you have the JBoss IDE plug-ins installed, the first thing you need to do is configure the JBoss server instance. To do this, you need to open the Server Navigator view by going to Window ➤ Show View ➤ Other and selecting the view from the JBoss IDE category, as shown in Figure 9-1.

Figure 9-1. *Eclipse view browser*

Once the Server Navigator is displayed, right-click it and choose Configuration. When the Configuration dialog box appears, right-click the appropriate icon for your version of JBoss and choose New from the pop-up menu. Enter a meaningful name for your server and then enter the path to the JBoss home directory in the corresponding box, as shown in Figure 9-2. The home directory is the one containing the bin directory, not the bin directory itself.

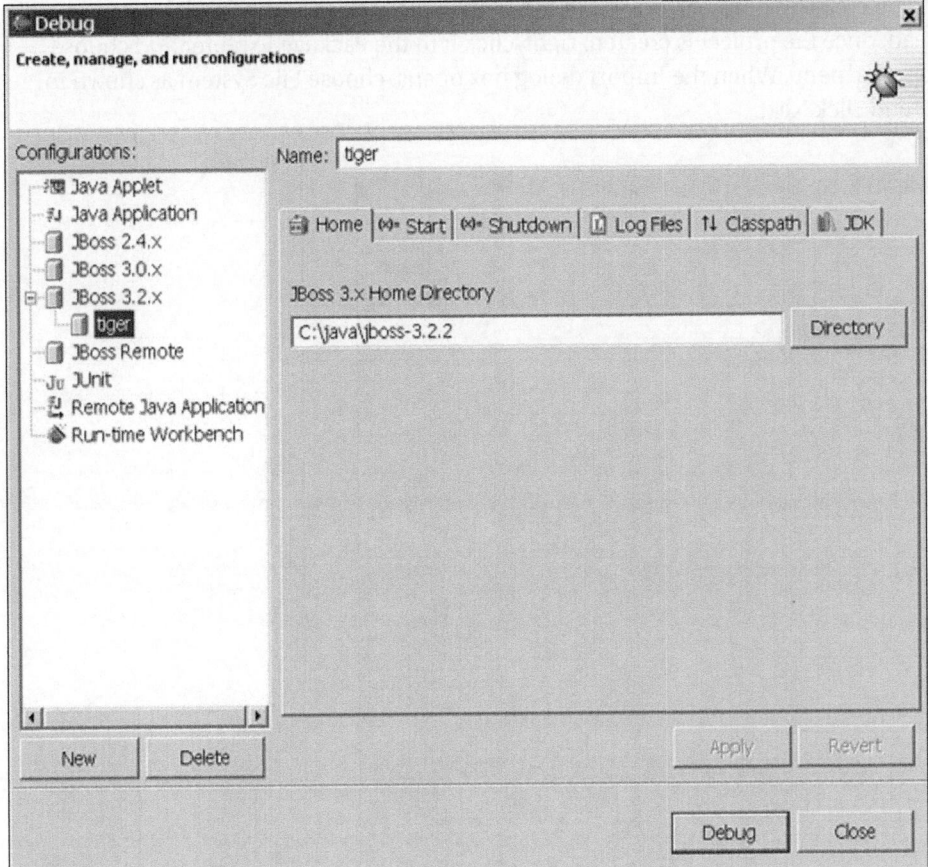

Figure 9-2. *JBoss IDE server configuration*

Under the JDK tab, make sure that the JDK selected is actually a full JDK and not just a JRE. When we first installed the plug-in on our Windows machine, it picked up the Sun JRE instead of our BEA JDK. Once that is done, click Apply and then Debug.

When the Configuration dialog box closes, the JBoss application server will start up inside the Eclipse IDE. You will see all the messages that usually go to the console being streamed through the Eclipse Console window.

Debugging the JavaEdge Application

To start debugging, you need to create a new project in Eclipse to hold the JavaEdge source code. To create a new project, go to File ➤ New ➤ Project and select Java Project from the dialog box.

When you create the project, don't create it in the same folder as the JavaEdge source code. Instead, once the project is created, right-click it in the Package Explorer and choose Import from the menu. When the Import dialog box opens, choose File System as shown in Figure 9-3, and click Next.

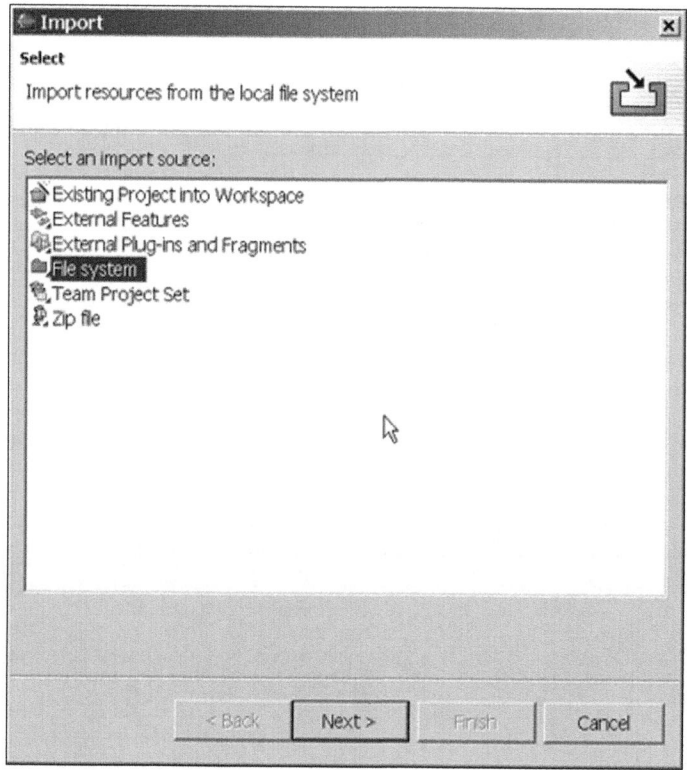

Figure 9-3. *Eclipse Import dialog box*

You are now prompted to choose the folder to import, so select the folder containing the JavaEdge source code. You need to check the box displayed next to the source folder as shown in Figure 9-4 to make sure Eclipse includes all the source files.

Once the source code is imported, make sure that JBoss is running by checking the status on the Server Navigator. If JBoss is not running, you can right-click the icon for your server and choose Start to run it. Now open up the source file for HomePageSetupAction and set a breakpoint inside the execute() method as shown in Figure 9-5 by double-clicking the margin of the code editor.

Now fire up your browser and point it to the JavaEdge application running in JBoss. Once the home page executes, the code will stop at the breakpoint you defined, and Eclipse will switch into Debug mode. From here you can step through your code in the standard way you would with any debugger. You will find the debugger commands under the Run menu along with the particular shortcut keys for your platform.

You can set breakpoints at any point in your code, enabling you to analyze exactly what is going on within your application.

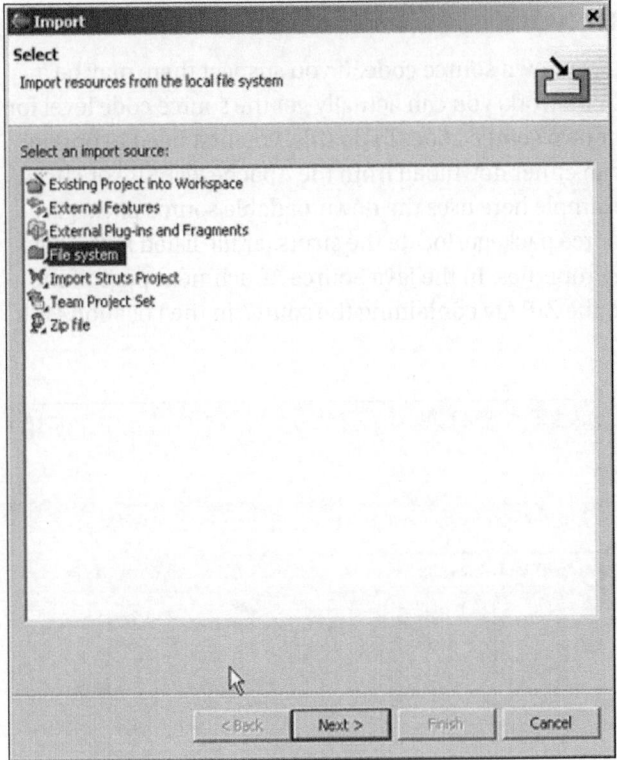

Figure 9-4. *Eclipse Import wizard*

```
HomePageSetupAction.java   ×
    public ActionForward execute(ActionMapping mapping,
                                 ActionForm      form,
                                 HttpServletRequest request,
                                 HttpServletResponse response) {


    IStoryManager storyManagerBD = StoryManagerBD.getStoryManagerBD();
    Collection topStories = storyManagerBD.findTopStory();
    request.setAttribute("topStories", topStories);

    return (mapping.findForward("homepage.success"));
    }
}
```

Figure 9-5. *Breakpoints in Eclipse*

Hot-Deploy

One really nifty feature of running the JBoss application server from within Eclipse is hot deployment of code. Provided you are running a JVM that supports in-VM replacement, such as the Sun JVMs 1.4.1 and 1.4.2, then when you are running JBoss and your J2EE application from within the Eclipse IDE, any time you recompile a class it will replace the current version in the JBoss VM. This allows you to make lots of changes while debugging your application without having to perform a full rebuild and redeploy each time.

Debugging the Struts Framework

You're not only restricted to debugging your own source code. If you suspect there may be a problem with some part of the Struts framework, you can actually get the source code level for the framework at the same level as your own source code. To do this, you first need to obtain the source code for Struts, which you can either download from the Apache web site or check out from the Apache CVS server. The example here uses the downloadable source package.

Once you have downloaded the source package, locate the struts.jar file listed in the Package Explorer, right-click it, and choose Properties. In the Java Source Attachment page of the Properties dialog box, enter the path to the ZIP file containing the source in the Location Path box, as shown in Figure 9-6.

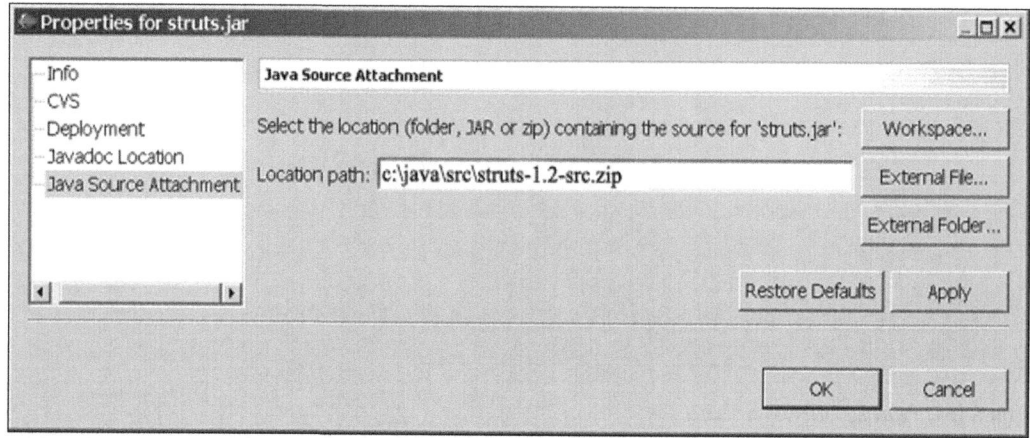

Figure 9-6. *Source code attachment for Struts*

Once you have mounted the source code, expand the struts.jar node in the Package Explorer, and then expand the org.struts.action node. Under this node you will find the RequestProcessor class. If you expand this node, all the methods are listed. Clicking the process() method will bring up the source code, and you can place a breakpoint directly inside the process() method. When you next request a page from the JavaEdge application, JBoss will halt execution at your breakpoint, and the Eclipse IDE will switch into debug mode with the Struts RequestProcessor source code in the current view.

Summary

In this chapter, we have given you an in-depth look at logging technologies, addressing exactly what makes a good logging tool and looking at tools that meet the required criteria. Specifically, this chapter has focused mainly on Commons Logging and log4j, as together these tools provide the most flexible and complete logging solution currently available.

We have addressed issues related to the design of a logging strategy, as well as the performance of Commons Logging and log4j. We discussed at length some of the best practices that you should take into consideration when adding logging support to your application. Most of the concepts in this chapter have been backed up by practical demonstrations, so you should now have a sense of how these topics work in a real scenario, not just on paper.

Of course, we haven't neglected Struts; we have taken an extensive look at how to configure logging within Struts, and also at some specific issues related to the JBoss application server. To cement these ideas, we demonstrated how logging has been integrated into the JavaEdge application and also explained the decision-making process we went through when picking our logging strategy.

In the final part of the chapter, we presented a practical demonstration of how you can leverage the Eclipse IDE and JBoss application server to interactively debug not only your application, but the Struts framework as well.

Velocity Template Engine

All of the Struts examples you have seen so far in this book have used JSP as the view technology. Although JSP is sufficient for most applications, it can sometimes prove too complex to be handled by designers, and there is always the temptation to fix'a small problem by using a scriptlet within the JSP rather than returning to the Struts actions or business logic.

As with any good MVC framework, Struts is not coupled to a single view technology. In fact, one of the main reasons for using an MVC framework is so that the view technology can be easily changed and decoupled from the logic. The Velocity template engine is another project from the Apache Jakarta team designed to function as a view technology for web applications. Originally designed as a stand-alone project, Velocity is now integrated into many other projects, Jakarta and otherwise, including of course Struts.

In this chapter, we are going to look at how Velocity can simplify view creation, especially when working with designers who have little or no programming knowledge. We will also look at how Velocity can help you avoid some of the antipatterns, specifically the Tight-Skins antipattern, that have been discussed throughout the book. This chapter will introduce you to the basics of the Velocity template engine as well as how it is integrated into the Struts framework.

What Is a Template Engine?

If you have had no experience working with a template engine, then you may be wondering what exactly a template engine is. Essentially, a template engine forms a simplified version of JSP. Most template engines allow you to create output based on a set of rules and operations. Unlike JSP, a template engine does not allow for complex business logic to be embedded in the template; there are just enough logic constructs to support the creation of the content.

Using a template engine offers some distinct benefits over using something like JSP:

Ease of use: You will generally find that template engines, Velocity included, are extremely easy to use. This is especially true when you are working alongside nontechnical team members such as designers, who should be able to get to grips with Velocity within a few hours.

Simplicity: A good template engine contains few constructs for its template language, making the construction of templates a simple matter. Since most template languages simply focus on their ability to generate text output, the learning curve is much more relaxed than that with technologies such as JSP, which has all the complexity of the Java language behind it.

Flexibility: Template engines are simply mechanisms for generating dynamic output. Although JSP is capable of producing output that is not HTML based, it is certainly most suited to the creation of HTML for web pages. A template engine, on the other hand, is equally comfortable creating HTML, XML, SQL, or text-based output. Using a template engine, you can create the layouts for not only your web pages, but also any other output your application might generate such as e-mails, invoices, or reports.

Reusability: A particularly useful feature of a template engine is that your templates are not coupled to output to a browser. A template that generates an order confirmation e-mail can be used in multiple applications and does not even need to be sent as an e-mail.

Template engines are not without their disadvantages, however:

Power: Although you will find that most template engines are quite powerful, they are not quite as powerful as JSP. You have no ability to place scriptlets in your code, so you cannot leverage any kind of advanced logic within your view. While many, including ourselves, would consider this a good thing, if your application or development team relies extensively on scriptlets, then this may pose a problem for you. On the other hand, if you have gotten into the bad habit of using scriptlets, a template engine is a good method of enforcing a clean separation of code and layout.

Tool support: Our biggest problem with using a template engine is the lack of integration with other technologies. In the current release of Velocity, the integration of tiles isn't as good as the Tiles framework support in Struts when using JSP. Currently you can only use Velocity as an individual tile, not to create the root layout of a Tiles framework application. However, as we mention later on, this is changing, and many different tools are in the process of being integrated with the Velocity engine.

Familiarity: Perhaps the least worrying of the disadvantages of a template engine is the lack of familiarity you may have with it. If your team is made up solely of programmers who are already proficient with JSP, then learning another mechanism for something to which you have a perfectly good solution may not seem like a good use of your time. When considering this, you should remember that the learning curve for a template engine is especially low when compared with the likes of JSP.

Getting Started

At the core of Velocity is the template. You can't really do much in Velocity without first building a template. Velocity templates are written using the Velocity Template Language (VTL) and are then passed into the Velocity engine along with a `Context` object that contains all the variable data that is needed to render the content for that template.

Before we take a look at the Velocity internals and the VTL syntax in some detail, let's build a simple example to highlight how Velocity works. To start with, you will need to obtain the Velocity jar file from the Jakarta web site at `http://jakarta.apache.org/velocity`. At the time of writing, the current release of Velocity is 1.4.

The Velocity distribution contains two separate jar files, one containing Velocity and the other containing all the dependencies. You can either obtain all the classes that Velocity requires separately or use the dependencies jar file instead.

This next section discusses Velocity in general and makes very little reference to its use in a web environment. All the samples are run from the command line and are intended to provide an overview of Velocity without the added complexity of the web environment.

To start with, you need a template. A template is simply a plain text file that contains the static content combined with VTL constructs that define how the template will be constructed. For the first template in this chapter, you will start small. Create a text file called HelloVelocity.vm and add the following text to it:

```
Hello $who!
```

Don't worry too much about the template syntax just yet; we will cover that in more detail soon. Now you need to create the code to utilize this template. You want to load the template into a simple console application and create some output based on it. The code to do this is quite simple:

```
import java.io.StringWriter;

import org.apache.velocity.VelocityContext;
import org.apache.velocity.app.Velocity;

public class HelloVelocity {

    public static void main(String[] args) throws Exception{

        Velocity.init();

        VelocityContext context = new VelocityContext();
        context.put("who", "Velocity");

        StringWriter writer = new StringWriter();

        Velocity.mergeTemplate("HelloVelocity.vm", "ASCII", context, writer);
        System.out.println(writer);
    }
}
```

In the main() method you initialize the Velocity engine with default parameters with a call to Velocity.init(). Next you create a new VelocityContext object and set the value of the who variable to Velocity. The final part of the code merges the content of the HelloVelocity.vm template with the content stored in the VelocityContext object and places the resulting text in the supplied StringWriter instance. When you run this example, you see the following output:

```
Hello Velocity!
```

From the output you can see that content from the HelloVelocity.vm template was merged with the parameters you set in the VelocityContext. You are probably thinking that was an awful lot of code just to display Ḧello Velocityẗo the console window, and certainly in this case you are correct. However, when you are outputting a large amount of content, especially lots of static and dynamic context mixed together, such as on web pages, you will save a great deal of time using this method.

Velocity and VelocityContext Classes

The Velocity class is the core class used to parse and execute your Velocity templates. Internally, the Velocity class is a simple wrapper around the RuntimeSingleton class, which in turn maintains a singleton instance of the actual engine. Starting from version 1.2 of Velocity, you can now create separate instances of the Velocity engine using the VelocityEngine class, which provides a simple wrapper around the runtime. You should avoid invoking the runtime directly, since the implementation details may change dramatically, but the Velocity and VelocityEngine classes will maintain a consistent, if evolving, interface.

Velocity wouldn't be much use if you couldn't pass in data from your Java applications to be used when executing a template. To this end, the Velocity engine introduces the notion of a Context. To execute a template, you are required to create a Context, usually in the form of the concrete VelocityContext class, and pass this to the Velocity engine along with the template. The Context forms the container for all the data available to your template. When building the VelocityContext in your Java application, each piece of data is associated with a key name that you can use to refer to that data from within your template. In the previous example, you add the value "Velocity" to the VelocityContext under the key "who". Then in the template you are able to use the $who variable to access the value stored in VelocityContext.

Velocity Template Language

In the previous section, we showed you a simple demonstration of Velocity, but in reality you wouldn't want to use Velocity for something that simple, as you would just end up writing more code than you need to. In this section, we are going to take you through a detailed look at VTL and present some more complex examples along the way as well.

Comments

No programming language, VTL included, would be complete without comments. If you decide to leverage Velocity extensively throughout your application, you will no doubt end up with some very complex templates. Without the ability to annotate your templates, you will find it very difficult to maintain your applications.

As in Java, Velocity supports single-line and multiline comments. A single-line comment is denoted by two # characters at the beginning of your comment text. The comment then runs to the end of the line:

```
## say hello
Hello $who
```

unlike in Java, where something like this would be acceptable:

```
int x = 0; // end of line comment
```

You cannot use single-line VTL comments at the end of a line in your template. So something like this:

```
Hello $who ## end of line comment
```

would throw up a `ParseException` and your code will come to an abrupt stop. For multiline comments, you simply need to start your comments with #* and end with *#for example:

```
#* say hello
okay then I will *#
Hello $who
```

Unlike single-line comments, you can use multiline comments at the end of a line in your template:

```
#* say hello
okay then I will *#
Hello $who #* end of line *#
```

Be careful with multiline comments as they can sometimes be responsible for undesirable output in your template. If you run one of the previous templates with multiline comments through the code example previously shown, you will notice that you get a stray line *before* the "H ello Velocity"line. It seems that Velocity will ignore the multiline comments when processing a template but not the trailing newline characters that follow the *# at the end of the comment. You can get around this by doing something like the following:

```
#* say hello
okay then I will
*#Hello $who
```

In this case, there is no newline in the space between where the comment ends and the template content starts, so you will get the desired behavior of a single line reading "Hello Velocity."

Variables

You can probably guess by now what a VTL variable looks like; all the previous examples have contained a single variable, $who. Variables are passed to the Velocity engine via the `VelocityContext` class. Without variables, you wouldn't be able to create many useful templates because you would be restricted to using the content that was predefined in your templates.

Accessing Variables

To access a variable within your template, you simply use the name of the variable prefixed with the $ symbol as follows:

```
Hello $who
```

When you are passing a variable to the Velocity engine as part of a `VelocityContext`, you should exclude the $ character:

```
VelocityContext context = new VelocityContext();
context.put("who", "Velocity");
```

You are not limited to using variables that are passed into your template for Java. Within a template you can create your own variables and utilize them in the same way throughout your template. For instance, this template:

```
#set ($greeting = "How are you?")
Hello $who. $greeting
```

gives the following output:

```
#set ($greeting = "How are you?")
Hello $who. $greeting
```

In the first line of this template, you use the #set directive (more on directives in the next section) to create a new variable called $greeting, and you give it the value "How are you?" On the second line of the template, the value of the $greeting variable is substituted in the same way as the $who variable.

Variable Values

When you are passing variables into Velocity from Java, you can use any primitive or object that you want. For primitives, the corresponding String value will be displayed in the output. For an object, Velocity calls the toString() method to get a String value for output, so you should make sure that any objects you pass to Velocity return valid data from their toString() method.

When declaring variables internally, you are limited to using any of the following:

- *String literals*: You can use any kind of string literal such as "Hello World".

- *Number literals*: You can use any integer literal such as 12 or 123456. You cannot use floating-point numbers when declaring a variable internally.

- *Boolean literals*: You can declare a Boolean variable using either true or false (no quotes).

Quiet References

If you have added a variable to your template as part of the output, but you neither give it a value inside the template nor pass in a value from Java, then the actual variable name will be displayed instead. To see this in action, add an extra variable to the template from the previous example:

```
#set ($greeting = "How are you?")
Hello $who. $greeting $question
```

If you run the example now, you are presented with the following output:

```
Hello Velocity. How are you? $question
```

In most cases, this output is desirable, as it helps you to debug your templates. But there may be some cases where you want to have an optional value that may or may not be passed to your template from Java. In this case, you can use a quiet reference to prevent the variable name from being displayed if no value is present. To use a quiet reference, you simply prefix your variable name with $! instead of $:

```
#set ($greeting = "How are you?")
Hello $who. $greeting $!question
```

So when you run this example again, the output now reads:

```
Hello Velocity. How are you?
```

Variable Concatenation

Within a template, you will often find the need to concatenate the values of two or more variables together. If all you need to do is concatenate the values of the variables together for output, you can just place the variable names next to each other in your template:

```
#set ($firstName = "Gandalf ")
#set ($lastName = "Stormcrow")
Hello $who. My name is $firstName$lastName
```

Notice in the last line of this template you place the $lastName variable directly after the $firstName variable. When you run this template, you get the following output:

```
Hello Velocity. My name is Gandalf Stormcrow
```

Notice that you add a space to the end of the $firstName variable declaration, which is why it was included in the output. If you plan to use the concatenated value more than once throughout the template, then you will probably want to create a new variable to hold the concatenated value. To achieve this, you simply need to add the variable names inside of the new variable declaration:

```
#set ($firstName = "Gandalf ")
#set ($lastName = "Stormcrow")
#set ($fullName = "$firstName$lastName")
Hello $who. My name is $fullName
```

This template gives the exact same output as the previous template. Notice that you still have to include the quotes around the variable names. In this case, you could have added some static text in between the variables to modify the variable that was created:

```
#set ($firstName = "Gandalf ")
#set ($lastName = "Stormcrow")
#set ($fullName = "$lastName. $firstName$lastName")
Hello $who. My name is $fullName
```

Notice that you add the $lastName variable again but also a static period character followed by a space. When this template is run, both static characters are carried throughout the (very James Bond) output:

```
Hello Velocity. My name is Stormcrow. Gandalf Stormcrow
```

The problem with concatenation arises when you want to concatenate the value of a variable with some static content. Consider this version of the previous template:

```
#set ($firstName = "Gandalf ")
#set ($lastName = "Stormcrow")
#set ($fullName = "$lastName. $firstName$lastName")
Hello $who. My name is $firstNameStormcrow
```

Notice how you add the last name as static content. When this runs, the content actually displays $firstNameStormcrow rather than Gandalf Stormcrow because Velocity interprets this as a single variable name without a value. In a case like this, you need to use the formal Velocity notation to reference the variable:

```
#set ($firstName = "Gandalf ")
#set ($lastName = "Stormcrow")
#set ($fullName = "$lastName. $firstName$lastName")
Hello $who. My name is ${firstName}Stormcrow
```

In the preceding example, you wrap the variable name for $firstName in curly braces, which Velocity uses to denote a variable. In most cases, you can leave these braces off, as in the previous template examples, but here they are required to get this template to function.

Escape Characters

Consider the following template example:

```
#set ($widgetCost = "12.99")
#set ($wotsitCost = "13.99")
Price List
----------

$widgetCost = $widgetCost
$wotsitCost = $wotsitCost
```

While it is clear you want to display the variable name and the value, it is also clear that the actual output will be:

```
Price List
----------

12.99 = 12.99
13.99 = 13.99
```

To display the name of the variable that has a value, you need to prefix the variable name with the escape character, which in keeping with Java is a \. So to correct your previous template, you would simply need to prefix each variable name with a \ when you want the name to be displayed:

```
#set ($widgetCost = "12.99")
#set ($wotsitCost = "13.99")
Price List
----------


\$widgetCost = $widgetCost
\$wotsitCost = $wotsitCost
```

Now that the template is corrected, the output is as desired:

```
Price List
----------


$widgetCost = 12.99
$wotsitCost = 13.99
```

To display the \ character itself, you can just include it in the template. Displaying the $ character is not as simple, however. In the case where you want to display the $ character immediately before a variable value, you can include the $ character before the variable in your template:

```
#set ($widgetCost = "12.99")
#set ($wotsitCost = "13.99")
Price List
----------


\$widgetCost = $$widgetCost
\$wotsitCost = $$wotsitCost
```

Notice that where you are getting the values of the $widgetCost and $wotsitCost variables you need to add an additional $ character before the variable. When you run the example now, you get this output:

```
Price List
----------


$widgetCost = $12.99
$wotsitCost = $13.99
```

In fact, you can place the $ character on its own anywhere in the template, and it will display just fine. The only place you cannot have a $ character is as the last character in your template. So while this template will work fine:

```
#set ($widgetCost = "12.99")
#set ($wotsitCost = "13.99")
Price List
----------
```

```
\$widgetCost = $$widgetCost
\$wotsitCost = $$wotsitCost
```

```
All prices in USD ($).
```

if you remove the trailing) and . characters, you will get a ParseException. The only way around this is to declare a variable with $ as its value and use that as the last value in your template:

```
#set ($widgetCost = "12.99")
#set ($wotsitCost = "13.99")
#set ($dollar = "$")
Price List
----------


\$widgetCost = $$widgetCost
\$wotsitCost = $$wotsitCost

All prices in USD $dollar
```

Variables are an important part of how Velocity works, and understanding them will enable you to get the most of the Velocity engine. We have pretty much exhausted the variable topic now, but you will find a much more in-depth discussion of escaping on the Velocity web site at http://jakarta.apache.org/velocity.

Object Methods

If you want to pass an object to the Velocity template from your Java code, you are not limited to accessing only the value of that object's toString() method. Velocity supports the ability to access any of the methods on the object as well. For instance, consider the first example in this chapter. The Java code in that example adds a single String object to VelocityContext. The template used for that example simply displayed the value of the String object and nothing more, but what if you wanted to find out the length of String? You can simply access the String.length() method from within your template:

```
Hello $who!
Your name has $who.length() characters in it.
```

Obviously this would throw an error if the object passed in as the $who variable didn't have a length() method, but since $who is a String, you get this output:

```
Hello Velocity!
Your name has 8 characters in it.
```

Velocity also supports chaining of method calls so you can have something like this in a template:

```
Hello $who!
The who variable is a $who.getClass().getName() instance.
```

which creates this output:

```
Hello Velocity!
The who variable is a java.lang.String instance.
```

JavaBean Properties

Velocity has been designed with simplicity in mind, and for that reason it provides a simple syntax for dealing with classes that expose properties as methods that conform to the JavaBean naming conventions. You can modify the previous example to make use of this simplified syntax as follows:

```
Hello $who!
The who variable is a $who.Class.Name instance.
```

In this case, the Velocity engine interprets $who.Class to match the $who.getClass() property as per the JavaBeans specification. You can also refer to properties within a set statement:

```
#set ($customer.FirstName = "Gandalf")
```

If there is no corresponding setFirstName() method on the $customer object, then this throws an error; otherwise, the value of Gandalf would be stored in that property.

Arithmetic

Along with support for integer primitives inside of your templates, Velocity provides support for simple integer arithmetic. The arithmetic support is very basic, supporting only five operators: +, -, *, /, %. You are no doubt more than familiar with the first four operators, but you may not be as familiar with the fifth. The modulo (%) operator returns the remainder of a division. As an example, 20 / 3 equals 6 with 2 remaining, so 20 % 3 equals 2. All arithmetic works on integers, and the results will only ever be an integer, so 20 / 3 would return 6 as the answer when executed inside a Velocity template.

In this example, we show you how to use the arithmetic support of Velocity to add the shipping costs to your list of products:

```
#set ($widgetCost = 13)
#set ($wotsitCost = 14)
#set ($shipCost = 2)
#set ($widgetTotal = $widgetCost + $shipCost)
#set ($wotsitTotal = $wotsitCost + $shipCost)
Price List
----------

\$widgetCost = $$widgetCost $$widgetTotal
\$wotsitCost = $$wotsitCost $$wotsitTotal

All prices in USD ($).
```

Notice that $widgetCost and $wotsitCost variables have been changed to integer literals as opposed to string literals. The arithmetic functions will only work on integer literals and not numbers contained within a string. You should also note that you have to change the item costs to integers, as Velocity does not support floating-point literals inside its templates. This template gives the following output:

```
Price List
----------


$widgetCost = $13 $15
$wotsitCost = $14 $16

All prices in USD ($).
```

Directives

This is where it gets interesting. Using directives, you can make your templates much more dynamic and appealing. In the previous examples, you use the #set directive to set a variable value within the template. The #set directive is only one of the many directives available in VTL. In this section, we are going to look at the most commonly used directives that you can include in your templates.

Including Static Content with #include

If you are planning on building a web site with Velocity, then you will no doubt have a large amount of content that is going to be common across your templates. Thankfully you are not forced to include this content in every single template. Instead, you can place the common content in a separate file and use the #include directive to have Velocity include it in another template. For example, say you have a main HTML page in a template like this:

```html
<html>
    <head>
        <title>Legolas Industries Homepage</title>
    </head>
    <body>
        <h1>Welcome!!</h1>
        #include("templates/HTMLFooter.vm")
    </body>
</html>
```

Notice the #include directive near the bottom. If you couple this with the HTMLFooter.vm template:

```html
<h3>Copyright &copy; Legolas Industries 2003</h3>
```

and run it through Velocity using the following code:

```java
import java.io.StringWriter;

import org.apache.velocity.VelocityContext;
import org.apache.velocity.app.Velocity;
public class ImportDemo {

    public static void main(String[] args) throws Exception {
        Velocity.init();

        VelocityContext context = new VelocityContext();

        StringWriter writer = new StringWriter();

        Velocity.mergeTemplate(
            "templates/HTMLBody.vm",
            "ASCII",
            context,
            writer);
        System.out.println(writer);
    }
}
```

you end up with this output:

```html
<html>
    <head>
        <title>Legolas Industries Homepage</title>
    </head>
    <body>
        <h1>Welcome!!</h1>
        <h3>Copyright &copy; Legolas Industries 2003</h3>
    </body>
</html>
```

Notice from the Java code that you only specify the HTMLBody.vm template in your call to Velocity.mergeTemplate(), but the code from the HTMLFooter.vm template still finds its way into your final output. This is the #include directive at work. With #include the contents of the include file are substituted for the directive itself. You can also pass multiple arguments to the #include directive to import multiple files in one go:

```
#include("HTMLFooter.vm", "HTMLLinkBar.vm")
```

The drawback of the #include directive is that any VTL content in the include files is ignored by Velocity and treated as static content, so you can't change the content of the included files based on any of the variables in the current context. However, this leads us quite nicely into a discussion of the #parse directive.

Embedding Other Templates with #parse

The #parse directive is designed to overcome the drawbacks with the #include directive by
first running include files through the Velocity engine before including the fully parsed contents in the parent template. To highlight this, make a few small changes to the previous
templates. In the HTMLBody.vm template, replace the company name with a variable that
is defined in the first line of the template. Also replace the #include directive with a #parse
directive as shown here:

```
#set ($companyName = "Legolas Industries")
<html>
    <head>
        <title>$companyName Homepage</title>
    </head>
    <body>
        <h1>Welcome!!</h1>
        #parse("templates/HTMLFooter.vm")
    </body>
</html>
```

In the HTMLFooter.vm template, you replace the company name with the same variable
you use in the HTMLBody.vm template, but notice that this template does not define the
value of the variable, as you want to use the value that is defined by the parent template (in
this case HTMLBody.vm):

```
<h3>Copyright &copy; $companyName 2003</h3>
```

When you run this through the same Java code as before, you get the following output:

```
<html>
    <head>
        <title>Legolas Industries Homepage</title>
    </head>
    <body>
        <h1>Welcome!!</h1>
        <h3>Copyright &copy; Legolas Industries 2003</h3>
    </body>
</html>
```

As you can see, not only have the contents of the HTMLFooter.vm template been included
in place of the #parse directive, but the value of the $companyName variable has been replaced in
both templates by the variable defined in HTMLBody.vm.

When using the #parse directive, the template containing the directive is considered
the parent, and the template being parsed is considered the child. In this case, the child has
access to all of the variables in the parent template's context. When you define a variable in the
child template, it is actually added to the parent template's contextessentially all the templates in the tree share the same context. This may trip you up a little if you try to access a
variable that is defined in the child template from the parent template *before* the child template has been parsed. In this case, the variable has no value, and the name will be outputted;

but if the child template has already been parsed, then the variable value will be outputted. We know this is quite a complex topic to understand, so being the kind people we are, we will walk you through another example. In this example, change the HTMLFooter.vm template and add a single variable declaration:

```
#set ($innerVar = "This is an inner variable")
<h3>Copyright &copy; $companyName 2003</h3>
```

In the HTMLBody.vm, you add two references to this variable, one before the #parse directive and one after it:

```
#set ($companyName = "Legolas Industries")
<html>
    <head>
        <title>$companyName Homepage</title>
    </head>
    <body>
        <h1>Welcome!!</h1>
        $innerVar
        #parse("templates/HTMLFooter.vm")
        $innerVar
    </body>
</html>
```

If you run this example, you will be presented with the following output:

```
<html>
    <head>
        <title>Legolas Industries Homepage</title>
    </head>
    <body>
        <h1>Welcome!!</h1>
        $innerVar
        <h3>Copyright &copy; Legolas Industries 2003</h3>
         This is an inner variable
    </body>
</html>
```

Notice that before the #parse directive the variable has no value, so the name is outputted; but after the #parse statement, when the child template has been parsed, $innerVar has a value, and this is included in the output.

You may be wondering what the point of the #include directive is when you have the #parse directive at your fingertips. Well, the answer is simple: performance. When you use the #parse directive, the Velocity engine will treat the file as another Velocity template and will parse it for variables and directives, whereas with the #include directive Velocity will just read in the file contents and insert them into the output stream. When all you need to do is include the contents of a static resource, then use #include to avoid the overhead introduced by the Velocity engine.

If you find yourself using #import or #parse often within Struts/Velocity applications, then you should consider refactoring to use Tiles, as you will find maintenance much easier.

Making Decisions with #if, #else, and #elseif

So far, all the templates you have seen in this chapter have been quite static. Aside from the occasional variable substitution or template import, nothing much has changed within the example templates—certainly the structure of the output hasn't changed dramatically.

Velocity has quite sophisticated support for conditional blocks within your templates, and without them it wouldn't prove to be such a useful tool. The idea of the conditional statements in Velocity is not to allow for complex business logic but more to support the logic needed to produce the kinds of complex views that are required by today's web applications. Can you imagine trying to build a web application without being able to change the interface that is displayed to your users? Even a relatively simple application like the JavaEdge application developed in this book requires this ability. How well would the login/logout functionality of the JavaEdge application work if you were unable to hide the logout button when a user is logged out and show it when that user is logged in?

You will be glad to hear that using the conditional directives in Velocity is no more complex than using any of the other VTL directives described previously.

At the most basic level, you have the #if directive, which is synonymous with the Java if statement. The #if directive is complemented by the #else directive, which will allow you to provide some alternative output if the #if directive evaluates to false. To see how this is done, add some extra directives to your previous template as shown here:

```
#set ($companyName = "Legolas Industries")
<html>
    <head>
        <title>$companyName Homepage</title>
    </head>
    <body>
        <h1>Welcome!!</h1>
        #if ($userType == "elf")
            <h2>You are an elf!</h2>
        #else
            <h2>I don't know what you are!</h2>
        #end
        #parse("templates/HTMLFooter.vm")
    </body>
</html>
```

Also change the Java code slightly to add the $userType variable to VelocityContext:

```
public static void main(String[] args) throws Exception {
        Velocity.init();

        VelocityContext context = new VelocityContext();
        context.put("userType", "elf");

        StringWriter writer = new StringWriter();
```

```
        Velocity.mergeTemplate(
            "templates/HTMLBody.vm",
            "ASCII",
            context,
            writer);
        System.out.println(writer);
    }
```

When you run this example, you get the following output:

```
<html>
    <head>
        <title>Legolas Industries Homepage</title>
    </head>
    <body>
        <h1>Welcome!!</h1>
                <h2>You are an elf!</h2>
                <h3>Copyright &copy; Legolas Industries 2003</h3>
    </body>
</html>
```

You should also try running this example with a different value set for $userType. Of course, you are not just limited to simple conditional statements like this one. Velocity also supports the #elseif directive, allowing you to make more complex decisions within your templates. For example:

```
#set ($companyName = "Legolas Industries")
<html>
    <head>
        <title>$companyName Homepage</title>
    </head>
    <body>
        <h1>Welcome!!</h1>
        #if ($userType == "human")
            <h2>You are a human!</h2>
        #elseif ($userType == "orc")
            <h2>You are an orc. Damn, you're ugly!</h2>
        #elseif ($userType == "elf")
            <h2>You are an elf! How go the pointy ears?</h2>
        #else
            <h2>I don't know what you are!</h2>
        #end
        #parse("templates/HTMLFooter.vm")
    </body>
</html>
```

Try running this one with different values set for the $userType variable. You've seen the examples, now comes the science. When building your conditional statements you should follow these three guidelines:

- I f you pass in a primitive Boolean, a Boolean object either as a variable or as an expression that evaluates to a Boolean value, then the Velocity engine will, quite obviously, use the appropriate true or false value.

- I f you pass in a variable that is not a Boolean, then the condition will evaluate to true if that variable exists in the current context and false if it does not.

- Y ou can pass in the literals true or false to represent their appropriate values.

Working with Collections Using #foreach

Building a web application usually means working with a database, and this in turn usually means one thing: lists. The main reason you would use a database is to store data, and since you are using a database to store the data, you are probably storing large lists of data rather than individual items. No view technology would be complete without the ability to output lists in a quick and efficient manner, and in Velocity this is executed with typical simplicity.

Using the #foreach directive, you can repeat a block of your template for each item in a list of data, changing the output based on the current item in the list. When it comes to the actual lists, you have three options:

- V elocity arrays

- V elocity ranges

- J ava collections

Velocity provides a simple syntax to build arrays internally that can then be used with the #foreach directive to output a list of data. To declare an array variable, you use the #set directive with a different syntax for the variable value:

```
#set (myArray = ["one", "two", "three"])
```

Notice that for the value you add three separate values, delimited by commas, and wrap the whole thing in square brackets. Once you have an array available in the active context, you can use the #foreach directive to loop through the elements and output them:

```
#set ($myArray = ["one", "two", "three"])
#foreach($item in $myArray)
    List Item: $item
#end
```

When you run this through Velocity, you get the following output:

```
List Item: one
List Item: two
List Item: three
```

You should note that you don't have to declare the array as a variable; instead, you can use the array syntax in place of the array variable in the #foreach directive. The range operator in Velocity provides a simple way to declare an array of integers without having to specify every single integer; you simply specify the beginning and end of the range:

```
#foreach($number in [1..5])
    Current Index: $number
#end
```

In this example, the range is declared using [1..5] with 1 being the start of the range and 5 being the end. You can, of course, specify any integer for the start and end of the range. This example will create this output:

```
Current Index: 1
Current Index: 2
Current Index: 3
Current Index: 4
Current Index: 5
```

Note that in the preceding example you could have assigned the range to a variable instead of creating the array directly inside of the #foreach directive. If you need to use a range of numbers or an array more than once in the same template, then you should consider creating a variable to hold it rather than re-creating it each time you use the #foreach directive.

Of course, both of these features are quite useful, but the real power comes from being able to pass in a Collection from your Java code and access the objects contained in it. Using this capability, you can load the data from your database and package it up using the Value Object pattern in a similar manner to the way we have demonstrated loading the data for the JavaEdge application. Once you have a Collection of value objects, you can pass them into Velocity and have the template render the data as appropriate.

This next example is slightly more involved than the previous ones and returns to the earlier example of a price list. What you want to achieve is a list of products and their prices. The products are described in Java as the Product class and are loaded from some data store and passed to the presentation tier in a Collection. You want to use Velocity to take this Collection of objects and build an HTML price list.

So first you need the Product class in Java to hold the product details:

```
public class Product {

    private String name;
    private double price;

    public Product(String aName, double aPrice) {
        name = aName;
        price = aPrice;
    }

    public String getName() {
        return name;
    }
}
```

```
    public double getPrice() {
        return price;
    }

    public void setName(String val) {
        name = val;
    }

    public void setPrice(double val) {
        price = val;
    }
}
```

This is a very basic class to hold the data for one product. It has two properties, Name and Price, with the corresponding get() and set() methods. The next thing you need to do is to create a Collection of Product objects and store the Collection in the VelocityContext:

```
public static void main(String[] args) throws Exception {
        Velocity.init();

        VelocityContext context = new VelocityContext();

        Collection products = new ArrayList();
        products.add(new Product("Widget", 12.99));
        products.add(new Product("Wotsit", 13.99));
        products.add(new Product("Thingy", 11.99));

        context.put("products", products);

        StringWriter writer = new StringWriter();

        Velocity.mergeTemplate(
            "templates/Foreach.vm",
            "ASCII",
            context,
            writer);
        System.out.println(writer);
    }
```

As you can see, constructing the Collection and storing it in the VelocityContext is pretty basic stuff, although in real life you would probably load the Product objects from a database rather than having them hard-coded into your application. The final piece for this example is the template shown here:

```
<html>
    <head>
        <title>Gimli's Widgetarium</title>
    </head>
    <body>
```

```
    <table>
        #set ($rowCount = 1)
        #foreach($product in $products)
            #if ($rowCount % 2 == 0)
                #set ($bgcolor = "#FFFFFF")
            #else
                #set ($bgcolor = "#CCCCCC")
            #end
            <tr>
                <td bgcolor="$bgcolor">$product.Name</td>
                <td bgcolor="$bgcolor">$product.Price</td>
            </tr>
            #set ($rowCount = $rowCount + 1)
        #end
    </table>
    </body>
</html>
```

This template is quite complex and requires a little bit of explanation. Ignoring the static content, the bulk of the content in this template is created in the #foreach loop. The #foreach loop looks at each Product object stored in the $products Collection and outputs a table row for each one. If you look at the table cells, you will notice that the actual properties of the Product objects are accessed using the shortcuts discussed earlier. The other interesting part of this template is the use of the modulo operator coupled with the #if and #else directives. Using these constructs, you can differentiate between odd- and even-numbered rows in the table and color them accordingly.

As you can see, using the #foreach directive is actually very easy—you are only really limited by your creativity. As with all of the directives in Velocity, #foreach has a very simple syntax that provides enough power to support the creation of your view, but is of little use for performing any kind of business logic. Most people, ourselves included, would find this to be a godsend, as it prevents any lax developers on your team from breaking your strict architecture.

Macros

In the previous section, we looked at Velocity directives, but if you are familiar with Velocity, you will have noticed that we missed one. Velocity provides excellent support for macros, sometimes called *Velocimacros*, using another directive, #macro. We have decided to separate our discussion of the #macro directives from that of all of the other directives, because you will rarely use the #macro directive within the body of your template; it tends to be something that you use once or twice near the top of your template or in a separate include file, instead of referring to your defined macros in the body of your template.

If you aren't familiar with the concept of macros, they are a way of packaging up bits of functionality into a reusable unit. Macros in Velocity are simply a way of reducing the amount of code you need to type and maintain. When your template is parsed, any calls to a macro are expanded into the full code of that macro at the point in the template where the macro call exists. Sort of like automatic find and replace!

To declare a macro within your code, you use the #macro directive. Rather than give you a trivial example, take a look at a rewritten version of the previous example that uses a macro to output the table of products. The Java code for this example is the same; all that changes is the template:

```
#macro (writeTable $productList)
    #set ($rowCount = 1)
    #foreach($product in $productList)
    #if ($rowCount % 2 == 0)
        #set ($bgcolor = "#FFFFFF")
    #else
        #set ($bgcolor = "#CCCCCC")
    #end
        <tr>
            <td bgcolor="$bgcolor">$product.Name</td>
            <td bgcolor="$bgcolor">$product.Price</td>
        </tr>
        #set ($rowCount = $rowCount + 1)
    #end
#end
<html>
    <head>
        <title>Gimli's Widgetarium</title>
    </head>
    <body>
        <table>
            #writeTable($products)
        </table>
    </body>
</html>
```

Notice how you create a macro with the #macro directive. Inside of the parentheses the first argument for the #macro directive is the name of the macro you want to create, in this case writeTable. All the remaining arguments are the names of arguments that you can pass to the macro; in this case, you see just one argument, $productList, but you can have as many arguments as you like. Inside the macro body you use the #foreach directive to output the list of Product objects contained in the $productList argument. As you can see, the code inside the macro body is identical to the code used in the body of the previous example. Whereas before you had the code to render the table, here you call the macro using the #writeTable directive, which is created by the macro declaration instead. In this particular case, using a macro has no particular benefit; it would have been simpler to render the table directly. However, if you want to render the table again, then you could reuse the macro, or you could place the macro in an external file and include it in multiple templates using #parse. In this way, Velocity provides a mechanism for you to centralize your presentation logic.

Struts and Velocity

Up to now, none of the examples have used Struts in any way. Instead, they have all run inside a simple Java class and written their output to the console. In this section, we are going to show how you can use Velocity alongside Struts in the JavaEdge application to build printer-friendly output for a story.

VelocityTools

On its own, Velocity does not have support for working with Struts; that support is introduced by another Jakarta project: VelocityTools. As part of the Velocity project, the Jakarta team added a mechanism to extend the capabilities in a standard way without affecting the core code base. This mechanism involves building a kind of plug-in called a *tool* and then configuring this within Velocity so that it runs within your application. As well as building the model, the Velocity team started a separate project, VelocityTools, to build a set of standard tools to provide integration with other projects, one of these being Struts. The result of this is the VelocityStruts toolset that enables your Velocity templates to work alongside Struts. This includes, amongst other things, support for working with `ActionForms`, the Validator, and more recently the Tiles framework.

For the next example, you will need to download VelocityTools from the Jakarta web site at `http://jakarta.apache.org`. The JavaEdge application was built using version 1.0 of Velocity-Tools and version 1.3.1 of Velocity.

Printer-Friendly Pages

The aim of this example is to demonstrate how you can replace JSP with Velocity as the view layer in your application. We also want to show that you can quite happily run Velocity alongside JSP in your application; you are not restricted to using one technology or the other. To this end, we have decided that rather than showing you how to create a version of the JavaEdge application that uses Velocity as the view technology, we will demonstrate creating an additional feature within the existing application, namely printer-friendly pages for the stories. At the end of this example you should have a good understanding of how Velocity and Struts interact and how you can leverage the Velocity engine in your own applications.

Getting Started

To start with, you need to add the Velocity, Velocity Dependencies, and VelocityTools jar files to the lib directory of the JavaEdge application. You also need to add the dom4j jar file that is included with the VelocityTools download, since the VelocityTools project won't run without it. The Ant build file that you use to build the JavaEdge application will automatically include these new jar files in the war file when the application is assembled for deployment.

Configuring the Velocity Servlet

In the previous examples, all processing of the Velocity templates has been done by manually constructing `VelocityContext` and manually configuring and executing the Velocity engine. With Struts, you don't want to have to go through this process every single time you build a view using Velocity. Thankfully, you don't need to. With the VelocityTools project comes the `VelocityViewServlet`, which you can map to the *.vm extension to have all-out Velocity templates processed automatically by Velocity. Configuring the VelocityViewServlet is a fairly simple matter of adding the servlet declaration and mapping options to the JavaEdge web.xml:

```
<!-- Velocity Template Engine Servlet -->
  <servlet>
      <servlet-name>velocity</servlet-name>
      <servlet-class>
        org.apache.velocity.tools.view.servlet.VelocityViewServlet
      </servlet-class>

      <init-param>
        <param-name>org.apache.velocity.toolbox</param-name>
          <param-value>/WEB-INF/toolbox.xml</param-value>
      </init-param>

      <init-param>
        <param-name>org.apache.velocity.properties</param-name>
        <param-value>/WEB-INF/velocity.properties</param-value>
      </init-param>

      <load-on-startup>10</load-on-startup>

  </servlet>
<servlet-mapping>
      <servlet-name>velocity</servlet-name>
      <url-pattern>*.vm</url-pattern>
  </servlet-mapping>
```

Two initialization parameters are passed to the VelocityViewServlet: one to specify an optional configuration file (org.apache.velocity.properties), and one to specify where the toolbox configuration file is (org.apache.velocity.toolbox). The properties file is unimportant, as you are sticking with the default settings for the servlet, but we usually add this in anyway and create the file as it makes it easier to change the settings later on. The toolbox configuration file is much more important, as this is how you configure additional tools within the Velocity engine. The VelocityViewServlet takes care of instructing the Velocity engine to read the file—you just need to tell the servlet where the toolbox configuration file is situated.

The toolbox configuration file is a simple XML file that is used to load additional tools into the Velocity engine. To use Velocity with Struts, you are going to need to expose your Struts objects to the Velocity templates, and to do this you need to use the four core Struts tools:

- MessageTool: This tool gives your template access to the resources stored in your Struts resource file; in the case of the JavaEdge application this is the ApplicationResources.properties file.

- FormTool: This tool allows you to access ActionForm beans that are accessible within the current scope. You also use FormTool to build HTML forms that work with the Struts framework from within your templates.

- ErrorsTool: Using this tool, you can work with Struts error messages within your templates in a manner similar to that by which the `<html:error>` tag works in JSP.

- StrutsLinkTool: This tool helps you to build links to other Struts actions from within your templates. This is synonymous with the `<html:link>` tag used in JSP.

The toolbox.xml file looks like this:

```
<toolbox>
  <tool>
    <key>link</key>
    <scope>request</scope>
    <class>org.apache.velocity.tools.struts.StrutsLinkTool</class>
  </tool>
  <tool>
    <key>msg</key>
    <scope>request</scope>
    <class>org.apache.velocity.tools.struts.MessageTool</class>
  </tool>
  <tool>
    <key>errors</key>
    <scope>request</scope>
    <class>org.apache.velocity.tools.struts.ErrorsTool</class>
  </tool>
  <tool>
    <key>form</key>
    <scope>request</scope>
    <class>org.apache.velocity.tools.struts.FormTool</class>
  </tool>
</toolbox>
```

Notice that all four tools we discussed previously are defined here along with the scope in which they are stored, in this case the request scope, and a name. The name you give the tools here is the name of the variable with which you can access them inside of your templates. While we will be demonstrating a selection of the methods available on these tools, we will not be showing them all; you can find the list of methods in the documentation included with the VelocityTools download.

So to recap, in this section you have seen how to map requests for any resource ending with .vm to the `VelocityViewServlet` and also configure the four key Struts tools within the Velocity engine. At this point, you can use a Velocity template as the destination for any `ActionForwards` defined within Struts.

Creating the Struts Action

Typically, when creating a new feature in a Struts application, you have to create one or more `Action` classes to hook up the user interface to the business logic behind. However, the whole point of Struts is that your `Action` classes have nothing to do with the *actual* user interface; instead, they are merely the control logic that sits behind the user interface. In this case, the action you want the JavaEdge application to perform is to display a story and the list of associated comments. From a Struts point of view, you already have an action that does that: StoryDetailSetupAction. Okay, so when this action is used now, the resultant output isn't particularly printer friendly, but that has nothing to do with the Action class; it simply gathers the data required and then passes off responsibility to the view.

StoryDetailSetupAction gathers all the data that you need for your printer-friendly view, since all you are really doing is creating a different view of the same action within the web site, that is, viewing a story. So you don't actually need to create a new Action class; instead, all you need to do is create a new ActionMapping in the struts-config.xml file and configure the ActionForward for that mapping to use your Velocity template instead of the JSP page. So where the mapping for the standard web view looks like this with a JSP view:

```
<action path="/storyDetailSetup"
type="com.apress.javaedge.struts.storydetail.StoryDetailSetupAction">
<forward name="storydetail.success" path="/WEB-INF/jsp/storyDetail.jsp"/>
    </action>
```

your new mapping for the printer-friendly view looks like this, with a Velocity view:

```
<action path="/printFriendly"
type="com.apress.javaedge.struts.storydetail.StoryDetailSetupAction">
<forward name="storydetail.success" path="/WEB-INF/velocity/printFriendly.vm"/>
    </action>
```

Notice that both actions are using the same Action class, because they are essentially two different views of the same data.

Linking to the Action

It won't surprise you to know that linking to your new action is no different than linking to any other Struts action, because that is exactly what it is just a standard Struts action. The important point here is that the view technology has absolutely no bearing on how you interact with your Struts actions. The following adds a link to the print-friendly story page from the standard story page using the Struts <html:link> tag:

```
<html:link action="/printFriendly" paramId="storyId"
paramName="storyVO" paramProperty="storyId">
Printer Friendly
</html:link>
```

Building the View

Now comes the fun part! The template that you build is fairly simple; we'll include it completely here and then explain the individual parts separately:

```
<html>
    <head>
        <title>Print Friendly</title>
    </head>
    <body>
    <a href="$link.setAction("/storyDetailSetup")?storyId=$storyVO.storyId">
```

```
[back]</a>
        <table border="0" cellspacing="2" cellpadding="1">

            <tr>
                <td colspan="2">
                    <font size="10">$storyVO.StoryTitle</font>
                </td>
            </tr>
            <tr>
                <td bgcolor="#CCCCCC">Posted By:</td>
                <td>$storyVO.StoryAuthor.FirstName
                $storyVO.StoryAuthor.LastName</td>
            </tr>
            <tr>
                <td bgcolor="#CCCCCC">On:</td>
                <td>$storyVO.SubmissionDate</td>
            </tr>
            <tr>
                <td colspan="2">
                    <font size="4">
                        <i>$storyVO.StoryIntro</i>
                    </font>
                </td>
            </tr>
            <tr>
                <td colspan="2">
                    <font size="4">
                        $storyVO.StoryBody
                    </font>
                </td>
            </tr>
            <tr>
                <td colspan="2">
                    <br><i>Comments</i><hr>
                </td>
            #foreach ($comment in $comments)
            <tr>
                <td width="30"> </td>
                <td>Posted By: $comment.CommentAuthor.FirstName
$comment.CommentAuthor.LastName<br>
                On: $comment.SubmissionDate</td>
            </tr>
            <tr>
                <td width="30"> </td>
                <td>$comment.CommentBody</td>
            </tr>
            <tr>
```

```
                    <td colspan="2"><hr></td>
                </tr>
                #end

        </table>
    </body>

</html>
```

We'll start with the simple bits. First off you render the details of the story and its author. The code for this should look fairly familiar; just be aware that whatever beans were placed into the request context by the StoryDetailSetupAction were transferred into the VelocityContext by the VelocityViewServlet before it processed the view template.

```
<tr>
    <td colspan="2">
        <font size="10">$storyVO.StoryTitle</font>
    </td>
</tr>
<tr>
    <td bgcolor="#CCCCCC">Posted By:</td>
    <td>$storyVO.StoryAuthor.FirstName $storyVO.StoryAuthor.LastName</td>
</tr>
<tr>
    <td bgcolor="#CCCCCC">On:</td>
    <td>$storyVO.SubmissionDate</td>
</tr>
<tr>
    <td colspan="2">
        <font size="4">
            <i>$storyVO.StoryIntro</i>
        </font>
    </td>
</tr>
<tr>
    <td colspan="2">
        <font size="4">
            $storyVO.StoryBody
        </font>
    </td>
</tr>
```

Notice that the variable name for the StoryVO object matches the name given to it when it was placed in the request context by the StoryDetailSetupAction:

```
public ActionForward execute(ActionMapping mapping,
                             ActionForm    form,
                             HttpServletRequest request,
                             HttpServletResponse response){
```

```
        String storyId = request.getParameter("storyId");

        IStoryManager storyManager = StoryManagerBD.getStoryManagerBD();
        StoryVO storyVO = storyManager.retrieveStory(storyId);

        request.setAttribute("storyVO",storyVO);
        request.setAttribute("comments", storyVO.getComments());

        return (mapping.findForward("storydetail.success"));
    }
```

Also notice from the template that you access the properties of the StoryVO and MemberVO (the author) objects using the quick notation. This is because you use the JavaBean naming conventions for all the value object classes in the JavaEdge application. When using Velocity, this makes your templates much easier to read and maintain, especially by nonprogrammers.

The next part of the template renders the list of comments. If you look at the code for StoryDetailSetupAction, you will see that the comments are stored as a vector instance in the request scope. Before VelocityViewServlet parses the template, it will transfer this vector to VelocityContext, and subsequently you can use the #foreach directive in your template to output the list of comments.

```
#foreach ($comment in $comments)
<tr>
    <td width="30"> </td>
    <td>Posted By: $comment.CommentAuthor.FirstName
$comment.CommentAuthor.LastName<br>
        On: $comment.SubmissionDate</td>
</tr>
<tr>
    <td width="30"> </td>
    <td>$comment.CommentBody</td>
</tr>
<tr>
    <td colspan="2"><hr></td>
</tr>
#end
```

The last part of the template we wish to touch on is the back link that is rendered at the top of the page. For this you use StrutsLinkTool to avoid having to know in advance any of the details about what URL mapping method is used in Struts or what the name of the context is in which the JavaEdge application is deployed.

```
<a href="$link.setAction("/storyDetailSetup")?storyId=$storyVO.storyId">[back]</a>
```

Notice the call to $link.setAction; the $link variable was mapped to StrutsLinkTool earlier on in the toolbox.xml file. In this call, you simply pass in the name of the action you wish to link back to. StrutsLinkTool takes care of making sure that the link is rendered correctly, with the correct context name and correct URL format. And last of all, you simply append the storyId parameter to the link using standard VTL so that the user is sent back to the correct story page.

Struts and Velocity

As you can see, getting Struts and Velocity working together is very easy; in fact, it has taken us more time to write this single section than it did to put the example together.

This section has shown a practical example of how you can couple Struts and Velocity to create powerful web applications quite simply. As we demonstrated, using a Velocity view with a Struts action requires little or no work on your part, as your existing Struts actions will continue to function just as well with Velocity templates as they did with JSP. Most of the hard work in connecting the two together is taken care of by the `VelocityViewServlet`.

The four core tools included in the 1.0 release of `VelocityStruts` provide all the extensions you will need within your templates to rival most of your JSP view pages. We say "most" because Velocity is missing integration with some of the more advanced features, such as integration with the Tiles and the Validator frameworks. However, as we write this, the next version of VelocityTools is in development, and we were able to preview tools that added support not only for Tiles and Validator, but also for manipulating `ActionMessages` and links in an SSL-enabled environment.

The integration between Velocity and Struts is still very much in its infancy, but already the project offers plenty of powerful features that enable you to build elegant solutions to your problems. You can watch for the emergence of the next version of VelocityTools at the Velocity web site.

Best Practices for Velocity Use

Before we close this chapter, we want to cover the practices that you should follow when using Velocity.

Use Macros

If you decide to build your entire web application using Velocity, or even just a small part of it, you should try and use as many macros as you can to centralize your layout logic. Doing this will enable you to make and test any changes easily. You can move your macros into a separate file and include them in your templates using #parse, or you can even create one or more global macro files that are available to your entire application. By default, Velocity will look for VM_global_library.vm in the root of your classpath as the default file for global macros. If you have macros contained in separate files that you want to reuse in multiple applications, you can make these available globally by setting the value of the `velocimacro.library` property to a comma-separated list of the filenames. You can set this property either with a call to `System.setProperty()` or via the velocity.properties file.

Know When to Use #parse and When to Use #include

It is good practice to split your templates into multiple files so that you can reuse the content in multiple templates. Most web sites have some kind of header and maybe a footer—these make ideal candidates to be placed in a separate template of their own. When importing external files into a template, take care to use #include whenever you don't require the file to be processed by Velocity. By using #parse on files that have no VTL content, you are adding unnecessary overhead to your application that is easily removed by using #include.

Use JavaBean Property Names

To make your template easier to read and maintain, especially by others who may have to make changes in your absence, you should stick to using property name shortcuts such as $customer.EmailAddress as opposed to $customer.getEmailAddress(). This is especially true if you are working with web designers who are unfamiliar with Java, as Velocity is very easy to understand and learn.

Summary

In this chapter, we have introduced the key concepts behind the Velocity template engine as well as provided an in-depth look at the Velocity template language. Along with the many console-style examples herein, we have demonstrated with a full working example how the Velocity template engine can be integrated with the Struts framework as an alternative view component to JSP. Finally, we have discussed some of the best practices you can employ when developing your Struts- and Velocity-based applications.

## CHAPTER 11

Extending the Struts Framework

Any framework is only as good as what you can accomplish with it. To this end, most good frameworks, Struts included, provide some mechanism to extend the features provided by the framework, so that you are pretty much limited only by your own imagination.

Struts has more than one extension mechanism, each of which fits a specific purpose. In this chapter, we are going to look at each method in turn, and take you through the key features that will allow you to extend the Struts framework to provide extra services for your application.

Specifically, this chapter addresses four main extension methods:

- *Extending* Action *and* ActionForm: The simplest method of extension within Struts is to provide your own classes that override the Action and ActionForm classes. In this way, you can provide standard services to your application's presentation layer through the Struts framework.

- *Extending* RequestProcessor: By extending RequestProcessor, you can hook into the Struts request processing flow and perform your own processing during the request cycle.

- *Creating configuration beans*: Using custom configuration beans, you can provide additional information about your actions that can be used by a custom Action or a custom RequestProcessor.

- *Building a plug-in*: Using Struts plug-ins, you can provide application-level or background services to your application that allow you to perform processing outside the context of a request.

Each topic is covered in its own section, and we provide the pros and cons for each mechanism along with guidelines for when best to employ a particular mechanism.

Extending Action and ActionForm

Most of the processing carried out by your application within the context of the Struts framework happens inside an Action- or ActionForm-derived class. Quite often you will perform repetitive tasks within your Action or ActionForm classes that you would like to refactor out into a separate helper class. In cases like these, you can extend the Action and ActionForm classes provided by Struts, creating your own base `Action` and `ActionForm` classes that are used by the remaining actions in your code.

For the remainder of this section, we will focus on extending the `Action` class, but you should remember that most of the principles still apply when you want to extend the `ActionForm` class.

There are two main reasons to provide your own base `Action` class: You want to provide some standard services to your actions, and you want to hook into the execution of your actions to provide some form of preprocessing.

Providing Common Services to Your Actions

In any application, you will have common logic within the presentation tier that you would like to avoid duplicating throughout the code. When using the Struts framework, the perfect place for this is in a common base class shared by all your `Action` classes. Using this method, you can make the code within your actions cleaner by avoiding the need to reference one or more helper classes just to perform some standard logic processing. In some cases, such as the one we demonstrate shortly, you will find that providing your own base actions makes sense semantically when you look at the logic being performed.

Before we jump into the example, we want to give you some guidelines for using a base `Action` class to provide application services:

- *Avoid heavy processing*: Try to avoid putting any heavy processing or large amounts of logic inside a base `Action` class. In most cases, the logic you encapsulate within the `Action` class should be short and sweet, such as providing typed access to session properties, not authenticating a user against an LDAP directory server.

- *No business logic*: You should avoid at all costs placing your business logic in the base `Action` class. This is a classic exhibit of the Tier Leakage antipattern discussed in Chapter 2 and will cause the logic to become very tightly coupled to the Struts framework. Restrict the logic to presentation- or web container–specific issues.

- *No side effects*: Try to avoid making the logic have any major side effects. With this mechanism you are encapsulating lightweight logic to reduce the amount of code you need to write and maintenance you need to do. If your logic has side effects that are not apparent by the method name, then your logic is in the wrong place and you should consider refactoring.

Now for the example.

Accessing Session Properties

One of the common purposes for which we like to use a standard base `Action` class is to provide typed access to data stored in the session. In this way, we can avoid checking for a property's existence and casting every time we want to access the property. In the JavaEdge application, you store the current identity of the current user, as a `MemberVO` object, in the user's session. Every time you want to access it, you have to retrieve it from the session and cast it to the correct type. This is certainly not a massive amount of logic, but it is enough to drive you insane when you have typed it in hundreds of times in a big application. Consider the maintenance of those hundreds of lines of code time to try on your new wraparound jacket. But you can encapsulate this logic as a set of get() and set() methods in the base Action class and then use those methods from the actual Action class that performs the processing.

Currently you have the PostComment Action which processes any user requests to post a comment about a story. The code for this class is as follows:

```java
public class PostComment extends Action {
    // Create Log4j category instance for logging.
    static private org.apache.log4j.Category log =
                org.apache.log4j.Category.getInstance(
                    PostComment.class.getName());

    public ActionForward execute(ActionMapping mapping,
                                 ActionForm      form,
                                 HttpServletRequest request,
                                 HttpServletResponse response) throws Exception {

        if (this.isCancelled(request)){
            System.out.println("*****The user pressed cancel!!");
            return (mapping.findForward("poststory.success"));
        }

        PostCommentForm postCommentForm = (PostCommentForm) form;
        HttpSession session = request.getSession();

        MemberVO      memberVO    = (MemberVO)
                session.getAttribute("memberVO");
        String        storyId     = (String)
                request.getParameter("storyVO.storyId");


        IStoryManager storyManagerBD = StoryManagerBD.getStoryManagerBD();
        StoryVO storyVO = storyManagerBD.retrieveStory(storyId);

        StoryCommentVO storyCommentVO = postCommentForm.getStoryCommentVO();
        storyCommentVO.setCommentAuthor(memberVO);
        storyCommentVO.setSubmissionDate(
                new java.sql.Date(System.currentTimeMillis()));
        storyVO.getComments().add(storyCommentVO);
        storyManagerBD.updateStory(storyVO);

        return (mapping.findForward("postcomment.success"));
    }
}
```

Notice the code to retrieve the MemberVO from the session:

```java
MemberVO      memberVO    = (MemberVO) session.getAttribute("memberVO");
```

It's only one line of code, but it doesn't do anything spectacular; there is no check to see if the object exists, and there is no code to handle the nonexistence of the object at all—the code simply assumes that the MemberVO will be there. In this case, it most likely will be there, because the JavaEdge application uses a Filter to make the current user the anonymous user if they have not logged in or their session has expired.

Consider what would happen if the Filter were not used, and JavaEdge did not support the anonymous user. To get around this, you would have to go back through all the code and add checks everywhere that the MemberVO is loaded from the session. However, if it were the case that the JavaEdge application would not always have a MemberVO in the session, you would be able to encapsulate all the logic for retrieving the MemberVO in a base Action class.

So that is the theory behind it; now on to the code. We will show you the full code here and discuss each part separately in the following text:

```java
public class ActionBase extends Action {

    private static final String MEMBER_VO_KEY = "memberVO";

    private HttpServletRequest _request = null;
    private HttpServletResponse _response = null;

    public ActionForward execute(
        ActionMapping mapping,
        ActionForm form,
        HttpServletRequest request,
        HttpServletResponse response)
        throws Exception {

        _request = request;
        _response = response;

        return super.execute(mapping, form, request, response);
    }

    protected void setMember(MemberVO member) {
        _request.getSession().setAttribute(MEMBER_VO_KEY, member);
    }

    protected MemberVO getMember() {
        HttpSession session = _request.getSession();

        if (session.getAttribute(MEMBER_VO_KEY) == null) {
            throw new ApplicationException("Not Logged In");
        } else if(!(session.getAttribute(MEMBER_VO_KEY) instanceof MemberVO)) {
            throw new ApplicationException("Session Corrupted");
        } else {
            return (MemberVO) session.getAttribute(MEMBER_VO_KEY);
        }
    }
}
```

First and most obvious is the class declaration. You define the Struts Action class as the base class for this class:

```
public class ActionBase extends Action {
```

The next part is where it gets slightly tricky. If you want to capture data from the session or from the request in your base action, then you need to override execute() so that you can store the HttpServletRequest and HttpServletResponse objects. The Action class has no properties that allow you to access these, hence they are passed as arguments to the execute() method.

```
public ActionForward execute(
        ActionMapping mapping,
        ActionForm form,
        HttpServletRequest request,
        HttpServletResponse response)
        throws Exception {

    _request = request;
    _response = response;

    return super.execute(mapping, form, request, response);
}
```

The code itself for this is nothing spectacular. You just store the objects in private fields within the class. The next step is to define the property for the MemberVO object. The set() method is very simple—you just store the object in the session. You don't need to check the type, because the method will only accept a MemberVO object or a derived type as the argument.

```
public void setMember(MemberVO member) {
    _request.getSession().setAttribute(MEMBER_VO_KEY, member);
}
```

The get() method is slightly more complex, as this is where you perform most of the checks to make sure that the MemberVO object exists in the session:

```
public MemberVO getMember() throws Exception {
    HttpSession session = _request.getSession();

    if (session.getAttribute(MEMBER_VO_KEY) == null) {
        throw new ApplicationException("Not Logged In");
    } else if(!(session.getAttribute(MEMBER_VO_KEY) instanceof MemberVO)) {
        throw new ApplicationException("Session Corrupted");
    } else {
        return (MemberVO) session.getAttribute(MEMBER_VO_KEY);
    }
}
```

Notice that you need to check both that MemberVO exists and that it is of the correct type. If either of these conditions is false, then an ApplicationException is thrown. Don't try to forward the user to somewhere from this code—it won't work. The request will be committed, but the control will return to the subclass, which will then try to forward again via an ActionForward, causing an Exception. Instead, use an Exception such as ApplicationException and configure a global exception handler for it. You may want to build a specific Exception class to handle this behavior so that you can handle the nonexistence of the MemberVO differently in the case of a real error.

That is it for the base Action class; however, the solution does not yet work. Since Java does not call overridden methods on parent classes by default, when you make PostComment derive from ActionBase, the execute() method in ActionBase does not get executed, so the request and response objects are unavailable to the getMember() and setMember() methods. To remedy this, you simply need to add a call to super.execute() as the first line in the PostComment.execute() method, remembering to allow for thrown exceptions. The modified code for the PostComment action now looks like this:

```
public class PostComment extends ActionBase {
    // Create Log4j category instance for logging.
        static private org.apache.log4j.Category log =
                org.apache.log4j.Category.getInstance(
                    PostComment.class.getName());

        public ActionForward execute(ActionMapping mapping,
                            ActionForm     form,
                            HttpServletRequest request,
                            HttpServletResponse response) throws
                            Exception {
    super.execute(mapping, form, request, response);
    if (this.isCancelled(request)){
        System.out.println("*****The user pressed cancel!!!");
        return (mapping.findForward("poststory.success"));
    }

    PostCommentForm postCommentForm = (PostCommentForm) form;
    HttpSession session = request.getSession();

    MemberVO       memberVO      = getMember();
    String         storyId       = (String)
            request.getParameter("storyVO.storyId");


    IStoryManager storyManagerBD = StoryManagerBD.getStoryManagerBD();
    StoryVO storyVO = storyManagerBD.retrieveStory(storyId);

    StoryCommentVO storyCommentVO = postCommentForm.getStoryCommentVO();
    storyCommentVO.setCommentAuthor(memberVO);
    storyCommentVO.setSubmissionDate(
        new java.sql.Date(System.currentTimeMillis()));
```

```
        storyVO.getComments().add(storyCommentVO);
        storyManagerBD.updateStory(storyVO);

        return (mapping.findForward("postcomment.success"));
    }
}
```

With this solution, you have a simple mechanism for building your own base Action classes. If you follow this simple pattern, you will be able to encapsulate much of the repetitive state management and presentation within the base Action class.

Hooking into the Action Execution

Another reason you might want to extend the Action class is to hook into the execution process to perform some kind of preprocessing before the Action class executes. In most cases, this kind of behavior would be better handled by implementing your own RequestProcessor, because you have to manually derive each Action class from the base Action class and also remember to call super.execute(). However, as with anything else, there are some cases where you may find the ability to hook into the execution of an action useful. For instance, what if you want to build an application where certain pages can only be viewed by the local machine? You may be building a web application, and you want to make sure that the configuration pages are only accessed from the local host. Since you don't want to do this for every page, the simplest solution is to provide a standard base class that will restrict the access of the action.

We don't have any pearls of wisdom for this approach, because it is not something we would often use. Even in this example, we would have preferred to implement RequestProcessor and build some kind of configuration tool so that we could selectively choose which actions could and couldn't be viewed externally. The code for this example is quite simple:

```
public class LocalAction extends Action {

    public ActionForward execute(
        ActionMapping mapping,
        ActionForm form,
        HttpServletRequest request,
        HttpServletResponse response)
        throws Exception {

        if (!(request.getRemoteHost().equals("127.0.0.1"))) {
            throw new ApplicationException("Access Denied!");
        }

        return super.execute(mapping, form, request, response);
    }
}
```

Again notice that you throw an ApplicationException instead of trying to redirect the user to a specific page. You could have used a global forward here, but that would mean a check in the subclass to see if this method returned a meaningful ActionForward, which would then be used by the subclass. This defeats the point really, since you end up with just as much code in your Action classes as you would if you had checked the host address specifically. Anyone trying to log on to this page from a machine that is not the local host will receive the access denied message.

Of course, you still have to add an explicit call to super.execute() within your derived Action class, so if you wanted to secure the home page, your code for the HomePageSetupAction.execute() method would look like this:

```
public class HomePageSetupAction extends LocalAction {
public ActionForward execute(ActionMapping mapping,
                             ActionForm     form,
                             HttpServletRequest request,
                             HttpServletResponse response)
                             throws Exception {

        super.execute(mapping, form, request, response);
        IStoryManager storyManagerBD = StoryManagerBD.getStoryManagerBD();
        Collection topStories = storyManagerBD.findTopStory();
        request.setAttribute("topStories", topStories);

        return (mapping.findForward("homepage.success"));
    }
}
```

The class is derived from LocalAction, and the first call in the execute() method is super.execute(), meaning the security of this page will be checked. As you can see, this isn't the most elegant solution, as there are a lot of things to remember to do to use the security; it is not something that, once it is implemented, just works. Later in the chapter, we will look at a much more elegant solution to this problem using the RequestProcessor class.

As you can see from the examples, providing your own base Action class is quite a simple thing to do; however, you will find that for anything more advanced than providing typed access to simple parameters, much more elegant ways exist for achieving the goal. Overall you will find this method of extension useful because it is quick and easy to implement, but in the long term the solutions you build using this method may prove to be just as much hassle as the problems they are intended to solve.

Extending RequestProcessor

Although from the outside it would appear that the ActionServlet class is the controller in Struts' MVC arsenal, in actual fact it is the RequestProcessor class. Since version 1.1 of Struts, all request processing was moved from the ActionServlet into the RequestProcessor class (or TilesRequestProcessor if using the Tiles framework). This mechanism of decoupling Struts from the actual presentation technology, in this case servlets, is intended to allow Struts to be used in many more areas in the future. For now, however, it makes extending core request processing of the framework extremely easy.

Every time you make a request for a Struts action within your application, it is processed by the RequestProcessor. It is important to note that the RequestProcessor will not handle requests for images, HTML, or plain JSP pages unless you have configured the servlet container accordingly. By replacing the default RequestProcessor class with an implementation of your own, you are able to hook into the request process and provide your own behavior. In this section, we are going to provide two separate examples. First, we are going to demonstrate how you can use the RequestProcessor to replace the functionality of a Filter, and second, we are going to revisit the security examples from the Extending Action and ActionForm section and show you how to restrict host access using the RequestProcessor.

Building a RequestProcessor

Before we move on to the examples, we want to take some time to discuss the main techniques for implementing a RequestProcessor and discuss some patterns that you may find useful in building your RequestProcessor.

When building your own RequestProcessor class, the first decision you have to make is whether or not you want to support the Tiles framework in your application. If you are not too concerned about Tiles framework support, then your customer RequestProcessor should derive from the org.apache.struts.action.RequestProcessor class, whereas for Tiles framework support you should derive from org.apache.struts.tiles.TilesRequestProcessor. If you are unsure about whether or not your application will support the Tiles framework, then you should refactor all your RequestProcessor code into a helper class and build two separate RequestProcessors, one with Tiles framework support and the other without. Avoid the temptation to automatically derive from TilesRequestProcessor, since you will have unnecessary overhead in applications not using tiles.

The second thing to consider when building a RequestProcessor is which methods you are going to use to hook into the request flow. The three most useful methods are process(), processActionPerform(), and processPreprocess().

As its name implies, processPreprocess() is called before any of the actual request processing begins. This method is a great place to manipulate the session or request scope, but you can't throw any exceptions from the method, so you have to catch and handle all the exceptions within the method body. This only proves to be an issue when you have to start catching and handling ServletExceptions or IOExceptions, which are thrown by the RequestDispatcher class explicitly, as in most cases these will be caught and logged globally.

In the process() method, you are running at the root of the processing tree. You can choose to perform your processing before a call to super.process(), effectively performing some kind of preprocessing, or after super.process() to perform postprocessing; or you can choose to replace the processing logic altogether with no call to super.process(). In most cases, we advise you to use process() over processPreprocess(), since it has ServletException and IOException in its signature; this means you don't have to handle these exceptions explicitly within the process() code—you are free to leave them to be handled globally. Also, with process() you can do everything that you can with processPreprocess() and more, all within a single method.

The process() method is great because you get access to the request before Struts has had anything to do with it. However, there are some occasions when you want to perform some processing on the actual actions or their configuration data. In this case, you can hook into processActionPerform(), which will allow you to see the request almost at its final stage in Struts, when the configuration has been parsed, the appropriate Action and ActionMapping classes have been created, and Struts is ready to create the ActionForward to handle the final response.

In the examples that follow, we will implement one example using process() and the other using processActionPerform() so you can see the differences in how they work. We have decided not to use processPreprocess() for two reasons: There are more powerful options available to you, and if you do choose to use it, it is very easy to understand if you understand process().

Using RequestProcessor Instead of Filter

Let's first start off this section by saying that whenever you can use Filter, do. The Filter class is now part of the official servlet specification, and as such, the code you write will be usable on any 2.3 or above servlet container with or without Struts. However, our last statement contained the one caveat to using Filter that makes RequestProcessor viable: Filter only works on 2.3 servlet containers. If you are using an older container, then you can build your own RequestProcessor to implement pre- and postprocessing of the requests going into your application.

For this example, we are going to show you how to replace the MemberFilter class with a custom implementation of RequestProcessor. The MemberFilter checks the session to see if a MemberVO exists, signifying that the current user is logged in. If the MemberVO does not exist, then the MemberFilter adds the anonymous MemberVO to the session, making the user appear as an anonymous user. The MemberFilter only works on 2.3 servlet containers; the next example will run on any container capable of running Struts 1.1.

To start, you create three basic classes: RequestProcessorHelper, JavaEdgeRequestProcessor, and JavaEdgeTilesRequestProcessor. Normally you wouldn't include the name of the application in a class name, but not having two different classes sharing the same name will make perusing the examples in this chapter easier. The JavaEdgeRequestProcessor and JavaEdgeTilesRequestProcessor defer all processing to the RequestProcessorHelper but derive from different base classes.

First off, here is the code for RequestProcessorHelper:

```
package com.apress.javaedge.struts.controller;

import java.io.IOException;

import javax.servlet.RequestDispatcher;
import javax.servlet.ServletException;
import javax.servlet.http.HttpServletRequest;
import javax.servlet.http.HttpServletResponse;
import javax.servlet.http.HttpSession;

import org.apache.commons.logging.Log;

import com.apress.javaedge.common.DataAccessException;
import com.apress.javaedge.common.MemberFilter;
import com.apress.javaedge.common.ServiceLocator;
import com.apress.javaedge.member.MemberVO;
import com.apress.javaedge.member.dao.MemberDAO;

public class RequestProcessorHelper {
```

```
//    Commons Log for this class.
private static Log log =
    ServiceLocator.getInstance().getLog(MemberFilter.class);

public boolean checkMember(
    HttpServletRequest request,
    HttpServletResponse response)
    throws IOException, ServletException {

    HttpSession session = request.getSession();

    MemberVO memberVO = (MemberVO) session.getAttribute("memberVO");
    memberVO = null;

    /*If a session cannot be found, give the user one.*/
    if (memberVO == null) {
        try {
            MemberDAO memberDAO = new MemberDAO();
            memberVO = (MemberVO) memberDAO.findByPK("1");

        } catch (DataAccessException e) {
            log.error(
          "DataAccessException thrown in RequestProcessorHelper.checkMember(): "
                + e.toString(),
            e);

            RequestDispatcher rd =
                request.getRequestDispatcher(
                    "/WEB-INF/jsp/systemError.jsp");
            rd.forward(request, response);

            return false;
        }

        session.setAttribute("memberVO", memberVO);
    }

    return true;
    }
}
```

This code should seem fairly familiar; you define a static log instance to allow yourself to log any errors that occur within the code. The checkMember() method accepts HttpServletRequest and HttpServletResponse arguments. From there the code in that method is almost identical to the code in the MemberFilter.doFilter() method, except the checkMember() has no call to FilterChain.doChain() because it is not a Filter. Also, the checkMember() returns true if everything goes through okay; otherwise, it returns false. You will see why this is important when we get to the RequestProcessor hooks.

Now on to the implementation of JavaEdgeRequestProcessor:

```
package com.apress.javaedge.struts.controller;

import java.io.IOException;

import javax.servlet.ServletException;
import javax.servlet.http.HttpServletRequest;
import javax.servlet.http.HttpServletResponse;

public class JavaEdgeRequestProcessor
    extends org.apache.struts.action.RequestProcessor {

    private RequestProcessorHelper helper = null;

    public JavaEdgeRequestProcessor() {
        super();
        helper = new RequestProcessorHelper();
    }

    public void process(
        HttpServletRequest request,
        HttpServletResponse response)
        throws IOException, ServletException {

        if(helper.checkMember(request, response)) {
            super.process(request, response);
        }
    }
}
```

First off, notice that this class extends org.apache.struts.action.RequestProcessor and also that you need to define a private field to hold an instance of RequestProcessorHelper, which is actually instantiated within the constructor. The important part of this class is the process() method. Within process(), you use the RequestProcessorHelper class to check for the existence of the MemberVO in the session and to create one as appropriate. The important thing to notice here is that if checkMember() returns true (that is, it executed successfully), then you allow the request chain to continue with a call to super.process(). If the checkMember() method does not succeed, most likely because the anonymous user is not in the database and there is no MemberVO in the session, then checkMember() sends the request elsewhere with this code:

```
RequestDispatcher rd = request.getRequestDispatcher(
                          "/WEB-INF/jsp/systemError.jsp");
rd.forward(request, response);
```

If this code executes and the request chain is executed further by Struts, then a ServletException will be generated because when Struts comes to redirect to the view, it will find that the response has already been committed by the RequestDispatcher in checkMember(). So to recap this, if you want to send the user somewhere else within the process() method, do not call super.process(); simply set the response as appropriate with RequestDispatcher and then allow the process() method to end. The code for the JavaEdgeTilesRequestProcessor is almost identical, other than the obvious difference in parent class.

That is the actual code; now on to how to configure it. First off, you want to remove the <filter> and <filter-mapping> tags for MemberFilter in the web.xml file so you can test the processor. Now all you need to do is change the controller definition within struts-config.xml depending on which controller you plan to use. If you want to use tiles, then you must have the Tiles plug-in defined in the configuration file and you need to change the controller definition to

```
<controller
processorClass=
    "com.apress.javaedge.struts.controller.JavaEdgeTilesRequestProcessor"
/>
```

If you just want to use Struts without the Tiles framework, then use the following controller definition:

```
<controller
processorClass="com.apress.javaedge.struts.controller.JavaEdgeRequestProcessor"
/>
```

Now start up the application and it should work just fine—RequestProcessor now takes care of the MemberVO class in the session and not the MemberFilter class.

Verifying Host Access with RequestProcessor

Earlier on in the chapter we presented a solution to restrict access to the web application based on the host address. The solution used a customized base Action class to perform the check before the execute() method of an Action was run. There were two main problems with this solution. First, it required almost as much code to hook into the base Action as to perform the check manually within each Action. Second, it relied on developers to remember to derive their actions from the correct base class and to call super.execute() before any other processing. As we promised, we will be showing you a better solution to this problem; however, before we continue along the road with the RequestProcessor class, we want to show you how to provide custom configuration handling for your Action classes so you can then use this knowledge to provide a much more reusable solution to the secure page problem.

Creating Configuration Beans

If you have read this book from the beginning, it may not have escaped your notice that in Chapter 2 we described the configuration attributes for the <action> tag and left one of them with no more than a cursory description, the className attribute. Well, now we're going to explain exactly what it is for.

Struts uses another Jakarta project called Commons Digester to handle the reading of the configuration file and its transformation into a set of Java objects. The Digester project actually started out as part of Struts, but proved so useful that the Struts team separated it out into a entirely new project.

The Struts team realized that extension capabilities in the world would be of no use without some way to provide additional configuration details for the extensions people were building. To this end, when integrating Digester into Struts, the Struts team left an extension point in the configuration logic so that you can replace the configuration beans with your own implementation and provide them with additional parameters.

In this section, we are going to build a configuration bean that will be used in conjunction with the RequestProcessor code in the next section to provide pages that are accessible only from the host machine.

Building the JavaEdgeActionMapping

As of Struts 1.1, the default configuration bean for an <action> node is the ActionMapping class. By extending this class, you can provide additional configuration data to your custom RequestProcessors or actions.

Okay, so that's the theory behind it; now for an example. In this example, we are going to show you how to build a configuration bean that will allow you to specify whether or not a particular action mapping should be restricted to the local host only.

The code for the actual configuration bean is fairly basic, so here it is in full:

```
package com.apress.javaedge.struts.config;

import org.apache.struts.action.ActionMapping;

public class JavaEdgeActionMapping extends ActionMapping {

    private boolean secure = false;

    public JavaEdgeActionMapping() {
        super();
    }

    public boolean isSecure () {
        return secure;
    }

    public void setSecure(boolean isSecure) {
        secure = isSecure;
    }
}
```

The JavaEdgeActionMapping class derives from org.apache.struts.action.ActionMapping, which is the default configuration bean for <action> nodes. Other than an explicit call to the parent constructor, the only thing this class has is a single boolean property, secure, with both get() and set() methods.

That's all there is to the Java code. Now all you need to do is add the appropriate configuration details to the struts-config.xml file. To secure the home page, you just set the className attribute to the full name of the custom configuration bean, in this case com.apress.javaedge.

`struts.config.JavaEdgeActionMapping`, and then use the `<set-property>` tag set the secure property to true.

```
<action path="/homePageSetup"
type="com.apress.javaedge.struts.homepage.HomePageSetupAction"
 unknown="true"
className="com.apress.javaedge.struts.config.JavaEdgeActionMapping">
        <set-property property="secure" value="false" />
        <forward name="homepage.success" path="/WEB-INF/jsp/homePage.jsp" />
  </action>
```

Now when you request the home page from a remote machine, what happens? It is still displayed. At this point, all you have done is provide the configuration data, nothing more. In the next section, we are going to revisit the `RequestProcessor` classes, this time to implement the `processActionPerform()` method to make use of this additional configuration data.

Revisiting RequestProcessor

At this point, we have taken you through the basic mechanics of extending the `RequestProcessor` class and through building custom configuration beans. In this section, we are going to combine that knowledge to build a much more comprehensive solution to the secure page problem that was highlighted in the "Extending Action and ActionForm" section.

To recap the last section, we showed you how to build a custom configuration bean that allows you to specify whether or not a page should be restricted to being viewed on the host machine, by setting the `secure` property accordingly. Now you need to implement the code within your `RequestProcessor` to read this configuration data and act appropriately.

You already have the basics of the `RequestProcessor` classes in place for both Tiles-based and non–Tiles-based applications. All you need to do is extend these classes to provide the desired features. To start, implement the `checkHost()` method in the `RequestProcessorHelper` class:

```
public boolean checkHost(
        HttpServletRequest request,
        HttpServletResponse response,
        ActionMapping mapping) throws IOException, ServletException {

    if (mapping instanceof JavaEdgeActionMapping) {

        JavaEdgeActionMapping jeMapping = (JavaEdgeActionMapping) mapping;

        if (jeMapping.getSecure()) {

            String hostAddress = request.getRemoteHost();

            if (!hostAddress.equals("localhost")) {

                RequestDispatcher rd =
```

```
            request.getRequestDispatcher(
                    "/WEB-INF/jsp/accessDenied.jsp");
            rd.forward(request, response);

            // Secure action and different host.
            // Deny access.
            return false;
        } else {
            // Host address matches, allow access.
            return true;
        }
      } else {
          // Not a secure action, allow access.
          return true;
      }

    } else {
        // Not a secure action, allow access.
        return true;
    }
  }
```

This method is quite complex, so we'll take you through it step by step. First off is the list of arguments the method accepts and its return type:

```
public boolean checkHost(
        HttpServletRequest request,
        HttpServletResponse response,
        ActionMapping mapping) {
```

You define the checkHost() method as returning a boolean, which will be true if the users are allowed access to the resource and false if they are not. In this way, you indicate when calling the method from your custom RequestProcessor class whether to allow Struts to carry on processing or not. As you can see, you include HttpServletRequest and HttpServletResponse arguments, along with an ActionMapping argument. If you recall from the previous section, "Creating Configuration Beans," ActionMapping is the default configuration class for all action mappings in the Struts framework. As such, Struts will pass this argument to the RequestProcessor; it is up to you to check it to see if it is actually your custom configuration bean, which is exactly what occurs as the first line of code for this method.

```
if (mapping instanceof JavaEdgeActionMapping) {

    JavaEdgeActionMapping jeMapping = (JavaEdgeActionMapping) mapping;        ...
} else {
    // Not a secure action, allow access.
    return true;
}
```

If ActionMapping is an instance of JavaEdgeActionMapping, then you cast it to that type, ready for additional checks; if not, then you assume that the resource the user is requesting is not intended to be secure, so you return true, indicating that the user is allowed access. If you are dealing with an instance of JavaEdgeActionMapping, then you first check the return value of getSecure().

```
if (jeMapping.getSecure()) {
    String hostAddress = request.getRemoteHost();

    if (!hostAddress.equals("localhost")) {

        RequestDispatcher rd =
            request.getRequestDispatcher("/WEB-INF/jsp/accessDenied.jsp");
        rd.forward(request, response);

        // Secure action and different host.
        // Deny access.
        return false;
    } else {
        // Host address matches, allow access.
        return true;
    }
} else {
    // Not a secure action, allow access.
    return true;
}
```

If getSecure() returns false, then although the configuration bean has been set to JavaEdgeActionMapping, the secure property is false, and this resource is intended for public access. If, however, getSecure() returns true, then you perform further checks to see if the host name of the requesting user is localhost. If the user is requesting from localhost, then you return true to allow that user access; otherwise, you forward the request to the accessDenied.jsp page and return false.

As far as explanations go, that was pretty intense, so just to recap: checkMember() will be passed an instance of ActionMapping. If this ActionMapping instance is in fact an instance of JavaEdgeActionMapping, then the method will perform further checks on the request; otherwise, the method returns true. If the ActionMapping argument is a JavaEdgeActionMapping instance, then the method checks to see if the getSecure() method returns true or false. If getSecure() is false, then the user is cleared to view the resource and the method returns true. If getSecure() is true, then checkMember() checks the host address of the requesting user. If the user is requesting from localhost, then they are allowed access and checkMember() returns true; otherwise the request is forwarded elsewhere and checkMember() returns false.

Now all that is left for us to do is hook into the appropriate method in the JavaEdgeRequestProcessor and JavaEdgeTilesRequestProcessor classes. If you use forwards or includes in your application as well as normal actions, then you will actually want to hook into three methods in the RequestProcessor: processActionPerform(), processForward(), and processInclude(); since processActionPerform is only called for actions, includes and forwards have their own methods to hook into. Here is the code for processForward() and processInclude() taken from JavaEdgeRequestProcessor:

```
protected boolean processForward(
        HttpServletRequest request,
        HttpServletResponse response,
        ActionMapping mapping)
        throws IOException, ServletException {

    if (helper.checkHost(request, response, mapping)) {
        return super.processForward(request, response, mapping);
    } else {
        return false;
    }
}

protected boolean processInclude(
        HttpServletRequest request,
        HttpServletResponse response,
        ActionMapping mapping)
        throws IOException, ServletException {

    if (helper.checkHost(request, response, mapping)) {
        return super.processInclude(request, response, mapping);
    } else {
        return false;
    }
}
```

As you can see, the methods are very similar, only differing in which method of the super-class they call internally. The logic here is quite simple. If checkHost() returns true, then the user is allowed access to the resource, and the method defers control to the superclass; this allows Struts to process as normal and will return the value of the corresponding method of the superclass. However, if checkHost() returns false, then the method returns false to stop Struts from performing any more processing and causing an error, since the response has already been committed by the call to RequestDispatcher.forward() in the checkHost() method.

The code for processActionPerform() does not differ that much:

```
protected ActionForward processActionPerform(
        HttpServletRequest request,
        HttpServletResponse response,
        Action action,
        ActionForm form,
        ActionMapping mapping)
        throws IOException, ServletException {

    if (helper.checkHost(request, response, mapping)) {
```

```
        return super.processActionPerform(
            request,
            response,
            action,
            form,
            mapping);
    } else {
        return null;
    }
}
```

Aside from the noticeable increase in method arguments, the only difference here is that the method returns ActionForward instead of boolean. So, as with the previous method, if the user is allowed to view the resource, then control is passed to the superclass and the appropriate result is returned from the method, resulting in Struts carrying on processing as normal. However, if the user isn't allowed to view the resource, then the method returns null, which will instruct Struts to stop any more processing, thus avoiding any errors.

As you can see from the code examples, you don't actually need very much code to build your own RequestProcessor and custom configuration beans. If you follow the patterns for managing the response, then you shouldn't come across any errors in which Struts tries to manipulate a response that you have already committed earlier on. Just remember in this situation that if you send the request elsewhere, then you have to instruct Struts to stop processing using the methods described.

One point of interest before we move on to the recap is that the process() method executes before the processActionPerform, processForward(), and processInclude() methods. In fact, the process() method is responsible for calling those methods. So in the case of the JavaEdge application, the session will be checked for the MemberVO and have one added if appropriate well before the user's right to access the resource is verified. You may find that this could have an impact on your application, in which case you can move any logic from process() into processActionPerform(), processForward(), and processInclude().

The last few sections have given you an in-depth look at how to extend the Struts RequestProcessor class and how to provide additional configuration data to your custom RequestProcessor classes using custom configuration beans. The next section describes the fourth and final method of extending the Struts framework.

Building a Plug-In

Perhaps the most widely known method of extension in Struts is the plug-in method. In fact, many of the additional features for Struts, such as Validator and the Tiles framework, use plug-ins to add their functionality to the framework. Building a plug-in differs from building a RequestProcessor in that you are not intercepting each individual request; instead, you are hooking into the framework as it loads. Generally, plug-ins are used to load in some kind of application-specific data or to perform startup actions that are needed to ensure that the application will run correctly. We have also found that using plug-ins is an ideal way to run some background processes within the context of the servlet container, without having to fudge some kind of solution in which you have a scheduled task on the OS that requests a specific URL at a specific interval.

In this section, we are going to take you through the entire process of building a plug-in and configuring it within the Struts framework. The plug-in we are going to show you how to build will send out an e-mail newsletter of the top stories to all members in the JavaEdge application at a set interval.

Newsletter Service Basics

Before we get to the details of the actual plug-in implementation, we want to discuss the exact behavior of the Newsletter Service and look at the classes that actually implement the service before demonstrating how to hook these classes into Struts with a custom plug-in implementation.

The basic aim of the Newsletter Service is to send the list of top stories, via e-mail, to each member registered in the JavaEdge database. The logic for loading the top stories from the database is already built and is explained in Chapter 2. On top of this, we want to make the interval between sending the e-mails, the address of the SMTP server used, and the sender address of the e-mail externally configurable so they can be changed without having to go back to the code.

Thankfully, the Struts plug-in model makes it quite easy for you to create the implementation that you want. As you will see, building the logic for the actual Newsletter Service is much more complex than building the plug-in.

NewsletterManager

When you are building a plug-in, you should really consider refactoring the logic that plug-in is intended to perform into a separate class. If you have to use the logic elsewhere or for some reason you want to move from Struts to another technology, then you will have a much easier time of it. For the Newsletter Service, you create the NewsletterManager class to take care of the newsletter construction and the sending of e-mails.

The code for NewsletterManager is quite long, so we will go through each method separately, instead of giving one big block of code and attempting to explain it in one go. The basic class looks like this:

```
public class NewsletterManager {

    private static Log log =
        ServiceLocator.getInstance().getLog(NewsletterManager.class);

    private String _smtpServer = "";
    private String _fromAddress = "";

    public NewsletterManager(String smtpServer, String fromAddress) {
        _smtpServer = smtpServer;
        _fromAddress = fromAddress;
    }
}
```

Notice that you define a Commons Log instance so that you can log any errors that occur when trying to build or send the mail. Also note that there are two private fields to hold the address of the SMTP server and the e-mail address to use as the sender address for the outgoing

mail. The class has a single constructor that is used to pass in values for the _smtpServer and
_fromAddress fields.

The class contains one public method, sendNewsletter(), which when called by the client
application will build the newsletter and send it via e-mail to the JavaEdge members:

```java
public void sendNewsletter() throws ApplicationException {

        String mailContent = getNewsletterContent();

        Session mailSession = getMailSession();

        Collection recipients = loadRecipients();

        Message msg = new MimeMessage(mailSession);

        try {
            // From address
            Address fromAddress = new InternetAddress(_fromAddress);
            msg.setFrom(fromAddress);

            // Subject line
            msg.setSubject("JavaEdge Newsletter");

            // Body content
            msg.setText(mailContent);

            // Recipient addresses
            Iterator iter = recipients.iterator();
            while(iter.hasNext()) {
                MemberVO member = (MemberVO)iter.next();

                if(member.getEmail().length() > 0) {
                    Address bccAddress = new InternetAddress(member.getEmail());
                    msg.addRecipient(Message.RecipientType.BCC, bccAddress);
                }
            }

        // Send.
        Transport.send(msg);
    } catch (AddressException e) {
        log.error("AddressException in NewsletterManager", e);
        throw new ApplicationException("AddressException in NewsletterManager", e);
    } catch (MessagingException e) {
        log.error("MessagingException in NewsletterManager", e);
        throw new ApplicationException("MessagingException in NewsletterManager", e);
    }

}
```

The first line of this method creates the content for the newsletter with a call to getNewsletterContent():

```java
private String getNewsletterContent(){

    // Load the top stories.
    IStoryManager manager = StoryManagerBD.getStoryManagerBD();
    Collection stories = manager.findTopStory();

    // Now build the content.
    StringBuffer buffer = new StringBuffer();

    // Header
    buffer.append("Dear Member,\n\n")
        .append("Here are the top stories from the JavaEdge web site:\n\n");

    // Body
    Iterator iter = stories.iterator();

    while(iter.hasNext()) {
    StoryVO story = (StoryVO)iter.next();

    buffer.append("**************************************************\n")
      .append(story.getStoryTitle())
      .append("\n")
      .append(story.getStoryIntro())
      .append("\n")
      .append("<http://localhost:8080/JavaEdge/execute/storyDetailSetup?storyId=")
      .append(story.getStoryId())
      .append(">")
      .append("\n");
    }

    // footer
    buffer.append("**************************************************");

    return buffer.toString();
}
```

The getNewsletterContent() method retrieves the list of top stories from the JavaEdge database with a call to IStoryManager.findTopStory(). Once the list is loaded, the getNewsletterContent() method builds the newsletter content in a StringBuffer object.

Note In a real application, you would probably use something like Jakarta Velocity to externalize the mail content and make maintenance much easier. For more information on Jakarta Velocity, see Chapter 10.

The content itself is fairly basic: Each story has the title and intro listed along with the link needed to launch the JavaEdge application on the local machine with the appropriate story displayed. Back to the sendNewsletter() method, the next line constructs a mail session with a call to getMailSession():

```
private Session getMailSession() {

        // Set properties
        Properties mailProps = new Properties();
        mailProps.put("mail.smtp.host", _smtpServer);

        return Session.getDefaultInstance(mailProps);

}
```

This method is very basic—it simply sets the required property for the SMTP server using the value stored in the _smtpServer field, and then returns a standard instance of javax.mail. Session configured with the SMTP server address. Back in the sendNewsletter() method, the next line retrieves a collection of MemberVO objects representing the entire list of members in the JavaEdge application with a call to loadRecipients():

```
private Collection loadRecipients() throws ApplicationException {
        MemberManagerBD manager = new MemberManagerBD();
        Collection result = null;

        result = manager.getAll();

        return result;
}
```

The loadRecipients() method simply gets the list of recipients with a call to MemberManagerBD.getAll().

Note If you choose to implement something like this in your own application, you will probably have to implement some kind of opt-in/opt-out feature, as most people expect it and many countries now require it by law.

The MemberManagerBD.getAll() method was not created in previous chapters, so we have included it here:

```
public Collection getAll() throws ApplicationException{
        MemberDAO dao = new MemberDAO();

        try {
            return dao.findAll();
        } catch(DataAccessException e) {
```

```
        log.error("Error in MemberManagerBD.getAll()", e);
        throw new ApplicationException(
   "An application exception has been raised in MemberManagerBD.getAll()",e);
        }
    }
```

And here is the code for findAll():

```
public Collection findAll() throws DataAccessException {
        log.debug(
        "*******************Starting MemberDAO.findAll()*******************");
        PersistenceBroker broker = null;
        Collection result = null;

        try {

            Query query = QueryFactory.newQuery(MemberVO.class, new Criteria());

            broker = ServiceLocator.getInstance().findBroker();

            result = broker.getCollectionByQuery(query);

        } catch(ServiceLocatorException e) {
            log.error("ServiceLocatorException thrown in MemberDAO.findAll()", e);
            throw new DataAccessException(
                    "DataAccessException error in MemberDAO.findAll()", e);
        } finally {
            if(broker != null) broker.close();
        }
        log.debug(
    "****************Leaving MemberDAO.findAll()****************");
        return result;
    }
```

You will find an explanation of the code in these methods in Chapters 4 and 5, respectively. Back in the sendNewsletter() method, the newsletter content has now been created, a mail session instance has been created, and the list of recipients has been loaded from the database. The final block of code in the sendNewsletter() method builds a MimeMessage instance, populates the sender address and subject fields, and adds a bcc recipient for each MemberVO loaded from the database with a valid e-mail address. Once the body content is added to the MimeMessage, all that remains is for the e-mail message to be sent with a call to Transport.send().

Notice that all exceptions generated by JavaMail are caught, wrapped, and rethrown as ApplicationExceptions. This will simplify the exception-handling code within the client code. It also means that if you want to use a different mail implementation than JavaMail, you can do so without having to worry about editing client code to capture additional exceptions.

NewsletterTask

Since the newsletter will be sent automatically at set intervals, you need some way to schedule a task to execute the NewsletterManager.sendNewsletter() method at the appropriate time. As of version 1.3, Java has included the Timer and TimerTask classes to allow for scheduled tasks. By deriving a class from TimerTask and implementing the run() method, you can build a task class that can then be scheduled to run using the Timer class. For the Newsletter Service, you need to build the NewsletterTask class, which implements TimerTask.run() to create an instance of NewsletterManager and call its sendNewsletter() method:

```java
package com.apress.javaedge.struts.plugin;

import java.util.TimerTask;

import org.apache.commons.logging.Log;

import com.apress.javaedge.common.ApplicationException;
import com.apress.javaedge.common.ServiceLocator;

public class NewsletterTask extends TimerTask {

    private static Log log =
                ServiceLocator.getInstance().getLog(NewsletterTask.class);

    private NewsletterManager manager = null;

    public NewsletterTask(String smtpServer, String fromAddress) {
        manager = new NewsletterManager(smtpServer, fromAddress);
    }

    public void run() {
        log.info("Newsletter.run() started");

        try {
            manager.sendNewsletter();
        } catch(ApplicationException e) {
            log.error("Could not send newsletter", e);
        }

        log.debug("Newsletter.run() completed");
    }

}
```

Notice that the constructor for the `NewsletterTask` class accepts the same set of arguments as the `NewsletterManager` class, and in fact simply uses the arguments to create its own internal instance of `NewsletterManager`. In the `run()` method, you log the start and end of the method to ease debugging and wrap the `sendNewsletter()` call in a `try/catch` block. You don't want any exceptions to escape the `run()` method; instead, they are all caught and logged. If you don't catch and log the exceptions here, Struts will do it anyway, so you can't crash your application with a plug-in; but you want to be able to reuse this task in any framework, and you cannot rely on that behavior existing in every framework.

NewsletterPlugIn

Now that you have the code to perform the actual logic of sending the newsletter and a `TimerTask` class to enable this logic to be scheduled, we can move on to the actual plug-in. To implement a Struts plug-in, you need to create a class that implements the `org.apache.struts.action.PlugIn` interface. The interface has only two methods, `init()` and `destroy()`, both of which return `void`.

The `destroy()` method will be called whenever your application is stopped or your application server shuts down, provided that this occurs via the normal process and not because of a crash. You can use the `destroy()` method to tear down any resources that you have open in an orderly manner, but you cannot guarantee that this method will actually execute.

The `init()` method will always be executed each time your application starts up. You can be sure that the `init()` method will have executed before any actions are processed since it is indirectly called via the `ActionServlet.init()` method. The `init()` method is passed two arguments: a reference to the `ActionServlet` instance for your application, and a reference to the `ModuleConfig` instance for your application that contains all the configuration data for the entire Struts application and can be used to get the properties specified for your plug-in. Since all the logic for actually sending the e-mail is contained within the `NewsletterManager` class, the `NewsletterPlugIn` class simply has code to read in the configuration data and to initialize a `Timer` with the `NewsletterTask` class.

```
package com.apress.javaedge.struts.plugin;

import java.util.Map;
import java.util.Timer;

import javax.servlet.ServletException;

import org.apache.commons.logging.Log;
import org.apache.struts.action.ActionServlet;
import org.apache.struts.action.PlugIn;
import org.apache.struts.config.ModuleConfig;
import org.apache.struts.config.PlugInConfig;

import com.apress.javaedge.common.ServiceLocator;

public class NewsletterPlugIn implements PlugIn {

    private static Log log =
```

```
        ServiceLocator.getInstance().getLog(NewsletterPlugIn.class);

    private Timer timer = null;

    private long intervalFactor = 1000 * 60;

    private long interval = (60 * 72);

    private String smtpServer = "localhost";

    private String fromAddress = "javaedge@apress.com";

    public void init(ActionServlet servlet, ModuleConfig config)
        throws ServletException {
        log.info("NewsletterPlugIn.init() called");

        loadConfigData(config);
        startTimer();
    }

    public void destroy() {
        log.info("NewsletterPlugIn.destroy() called");
    }

    private void loadConfigData(ModuleConfig config) {

        PlugInConfig[] pluginConfigs = config.findPlugInConfigs();

        for(int x = 0; x < pluginConfigs.length; x++) {
            if(pluginConfigs[x].getClassName().equals(this.getClass().getName())) {
                log.debug("Found Plug-In Configuration");

                Map props = pluginConfigs[x].getProperties();

                // Load in the interval property.
                if(props.containsKey("interval")) {
                    try {
                        interval = Long.parseLong(props.get("interval").toString());
                        log.debug("Interval set to: " + interval);
                    } catch(Exception ignored) {
                        log.debug("Specified Interval was not a valid log value");
                    }
                }

                // Load the smtp server property.
                if(props.containsKey("smtp.server")) {
                    smtpServer = props.get("smtp.server").toString();
```

```
                    log.debug("smtpServer set to: " + smtpServer);
                }

                // Load the from address property.
                if(props.containsKey("fromAddress")) {
                    fromAddress = props.get("fromAddress").toString();
                    log.debug("fromAddress set to: " + fromAddress);
                }

                break;
            }
        }
    }

    private void startTimer() {
        timer = new Timer();

        long timerInterval = (interval * intervalFactor);

        timer.schedule(
                    new NewsletterTask(
                        smtpServer, fromAddress),
                    timerInterval, timerInterval);
    }

}
```

The NewsletterPlugIn class has a variety of field variables to store the configuration details for the NewsletterManager, the Commons Log instance used for logging within the class, and the Timer instance that the plug-in will use to schedule the sending of the newsletter. Notice that you also need to define a private field, intervalFactor. The reason for this field is that in the configuration you want to be able to specify the interval between newsletters in minutes, but the Timer works in milliseconds. The intervalFactor stores the number of milliseconds in a minute and is used to convert the interval value from the configuration into milliseconds for the Timer. Both the init() and destroy() methods write log entries to enable you to verify that the plug-in is actually being loaded into Struts. The init() method loads the configuration data with a call to loadConfigData() and then starts the Timer with a call to startTimer().

For loadConfigData(), the init() method passes in the ModuleConfig for the Struts application. The ModuleConfig object contains the configuration details for the entire application, not just the plug-ins. To get at the plug-in configuration, you need to call ModuleConfig.findPlugInConfigs() to get an array of PlugInConfig objects, one for each plug-in configured within the application. You can then loop through this array to find the PlugInConfig object for your plug-in by comparing the getClassName() property of the PlugInConfig object with the full name of your plug-in class. Once you have the correct PlugInConfig object, you can call getProperties() to retrieve a Map of the configuration properties specified for the plug-in. With the Map of configuration properties retrieved, getting the configuration data is a simple matter of accessing the elements in the Map. The loadConfigData() method follows this pattern and reads in three properties from the configuration: one for the SMTP server address, one for the sender address, and one for the interval between newsletters.

The last method of the NewsletterPlugIn class is startTimer(). This method doesn't really have much to do other than to create the Timer instance and then schedule the NewsletterTask to run. In the call to Timer.schedule(), you will notice that the interval is specified twice. The first interval is the delay before the Timer runs the task the first time, and the second interval is the delay between runs thereafter. This means that you set the task to run five minutes after the plug-in starts and then maybe once an hour after that.

As you can see, the actual plug-in code is very simple; the main bulk of the code for this plug-in was the logic required to actually send the newsletter. Creating the plug-in and starting the Timer requires very little code—in fact, the largest amount of code for the plug-in is the configuration load code. All that remains now is to configure the plug-in within the Struts application.

Configuring the Plug-In

If you have read either Chapter 6 or 7, then you will no doubt recognize the syntax used to configure the plug-in. To configure the basic plug-in, you simply need to add the following entry to the struts-config.xml file:

```
<plug-in className="com.apress.javaedge.struts.plugin.NewsletterPlugIn"/>
```

This will run the plug-in with the default set of parameters. Since you have specified the default period between newsletters to be 72 hours, you need to specify a much smaller period than this for debugging. Also, you don't use localhost as the SMTP server, so you can use the configuration properties to set the values without having to change the code.

```
<plug-in className="com.apress.javaedge.struts.plugin.NewsletterPlugIn">
    <set-property property="smtp.server" value="tiger"/>
    <set-property property="interval" value="1"/>
</plug-in>
```

As you can see, configuring the plug-in is very easy, and you are free to configure as many plug-ins as you like within your application.

Summary

Throughout this chapter, we have taken you through various extension mechanisms for the Struts framework, each with its own distinct advantages and disadvantages. First we presented a simple solution for providing typed access to session parameters using a base Action class, and also a method of securing resources using the Action class. From this discussion, you have seen that extending the Action class does not provide the most flexibility when extending Struts, nor does it reduce the amount of code needed to implement simple tasks in every action.

Next, we introduced custom RequestProcessor classes and how they can be used to hook into the request processing flow for Struts. We combined the knowledge of RequestProcessors gained earlier in the chapter with that of building custom configuration beans in order to provide a much more elegant solution to the problem of secure pages. From this, we have demonstrated that for the most part using a custom RequestProcessor is a much more desirable solution than using a custom Action class when you want to hook into the request flow within your Struts application.

Lastly, we focused on providing applicationwide startup or background services using the Struts plug-in model. The plug-in model is a very simple mechanism for you to provide services within your application that run outside the context of a user request. Any automated processes such as cleanup operations, marketing, or auditing that you would normally do via some kind of OS scheduled task can now be done using a Struts plug-in.

CHAPTER 12

■ ■ ■

Struts and Ajax

Ajax, or Asynchronous JavaScript and XML, was introduced in 2005 by Jesse James Garrett, sometimes referred to as the "father of Ajax." Ajax is not a single technology; rather, it is a collection of concepts and technologies that allow richer, more interactive user interactions with web applications. The term *Ajax* has now grown to refer to any native browser technologies that allow for asynchronous communication with a back-end server.

The fundamental concept behind Ajax is that when a portion of a web page changes, the entire page does not need to be refreshed. For example, when a user selects a country from a Country drop-down list, the States drop-down list is automatically populated with the appropriate list of states for that country. In a typical web application, this would require a round trip to the server and a page refresh. Using Ajax, the round trip to the server is done asynchronously and only the section of the page is refreshed behind the scenes. The fundamental technologies that allow this to happen are XML, JavaScript, and XHTML.

In this chapter, we will expose you to the new Ajax technology that takes web application development to a completely new level. We will show you how Ajax can be used in your Struts applications. Let us first describe what Ajax is in a little more detail.

Ajax Dissected

The basic technology behind Ajax is JavaScript. It allows

- D ata to be exchanged with a server using XML or other technologies such as JavaScript Object Notation (JSON)

- D ynamic display of new or changed data using DHTML and the Document Object Model (DOM)

- The use of data display standards such as Cascading Style Sheets (CSS)

Let's look at a few examples of applications in which Ajax is being used today, just to give you a flavor of what Ajax can really do.

Ajax on Google

Of course, as one might expect, Google is one of the biggest users of the new Ajax technologies. Google Gmail, Google Calendar, and the Google Personalized Home page are some prime examples of web applications that implement Ajax.

Google Calendar, for example, uses Ajax to quickly add and update calendar entries. If you use Gmail, it uses Ajax to display the little "loading" text in the top-right corner.

Ajax on Yahoo

Yahoo's new home page also implements Ajax. A lot of personalization capabilities, and features such as quick preview of e-mail, have been added to it recently, using the Ajax technologies.

Where Should I Use Ajax?

Here are several ideas about where Ajax might be worth using:

- *Forms*: This is a given. Web-based forms are slow! It should be a no-brainer to see how and why Ajax can dramatically improve the performance of web-based forms.

- *User communications*: Ajax can be a very useful technology in designing user communication features such as chat pages, voting buttons, message threads, ratings, etc. An example of this sort of feature is the Netflix movie ratings buttons.

- *News*: RSS feeds is another popular concept that can really leverage Ajax technologies. A few examples of this have emerged on the web recently, such as Google News.

- *Data manipulation*: An example is sorting or filtering on columns in a table. Another example is form completion with hints, such as the Google Suggest feature (you will see some code for this later in the chapter).

Note Ajax should not be thrown at every problem. Replacing large amounts of data with Ajax can lead to performance and other issues. Use Ajax only when traditional JavaScript widgets don't suffice, and when you have to do data manipulations involving round trips to the server.

Here is a good blog you can read to find out when *not* to use Ajax: http://alexbosworth.backpackit.com/pub/67688.

Ajax and Web 2.0

The Internet has grown exponentially in the last decade. Web 1.0 is and was the era of primarily static web sites transforming themselves to business processes/dynamic web applications, content management driven sites, and more recently portals. Even in the best of portals, there is still some level of intermixing between the layers (presentation, logic, business process, and so forth).

Web 2.0 is the new buzzword. This concept is truly separating out the presentation from the business logic. Ajax is one technology that really enables this vision by allowing the presentation to be driven by asynchronous calls to the server for data. Web Services technologies and Service Oriented Architecture (SOA) make this vision even easier to implement.

Ajax and SOA

So what does Ajax have to do with SOA? Ajax allows pieces of a web page to be asynchronously refreshed with new data. This data is typically retrieved by making a call to some back-end server, such as a WebLogic or Tomcat server. The code running behind the scenes can be non-service oriented and this would still work. However, if implemented as services, the boundaries for the use of Ajax become close to limitless. It opens up a whole new level of data presentation options and gives birth to a new generation of aggregated portal capabilities.

We have spent some time going over the basics of Ajax—what it is and what is does. Let's dive in and talk technology. In the next section, we explore the internals of Ajax.

Ajax Internals

Ajax is not a single technology, as mentioned earlier in this chapter. It is important to remember that Ajax is not Java or .NET dependent. You can write Ajax code (in JavaScript) to communicate with any sort of back-end code—Java, .NET, PHP, or just about anything else. From a technical perspective, the single biggest benefit of Ajax is that it helps speed up your web application. It does this in three basic ways:

- Better utilization of the browser cache

- Batching up of network requests in a single packet to reduce network latency issues

- Decreasing the workload on the server by not requiring it to process the entire page

Let's look at a typical Ajax request-response cycle.

Ajax Request-Response Cycle

Figure 12-1 shows a typical user request-response cycle when using Ajax.

In this example, the user initiates a request by moving their mouse over some element onscreen (let's say they moved their mouse over the Password field, and you want to provide a tool tip that displays the password rules that you would like to enforce). Using JavaScript, the application would recognize the mouseOver and create an XMLHttpRequest object. This would then interact with your back-end server and respond in XML. The client browser then parses this XML and shows the tool tip to the user.

This is a typical request-response cycle using Ajax. The key thing here is the XMLHttpRequest object, which we will examine next.

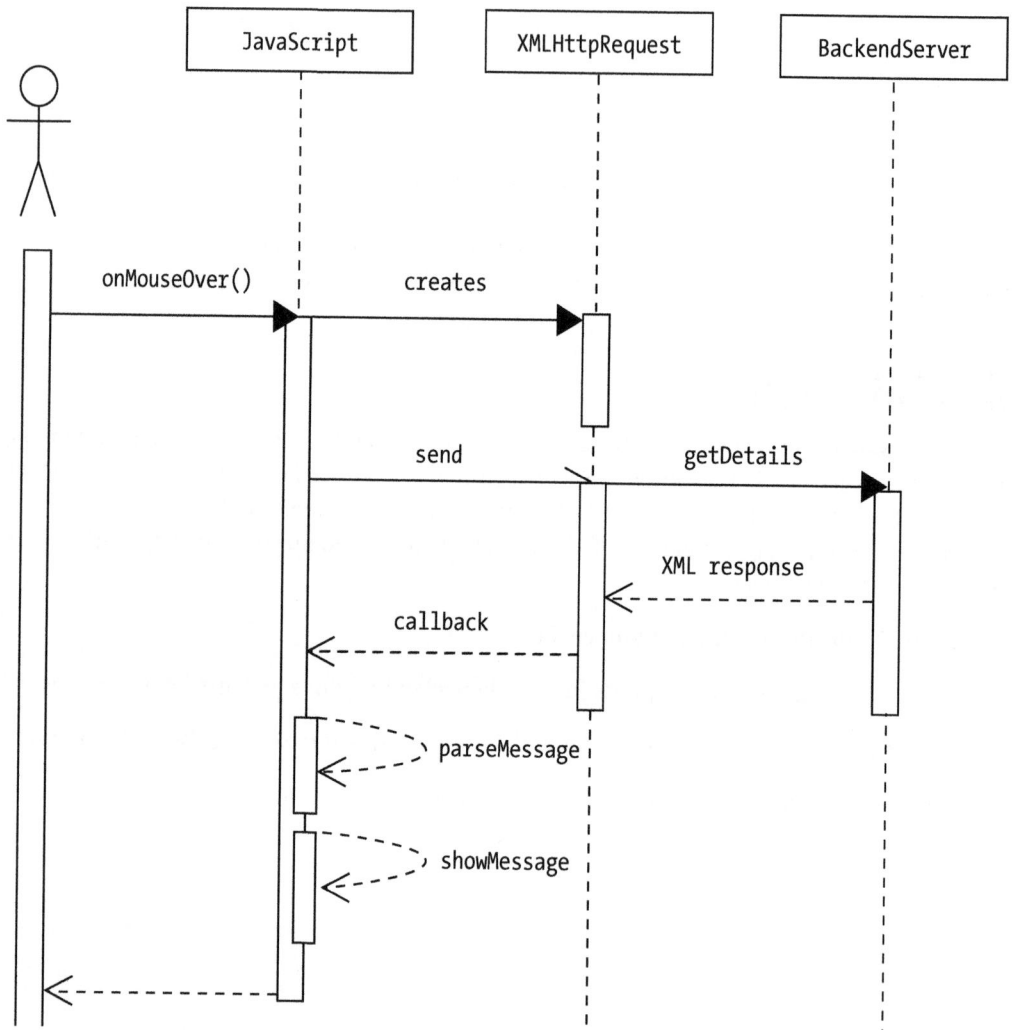

Figure 12-1. *Ajax request-response cycle*

XMLHttpRequest Object

The XMLHttpRequest object was introduced by Microsoft in Internet Explorer 5.0. Recently, Mozilla and Apple have included support for this in their web browsers (Firefox and Safari, respectively). This object is the fundamental basis for Ajax. Microsoft's implementation is different from that of other browsers, so when you create this object in your code, you need to do a typical browser check. For Internet Explorer, create this object using

```
var req = new ActiveXObject("Microsoft.XMLHTTP");
```

For Firefox and Safari, it's just a native object:

```
var req = new XMLHttpRequest();
```

You will see detailed code samples in the next section.

There is now a working draft in the W3C to make XMLHttpRequest a standard. The following is the interface definition that is proposed by W3C as the standard:

```
interface XMLHttpRequest {

            attribute Function        onreadystatechange;
  readonly attribute unsigned short   readyState;
  void              open(in DOMString method, in DOMString uri);
  void              open(in DOMString method, in DOMString uri, in boolean async);
  void              open(in DOMString method, in DOMString uri,
      in boolean async, in DOMString user);
  void              open(in DOMString method, in DOMString uri,
          in boolean async, in DOMString user, in DOMString password);
  void              setRequestHeader(in DOMString header, in DOMString value)
                                    raises(DOMException);
  void              send(in DOMString data)
                                    raises(DOMException);
  void              send(in Document data)
                                    raises(DOMException);
  void              abort();
  DOMString         getAllResponseHeaders();
  DOMString         getResponseHeader(in DOMString header);
            attribute DOMString       responseText;
            attribute Document        responseXML;
            attribute unsigned short  status;
                          // raises(DOMException) on retrieval
            attribute DOMString       statusText;
                          // raises(DOMException) on retrieval
};
```

This should give you some idea of what features are available as part of the XMLHttpRequest object. Enough fun and games, let's look at an example of Ajax using Struts and see how the XMLHttpRequest object is really used.

Ajax and Struts in Action

In this section we will build an example of a simple Struts application that uses Ajax. This application is similar to the Google Suggest feature, which offers to the user search keywords as they start typing. Think of a City text field in your web application. Imagine how much easier it would be for your users if you could "suggest" a list of cities as they started typing. For example, if they typed "Ba" you could show them all the cities that started with "Ba," as shown in Figure 12-2, which assumes that the country is India.

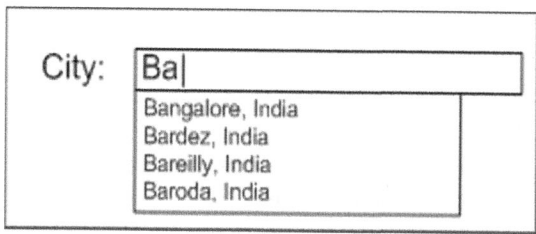

Figure 12-2. *Ajax "suggest" drop-down list*

The rest of the chapter focuses on the code to build this feature using Ajax and Struts. We will build some basic Struts code that performs the same functions as shown in Figure 12-2. It will use the same request-response cycle for Ajax invocation as shown in Figure 12-1.

Cities.jsp

Cities.jsp, shown next, is the JSP file that we will use to invoke the Ajax code to get the list of cities as the user types more characters into a text field:

```
<html>
<script language="javascript">
/*
 * Returns an new XMLHttpRequest object, or false if the browser
 * doesn't support it
 */
var availableSelectList;
function newXMLHttpRequest() {

  var xmlreq = false;

  // Create XMLHttpRequest object in non-Microsoft browsers
  if (window.XMLHttpRequest) {
    xmlreq = new XMLHttpRequest();

  } else if (window.ActiveXObject) {

    try {
      // Try to create XMLHttpRequest in later versions
      // of Internet Explorer
```

```
        xmlreq = new ActiveXObject("Msxml2.XMLHTTP");

    } catch (e1) {

      // Failed to create required ActiveXObject

      try {
        // Try version supported by older versions
        // of Internet Explorer

        xmlreq = new ActiveXObject("Microsoft.XMLHTTP");

      } catch (e2) {
        // Unable to create an XMLHttpRequest by any means
        xmlreq = false;
      }
    }
  }

  return xmlreq;
}

  /*
   * Returns a function that waits for the specified XMLHttpRequest
   * to complete, then passes it XML response to the given handler function.
   * req - The XMLHttpRequest whose state is changing
   * responseXmlHandler - Function to pass the XML response to
   */
  function getReadyStateHandler(req, responseXmlHandler) {

    // Return an anonymous function that listens to the XMLHttpRequest instance
    return function () {

      // If the request's status is "complete"
      if (req.readyState == 4) {

        // Check that we received a successful response from the server
        if (req.status == 200) {
          // Pass the XML payload of the response to the handler function.
          responseXmlHandler(req.responseXML);
        } else {

          // An HTTP problem has occurred
          alert("HTTP error "+req.status+": "+req.statusText);
        }
      }
    }
  }
}
```

```
function search(searchKey) {
    var form = document.forms[0];
    var keyValue = document.getElementById("getCities").value;

    keyValue = keyValue.replace(/^\s*|\s*$/g,"");
    if (keyValue.length > 1)
  {

    availableSelectList = document.getElementById("searchResult");


    var req = newXMLHttpRequest();

    req.onreadystatechange = getReadyStateHandler(req, update);
    req.open("POST","<%=request.getContextPath()%>/searchCity.do", true);
    req.setRequestHeader("Content-Type", "application/x-www-form-urlencoded");

    req.send("getCities="+keyValue);
  }
}


function update(cartXML)
{

    var countries = cartXML.getElementsByTagName("cities")[0];

   var country = countries.getElementsByTagName("city");
   availableSelectList.innerHTML = '';
   for (var i = 0; i < country.length ; i++)
   {
     var ndValue = country[i].firstChild.nodeValue;
     availableSelectList.innerHTML += ndValue+"\n";

   }

}
function searchByCountry()
{
    var form = document.forms[0];
    alert("This gets the city names");

}
</script>

<form action="searchCity" id="searchByCityForm">
    <table border="0" cellpadding="3" cellspacing="0" width="100%">
      <tr>
```

```
        <td ><B>By Country</b></td>
      </tr>
      <tr>
        <td class="promo">
        <table border="0" cellpadding="3" cellspacing="0">
              <tr>
              <td valign="top">
              <input type="textbox" id="getCities" size="20"
                      onKeyDown="search(this);" style="width:300px;"
                          autocomplete="off" >
              <div align="left" id="searchResult"  style="width:300px;➡
border:#000000; "></div>
              <a href="javascript:searchByCity();">
                      <img src="<%=request.getContextPath()%>/b_go.gif" alt="go"
                          width="23" height="15" border="0"></a>
                </td>
              </tr>
        </table>
          </td>
      </tr>
    </table>
</form>
</html>
```

The preceding code uses the XMLHttpRequest object to post to a Struts action to get a list of cities. Let's look at the Struts action next.

GetCitiesNamesAction

GetCitiesNamesAction is a typical Struts action class that calls a back-end data access object (DAO) to get a list of cities:

```
package com.apress.strutsbook.ch12;

import javax.servlet.http.HttpServletRequest;
import javax.servlet.http.HttpServletResponse;
import org.apache.struts.action.ActionForward;
import org.apache.struts.action.ActionMapping;
import org.apache.struts.action.*;

/**
 * Struts action class
 */
public class GetCitiesNamesAction extends Action {

    public ActionForward execute(ActionMapping mapping,
        ActionForm form,HttpServletRequest request,
            HttpServletResponse response)
```

```
            throws Exception {
        CitiesDAO citiesDAO = new CitiesDAO();
        String searchText = request.getParameter("getCities");
        String cities = citiesDAO.getCitiesByName(searchText);
        response.setContentType("application/xml");
        response.getWriter().write(cities);
        return null;
    }
}
```

As you can see, there is nothing really fancy about the Struts action itself. Let's look at the DAO next.

CitiesDAO

The DAO class is also no different than it would be in a non-Ajax, or even a non-Struts, application. Its function is to get the data from the database and, because it is Ajax based, return XML. As a good programming practice, the DAO probably should return a String or StringBuffer. The conversion to XML should be done in a separate helper or delegate class (but hey, we are not here to study object-oriented design patterns).

```
package com.apress.strutsbook.ch12;
import java.sql.*;
import javax.naming.InitialContext;
import javax.sql.DataSource;

public class CitiesDAO {

    /**
     * Get a connection from a specified datasource
     * @param dataSourceName name
     * @return Connection
     */
    public Connection getConnection(String dataSourceName) {
        InitialContext context = null;
            try {
                context = new InitialContext();
            DataSource dataSource = (DataSource) context.lookup(dataSourceName);
            return dataSource.getConnection();
        }       catch(Exception ex) {
            ex.printStackTrace();
            return null;
        }
    }

    /**
     * constructs the xml string to be sent to the browser
     * @param prefix
```

```
    * @return
    */
   public String getCitiesByName (String prefix) {
       Connection conn = null;
       PreparedStatement psmt = null;
       ResultSet rs = null;
           StringBuffer cities = new StringBuffer();
       String sql = "select city_name from city where city_name like ?";
       try {
               conn = getConnection("dsDB");//substitute dsDB with your datasource ➥
name

               psmt = conn.prepareStatement(sql);
               psmt.setString(1,searchText+"%");
               rs = psmt.executeQuery();
               //construct the xml string.
               cities.append("<cities>");
               while(rs.next()) {
                       cities.append("<city>"+rs.getString("city_name")+"</city>");
               }
               cities.append("</cities>");
                       rs.close();psmt.close();


       }
               catch(SQLException se) {
               se.printStackTrace();
       }
               finally {
               try {
                               conn.close();
                       }
                       catch(Exception e) {
                               e.printStackTrace()
                       };
       }
       return cities.toString();
   }
}
```

That's it. That's all the code that you really need. Setting this up within a Struts application will be left for you as an exercise to complete on your own. You need to register the action in the struts-config.xml file and set it up like you would with any other struts JSP and action classes. Run it, and see what you get.

Summary

Ajax is a cool new technology and is probably here to stay. It truly opens up a new avenue for user interfaces for web applications. However, be cautious. Until the W3C standard is finalized and then adopted, you need to deal with cross-browser issues when programming in Ajax. Also, don't abuse the use of Ajax. For example, persist only useful data in the background; don't use it to skip confirmation dialog boxes, and so on. Be wise about when you really need the power of Ajax. Have fun with it!

APPENDIX A

■ ■ ■

JavaEdge Setup and Installation

Throughout the book, we have used the example application, JavaEdge, to provide a practical demonstration of all the features discussed. In this appendix, we will walk you through setting up the tools and applications required to build and run JavaEdge, as well as take you through the steps needed to get the JavaEdge application running on your platform.

Environment Setup

Before you can get started with the JavaEdge application, you need to configure your platform to be able to build and run JavaEdge. Specifically, you need to configure Apache Ant in order to build the JavaEdge application and package it up for deployment. In addition, the JavaEdge application is designed to run on a J2EE application server and to use MySQL as the back-end database. You also need to have a current JDK installed; the JavaEdge application relies on JVM version 1.5 or higher, so make sure your JDK is compatible. We haven't included instructions for this here, since we are certain that you will already have a JDK installed if you are reading this book. However, if you do need to download one, you can find it at http://java. sun.com/j2se/1.5.0/download.jsp.

Installing MySQL

The JavaEdge application uses MySQL as the data store for all user, story, and comment data. If you don't already have the MySQL database server, then you need to obtain the version applicable to your platform. You can obtain the latest production binary release of MySQL for your platform at http://www.mysql.com. The code with this application has been tested with the 4.0 release of MySQL, however, it should work just fine with a later release.

Windows Setup

The Windows distribution of MySQL comes complete with a Windows Installer package that will automatically install and configure MySQL on your system. If you are running on Windows NT, 2000, or XP, you need administrative privileges in order to get the installation to succeed.

Once you have downloaded the MySQL setup file, unzip it to a temporary directory and then run the setup.exe file. The setup program will take you through a series of steps that will allow you to choose which components are installed and where they are installed to. When choosing an installation directory, try to avoid any paths that contain spaces, as these have been known to cause problems.

Once the installation is complete, the easiest way to start and manage the MySQL server is to use the WinMySQLAdmin tool. You will find this tool in the {mysql_home}\bin directory, and once you have run it for the first time, it will run each time the machine starts. WinMySQLAdmin puts a small icon in the taskbar, and by right-clicking this icon, you can easily start and stop the MySQL server.

Linux RPM Setup

The simplest way to install MySQL is to use the RPM packages supplied on the download site. If your system doesn't support RPM packages, then read the instructions in the next section.

If you choose to install from the RPM package, then you need to obtain two separate RPM files, one for the server and one for the client tools. The filenames for these packages are MySQL-server-VERSION.i386.rpm and MySQL-client-VERSION.i386.rpm, respectively, where VERSION is the version number of MySQL you are downloading.

Once you have obtained the correct files, you can use the RPM package manager on your system to install MySQL. Many modern Linux distributions will allow you to do this graphically, but if you prefer to use the shell or you have to use the shell, then you can install with this command:

```
rpm -i MySQL-server-VERSION.i386.rpm MySQL-client-VERSION.i386.rpm
```

This will install MySQL in the /var/lib/mysql directory and will also configure the system to start MySQL automatically at boot time with the appropriate entries in the /etc/init.d file. Now that the database server is installed, all that remains is to configure the basic mysql database and to test that the installation runs. To install the mysql database, you need to switch to the installation directory and run the following command:

```
./scripts/mysql_install_db
```

Then you can start up the server in a background process using the mysql_safe tool:

```
./bin/mysql_safe –user=mysql &
```

You can start mysql directly if you choose, but using the mysql_safe wrapper tool is the preferred mechanism. If the server won't start or you experience any installation issues, then you should check out the MySQL web site at http://www.mysql.com.

Linux Non-RPM Setup

If you are running a Linux distribution that does not support RPM packages, you can install MySQL directly from a binary distribution. The binary distribution is packaged as a tar file. Installing the binary distribution directly involves performing many tasks such as configuring the group and user for MySQL and setting permissions that were performed automatically by the RPM installation. After downloading the tar file, you should issue the following commands at the shell prompt:

```
shell> groupadd mysql
shell> useradd -g mysql mysql
shell> cd /usr/local
shell> gunzip < /path/to/mysql-VERSION-OS.tar.gz | tar xvf -
shell> ln -s full-path-to-mysql-VERSION-OS mysql
shell> cd mysql
shell> scripts/mysql_install_db
shell> chown -R root  .
shell> chown -R mysql data
shell> chgrp -R mysql .
shell> bin/mysqld_safe --user=mysql &
```

This will configure a specific user and group for MySQL ownership and configure the appropriate permissions with the OS to enable MySQL to run. You will find a much more detailed explanation of this setup at http://www.mysql.com/documentation/mysql/bychapter/manual_Installing.html#Installing_binary.

Other OS Setup

Windows and Linux are not the only operating systems that will run the MySQL database server. Most Unix-based operating systems such as Solaris, FreeBSD, and even Mac OS X will run MySQL. The MySQL web site has full installation instructions for all these operating systems.

Changing the MySQL Root Password

After installing the MySQL database server, the root password for the server is blank. You should change this as soon as you have started the server to prevent any security issues. By default, you can log in to the MySQL server as the root user by simply using this command:

```
mysql --user=root
```

You will not be prompted for a password, so anyone could gain full access to your database. To rectify this, log on as a root user and issue the following commands to give the root user a password:

```
use mysql;
UPDATE user SET Password=PASSWORD('mypassword') WHERE user='root';
FLUSH PRIVILEGES;
```

Log out of the server and try logging in again. You can't. Now you need to use the following command to log in:

```
mysql –user=root –p
```

at which point MySQL will prompt you for the password you provided when modifying the user table in the mysql database.

With that change made, you are all ready to go on the MySQL front. Now for JBoss.

Installing JBoss

With the database server ready and running, you now need to configure the application server on which to run the JavaEdge application. For this book, we have used the JBoss application server, and the JavaEdge application has been fully tested on JBoss. JBoss is a freely available open source package used by many developers worldwide. You can obtain the latest version, or any version above 3.2.2, from the JBoss web site at `http://labs.jboss.com/portal/`.

Setting up JBoss is actually quite easy and requires very little effort. There are no OS-specific distributions of JBoss since it is all written in Java, but you can obtain the system in either a zip file or a tar file. Once you have downloaded the appropriate archive file, simply extract the files to a directory on the system.

■**Caution** Windows users: Avoid installing JBoss in a path that has spaces in the name and try to keep the path names as short as possible, because long path names may cause some problems with certain JDKs.

Before running the JBoss application server, you should make sure that the `JAVA_HOME` environment variables point to the installation directory of your Java SDK; otherwise, JBoss will be unable to find the tools.jar file that it requires.

Once you have set the `JAVA_HOME` environment variable, you can run the JBoss server. Windows users should run the run.bat file in the {jboss_home}\bin directory, whereas Unix and Mac OS X users should run the run.sh file in the same directory.

■**Tip** Unix users: Although Windows users will have to put up with the JBoss console window staying onscreen while the server is running, Unix users can run the JBoss start-up script as a background process using this command: `{jboss_home}/bin/run.sh &`.

Once JBoss has started, you will see a message in the console indicating a successful start-up and how long it took. If this message does not appear, you will instead see the stack trace of the error. Visit the JBoss forums at `http://www.jboss.com/index.html?module=bb` to get some assistance with the problem.

Installing Apache Ant

The last tool you need to get up and running with the JavaEdge application is Apache Ant. As with JBoss, there is no platform-dependent distribution; you simply download either a zip or tar archive as you prefer. The latest version of Ant is available from `http://ant.apache.org`; for this book, we used version 1.6.5. Setting up Ant is very similar to setting up JBoss—you simply extract the downloaded archive into a directory, preferably with no spaces in the name. To make running Ant easier, you will probably want to add the Ant bin directory to the `PATH` environment variable so you can run it easily from any location. Also, you need to configure the `ANT_HOME` environment variable to point to the Ant installation directory, since a lot of tools, including the JavaEdge build script, use this environment variable.

Application Setup

Now that your environment is configured correctly, it is time to build the JavaEdge application and deploy it on the application server.

Obtaining the JavaEdge Code and Dependencies

You can download all the source code for the JavaEdge application from the Apress web site at http://www.apress.com. The download includes all the jar files needed to run the JavaEdge application such as Struts, Velocity, and OJB. You are free to download these tools yourself, and you will find instructions for each tool in its corresponding chapter in this book. Once you have downloaded the JavaEdge archive file, extract it to a directory on your machine.

Installing the JavaEdge Database

The first task to get the JavaEdge application up and running is to create the JavaEdge database in your MySQL server. Make sure the MySQL server is running, and if it isn't, start it up using the commands described earlier.

Installing the JavaEdge Database and Tables

Provided with the code download is a script for creating the JavaEdge database and its tables, along with some sample data to get you started. To run the script, connect to MySQL as a root user and run the following commands, using the correct script path for your environment:

```
\. d:\javaedge\src\sql\create_java_edge.sql
\. d:\javaedge\src\sql\mysql_user_setup.sql
\. d:\javaedge\src\sql\insert_data.sql
```

Don't forget the leading \. characters at the beginning of each line. These scripts will create the JavaEdge database, the tables in it, the data for those tables, and the user name used by the JavaEdge application to connect to MySQL. To verify that the scripts succeeded, swap to the JavaEdge database, which is named waf, using the following command:

```
use waf;
```

Now verify that the tables were created by using the following command:

```
show tables;
```

This should show three tables: member, story, and story_comment. You should check that the story table has its initial data by running the following command:

```
select * from story;
```

To make sure that the JavaEdge user account was created in MySQL, run the following commands:

```
use mysql;
select user from user where user = 'waf_user';
```

If this command returns zero results, then the user account is missing, and you should run the mysql_user_setup.sql script again. The database is almost ready to go now; all that is left is to configure OJB.

Installing the OJB Tables

The JavaEdge application takes advantage of the auto-increment features of OJB for which you need to add the OJB tables to your database. To do this, you need to obtain the full OJB distribution from http://db.apache.org/ojb. Once you have the OJB distribution, extract the files to a directory on your machine.

With the OJB distribution extracted, open up the build.properties file in the main OJB directory and find the database profiles at the top of the file. Uncomment the MySQL profile and comment out any other database profiles that are currently uncommented.

Next, open up the mysql.profile file and change the configuration to point at the waf database. The configuration file will look similar to this:

```
dbmsName = MySql
jdbcLevel = 2.0
urlProtocol = jdbc
urlSubprotocol = mysql
urlDbalias = //localhost:3306/waf
createDatabaseUrl = ${urlProtocol}:${urlSubprotocol}:${urlDbalias}
buildDatabaseUrl = ${urlProtocol}:${urlSubprotocol}:${urlDbalias}
databaseUrl = ${urlProtocol}:${urlSubprotocol}:${urlDbalias}
databaseDriver = org.gjt.mm.mysql.Driver
databaseUser = apress
databasePassword = pwd
databaseHost = 127.0.0.1
```

The user name you give OJB to connect to the database must have the CREATE TABLE permission, as it won't be able to create the OJB tables otherwise.

Now from the command line, run the following command within the OJB directory:

```
ant prepare-testdb
```

This generates the script necessary to create the OJB tables within MySQL and executes them against the database. You can check that the tables have been created by logging into the waf database with the MySQL client and running the show tables command as detailed earlier.

Building JavaEdge

Now that the database is configured, all that is left is to build the application and deploy it. Provided that you have configured Ant correctly, building JavaEdge is simple. The JavaEdge application comes complete with build scripts for both Windows and Unix that provide an extra level of error checking above that provided by the Ant scripts. Simply run the script appropriate to your environment, build.bat for Windows and build.sh for Unix, and the application will be built, the documentation generated, and the war file created for deployment.

Deploying JavaEdge

Once you have built the application, you are ready to deploy it to the application server and test it out. There are two methods of deployment in JBoss, each with its own merits. Before you start with the deployment of the JavaEdge application, make sure that the JBoss application server is running; if it isn't, you can start it using the run scripts detailed earlier.

Tip JBoss and Apache users: If you have JBoss hosting provided by an external company that uses Apache as the front-end web server, then you have to request that your hosting provider set up an additional mount point to direct all Struts traffic to the JBoss container. The mount point required will differ based on the URL mapping that you used for the Struts servlet.

War Deployment

The simplest method of deployment in JBoss is war deployment. With this method, you simply drop the war file for your application into the {jboss_instance}/deploy directory, and JBoss takes care of deploying the application and setting up the servlet container, in most cases Tomcat, to run it. Try dropping the JavaEdge war file into the JBoss deploy directory. If you have JBoss running in an active console, you will see the deployment messages streaming by. Once the deployment has finished, point your browser at http://localhost:8080/JavaEdge to try out the application.

The war deployment method makes the initial deployment of your application very easy, but from a maintenance point of view it is a nightmare. To make any changes to the JSP files or Struts configuration of your application, you have to rebuild the war file and then redeploy it as a whole to the JBoss server. If you just want to make a simple change, this is quite a limiting factor. Also, if you have a design team working on the layout of the JSP files, then it needs to be familiar with Ant or some other build tool in order to build the war file.

Tip Regarding war deployment and FTP: If you use FTP to deploy your applications in JBoss, you may find that dropping the war file into the deploy directory over FTP throws up some problems. It seems that for a big war file, JBoss will start to deploy the application before the entire war file has uploaded, resulting in numerous spurious errors. There are two ways to get around this. The first is to stop the JBoss server, upload the war file, and start JBoss again once the file is uploaded. The other is to FTP the war file to a temporary directory and then use SSH to move the war file to the deploy directory.

Another issue with using the war deployment mechanism is that you can't use any features that are intended to create or update files within the scope of your applications. Because the application does not have an actual directory structure, everything is accessed from the war file; you cannot, for instance, upload files into the images directory for your application since there is no images directory. Any calls to ServletRequest.getRealPath() or HttpServletRequest.getContextPath() will return null, as no physical OS location exists for your application files. Thankfully, a solution to both of these problems is available.

Directory Deployment

JBoss supports another method of application deployment that allows for simple changes to be made without having to re-create the war file each time. It also allows you to create files within the subdirectories of your application and will return the correct results for calls to ServletRequest.getRealPath() and HttpServletRequest.getContextPath().

This method of deployment is no more complicated than the war file method; it is just not quite as clean. To start with, you need to create a directory within the JBoss deploy directory. The name of this directory should be the intended name of the application context followed by .war, so for the JavaEdge application the name of the directory would be JavaEdge.war. Once the directory is created, you simply copy the files for your application, in the correct structure, into the application directory in JBoss. JBoss will then pick up the application and deploy it.

We have found that it is still much easier to package the application up as a war file, because it makes transporting the application between servers much easier and results in fewer lost files. However, when deploying, you can simply extract the files from the war file manually and place them in the directory. To extract files from a war file, you can use the jar command-line tools supplied with your JDK. The following command will extract the files from the JavaEdge war file:

```
jar-xf JavaEdge.war
```

If you make any changes to your application, you can force JBoss to reload the application by simply updating the modified date of the web.xml file using the touch command in Unix, or by opening the file and saving over it in Windows.

Summary

At this point, you can run the JavaEdge application and test it out. You will find that many of the points discussed here will apply to applications that you develop yourself, and you should now have a better understanding of what is involved in building and deploying an application such as JavaEdge. If you make any changes to the JavaEdge application, provided that you follow the same directory structure that we have, the build file will automatically compile and include your changes, so you should have no problem deploying the changes to JBoss.

APPENDIX B

■■■

Struts Development Tools

An amazing and highly encouraging aspect of the Struts framework is the massive amount of support it is given from tool vendors. The many, many different tools available to help you develop with the Struts framework range from testing tools, to configuration file editors, to full-on graphical designers for Struts. What is also remarkable is that not all the vendors for these tools are small companies or open source developers. In fact, both Borland and IBM have included Struts support in their mainstream IDEs.

In this appendix, we are going to explore a selection of tools that you will find useful when developing applications with the Struts framework. Many of the tools would warrant entire books to themselves, so instead of trying to cover all their features here, we will concentrate mainly on using these tools with Struts, and provide sign-posting details so you can find out more about each tool.

The tools we are going to cover are

- *Eclipse IDE*: An open source IDE project, originally started by IBM. Eclipse is a great IDE that we use for most of our development. We have included it here for two reasons: A good IDE can help increase your productivity greatly, and one of the other tools described here is a plug-in for Eclipse.

- *NetBeans IDE*: Another open source IDE, this time started by Sun Microsystems. NetBeans IDE forms the core of the Sun ONE Studio, but the open source version is available for download from the Web. Not quite as fast as Eclipse, NetBeans does, however, have quite a nifty JSP editor that you might find useful. We have included this for the same reasons as Eclipse.

- *IBM WebSphere*: A commercial IDE available from IBM. WebSphere is based on Eclipse but adds many extra features, such as a full JSP editor and integrated support for Struts 1.1.

- *Borland JBuilder 2006*: Newly released from Borland, has, in our opinion, one of the best JSP editors available. Struts support in JBuilder has been available since the JBuilder X release.

- *Struts Console*: A cool open source project built by James Holmes that provides a Swing-based editor for the most common Struts configuration files. This tool is available as a plug-in for many different IDEs, including Eclipse, NetBeans, WebSphere, JBuilder, and Oracle JDeveloper.

- *Exadel Studio*: Available from Exadel, Inc., a full graphical modeling tool for your Struts applications. It allows you to model your Struts applications using a drag-and-drop graphical environment and will generate all the configuration files and stubs for `Action` and `ActionForm` classes.

- *XDoclet*: The now ubiquitous code-generation tool. XDoclet is covered in much greater detail in Chapter 8, but we have included it here for completeness.

- *Apache JMeter*: Another project from the Apache Jakarta team, a load testing tool that you can use to make sure your Struts application will handle the load you want it to.

With this selection of tools, you have everything you need to design, build, test, and profile your entire Struts-based application.

Eclipse

It's likely that you are already familiar with the Eclipse project and the resulting IDE. While Eclipse itself does not include any tools specific to Struts development, it does serve as the host for many of the plug-in–based tools we are going to look at.

The current version of Eclipse as of the time of writing is 3.1.2. Eclipse is not only a good plug-in host, but also has excellent support for refactoring, JUnit testing, and Ant. When building our sections of the JavaEdge application, we used Eclipse as the IDE. Eclipse works particularly fast and is based on its own UI class library called the *Standard Widget Toolkit* (SWT).

One the most useful features in Eclipse for any kind of development is its support for Ant. For the JavaEdge application, we used Ant to build the entire application, package up the code for distribution, control XDoclet, and generate the documentation. Of course, you can do much more with Ant, but you will find that managing the Ant build file can quickly become unwieldy and sometimes remembering a parameter for a certain task can prove to be a headache. Fortunately, Eclipse comes with a fantastic Ant build file editor, shown in Figure B-1, that has code insight and code completion to make creating and updating your build files a breeze.

As demonstrated in Figure B-2, you can also entirely control Ant from within the Eclipse environment, so there is no need for you to open up a separate console window to control your build process. Couple this with Eclipse's support for incremental compilation, and you can rapidly reduce the time taken in the code, build, and test cycle that most developers go through.

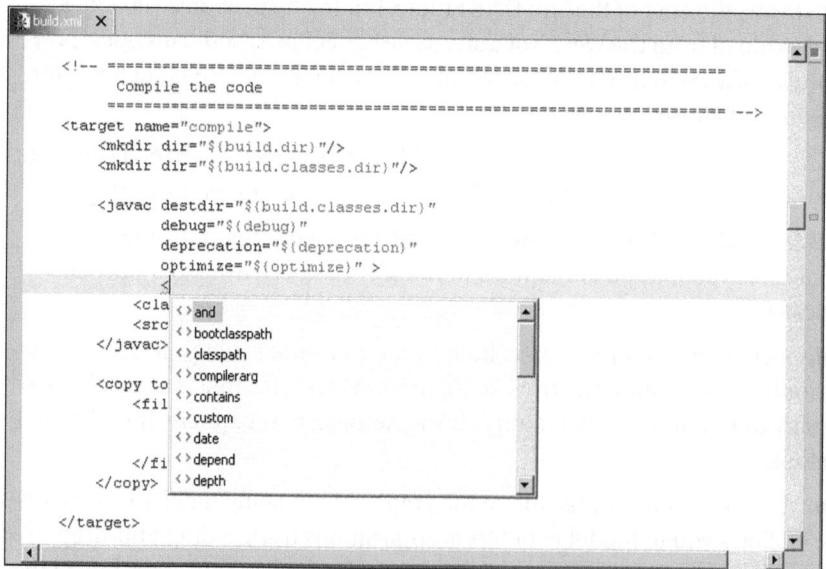

Figure B-1. *Editing Ant build files with Eclipse*

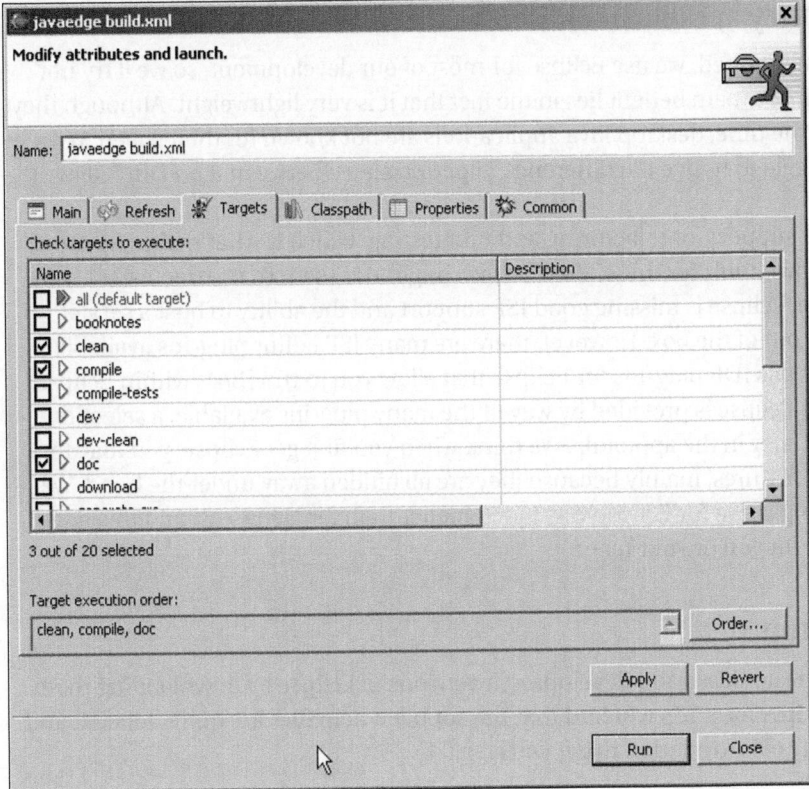

Figure B-2. *Running Ant from Eclipse*

Where Eclipse really excels is in its support for unit testing. The JUnit testing tool is heavily integrated into Eclipse, as you can see in Figure B-3, providing a fully integrated testing environment. Eclipse provides simple shortcuts in your code for building JUnit TestCases as well as an in-IDE test runner to enable you to run your tests easily while building your code.

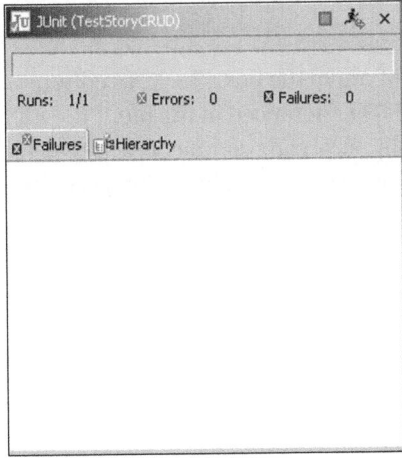

Figure B-3. *Eclipse and JUnit—strong integration*

Eclipse Summary

As we have already mentioned, we use Eclipse for most of our development, so we'll try not to be too biased! Eclipse's main benefit lies in the fact that it is very lightweight. Although they are getting better all the time, desktop Java applications are not known for their speed. With Eclipse, you will struggle to notice the difference in performance between it and an IDE written in native code.

Eclipse has great support for refactoring and unit testing, which is what makes us use it, but if you have your own tools for these, then Eclipse might not seem that attractive.

On the downside, Eclipse is missing good JSP support and the ability to host a servlet container in-process out of the box. However, there are many JSP editor plug-ins available for Eclipse, and JBoss has IDE plug-ins for Eclipse that allow you to run JBoss within Eclipse.

Struts support in Eclipse is provided by way of the many plug-ins available, a selection of which are detailed later in the appendix. We think when you first get Eclipse, you may feel it seems a bit thin on features, mainly because they are all hidden away under the hood. We found that the learning curve for Eclipse was much higher than for NetBeans, and this may be a restrictive factor for you or your team.

Eclipse Next Step

You can try out the latest release and development versions of Eclipse by downloading them from `http://www.eclipse.org`. You will find that the supplied help files are quite detailed and should give you plenty of information to get you started.

NetBeans

NetBeans is the open source IDE offering from Sun and forms the basis of its Sun ONE Studio product. NetBeans is a traditional Swing-based application, in contrast to the SWT-based Eclipse IDE. While NetBeans doesn't offer the same support for refactoring and unit testing as Eclipse, it does have better support out of the box for building web applications.

JSP, HTML, XML, and DTD Editors

NetBeans comes with an impressive array of editors straight out of the box. The XML editor, shown in Figure B-4, supports code completion using the DTD referenced in the file.

As shown in Figure B-5, the JSP and HTML editor also supports code completion, although it won't read the tag library descriptors for any tag libraries you have defined in your page, unlike the JSP editor in Exadel Studio.

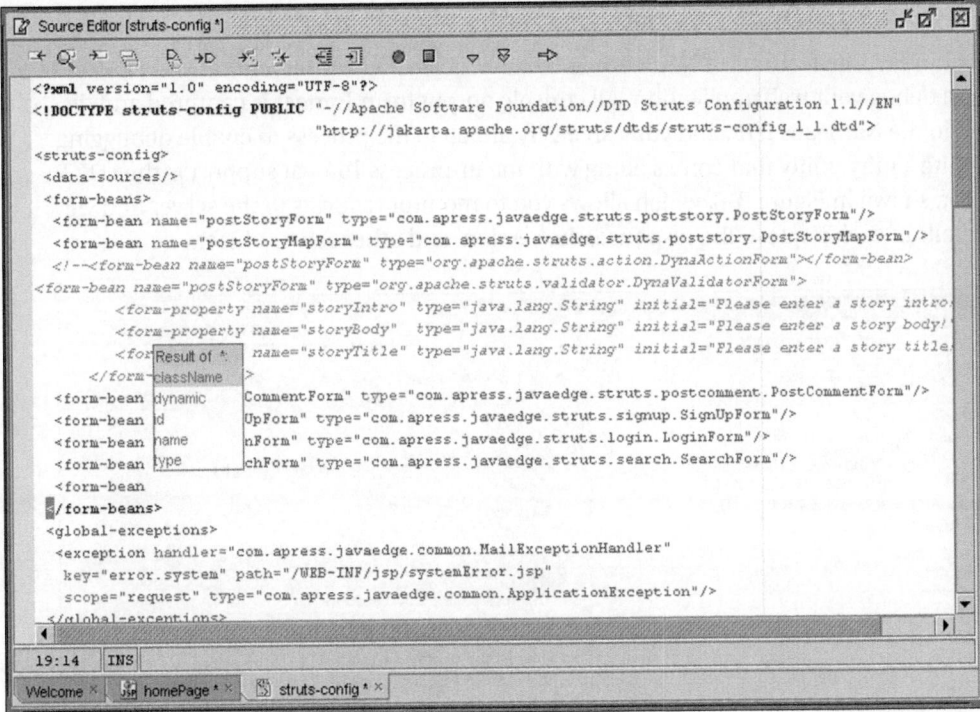

Figure B-4. *Editing XML with NetBeans*

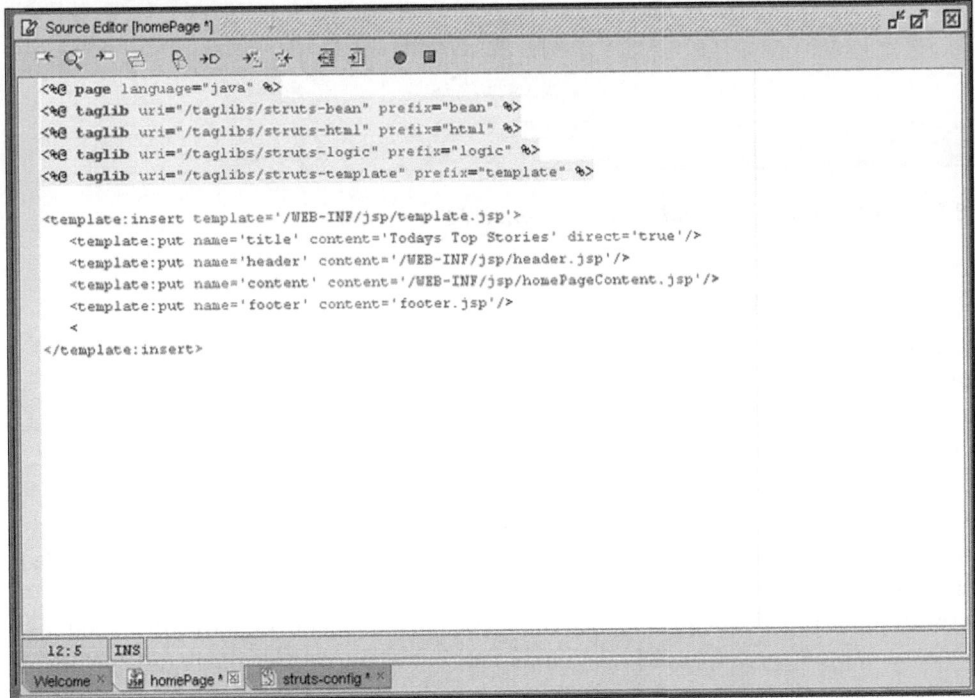

Figure B-5. *NetBeans has fantastic JSP support.*

In-Process Tomcat Server

One of our favorite features of NetBeans is the in-process Tomcat server that you can use to test and debug your web application. All console output from Tomcat is captured and displayed in the NetBeans IDE, and you can easily attach to the process to enable debugging.

Quite a nifty utility that comes along with the in-process Tomcat support is the HTTP Monitor, shown in Figure B-6, which allows you to monitor requests to the server and view the details of each request, the response, the session, and other server objects.

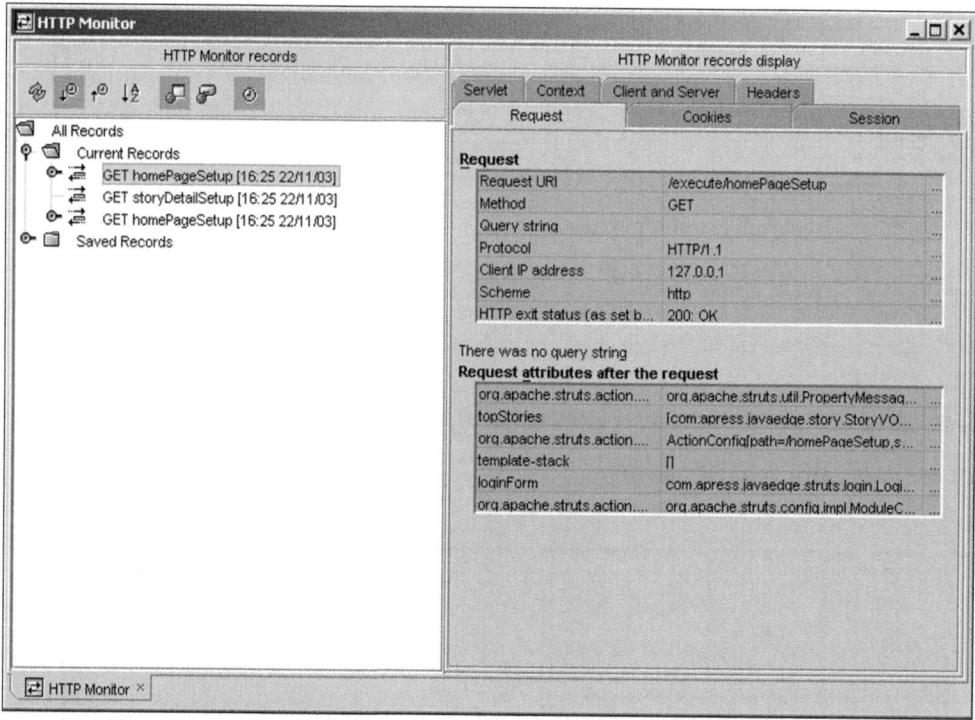

Figure B-6. *Monitoring requests and responses with HTTP Monitor*

NetBeans Summary

NetBeans was the first Java IDE we used. Before that, we were in 'text editor land,' and the main reason we started using NetBeans was because it was, and still is, so easy to pick up. A couple of hours and you can be up and running building your project. The support for JSP and HTML out of the box is great, although the Java code editor is not quite as good as the others we have tried.

NetBeans is seriously lacking in its support for refactoring and unit testing, which we value quite highly. NetBeans attempts to make up for this with the inclusion of the embedded Tomcat engine and the nifty and infinitely useful HTTP Monitor.

NetBeans doesn't perform quite as well as Eclipse or WebSphere, but it isn't slow; and the memory consumption is relatively low, so it functions quite happily on a medium-specification machine.

As with Eclipse, the Struts support in NetBeans comes in the form of plug-ins such as Struts Console, which is discussed later in this appendix.

NetBeans Next Step

You can download the latest version of NetBeans from http://www.netbeans.org and, as with Eclipse, the help documentation is actually quite good. We used version 5.0 for the discussion in this appendix, which is the latest release at this time. You will find a full release roadmap along with test builds on the NetBeans web site. Among the large amount of information on the NetBeans web site, you will find information about some of the plug-ins to enable Ant support, JUnit testing, and many other features.

IBM WebSphere

WebSphere is IBM's commercial IDE based on the Eclipse project that IBM started. It seems to be a rare occasion when you can say honestly that a commercial IDE that is also available as an open source project is worth buying. But this IDE comes jam-packed with features that could fill this book ten times over. In this next section, we are going to give you a whirlwind tour of the Struts support available in WebSphere. You should note that the Struts support in WebSphere is extensive and would warrant an entire book just to itself, so this is just a taster! For the examples in this section, we used WebSphere Studio Application Developer 5.1.

Creating a Struts Project

With WebSphere, IBM has decided against just adding a few editors to ease Struts development, opting instead to have a whole project type dedicated to Struts. In fact, you will find a project type for Struts 1.2, with the IDE adapting to the features specific to that release of Struts (see Figure B-7).

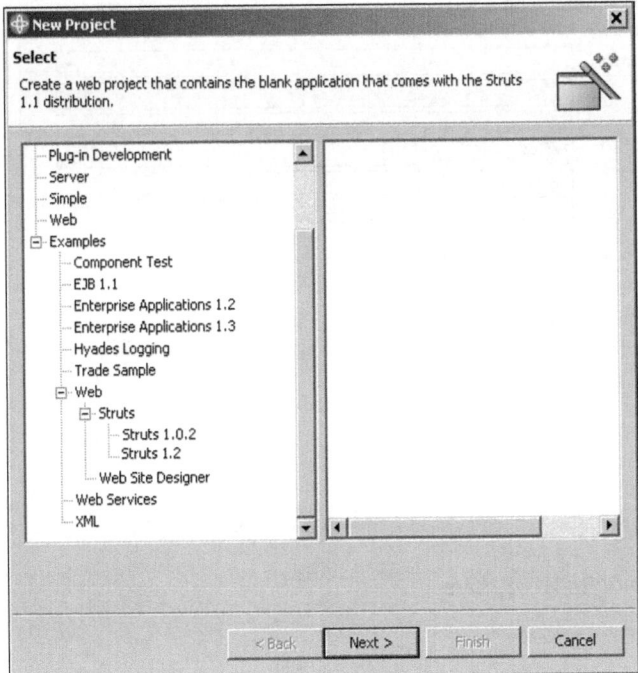

Figure B-7. *Creating Struts applications with WebSphere*

The basic Struts project type is essentially the sample included with the Struts distribution, but it is an excellent starting point if you are just starting out with Struts; the blank project will save any Struts developer new or old the hassle of setting up the basic files. You can, of course, just use a web project, and you still get full Struts support, but the blank project gives you a skeleton struts-config.xml file, a basic Ant build script, and basic files for Tiles framework and Validator support.

Managing Configuration

WebSphere has extensive support for managing the configuration of your Struts applications. As you can see in Figure B-8, the struts-config.xml editor goes beyond a simple user interface for editing the underlying XML and provides full integration with your Struts project.

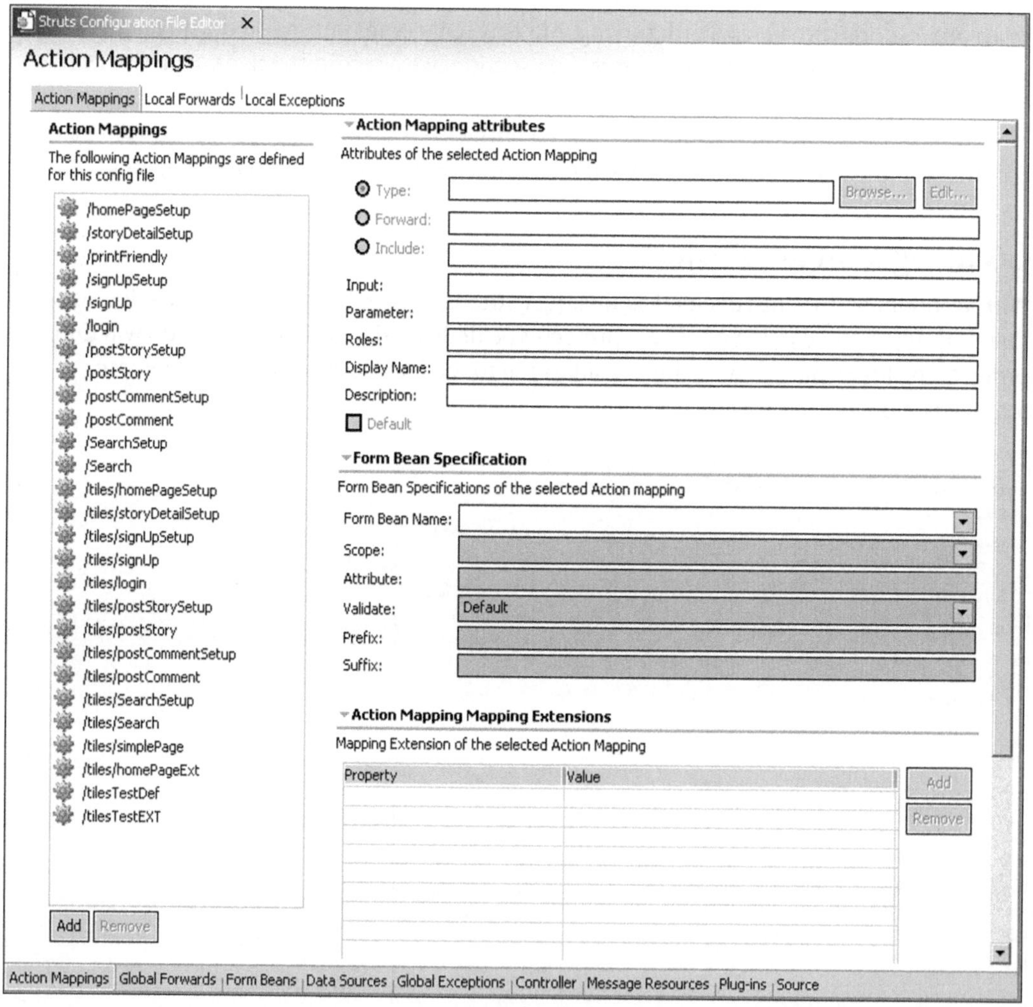

Figure B-8. *Editing Struts configuration with WebSphere*

For instance, when setting up an action mapping, you don't have to enter the name of the Action class; instead you pick it from a list of Action classes that WebSphere builds from your project and the referenced libraries. This is supported throughout from ActionForm configuration to controller configuration and can really help iron out annoying errors due to typos. On top of this, you get full error checking on the configuration file, which is useful if you have changed some of the file by hand or imported it from elsewhere.

You will also find a similar editor for the web.xml file. While this isn't specifically a Struts configuration file, you won't get very far without it, and the WebSphere editor really reduces the amount of coding you have to do within this file.

The only downside we can see is that there is no editor for Tiles and Validator configuration files; and while the XML editor is very smooth, it would have been nice to see these two types of files get their own editors. However, you can get around this by using a plug-in such as Struts Console, detailed later on, to add a Tiles and Validator configuration file editor.

Creating Actions and ActionForms

Despite having such a good configuration file editor, you will find that in the day-to-day activity of creating actions and ActionForms, you rarely have to use it. WebSphere provides simple file wizards for creating actual actions and ActionForms that automatically add the appropriate configuration details to the struts-config.xml file (see Figure B-9).

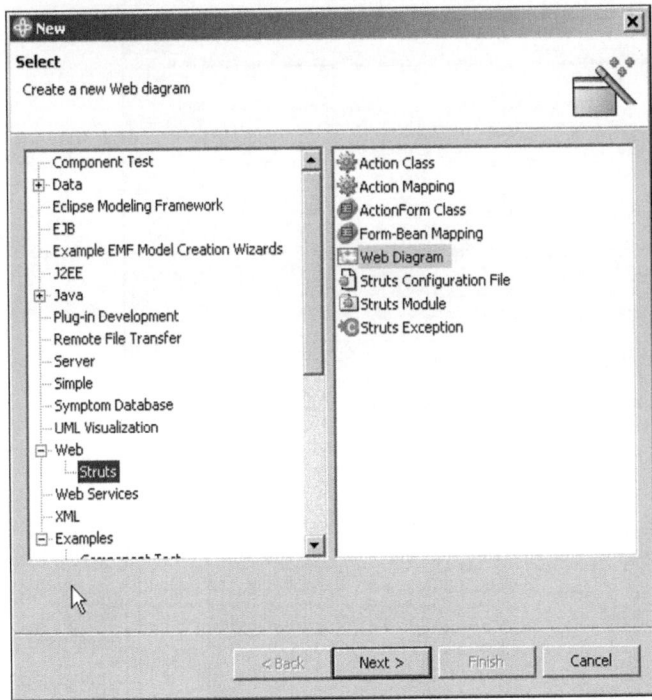

Figure B-9. *Creating Struts application components in WebSphere*

With the wizards, you can create new classes or reuse existing ones and at the same time specify all the configuration details possible. In keeping with the rest of the Struts support, wherever possible the information required is presented in list form derived from the rest of your project data. For example, in the New Action Mapping wizard, shown in Figure B-10, you can choose a form bean from the list of those configured in the struts-config.xml file.

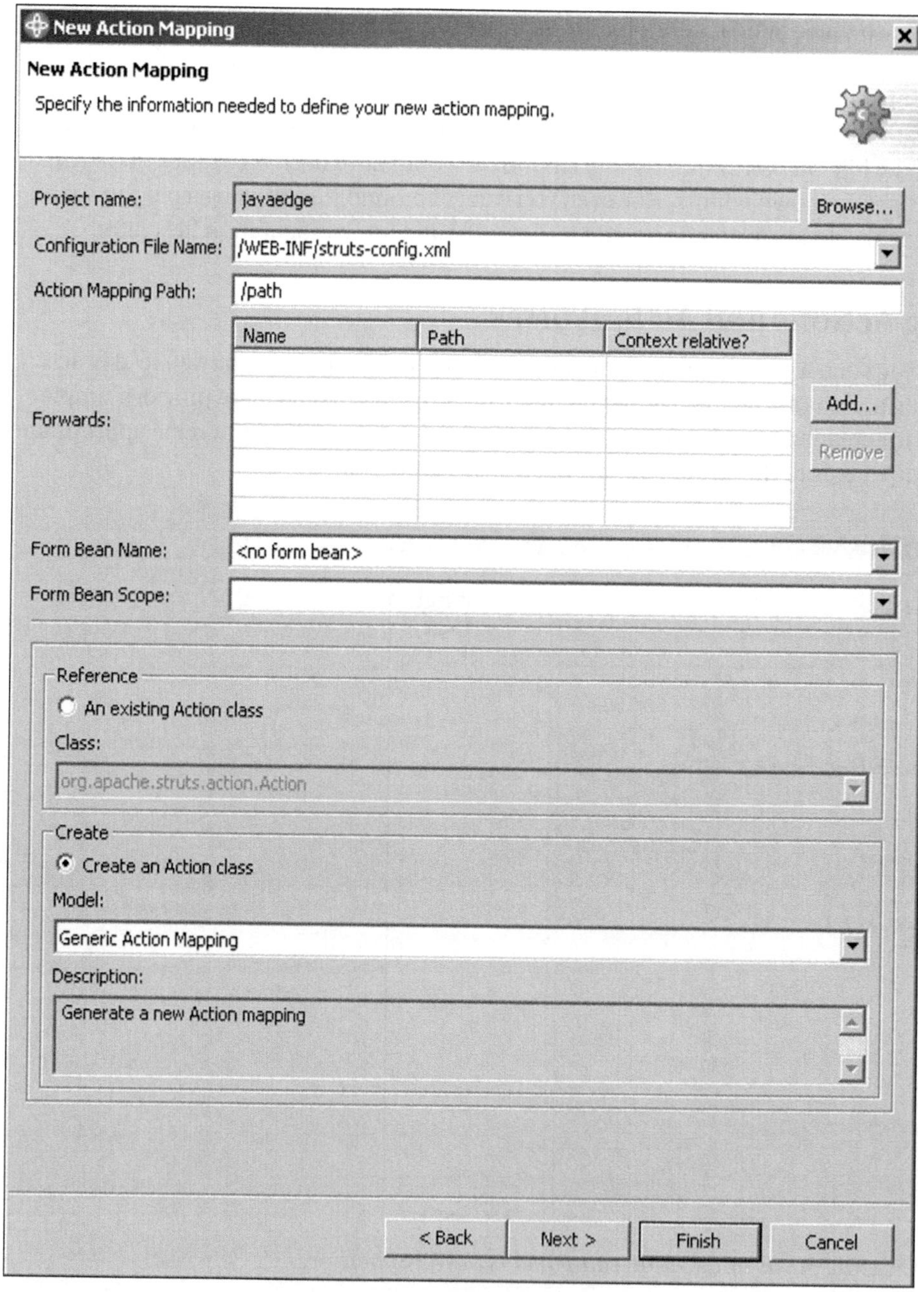

Figure B-10. *Action mapping with WebSphere*

One thing we were particularly impressed with was the code the wizards generate. Instead of just giving you a basic class derived from `Action`, you instead get the class with the appropriate methods already overridden and complete with usable skeleton code into which you can add your `Action` code.

Web Diagrams

WebSphere comes complete with a Web Diagram Editor, shown in Figure B-11, that allows you to graphically model a web application. As you draw the individual pieces and link them together, the underlying code is generated in your project. IBM has fully integrated Struts support into the Web Diagram Editor, allowing you to graphically design your Struts applications.

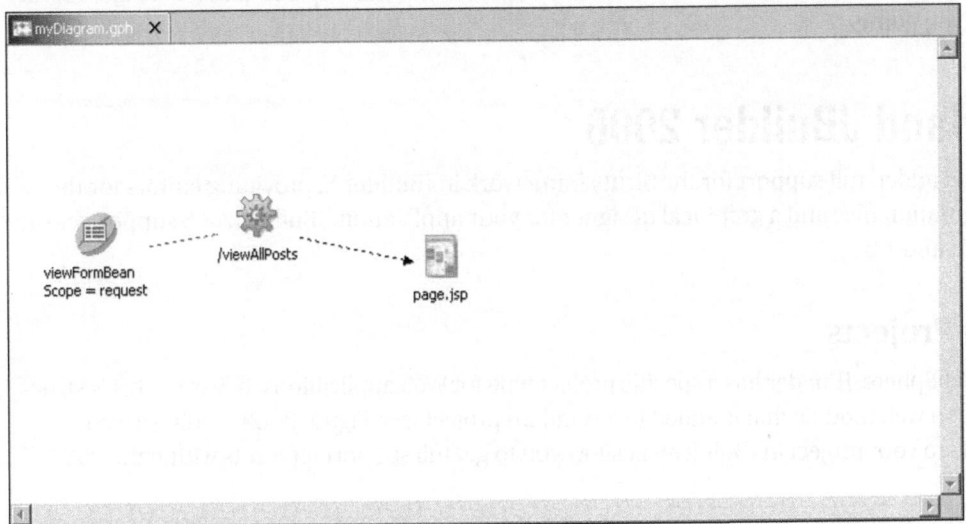

Figure B-11. *Modeling your Struts applications graphically using WebSphere*

Essentially the Web Diagram Editor is a graphical wrapper around the wizards discussed in the previous section. Although this is a nifty little feature, we have found that we get no productivity benefit from using this method; instead, we prefer to stick with the wizards that give us a productivity boost but allow us to think about our applications in a more traditional way. Perhaps we're stuck in our ways!

WebSphere Summary

We have found that WebSphere is a very useful and usable IDE. It has strong support for a lot of the things that we value such as refactoring and unit testing. However, the support for JSP editing is not quite as good as that in JBuilder, and we feel that while the UML support is there, in JBuilder it is much better.

Struts support is, of course, excellent. We think the WebSphere configuration file editor is our favorite, and we like the fact that the Struts examples come prepackaged as WebSphere projects, making it easier for people who are learning Struts to get started.

WebSphere's biggest plus point is that for such a large IDE, it is not particularly resource intensive; you certainly don't need a high-powered machine to run the IDE comfortably. We think this performance gain comes from the underlying use of the SWT library for graphics as opposed to traditional Swing.

WebSphere Next Step

As we mentioned earlier, Struts support in WebSphere is a huge topic, and WebSphere itself is even larger. Your first port of call should be the IBM web site (http://www-306.ibm.com/software/websphere/) where you can download a 60-day evaluation of the software to get yourself started. You can also get plenty of good books on WebSphere: try *WebSphere Studio Application Developer 5.0: Practical J2EE Development* (Livshin, Apress, ISBN: 1-59059-120-8) to get you going.

Borland JBuilder 2006

Borland added full support for the Struts framework in JBuilder X, providing editors for the configuration files and a graphical designer for your application. JBuilder 2006 supports Struts 1.0, 1.1, and 1.2.

Web Projects

Like WebSphere, JBuilder has a specific project type for Web applications; however, this is structured as a web module that is added to a standard project (see Figure B-12). Adding a web module to your project in JBuilder will allow you to get full support for Struts within the IDE.

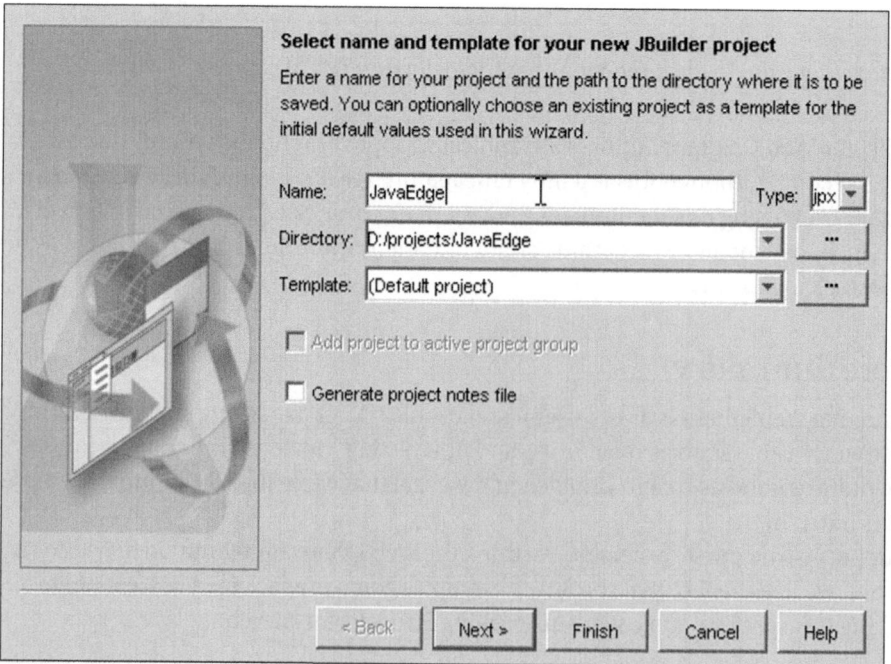

Figure B-12. *Creating projects with JBuilder*

Configuration File Editor

As with most of the Struts tools in this appendix, JBuilder provides a graphical means for editing the Struts configuration files. JBuilder uses a tree view to navigate the struts-config.xml file, as you can see in Figure B-13, but presents the details for each section in a full window within the IDE.

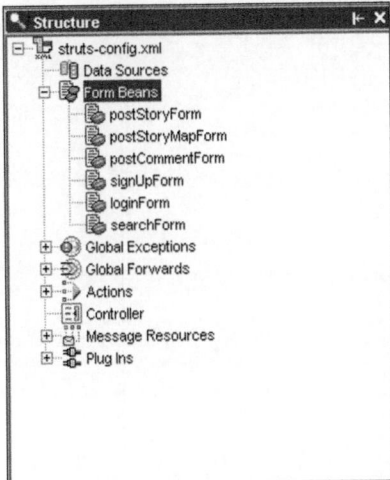

Figure B-13. *Tree navigation for Struts configuration file in JBuilder*

You can also completely skip using the tree view for the configuration file, instead using the tabs across the top of the display pane, which allows you to switch in and out of different sections of the configuration file (see Figure B-14).

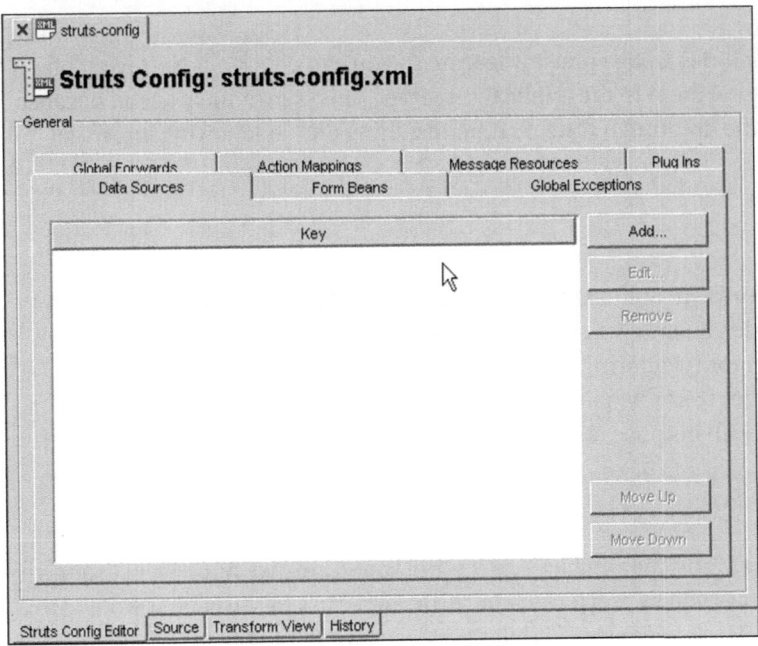

Figure B-14. *Configuring your Struts application with JBuilder*

JSP Editor

Anyone who has already used JBuilder in the past will know it has one of the best JSP editors on the market. It supports full code completion for HTML and JSP, including support for the JSP and any tag libraries defined within your page (see Figure B-15).

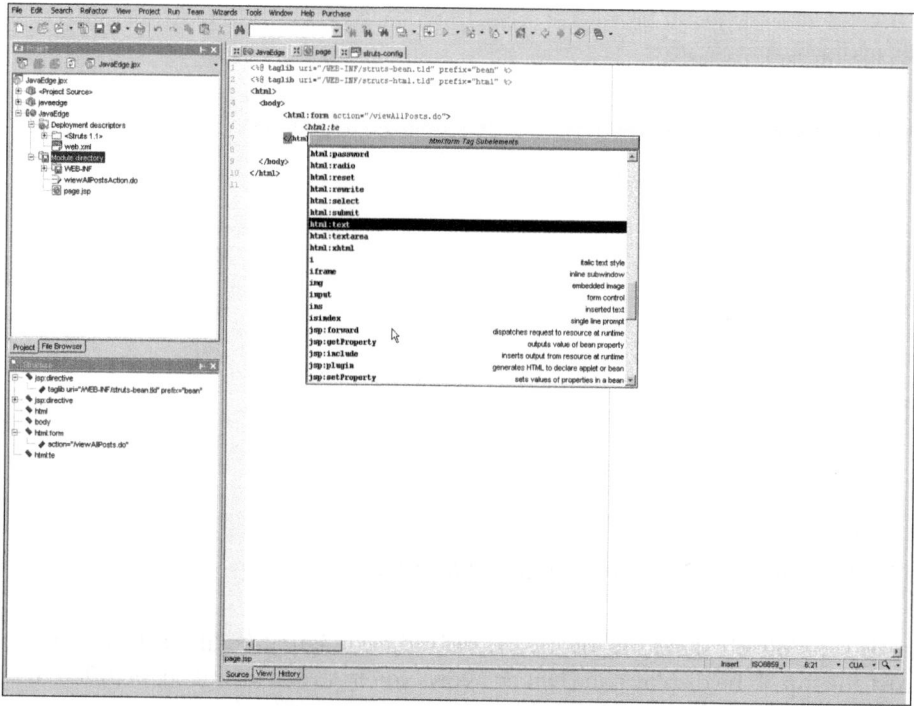

Figure B-15. *Fantastic JSP support in JBuilder*

The JSP editor also includes a page preview feature so you can check out the layout of your pages before you deploy them to the application server. This is extremely useful because it will help you to reduce the amount of time you spend editing and redeploying just to get the layout of a page correct.

UML Designer

JBuilder has full support for UML built in, allowing you to model your code directly in the IDE and then have the code generated. You can also manipulate existing code in the UML with some limited support for refactoring, as shown in Figure B-16.

While the UML designer is a very handy function, we would have liked to see better support for refactoring as well because that is the area that JBuilder really shines in.

JavaDoc Preview

We have included mention of this feature because it is not something we have ever seen in an IDE. Basically, JBuilder allows you to preview the JavaDoc for a class to see what it would look like when converted to HTML (see Figure B-17). It provides a simple way to make sure that your documentation is up to scratch without having to go through the generation process.

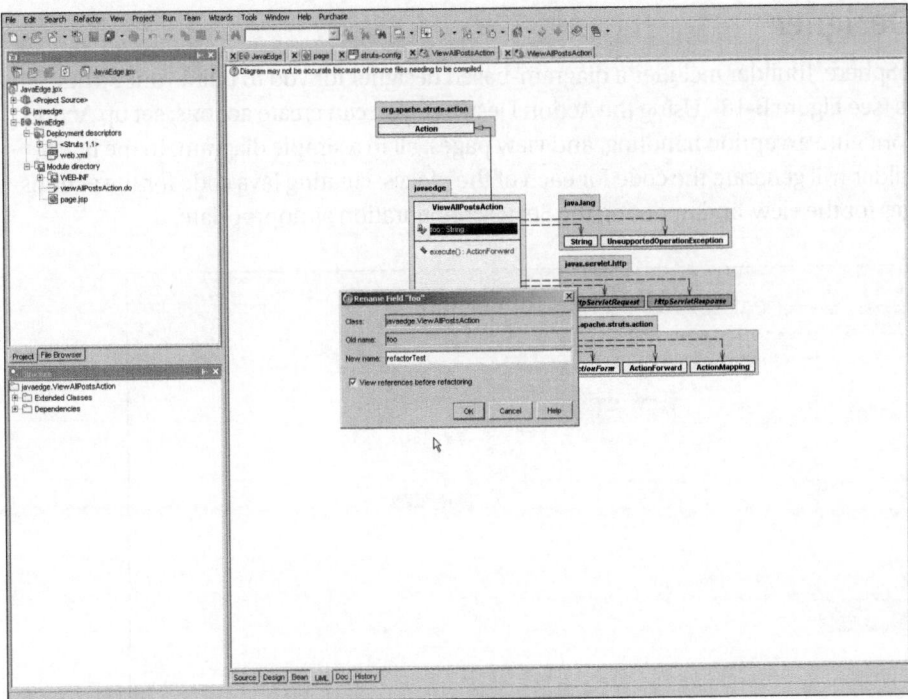

Figure B-16. *Refactoring code with UML*

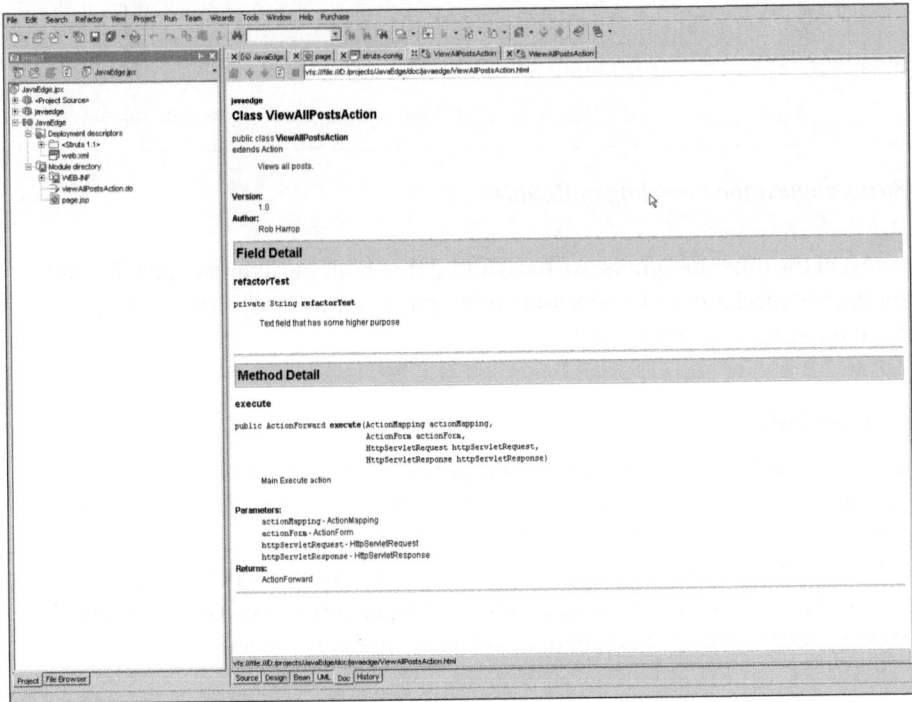

Figure B-17. *Previewing your JavaDoc with no lengthy generation process*

Action Designer

As with WebSphere, JBuilder includes a diagram-based designer for you to build your Struts applications (see Figure B-18). Using the Action Designer, you can create actions, set up Action Forwards, configure exception handling, and view pages, all in a simple diagram. In the background, JBuilder will generate the code for each of the pieces, creating Java code for the actions and JSP pages for the view, and updating the Struts configuration as appropriate.

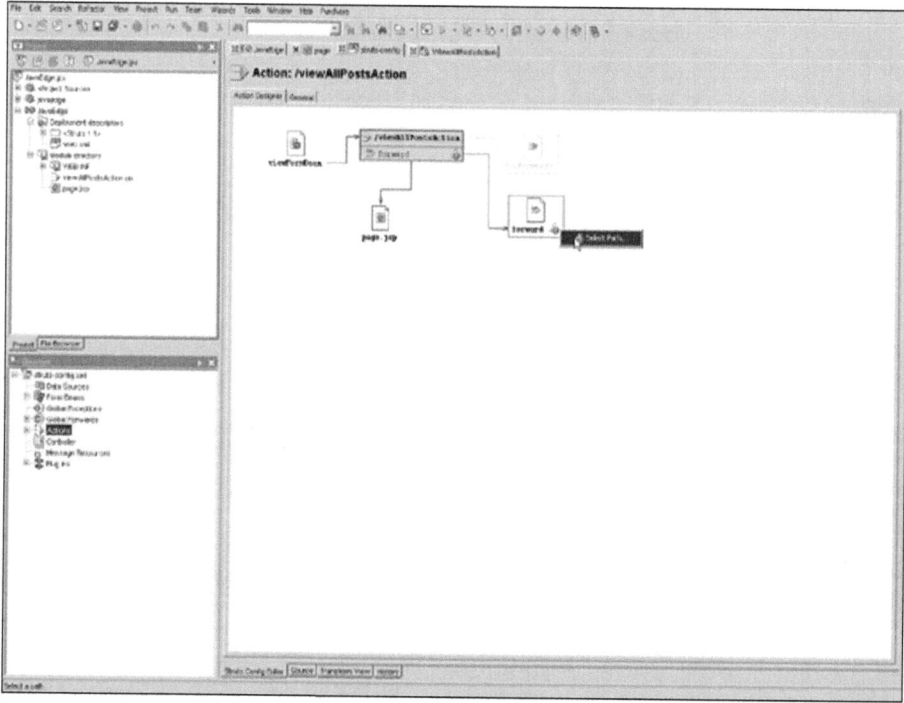

Figure B-18. *Struts application modeling in JBuilder*

As with most of the other designers, we have found that building a project like this can quickly get messy, but this kind of view does serve as a great way to verify that the code you have written is connected as you expected.

JBuilder Summary

Overall, JBuilder is a strong IDE; it has excellent support for JSP editing and some good UML tools. We really miss the refactoring support when using this IDE, but not everyone will. The Struts support is excellent; it is certainly not something Borland bolted on as an afterthought.

What we like about JBuilder and Borland is that they now have the whole suite of tools available, and they integrated everything very well. So, in large projects you can have your IDE, issue tracking, source control, and change control all integrated together.

The main drawback we found with JBuilder is that it is a mammoth to run. We are running on 1.5GB of RAM, so for us it is not so bad, but we used it on a friend's machine once with just 512MB RAM, and it was ridiculously slow. We have noticed that the memory usage will slowly creep up through a session, so you may find yourself stopping and starting the IDE once or twice a day on slow machines.

JBuilder is definitely worth a try; you might even feel that this is the IDE for you. We have certainly found that people love or hate JBuilder in equal measure just as people love or hate Eclipse/WebSphere. We know a lot of developers who use JBuilder X or JBuilder 2006 and love it.

JBuilder Next Step

Go get a copy! You can download a 30-day trial of the Enterprise Edition from http://www.borland.com, and it is also giving away the Foundation Edition for JBuilder 2006, although that doesn't have support for Struts. Borland has an active, developer-focused web site at http://bdn.borland.com, where you will find a mass of information about all its products.

Struts Console

Struts Console is a tool developed by James Holmes that provides a Swing-based editor for the majority of the Struts configuration files. You can use Struts Console either as a stand-alone or as a plug-in to one of the following IDEs:

- E clipse
- IBM WebSphere
- I ntelliJ IDEA
- N etBeans
- S un ONE Studio
- B orland JBuilder
- O racle JDeveloper

We prefer to use it within Eclipse, since that is the IDE that we use for most of our development.

Getting Started

To get started with Struts Console, you need to download the current distribution from James Holmes' web site at http://www.jamesholmes.com/struts/console/index.html. As of the time of writing, the current version of Struts Console was 4.8.

We are only going to discuss setting up Struts Console in an Eclipse environment; you will find instructions for running Struts Console stand-alone or in one of the other IDEs on James Holmes' web site. So once you have Struts Console downloaded, you need to shut down your copy of Eclipse if it isn't already closed and open up the directory where you installed Eclipse.

In this directory you will find another directory called plugins. Copy the com.jamesholmes.
console.struts directory from the Struts Console directory into the plugins directory in your
Eclipse installation directory, and then restart Eclipse. To verify that the Struts Console plug-in
has been correctly installed, open the Preferences dialog box from the Window menu and you
should see Struts Console listed on the left side, as shown in Figure B-19.

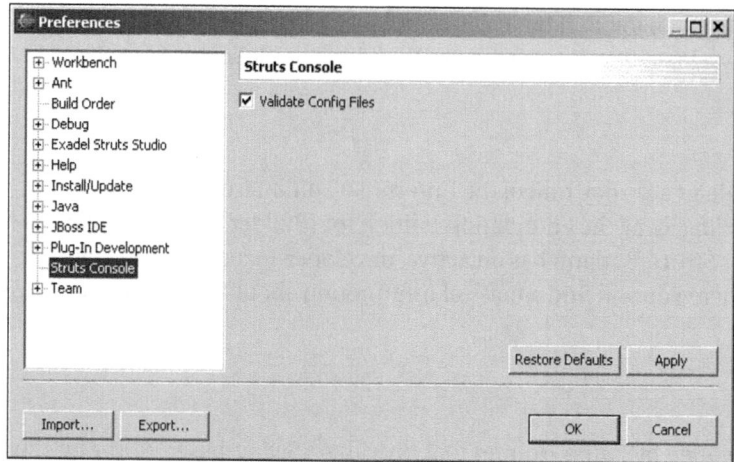

Figure B-19. *Struts Console installed in Eclipse*

With that done, you can now start using Struts Console to edit the Struts configuration files.

Editing the Struts Configuration File

The file we want to look at editing with Struts Console is struts-config.xml. To open the
struts-config.xml file in Struts Console, locate it in the Navigator, right-click it, and choose
Open With ➤ Struts Console. Struts Console will now open up, and the sections of the struts-
config.xml file will be listed on the left side (see Figure B-20). If Struts Console reports that the
file doesn't match the Struts DTD but your application still runs, then you may have some of
the elements in the wrong order. At one point, we had the `<global-exceptions>` tag after the
`<global-forwards>` tag, but the DTD defines that they should appear the other way around.
Struts Console will enforce strict adherence to the DTD.

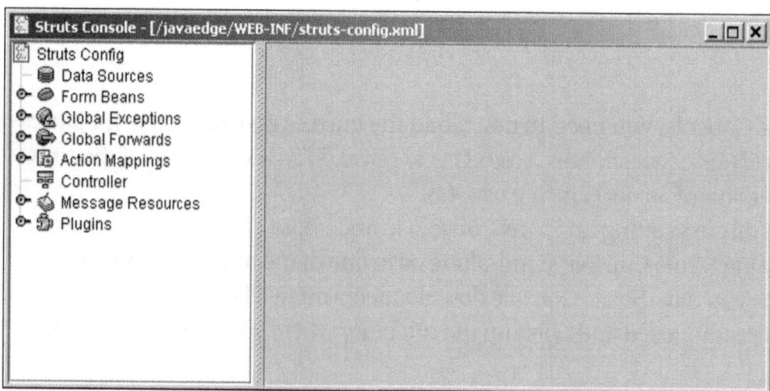

Figure B-20. *Struts Console configuration editor*

To start with, try editing the configuration of one of your form beans. Notice that we have used the JavaEdge application for our examples. To open up the configuration screen for your form bean, collapse the Form Beans node in the left-hand tree view, and you will see a list of all the defined form beans. Select the form bean you want to edit, and the details for the bean will appear in the right-hand pane (see Figure B-21).

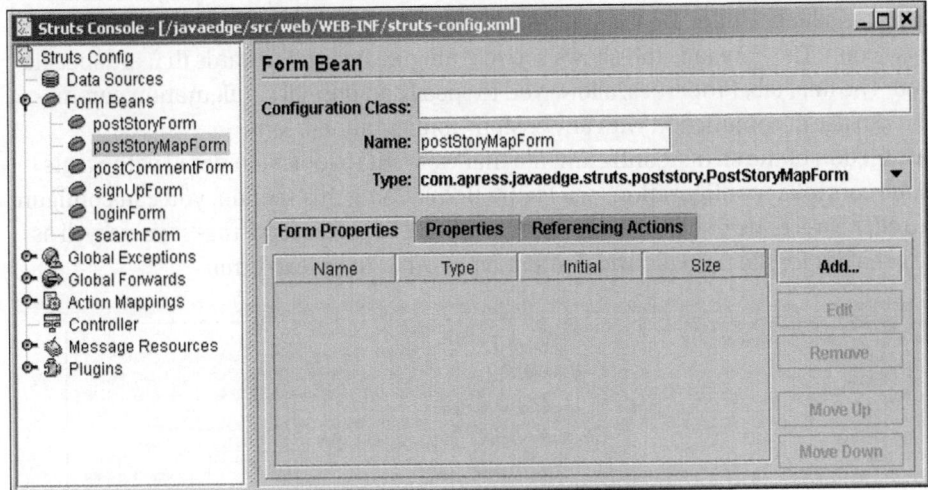

Figure B-21. *Manipulating form bean configuration with Struts Console*

In addition to specifying a name and type for your form bean, you are able to specify a different configuration bean to use when reading in the configuration details for this form bean. In the Type drop-down box, you will find that the three types of DynaActionForm are listed already; using the Form Properties tab at the bottom, you can build up a dynamic action form. The last tab, Referencing Actions, shows a list of all action mappings that use this particular form bean.

Now take at look at the configuration for one of your actions. Collapse the Action Mappings node in the tree and select the action you want to configure, as shown in Figure B-22.

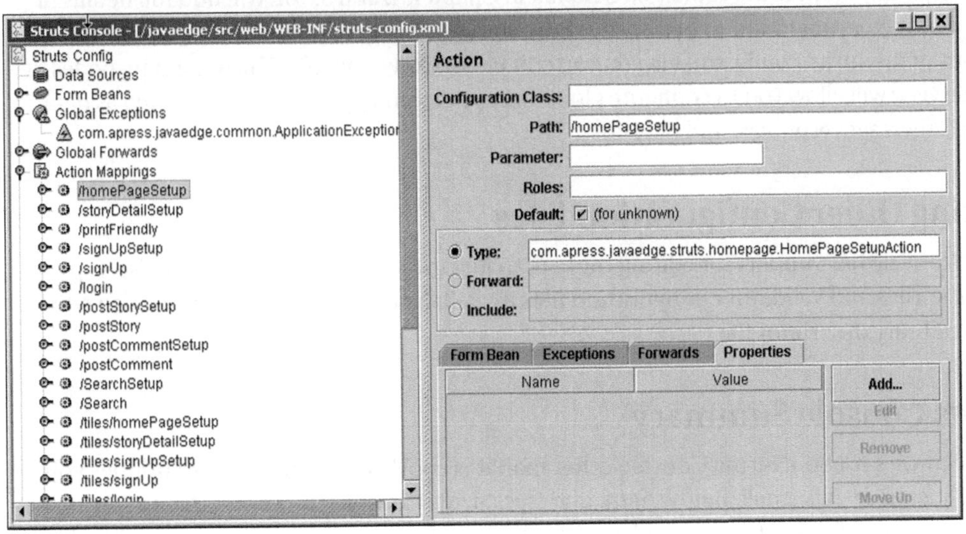

Figure B-22. *Setting up action mappings with Struts Console*

As with the form bean configuration, you are able to specify the name of the action as well as a configuration bean to change the way in which the configuration is processed by Struts. You have three options for what the action is mapped to: You can choose an Action class, you can choose to forward to a resource, or you can choose to include a resource in the response stream. These three choices are mutually exclusive.

Under the Form Bean tab at the bottom of the screen, you configure, if required, the form bean used for this action. Under the Exceptions tab, you can configure specific exception handling for this action. The Forwards tab allows you to configure Action Forwards that are specific to this action. The final tab, Properties, allows you to specify additional configuration parameters that you can use in conjunction with any custom configuration beans.

The last section of the struts-config.xml file that we want to look at in detail with Struts Console is the controller configuration (see Figure B-23). Using this section, you can configure which controller class to use, such as RequestProcessor or TilesRequestProcessor, as well as specify the behavior for file uploads and content types other than text/html.

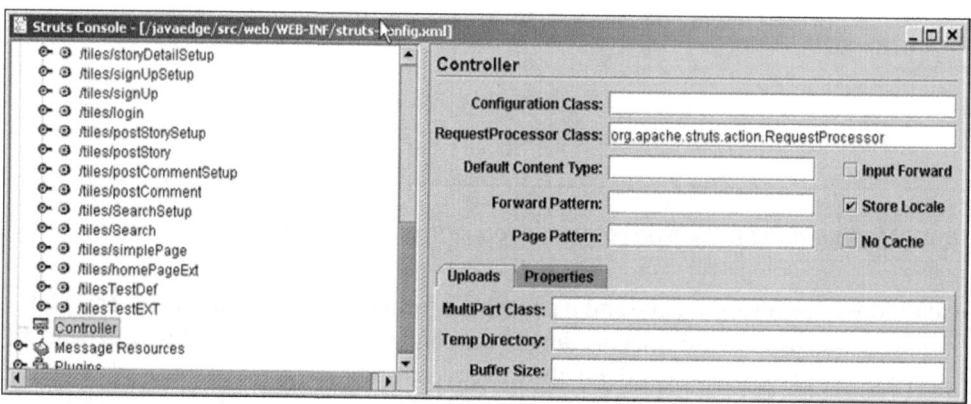

Figure B-23. *Configure the Struts controller with Struts Console*

We're sure you noticed many more configuration options as you browsed the Struts Console interface. Many of these are explained in detail in Chapters 2 and 3. You will find full details of those parameters not found in this book on the Struts web site. Of course, these are not the only sections of the struts-config.xml file you can edit using Struts Console. The remaining nodes of the tree view will allow you to configure global exceptions and global forwards as well as data sources, message resources, and plug-ins.

Editing Other Configuration Files

Struts Console has support for editing more than just the struts-config.xml file—it also supports the Tiles and Validator configuration files as well. Not only that, but you can also edit any tag library descriptor file.

Struts Console Summary

What can we say about Struts Console other than it is cool? This is one of those utilities you should just have. It is small, lightweight, and free. Struts Console allows you to edit all the possible parameters for Struts you could ever think of and few you didn't know existed. The XML it generates adheres 100 percent to the Struts DTD, so there will be no problems having Struts load it into the servlet container. There are no real downsides to this tool—we encourage you to go and get it as soon as you finish reading this book.

Struts Console Next Step

We're sure you can see that Struts Console is a useful tool that can take a lot of the drudge work out of configuring your Struts application. It is really very simple to use, especially if you are already familiar with the Struts framework, which by getting this far into the book we'll assume you are.

Exadel Studio

Exadel Studio is a full Struts development tool from Exadel, Inc. (`http://www.exadel.com/web/portal/home`). It comes in two versions: either as a plug-in for Eclipse or as a stand-alone version. There is no real difference between the two, since the stand-alone version is just the basic Eclipse distribution and the plug-in packaged together.

The whole idea behind Exadel Studio is that you have a full environment in which to develop your Struts-based applications. To this end, Exadel Studio comes with a massive number of features that aren't directly related to Struts but will make your development life easier.

If you want to try out Exadel Studio, you can download a 30-day trial from the Exadel web site. For this book, we used Exadel Studio 4.0.

Struts Projects

Exadel Studio adds a new project type to Eclipse, the Struts project, which you must use in order to take advantage of most of the features. When you start a Struts project, you get the base files you need such as struts-config.xml and web.xml.

Configuration File Editors

As with most of the tools discussed here, Exadel Studio provides an editor for the struts-config.xml file, but chooses to use a different approach. In Exadel Studio, the struts-config.xml file node in the project tree is collapsible and shows all the subsections of the files (see Figure B-24). Each section of the file can be collapsed further to show the composite parts.

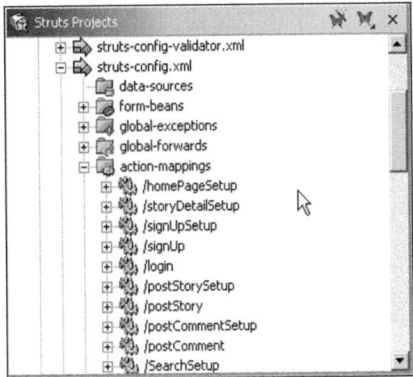

Figure B-24. *Exadel Studio configuration navigator*

Selecting one of the nodes highlights the detail for that node in the Properties window, where you can edit them directly (see Figure B-25).

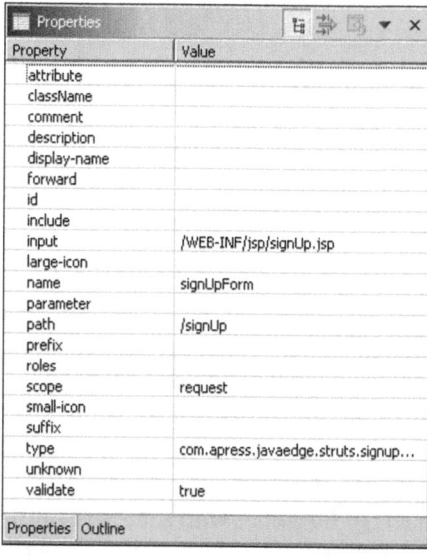

Figure B-25. *Configuration properties view in Exadel Studio*

If you right-click a node, you get the options for that particular node, allowing you to view the properties in a separate, more organized dialog box or to perform configuration actions specific to that node. For instance, if you right-click the action-mappings node, you can choose to add a new action. This will bring up an action mapping wizard, as shown in Figure B-26.

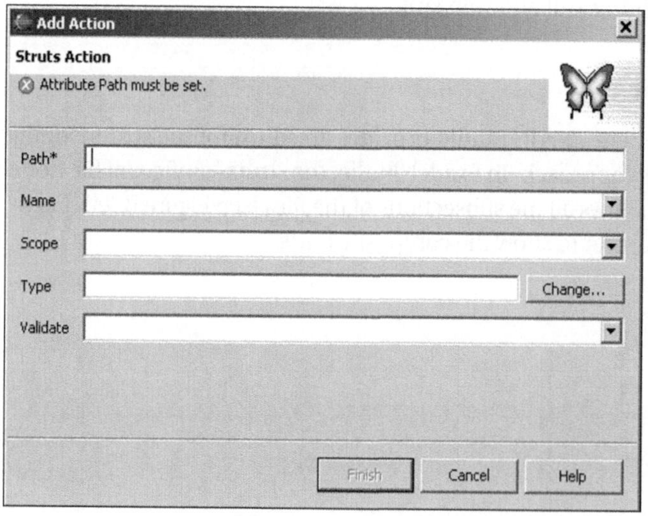

Figure B-26. *Adding a new action with Exadel Studio*

If the Action class doesn't already exist, you can enter the name of a new class that will be created later on. While Exadel Studio won't automatically create a new Action class for an action mapping, you can right-click the action mapping and choose Generate to create the Action class. Once the action mapping is created, you can then right-click and add forwards, exceptions, and properties. This behavior is carried out through the entire configuration file editor.

Along with support for the struts-config.xml file, the Professional Edition of Exadel Studio includes editors for Tiles framework configuration, Validator configuration, and TLD files.

Exadel Studio also comes with an editor for the web.xml file that works in a similar way to the struts-config.xml editor (see Figure B-27).

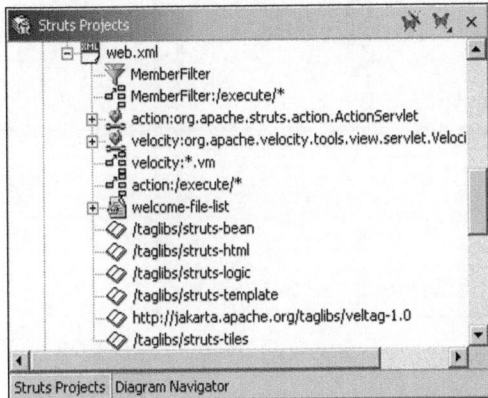

Figure B-27. *Editing web.xml with Exadel Studio*

One last point on the Exadel Studio configuration file support in the Professional Edition is that it has fully integrated support for Struts modules. With more and more applications using multiple modules in their implementation, this is an important feature for any Struts tool.

XML Editor

For those times when an editor is not available or when you want to get down and dirty with the configuration, Exadel Studio provides a simple XML editor with support for code highlighting and basic code completion. Eclipse developers will find this quite useful due to the lack of an XML editor out of the box with Eclipse.

JSP Editor

Another thing that is sadly lacking in Eclipse is a good JSP editor. Exadel Studio includes quite a good editor that has customizable code highlighting and good support for code completion, as shown in Figure B-28. A useful feature of the code completion is that it is not just limited to HTML but also reads the TLD for any tag libraries specified in your JSP file and provides code completion for those as well.

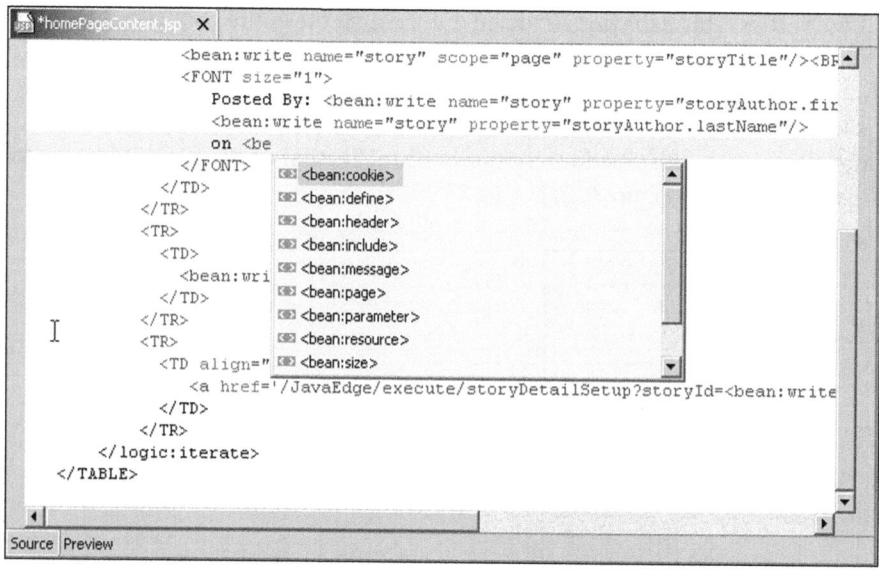

Figure B-28. *Excellent JSP editing support in Exadel Studio*

On top of this, Exadel Studio includes what has got to be one of our favorite features available: JSP Preview. If you are like us, then you will hate having to tune designs by making a change and then redeploying to the application server. Using JSP Preview, you get a good idea of how the page will look before you have to deploy (see Figure B-29).

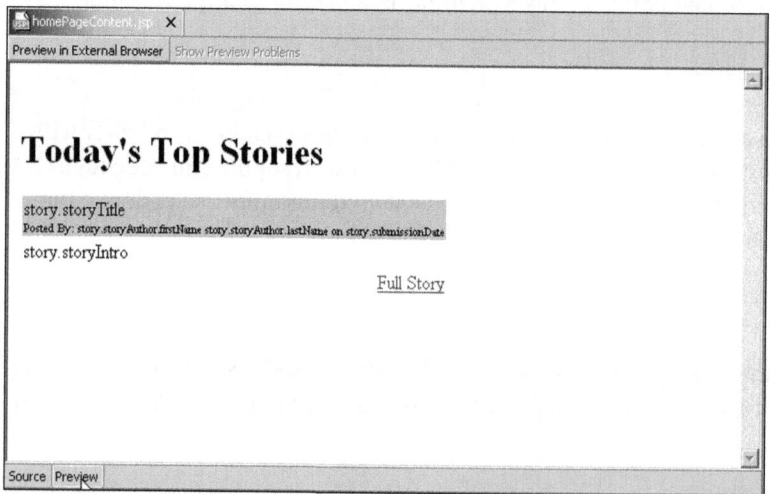

Figure B-29. *Quickly previewing JSP views in Exadel Studio*

Web Flow Designer

Exadel Studio also provides a diagram-based view of your Struts application, as shown in Figure B-30, allowing you to manipulate the application graphically. The actual editor works in a similar way to the configuration file editor in that as you create actions and ActionForms, it won't actually create the code for nonexistent classes until you explicitly instruct it to by right-clicking the item you want to generate code for and choosing Generate.

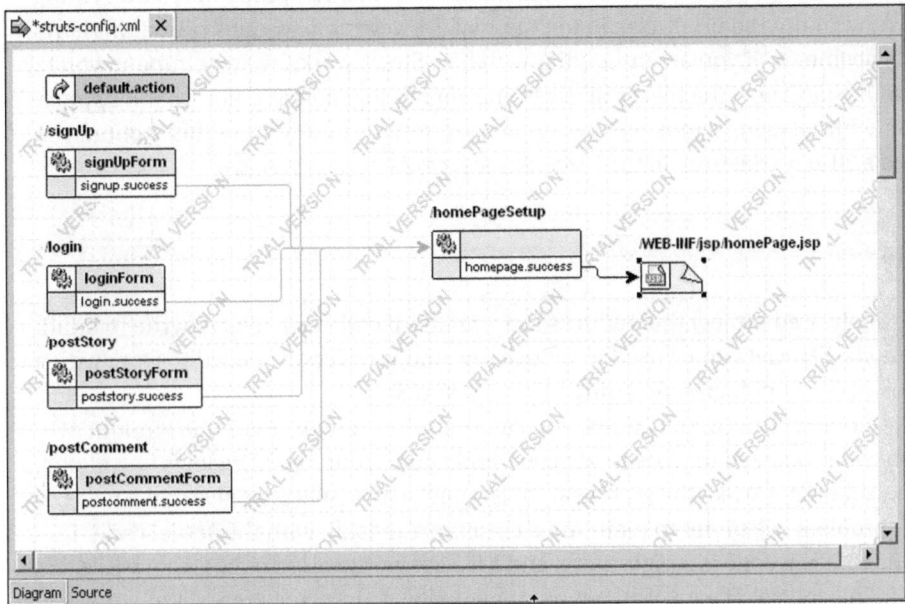

Figure B-30. *Full graphical modeling for Struts applications in Exadel Studio*

In this case, this works quite well, since you can play around with the design until you are happy with it and then generate the code in bulk by simply right-clicking a blank part of the canvas and choosing Generate.

Connecting up the pieces of your application is simply a matter of dragging a connector from one piece to another. Any changes you make, such as creating Action Forwards or exceptions, are automatically added to the diagram and the tree editor regardless of where you make them. However, changes are not written to code until you choose to generate the code, and they are not written to the struts-config.xml file until you explicitly choose Save from the context menu. In this way, you are free to experiment with the design without worrying about affecting something that is already working correctly.

Exadel Studio Summary

Exadel Studio will prove really useful to anyone who does a lot of Struts development. What we like about Exadel Studio is that the developers have thought to include all the additional functionality, such as a JSP editor, that you will need to build Struts applications and haven't just built a simple configuration file editor that you can get for free.

The graphical editor is the best we have seen, beating those in WebSphere and JBuilder hands down, and the support for advanced features such as tiles and modules means that you won't be left with a tool that does just half of the job you want.

On the downside, this tool may not prove useful to everyone. If all you want is a simple configuration file editor, then you'd be better off sticking with Struts Console; but if you want a full suite of tools for Struts development, then this is the tool for you.

Exadel Studio Next Step

As far as we know, there are no books available for Exadel Studio~~just~~ as well then that the manual supplied with the product is very detailed. You will find that pretty much everything you need to know about the product is in the manual. However, we would say that this isn't a tool for Struts beginners. If you are unfamiliar with how Struts works, we recommend you take the time to understand how the pieces of the framework fit together and how to put applications together without using a tool like this. As we mentioned at the start of this section, you can download a 30-day trial from `http://www.exadel.com/web/portal/home`.

XDoclet

XDoclet is a widely used project that reduces the amount of code you need to write to build your applications. XDoclet can be used to reduce the amount of code needed to work with a variety of tools and technologies including EJB, JMX, and Struts.

When developing Struts applications, you can use XDoclet to decrease the amount of configuration code you need to write to get your application running. XDoclet is one of our favorite tools. Although we like the graphical tools, which can sometimes give you a new perspective on a problem, we prefer to maintain a closer relationship with the actual code. However, configuration code is a nightmare, and XDoclet helps you to reduce that while still keeping you in full control of a project. We are not going to go into any more detail on XDoclet here, as we have included a full rundown on XDoclet in Chapter 8.

Apache JMeter

JMeter is a load testing tool, written entirely in Java, that you can use to test and analyze the performance of your application under a heavy load. JMeter is ridiculously easy to use and provides you with a simple mechanism to verify whether your application will handle the loads you expected it would.

Getting Started

The first thing you need to do is download JMeter from the Jakarta web site at `http://jakarta.apache.org/jmeter/`. Once you have obtained JMeter, unpack it and then start it up. The distribution contains a batch file and shell script to start the tool on both Windows and Linux systems. For this book, we used the latest version at the time, which was 2.1.1.

Features

JMeter allows you to load many different application types. Core to JMeter is the concept of a *sampler*. This is a class that will perform a single test and return some data about that test. JMeter comes complete with samplers for making HTTP and FTP requests as well as samplers for Web services, JDBC databases, and LDAP directories.

With JMeter, you are not limited to making simple requests to a sampler one after the other. You can have multiple threads running at the same time, processing many different request patterns. Using logic controllers, you can control how requests are made and in what order.

Of course, sometimes you do not want to simply bombard the system with request after request. In this case, you can use timer components to submit a limited number of requests in a certain period of time, or you can use a timer to ensure that a uniform number of requests are submitted within a given period of time. JMeter even has support for random pauses between request submissions so you can add some level of uncertainty to your load testing.

Sometimes it can be useful to ensure that the data that is being returned from a request is correct. To support this, you can perform assertions on the data returned from a request, and JMeter will track the number of successful and unsuccessful requests. This is useful for web sites, as you can watch for valid data that you know the page will return, and then when this stops appearing, you can tell that some kind of server error has occurred.

The final piece in the puzzle is how exactly you view your results. Well, JMeter has a wide variety of analysis tools ranging from simple data tables, to aggregate reports, all the way up to graphs of throughput displaying highs, lows, averages, and deviations.

Creating a Sample Test

So now that you know what JMeter does, in this section we're going to give you a demonstration of how it works. For this example, we want to test the response time of the home page and the View All Stories page. We also want to make sure that in each cycle the home page is requested first, followed by the View All Stories page, as would most likely happen in a standard user scenario.

Once you open JMeter, you will see two nodes in the left-hand tree, one for the WorkBench and one for the test plan, as shown in Figure B-31. We have renamed our test plan to JavaEdge Test.

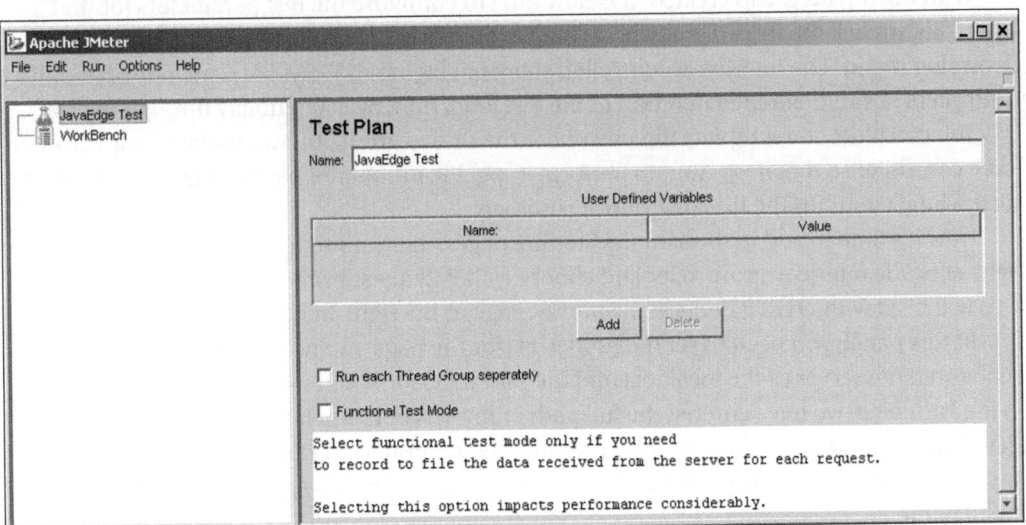

Figure B-31. *Renaming the test plan to JavaEdge Test*

The next step is to create a thread group to control execution of the requests. To do this, right-click the JavaEdge Test node and select Add ➤ Thread Group from the pop-up menu. This will create a Thread Group node underneath the JavaEdge Test node in the tree and bring up the Thread Group properties page in the right-hand pane (see Figure B-32).

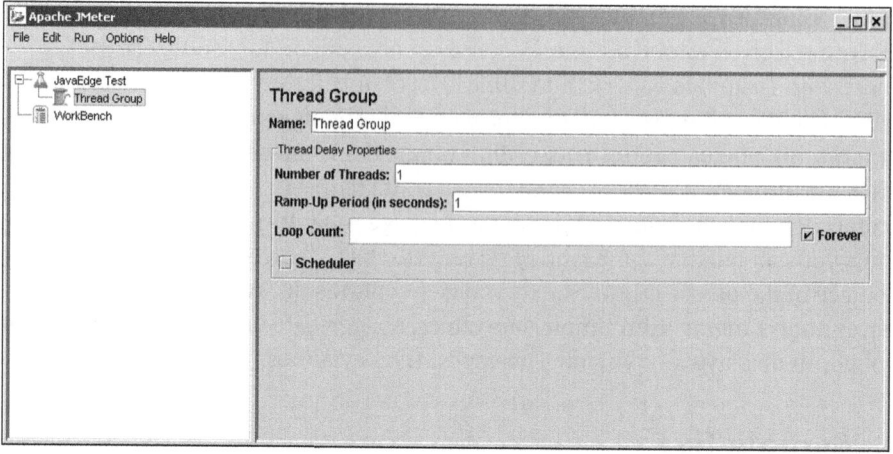

Figure B-32. *Creating a thread group for the tests*

Give your thread group a meaningful name and choose the number of threads you want to run your tests. We have chosen to limit our group to one thread, since that should be plenty for what we want to do. You can choose to limit the number of times the thread group will loop through the controllers and samples contained in it, or leave the loop to run until it is manually stopped. We have left the loop to run indefinitely.

With the thread group created, it is now time to configure the test parameters for that group. Right-click the thread group and choose Interleave Controller from the Add ➤ Logic Controller menu. The interleave controller, shown in Figure B-33, will execute one of its sub-controllers or samplers each iteration of the test loop, moving sequentially through the list.

You can place the samplers directly under the thread group, but we prefer to use the inter-leave controller so that if we want to perform a specific number of page requests, we can just set the loop count for the thread group accordingly.

Now it's time to add in the samplers for the pages you want to test. To do this, you need to right-click the interleave controller and choose HTTP Request from the Add ➤ Sampler menu. This will display the HTTP Request properties page in the right-hand pane (see Figure B-34).

In this panel, you need to set the properties for the page you want to request. We have configured the server as the localhost and the port to 8080, which we are running JBoss on. In the Path field, we have entered the full path of the server to the JavaEdge home page action, /JavaEdge/execute/homePageSetup. Don't add the server name or port to the path, since they are already included in the configuration for this request. Finish by giving the request a mean-ingful name.

When you are specifying the HTTP request settings, you're not limited to testing against an application running on your local machine. In fact, in most cases you will want to test against a live application to take into consideration Internet traffic and the live server hardware.

Repeat this process to create a request for the All Stories page. Now create an assertion as shown in Figure B-35 to make sure that the page returned when the home page request is processed is in fact the home page.

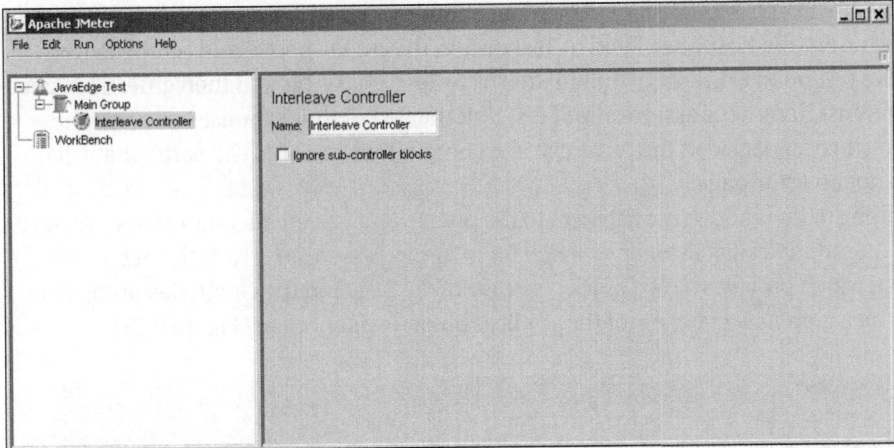

Figure B-33. *Adding an interleave controller to control requests*

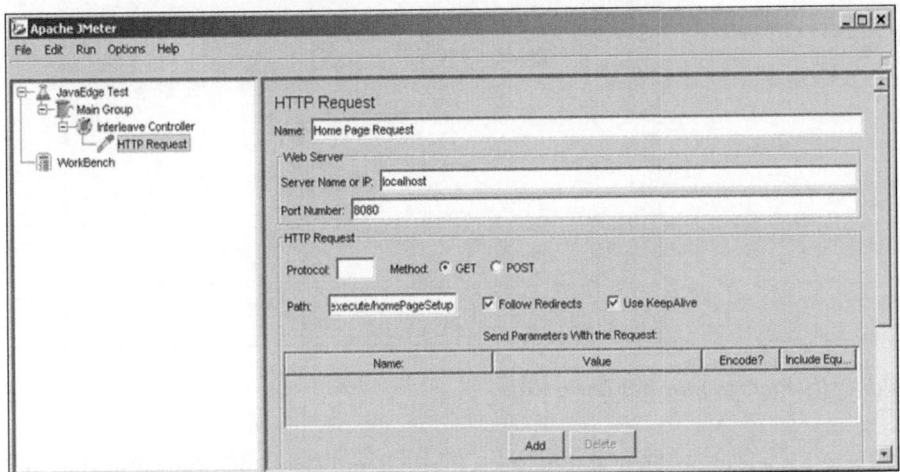

Figure B-34. *Adding an HTTP request for the JavaEdge home page*

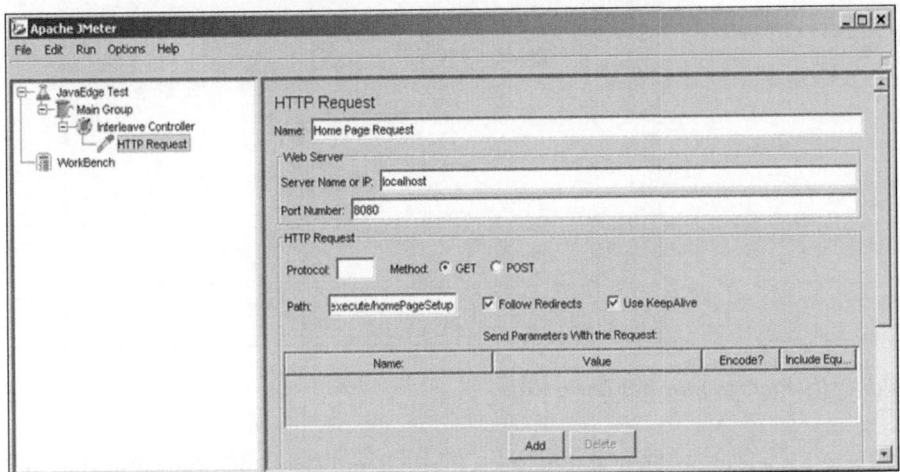

Figure B-35. *Creating a response assertion to verify response data*

Right-click the Home Page Request node and choose Response Assertion from the Add ➤ Assertions menu. Set the Response Field to Test option to Text Response and set the Pattern Matching Rules option to Contains. Under Patterns to Test, click Add and then enter **The Java Edge** in the new list item. This assertion will test that the text of the response contains The Java Edge,"and since all pages on the JavaEdge site contain this text, this will verify that what is returned is not an error page.

The last thing to do is add some listeners to the plan to analyze the incoming data. We have opted for the Assertion Results listener to watch for incoming assertion errors; the Aggregate Report listener, which provides a nice quick overview of the test; and the Graph Results listener, which gives a nice graphical overview of the application performance (see Figure B-36).

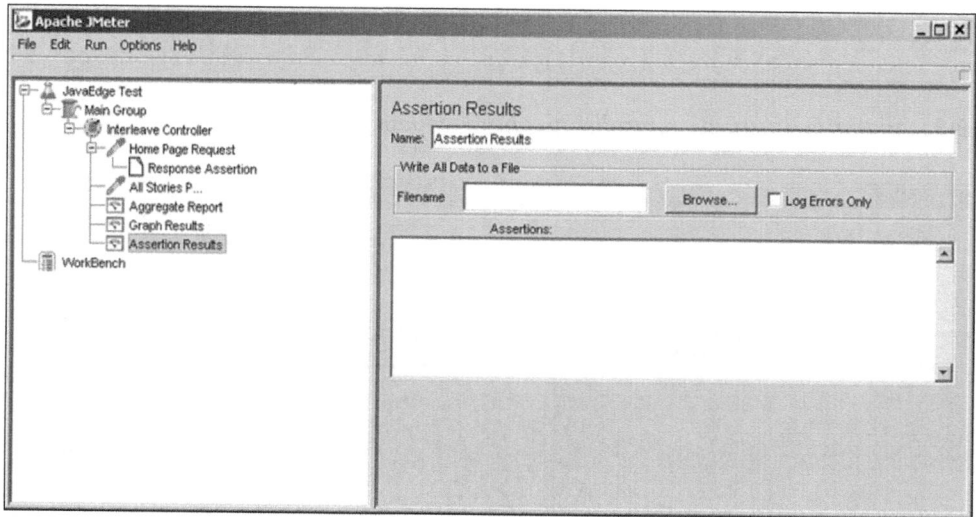

Figure B-36. *Adding listeners to monitor test results*

Now that the test is all set up, all that remains is to run it and view the results. You should save the test plan first in case anything crashes during the test run. This is especially true when you know that you will see an average of 95 percent CPU usage when running the test.

To start, select Start from the Run menu. If you want to watch the test in progress, then you can monitor any of the listeners to see what is happening. For instance, you watch the graph to monitor average throughput and response times. Once you are happy that you have enough test data, then it is time to stop the test and analyze the data. To stop the test, simply select Stop from the Run menu. Once the test is finished, you can take the time to look at the results in detail. Be careful, because some of the results visualizers are very memory intensive and may crash the JMeter tool—these particular tools are noted in the JMeter manual.

JMeter Summary

JMeter is a must-have tool. The features that we have discussed in this section are just a small part of what JMeter can do. Every single web application that you build will have some kind of performance expectations surrounding it. Using JMeter, you can test your code until it meets these criteria, and also verify that the final deployed version of the software hits the criteria too.

JMeter Next Step

The obvious starting point for more information about JMeter is the Jakarta web site at `http://jakarta.apache.org/jmeter`. Currently no books are available on the JMeter topic; however, there is mass of information about it on the Internet, so fire up the browser and hit Google for more information.

Summary

Okay, so by this time we know that you are probably chomping at the bit to get to grips with some more of these tools. We're sorry we couldn't give you more details about each tool (like any normal programmer we were bursting to tell you about every single one), but we also had to avoid making a single appendix that was longer than the rest of the book while still giving each tool a fair amount of coverage.

Most of the tools detailed in this appendix are mutually exclusive. It is our feeling that if you use IBM WebSphere, then you are unlikely to use JBuilder or Exadel Studio. If you are using Eclipse or NetBeans, then you probably won't be parting with the cash for one of the commercial IDEs, although you may find that Exadel Studio or Struts Console fit nicely into your development environment. This should not stop you from trying out each of these tools to see which fits you the best—you may be surprised.

One thing we'd really like to drive home about the IDE tools is that they are not a replacement for a good understanding of the Struts framework. Even for experienced Struts developers, using the RAD tools such as the designer from WebSphere, JBuilder, or Exadel Studio can quickly get messy, but such developers have the knowledge to fix it. If you are just starting out in Struts, then we strongly recommend that you do some work without using the configuration file editors and without the diagram tools so you can build up a thorough understanding of how the framework ticks. Then when you start to use the time-saving tools and something goes wrong, you will have the knowledge required to fix it.

■ ■ ■

Struts and Strecks

Strecks is an extension to Struts that can only be used with Java 1.5 (Tiger) or later. It is built on top of the 1.2.x codebase. Strecks is not a replacement to Struts, but rather a layer of abstraction on top of it. All the inherit concepts of Struts such as Action and Action Forms are still present, but in Strecks they are enhanced with some new functionality or are simplified with annotations.

The goal of the Strecks project is to improve developer productivity and the overall maintainability of the code. It is based on the concept of JSR 175 (Java Language Metadata Technology)' annotations that allow you to use a java.doc paradigm to generate some code in the background, or enforce certain types of rules. This hides the inner workings of Struts from developers, allowing them to focus on the business code that they need to write.

If you are a fan of BEA products, you might have heard of BEA WebLogic Workshop. The first web application framework to use annotations was the Java Page Flow Controller framework, a feature of WebLogic Workshop. BEA then donated the framework to open source, now known as the Apache Beehive project. *Pro Apache Beehive* (Apress, 2005) is a good starting place if you are interested in this framework. It is built on top of Struts and based totally on JSR 175 annotations.

Strecks is yet in a nascent stage, with 1.0-beta-3 being the latest release (released on July 7, 2006). Since a lot of the technology is bound to change as people start using it, this appendix will not cover it in much detail. Keep an eye on the Strecks home page for the most up-to-date information (`http://strecks.sourceforge.net//index.php`). This appendix shows you one high-level example to whet your appetite and get you excited about trying out Strecks.

Using Strecks

To get started with Strecks, first download the latest version from `http://strecks.sourceforge.net//download.php`. Take the Strecks jar file and place it in WEB-INF/lib. Add the following line to your struts-config.xml file to enable Strecks:

```
<controller
      processorClass="org.strecks.controller.ControllerRequestProcessor"
      contentType="text/html;charset=utf-8" inputForward="true"
      nocache="true" />
```

Note You must be using Java 1.5 or later to use Strecks.

You also need to make sure that your strecks.properties file is in the application classpath somewhere (such as APP-INF/lib). This file is used to configure interceptors (think of them as ServletFilters) and extension points, as follows:

```
form.handler.impl=org.strecks.form.handler.SessionErrorFormHandler
before.interceptor.1=org.strecks.interceptor.ActionLoggingInterceptor
before.interceptor.2=org.strecks.interceptor.RedirectBeforeInterceptor
after.interceptor.2=org.strecks.interceptor.ActionLoggingInterceptor
```

Let's look at several basic annotations.

@Controller and @ActionInterface

The @Controller annotation is used to identify the controller action, which will execute the ActionBean's methods:

```
@Controller(name = MyController.class)
public class MyAction implements BasicAction
{
    public String execute()
    {
        return "success";
    }
}
```

This annotation goes hand in hand with the @ActionInterface annotation. In this case, MyAction implements BasicAction, which is an ActionInterface, declared as follows:

```
@ActionInterface(name = BasicAction.class)
public class MyController extends BaseBasicController
{
    protected ViewAdapter executeAction(Object actionBean, ActionContext context)
    {
        //implementation omitted
    }
}
```

Note Every ActionBean needs to have the @Controller annotation because it defines the controller instance that will execute these actions.

@NavigateForward

This annotation provides a mechanism to decouple navigation logic from the business code. For example, in an ActionBean, you can have a method that looks like this:

```
@NavigateForward
public String getResult()
{
    return "success";
}
```

This annotation helps decouple navigation from the processing of the request. It ties to the `ActionMapping.findForward(String)` to find the appropriate ActionForward.

@BindSimple and @ValidateRequired

The annotations we have described thus far are related to the ActionBean. The `@BindSimple` class of annotations is for data binding and validation. The following is an example:

```
@BindSimple(expression = "myObject.integerValue")
public String getQuantity()
{
    return quantity;
}
@ValidateRequired(key = "number.required")
@ValidateInteger(key = "field.must.be.number")
public void setQuantity(String quantity)
{
    this. quantity = quantity;
}
```

This example shows you how to use the `@BindSimple` annotation to bind a getter method to a variable. The setter method shows you an example of data validation using the `@ValidateRequired` and `@ValidateInteger` annotations. This really highlights the power of annotations. You do not have to write all the logic to perform the validation. Upon execution two validations will be performed: the first to make sure that some value has been provided (`@ValidateRequired`) and the second to make sure that the value entered is an integer (`@ValidateInteger`). As a developer, you do not need to see an example to appreciate how much code you have just saved yourself from writing.

What You Can Do with Strecks

The preceding examples have shown you some very basic annotations. Strecks contains a whole bunch of different annotations, which fall into the following categories:

- A ctionBean annotations

- D ata binding and conversion annotations

- V alidation annotations

- D ependency injection annotations

In addition to many out-of-the-box annotations, Strecks comes with a complete framework to extend and create your own annotations. For example, Strecks does not have an annotation to validate currencies, something like @ValidateCurrency. If your application involves many currency calculations, you might want to write this as a Strecks extension. Another example could be a currency conversion extension that would convert U.S. dollars to British pounds or Indian rupees.

Is Strecks for Me?

The concept of annotations is catching on fast. It is the new way to write Java code. So, sooner or later you will be using some framework or technology that uses annotations. Strecks is an excellent extension to Struts, and if you are already on Java 1.5, there is little to no reason why we would recommend against Strecks.

If you are working in a Java 5 and Struts shop, you will definitely benefit from using Strecks. Strecks represents the new set of best practices programming techniques for Java web application development. However, if you still are not on Java 1.5, your obvious first move needs to be to migrate to Java 1.5. Understandably, this might be a bigger undertaking than your team might have the time and money for, but it probably is on your roadmap somewhere.

Index

You Need the Companion eBook

Your purchase of this book entitles you to buy the companion PDF-version eBook for only $10. Take the weightless companion with you anywhere.

We believe this Apress title will prove so indispensable that you'll want to carry it with you everywhere, which is why we are offering the companion eBook (in PDF format) for $10 to customers who purchase this book now. Convenient and fully searchable, the PDF version of any content-rich, page-heavy Apress book makes a valuable addition to your programming library. You can easily find and copy code—or perform examples by quickly toggling between instructions and the application. Even simultaneously tackling a donut, diet soda, and complex code becomes simplified with hands-free eBooks!

Once you purchase your book, getting the $10 companion eBook is simple:

❶ Visit **www.apress.com/promo/tendollars/**.

❷ Complete a basic registration form to receive a randomly generated question about this title.

❸ Answer the question correctly in 60 seconds, and you will receive a promotional code to redeem for the $10.00 eBook.

2560 Ninth Street • Suite 219 • Berkeley, CA 94710

eBookshop

THE EXPERT'S VOICE™

Offer valid through 5/07.

GPSR Compliance

The European Union's (EU) General Product Safety Regulation (GPSR) is a set of rules that requires consumer products to be safe and our obligations to ensure this.

If you have any concerns about our products, you can contact us on ProductSafety@springernature.com

In case Publisher is established outside the EU, the EU authorized representative is:

Springer Nature Customer Service Center GmbH
Europaplatz 3
69115 Heidelberg, Germany

Batch number: 09485245

Printed by Printforce, the Netherlands